ADVANCED
EARLY YEARS

FOR FOUNDATION DEGREES & LEVELS 4/5

2nd edition

Editors:

Iain Macleod-Brudenell
Janet Kay

www.heinemann.co.uk
✓ Free online support
✓ Useful weblinks
✓ 24 hour online ordering

01865 888118

Heinemann is an imprint of Pearson Education Limited, a company incorporated in England and Wales, having its registered office at Edinburgh Gate, Harlow, Essex, CM20 2JE. Registered company number: 872828

www.heinemann.co.uk

Heinemann is a registered trademark of Pearson Education Limited

Text © Pearson Education Limited 2008

First published 2008

12 11 10 09 08
10 9 8 7 6 5 4 3 2 1

British Library Cataloguing in Publication Data
A catalogue record for this book is available from the British Library

ISBN 978 0 435401 00 9

Typeset by Tek-Art, Croydon, Surrey
Original illustrations © Pearson Education Limited, 2008
Illustrated by Katie Mac co NB Illustration
Cover design by The Wooden Ark Studio
Picture research by Alison Prior
Cover photo © Joe Polillio/Getty Images
Printed in the UK by Scotprint

Acknowledgements
The authors and publisher would like to thank the following individuals and organisations for permission to reproduce photographs:

©Alamy/AM Corporation, p71; ©Alamy/Bubbles Photolibrary, p71; ©Alamy/Peter Banos, p71; iStockphoto/Jaroslaw Wojcik, p71; ©iStockphoto/Michael Pettigrew, p153; ©Pearson Education Ltd/Jules Selmes, p34, p71, p98; ©Photodisc, p19, p71

Every effort has been made to contact copyright holders of material reproduced in this book. Any omissions will be rectified in subsequent printings if notice is given to the publishers.

Websites
The websites used in this book were correct and up-to-date at the time of publication. It is essential for tutors to preview each website before using it in class so as to ensure that the URL is still accurate, relevant and appropriate. We suggest that tutors bookmark useful websites and consider enabling students to access them through the school/college intranet

Contents

About the authors

Janet Kay originally trained as a social worker working with children and families and specialising in child protection. She is currently a Principal Lecturer in Children and Childhood at Sheffield Hallam University. Janet is the author and co-author of several publications on Early Years subjects, including child protection, behaviour management, multi-agency working and Early Years policy.

Iain MacLeod-Brudenell has had teaching, advisory, inspection, teacher training and professional development (Inset and research supervision) experience in Early Years education. Prior to this his experience was very varied, having been a Head of an Art Department in secondary education, a curriculum and professional development teacher in multicultural education and involved in anti-racist teaching in nursery, primary and secondary schools and a design and technology adviser. Iain was involved in initiating and developing HND and multidisciplinary BA and Foundation Degree courses in Early Childhood Studies at the University of Derby. Recent experience includes senior management posts in Further and Higher Education.

Vicky Cortvriend holds both a degree in Nursing Management and Education and a Masters in Education. She worked initially as a midwife in South Africa, returning to the UK in 1990 and then worked as a psychiatric nurse where she was involved in both student and client education. From 1994 to 2004 she was a lecturer in Early Childhood Studies working with students from level 2–6. Vicky is currently working for CACHE, the awarding body that specialises in qualifications for childcare and education.

Elaine Hallet is a Teaching Fellow for Foundation degrees and the Early Years Research Leader at the University of Derby. She has taught and worked widely in the Early Years and school settings, the Advisory Service, Further and Higher Education, and as a QAA Foundation Degree Reviewer. Publications and conference papers are from her particular interests of early literacy; work-based learning and reflective practice; widening participation and lifelong learning; and the development of a graduate Early Years workforce. Her current doctoral research concerns the experiences of women Early Years Sector – Endorsed Foundation Degree graduates and the impact of their studies upon personal and professional development and professional practice.

Melanie Henshaw has owned and managed Little Scholars, Private Day Nursery, for eleven years. She also lectures on the Foundation Degree – Children's and Young People's Services – and the BA (Hons) Early Childhood Studies at the University of Derby. She has a diploma in Child Psychology and a BA (Hons) in Early Childhood Studies.

Dr Vivienne Walkup leads teams providing Early Childhood and Education Studies at the University of Derby. She was previously a teacher and lecturer in English before becoming a lecturer in psychology and education. She is a practising counsellor and has a particular interest in child psychology; she has recently published a co-authored text which applies psychology to education. She is the mother of five children.

Candida Brudenell is Head of Targeted Services 0–7 years at Nottingham City Council, with responsibility for the development, delivery and sustainability of all of Sure Start Children's Centres in the city.

Caron Carter is Senior Lecturer in Early Childhood at Sheffield Hallam University, with research interest in children's friendships, social and emotional development and children's participation.

Acknowledgements

Janet Kay wishes to thank:
my friend and colleague Pam Dewis for her contributions to the Health Policy section of Chapter 13 and for her patience and persistence in explaining the complexities of children's health policy to me.

Iain MacLeod-Brudenell wishes to thank:
Jo and Eva for their support while writing for this edition, and George, Flora and William for age-related inspiration. Special thanks to my daughters, Candida Brudenell, for critical review and contributions to several chapters, and Tamsin Bowers-Brown (Sheffield Hallam University) for her assistance with aspects of research practice. Also thanks to Janet's daughter Amie for her help with electronic communication in Chapter 7.

Vicky Cortvriend wishes to thank:
husband Martin and children Steven, Shaun and Lyndall for their continued support and encouragement.

Elaine Hallet wishes to thank:
all Foundation Degree in Educare and Early Childhood graduates at the University of Derby for helping my understanding of work-based learning and reflective practice.

Melanie Henshaw would like to dedicate this chapter in memory of her sister Tina and in celebration of her grandson Shaun. She wishes to thank Elaine Hallet for opening the door to HE, her husband for proofreading hundreds of essays and all her family, especially mum, dad and daughter Kirstie, for their support and encouragement.

Vivienne Walkup wishes to thank:
all those who have continued to encourage me and to my daughters, sons, granddaughters and grandsons who continue to inspire me.

Introduction

This new edition of our popular book has been updated to cover recent developments in policy and practice relevant to students and practitioners in Early Years contexts. The book continues to provide a sound basis for promoting understanding of key Early Years issues for Foundation Degree students and others at Levels 4 and 5 and on degree courses in Early Years. The contents, however, are also of interest for those in practice who may not be studying formally but who wish to be well informed about issues in Early Years contexts and services and who want to develop their own ability to analyse and reflect on these issues. Foundation Degrees in Early Years aim to equip students with a combination of the technical abilities, academic knowledge and transferable skills that employers in the Early Years sector require. Many practitioners on Foundation Degrees and other courses will already have a range of rich and varied experiences of working with children and families, although students may be beginning academic study from different starting points. This new edition will focus on aiding you to fully recognise your existing academic and practice skills, to further develop these skills, and to extend your knowledge and understanding of many of the key issues within Early Years settings and services.

Students on Foundation Degrees may also be considering further study on completion. Although the Foundation Degree is a valuable higher education qualification in its own right, it is also seen by the government as making a significant contribution to the 'ladder of lifelong learning', providing opportunities for students to progress to an Honours Degree and further professional qualifications such as the Early Years Professional Status (EYPS).

Early Years Foundation Degrees aim to integrate study and work in order to enhance practice, often through work-based modules and projects, but also through assessment by means of reflecting on practice-based application of theory. This updated edition will help you to become more aware of developmental approaches to learning and to reflect upon practice, which will extend your professional competence and effectiveness in supporting the well-being of children.

Encouraging equity

Effective communication between adults and children involves critical analysis of one's own interpersonal interactions with adults as well as children. This should include the ability to evaluate the effect of one's actions on other people in the environment in which you work. A central theme within this book is reflection on factors that contribute to effective communication with others, including children, parents and other professionals. The practitioner's awareness of equity, anti-discriminatory practice and equality of opportunity should permeate every area of practice.

We use the term 'equity' throughout this book in preference to the broad and less defined term 'equal opportunities'. Equity is a proactive approach, concerning 'doing' rather than 'offering'. In order to provide equality of opportunity, individual children may require different and often unequal treatment so that they have complete access to opportunities offered to other children. For example, a child who has difficulty developing social skills may require additional support. A child who is learning to use English when it is not his or her first language will also require support in order to access the curriculum. Equitable approaches will therefore reflect developmentally appropriate Early Years practice.

About this book

This edition has been updated to reflect radical changes in Early Years policy and practice since the Every Child Matters agenda was first published in 2003. The book reflects the integrated approaches to health, care and education of young children in the context of promoting well-being for all children and specialist services for some, which is at the heart of that agenda. Changes to Early Years policy and practice have been discussed in the context of changes to services for all children and families where appropriate. The book also supports the reader to develop reflective skills in order to evaluate, analyse and question the policy that guides their work and the practices in their own workplace and the wider context. Reflective practice is a theme running through the book as we see this as a key factor in improving quality for children and families. The book also promotes your ability to reflect on workplace practice in the context of theoretical issues, to support your growth as a reflective practitioner with a commitment to lifelong learning.

A new first chapter has been added to focus your thoughts on study skills and your ability to study effectively and develop academic writing skills in order to balance work, life and study successfully. Chapter 2 has been updated to include newer developments in trends and traditions in Early Years care and education to provide a context for the rest of the chapters in the book.

This new edition has updated and developed key chapters on children's development which support your understanding of children's developmental processes and needs across the range. Chapter 4 (Physical development) and Chapter 9 (Supporting children's healthy development) focus on children's physical development and their physical and mental health and well-being respectively.

Understanding children's developmental processes and the additional needs which can arise from these also requires practitioners to study and develop a good understanding of aspects of cognitive, language and emotional and social development. We address these issues in Chapters 5, 6 and 7.

Development and learning through play and more structured learning processes are discussed in Chapter 8 (Playing) and Chapter 11 which looks at developing strategies for supporting learning within the Early Years Foundation Stage (EYFS). This chapter also looks at supporting children with additional needs, a theme which runs throughout the whole new edition.

Reflection upon your own personal and professional growth will require consideration of your own attitudes to working in Early Years services and the development of reflective skills are discussed in Chapter 3 (The reflective practitioner). Evaluation of practice often involves the practitioner in research. In this book, Chapter 12 covers observation, and Chapter 16 focuses on helping the reader to develop research skills in order to complete a small-scale research study of their own, and to conduct research and evaluation in their own setting to get feedback from children and families and to inform improvements in practice.

As mentioned above, this new edition clearly addresses the implications of the current policy strategy and the changes in practice and services stemming from this agenda. New ways of working, cultural change and new concepts driving integrated service provision have all changed the landscape of children's services in recent years and continue to dominate policy and practice in the area. Chapter 13 in this new edition provides the background and context to the current policy and legislative framework for Early Years services and evaluates how this policy was developed and implemented. Policy and practice issues specific to the key issue of safeguarding are discussed in Chapter 14.

Principles underpinning ways of working with others are the key issues in Chapters 10 (Parenting and parent partnership) and 15 (Leading and working in multi-professional teams). Working with parents and families has become a much stronger theme in Early Years services in recent years, both in terms of developing partnerships and in understanding that quality services to children need to include support for parents in their difficult and demanding role. The new Chapter 10 discusses the parenting role and how parenting style may impact on children's development to support your understanding of the significance of parenting for children's healthy development. The chapter also discusses how Early Years settings and practitioners can support good standards of parenting and promote parent partnership. The new Chapter 15, dealing with multi-professional teamwork and leadership, reflects the role of many students whose study at Levels 4 and 5 is reflected in new responsibilities in this area or who require better understanding and practices relating to existing leadership responsibilities.

Features of this book

Most Early Years Foundation Degree students will be undertaking their course through part-time study and will find that their academic studies complement and inform skills in their current jobs. Other students who may have less practice-based experience will undertake work experience placements as part of their course. The book offers a range of features to support understanding and application of the links between theory and practice based on a variety of learning modes to help you to progress at your own pace, using methods that are best suited to you.

The learning that takes place during work experience is invaluable, not simply for improving and enhancing practice, but also for the place it has in contextualising the taught elements of the programme of study. In this book, case studies provide examples from practice that illustrate key learning points. In some cases there are activities related to these for you to develop your understanding of the issues further. By posing questions for your consideration and by presenting contentious issues for you to address through activities and discussion points, we aim to prepare you for assessment on your course and progression to further qualifications by helping you develop critical thinking and analytical skills. You are also encouraged, through the use of these discussion points and activities, to evaluate and monitor your developing skills. The new edition also has, in addition to comprehensive reference lists, a section on 'How to move on in your research' at the end of each chapter for you to use to extend your knowledge and understanding of the topic. In other parts of the book we continue to signpost you to key readings and significant documents, often available online.

It is strongly recommended that you keep a log, journal or a reflective diary during your programme of study. This is where you can record all your new learning, such as your developing skills in time management, your thoughts and reflections on practice, and the links you are making between theory and practice. Many Foundation Degrees now use this as a basis for assessments that focus on self-development and evaluation. Each chapter in this book will encourage you to consider the importance of becoming aware of important issues in the Early Years. As such, we will provide you with some ideas for developing platforms for self-knowledge and devising a programme of personal development.

Finally...

...we hope that you will find this new edition a valuable support in your studies and in your work practice. Good luck with your course!

Iain MacLeod-Brudenell and Janet Kay

Study skills

Vicky Cortvriend

This chapter is designed to encourage you to develop the study skills that will enable you to successfully complete your chosen course, whether it is a Foundation Degree, a National Vocational Qualification (NVQ), Scottish Vocational Qualification (SVQ) or other Early Years-related course at Level 4 or 5. All of these qualifications seek to:

➤ encourage students to explain and evaluate theoretical issues in the chosen field of study

➤ help students apply their critical understanding of such issues in appropriate practice settings.

There are two key strands in studying for an Early Years qualification: theory and practice. In order to better understand Early Years theory we believe that students should be encouraged to reflect upon practice as well as engage in practice – to think as well as do.

The purpose of this chapter is therefore to demonstrate that with a little practice and organisation it is possible to study at the same time as engaging in practice. The chapter offers advice on how to balance your life with your study and how to make the most of your study time. It also gives guidance on academic writing, including planning and preparation and the difference between analysing and evaluating.

This chapter addresses the following areas:

➤ Time management
➤ How to make the most of your course
➤ Academic writing

By undertaking the suggested study within this chapter it is hoped that you will be able to:

1 use your time effectively and find an acceptable balance between work, life and study
2 maximise all relevant resources including electronic and technological ones
3 understand what is required at your particular level of study
4 successfully complete your chosen course.

Time management

How to begin

One of the burning questions for students is 'How much time must I put aside for study?' This is a very difficult question to answer because everyone works and reads at different speeds, and some people like to write or type notes while others prefer to read notes and books over and over again.

As a rough guide, you should expect to spend the same amount in personal study time as you do in formal taught sessions, although there will be times when you would expect to spend longer, for example coming up to deadlines. On some courses the amount of time you are expected to spend in personal study is outlined in the course documents.

Some students studying Early Years and related courses at Levels 4 and 5 are mature students who may have lots of experience of working with children in a range of settings, but who may also have not had to study for some time. For these students, returning to study can seem quite daunting. They may ask themselves 'Can I do it?' and 'Why am I doing it?', particularly during the first few weeks of their course. Often when such students get back their first assignment with their grade and tutor feedback their confidence and self-belief is restored.

Whether you are returning to study or not, it is important to remember your long-term goals if you feel apprehensive. Picture yourself in cap and gown receiving your degree certificate on a stage in front of your family and friends. A very real sense of achievement!

What does it take to be a successful student and an independent learner?

Getting started

Find a place or places where you can study and store your materials. Some people need peace and quiet whereas others are happy to study with background noise.

An ideal place would be a well-lit corner of a room with a table to work on and a plug socket within reach. Once you have determined where you will do most of your studying you will feel able to begin. It is worth spending some time at the start of your course making sure you are comfortable with your chosen spot and that it is in a place where other people such as family members will not interrupt you regularly.

Case Study 1

Individual study choices

I found that when I was revising for an exam I needed peace and quiet but when writing assignments I could manage quite easily in a noisy environment. I would keep the materials required for the latest assignment or task in a case which I took with me wherever the family was going and often would be beavering away in the car or even in the swimming pool café while the children swam.

It is useful to keep all your study resources in one place, especially all the correspondence that goes with your course. Have one file or folder for correspondence and be quite strict about putting items in as they arrive. That will prevent the frustration that occurs when you cannot put your hands on a letter that you know you received but that someone has tidied (or thrown) away. If you are sharing space and a computer with other people, work out rules for respecting each others' needs and ensuring that work can be stored safely for each person, whether paper-based or electronic – there is nothing worse than having half an assignment accidentally deleted by a child doing homework in a hurry.

Prioritise

In order to achieve any goal there needs to be a sequence of events. In the case of achieving a qualification, the sequence begins when you register for your course of study, or perhaps when you decide that you want to study. A major part of your work towards the goal of achieving a qualification is learning through independent study, so it is important that you make time for study. There has been much written about how to find time in a busy schedule without giving something up, and although it is possible to balance your life it is a fact that you must learn to prioritise and quite probably 'give something up' or 'put something on hold'.

The first thing to do is decide upon your priorities. Once you have taken the decision to embark on a course of study you need to decide what else in your life you feel has to be done by you, what can be done by or shared with someone else and what can be put on hold. It is a good idea to write these down and discuss them with your family and friends where appropriate.

Time

A few tips on how you may manage your time are given in Figures 1.1 and 1.2. Activities 1 and 2 on page 4 will help you to do this.

It is important to balance your work, home, social and study life. You should not be studying to the detriment of the other aspects of your life. The quality of time you give to study is more important than the quantity of time.

Becoming an independent learner	
Managing your time	Each of us has a busy life. We may have a work life, a family life and a social life. Becoming a student means fitting in a study life. How can this be done? The key to this is being able to manage your time, to prioritise and to make effective use of the time available.
Gaining control of your time	Time is precious; it can easily get out of control and your time can disappear. Time can never be regained so you need to control it by planning and organising it.
Creating study time	It is important to identify the time you have available for your studies. This can be done by researching your own weekly timetable and finding out how you will spend your time in a typical working week.

Figure 1.1 Independent learning: managing your time

Your time	
Committed time	This is time allocated on a regular basis that cannot be altered: for example, time spent at work, travelling time, childcare arrangements, regular social commitments, meetings and other activities.
Provision time	This is time spent in maintaining the personal needs of your life: for example, shopping, cooking and eating meals, washing, cleaning and sleeping.
Adaptable time	The space left on your timetable is adaptable time. This is time that you can use as you wish. In the life of a student some of this becomes study time. How you plan and organise this time determines the effective use of it and your success as a student.

Figure 1.2 Your time: its components

Activity 1

Sharing and prioritising

Activity	By	Timescale
Coursework	Self	Hand in dates on calendar
Weekly shop	Partner	Saturdays
Cooking	Shared	Self weekdays, partner weekends, son Fridays.
Washing and Ironing	Children share	Saturday morning
Garden	Share	Depends on weather and time of year

Reward/Balance

It is also important to reward yourself for working hard to achieve your goals.

Activity 2

Plan a timetable

Plan a timetable of tasks you would like to achieve, the date you want to complete them and the reward for completing the task

Task	Timescale	Reward

Keep a list of things you need to complete and update it regularly.

Case Study 2

Managing time

I always put assignment hand-in dates on the calendar with a week to spare so if it was due on the 10th of the month I would put the 3rd, then I was always on time. I might also use the reminder facility on a mobile phone or a computer for this. The more places you have reminders the less likely you are to forget.

Do a little often rather than leaving everything to the last minute – the old adage 'a stitch in time saves nine' really works. Although some people say they work best under stress and always leave things until the last minute it is often true that these people do not submit their best efforts. They make mistakes and just do not leave themselves enough time to complete work correctly. See activities 3 and 4 on page 5 that will help you to balance your time.

Have a contingency plan in case of emergencies. For example, arrange with someone you trust to babysit or cook a meal for you if you do get behind with work and need to catch up.

Activity 3

The best time to study

1 What is the best time for you to study?
Tick the most appropriate statements.

I need to work for at least 2 hours to achieve anything. ☐
I can only concentrate for 2 to 3 hours maximum. ☐
I can think and study better in the morning. ☐
I can think and study better in the evening. ☐
I can think and study better at night-time and very early in the morning. ☐
I work better before meals. ☐
I work better after meals. ☐
I find it hard to work in the evenings after work. ☐
I find it better to work for longer periods at the weekends. ☐
I have to be at home to study. ☐
I prefer to study in a library. ☐
I find it easier to study with a friend. ☐

2 Now think about how you are going to organise your study time for successful studying.

Activity 4

Designing a study calendar

Design a study calendar which takes into account your personal preferences as to when you feel you study best and the requirements of work and family life. Are you a person who leaves things until the last minute? Or do you prefer to do a bit at a time? Do you work best in the early morning or late at night? Either way a study calendar will help you feel organised and in control.

	Dawn	Morning	Afternoon	Evening	late
Monday		Work	Work	Gym	
Tuesday		Work	Work	Study	
Wednesday	Study	Work	Work	Walk	
Thursday		Work	Work	Pub	
Friday		Work	Study	Running	
Saturday		Study	Shop	Walk	
Sunday	Church	Garden	Relax	Study	

Exercise

Do build in some time for regular exercise, it will make you feel better and is a very good way of getting rid of stress.

Avoid substitute activities

These are all things that you might do before settling down to the main study task in hand. It is easy to be tempted to do the washing up, phone a friend or watch a television programme, substituting the planned task with other activities. Rank the activities in order of importance or urgency and do the most important first. The substitute activities can be done after the main task. Discipline is needed for this.

Compile a 'Not to do' list

A 'Not to do' list might include jobs or temptations that should not be undertaken as they will use up time allocated for your study time. For example, you may choose not to answer the phone during your studying. This list will help you focus on your studying and use the time effectively.

Establish short-term tasks and long-term goals

You will read a lot of academic material and write a great deal as an undergraduate student. And it is likely that you will study across several areas. Hand-in dates and deadlines are crucial at university and failure to meet them can result in your failing a module. All this can seem overwhelming so it is important to break your goals down into small and achievable tasks.

Break things down into bite-size chunks you can deal with. This really does help, particularly if you put them on the calendar and strike them off as you complete each one.

In setting a long-term goal, identify what you ultimately want to achieve. It may be to hand in a module on time. Your short-term tasks will give you an idea of what you are trying to achieve over the next week and tell you what you need to do when you start a study session. This will stop you wasting time when you sit down because you do not know what to do in the time available. For example, a goal of 'I will do the assignment by the end of the week,' can seem overwhelming and unachievable. The shorter task 'I will do Question 1 of the assignment in my study time this week,' is realistic and achievable.

Don't set yourself up to fail. If you know that you will not be able to achieve a task by a certain date then negotiate a date that you know you will be able to achieve. You may need to adjust your calendar if you have been too optimistic about the time you do have available. After a time you may find that studying becomes a habit and you no longer require a calendar. It just all falls into place.

Get help and support

Enlist the support of your colleagues. For example, you may find that people are willing to share books and articles, engage in debate and discussion and generally become involved in what you are studying. This can prove beneficial for the whole team as current practice is discussed and debated and will help you in your reflection, analysis and evaluation.

Find a mentor or buddy who you can bounce ideas off and who will listen to your presentations and proofread your work. This may be a colleague, partner, sibling, child or friend. A knowledge of Early Years is not essential because what you are looking for is someone who will be able to hear and read if you are expressing yourself clearly and will be confident enough to give you constructive feedback. If your buddy is a person on your course then they could also pick up notes if you happen to miss any taught sessions, and of course you would do the same for them. If they are not on your course it is a good idea to strike up a reciprocal agreement with someone who is so that you do not miss anything should you be absent at any time.

Family life can be unpredictable and events may occur that may easily disrupt a well-organised study pattern. Make contingency plans with partners, friends and/or family to help with childcare or give support if a deadline is looming. Promise children that the attention they are not getting now will be available after a certain date and put aside some time to spend with them even when you are studying hard. Make sure those close to you understand how important your studies are to you and that they know how to best support you (which may just mean leaving you alone at times).

How to make the most of your course

Lectures, seminars and tutorials make up a significant part of your course so it makes sense to make the most of them and attend as often as possible. Indeed, for some courses there is a minimum expectation of the numbers of sessions you are expected to attend. Make sure you are aware of any expectations at the start of your course. This is particularly important if you are planning any holidays during term time.

Make a 'To do' list

Quality use of time is more important than how much is available. It is possible to achieve a great deal in one hour of quality time, particularly if you use a 'To do' list. On this list place everything you have to do before you start. Place the items in order of priority. One of the easiest ways of doing this is to classify the items '1', '2', '3' as follows.

1　The most important items which have to be done in that day's study time.

2　The next important.

3　The least important.

Put a date by each item for when it has to be achieved. Tick or cross out items on the list as they are completed – this will give a great sense of achievement. Compile a 'To do' list at the end of every study time. This revised 'To do' list summarises the work achieved that day and prepares you for the next day's work.

What sort of a learner are you?

You might have come across David Kolb, who published his learning styles model in 1984. The model gave rise to related terms such as Kolb's experiential learning theory (ELT), and Kolb's learning styles inventory (LSI). In his publications – notably his 1984 book *Experiential Learning: Experience as the Source of Learning and Development* – Kolb acknowledges the early work on experiential learning by others, including Rogers, Jung, and Piaget.

There are many questionnaires and tests available relating to learning styles and it may help to do one to have an understanding of what style suits you best.

Remember that we often are a mix of several styles but one tends to be predominant. Understanding how you learn should help you get the best out of your course.

Activity 5

Learning styles

Using the table in Figure 1.3, identify the type of learning style that best describes you.

Activist	'Spotlight' people, chatterers, communicative, competitive, very good at convincing others of their point of view. People-orientated and dramatic. Always take an active part in any learning experience; often sitting at the front of the class.
Pragmatist	'Doers', tend to be more extrovert than introvert, get bored easily, focus on 'what can I get out of this'. Learn best by observing and then doing. Listening can be challenging for them. They tend to change careers, they need flexibility and autonomy. Will sit at the front unless bored, in which case they may move to the back and become disruptive.
Reflector	'Ideas people' and listeners, need time to prepare and like to know what the game play and the whole picture is, will avoid presentations if possible. Very good at paraphrasing and problem solving, they tend to sit in the middle of the room listening to what is going on around them and consider all the options.
Theorist	Often a 'loner' who likes own space. Can ask what appear to be bizarre questions, they are natural-born researchers but might come across as unresponsive and dismissive. They also like to consider all the options and once decided will dot all the i's and cross the t's. Often good at exams.

Figure 1.3 Learning styles

Experiential learning and how it might work for you.

Kolb described a four-stage cycle of learning in which **immediate or concrete experiences** from a lecture or seminar provide a basis for **observations and reflections** in reading over and editing your notes. These observations and reflections are assimilated and distilled into **abstract concepts** through assignments and revised practice, producing new implications for action which can be **actively tested** at work or placement, in turn creating new experiences.

Taught sessions enable you to develop an understanding of the course syllabus and material, they provide a rich debating field and help you explore and understand the latest ideas and concepts. They should encourage you to engage in further study giving you names and titles of relevant theorists, articles, research papers and books.

Take an active part during your taught sessions. This does not necessarily mean that everyone has to contribute to the discussions all of the time. Some people feel happier taking part in small group discussions rather than in class debate. But do try to remain focused on what is going on and relate what you are learning to your practical work and to previous learning. If and when you feel confident take part in the discussions and share your experiences with the group. This will help you develop the skill of comparing and contrasting opposing points of view while becoming practised at articulating your own opinion.

Preparation

Preparing for your taught sessions sounds a simple and logical idea but I was always surprised by the number of students who would begin each session with the question 'What are we doing today'?

If you come prepared by having read around the topic, and brought with you any tasks or work that you were asked to bring, you will feel able to concentrate and will really benefit from the session. It may be that not all taught sessions are very stimulating and exciting, but all should be relevant to your course and all will contain some information you were previously unaware of.

Your course tutor should have given you

a reading list and there may be specified readings for particular taught sessions – make sure you do this reading as the minimum you do to prepare for your session. You may need to read articles and chapters more than once and take notes in order to fully understand the topic and issues.

Using the relevant chapter of this book and completing some of the tasks included is one way of preparing for the coming lecture or seminar. You can use some of the ideas as topics for debate and discussion within your class or study group.

Other resources

The internet provides a rich source of information on every topic you will need to research or read around. However, it is important to be sure that internet sources are appropriate for academic work as some may be simply one person's uninformed opinion. Look for referenced journal articles and other publications such as government documents. If you cannot access an article on the web because you are not a subscriber, check with the learning centre catalogue and you may well find it there either as an electronic journal item or in a paper-based journal.

Resources in university learning centres can be accessed via the internet and a secure user password which you will be given once you have become a student. It may be possible to register online and receive books and journals through the post, rather than having to visit the learning centre itself.

Having said that, many people still enjoy visiting and studying in a library or learning resource centre. All libraries and learning resource centres have internet access that is cheap or free and accessible with technical support and expertise on hand. This can be an excellent resource for those who are not computer literate or who do not own their own computer.

Note-taking

It is not necessary to write down every word, but it is useful to make notes of important facts. Often the lecturer will guide you in that, advising you to 'make a note of that'. Be sure to include any references to books, journals, articles with the name of author, title of publication, publisher and year so that you can look it up and make reference to it if needed.

Some students may take notes directly onto a laptop. Notes still need editing at the end of the session and backing up in case of a crash. It is useful to label all notes with the lecturer's name, date and topic. Many tutors make PowerPoint slides available through the institution's intranet site specific to your course (such as Blackboard) and it is useful to download these to save note-taking.

If you have prepared for the session you will be able to recognise key facts and take notes accordingly. But however you decide to take notes it helps if you read over them that night to ensure they still make sense. It is frustrating if, when writing an assignment sometime later, you read over your notes and cannot make head or tail of them! In fact it is a good idea to put together any notes you have made with any handouts or downloaded material and write a summary of the topic with key points underlined or highlighted. The sooner this is done following the session the more beneficial it will be. This will ensure that you have a clear idea of the content of the session and be well prepared for the following one. It will also enable you to make notes of anything you would like to challenge or query during your next session.

Storing your references

When referring to other people's work in your assignments you will need to acknowledge sources by using the Harvard system of referencing (see the References and Further Reading sections at the end of the chapters in this book for example). There are variations within the Harvard system, however, so you will need to clarify the format preferred by the university you are attending.

It is a good idea to keep all such references in one place so when you are writing an assignment, study or dissertation you have a ready-made source of useful references.

In your list, include the author's name, date of publication, title of publication, place of publication and publisher's name. This information is then easily accessed for writing your assignment and producing a bibliography or reference list.

Case Study 3

References

One very organised student I knew had a system of filing cards that she used to great effect. On each card she listed all the information necessary to compile a bibliography and also some quotations she thought might come in useful. This could easily be emulated using a folder on a laptop, or indeed a notebook. List the references for books, journals and websites, either under the author or subject headings: for example, Play, The Early Years Curriculum, Special Educational Needs.

Keep a diary or journal

By keeping a reflective diary or journal you will be able to note down your study progress. You can jot down your thoughts, ideas, feelings, and any relevant work experiences and record references to articles you have read or put research materials in your journal and annotate with notes. This reflective diary or journal is a personal dialogue and a working notebook, a useful resource to help in writing your assignments. At the end of the course it will be interesting to look back at your journal to see your progress and the development of your ideas.

Cockburn (2001:108) describes how a journal is a useful tool and resource when studying.

A journal is a powerful part of an educator's professional development. A journal is a place for reflecting, speculating, wondering, worrying, exclaiming, recording, proposing, reminding, reconstructing, questioning, confronting, dreaming, considering and reconsidering. The journal holds experiences as a puzzle frame holds its integral pieces. The writer begins to recognise the pieces that fit together and, like a detective, sees the picture evolve. It is a space for thinking.

Research and finding information

As previously mentioned, learning resource centres and the internet are invaluable sources of information. Your course materials will include suggested reading materials and at the end of each chapter of this book you will find a list of resources such as useful books, articles and websites, each giving a synopsis of the content to enable you to easily decide which will be most useful for you.

If you do use the library make sure you are well prepared before you go with a list of topics you need to research and the titles and authors of the books written down. Learning resource centres often only stock a few copies of the most popular textbooks. However, they should have copies of the key texts as reference copies which cannot be borrowed.

Most learning centres are moving towards online rather than paper-based materials, including electronic books/journals and digitised material which can be accessed online. In most cases, specific module material is also available through the student intranet site for the relevant module. This may include basic course documents, links to online journals, government websites and other electronic material, and reading lists. It is very likely that your course will offer you an induction in the learning centre so you can familiarise yourself with how to access online materials.

Plagiarism

Plagiarism is representing someone else's work as your own, whether this is copying work from a fellow student or from a book, article or other published text. Don't be tempted to download information from the internet and pass it off as your own work as higher education institutions (HEIs) have sophisticated software such as TurnitinUK which can scan academic work and check for plagiarism. With the growth of this type of plagiarism, tutors can be very skilled at spotting changes in writing style and language. Copying from friends can be fatal to friendship if caught, as all parties will end up in plagiarism hearings whether 'guilty' or not. Plagiarism hearings are held to deal with infringements and as plagiarism is considered a serious academic offence, penalties can affect your academic progress significantly. On top of this, it is very unpleasant to be caught cheating. Check the plagiarism guidelines for your course or HEI and, if in doubt, ask your tutor for additional guidance.

It is also important to be really clear about referencing as failure to reference correctly can result in unintentional plagiarism (for example, if you do not reference a quote properly). You will have referencing guidelines to help you get this right and your tutor will help you. There may be support sessions on referencing on your course or through the learning centre so use these to make sure you have got the referencing right – and as referencing errors can sometimes affect your marks you will benefit in this way too.

Lots of mature students avoid finding out how to access online materials, yet they can benefit most, as using these resources reduces long trips to learning centres which may not work well with family life and work. It is well worth overcoming any fears you may have about this as with a little effort you can make your research a lot simpler and less time-consuming. Most learning centres also have helpdesks to support students who are struggling with any aspect of finding or retrieving materials.

Textbooks can be expensive to buy new so try the second-hand notice board (these are often online as well as on an actual board) or eBay, which has an increasing number of academic texts for sale.

Many students will want to purchase at least one seminal text for their course and with so many books available it is important you choose the one that is right for you. Have an idea what you would like it to include: key theorists, topics, research. Read the synopsis on the back cover, the list of contents, the introduction and at least part of one chapter to get a feel of the content and the style of writing. That should give you a good idea if it is the book for you. However, it is also important to check with your tutors which books will be worth buying and which may not.

Academic writing

Preparation

You will be given a list of assignment topics, titles and hand-in dates at the start of your course. This is to give you an idea of the assessment strategy, different topics covered and the timescale. One thing you should make sure you do is enter all the hand-in dates on your calendar and in your diary. If you use an electronic diary on your computer you can programme it to remind you a month, then a week before it is due. You can also use the reminder facility on a mobile phone for this.

However, few people start thinking about the actual writing until they begin the taught sessions for that particular module.

Once it is time to start do not put it off otherwise you will be rushing around panicking and wasting time. The time and effort you have already invested will start to pay dividends because you will have your notes labelled and filed and a ready-made list of references.

Collect all the information and resources you already have and make a list of anything missing. Decide where to find the missing information and either search carefully on the internet or access the learning centre resources. Make sure you also have to hand any assessment guidance, assessment criteria that you will need to cover and any notes you have made about what to include in the assignment or how to structure it.

Put all your ideas down on paper, perhaps using a 'mind map' or other diagrammatic approach. Working diagrammatically is one way of getting all your ideas down on paper quickly and you can then consider what you have written and refine accordingly. Some people find it useful to make further diagrams branching out from their original one which add detail such as references to use.

Writing

The introduction for an assignment should state what the reader can expect to discover in the main body of the essay. It should be short and concise. The main body is where you discuss the actual topic of the essay, putting forth various points of view and analysing and evaluating the evidence. The first paragraphs should introduce key points and you should always try to provide a balanced point of view. This section is where you might like to use quotations to illustrate your arguments. Remember, an academic piece of writing must be underpinned using the work of theorists and other authors; it is not made up solely of your own personal points of view. The conclusion should be a summing up of all the points made without introducing the reader to any new ideas.

You will probably find that you will want to go over what you have written more than once and will end up having more than one draft. This is where a computer can be very useful because you can save your first drafts and edit them without having to rewrite everything. Just remember to continually press 'Save' – it is immensely frustrating when you have just completed a piece of work without saving it and the computer crashes. Always back up your work on another piece of hardware such as a memory stick.

Expectations

Figure 1.4 gives you a clear idea of what is expected at the different levels for different terms and should help you to provide sufficient depth and breadth of information for the level you are studying. Another useful tool is to look at the grade criteria in your student handbook. It will explain what is expected for each grade in terms of detail. The higher the grade, the more complex discussion of the material is expected. An assignment that achieves a minimum pass grade may contain the same basic information as that which achieves a distinction but the assignment that has achieved a distinction will have demonstrated a real and genuine understanding of the topic and reflected upon the issues raised.

Term	Level 2	Level 3	Level 4	Level 5
Describe	Provide clear details about a topic	Provide clear details about a topic with examples and references	Provide clear in-depth details about a topic with examples and references	Provide clear in-depth details about a topic with examples and references
Evaluate		Review theory or practice in a way that shows clearly the points for and against, making a reasoned judgement in conclusion	Review theory or practice in depth from two or more perspectives giving clear concise reasons for your arguments	Critically review theory or practice in depth from a range of perspectives giving clear concise reasons for your arguments
Analyse	Provide clear details about a topic using one theory to illustrate your answer	Examine a topic in detail to explore the meaning, essential features and significance. This often requires providing more than one perspective or theory	Fully analyse a topic to explore the meaning, essential features and significance, giving reasons and references to support your conclusion. This will require describing more than one perspective or theory	Critically analyse a topic to explore the meaning, essential features and significance. This will require examining more than one perspective or theory in order to support your line of reasoning

Figure 1.4 The degree of information and understanding required at different levels of study (CACHE, Finding the Level, 2nd edition, 2006).

Conclusion

The advice given here on academic writing relates mainly to individual written assignments such as essays. You may find that assessment takes place through a range of different requirements such as individual and group presentations; case studies; reflective accounts; online discussions, blogs and wikis; poster presentations and film-making and other creative approaches to testing your knowledge. However, most of these still require you to be able to write academically and to use theory and referencing appropriately to support your discussion.

Finally, enjoy your studies! This is the main aim of your chosen course. Enjoy both your time as a student and your studies, reflect upon your practice, discover new knowledge and develop new understandings and skills within the Early Years field and gain some new friends.

References

Abbott, L. and Moylett, H. (1997), *Working with the Under Threes: Training and Professional Development.* Maidenhead: Open University Press

Abbott, L. and Pugh, G. (1998), *Training to Work in the Early Years: Developing the Climbing Frame.* Maidenhead: Open University Press

Anning, A. and Edwards, A. (2003), *Promoting Children's Learning from Birth to Five: Developing the New Early Years Professional.* Maidenhead: Open University Press

Cockburn, A. (2001), *Teaching Children 3–11: A Student's Guide.* London: Paul Chapman

Drake, P., Jackiln, A., Robinson, C. and Thorp, J. (2004), *Becoming a Teaching Assistant.* London: Paul Chapman

Dryden L., Forbes R., Mukherji P., Joshi U. (2005), *Essential Early Years.* Oxford: Hodder Education

Hilton, M. (1994), *Interpersonal Interaction.* London: Longman

Kay, J. (2002), *Teaching Assistant's Handbook.* London: Continuum

Kolb, D. (1984), *Experiential Learning: Experience As The Source Of Learning And Development.* New Jersey: Prentice-Hall Inc.

Traditions and trends in Early Years education and care
Iain MacLeod-Brudenell

This chapter is designed to encourage you to extend your knowledge of the work of some of those who have made significant contributions to the study of young children. Considering key ideas and following them through from their original conception to the present day will enable you to gain insights into current practice. This chapter also introduces the notion of combining care with education in working with young children. Although this approach has gained favour in the development of national frameworks to support early learning, and is now the central platform for provision for very young children, its origins were fundamental to the philosophical approach of many pioneers in the study of early childhood.

There is a strong tradition of combining early learning and care in an holistic approach to working with young children. 'Education' may not be the most appropriate term to apply to younger children in the home and pre-school as the word has associations for many people with more formal, planned approaches to learning.

This chapter does not attempt to look at each and every person who has influenced Early Years practice. Instead, it begins by focusing on a few aspects of the work of some leading theorists in early childhood studies – in particular Froebel, Montessori and Steiner. Emphasis is then given to the theories and work of two key practitioners – Robert Owen and Margaret McMillan; the focus on these two people is not because they are the most important theorists but rather because they are examples of practitioners who use an approach that draws on the combined provision of care and early learning.

This chapter addresses the following areas:

➤ Why we should be aware of historical traditions in care and education
➤ Major theorists and their influence
➤ Friedrich Wilhelm Froebel
➤ Maria Montessori
➤ Rudolf Steiner
➤ The traditions today
➤ The influences of Jean-Jacques Rousseau
➤ Traditions becoming trends
➤ The work of Robert Owen
➤ The work of Margaret McMillan

By undertaking the suggested study within this chapter it is hoped that you will be able to:

1 recognise the origins of some of the philosophical foundations of current methods and practices in Early Years education and care

2 identify the influence of key figures in the history of early childhood philosophy on present-day practice in Early Years education and care

3 make informed reflections upon recent issues in Early Years education and care provision.

Why we should be aware of historical traditions in care and education

Degree courses in the study of early childhood may vary in the focus they place upon the study of early learning, education and care. A common feature, however, is the emphasis placed upon a combined holistic approach to children's care and educational needs. All courses in early childhood studies seek to encourage students to explain and evaluate theoretical issues in the field of early childhood studies and to apply their critical understanding of such issues in appropriate practice settings.

Thus, there are two key strands in studying for a degree in early childhood studies: theory and practice. In order to better understand early childhood education and care theory we believe that students should be encouraged to reflect upon practice as well as engage in practice: to think as well as 'do'. This chapter presents ideas that were promoted by key thinkers in the study of early childhood which have shaped the provision of Early Years education and care today, and are present in many of the issues that appear in current legislation and practice.

Within recent years increased emphasis has been placed on an integrated approach to supporting young children's development, early learning and the care of young children. This model is promoted by recent legislation in England (Department for Children, Schools and Families) and Sure Start programmes and is central to the implementation of the Childcare Act 2006. The Scottish Government (Learning and Teaching Scotland), the Welsh Assembly (Learning Wales), the Department for Education and the Northern Childcare Partnership in Northern Ireland, and the Republic of Ireland (Department of Education and Science, Office of the Minister for Children) are all providing or developing similar approaches to integrated care and education.

The Scottish curriculum is currently reviewing guidance for those supporting children from birth to three – Early Years workers, social care and health practitioners and students preparing to work in Early Years settings – so that they may interpret and adapt the guidance as a framework for their own practice. The Republic of Ireland is also planning along similar lines. In 2004, the National Council for Curriculum and Assessment (NCCA) consultative document *Towards a Framework for Early Learning* was published. Since then, the NCCA has been developing a national framework to support all children's learning from birth to six years. Similar developments are taking place in Northern Ireland and Wales.

Curriculum guidance or statutory requirements will affect methods of working and these are usually well established. For some, the approach to early learning and care may also be offered using a particular approach such as High/Scope, or it may follow a particular philosophy such as is found in Steiner or Montessori nurseries and schools. In our expectations of children there may be close links to their performance in achieving the tasks outlined in such curricula.

We may also take for granted such ideas as 'parents as partners' and 'child-centred approaches'. Familiarity with such terms, or frequency of use, sometimes blurs the power of such statements. But where do these ideas originate? In your previous studies you may have looked at some of the main sources of Early Years curriculum and care theory; you may also be aware of such thinkers as Piaget and Vygotsky, of practitioners such as the McMillan sisters and Steiner. It may not be clear to you where the linkage between the theories expounded by these thinkers and present-day practice lies. This chapter aims to demonstrate some of these links.

Major theorists and their influence

Many seminal thinkers have influenced contemporary early childhood education and care. We regard these thinkers as important today, but they may have been seen very differently in their own time. For some of their contemporaries, these theorists appeared to reflect the values of a few people, but with hindsight we can see that they all functioned within the context of the values of the time. Their influence has not only been long lasting but has also influenced Early Years curricula throughout the world.

A starting point for any recent study of traditions in early education must be to acknowledge the work of Bruce (1987) in her comparison of the work of three leaders in the field of early childhood studies: Froebel, Montessori and Steiner. (Bruce further develops her discussion by comparing their work with that of more recent thinkers: Piaget, Vygotsky, Bruner and Mia Kelmer Pringle.)

Brief details of the work of Froebel, Montessori and Steiner are provided in this section. To discuss all aspects of the work of each theorist would detract from the key message that you should take from this discussion and, therefore, the aim is to illustrate some of the key aspects of their work only to enable you to compare and contrast ideas. You should refer to websites listed at the end of this chapter for more detailed information.

Friedrich Wilhelm Froebel (1782–1852)

Froebel developed the concept of focused early learning experiences, based on the idea of 'natural unfolding'. Through close observation of children, adults – both parents and teachers – could determine the child's readiness to learn and thus provide appropriate activities. The role of the mother in recognising the capacity for learning in their children and for nurturing this learning was an important underpinning feature of Froebel's vision. The role of the teacher was as a guide and support in developing children's inherent capacity for learning.

Froebel formulated the idea of the kindergarten as a means of educating young children. The term *Kindergarten* ('children's garden') reflects the metaphors he used to describe and explain his educational theory. In Froebel's view of early childhood, a child was likened to a seed, the process of learning 'unfolding' to the flower emerging from a bud and the educator likened to a gardener nurturing the plant.

To Froebel, both the child's own nature and the more universal aspect of nature were in close harmony. To enable the child to develop his/her inherent capacity for learning, the supportive adult had to be trained in this particular method. Froebel's curriculum was carefully planned. Children

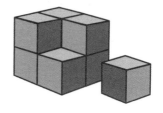

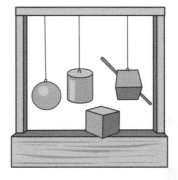

Froebel's gifts are intended to develop complex skills of perception, manipulation and combination

were encouraged to learn through playful activity and songs.

Froebel's 'gifts' were an essential aspect of his structure for learning. Gifts included balls of different colour and size, cubes, cylinders and spheres. The kindergarten teacher supported the child in using these objects, handling and considering them in order to acquire an understanding of shape, size and colour, and of concepts such as contrasting, counting and measuring. Occupations comprised materials for developing psychomotor skills: for example, cutting, folding, modelling, stringing beads and sewing.

Key points of Froebel's approach

Froebel's approach emphasised the following:

➤ that children are able to develop their unique capacity for learning 'unfolding' through play. Active learning is essential, as is the use of concrete manipulative materials in the learning process

➤ the importance of mothers in the education of young children

➤ that children learn through carefully structured play, matched to their readiness, with guidance, appropriate direction and an organised and prepared learning environment

➤ the importance of training for early childhood (kindergarten) teachers. The first kindergarten was established in England in 1851 and the first specific training establishment – the Froebel Training College – was opened in 1876.

Influence of Froebel's work on current practice

These points are as contentious today as they were in the early 19th century. The emphasis on active learning is well established within Early Years settings, but there is also emphasis upon meeting targets within current guidance from central government. It may be argued that targets are indicative of 'normal' expectations of children's development; however, there appears to be widespread misunderstanding and misinterpretation of the guidance in practice. Worksheets are regularly used in some pre-school settings, and yet there is no requirement or expectation for their use; it is a misunderstanding of the curriculum guidance. Supportive materials provided in the Curriculum Guidance for the Foundation Stage (QCA, 2000) emphasised the need to be aware of the differences in individual developmental rates, and yet in practice play appears to be subservient to the taught curriculum. Documents will, some may say, encourage a play-based curriculum. Evidence provided by interpretation of the inspection of Early Years settings would indicate that play-based learning is not a priority.

The role of mothers

The role of mothers in child rearing continues to be an issue for debate. Froebel believed that mothers should be encouraged to devote their time to caring for and educating their children.

In today's society, in the United Kingdom, it may be argued that there is subtle pressure from government and the media to encourage mothers of young children to work rather than to remain at home. Sure Start Children's Centres, for example, have had some success at engaging mothers in particular rather than fathers and so it is an emerging priority to concentrate on engaging fathers. Teaching and nurturing children in the home appears to be regarded as less effective or desirable than education in more formal, out-of-home settings.

It is an emerging priority to concentrate on engaging fathers

Training of practitioners for work in Early Years settings

Froebel believed that the training of workers for Early Years settings was essential. Children are now being admitted to out-of-home settings at a progressively earlier age than was formerly the case. The training of practitioners in Early Years education and care is, therefore, an area that has received some considerable attention in recent years. In effect, current practice is now trying to catch up with ideas that Froebel proposed many years ago. The requirement for courses leading to a wide range of specific childcare qualifications, at a variety of levels of academic and practice-based competence, particularly in the emerging role of Early Years professional, is crucial. Basic skills have been met in knowledge and understanding of childcare through, for example, the NVQ qualifications route. More rigorous study on BA Early Childhood Studies programmes has ensured that potentially a highly qualified workforce is available to work with young children. However, until recently there has been no significant change in the range of qualifications and training to fully match qualifications to the needs of children and parents and so has some way to go to meet Froebel's vision.

Current developments through new childcare and education programmes, such as the emergent Foundation Degrees, enhance practitioner confidence and skills through a mixture of academic and work-related study. These may prove to be an effective short-term solution to meeting government targets by supplying greater numbers of more highly qualified staff for Early Years settings than is presently available. The full implementation of the Childcare Act (2006) may significantly change the impetus for change around the focus of training for Early Years workers. The initial training of teachers in Early Years settings remains largely focused on meeting government agendas or political imperatives (and is controlled by inspection) rather than focusing on those areas of child development that are prominent in the curricula of similar training schemes in other parts of the world. The syllabus of Froebel's Training College has been largely superseded in English teacher education by emphasis on a much narrower curriculum, despite valiant efforts by a number of universities and colleges.

Activity 1

Varying practices in training practitioners for Early Years settings

Extend your awareness of different practice in the training of Early Years staff. Talk to colleagues about the content of their training course, for example:

➤ nursery nurses

➤ classroom teaching assistants

➤ play workers

➤ social workers working with young children

➤ teachers.

If you wish, you may combine this activity with some practice in using research methods (see Chapter 16), either now or at a later date.

Research activity

Devise a questionnaire or a schedule for informal interviews

Your questions may focus on issues such as:

➤ similarities in the content of the courses, the curriculum

➤ comparability between the length of the different courses and future roles and responsibilities

➤ the monitoring of work practice or placement

➤ assessment of practice-based study

➤ the proportion of time allocated to child development as part of training.

Devise a questionnaire, or a schedule, for informal interviews. Your questions may focus on issues such as:
- similarities in the content of the courses, the curriculum
- comparability between the length of the different courses and future roles and responsibilities
- the monitoring of work practice or placement
- assessment of practice-based study
- the proportion of time allocated to child development as part of training.

Comment on research activity

If you undertake this research, either informally through conversation with colleagues, or through a more focused interview or questionnaire, it will illustrate current variation in aspects of Early Years training. This research should provide some very interesting comparisons between training in different locations. The period in which training was undertaken will also reveal different emphases in curriculum content.

Maria Montessori (1870–1952)

Montessori's method drew on the ideas of Rousseau and Pestalozzi and the practical approaches to teaching devised by Froebel. Emphasis was placed on the child experiencing carefully organised preparatory activities, rather than repetition, as a means of developing competence in skills.

First the education of the senses, then the education of the intellect. The essential thing is for the task to arouse such an interest that it engages the child's whole personality.

Montessori (1967:206)

Montessori's first involvement with young children was as a medical practitioner and not as an educationalist. In fact, she was the first woman in Italy to qualify as a physician. Her work with those children who were regarded as difficult to educate, including those whom we would now classify as having special needs, prompted her initial interest in educational methodology.

Montessori method of training teachers

Montessori's method of teaching has been successful in a wide range of contexts. This is in part due to the emphasis placed on the training of teachers in the Montessori method. There is a particular emphasis on the need for good observational skills, in order to inform planning and support and guide children's learning. Montessori intended teacher intervention to be appropriately applied – children guided rather than over-directed. This approach has led to 'de-centring' of the teacher's role. Montessori settings strive to present a stimulating environment. They would also claim that they encourage children to participate more fully in taking responsibility for their own learning. (Such claims would also be made by those following a more mainstream curriculum and other methodological approaches such as High/Scope.) Montessori was one of the first to stress the importance of these aspects of early learning.

Rudolf Steiner (1861–1925)

A third key person, who is very influential on present-day practice in many countries, is Rudolf Steiner. As well as having influenced approaches used within 'mainstream' nursery and Early Years education curricula, Steiner educational theory is used in its complete form in Steiner Waldorf schools in over 40 countries. There are currently more than 800 schools, and, although each school is independently managed, they all conform to Steiner's principles. Often, these private schools provide an alternative to the national prescribed curricula present in mainstream education, within different cultural and social contexts.

Spiritual dimension to Steiner's approach

Steiner education, or Waldorf/Steiner education as it is often known, has its origins in a vision of education as a means of changing society. In this respect, there are many similarities between Steiner's intentions and those of Owen (see page 28) and McMillan (see page 31). Steiner differs markedly from the other two educational and social reformers in that the spiritual dimension was the key to his entire approach to life. His philosophy has at its core a view that the person is a threefold being of spirit, soul and body. These three aspects unfold in three developmental stages on the path to adulthood: early childhood, middle childhood and adolescence. In many ways, there are clear links to the perceptions of stages of childhood and adolescence that are reflected in the organisation of stages of teaching the curriculum: in England in the Key Stages, in nursery, first, middle and upper schools, or in nursery, primary and secondary schools. This staged approach has been reflected in curricula throughout the world and at different times.

The origins of Waldorf/Steiner schools have links with industry and philanthropy. In the period following the First World War, Europe was suffering from political instability, economic uncertainty and great social problems. In 1919, Rudolf Steiner was asked by Emil Molt, the owner of the Waldorf Astoria cigarette factory in Austria, to open a school for the children of his employees. This type of philanthropy was not uncommon: schools linked with factories, the most notable of which was Owen's ground-breaking venture at New Lanark in Scotland, were well established. The link with workplace nurseries today is obvious.

Conditions set by Steiner

Steiner's Waldorf School, *Die Freie Waldorfschule*, was free in more than name. The four conditions set by Steiner were:

➤ that the school be open to all children

➤ that it be co-educational

➤ that it be a unified twelve-year school

➤ that the teachers, those individuals actually in contact with the children, have primary control of the school, with minimum interference from the state or from economic sources.

These preconditions indicated a philosophical approach to teaching and learning that was very different from those employed in Austria at that time.

The Waldorf/Steiner curriculum aimed then, and continues, to develop an approach to learning which draws fully on three dimensions: the body, the mind and the spirit. Although much of the language used in Steiner's approach may appear to be exclusive and rooted in theological dogma, in essence there are many aspects of his theory which most early educators would strive to attain a balance between: sound skills in literacy, languages and numeracy, and confidence in aesthetic awareness and practice (in music, art, craft and physical development).

Steiner's approach to the education and care of young children has a strong emphasis on the spiritual dimension. There is an attempt in the Waldorf/Steiner method to 'unfold', to develop the full potential of every child. Childhood is seen as a stage but within a much broader perspective than in other theoretical approaches. Steiner's philosophy, **Anthroposophy**, acknowledges existence before birth and after death.

Stages of Waldorf/Steiner education match children's developmental stages with a broad and child-focused curriculum. 'Rhythm' and 'balance' are frequently used terms in the curriculum. This is manifest in the respect given to seasons and times of the year, as well as times of life. The balance of skills and knowledge is fostered by equal emphasis on artistic, practical and intellectual work throughout the school curriculum. At the heart of this approach is the child and a recognition that, in order to promote the inner development of the child, it is necessary to provide appropriate experiences for each determined stage of development.

Values feature prominently in Waldorf/ Steiner education: social awareness is fostered, and empathy and sensitivity to others are promoted. Individual aptitudes and needs are nurtured by the sustained, ongoing and supportive relationship between a child and his or her teacher.

Steiner's approach to training teachers is very well supported with a rigorous training programme in theoretical and practice-based child-centred education. There are 50 teacher training centres around the world. In Waldorf/

Steiner teacher training, one course offers two years of college-based work, followed by one year in placement. A range of pre-service and in-service courses ensures that teaching methods are consistent and conform to the Waldorf/Steiner model.

Key points of Steiner's approach

Steiner's approach emphasised the following.

➤ A broad curriculum is offered. There is a balance of aesthetic, social, emotional, spiritual and cognitive development within the taught curriculum.

➤ The curriculum responds to developmental stages.

For a recent report on Steiner schools in England see Woods, P., Ashley, M. and Woods, G. (2005).

Activity 2

Research the contributions made by Froebel, Steiner and Montessori

1 Undertake a web search to find out more about Froebel, Steiner and Montessori.

2 Look at some of the websites of Montessori and Waldorf/Steiner schools.

3 Based on the very brief summaries offered here and your web-based research, what do you consider to be the most important contribution of each of these thinkers to current practice in your workplace?

The traditions today

Although Bruce's discussion (1987) is limited in range to only three 'leading theorists', these people are probably the most important in terms of influencing current educational thought and practice. Bruce has provided a valuable and influential framework.

The Early Years Curriculum Group (EYCG, 1992), who adapted Bruce's principles (Fisher, 1996:32), have in turn been very influential in curriculum development, the effects of which can be seen in the documentation for the Early Years Foundation Stage (available to view on many websites, such as TeacherNet). The child-centred approaches to early childhood education and care outlined by Rousseau and Pestalozzi can be seen clearly in the theories of other early childhood educators such as Robert Owen as well as later figures such as Margaret McMillan and Susan Isaacs. It is well to recognise their contributions, while not diminishing the roles of those whom Bruce has chosen to discuss.

The Ten Common Principles

The Ten Common Principles of early childhood education (Bruce, 1987:10) are based on the philosophical approaches of the three figures that Bruce considers to be the most important influential pioneers in this field: Froebel, Montessori and Steiner (see Figure 2.1).

Childhood is a part of life, not simply a preparation for the future.

The whole child is considered to be important.

Learning is not compartmentalised, for everything links.

Intrinsic motivation, resulting in child-initiated, self-directed study, is valued.

Self-discipline is emphasised.

There are specially receptive periods for learning at different stages of development.

What children can do (rather than what they cannot do) is the starting point in the child's education.

There is an inner life in the child which emerges especially under favourable conditions.

The people (both adults and children) with whom the child interacts are of central importance.

The child's education is seen as an interaction between the child and the environment the child is in including, in particular, other people and knowledge itself.

(Bruce, 1987:10)

Figure 2.1 Principles of early childhood education

The influences of Jean–Jacques Rousseau
(1712–1778)

In your reading you will begin to identify how thinkers influence each other and how their ideas are modified to meet the needs of children in different social, historical and geographical contexts. One of the earliest and most influential thinkers was Jean-Jacques Rousseau, a man of many talents: a philosopher with an interest in social and political ideas, a musician, a botanist and, above all, an influential writer. In the sphere of early childhood study, his novel *Émile* (1762) introduced a new theory of education. This approach emphasised the nurturing of the child to encourage free expression rather than repression, a common response to children in his time.

Rousseau's theory of education can be viewed on numerous websites (information is provided at the end of this chapter). His psychologically orientated method of education led to new methods of education and care and his influence can be seen in the theories and practice of Johann Heinrich Pestalozzi, Robert Owen and Friedrich Froebel. Their influence continues to be felt in the present day through figures such as the McMillan sisters, Susan Isaacs, John Dewey and other pioneers of modern early childhood education and care. Rousseau was probably the first widely read writer to identify the link between emotional/physical care and education in the context of effective learning.

Traditions becoming trends

There are two main responses to early childhood education and both are recorded in Roman times. One view, recorded by Plato in *The Republic*, sees early childhood as a special stage in life and recommends that adults take particular care when educating the young, as 'in all things the beginning is the most important part'.

The second view, which sees children being in need of training by submission of the will, is recorded by Seneca. This approach to education viewed the child as 'an empty vessel' to be filled with knowledge. The teacher instructed and the child would learn. If learning was not successful the problem lay with the child rather than the teacher.

These two traditions have run parallel through history and can be discerned in present-day practice, particularly in later primary education. Generally, most educators regard the earliest years of education as different from the later years in that practice is more child-focused in the earliest years. It may be argued that the drive to a narrower skills-based curriculum may eventually displace a child-focused one.

Child-centred learning

Johann Pestalozzi (1746–1827) advocated teaching through kindness and he was the first to apply Rousseau's ideas of child-centred learning approaches in practice. A child-centred curriculum was also fundamental to the teaching method of Robert Owen. (See page 28 for a discussion of Owen's work.)

In Owen's time it was not unusual for children to be exploited and maltreated; they were employed in mills and other industrial settings where mortality rates were high. The living conditions of the working poor were also appalling. The kindness with which the teachers at Owen's school at his factory complex at New Lanark treated the children was, therefore, in marked contrast to the usual life experiences of young children in the early 19th century. Another remarkable aspect of the teaching method at New Lanark was that children were not physically punished but were managed in their behaviour through kindness – a very unusual procedure in the 19th century.

Early Years education and 'crime'

The converse of this attitude is demonstrated by Samuel Wilderspin, who was active in the 1840s. He advocated infant schools chiefly as a means of combating child 'crime' (Cusden, 1938:3).

This approach is not far removed from some more recent responses to socio-educational issues. The National Commission on Education report *Learning to Succeed* (1993) emphasised the importance of nursery education and the dangers of admitting children to formal schooling at too early an age. The report urged expansion of nursery education, with provision in priority areas being seen as the most urgent need. The argument proposed within the document, however, was that the cost of such expansion would be offset by reduction in the costs of remedial action in adolescence and by reduced social costs, which arise from youth unemployment and juvenile crime (National Commission on Education, 1993:137).

Divergence of opinion

One of the main reasons why there is such divergence in opinion on the methods of caring for and educating young children is the recognition that young children up to the age of 8 are impressionable and can be moulded to conform to particular social patterns.

McMillan considered that the natural end of early childhood was reached at the age of 7, which corresponds with the traditional end of infant education in England and Scotland. At this age, too, many other countries begin their formal education of children.

The claim by the Jesuits that the period from birth to 7 is of crucial importance to a child's education is well known. It has a basis in fact, as the rates of development and learning are at their most rapid during this stage of childhood. It may be argued, therefore, that the young child needs to be encouraged and stimulated through the provision of a wide range of experiences.

Developmentally appropriate curriculum

Much has been written about the **developmentally appropriate curriculum**. Blenkin (1994) indicates the extent to which international research studies in early learning and early childhood education have been remarkable for the consistency of their recommendations and findings. This is demonstrated in, for example, the New Zealand ECCE Working Group, the work of the Canadian Ministry of Education in their Early Years papers and in policies and practices emerging in European countries (Mills and Mills, 1998). This research has helped to clarify what a developmentally appropriate curriculum for young children would look like and to identify the demands that such a curriculum would make on practitioners in Early Years settings, thereby clarifying their training needs (Blenkin, 1994).

There is very little current training at higher level for those working with very young children. The needs of those working with babies and toddlers are not well served by publications that often focus on the Early Years of childhood from 3 years and upwards. Until recently, little attention was paid to the age range from 3 to 5 years, where a developmentally appropriate curriculum may be seen as having the greatest potential impact. As Bruce's published works drew on the work of key early childhood thinkers and presented them for the 1980s, Hurst and Joseph (1998) have interpreted these theories for the turn of the 21st century. These Principles for a Developmental Curriculum are now widely recognised as an appropriate theoretical underpinning for early childhood curriculum programme development (see Figure 2.2).

For articulate and compelling arguments, see Hurst and Joseph (1998), Blenkin and Kelly (1994), and Siraj-Blatchford (1997:17) for some cautionary comments. It can be seen that there are strong similarities between these principles and those outlined by Bruce (1997: see Figure 2.1).

Guidance on supporting early childhood development

There are many different visions of what is required of the adult in supporting early childhood development and yet there are also some common themes. The curriculum guidance documentation of Scotland, Ireland, Northern Ireland, Wales and England all draw on the themes indicated within Figures 2.1 and 2.2. However, the interpretation of such guidance by managers of childcare and teachers may result in very different experiences for children.

The curriculum method devised by Owen in 1816 indicates that he was conscious of the need to devise a programme that was appropriate to the needs he perceived young children to have. This appeared to work. But given enthusiastic practitioners, it may be argued that even more formal approaches to education may also work. Perhaps the key to success is the respect for children by those who care for and educate them.

The youngest, or infant class, under the age of five, … (were under the) charge of a male and female superintendent, and whose principal office it is to encourage amongst them habits and feelings of good-will and affection towards each other.

Our party walked down to the village, and entered the children's play ground. God bless their little faces, I see them now. There were some bowling hoops, some drumming on two sticks – all engaged in some infantine amusement or other. Not a tear – not a wrangle. Peaceful innocence pervaded the whole group. As soon as they saw us, curtsies and bows saluted us from all quarters.

(from a report by the Duke of Kent's personal physician in McNab (1819), quoted in Siraj-Blatchford (1997))

Anyone familiar with young children in nursery settings will recognise the responses of these children. A new face in the nursery is soon accosted and questioned; we may no longer have curtsies and bows, but the personal response is the same.

> ➤ Each child is an individual and should be respected as such.

> ➤ The Early Years are a period of development in their own right, and education of young children should be seen as a specialism with its own valid criteria of appropriate practice.

> ➤ The role of the educator of young children is to engage actively with what most concerns the child, and to support learning through these preoccupations.

> ➤ The educator has a responsibility to foster positive attitudes in children to both self and others, and to counter negative messages which children may have received.

> ➤ Each child's cultural and linguistic endowment is seen as the fundamental medium of learning.

> ➤ An anti-discriminatory approach is the basis of all respect-worthy education, and is essential as a criterion for a developmentally appropriate curriculum (DAC).

> ➤ All children should be offered equal opportunities to progress and develop, and should have equal access to good-quality provision. The concepts of multiculturalism and anti-racism are intrinsic to this whole educational approach.

> ➤ Partnership with parents should be given priority as the most effective means of ensuring coherence and continuity in children's experiences, and in the curriculum offered to them.

> ➤ A democratic perspective permeates education of good quality and is the basis of transactions between people.

(Hurst and Joseph, 1998:xi)

Figure 2.2 Principles for a Developmental Curriculum

The theorists discussed in this chapter did not have a unified approach to every aspect of early childhood education and care; often their vision and their priorities differed markedly from one another. Four key aspects, however, are present in the educational ideology of every one of these thinkers. These are illustrated in Figure 2.3.

Key aspects that are common to the theoretical approaches to the care of young children are shown in Figure 2.4.

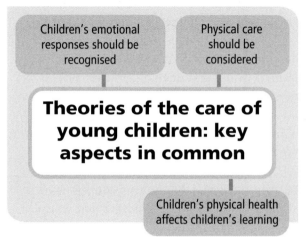

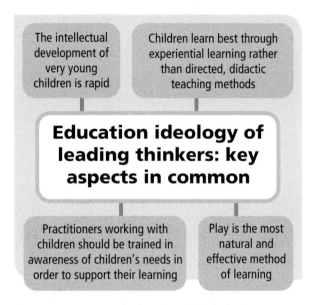

Figure 2.3 Aspects of educational ideology that are common to leading thinkers

Figure 2.4 Aspects that are common to theoretical approaches to the care of young children

To illustrate the link between the aspects of education and care illustrated in Figures 2.3 and 2.4, the work of two important pioneers in the field of 'Early Years education and care', Robert Owen and Margaret McMillan, is briefly examined.

The work of Robert Owen (1771–1858)

Owen lived in times of great change. This was a period of rapid industrial development, with the exploitation of the workforce of women and young children as well as men. It was a time of great social and political unrest in Britain and revolution in Europe. His motives for developing an interest in early childhood education reflect his political values. A free thinker in an age when religious practice was the norm, Owen was a philanthropist and a political theorist who was not driven by religious imperatives. He was self-educated, a draper's assistant who had become a successful and very wealthy businessman as an owner of cotton mills.

In 1816, Robert Owen established the first school for infants in Britain, at New Lanark in Scotland, a fact that is often overlooked. The age range of the children is also of interest: 1 to 10 years. The novelty of his approach was attractive to those who were interested in industrial productivity as well as education. He claimed that the substantial profits generated by his cotton mills were due to the type of education he provided for the children of his workers. The school had visitors from across the world, many of whom commented on the happiness of the children.

It was unusual at this time for employers to be concerned about the welfare of their employees. Owen's motives for establishing a school were to promote social improvement. He was appalled by the conditions of working people and particularly of children. He is credited as one of the founders of the co-operative and socialist movements in Britain.

Educational environment is key

In your previous studies you will doubtless have encountered the nature/nurture debate – that is, the extent to which children are influenced by genetic inheritance or by the environment. Robert Owen firmly believed that the educational environment was a main contributing factor in shaping the ways in which children responded to educative experiences, social behaviour and value systems. Owen was scathing about any influence that heredity might have on a child's development.

He believed that by the use of good role models and appropriate educative and social experiences, children's individual characters could be shaped at a very early age. To this end, he employed male and female teachers who were required to have 'a great love for and unlimited patience with infants'.

A stimulating curriculum

Owen's emphasis was on a stimulating curriculum that offered freedom for the child from the pressures commonly associated with childhood at that time. Singing and dancing featured within the curriculum and he employed a small group of musicians to play to the children from a musicians' gallery. Music has always been a strand of child-centred curricula.

Activity 3

The role of music in children's development

Consider the role of music in your workplace setting. What is its purpose? How does it help children's cognitive, social and emotional development?

Owen's curriculum did not include craft, now more commonly referred to as design technology. We may think this highly unusual, given young children's propensity for creativity, but Owen considered that there would be time enough for such activity in later employment!

Where Owen's approach differs from the current Foundation Stage curriculum (QCA, 2000) is in the pace at which the curriculum is experienced as well as the content.

The children were not to be annoyed with books, but were to be taught the uses or nature of common things around them by familiar conversation when the children's curiosity was excited so as to induce them to ask questions.

Owen, quoted in Silver (1969: 65)

Blenkin (1994:29) indicates a remarkably similar approach to Owen.

Rates of development and learning are at their most rapid during this stage of education, and they are highly susceptible to environmental constraints or advantages. The young child, therefore, needs to be stimulated by a wide range of experiences rather than confined to a narrow and restrictive program.

The following extract is from a report written by the Duke of Kent's personal physician following a visit to Owen's school at New Lanark.

The youngest, or infant class, under the age of five, are of course occupied only in the amusements which are suitable to their age, playing about in the area before the school, when the weather admits it, under the charge of a male and female superintendent, and whose principal office it is to encourage amongst them habits and feelings of good-will and affection towards each other.

(McNab, 1819)

There are many aspects of Owen's curriculum that will be familiar to those who have worked in settings where children have choice over the pace and areas of their learning; where there is an emphasis on outdoor as well as indoor activity; and where there is an emphasis on the development of social skills and support for individual needs.

Social development as an essential element of child-centred models

Social development has been regarded as an essential element of many child-centred curriculum models, as it is now in many of the curricula, most notably that of New Zealand. Owen advocated this and there is some evidence to support the success of his methods, as in the following extract from a report produced by Leeds Poor Law Guardians of 1819.

In the education of the children the thing that is most remarkable is the general spirit of kindness and affection which is shown towards them, and the entire absence of everything that is likely to give them bad habits, with the presence of whatever is calculated to inspire them with good ones; the consequence is, that they appear like one well regulated family, united together by the ties of the closest affection. We heard no quarrels from the youngest to the eldest; and so strongly impressed are they with the conviction that their

interest and duty are the same, and that to be happy themselves it is necessary to make those happy by whom they are surrounded, that they had no strife but in offices of kindness.

Podmore (1923:148)

Owen's vision: a lasting contribution

Many of Owen's social experiments were short-lived, but as Silver (1969) indicates, his vision of education inspired generations of activists. Owen was undoubtedly a man ahead of his time, and his principles could not be sustained at a time of rapid industrialisation when many cared little for the welfare of workers. Owen is reported to have said the following on his death bed.

My life was not useless; I gave important truths to the world. And it was only for want of understanding that they were disregarded. I have been ahead of my time.

(quoted in Siraj-Blatchford (1997:62)

Owen was undoubtedly a difficult and, at times, pompous man; his responses to issues were sometimes autocratic and paternalistic. Although his approach was soon eclipsed by other more formal and didactic approaches to early childhood education and care, his vision did not vanish. Nursery and infant education was established as a sociological need. The informal approach to early childhood education initiated at New Lanark emphasised early childhood and nursery education as a distinct phase. This obviously has parallels with the thinking of Froebel, Montessori and Steiner. Owen put this into action in Great Britain. The development of the Foundation Stage, drawing the reception year of infant education once more into an early childhood framework with nursery education and care, may be seen as a tribute to Owen's life work.

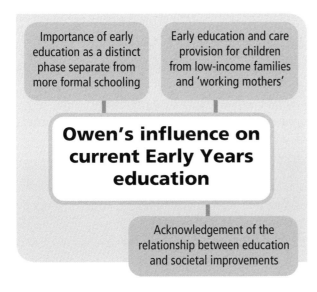

Importance of early education as a distinct phase separate from more formal schooling	Early education and care provision for children from low-income families and 'working mothers'

Owen's influence on current Early Years education

Acknowledgement of the relationship between education and societal improvements

Figure 2.5 Current practice in early education and care: Owen's influence

Activity 4

Owen's work in the social context

Undertake a web-based search to find out more about Owen's work in the social context. Based on the findings of your research and your own practice in the workplace, answer the following questions:

1 Owen recognised the link between children's social welfare and early learning. Is this still important today?

2 Which aspect of Owen's work do you find most attractive or interesting?

The work of Margaret McMillan (1860–1931)

Margaret McMillan, like Robert Owen, was distressed by the living conditions of the poor. Although they lived at different times, both saw education and social care as being the answer to a changed order in society. Neither was 'typical' of his or her time and social group; both could be regarded as 'outsiders'.

Margaret McMillan, who was influenced by Froebel's teaching, saw nursery education, health and social care as of equal importance. With her sister, Rachel, she founded the first school clinic in 1908 and the first 'open-air' nursery school in 1914. The nursery school proposed by McMillan was intended to address the physical, health and educational needs of disadvantaged children. In both the curriculum and the design of the buildings, these 'open-air' nurseries were seen as a means of offsetting the appalling conditions that many children suffered in urban industrial areas.

McMillan was a Christian Socialist at a time when social class was breaking down but society was still rife with social convention. Although McMillan was a member of the Froebel Society, the most active group in her time for those interested in early childhood, her agenda was very different from many other members of the group (Steedman, 1990). Her approach was regarded as radical and socially orientated, which contrasted with the 'safe' and socially conventional approach to change promoted by other members of the group.

The equal importance of nursery education, health and social care

Concern for children's health and well-being as well as their educational development features as a prominent strand, with different levels of emphasis, in the work of both Owen and McMillan. Social and health care for young children is now readily available and is taken for granted and yet the need for vigilance is still present, as recent media coverage indicates.

Margaret McMillan saw nursery education,

health and social care as being of equal importance. Recent trends in educational and care provision in England have taken a more unified approach to meeting the needs of young children. Sure Start initiatives have spiralled from small-scale intervention projects to major training and implementation initiatives. This unified approach so central to McMillan's approach was clearly seen in the Sure Start (2003) Framework to Support Children in their Earliest Years, as below.

Support, information, guidance and challenge for all those with responsibility for the care and education of babies and children from birth to three years.

Sure Start (2003:4)

Interestingly, the Core Offer for Sure Start Children's Centres, which should be fully implemented in every community by 2010, is expected to provide: early education integrated with daycare, family support and outreach, child and family health services and advice and information for parents/carers (DCSF, Nov. 2006).

As a member of the Independent Labour Party, McMillan was on the School Board in Bradford, which in her time was an industrial city with extensive slums. The School Board, a precursor of the Local Education Authority, provided a platform for McMillan to promote the welfare as well as the education of poor children. Free school meals and health checks were seen as essential prerequisites of education. Children could learn effectively only once they were healthy and adequately nourished.

Open-air nursery schools

Sometimes there is a tangible link with some of these early educators. Schools visited or founded by McMillan are still in active operation. Margaret and her sister Rachel devised, developed and promoted the idea of the 'open-air nursery school'. The purpose of the school was to promote the health and well-being of the child. Those who work in

these school buildings today will not have experienced the full force of the elements as those first pupils did, as the verandas have been largely closed up! Cusden (1938) provides good graphic evidence of the layout of these schools, which were designed to provide space; the schools were 'open' in spatial terms as well as open to the air.

Children want space at all ages. But from the age of one to seven, ample space is almost as much wanted as food and air. To move, to run, to find things out by new movement, to feel one's life in every limb, that is the life of early childhood... In the open-air Nursery Schools nine hours is a reasonable nurture day. Not five out of the twenty-four but nine; and this is the minimum if the work is to be really effective.

McMillan (1930:10–11)

Concern with health was evident in the design of school buildings; for example, as can be seen from Figure 2.6, each room had its own bathroom.

Margaret McMillan drew together ideas she had shared through articles and lectures in *The Nursery School*. This book was first published in 1919 and it is important to place this in the context of its time. After the First World War social conditions were changing. There were huge numbers of young widowed women, and women had taken more responsibility for many aspects of life previously undertaken by men because of their absence during the war.

The relationship between the community and school was crucial. The London County Council Annual Report of the School Medical Officer (1930:44) indicates that the Rachel McMillan Nursery School closed for only six days during the summer period. It was noted that this strategy resulted in much healthier children at the end of the usual summer holiday period than was previously the case.

Margaret McMillan was also unconventional in her view of the size of a school. In rural areas, schools would be small and serve the local community, but in urban areas

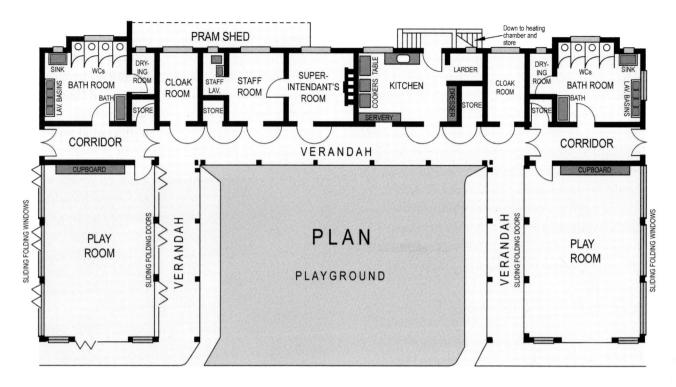

Figure 2.6 A plan of a McMillan open-air nursery school

schools could be very large; McMillan had no objection to schools catering for as many as 300 children. Classes would necessarily be small because of the age of the children, and the need for sufficient and well-trained staff was recognised. Large schools were seen as an opportunity to build links with the community. The schools proposed by McMillan would not only provide support for children's well-being, health and education, but also act as a means of helping to rejuvenate the area surrounding the school. Comments made by McMillan in her talks and in her writing indicate her commitment to social change. As a means of promulgating her approach to community enhancement, McMillan was not averse to overemphasis, what we would regard today as 'hard sell promotion and publicity', as the following quotation demonstrates.

No one passes the gate without looking in. All day there are groups near the entrance and eyes watching through the paling. They make me think always of the queues waiting to go into a theatre.
McMillan (1930:13)

Parents were encouraged to come into school, to watch their children at work and play. She encouraged parents to learn from teachers and teachers to draw on the additional knowledge parents have of their own children. Frequent parents' meetings and the use of the school as a community base were important elements in McMillan's approach to interaction between the school and the community it serves. It could be argued that we would do well to revisit some of these ideas; that rather than using parents either as information providers for assessment records, or as recipients of the records, a more meaningful interaction could be negotiated.

The curriculum

McMillan took Froebel's garden metaphors and related them to real gardening. The absence for many children of gardens from their lives (gardens were a rarity in many inner city areas) was felt to be a particularly serious shortcoming by McMillan. Gardens equated with fresh air and robust health. To this end,

McMillan proposed that schools be designed so that a veranda would run along the building and the rooms situated so that each would lead directly onto the garden. The garden would be a place to grow all manner of flowers and vegetables to stimulate the senses and provide a resource for experiential learning; it would also act as a place where gross motor skills could be developed. The absence of safe and appropriate play equipment in children's home environments would be compensated for by the provision of slides, swings and a playground constructed using many natural materials.

Like Owen, McMillan promoted the inclusion of music in the curriculum and encouraged staff to learn an instrument.

If as in one Nursery School some teachers learn the violin it will be a great joy. For very little children appear to have a love of stringed instruments. The flute is also a good instrument, and also the zither and the banjo.

McMillan (1930:19)

The love of song, rhyme and music is clearly demonstrated by most young children, particularly when gifted practitioners encourage it.

McMillan's influence on present-day practice

McMillan's approach to outdoor play can be seen as a precursor of practice in many mainstream nursery settings today. All-weather surfaces, large tyres, wooden climbing structures would no doubt be approved by McMillan. Finding a working garden is now a rarity, a missed opportunity, as children could experience all of the senses in growing, harvesting and eating produce. With a little imagination, this important aspect of science, health, technology, language, maths and physical development could be revived.

McMillan had an interesting approach to the use of outdoor areas: outside learning.

As well as the resource for areas which would now be linked to Knowledge and Understanding of the World and Physical Development, she also recommended that 'blackboards' (chalkboards) be placed on the outside, as well as the inside, walls of the school in case 'children want to draw or

McMillan's emphasis on outdoor play is continued in many modern nursery settings

scribble'. In the period before the child's fifth birthday, even in the more formal aspects of the curriculum, a naturalistic approach was taken, and reading and writing was seen as emerging from other activities in a natural and unhurried way. When the child's fifth birthday approached there was no sudden change to more formal methods but more a gradual transition. In some respects, the formation of the Foundation Stage now uses this approach.

Activity 5

Understanding McMillan's curriculum

1   Compare McMillan's curriculum with other Early Years curricula currently used in New Zealand, Scotland or other countries. Carry out your research using the internet (UNESCO is a good starting point) and professional journals such as *Nursery World*.

Consider the following questions.

2   How would you develop gardening as a means of promoting health and social development, and which areas of children's understanding and learning could be fostered?

3   How would you promote 'outside learning'?

McMillan's approach to nursery attendance is interesting in that it foreshadows some aspects of 'wraparound care'. In order that consistent and long-term provision of education and care could be provided, she insisted that the children should attend nursery full time.

A short nurture day is in great measure a waste of time and money. The great process which it exists to forward is not possible in short sessions broken by long intervals.

McMillan (1930:37)

Training of teachers

McMillan believed a three-year specialist training for those teachers intending to work with younger children (birth to age 7) was required. The link between theory and practice was promoted by the inclusion of supervised and monitored workplace practice. In McMillan's model can be seen aspects of training that have been used for many years in initial teacher education. The monitoring of practice has always been present in these courses, but the assessment of such practice has been subject to varying degrees of rigour. Teacher competencies, appropriate to different age groups, have been formulated to meet government criteria and curriculum targets.

Ideas for further research

McMillan saw nursery education as a means of addressing the terrible social ills of life in the inner city. To what extent is this view reflected in the way in which the Sure Start initiative is addressing the needs of children and families in similar locations today?

McMillan strongly promoted the belief that children should be provided with a suitable learning environment. Although aspects of the healthy lifestyle encouraged in nursery schools in McMillan's day may now have been relegated to peripheral importance, limited space for school rebuilding in inner city areas may encourage more innovative and child-friendly architecture to be considered. What efforts are being made in redesigning, modifying or 'new build' to meet current health needs in childcare and education?

McMillan proposed the view that all children should have access to a nursery with trained staff to look after them. Current trends in England require a minimum qualification for those working in settings with young children. This is currently under review. It would be useful to examine a qualification, for example an NVQ 2, and to consider, in the light of your experience in the workplace, whether the qualification provides adequate training. Justify your opinion.

In McMillan's time it was common for children attending nursery full time to have opportunity for a sleep during the day.

Conversations with students on Early Years education and care courses who are also nursery staff have indicated that many children do need opportunity for sleep and a quiet period during the day. What is your opinion? Is this based on your workplace experience?

Work-related activities: keeping a diary

The diary may be used to provide a commentary about your own personal development alongside your reading and thus support your course of study.

How you set it out will be a personal choice but it does need to be organised!

You need to be able to use it for reference – so write clearly and concisely.

Highlight the links between the ideas illustrated in this chapter and aspects of the practice within your workplace as you begin to identify them.

Illustrate your points by specific examples of experience in the form of short stories (vignettes). These may be developed as case studies at a later date (see Chapter 16, Research methods).

You may wish to focus on one aspect of practice in your setting that reflects the influence of a key figure in the history of early childhood (case study). This will help you to make informed reflections upon recent issues within educare provision.

Remember to reflect and to analyse – and to evaluate your progress.

Conclusion

Habits, in general, may be formed very early in children. An association of ideas is, as it were, the parent of habit. If, then, you can accustom your children to perceive that your will must always prevail over theirs, when they are opposed, the thing is done, and they will submit to it without difficulty or regret. To bring this about, as soon as they begin to show their inclination by desire or aversion, let single instances be chosen now and then (not too frequently) to contradict them. For example, if a child shows a desire to have any thing in his hand that he sees, or has any thing

in his hand with which he is delighted, let the parent take it from him, and when he does so, let no consideration whatever make him restore it at that time.

Witherspoon, quoted in Swann and Gammage (1993)

We have looked at what we may consider to be the positive influences of key educators and carers on current practice. Practices such as those advocated by Witherspoon, one of the key figures in the development of schools for infants in the 19th century, may be seen as reflecting the values present in Victorian England.

The priority given to values changes within a remarkably short time, as the numerous versions and variations of the National Curriculum illustrate. The fate of National Curriculum Foundation Subjects such as Physical Education, Art and Music demonstrates how a priority in the curriculum, supported by detailed and extensive guidance, may be reduced to a short indicative range of statements with alarming rapidity.

The introduction of the Foundation Stage Profile in 2003 (DfCSF 2003) and tests at the end of Key Stage 1 appeared to indicate an emphasis on rigorous formal assessment of young children. This may have been linked to the ever-changing imperatives of central government in England. Meeting self-imposed government targets may be one reason for such actions. One would hope that at the heart of these actions there is an aim to provide better life chances for children. A very different approach was presented almost ten years ago by the Royal Society of Arts report *Start Right: The Importance of Early Learning*. Christopher Ball, the author, argued for part-time nursery education for 3- and 4-year-olds, which could be part-funded by offering part-time nursery education, rather than full-time schooling, to 5-year-olds and raising the compulsory school age to 6. Nursery education was seen as providing a means of helping to prevent school failure and thereby promoting future success in life.

The report demonstrates the importance of early learning as a preparation for effective education to promote social welfare and social order, and to develop a world-class workforce.

Ball (1994:6)

Sure Start programmes have blossomed and the concept has now grown beyond its origins in compensatory support for children. However, some questions must still be posed: Is Early Years education simply compensatory? Is this connected with the emphasis placed on increasing the numbers of 3-year-old children entering educational settings in England? Are babies and children under three best served by curriculum guidance?

Such questions may appear unwarranted. Should not all children have access to 'quality' educational provision?

This chapter may have provided you with grounds for questioning and analysing current approaches to Early Years education and care in England. Academic criticism should not focus on negativity in its response to an issue. You are encouraged to reflect, to question and to analyse. Current practice in education and care reflects centrally driven policy and legislation and has an influence on many sector settings that were once independent: for example, the pre-schools (formerly play groups), the Pre-School Learning Alliance and Montessori schools. It may be argued that there is little difference between current government initiatives and other intervention strategies proposed by Owen, Steiner and McMillan, or initiatives such as those proposed by the Plowden Committee (DES, 1967).

Based upon your reading you should now be able to provide an argument to support your own views on this subject. What is early education for? What provision should be made? Social contexts have changed dramatically since 1816. Have the needs of children, the type of teaching required and the responsibility of parents in the process of education changed in the intervening time, or are there some trends that are constant? You may now have some answers to these questions.

Activity 6

Self-assessment

Select from your research one person or trend in the history of early childhood education and care.

1 Consider the era in which the person lived and worked or when the trend began.

2 What major events occurred during the lifetime of the person that may have affected his or her approaches to early childhood education and care?

3 What do you think was the most important personal influence in forming his or her approach to education and care?

4 What do you consider to be the person's/trend's major contributions to the development of young children and/or early childhood education?

5 What is the relevance of the trend/work of this person to us today?

6 What lasting aspect of this trend's/person's influence is visible in your workplace setting?

7 Which aspect of studying this chapter have you most enjoyed?

8 How has it affected your personal understanding of early childhood education and care?

9 Will it have an effect on your practice?

How to move on in your research

Developing your skills in research and reading for traditions and trends

You may find a suitable range of books available in your university or college library, but much material is also accessible on the internet.

Online indexes

Online indexes may be used to find books, journals and newspaper articles about historical aspects of Early Years education and care. The internet will also allow you to access media articles about emerging issues.

Keyword search

Use a keyword search. This will help you to locate broad areas of study.

Specific key thinkers can be found by searching, for example: Montessori.org.uk.

Use subject headings

The best method of undertaking an initial search is through the use of subject headings. For example:

> early childhood education+history
> early childhood education+philosophy
> early childhood educators+biography

Your research may then be extended by looking at specific thinkers. For example:

> pestalozzi+kindergarten
> robert owen+education
> margaret mcmillan+education

Journal articles

Journals are a good source of relatively current information about your topic. This includes professional journals such as *Nursery World* and the more academic ones, which are now available online.

References

Ball, C. (1994), *Start Right: The Importance of Early Learning*. London: Royal Society for the Encouragement of Arts, Manufacture and Commerce

Bertram, A. and Pascal, C. (2002), *Early Years Education: An International Perspective*. QCA/NFER

Blenkin, G. and Kelly, A. (eds) (1994), *The National Curriculum and Early Learning: An Evaluation*. London: Paul Chapman

Bruce, T. (1997), *Early Childhood Education*. London: Hodder and Stoughton
    An interesting book from an historical perspective to note how rapidly changes have occurred within Early Years education and care.

Cusden, P. (1938), *The English Nursery School*. London: Kegan Paul, Trench, Trubner & Co. Ltd
    This book provides an insight into the implementation of curriculum in the tradition of McMillan.

DES (1967), *Children and their Primary Schools*. London: HMSO

DfES (2002), *Early Years Sector-Endorsed Foundation Degree: Statement of Requirement*. Nottingham: DfCSF

DfES/DfWP (2003), *Birth to Three Matters*. London: Sure Start/DfCSF

Education Enquiry Committee (1929), *The Case for Nursery Schools*. London: George Phillip

EYCG (1992), *First Things First: Educating Young Children*. Oldham: Madeleine Lindley

Fisher, J. (1996), *Starting from the Child*. Maidenhead: Open University Press
    A very accessible book which provides an overview of Early Years practice and theory.

Hurst, V. and Joseph, J. (1998), *Supporting Early Learning: The Way Forward*. Buckingham: Open University Press
    Hurst and Joseph are proponents of a developmentally appropriate curriculum. This book provides the theoretical basis for a series of Early Years curriculum related books.

Kramer, R. (1978), *Maria Montessori: A Biography*. Oxford: Blackwell.

Learning and Teaching Scotland (2005), *Birth to Three: Supporting our Youngest Children*, Scottish Executive

London County Council (1930), *Report of the School Medical Officer*. London: LCC

McAvley, H. and Jackson, P. (1992), *Educating Young Children*. London: David Fulton

McMillan, M. (1930), The *Nursery School*. London: Dent

McNab, H. (1819), *The New Views of Mr Owen, Impartially Examined*. SCCC

Mills, C. and Mills, D. (1998), *Dispatches: The Early Years*. London: Channel 4 Television

Montessori, M. (1916), *The Montessori Method* (1964 edn). New York: Schocken Books

Montessori, M. (1949), *The Absorbent Mind* (1967 edn). New York: Dell

Podmore, F. (1923), *Robert Owen: A Biography*. London: George Allen and Unwin

QCA (2000), *Curriculum Guidance for the Foundation Stage*. London: HMSO

QCA (2003), *Foundation Stage Profile.* London: HMSO

Roberts, R. (1995), *A Nursery Education Curriculum for the Early Years.* Oxford: National Primary Centre

Silver, H. (1969), *Robert Owen on Education.* Cambridge: Cambridge University Press

Siraj-Blatchford, J. (1997), *Robert Owen: Schooling the Innocents.* Nottingham: Educational Heretics Press

Steedman, C. (1990), *Childhood, Culture and Class in Britain: Margaret McMillan 1860–1931.* London: Virago

Swann, R. and Gammage, P. (1993), 'Early Childhood Education – Where are we now?', in **Gammage, P. and Meighan, J. (1993)**, *Early Childhood Education: Taking Stock.* Nottingham: Education Now Publishing Co-operative

Wells, G. (1987), *The Meaning Makers: Children Learning Language and Using Language to Learn.* London: Hodder Arnold

Woods, P., Ashley, M. and Woods, G. (2005), *DfES Steiner Schools in England Research Report No 645.* Nottingham: DfES Publications
    An accessible report providing a good starting point for understanding how the Steiner approach is being implemented in England.

Useful websites

McMillan
www.spartacus.schoolnet.co.uk/WmcmillanR.htm
www.unesco.org

Montessori
www.montessori.org
www.montessori.org.uk
http://edheretics.gn.apc.org/EHFHome.htm

Owen
www.robert-owen.com/
www.robert-owen.midwales.com/rowen/
http://archive.co-op.ac.uk/owen.htm

Steiner
www.emerson.org.uk
www.steinerwaldorf.org

High/Scope
www. high-scope.org.uk
    Website run by High/Scope UK, a charitable organisation promoting the High/Scope approach to teaching young children.

England
www.nc.uk.net
    The National Curriculum website, run by the QCA. Includes programme of study requirements and teaching resources.

www.opsi.gov.uk/ACTS/acts2006/20060021.htm
    The Childcare Act 2006

Republic of Ireland
http://www.ncca.ie

Scotland
http://www.ltscotland.org.uk

Sure Start
http://www.surestart.gov.uk/

TeacherNet
www.teachernet.gov.uk

3 The reflective practitioner

Elaine Hallet

This chapter explores and discusses the role of the practitioner in the Early Years and how, through reflective thinking and behaviour practitioners can develop their knowledge, skills and professional practice. This process enables practitioners to meet new employment opportunities and implement emerging policy into practice within the changing Early Years sector and the evolving integrated Children's and Young People's Services.

By undertaking the suggested study within this chapter it is hoped that you will be able to:

1   be aware of the emerging work role opportunities open to Early Years practitioners

2   understand the concept of reflection and reflective practice

3   engage in activities to help your own reflective practice

4   appreciate the significance of becoming a reflective practitioner as a service provider for children and families

This chapter addresses the following areas:

➤ The changing role of the Early Years practitioner

➤ The concept of reflective practice

➤ Continuing professional development as a key enabler for reflective practice and practitioner's career progression

➤ The value of work-based learning for reflection

➤ Developing a reflective learning environment

➤ Becoming and being a reflective practitioner

The changing role of the Early Years practitioner

Many practitioners working within Early Years settings qualified as nursery nurses or teaching assistants. The term 'nursery nurse' emerged from the workforce of women who worked in children's nurseries during Victorian times. Their role was a nursing and caring one, providing for the physical and health care needs of babies and children who attended the nurseries. Originally they were nurses who worked in nurseries, hence the name. The role of teaching assistants developed through practitioners working in schools by assisting teachers with general classroom duties. A nursery nurse or a teaching assistant working in a nursery or school would carry out tasks to support the nursery or class teacher's role of teaching the children. These daily tasks may have included setting out activities, displaying children's work, cutting paper, sharpening pencils, tidying up, washing the paint pots and changing children's clothes after an 'accident'.

Practitioners still undertake these tasks but the roles of the nursery nurses and teaching assistants have evolved significantly within the last five years as Early Years settings provide a broader raft of services to meet children's and family needs, and children's special educational, literacy and numeracy needs. As a result, the nursery nurse's or teaching assistant's role has developed into that of a practitioner with a diverse range of responsibilities, working with parents, children, families, and health, educational and social professionals. School and Children's Workforce Reform initiatives (2006) are reforming work roles with clearly defined roles and responsibilities. These roles are often multidisciplinary, crossing health, social and educational areas. The following list shows the different job roles Early Years practitioners undertake in daycare and nursery settings and classroom settings within schools after qualifying as nursery nurses and teaching assistants.

➤ Childminder
➤ Children's Centre Manager
➤ Creche Leader
➤ Deputy Nursery Manager
➤ Early Years Professional
➤ Further Education College Tutor
➤ Health Visitor Assistant
➤ High Level Teaching Assistant
➤ Integrated Service Development Officer
➤ Key Person
➤ Learning Mentor
➤ Local Authority Workforce Training Manager
➤ Local Authority Children's and Young People's Service Officers
➤ Nanny
➤ Nursery Manager
➤ Nursery Nurse
➤ Nursery Officer in Charge
➤ NVQ Assessor
➤ Outreach and Community Development Worker
➤ Parent Partner Development Worker
➤ Portage Worker
➤ Pre-school Leader
➤ Senior Nursery Nurse
➤ Senior Playworker/Coordinator
➤ Special Needs Support Assistant
➤ Sure Start Practitioner/Manager
➤ Teaching Assistant
➤ Teaching Assistant Team Leader
➤ Toy Library Leader

Practitioners working in these job roles are undertaking a range of different responsibilities.

➤ Practitioners working in Sure Start projects and as Outreach and Community Development Workers work closely with parents in supporting and enhancing parenting skills.

➤ Nursery nurses working with Health Visitors assist with parents and their babies in clinics and during home visits.

- Practitioners working in Children's and Young People's Services are involved in developing and implementing policy and practice such as, for example, the Every Child Matters agenda.

- Practitioners working in schools in the Extended Schools provision run breakfast clubs, out-of-school clubs and play schemes.

- Practitioners working in schools as learning mentors, teaching assistants and nursery nurses monitor children's attendance, work with parents in developing strategies to improve children's behaviour, and support 'looked after' children in the Early Years setting.

- Special needs support assistants work with children who have specific needs, to enable them to access the curriculum and implement Individual Education Plans (IEPs) to meet children's individual and particular needs.

- Teaching assistants and nursery nurses plan and implement activities to help children's literacy and numeracy development.

- High-level teaching assistants cover teachers' classes to enable them to have preparation time.

- Some senior nursery nurses are responsible for the daily running of the nursery class.

- Early Years professionals lead the Early Years Foundation Stage and support other professionals within it.

These roles and responsibilities have emerged in response to the recognition that the early years of a child's life are a significant phase in his or her development. Children's learning and development in these early stages of life underpin much of their future achievements. This has been recognised by those governments that have given a high priority to education, for example in Scandinavian countries.

The introduction of the Labour party into government in 1997 put education high on the government agenda. Policies and initiatives for integrated multi-agency working, developing the Early Years as a significant phase of education, learning and development, raising educational standards in schools were introduced. Since 2000, the government (DfES/DCFS) recognised the Early Years as an important foundation for children's learning and development. Initiatives to implement policy have been supported by financial funding and are established to provide standards of provision for children and families. These include those shown in Figure 3.1.

Government initiatives	Aims and objectives
The National Childcare Strategy	Provides a national approach and framework for childcare provision.
Early Years Development Partnerships	Provide a local base to develop policy and practice within local authorities. (No longer in use)
Sure Start	Provides funding for projects in deprived areas for parent and family support.
Beacon Schools and Early Excellence Centres	Provide professional development opportunities for practitioners to observe best practice.
The National Day Care Standards and Ofsted	Provide a benchmark standard for high-quality provision in all Early Years settings.
Neighbourhood Nurseries	Provide locally based nurseries to serve the needs of a particular community.
Children's Centres	A 'one stop' resource for parents and families.
An integrated Children's Service	A multi-professional service to meet the holistic needs of children.
Common Assessment Framework	An assessment process that crosses education, social and health services for children's safety and well-being.

Figure 3.1 Early Years initiatives for policy and practice

The concept of reflective practice

The recognition of the Early Years as a vital phase of development was highlighted in the Rumbold Report (1990). This report recognised the importance of the Early Years as a period of 'rapid growth and development, both physical and intellectual. At this stage children's developmental needs are complex and interrelated' (1990:7). The Effective Provision for Pre-School Education Project (EPPE Project, 1999, Sylva et al, in Pugh, 2001), the largest project on pre-school education in the UK, also found marked differences in equality of provision and diversity of practitioners working in Early Years settings. Both these reported upon the quality of educational experience offered to young children. Significant recommendations were made in relation to a pre-fives curriculum, the initial training of practitioners and the continuing professional development of Early Years practitioners. These are now evident in the evolving Early Years field with the introduction of the Early Years Foundation Stage curriculum (2008), the reform of the workforce (2006), the introduction of a graduate workforce and the introduction of professional status recognition in the High Level Teaching Assistant and the Early Years Professional awards (2002 onwards).

The Rumbold Report recognised that the role of the practitioner who works with young children is 'a demanding and complex task. Those engaged upon it need a range of attributes to assure a high-quality experience for children' (1990:19). Every child has an entitlement to high standards of care and education. Quality in education and care does not depend solely on government policy, purpose-built schools and nurseries or even funding. The decisive factor in determining it is the quality of the educators (Abbott and Rodger, 1994). There is a strong link between the quality of training and professional development and the quality of provision for children. The impact of the research undertaken in the EPPE Project (1999) showed evidence of the effectiveness of early education upon children's learning and development. The project findings have influenced 'evidence-based policy' at national and local authority levels, including the development of a graduate workforce to raise the qualifications and standards of practitioner's practice (Pugh and Duffy, 2006:176).

The training and professional development needs of those responsible for the care and education of young children are a key issue. The Rumbold Report proposed multidisciplinary courses in which child health care and education professionals come together. In 2001 the government identified a national lack of a highly skilled workforce qualified to Level 4 and beyond. Foundation Degrees were introduced to provide this, of which work-based learning and assessment forms an integral part of the degree. Articulated progression routes enable Foundation Degree graduates to progress to the final stage of a BA undergraduate award at an ordinary or honours degree level. These academic and vocational degree courses in Early Childhood Studies and Early Years not only provide professional development opportunities, but raise the status of Early Years practitioners and signal that high-level qualifications are necessary for working with young children.

Degree-level courses provide long-term professional developmental opportunities, but there is also a need for Early Years practitioners to have an entitlement to short courses in order to update their knowledge, skills and understanding to meet the changing needs of the Early Years field. Long- and short-term continuing professional development underpins the various Early Years roles and responsibilities discussed earlier. Long-term professional development courses support the emerging leadership roles within the Early Years sector and Integrated Children's and Young People's Service. These include Senior Practitioners (the Department for Education and Skills, DfES, 2002), High Level Teaching Assistants (Teacher Training Agency TTA, 2003), Early Years Professionals (Children's Workforce Development Council, the CWDC, 2006) and Centre Leaders with the National Professional Qualification in Integrated Centre Leadership award (National College for School Leadership, 2005/6). These awards not only provide practitioners with graduate and postgraduate levels of study but give professional recognised status for knowledge, skills and experience. Many practitioners are progressing in their career by climbing up this professional 'climbing frame of qualifications' (Abbott and Pugh, 1998). Figure 3.2 illustrates the range of academic and vocational long- and short-term courses available to practitioners.

Professional status awards National Professional Qualification in Integrated Centre Leadership (NPQICL) (level 7) Early Years Professional (EYP) (graduate, level 6) Senior Practitioner (level 5) High Level Teaching Assistant (level 4 equivalent)
Postgraduate awards Doctoral (PhD, EdD) Masters (MA, M.Ed, MSc)
Degree awards Bachelor of Arts – ordinary or honours degree Foundation Degree DfES Surestart Recognised Early Years Sector – Endorsed Foundation Degree
Level 4 qualification CACHE NVQ 4 in Children's Care, Learning and Development (NVQCCLD-L4)
Initial training Level 3 qualifications CACHE Level 3 awards Diploma in Child Care and Education (DCE-L3) Diploma in Pre-school Practice (DPP-L3) Certificate in Children's Care and Learning and Development (CCCLD-L3) Certificate in Early Years Foundation Stage Practice Award in Early Years and Child Care for Playworkers (AEYCCP-L3) Level 3 in Playgroup Practice in Wales (DPPW-L3) Level 3 Diploma in Early Years Care and Education, Welsh medium (W-DEYCE-L3) NVQ level 3 in Children's Care, Learning and Development (NVQCCLD-L3) BTEC level 3 award National Diploma in Early Years
Short courses for professional updating For example, child protection, health and safety

Figure 3.2 Long- and short-term professional development opportunities

Continuing professional development as a key enabler for reflective practice and practitioner's career progression

As identified in Figure 3.1, practitioners working in the wide range of work roles are in the forefront of developing, managing and leading the significant changes in the Early Years sector for children and families. In order to achieve this practitioners need to have relevant knowledge, skills and attributes. Reflective practice enables practitioners to develop these attributes. As reflective practitioners working within the sector they are forming new ways of working with other professionals, children and families. The government recognises the need for professional development for employees and is currently, at the time of writing, funding curriculum professional development opportunities through the Transformation Fund and the Home Grown Graduate incentive for providers (2007). The government encourages and promotes the development of 'reflective skills in practice' (Leeson, 2007:180 in Willan et al, 2007) through professional awards as the National Professional Qualification in Integrated Centre Leadership (NPQICL) in which reflective practice is a key component within the programme so that the leaders of the integrated Children's Centres are reflective practitioners and leaders. This emphasis on 'reflection' as a key professional practice skill and attribute poses the following questions which will be discussed in the next part of the chapter.

➤ What is reflective practice?

➤ Who is a reflective practitioner?

➤ How do I become a reflective practitioner?

Bolton acknowledges that reflective practice has become a standard in initial and continuing professional education and development and states that it is a 'state of mind, an attitude, an approach. An educational approach that makes the difference between twenty years of experience or one year of experience twenty times.' (2006:3)

Becoming a reflective practitioner through reflective practice

It is first important to understand what reflective practice is and how being reflective enables an Early Years practitioner to be a reflective practitioner. Donald Schon's work (1983) has been instrumental in developing the concept of 'the Reflective Practitioner' in professional practice (Moon, 2007:39). Schon defines two processes of reflection in reflective practice. These are 'reflection-in-practice' and 'reflection-on-practice', so describing levels of reflective practice. A practitioner in the course of their daily work 'reflects in' on their tasks. However, a practitioner who 'reflects on' their practice takes the reflective process to a higher level by linking practice to theories and developing 'theories in use' and new ways of working. Schon describes this professional ability as 'artistry', a 'kind of knowing' that develops and expands professional knowledge and practice (Moon, 2007:40). The following example shows a daily task in which reflection-in-practice takes place.

During an inspection of an infant school, the inspector observed a boy carrying out his daily task of watering the plants in his classroom, which he did before home time each day. The boy came to the last plant in the classroom, which did not have any leaves or flowers on and looked remarkably like a stick in a pot. 'Why are you watering that?', he asked. 'Cos I always do', answered the boy.

Gervase Phinn, 2002

The boy's task can be compared to the work of a practitioner in an Early Years setting. As practitioners we may choose to carry out daily work tasks in a routine way without thinking or considering the impact on the children's learning and development; or we can stop to question and reflect upon our interactions with children, parents and staff and consider how they affect provision for children and, in doing so, be reflective practitioners. The need for reflection, review and evaluation is based upon the changing and evolving job roles derived from internal and external changes. Reflective practice is a process of regularly reviewing our own work and the provision within the work setting, looking for and making improvements. Long-term professional development courses enables this. This is shown in the following example of reflection-on-practice from a Foundation Degree graduate.

Reflective conversations with other professionals and students, sharing their experiences, listening to their ideas and understanding of education will help me to support or challenge my own perspectives. The way I reflect on my reflections will change as I change and the more I will learn about my professional development. Contact with children and their families, reading relevant publications, examining research reports and engaging in discussions with my tutor, mentor and students will aid my development as a learner, carer and educator. Through self-evaluation, investigating my own practice and developing ways to improve it I will find a way through difficult situations, resolve problems and help to make my work with children and families more successful.

Shirley Collier, Foundation Degree Educare and Early Childhood, University of Derby

To become a reflective practitioner who influences emerging Early Years policy and practice means making reflective practice a way of behaving, thinking and doing. 'Being reflective' and being a 'reflective practitioner' refers to a long-term characteristic of a person's behaviour rather than a cognitive activity' (Moon, 2007:5). To become a reflective practitioner the practitioner has undertaken a learning process in which their behaviour has changed, developed and modified. It is difficult to know if and when this cyclical process ends. The concept of lifelong learning implies that it is a continuous process. Reflective practice is not a natural process to all. Practitioners need to learn how to be reflective and develop reflection on practice, engaging their own practice to theories and experts within the Early Years field. This chapter includes ways of learning to reflect with activities for practitioners to engage in reflection based upon their own work setting.

The value of work–based learning for reflection

Work-based learning is central to the Foundation Degree. These vocationally focused degrees equip learners with the skills and knowledge relevant to their employment and the needs of employers. They integrate work-based learning with academic rigour.

Foundation Degree Benchmark statement (2002:3)

Foundation Degree students use their everyday work with children, families and colleagues as a reflective evaluation and research base on which to modify and develop their practice. This contextualised work activity enables practitioners to start with their own professional practice and then engage with other knowledgeable experts within the field and relevant theories. This enables them to develop their professional learning and practice in a concrete way that feed back into the setting or service in which they work.

Work-based mentors play an important role in supporting this learning process within the work setting by sharing their expertise and experience with the student. This approach enables students to reflect upon their practice in a relevant and meaningful way, building upon and extending their practice with theory, so embedding new and developing knowledge and practices within their everyday work. This work-based learning integrated with academic study helps the student to become a reflective practitioner or an 'inquiring professional', as Anning and Edwards (2003:34) describe this new practitioner working in the Early Years.

The following Work-based Learning Reflective Activity will enable you to undertake some reflective learning based upon a daily activity undertaken in your work setting. Use the heading and question prompts to think reflectively about your engagement within the activity and how through reflection you can develop this.

Activity 1

Work-based Learning Reflective Activity

➤ Describe the work-based activity.

➤ What have you learnt?
(What went well? What did not go well?)

➤ What have you read?
(What do I know about this area/topic? Who are the experts within this area? What are the theories in this area?)

➤ How does this knowledge and understanding help you to improve the activity and future practice?

➤ What does your work-based mentor think?
(Has she or he any experience or expertise they could share with me to affirm or improve my practice?)

Developing a reflective learning environment

For practitioners to become reflective they need to have access to an environment in which reflective learning can take place. The following activities explore ways of creating such an environment. During undertaking long- and short-term professional development courses, an Early Years practitioner becomes part of a community of learning practitioners. These may include their work-based mentor, work colleagues within and beyond their own work setting, other professionals they meet and work with, for example on short courses, students they are studying their degree with in college or university and academic tutors and lecturers. This learning network of vocational and academic professionals produces a unique community of learners for each individual practitioner who:

➤ support each other through their study

➤ exchange ideas

➤ share knowledge, experience and practice

➤ enquire about and challenge concepts, theories, knowledge and understanding in order to reflect upon and develop their provision for children, parents and families.

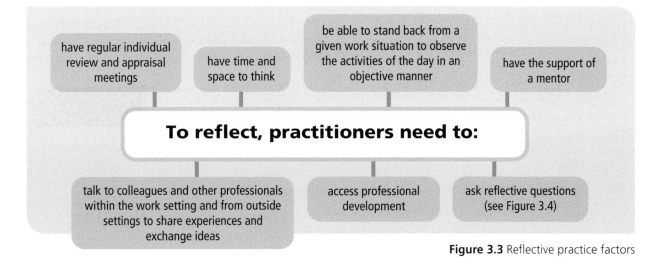

Figure 3.3 Reflective practice factors

Activity for reflective learning

Reflect upon your own work environment. Does it allow for reflective learning?

I need	Do I have this? (yes/no)	Does this allow me to reflect? Do I need to improve this? How can I improve this?
Reflection time To have time and space to think about my work with children, families, parents and colleagues.		
Observation time To be able to stand back from a given work situation to observe the activities of the day in an objective manner.		
Reflective questioning To be able to ask colleagues questions about their practice and for others to question me about my practice.		
Engage with other colleagues To talk to colleagues and other professionals within my work setting and from other settings and services to share experiences and exchange ideas.		
Access professional development To identify my own professional needs and access relevant professional development courses.		

continued ▶

I need	Do I have this? (yes/no)	Does this allow me to reflect? Do I need to improve this? How can I improve this?
A work-based mentor To have the support of a work-based mentor to discuss personal and professional issues with.		
Appraisal To have regular individual review and appraisal meetings with clear achievable targets to develop my practice.		

A key component within a reflective learning environment are questions. For an Early Years practitioner it is important to work in a questioning culture in which professional practice is questioned, discussed and developed through critical learning dialogue. The following examples in Figure 3.4 and Figure 3.5 would enable this to occur.

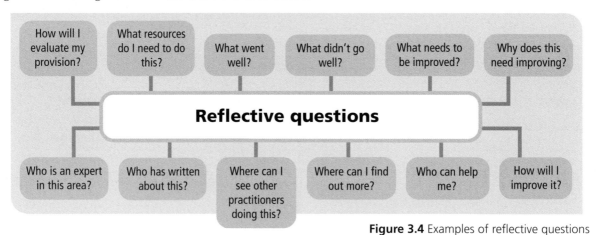

Figure 3.4 Examples of reflective questions

The use of open-ended questions is key in the reflective learning process. The Johns Model of Reflection (1994) of guided reflection through questioning is used within the nursing profession and provides a way to help practitioners access, make sense of and learn through experience. The questions in Activity 3 have been adapted from this model to enable Early Years practitioners to develop reflective learning from their everyday work experience.

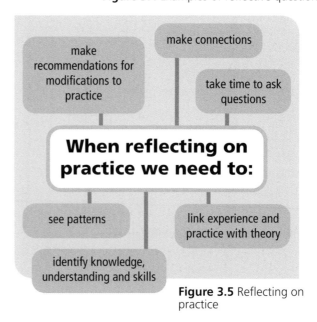

Figure 3.5 Reflecting on practice

Developing reflective learning from work experiences

Write a description of a work experience, asking yourself the open-ended questions below.

What are the key issues that I need to pay attention to?

Reflection
What was I trying to achieve?
Why did I act as I did?
What were the consequences of my actions?
for the child/children, the parents, myself,
the people I work with?
How did I feel about this experience when it
was happening?
How did the child/parent/colleague feel?
How do I know how the child/parent/
colleague felt?

Influencing factors
What internal factors influenced my decision-
making actions?
What external factors influenced my
decision-making actions?

What sources of knowledge did or should
have influenced my decision-making actions?

Alternative strategies
Could I have dealt better with the situation?
What other choices did I have?
What would be the consequences of these
other choices?

Learning
How can I make sense of this experience in
light of past and future practice?
How do I now feel about this experience?
Have I taken effective action to support
myself and others as a result of this
experience?
How has this experience changed my way of
knowing in practice?

Becoming and being a reflective practitioner

In order to reflect we need to create time from a busy personal and professional life to think about and evaluate our actions. Reflection as a learning process helps us to make better sense of our practitioner's role and its contribution to the children, parents and families within our work and the setting itself. Being a reflective practitioner helps us to increase our skills, understanding and professional practice. It results in our being more effective practitioners. Drummond (in Fisher, 2002:194) highlights the importance of self-knowledge for the educator and practitioner. She defines effective practitioners as those who understand themselves, their knowledge, their feelings and the framework within which they understand children.

Practitioners regularly assess children and it is important that practitioners assess themselves also. Being reflective professionals requires that we continually review and develop our own practice. Reflective conversations are an important part of this evaluation. These can take place at university or college with tutors or within the work setting with colleagues and work-based mentors. Work-based mentors can contribute to the reflective process by sharing their experience and expertise by asking questions and challenging workplace practices in a supportive way. Pollard and Tann (in Fisher, 2001:199) suggest that reflective practice, professional learning and personal fulfilment are enhanced through collaboration and dialogue with colleagues.

By reflecting on our thoughts and actions, relating them to those of other theorists and practitioners and taking advice from more experienced practitioners, our workday practice becomes more skilled and 'knowing-in-action', as described by Schon in Cockburn (2001:103). On a daily basis, practitioners make innumerable judgements based upon their understandings, judgements and skilful performances. As practitioners gain experience in their work role they are able to read signs and carry out successful activities based upon their experience. They use their experiences, knowledge, skills and understanding to refine and modify their practice, adapt and make changes as appropriate to meet the needs of children, parents and staff they work with. They will evaluate and reflect upon their work in an ongoing process of review and development. The use of questions and questioning to discover and to challenge knowledge and practice is part of this review process. Reflective questions may include considerations about children's learning. They enable practitioners to agree, disagree and challenge provision where necessary. Examples of these are shown in Figure 3.6.

Similar questions are key to ask yourself in order to review and evaluate your own practice, identifying areas of strength and areas for development in an action plan. The following section will help you to reflect on your own personal and professional needs and your role within your work setting.

The words What, Why, How, Can, Where, When and Who are helpful in forming reflective questions in order to review and evaluate your practice.

➤ What am I doing?

➤ Why am I doing it?

➤ How am I doing it?

➤ Can I improve it?

➤ Where can I improve?

➤ When can I review my practice?

➤ When can I plan, based upon my review?

➤ Who can help me to reflect?

➤ What resources will help me?

Activity 4 has been designed to help you to evaluate a specific task using these questions as a starting point for reflection and evaluation.

Reflective writing

The experience of reflective writing is an effective way for reflective thought. Bolton (2006:23) describes reflective practice writing as 'a way of expressing and exploring our own and others' stories: crafting and shaping to aid understanding and development'. Practitioners share their practice verbally over coffee or a sandwich at break times but 'we do not tell each other or ourselves the things at our cutting edge of difficulty'. By sharing reflective writing and discussing with others enables the development of practice because the outcomes of reflection are taken back into practice, improving and developing. Practitioners' 'stories are a bank of knowledge, skills and experience: much of our knowing is in our doing. We learn from our own and others' mistakes and successes, each other's ideas, experience and wisdom, and tackle and come to terms with our own problem areas.'

A Reflective Learning Journal in which daily notes and pieces of writing are made is a type of reflective writing. It may include writing about work issues, professional practice, readings, research, personal thoughts, feelings and ideas. This creates a personal dialogue for reflective thought and development. This can be shared

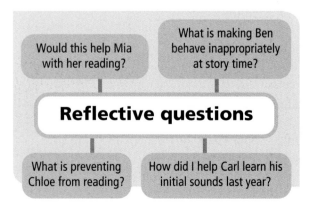

Figure 3.6 Reflective questions about children's learning

with others or kept as a personal document. Cockburn (2001:108) describes how a reflective journal is 'a powerful part of an educator's professional development. A place where he or she can reflect, speculate, wonder, worry, exclaim, record, propose, remind, reconstruct, question, confront, dream, consider and reconsider. The journal holds experiences as a puzzle frame holds its integral pieces. The writer begins to recognise pieces that fit together and, like a detective, sees the picture evolve. It is a space for thinking.' Activity 5 will help you begin your Reflective Learning Journal.

Action planning

Action planning is an important tool for prioritising and planning. Once you have begun to reflect upon your work role you will begin to identify areas of strength and areas for personal and professional development. Action planning is a useful way to plan for personal and professional development. Professional and work activity can be interrelated for the benefit of the practitioner and their work setting. Activity 6 shows this but also enables you to complete the action plan for your own personal and professional development needs.

Activity 6

Professional Needs Action Plan

From the questions above, identify four to six professional needs in an action plan.

Professional need (PN)	Long-term target date	Short-term targets	Completion date	Evidence of monitoring and evaluation
Example PN 1 Implement Story Sacks in Early Years Foundation Stage	May 2008	Attended Story Sacks conference Review of relevant books and articles	12.09.08	Report of conference information to all EY Foundation Stage and Senior Management Teams
		Lead an Early Years Foundation Stage Team meeting about Story Sacks	14.11.08	Minutes of meeting
PN 2				
PN 3				
PN 4				
PN 5				
PN 6				

Reflecting upon your role

In reflecting upon your practice you will be reflecting upon your role also, your perception of it and how others perceive it. The next section of this chapter concerns some key aspects of an Early Years practitioner's work role and provides some activities for personal reflection.

➤ Supporting children's learning

➤ Effective communication skills

➤ Working in teams and groups

➤ Leadership

➤ Managing change

Figure 3.7 illustrates some of the questions you may ask yourself when considering your role.

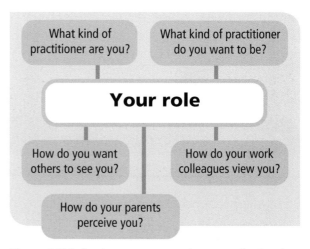

Figure 3.7 Reflecting upon your role as a professional working in an Early Years setting

Knowing yourself	
What roles do I have in my life?	I may be a parent, auntie, grandparent, governor, a teacher, nursery nurse, teaching assistant. How do these roles influence my role and work with children and parents?
What am I like as a learner?	What was my experience of learning at nursery and school? How has this influenced my approach to learning generally and in providing learning opportunities and experiences for children and parents?
What am I like as an educator and a carer?	Are these roles the same or different? What experiences have shaped me? Who has influenced me? Possibly a significant teacher, nursery nurse, a mentor or parents.
Who am I?	What experiences, influences and people have helped me to achieve as much as I already have? Where do I want to progress to? What do I need to do to achieve this? Some practitioners want to become a teacher; some don't, but do want to work with children in a role with more responsibility such as a Senior Nursery Nurse, a Learning Mentor, a Nursery Manager or an Early Years Professional.

Figure 3.8 Reflective questions about yourself

To answer these questions you need to know yourself personally and professionally. Some questions that may assist you in this process are given in Figure 3.8. Your role and responsibilities will vary according to the setting you work within. A practitioner working within a nursery may have responsibility as a key worker for a group of children, be involved in curriculum planning and work closely with parents. However, a practitioner working within an infant school may be involved in implementing curriculum activities and tasks planned by the teacher, rather than initiating them as a practitioner in a nursery may do.

In developing reflective practice, it is first important to identify the key knowledge and skills needed within a practitioner's role in working with babies and children under eight years of age, their parents and carers, and other professionals.

Figure 3.9 Requirements for working as a practitioner with babies and children under the age of 8

Supporting children's learning

A practitioner who works in an Early Years setting on a daily basis with children is a significant adult: a person who plans, supports, intervenes in and extends children's learning. There are many aspects to this role and many ways in which adults support and help children to interact with the environment around them to gain knowledge, skills and understanding from this interaction.

The E Framework shown in Figure 3.10 identifies seven ways in which adults support children's education and learning. You may like to reflect upon your own role in supporting children's learning using the E Framework.

Activity 7

Using the E Framework

Over the time span of one week reflect upon your role in supporting one child's or a group of children's learning using the seven headings in the E Framework.

1 Provide evidence.

2 Identify areas for development.

3 Write an action plan to develop your practice.

	Evidence	Area/s for development
EXPERIENCE		
EXTEND		
ENCOURAGE		
ENGAGE		
EDUCATE		
EXPLAIN		
EXAMINE		

The E Framework: a framework for the Early Years practitioner's role in supporting children's learning		
EXPERIENCE	Provide experiences, opportunities, resources inside and outside the learning setting.	For example: **Inside:** planned play areas, cafés, shops, literacy, numeracy, creativity areas **Outside:** chalking boards, walks in the local environment, big toys, playground apparatus
EXTEND	Question, listen, intervene in and extend children's learning where appropriate.	For example: **Adult during a local walk** Questioning and listening: 'What can you hear?' 'What sounds do the leaves make when we walk in them?' **Adult in the home corner** Intervening in and extending a child's play: 'Could you pour me a nice cup of tea, please?'
ENCOURAGE	Praise and value each child's progress in learning. Help children to achieve tasks and activities they may not be able to do on their own.	For example: **Adult writing with a group of children** 'Josh, I enjoyed reading your story so far. What might the dragon do next? I'll help you with any long words you may need so you can make your story more exciting.'
ENGAGE	Become involved in children's learning experiences. Provide for their individual needs.	For example: **Adult baking with children** 'You've made some lovely buns. I enjoyed making them with you. Grant wants to ice them, so shall we do that, Grant?'
EDUCATE	Be a role model for children by demonstrating knowledge, skills and understanding.	For example: **Adult at story time** 'Today I am going to read you one of my favourite stories. I hope you'll like it as much as I do.'
EXPLAIN	Listen to children, answer their questions.	For example: **Adult responding to a child's questions about where the water goes when the bath plug is pulled** 'The water goes down the plug hole into sewers, which are big tunnels under the street. It flows along pipes to the sewage works where it is cleaned.'
EXAMINE	Examine children's learning and development through observation and assessment in order to plan for their future development.	For example: Adults meet at the end of the day to review the observations of children they have carried out that day. This review informs planning of the next day's activities to meet children's individual needs.

Figure 3.10 The E Framework

Effective communication skills

A practitioner in an Early Years setting works in a people-centred service; the service users comprise parents, children and their families. The quality of this service is based upon effective relationships. Practitioners who work in this service are required to have effective communication skills in order to develop relationships with children, staff, parents and professionals. Rodd (1998:40) highlights the importance of practitioners communicating effectively, since 'the way in which early childhood professionals respond to children, parents and staff affects the quality of the interaction'. A people-centred service is built upon effective relationships, and the quality of interactions plays a vital part in this service.

Figure 3.11 indicates the range of people an Early Years practitioner working in a Sure Start Children's Centre communicates with and the context within which they do so. Work within a Children's Centre is varied and workers interact with a wide range of partners in order to deliver an 'integrated' service to families.

Communication is a two-way process, consisting of verbal and non-verbal interactions. Communication is about both giving and receiving messages. The message may give information or communicate feelings. The sender transmits a message through verbal and non-verbal interactions, selecting the form of communication which is most appropriate, with the intention that the receiver will accept it in the way it is intended. Figure 3.12 lists the forms of communication a practitioner can use.

Service users	Immediate context	Wider context
Children	Children accessing the Centre for play, health facilities, family learning or support.	Groups run within the Centre and as outreach in Community Settings. One-to-one work with individual families.
Parents	Parents accessing the Centre with their child/children, before their baby is born; as individuals to gain support as a parent or to be involved in the development of the Centre's activities.	Engaging parents out in the community to promote the Centre's services. Supporting parents to be involved in informing the development of activities within the Centre. Communicating at a one-to-one level and in group settings.
Staff	Teams within the Centre including workers from Health, Social Care and Early Years Education/Childcare backgrounds.	Wider team in a Centre would include admin, reception staff, facilities staff.
Other partners	A wider team of professionals including teachers and workers from local schools, specialist health providers, voluntary sector providers using the Centre to support the delivery of their own services.	Midwives, Health Visitors, social care professionals, JobCentre Plus workers, specialist workers such as speech therapists, paediatric nurses, teenage pregnancy workers, fathers' workers and community workers and volunteers.

Figure 3.11 The range of people working in a Children's Centre with whom a practitioner communicates

Forms of communication	
Pre-verbal	Music / Laughter / Sounds / Dance / Dress
Non-verbal	Body language / Sign language
Verbal	Spoken language / Listening / Singing / Recorded speech / Telephone
Written	Letters / Cards / Memos / Poetry / Literature / Fax / Email
Pictorial	Images / Logos and symbols / Sign language

Figure 3.12 Forms of communication

Verbal interactions

Verbal interactions are used throughout a practitioner's day. Carl Rogers (1961) (in Rodd, 1998:40) identified five response styles observed in 80 per cent of verbal communication engaged in by professionals working in human service occupations. These are shown in Figure 3.13.

Activity 8

Rogers' five response styles

1 Do any of the statements given as examples in Figure 3.13 sound familiar? You may like to listen to yourself during a day's work.

2 What kind of responses do you make in your interactions with parents, staff and children?

3 How many of Carl Rogers' five responses do you use?

4 Are there some you use more than others?

Non-verbal communication

Non-verbal communication, or body language, is used in conjunction with verbal communication and helps to convey a message in a positive or negative way.

Body language is just that, a non-verbal language. There are many languages in the world with different concepts and sounds; likewise body language is not the same in every country. It is dependent upon the culture of each country; for example, Maori children in New Zealand greet each other by rubbing noses, whereas this would not be the normally accepted greeting for children living in Liverpool. As practitioners it is important for us to be aware of the different cultural practices of the children we work with in order not to offend service users.

Some examples of non-verbal communication are given in Figure 3.14.

Rogers' five response styles (1961)	
Advising and evaluating responses	*What you should do now is …*
Interpreting and analysing responses	*The problem you really have here is …*
Supporting and placating responses	*Don't worry, they all go through that stage.*
Questioning and probing responses	*Is everything all right at home?*
Understanding and reflecting responses	*You appear to be pleased about how Vikram is progressing.*

Figure 3.13 Rogers' five response styles

Non-verbal communication	
Facial expressions	Facial expressions may indicate happiness, surprise, fear, sadness, anger, disgust or contempt, and interest.
Gestures	Gestures are used to elaborate or to expand upon speech. Some gestures are culture-specific; for example, greetings may involve shaking hands or kissing.
Body movements	While speaking, a person moves his or her hands, body and head continuously. These movements are closely coordinated with speech and form part of the total communication.
Body contact	This includes the use of touch and is used to show affection, support or anger.
Body posture	Attitudes to others are indicated by body posture; for example, a person with folded arms may be putting up a physical barrier to communication.
Physical proximity	The distance a person stands from another indicates intimacy or distance.

Figure 3.14 Non-verbal communication

Activity 9

Body language

1 During a session in a working day, write down how you used non-verbal language as part of effective communication in a situation with a parent, child or member of staff.

2 Reflect upon how the outcome could have been different if you had used negative body language.

Written communication

Practitioners in Early Years settings are often required to provide written communication to pass on information to parents, staff and other professionals. This type of communication can be chosen as the most appropriate form for that specific purpose or it can be a requirement of the setting. Practitioners are required to have adequate literacy skills in order to write effectively. Some examples of the different types of written communication produced by a practitioner working in an Early Years setting are shown in Figure 3.15.

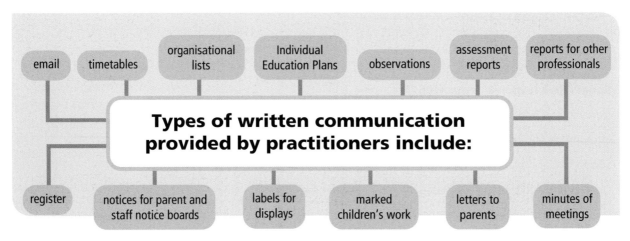

Figure 3.15 Some examples of written communication used in an Early Years setting

The practitioner's readers include:

➤ other staff

➤ parents

➤ professionals; for example, psychologist, Local Authority, Ofsted

➤ children.

Activity 10

Written communication

Consider your own use of written communication.

1 Has there been an occasion on which you chose written communication as a more effective means of conveying your message than verbal communication?

2 Do you use written communication in conjunction with verbal communication? If so, why? Does it make the communication more or less effective?

Active listening

Listening is the most important skill in the communication process. Early Years settings are busy places; as practitioners, we do not always have the time to listen attentively to children, staff and parents. Communication will be more successful if the sender gives as much attention to what they hear as to what they say. Being a good listener takes skill and practice. You not only have to hear the words children, staff and parents are saying, but you also have to understand them and then respond in an appropriate way. This means you make listening an active process. Hilton (1994:25) defines this as 'active listening'. Suggestions about how you may become an active listener are given in Figure 3.16.

Activity 11 has been designed to help you to reflect upon your listening skills.

Activity 11

Practise active listening

During the course of a working day select an interaction with a parent, child or member of staff and practise active listening.

1 How did you find this interaction?

2 How did the process of active listening develop positive interactions and relationships?

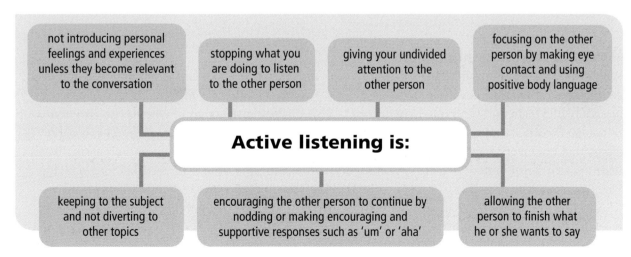

Figure 3.16 Practising active listening

Barriers to communication

There may be barriers to communication. Linguistic, cultural, physical and emotional issues can prevent effective communication. There may be:

➤ time constraints

➤ other stresses within the child's family

➤ English may be a second language for the child

➤ sensory difficulties, which may include hearing or sight disabilities.

Practitioners need to recognise possible barriers to communication and provide strategies to overcome them; for example, a bilingual support assistant could help parents to communicate with staff in their child's educational setting. Work settings serve a local community and are usually familiar with community needs. Practitioners working in an Early Years setting are in the front line of overcoming barriers to communication.

Activity 12

Overcoming barriers to communication

1 How do you and your work setting overcome any individual barriers to communication?

2 What strategies does your work setting use to overcome any community barriers to communication?

Working in teams and groups

Practitioners working within Early Years settings do not work in isolation but as members of a team and with others in groups or teams. Figure 3.17 illustrates the range of teams that may work together in supporting the learning and development of a child within an Early Years setting.

You may recognise some teams that you work in. Practitioners usually work in a number of teams and groups that vary in size. As a member of a team you will have different roles and responsibilities. Team members should have a common aim or aims and it is important for every member to cooperate and share his or her experience to maximise the efficiency of the provision. In order to operate effectively, all teams must have two dimensions.

➤ The Task – the job to be done or the problem to be solved.

➤ The Process – the way in which the task is carried out; it concerns how people bring their knowledge, skills and qualities together.

Jeffree and Fox in Taylor and Woods (1998:283)

Early Years practitioners need to develop effective relationships with individual team members in order to carry out their work effectively and for the team to work successfully within the organisation. This involves effectively communicating to all team members by actively listening, using clear verbal and non-verbal communication and supporting all members of the team. According to Woodcock (1986:44), building a team requires:

➤ clear objectives and agreed targets

➤ appropriate leadership

➤ sound policies and procedures

➤ sound inter-group relations

➤ individual development

➤ regular review of team performance

➤ cooperation and constructive conflict

➤ support and trust

➤ openness and confrontation.

Figure 3.18 illustrates some of the differences between effective and ineffective teamwork.

Within the team in which a practitioner works, members take on different roles and responsibilities, based upon their strengths and weaknesses. One team member may develop ideas, another may organise the team and another may actually implement the ideas generated. For successful teamwork, there needs to be a balance of different types of members to take on these roles and responsibilities.

Teams and groups within educational settings		
Staff team	Teaching teams	Early Years Foundation Stage/Key Stage 1 team/Year teams/Subject specialist teams
	Support teams	Nursery nurses/Teaching assistants/Classroom assistants/Special needs support assistants/Parent helpers
	Ancillary teams	School clerks/Premises/Mid-day supervisors/Catering
	Governors	Sub-committees
Outside agencies		Within the Local Authority and Integrated Services
Parents and carers		In Early Years or School settings and in liaison with the home
Children		Indoors and outdoors/in the Early Years Foundation Stage 1/Key Stage/Year groups and in different classes

Figure 3.17 Teams and groups working together in educational settings

Effective teamwork	Ineffective teamwork
The team should achieve more than the individuals working separately by using the individual talents, skills and specialisms of the team members to the best advantage.	The team may accomplish less than the individuals working separately and may be demotivated. This obviously affects the service the team provides.
Teams can promote creativity, morale and motivation.	Symptoms of less effective teamwork may include personality clashes, lack of openness, jobs duplicated or not completed and members failing to support each other.
An effective team may carry out tasks that individuals cannot complete on their own.	

Figure 3.18 Effective and ineffective teamwork

Activity 13

Working in a team

You may like to reflect upon your own experience of working in a team.
1 Was it an effective team, if so why?
2 Was it an ineffective team, if so why?

Reflect upon your own team work.
What teams or groups do you work in?
Select one of these teams and groups. Give an example of how you worked effectively in it.

Leadership

Leadership is a process whereby a person leads a number of other individuals to an agreed set of aims and objectives. There are now more women in leadership and management within Early Years settings than in many other professions. This reflects the percentage of female practitioners working within this field. Women leaders can give strong leadership within a collaborative framework. This female approach to power is based upon collaboration, inclusion and consensus building through reciprocal relationships, where the leader seeks to act with, rather than assert power over, others. The woman leader tends to see herself as a member of the team. Leadership becomes an holistic, inclusive and empowering process. Decisions are made in consultation. Issues are thoroughly discussed, with each group member participating fully until a basic agreement that is acceptable to everyone involved is reached. This is considered by many to be the most effective way of making decisions, as it produces 'innovative, creative and high quality decisions'.

(Rodd, 1998:92)

Women lead by empowering, teaching, providing role models and encouraging openness and questioning. Rodd (1998:11) describes four leadership behaviours in Figure 3.19.

Leadership behaviours	
Vision behaviour	Creating a vision and taking appropriate risks to bring about change
People behaviour	Providing caring and respect for individual differences
Influence behaviour	Acting collaboratively
Values behaviour	Building trust and openness

Figure 3.19 Four leadership behaviours, Rodd (1998:11)

Leaders should:
> inspire and motivate the staff team
> initiate change
> take decisions
> set objectives
> set the pace of the work setting
> develop a team culture
> facilitate and encourage the development of individuals
> inspire loyalty.

Successful leaders reflect, deliberate and plan the organisation of the work setting around values, philosophy, policies and the need to be responsive to change. Effective leadership in Early Years settings involves creating a community and providing a high-quality service. This involves:
> influencing the behaviour of others, particularly staff and parents
> supporting staff in their personal and professional development
> planning for, and implementing, change in order to improve the organisation.

Activity 14

Reflect upon leadership

You may like to reflect upon the leaders you have worked with and consider whether there has been one leader, for example head teacher, nursery manager, playgroup supervisor, who has particularly inspired and motivated you. If so:
1 What qualities did they have?
2 What did they help you achieve?

If there is a leader who has not inspired you:
1 What did he or she do or not do to support you?
2 How could he or she have helped you professionally?

66 Discussion point 1

Reflect upon your own leadership

What is your leadership style?
How do you lead others?
Give an example of a project you effectively led.

You may also want to read Chapter 15 of this book, 'Leading and working in Multi-professional teams'.

Managing change through action research

Early Years education is undergoing change and is evolving, as are other areas of education. External changes such as the introduction of the Early Years Foundation Stage has brought internal change to Early Years provision. Internal changes, too, arise from the needs of individual settings: for example, changing the snack routine or outdoor play provision. Managing change and surviving it are crucial for every practitioner working within the sector. Merchant and Marsh (1998:102) suggest that change should be carefully managed and well planned so that there are not too many demands on colleagues at any one time. Staff should take ownership of change by working in a collaborative way to implement it. Change should also be supported by appropriate staff development and discussion with relevant professionals. Successful change is likely to be lasting when there is a strong element of practicality. An example of this is the number of Early Years settings that have successfully implemented Story Sacks as a literacy resource to use with children and parents (Griffiths, 1997). This initiative began over ten years ago, it has been sustained over time and has become a common resource for children in their literacy development.

Action Research is a reflective cycle of research as it aims 'to improve and to involve' (Fisher, 2002:199) and 'practitioner research is increasingly important in developing and improving early childhood practice'. (Roberts-Holmes, 2005:5). Early Years practitioners are 'therefore increasingly recognised as important participants in the culture of childhood research' (Roberts-Holmes, 2005:5). Action research is an effective way of managing, implementing and reviewing change. When

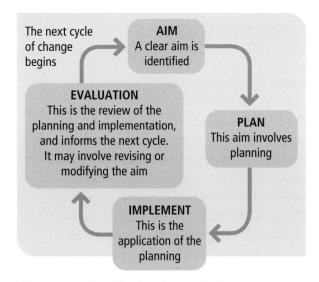

Figure 3.20 The Reflective Change Cycle

implementing change, there will be some staff that are resistant to it. The initiating practitioner should lead by example from a sound knowledge base and involve all staff in decisions of 'how' and 'when' the change should be implemented. Figure 3.20 shows a Reflective Change Cycle based upon Action Research as a useful way of approaching and managing change.

Activity 15

A personal role within change

You may like to reflect upon your role regarding any changes you have experienced.

1 Did you initiate the change?

2 Did you lead the team?

3 Were you a member of the team that implemented the change?

4 Did you resist the change?

5 Has the change been sustained?

Conclusion

There is a need for flexible services and a range of multi-professional roles to support the changing needs of children and families within the Early Years sector. The changing role of the practitioner and the importance of qualifications, personal and professional development to support this has been discussed in this chapter. An exploration of ways in which practitioners working within an Early Years setting may develop reflective practice through work-based learning and within a reflective learning environment is examined with interactive activities for practitioners to engage in. Practitioners who question, evaluate, research their professional practice and plan for their developing knowledge and skills in a reflective and evaluative manner become reflective practitioners. Practitioners can contribute to the new opportunities, roles and responsibilities that are available and emerging within the Early Years sector and integrated policy and practice. Reflective practitioners provide relevant and quality services for children and families.

How to move on in your research

The following are key texts to support this chapter.

Bolton, G. (2006) 2nd edition, *Reflective Practice, Writing and Professional Development*. London: Sage

Moon, J. (2007), *Reflection in Learning and Professional Development, Theory and Practice*. London: Routledge Falmer

Willan, J., Parker-Rees, R. and Savage, J., (eds) (2007) (2nd edition), *Early Childhood Matters*. Exeter: Learning Matters

References

Abbott, L. and Moylett, H. (1997), *Working with the Under Threes: Training and Professional Development*. Maidenhead: Open University Press

Abbott, L. and Pugh, G. (1998), *Training to Work in the Early Years: Developing the Climbing Frame*. Maidenhead: Open University Press

Abbott, L. and Rodger, R. (1994), *Quality Education in the Early Years*. Maidenhead: Open University Press

Anning, A. and Edwards, A. (2003), *Promoting Children's Learning from Birth to Five: Developing the New Early Years Professional*. Maidenhead: Open University Press

Cockburn, A. (2001), *Teaching Children 3–11: A Student's Guide*. London: Paul Chapman

Fisher, J. (2002), *Starting from the Child: Teaching and Learning from 3 to 8*. Maidenhead: Open University Press

Hilton, M. (1994), *Interpersonal Interaction*. London: Longman

Johns, C. and Graham, J. (1996), 'Using a reflective model of nursing and guided reflection', *Nursing Standard 11* (32) p39–41

Kay, J. (2002), *Teaching Assistant's Handbook*. London: Continuum

Merchant, G. and Marsh, J. (1998), *Co-ordinating Primary Language and Literacy: The Subject Leader's Handbook*. London: Paul Chapman

Pugh, G. (2001) (3rd edition), *Contemporary Issues in the Early Years: Working Collaboratively for Children.* London: Paul Chapman

Pugh, G., and Duffy, B. (2006) (4th edition), *Contemporary Issues in the Early Years.* London: Sage

Qualifications Assurance Agency (2002), *Foundation Degree benchmark (final draft).* London: QAA

Roberts-Holmes, G. (2005), *Doing Your Research Project.* London: Paul Chapman

Rodd, J. (1998), *Leadership in Early Childhood: The Pathway to Professionalism.* Maidenhead: Open University Press

Rumbold Report, Department of Education and Science (1990), *Starting with Quality: The Rumbold Report of the Committee of Inquiry into the Quality of Educational Experience Offered to 3 and 4 year olds.* London: HMSO

Taylor, J. and Woods, M. (1998), *Early Childhood Studies: An Holistic Introduction.* London: Hodder Arnold

Woodcock, M. (1986), *Team Development Manual.* London: Gower Press

4 Physical development from birth to 16 years

Vicky Cortvriend

This primarily theoretical chapter is designed to provide you with the knowledge and understanding required in order to enable you to support the physical development of the children and young people in your care. It discusses theories and stages of physical development to assist in your observations, which are crucial to the planning and provision of play and learning experiences that promote children's growth, development and learning.

An understanding of physical development is essential when studying the **holistic** (all-round or overall) development of children. Children's growth and development enables them to explore their environment, to make sense of their world, to achieve new skills, to change the way others perceive them, and, most importantly, it aids in their development of self. The child who successfully carries out various tasks and develops new skills can achieve a positive self-image. Conversely, children who constantly fail, or who are given the impression that they are failing, have difficulty in developing this positive sense of self. How and why children develop the way they do, and the factors that influence that development is discussed in some detail in this chapter. It is important to understand that children do not necessarily progress sequentially through stages/norms of development. Each child is a unique person who is a competent learner from birth, albeit within their own individual time frame. The challenge facing the practitioner is to meet the needs of the individual children in their care, by carrying out effective observations and then planning play and activities in order to enable each child to reach their potential.

This chapter addresses the following areas:

➤ Human development

➤ Theories of motor development

➤ Stages of physical development

➤ Factors influencing prenatal development

➤ Postnatal development

By undertaking the suggested study within this chapter it is hoped that you will be able to:

1 review and update your knowledge of the physical growth and development of children and young people

2 assess the physical development of babies/children/young people in your care

3 understand a range of theories of physical development.

Human development

Development is determined by the **genotype** of the child and is also influenced by various external factors, resulting in each child having his or her own personal **phenotype** and developing into a unique person. The genotype refers to the child's genetic makeup, and is entirely hereditary. Phenotype refers to the various environmental factors that influence the child's development.

Human development has, in the past, been studied from a compartmentalised point of view, which tended to lead to an unbalanced understanding of the developmental process. Development has been referred to in terms of **areas** or **domains** (cognitive, social, emotional, physical, normative, conative), and divided into periods (prenatal, infancy, childhood, adolescence, adulthood, old age). This unbalanced point of view can result in students concentrating on only one area to the detriment of others, without realising that each area impacts on the rest, and that each stage or period leads inexorably to the following one.

It is important to view development from a holistic stance, recognising that none of the areas develop in isolation; all areas influence and interact with each other and there is a continuous interaction between the individual's genotype and his or her individual environment. Development is a continuous process, beginning at conception and only ceasing when the person dies.

When studying human development you will come across the terms **growth** and **maturation**; there is a subtle difference between the two (see Figure 4.1).

Development per se has been defined as 'adaptive change toward competence' by Keogh and Sugden (1985). This suggests that during an individual's lifetime, he or she continually has to make adjustments in order to attain, or maintain, competence, as abilities develop and mature and then begin to change with age.

Physical development includes growth, increasing skill and functioning of the body whereas growth alone relates to a child's increasing height, weight and general size. Both growth and development depend on suitable nourishment, including a balance of the right foods and sufficient water to drink.

Increasing control and coordination is enabled by the maturing brain and nervous system, growing bones and muscles, a healthy diet, exercise and physical activity that includes both fine and gross muscle coordination.

Activity 1

Physical development

1 Think of a child who can crawl quite competently but who is now learning to walk. The child has to learn how to compensate for the change in the centre of gravity when he or she stands.

2 Write down some other examples relating to physical development where a child has achieved competence and is now making adjustments in order to develop a new competency.

Growth and maturation defined	
Growth	This is the increase in size, length, and weight (body mass).
Maturation	This is the development of the various systems that together form the human body. Examples are the nervous system, circulatory system, reproductive system and the endocrine system.

Figure 4.1 Development: growth and maturation

In carrying out Activity 1, some examples you may have thought of are:

➤ walking then being able to hop

➤ climbing the stairs on hands and knees, then beginning to put both feet on one stair, before finally climbing up as an adult would

➤ learning how to ride a two-wheeler bicycle after using stabilisers

➤ scribbling then mastering the art of forming letters.

The Early Years Foundation Stage (EYFS) describes how it is important that children should be supported in using all of their senses to learn about the world around them and to make connections between new information and what they already know. It also states that 'They must be supported in developing an understanding of the importance of physical activity and making healthy choices in relation to food' (EYFS, 2007:90).

In normal circumstances, growth and development are continuous and proceed in a typical, usual, or expected pattern. The term **normal** is used loosely to describe a child who is developing typical characteristics for his age and whose height and weight conform to the average.

There are theories, scales and charts that assist childcare workers in determining whether a child is, in fact, developing according to accepted norms. These include:

➤ Jean Piaget's developmental milestone theory (see Chapter 6)

➤ Mary Sheridan's age-related sequences of development (Sheridan, 1975)

➤ growth charts such as the WHO child growth standards

➤ the EYFS Learning and Development principles (2007) which describe the tasks/competencies a child should be able to achieve at 5 years of age.

The National Service Framework for Children, Young People and Maternity Services (2004) establishes clear standards for promoting the health and well-being of children and young people; and for providing high-quality services that meet their needs. One of their stated markers for good practice is that by the child's first birthday a systematic assessment of their physical, emotional and social development and family needs is carried out.

Most developmental scales are based on the work of Arnold Gesell, an American developmental psychologist who researched the development of children in the 1930s (see Theories of motor development on page 73).

However, the World Health Organization (WHO) has issued new guidelines on measuring the growth rates of babies. The summary of the WHO publication *WHO Child Growth Standards* states that 'a comprehensive review of the uses and interpretation of anthropometric references undertaken by WHO in the early 1990s concluded that new growth curves were needed to replace the existing standards' (WHO, April 2006).

With these new WHO Child Growth Standards it is now possible to show how children **should** grow. They demonstrate for the first time ever that children born in different regions of the world and given the optimum start in life have the potential to grow and develop to within the same range of height and weight for age.

Today in the UK, when carrying out their routine checks to record the child's progress, health professionals commonly use a personal child health record to record their findings. These usually contain pictures of 'milestones' alongside which the parent or health visitor can record when the baby/child first achieved each one.

Practitioners who work in Early Years settings observe children's physical development and their developing skills as an ongoing integral part of their practice. Should either a parent or an Early Years practitioner have concerns about a child's development (in any developmental area), then the practitioner needs to be able to provide some evidence that

Figure 4.2 Chart showing the WHO Child Growth Standards 1 to 5 years

Your child's developmental firsts

Your baby grows and learns faster in the first year that at any other time.

rolls over		sits with support		sits alone	
moves around or crawls		stands holding on		stands alone	
walks holding on		walks alone		first outdoor walk	

Figure 4.3

will either refute, or demonstrate, the reasons for these concerns.

Practitioners or parents may express concerns that a child's development is:

➤ slow

➤ delayed

➤ advanced

➤ precocious.

Carrying out a series of observations on the child, and then evaluating the observations against developmental stages/norms can, in part, provide the evidence for these concerns (see Chapter 12). The practitioner will then be in a position to discuss the issues with the child's parents or carers and have relevant evidence to pass on to other professionals such as child psychologists, paediatricians and health visitors, should the need arise. In addition, this information would be used to plan appropriate activities to support or extend the child's development.

When comparing a child's physical development with the norm, the practitioner observes the child's ability to move and to perform different tasks; this is an important part of the practitioner's role in an Early Years setting because it enables him or her to know how each individual child is developing, which in turn enables the practitioner to plan and carry out appropriate activities that are designed to allow the child to consolidate skills and extend his or her development (see Chapters 11 and 12). The practitioner in an Early Years setting is also in a position to provide valuable feedback to the child's parents or carers, and information for other professionals.

Terms commonly referred to when discussing motor skills are **gross motor skills** and **fine motor** or **manipulative skills** (see Figure 4.4).

Motor skills	Abilities
Gross motor skills	The ability to move using whole body movements
Fine motor, or manipulative, skills	The ability to perform skills that require hand and eye coordination

Figure 4.4 Terms that describe motor skills

Activity 2

Observe children or young people playing

1 Observe a group of children playing for a short period (see Chapter 12 for more information about observations).

2 Describe what they are doing, then evaluate your observation by picking out the fine and gross motor skills used.

3 Explain how the use of these skills enabled the children to socialise with their peers and how they aided the children's developing self-esteem (or not, as the case may be).

4 Plan suitable activities using the sources suggested below, that are designed to consolidate their skills, or, should a child not be progressing as you would expect, plan activities to support him or her in this area of development.

5 Use information from Chapter 5, and, if the children are aged 0–5 years, the Practice guidance for the Early Years Foundation Stage (DfES, 2007). Use other sources such as the WHO growth charts and texts such as the Meggitt (2007) book *Child Development Birth to 16 years*.

6 If the children are older than 5 years, refer to Key Stages 1 and 2 of the National Curriculum. If they are younger than 3 years, refer to developmental milestones. If the children are older than 7, refer to Key Stages 3 and 4 of the National Curriculum.

Theories of motor development

Theories attempt to organise accepted facts in order to give them meaning. They do this by testing known facts, and formulating theories to explore and advance new facts. They try to answer the question why. Theorists are people who conduct research in order to test existing theories or to develop new ones.

It is usually recognised that physical development follows a pattern from simple to complex, from head to toe, from inner to outer and from general to specific. Although there are a range of theories that relate to the physical development of children, the three main perspectives are the maturational theories, the systems theories and the ecological theories.

Maturational theories

These represent the nature side of the nature-nurture debate; they assume that as the brain, nervous system and muscular systems mature and develop, the infant will automatically develop increasingly complex gross and fine motor skills.

Gesell and Ames (1940, quoted in Slater and Lewis, 2002) carried out a longitudinal research programme that followed a group of infants from birth to 9 years of age. They produced findings that concluded that motor development proceeds in an invariant sequence, controlled by a maturational timetable that is present in the central nervous system. These studies still remain an important point of departure for empirical research and formed the basis for the developmental checklists (growth charts) used today.

Their research, however, failed to account for individual differences and also led to the assumption that the entire developmental sequence is predetermined. McGraw (1945) challenged these assumptions, following her own research on newborn babies and longitudinal studies on 82 healthy infants. She also carried out research on sets of twins, where only one twin received enriched motor training. McGraw concluded that walking develops in four major steps (see Figure 4.5).

Phase	Development
First (under 4 months)	During the first phase, sub-cortical reflexes largely control limb movements.
Second (under 4 months)	These reflexes become inhibited by higher cortical mechanisms during the first 4 months and the controlling influence of the sub-cortical reflexes diminishes or disappears.
Third (between 4 and 8 months)	Discrete muscle control is achieved under the direction of the higher cortical mechanisms.
Fourth (between 8 and 14 months)	All sub-cortical and cortical components integrate and the infant achieves the mature walking pattern.
Note: sub-cortical and cortical refer to areas of the brain.	

Figure 4.5 Stages in the development of walking in young children (McGraw, 1945)

Systems theories

Detailed animal experiments conducted by Waddington (1971) provide a strong argument against the maturational theories. His studies, based on the idea that any complex organism is made up of many subsystems, show that each subsystem develops according to its own timetable. Even a minor change in the developmental timing of a subsystem can (under some conditions) result in the emergence of a new species during evolution (quoted in Gould, 1992). This implies that differential growth rates across subsystems, together with other biological variants, may result in the induction of new patterns of motor coordination.

Dynamical systems

These theories concern systems that are influenced by a combination of different factors (similar to the idea of the phenotype) that ensure that the system is inherently unpredictable.

Researchers who are concerned specifically with human locomotion, that is, the way humans move, have utilised this idea (Thelen, 1989; Thelen and Smith, 1994). Their results showed that there is an important contribution to be made by positive environmental factors in the development of coordinated motor action, such as walking. This development is always the outcome of a complex interplay between all the variables: the central nervous system, musculo-skeletal system, and the environment (Goldfield and Wolff, 2002).

The Ecological Systems Theory

Urie Bronfenbrenner (1979) developed this theory to explain how everything in a child and the child's environment (the phenotype) affects how a child grows and develops. He described different aspects or levels of the environment that influence children's development. These are the microsystem, the mesosystem, the exosystem, and the macrosystem. The microsystem is the immediate environment that the child lives within and the interactions that take place within that environment. Children's microsystems will include any immediate relationships or organisations they interact with, their immediate family or carers and their school or daycare. How these groups or organisations interact with the child will have an effect on how the child grows; the more encouraging and nurturing these relationships and places are, the better the child will be able to grow. Furthermore, how a child acts or reacts to these people in the microsystem will affect how they treat her in return. Each child's special genetic (genotype) and biologically influenced personality traits, what is known as temperament, end up affecting how others treat them. The mesosystem includes the links between the different aspects of the microsystem, the exosystem are those influences outside the individual's microsystem so the individual is not directly involved but they have an influence on the experiences of that individual. A good example would be working mothers/primary caregivers' experiences. The macrosystem is the society, culture, norms and values of the world in which the individual lives.

Other theoretical approaches are discussed elsewhere in this book and include the phase stage theory of which the most well-known proponents are Sigmund Freud, Erik Erikson and Jean Piaget; the developmental task theory, developed by Robert Havighurst; and the behaviour setting survey of Roger Barker, which is generally recognised as the first major effort to bring physical and social contexts into psychological methodologies for studying human behaviour.

Discussion point 1

Is development continuous or discontinuous?

(See Theories of motor development, page 73)

This question, together with the nature-nurture debate (nature denoting the effects of genes, and nurture denoting the effects of the environment), has been vigorously discussed and has formed the basis for much research.

Conduct your own research into this area by studying the works of Arnold Gesell (1928) and Myrtle McGraw (1935), who are considered to be pioneers in the study of motor development, and later theorists such as Jean Piaget (1954) Keogh and Sugden (1985) and Urie Bronfenbrenner (1979) to help you to decide which point of view you favour.

One point to consider is when exactly do newborn abilities begin? It was previously thought, for example by the philosopher John Locke (1632–1704), that at the moment of birth the abilities of the baby were suddenly switched on (perhaps in the same way that the lungs begin to work). But it is quite possible that these abilities originate during the prenatal period, thus implying continuous development (Hepper, 1994). Bronfenbrenner (1992) believes that the various systems have an influence on the foetus from conception which again would support the continuous development argument.

Foetal behaviour

Another area that is now under discussion is that of the function of foetal behaviour. This is the way that foetuses move around in the womb in reaction to certain stimuli, or the way they suck their thumbs, blink their eyes, or move their mouths. You may have seen scans of foetuses demonstrating such behaviour. Why do they do this? This is the question being asked by some researchers. Are there reasons (stress, excitement, pain) for the foetus reacting and behaving as it does, or are the behaviours the result of the maturing of its systems?

Research carried out by Drachman and Sokoloff (1966) suggests that the movements the foetus makes are important for its structural development. It is also thought that the behaviour of the foetus may influence the development of the sensory system and brain. This is an interesting area for further reading and one that has been repeatedly researched by Hepper.

Stages of physical development

For many years it was thought that the development of the child only really began at birth, and events preceding the birth had little, if any, influence on the child's future development. It is now recognised that the immediate internal environment of the foetus, as well as the development and growth of the foetus, can be influenced by both sociocultural factors, and teratogens (a teratogen is an environmental agent that causes disruption in the normal development of the foetus). This results in prominent differences in newborn babies. Even at birth, therefore, babies can differ in their ability to cope with, and adapt to, their new environment.

Cigarette smoke and stress are two factors that are considered to have an influence on the foetus (see Teratogens, page 77). In the author's experience as a midwife, the babies of the women who had smoked during pregnancy were usually small and the placentas showed signs of calcification on examination after delivery. This is an indication that the baby was under stress while in the womb. Babies born to mothers who lived in poverty were also often small and looked like 'little old men' at birth. A midwife also described the difference between two babies born to the same mother, but ten years apart. The first, born during a time of great stress in the mother's life, when she was 20 years old, was rejected before his birth by the father; he was a very irritable baby, who spent the first year of life crying and did not sleep through the night until 3 years of age. The second baby, however, born 10 years later when the mother was going through a period of calm, and whom both parents wanted, was a quiet and relaxed baby who slept through the night from 6 weeks of age.

In the first part of this section, we look at the physical development of a child from conception through to birth.

Prenatal

The physical development of the child begins at conception. This period between conception and birth, which usually lasts for between 38 and 40 weeks, has been divided into three distinct phases (Moore, 1988). The first is known as the conceptual or germinal phase; this starts with the fertilisation of the egg and ends when the pregnancy is established. This is followed by the embryonic period, which begins during the second week and ends at the end of the eighth week, when the foetal period begins. This continues until the birth of the baby. The period as a whole is referred to as the prenatal period ('prenatal' means 'before birth').

Nature-nurture debate

The nature-nurture debate, genotype versus phenotype, is a continuing debate on the relevance and importance of genetic influences on the developing and maturing foetus compared to the influence of environmental and other factors. It is now suggested that development during the prenatal period involves an interaction between genes and the environment, with the environmental influences contributing more to the development of the foetus than was previously thought. It has also been suggested that the actions and reactions of the foetus (that is, its behaviour) will help shape its own development.

The function of foetal behaviour

Why does the foetus react and behave as it does in the womb and what is the significance of this behaviour? Does its behaviour relate to its development?

➤ At 7 weeks' gestation, the scan picture of the embryo shows quite clearly the large head, lack of neck, small trunk and tiny buds of growth where the limbs will grow. Movement is just discernible.

- At 8 weeks' gestation, the foetus, as it is now known, is fully formed with all organs present. A startle reflex can be seen and general movement is present.
- At 9 weeks' gestation, the foetus can hiccup and perform isolated arm and leg movements. In a male, the external reproductive organs begin to show.
- Foetal breathing movements begin at around 10 weeks' gestation. Between 8 and 12 weeks' gestation the fingernails, toe nails and hair follicles form. In a female, the development of the reproductive organs begins.
- Bones begin to grow; the foetus can flex arms and legs and can also suck. Sometimes scan pictures show foetuses sucking their hands.
- Between 13 and 16 weeks' gestation the foetus has developed unique handprints and footprints. The spinal cord begins to form and the foetus begins to make eye movements.
- Between 17 and 20 weeks' gestation the foetus becomes covered with the waxy substance known as vernix; its function is probably to protect the skin from the amniotic fluid that constantly surrounds it. The foetal heartbeat can clearly be heard through the woman's abdomen.
- The foetus continues to grow and develop and if born prematurely after 21 weeks' gestation can hear, see and produce crying noises.
- Between 22 and 24 weeks' gestation the foetus responds to sounds by moving.
- Between 26 and 29 weeks' gestation the lungs usually develop sufficiently to allow the foetus to breathe if birth occurs early.
- Between 30 and 38 weeks' gestation the foetus increases its weight by about a half. Fat accumulates, giving the full term 'chubby' appearance. The skin colour turns from red to white to bluish pink for all babies, regardless of their racial origin.

In the space of 38 weeks the baby has developed from a zygote (a bundle of cells) to a fully formed baby. This development, however, is not always straightforward as it is influenced by a number of factors. Examples include:

- environmental factors
- genetic factors
- health factors
- age of the mother
- nutritional factors and stress
- pregnancy with more than one foetus in the womb.

Development and maturation of the foetus

There appear to be three main factors that relate to the development and maturation of the foetus. These factors, which are outlined below, have dominated discussion, and continue to raise questions, prompting more research into the development of the embryo and foetus during the prenatal period.

Factors influencing prenatal development

Some of the main factors that affect prenatal development are outlined below.

Teratogens

Teratogens are agents that cause harm to the foetus during its development in the womb (see Figure 4.6).

Alcohol

Exposure to alcohol can lead to foetal alcohol syndrome as described by Abel (1989) and first recognised in the early 1970s during observations carried out on babies born to alcoholic mothers (Jones and Smith, 1973). These babies are characterised by growth

Teratogens	Effects on the foetus
Rubella	The first agent to be recognised as a teratogen was the rubella virus, commonly known as German measles. In 1941, McAllister Gregg, an ophthalmologist, confirmed that German measles in a pregnant woman often resulted in the baby being born with visual anomalies.
Radiation	The second teratogen to be described was radiation, following reports in the 1940s and 1950s about women who had been exposed to the atomic bomb, and who were reported to have given birth to babies who had birth defects. This, together with reports about research done on animals, implicated radiation as a teratogen (Warkany and Schraffenberger, 1947).
Thalidomide	The drug thalidomide given to pregnant women for nausea in the 1950s and early 1960s resulted in the birth of many infants who had severe arm and leg malformations (McBride, 1961, Lenz and Kapp, 1962).
Other substances	Other substances that are freely taken by mothers today have been identified as having harmful effects on the foetus – alcohol, cigarettes and drugs being the major culprits.

Figure 4.6 Some teratogens and their effects on the foetus

retardation, abnormal facial features and intellectual retardation. Heavy drinking throughout pregnancy, or binge drinking, is far more hazardous to the developing foetus than moderate drinking, although a safe dose for alcohol consumption during pregnancy has not yet been established. Reports have demonstrated that even moderate amounts of alcohol intake can result in spontaneous abortions, less alert babies and slower learning in newborns.

Foetal alcohol effect is considered to be a milder form of foetal alcohol syndrome, resulting in children who are born with less severe retardation than those with foetal alcohol syndrome, but who may suffer from behavioural difficulties and poor social skills.

In May 2007 the Department of Health advised that pregnant women and those trying for a baby should avoid alcohol completely. This replaced existing advice that one to two units such as a couple of glasses of wine per week is acceptable.

The change follows concern from some sectors that there is no safe amount of alcohol that mothers-to-be can drink. While heavy alcohol consumption during pregnancy is known to be damaging to the unborn child, the effects of more moderate intake are less clear. However, the Royal College of Obstetricians and Gynaecologists say there is no evidence that a couple of units once or twice a week will do any harm to the baby. The Department of Health said the revision was not based on new scientific evidence but was needed to help ensure that women did not underestimate the risks to their baby.

Cigarette smoking

Evidence published in the February 2004 report 'Smoking and Reproductive Life', produced by the BMA's board of Science and the Tobacco Control Resource Centre, states that smoking damages the health of both men and women throughout their reproductive life. It can lower fertility rates, and has a detrimental effect on the foetus during pregnancy. The evidence suggests that smoking may increase the risk of cleft lip and palate malformations in the developing foetus. The report confirms the findings from previous studies, suggesting that women who smoke are three times more likely to give birth to low-birth-weight infants. It appears that the number of cigarettes smoked and the length of time the woman smokes during pregnancy are linked to the size of the baby at birth. Spontaneous abortions, stillbirths and neonatal deaths are also more numerous in women who smoke during their pregnancy. Smoking can also compromise breast feeding because women who smoke produce less milk of a poorer quality. There is also substantial evidence to link passive smoking with reduced foetal growth and premature birth.

Prescription and other drugs

Legal and illegal drugs can also have an effect on the foetus. Pregnant women are advised not to take any over-the-counter or illegal drugs during pregnancy. If medication has to be taken, it should only be done so under close medical supervision.

There are various other factors that can have an influence on the effect that a teratogen will have on an unborn baby. You may perhaps cite an example of a woman who smoked 30 cigarettes a day throughout her pregnancy and gave birth to a baby who weighed more than nine pounds! The difficulty lies in predicting who will be affected. This is almost impossible to determine prior to a woman becoming pregnant, but the advent of ultrasound scans and other screening tests mean that it is easier to predict the birth of a healthy or possibly damaged baby. As a practitioner in an Early Years setting, you may be involved in offering advice and support to expectant parents.

Factors that determine the effect of a teratogen on an unborn baby

The factors outlined below play a part in determining the effect of a teratogen on an unborn baby.

The individual's genetic makeup or genotype

This may affect susceptibility.

The stage of development of the embryo/foetus

The stage of development of the embryo/foetus at the time it is exposed to the teratogen may be significant. There are periods of sensitivity during prenatal development when the

Prescription and other drugs	Effects
Tetracycline	If taken during the second or third trimester of pregnancy, it can cause staining of the baby's teeth.
Streptomycin	This has been associated with hearing loss.
Aspirin	There is a possibility of increased bleeding in mother and infant.
Benzodiazepines	Infants may display withdrawal symptoms at birth.
Vitamin A	Large amounts of vitamin A are known to cause major birth defects.
Retinoids (Roaccutane)	These anti-acne drugs have similar effects on the foetus as vitamin A.
Marijuana	It crosses the placenta and is found in the amniotic fluid surrounding the foetus. It is also probably present in the breast milk of heavy smokers.
Heroin and methadone	Babies suffer withdrawal symptoms at birth. Congenital defects have not been linked directly to either heroin or methadone, but stillbirths, infant deaths and low birthweight in newborns are common among users. Developmental difficulties in infants born to addicts are frequently observed but this may be due to the environment the infant is being raised in, rather than the effects of the drugs when in the womb.

Figure 4.7 Effects of legal and illegal drugs taken during pregnancy

embryo/foetus is more sensitive to teratogenic influences than other times. The third to eighth week of pregnancy is a period when many organs and systems are being formed. They are, therefore, very sensitive to toxic agents during this period. The brain, however, continues to grow and develop during the entire pregnancy, which is why exposure to teratogens at any time may have behavioural consequences for the child.

The amount of exposure

Does the type or strength of a teratogen affect the foetus in different ways? It has been documented that the damage tobacco smoke has on the foetus is linked to the amount of cigarettes the mother smoked. But the severity of a disease such as rubella does not always reflect the amount of damage to the foetus. Other factors such as the overall health of the mother play a part in determining the teratogenic effect.

Health conditions and illnesses

A number of health conditions can result in increased risk to the foetus. These include:

➤ Gaucher disease, an inherited condition affecting mainly Ashkenazic Jews

➤ diabetes

➤ hypertension

➤ eclampsia (occurs during some pregnancies)

➤ Rh incompatibility.

All pregnant women should have regular health checks, particularly if they have an underlying condition that may prove to be a risk factor (see Chapter 9, page 234, Screening during the antenatal period). German measles (rubella) is a potential hazard to the developing foetus, and other, severe, viral infections can also be dangerous to the foetus. It is important to refer expectant mothers to their doctor if they are at all at risk.

The websites listed at the end of this chapter provide further information about the above conditions.

Age of mother

Many women today, for a variety of reasons, choose to have children later in life. The likelihood of having a child with Down's syndrome increases markedly with the age of the mother. One in every 1,500 babies born to mothers aged 21 years will have Down's syndrome, whereas in mothers aged 49, the incidence rises to 1 in 10.

Teenagers, however, are also at risk of delivering less healthy babies, according to a study carried out by McAnarney (1987). This is thought to be due to the fact that the ova (eggs) are not fully mature in teenage girls. Teenagers are also still growing themselves and have their own nutritional needs as well as those of the developing foetus.

Nutrition

Nutritional factors can affect the well-being of the foetus, and the need for a woman to eat a well-balanced diet with sufficient protein, vitamins, minerals, and other nutrients during pregnancy is recognised by all health professionals. Women of normal weight for their height are typically advised to gain about 25–35 pounds during pregnancy.

The physical and neural development of the foetus can be severely impaired when a pregnant woman fails to eat a balanced diet. This was clearly demonstrated during the famines that occurred in parts of Holland and in Leningrad during World War Two following invasion by the Nazis. When the malnutrition occurred during the first trimester, death, premature birth and neural defects were recorded. When the malnutrition occurred later in the pregnancy, the babies were likely to be born small.

Each year up to 1,200 pregnancies in the UK are affected by Neural Tube Defects (spina bifida) – 85% of which result in abortions. Around 150 severely disabled babies are born with spina bifida, a severe birth impairment (Association for Spina Bifida and Hydrocephalus, 2007 (ASBAH)).

Government recommendations are that if you are pregnant or thinking of having a baby you should take a daily 0.4 mg (400 microgram) folic acid supplement from the time you stop using contraception until the 12th week of pregnancy.

The Association for Spina Bifida and Hydrocephalus supports the Food Standards Agency's decision to recommend to health ministers the mandatory fortification of UK flour with the vitamin folic acid. They consider that unnecessary severe disability will be prevented as a result of this initiative.

Discussion point 2

A woman's legal responsibility to her unborn child

Should a woman who is made aware of the possible teratogenic effects that using illegal substances can have on her unborn child, but continues to use them, be prosecuted for child abuse if the child is born with birth defects?

How far should the government go? Should it suggest limits relating to food/alcohol/smoking? Should it be allowed to fortify staple foodstuffs, for example fluoride in water and folic acid in flour? Or should all these aspects be up to individual choice?

Stress

Stress has been shown by several researchers to cause harm to the developing foetus (Wadha et al, 1993; Luke et al, 1995, in Bukatko and Daehler). Severe stress seems to result in premature births and babies of low birthweight. Anxiety during pregnancy seems to result in difficult births with a higher rate of complications during delivery.

The support given by family and friends has been shown to be a major factor in decreasing the effects of stressors on pregnant women, and so decreasing the harm done to the foetus (Norbeck and Tilden, 1983). Discussing concerns with supportive groups has been found to be an effective method of counteracting the harmful effects of stress.

Activity 4

Educating prospective parents

Consider the following questions.

➤ Would education help prospective parents to make the best choices for themselves and their unborn child?

➤ Would education help to reduce the incidence of unwanted pregnancies?

➤ Would education help to reduce the incidence of premature births and babies born affected by teratogens?

➤ Should the government take it upon themselves to remove our choice – as in smoking in public places, the addition of folic acid to flour? Even when the health benefits to our unborn children are clearly documented?

Think about what type of educational experience you would suggest – a series of talks by parents with first-hand experience, informal debates and discussion perhaps, or lectures by professional experts?

Reflect upon these suggestions then carry out the following activities.

1 Plan a series of antenatal sessions for a group of prospective parents. Include all the above information (and further research carried out by yourself) in a format designed to educate rather than frighten the clients.

2 Plan a series of sessions for 14–16-year-olds, again with the idea of educating them about the risks involved in smoking, drinking and drug taking while pregnant.

Postnatal development

A human infant's development in the womb can be influenced by the health, welfare, emotional state and physical well-being of the mother. The type, duration and environment of the birth can also influence both mother and baby. The mother's attitude can be influenced by factors including how the birth is planned, presence of complications, the level of pain and availability of pain relief, and the proximity of emotional support. A long and difficult birth is stressful for both the mother and her child.

As we saw earlier in the chapter, the baby can be highly active in the womb: in the final three months before birth, the baby moves spontaneously, can respond to sounds and light, and may suck thumb. At birth, although physically helpless, the baby has a set of reflexes that not only supports its interactions with its carers but also demonstrates that a 'template' for physical activity is in place. In order to understand this, we need to take a brief look at the brain.

The brain has two distinct hemispheres, which, together with the brain stem and spinal cord, are mirror images of each other, although function varies between the left and right hemispheres. There is only one gland – the pineal gland – not duplicated on each side of the brain. The hemispheres are joined by the corpus callosum, which transmits much of the communication between hemispheres. The surface of each hemisphere is covered by the cortex. Its most identifiable features are grooves (sulci) and ridges (gyri) that give the brain its characteristic wrinkled appearance but, more importantly, have characteristics which are unique to each human and which bear the imprint of experience. Each hemisphere is divided into four 'lobes'.

➤ The frontal lobe appears to deal with the most abstract and complex of brain functions, for example thinking, planning, conceptualising and in the conscious 'appreciation' of emotion.

➤ The parietal lobe appears to be mainly involved with movement, orientation, calculation and body image.

➤ The temporal lobe deals with hearing, language, comprehension, sound and some aspects of memory and emotion.

➤ The occipital lobe is mostly taken up with visual processing areas.

Our brains ultimately process all information they receive, developing over time. The lobes within the brain develop at different rates, depending on the particular skills they promote. In other words, our abilities and skills depend on the way our brain is 'wiring up'. The concept of physical development is often associated with large or gross motor movements such as walking, running, jumping and dancing, or fine motor movements made with the hands and fingers. However, smooth coordinated movements are impossible without support and feedback from our other senses, especially vision and touch. Movement and sensory information are so closely intertwined they should really be referred to as a sensorimotor system rather than being divided into the two areas.

One of the most interesting issues about movement is the existence in the brain of 'body maps', which include motor and somatosensory maps. Even though these 'maps' are arranged on a particular part of the cortex, the upward processing of information requires aspects of organisation across the entire cortex and subcortical brain areas (which lie underneath the cortex). A general 'rule of thumb' is that the more precise the movements generated by different parts of the body, the greater the area of the brain devoted to them. Greenfield (2000) describes the hands and the mouth as having an enormous allocation of space on the 'map' compared with the upper arm and the back, which have very little space devoted to them. It is also important to remember that, as Skoyles and Sagan (2002) point out, the brain's 'motor map' is built up by sensory information, including feedback from the position of our muscles and joints. For example, the pre-motor cortex (found in front of the motor cortex) guides movements via information from vision and other sensory feedback systems. The somatosensory maps and the 'motor map' (also known as the somatotopic map) lie close to each other on either side of the central sulcus, the deep ridge which roughly divides the frontal from the parietal lobes. The motor map lies in front of the sulcus and the somatosensory map lies just behind it. Each map displays the same distorted picture of the body, clearly illustrating the overall importance of each body area and the relationships between them.

Key developmental transitions in physical development: birth to three

The following section (page 87) concerns the physical changes that occur during childhood and adolescence. However, children develop at their own pace, achieving each milestone earlier or later than the general 'timeline' of development. In addition, the senses play a part in developing skills in movement: brains are maturing along with bodies.

The first part of this section has been divided into groups corresponding to the Birth to Three Matters initiative to provide a broad framework for thinking about the details of physical development. These groups are:

➤ heads up, lookers and communicators (0–8 months)

➤ sitters, standers and explorers (8–18months)

➤ movers, shakers and players (18–24 months)

➤ walkers, talkers and pretenders (24–36 months).

While the focus is on physical development across these age ranges, no aspect of development occurs in isolation and a child's social, emotional and physical environment will also influence the way in which a child develops. For example, a child given no opportunity to explore, or who is deprived of adequate nutrients or who receives little emotional encouragement may not develop optimal motor skills. The EYFS requires that the physical development of babies and young children should be encouraged through the provision of opportunities within an enabling environment to enable them to be active and improve their skills of coordination, control, manipulation and movement. They should also be encouraged to use all of their senses in developing an understanding of the importance of physical activity and developing healthy eating habits, (EYFS, 2007).

Heads up, lookers and communicators

At birth, infants are essentially helpless but by the time they are eight months old, they are able to sit steadily (or with minimal support) and often crawl or make some effort to move independently. While experience does influence development profoundly, a baby is given a 'head start' by the existence at birth of various reflexes. A reflex is an unconscious, spontaneous response to a stimulus. A classic example is if someone taps the knee in a certain place, the leg shoots out. Babies have a number of these reflexes including:

➤ palmar or grasp reflex

➤ rooting reflex

➤ sucking reflex

➤ moro or startle reflex

➤ plantar or foot reflex (stepping reflex)

➤ Babinski (curling of the toes).

The first three reflexes support immediate interaction with the mother through touch and feeding. The startle reflex suggests that the baby is 'primed' to respond to surprise or fearful situations, and the plantar and Babinski reflexes illustrate a potential 'wiring up' of basic motor movements that have been formed by the baby's actions in the womb. These reflexes all become less obvious over time as the brain matures and the baby becomes more discriminating in his or her responses. As babies get to know their world, they begin to respond more purposefully than the 'global' type of response seen in the newborn. For example, the stepping reflex occurs if the baby is held upright with the feet placed on a hard surface. The baby then moves his or her legs as if stepping or walking. Some research has indicated that this reflex does not totally disappear over the next few months but becomes integrated into the patterns of kicking, which in turn bear a similarity to the movements used when walking.

Babies' increasing control of their bodies follow a logical pattern. For example, by about six weeks after birth, babies can usually hold their heads up in line with their bodies when pulled to sit up. By the age of three months, a baby will spend a lot of time moving his or her arms and legs, and hand and finger exploration is notable. By the age of five months, the baby can actively grasp at attractive items such as toys but finds letting go difficult. Even by six months, letting go is usually accidental and the baby loses interest once the toy is out of sight. At the same time, control over the trunk is improving and by the age of four months, babies are able to roll from their backs to their sides. By the age of six months, babies can roll over from their back to their stomach, which incidentally puts the baby in the best position for the 'push ups' required for crawling. Sitting becomes increasingly steady and requires less support. By seven to eight months of age, the baby is usually very active and will change position, push up on his or her arms, move in circles and so on. The grasp is still fairly 'broad' although the baby can pick up objects of different shapes and weights and also start to modify the way in which hand actions are performed: not only banging but patting too.

As stated earlier, it is difficult to separate the child's development of muscular control from the impact of visual input. Newborn vision is limited to orientating to single targets, especially faces, but by the age of three months vision appears to be sufficiently integrated for the baby to switch attention from one 'object' to another. This is accompanied by the simultaneous development of such systems as orientation, motion and colour awareness, which all become more sensitive over time. Being able to see the position of a toy, both in relation to the other things around it, and relative to the position of the baby, helps children to learn to reach and grasp. Around the age of five to six months, the baby's visual control of reach and grasp suggests an awareness of 'near visual space', that is, the baby can reach for things close by reasonably accurately. Children of this age can also usually adjust the shape of their hands to accommodate the shape of the desired object. Over the next couple of months, the child's ability to reach with one hand appears to coincide with the child's control of the trunk; the child can usually sit steadily and unsupported by eight months of age.

By the time they reach eight months, therefore, most babies are able to move around freely and with choice and control. Incidentally, getting up is far easier for babies of this age than getting down! In the hands, the emergence of much finer muscle control develops with the emergence of the 'pincer grasp'. Most babies can also sit very steadily by this time and can therefore become involved in careful exploration of play materials. Babies can now also use their forefinger to point. Practitioners may find that babies go through a stage around this time when they do not like being on their backs and will try to sit up as much as possible.

Each child has two sets of teeth or dentitions (occasionally an individual may have one or three sets). At birth the teeth of both sets are present in immature form in the mandible and maxilla (jaw bones). There are 20 temporary teeth which begin to erupt when the child is about 6 months, and should all be present when the child reaches the age of 2 years.

Sitters, standers and explorers

From eight months onwards, both fine and gross motor movements are becoming steadily under the control of the baby. At this age, babies begin to look for an object they have dropped. The skill of letting go emerges at about the same time so babies will often practise this new knowledge by playfully dropping toys and hoping that obliging adults will pick them up so the baby can drop them again! This serves two important purposes. Firstly, the baby gets more practice in the skill of opening the hands in order to 'let go', and, secondly, it reinforces the idea of object permanence. Practitioners may also notice a change in the way the child can balance by no longer having to lean against a chair but standing unsupported and balancing using outstretched hands. Year-old babies have visual control of locomotion, which indicates an integration of physical action, attention, control and awareness of far and near visual space (Atkinson, 2000). It is only when muscles are sufficiently strong and sufficiently co-ordinated to both support the baby's weight and to follow a specific direction that babies begin to pull themselves up and take a step. The time at which a child walks alone depends on opportunity, the child's own determination, type of encouragement and muscle and balance development, but it is usually between 12 and 15 months (Hall, Hill and Elliman, 1990). It is interesting that it is at about a year old that a child can see clearly to the other side of a room and this coincides with greater mobility – the child can see where they are going. The ability to walk around obstacles requires practice, as does the child's ability to work out his or her body in relation to others. The child will therefore often try to crawl under and around things as well as walk towards desired objects or people. Practitioners may also notice that the child sometimes returns to crawling, as this may still be quicker and easier than the hard

work of walking. As the child approaches 18 months, walking becomes steadier and the child wants to climb. Again, this is a practice of motor skills and spatial skills as the child begins to get the idea of up and down. Children also have more control over their bodies by being able to kneel steadily and sit on an appropriately sized seat. All these skills allow for a growing sense of independence and an ability to interact at a number of physical levels.

As with the new skill of walking, fine motor movements require much trial and error. For example, attempts to use a spoon will often require some practice before the trajectory from plate to mouth is fully mastered. (Next time you use a spoon, slow your actions down and notice just how much skill is required to keep the spoon level and upright!) The ability to pick up small items using a pincer grasp also becomes more refined as the child becomes more able to let go of objects and begins to 'post' objects and handle toy bricks. By 18 months of age, children have usually achieved sufficient control over their hands to use them together and to build small towers, to scribble, to use a palmar (whole hand) grasp and to turn the pages of a book. In fact, these are examples of the kind of development test that health visitors often carry out on children aged between 18 months and two years.

Movers, shakers and players

Being able to run is the next step in the child's growing set of motor abilities. Running becomes less cautious and more confident as children approach their second birthday, although again there will be individual variations. Children need to feel safe walking before they start running. A new skill such as this engenders activity in various brain areas and as a child practises this skill and becomes more confident at it, the patterns of sensory information, cortical control, instructions to muscles and, ultimately, movements become more refined and so the activity becomes 'automatic'. Children are now confident with stairs but will probably still go downstairs on their bottoms and will need a helping hand or rail when going up. As the months pass, running becomes faster and can change direction. Most children can kick a ball without falling over, and bending down to pick up toys is now quite usual. Fine motor or hand movements are also much more developed, towers can be built higher, and objects can be placed more precisely, assuming, of course, that vision is developing normally too. The use of individual fingers rather than the whole hand is becoming more common. This increases independence as children can begin to try dressing themselves and eating with minimal support.

Walkers, talkers and pretenders

Overall, the next months show a growing refinement of the skills in both large muscle and fine muscle movement. Children aged three have been known to learn to ski or to play a musical instrument, and many children can pedal a tricycle, catch a ball and swim.

Again, individual children will vary considerably both in the type of activity they enjoy and the degree of skill they will reach. It is important that children are given the opportunity to try out their skills but practitioners must remember that children's confidence can be severely shaken if faced with something that they sense is beyond them and they are overly encouraged to accomplish it. The abilities to walk, run, climb, throw, catch, build, thread, make marks are all new or 'nearly new' and children will often want to consolidate their skills by repeating some actions over and over. The growing ability to engage in imaginative role play all support children in consolidating physical skills as they imitate domestic and adult activities, or pretend to be imaginary characters who can fly, fight, jump, hop and so on.

To summarise, from infancy onwards children develop motor control over their bodies, becoming increasingly able to move according to their own wishes. Improving physical development supports children in growing into being themselves just as much as any other aspect of development. However, physical development is only one part of development and the child's vision, the proper working of other sensory feedback mechanisms and the realisation that bodies move in space and in relation to other people and objects around them all takes time, practice, opportunity and, most of all, support from attentive adults.

The development of motor skills has important implications for the holistic development of the child. It is important that practitioners who work in Early Years settings are aware of the expected norms of development so that they will be aware of any deviation from the norm and can then share their concerns with relevant others (parents, carers, and other professionals).

The Early Years Foundation Stage (EYFS)

Figure 4.8 opposite illustrates the guidance provided by the **Early Years Foundation Stage** (EYFS) 2007, which has been developed as part of the Childcare Act 2006, in order to help young children achieve the five Every Child Matters outcomes of:

➤ staying safe
➤ being healthy
➤ enjoying and achieving
➤ making a positive contribution, and
➤ achieving economic well-being.

Activity 5

Skill development

Do early motor skills, that is, reflexes, pave the way for more complex voluntary activities?

Observe a young baby, then an infant of perhaps one year old. Can you see the link between the early reflexes of the baby and the skills that the one-year-old has developed? Write an account describing your findings.

30–50 months	Children are honing their large and fine motor skills and becoming stronger and more confident. They are playing with other children and learning to cooperate and share. Their increased confidence enables them to help adults and other children in everyday activities. They have good spatial awareness now and are able to walk backwards, sideways and can run around without running into each other or inanimate objects.
40–60 months	Children are now beginning to develop a stronger sense of 'me' and their understanding of their own world (Bronfenbrenner's microsystems). They are better able to plan and undertake more challenging activities and enjoy making and doing. Showing what they are able to 'do' running, dancing, ball games helps them to feel good about themselves and provides positive feedback for their development of self-worth. Children of 5 years are completely independent in the social skills of washing, dressing and eating. They should be able to use a range of small and large equipment (tools, construction and malleable materials) safely and with increasing control.

Figure 4.8 Early Years Foundation Stage guidance

The older child

5 to 8 years

The actual physical growth and development of children between the ages of 5 and 8 is less marked than during the early years. From the age of 6 years, children begin to lose their first set of teeth (commonly known as milk teeth). The permanent teeth start to appear around this age but the full complement of 32 teeth might not be present until the 24th year of age. Children are moving towards developing a good sense of balance and control and towards the end of this stage begin to enjoy activities such as climbing, ball and playground games that involve precise fine and gross movements.

8 to 12 years

This is a period of slow steady growth, followed by a period of rapid growth just before puberty, which usually occurs in girls between the ages of 9 and 13 years and boys between 10 and 16 years. The physical development of children does vary greatly and although some may reach sexual maturity around the age of 9 others mature much later during adolescence (Pappalia and Olds, 1993). Some children develop exceptional motor ability that enables them to excel, perhaps at some form of sport, for example netball,

swimming, running. All children during this period are refining their fine muscle coordination by enjoying activities such as building models, playing musical instruments, practising their computer skills and their gross muscle coordination by playing sport and team games.

Adolescence: 12 to 16/18 years

The onset of adolescence means that growth accelerates and children experience a series of changes both physical (external) and physiological (internal). They become taller and heavier and the proportions of their bodies change. There are changes in their strength, suppleness and stamina. They become sexually mature, developing primary and secondary sexual characteristics. Their nutritional requirements change accordingly in order to meet the changing needs of their bodies.

The acceleration of growth and maturation of the reproductive system is due mainly to the action of the pituitary gland. Physical change starts when the hypothalamus activates the pituitary gland to secrete growth and sexual hormones. These hormonal secretions trigger a rapid increase in height and mass as well as a change in the body's proportions. Girls start growing faster between the ages of 9½ and 14½, and are usually taller, heavier and stronger at this stage than boys of the same age. Boys start growing faster between 10½ and 16 years. This growth spurt lasts for around two years. On average girls reach adult height two years earlier than boys. Boys however then overtake the girls and end up taller and heavier as they reach young adulthood.

This rapid acceleration of growth can lead to a temporary decline in balance and coordination during early puberty. However, this awkwardness soon disappears and their bones harden and become heavier, their muscles develop strength and their stamina, motor skills and coordination continue to improve.

Sexual development

Primary sexual development refers to the sexual glands and the organs that are directly involved in reproduction. For boys these are the penis, testes and prostate gland; for girls the labia, vulva, vagina, uterus and ovaries. These organs grow bigger and mature during this period of accelerated growth.

Secondary sexual characteristics are those external characteristics that distinguish a child from an adult and a male from a female. They include male facial hair, female breasts, armpit and genital hair and voice and skin changes. Females begin menstruating and males have their first ejaculation.

Conclusion

Children and young people will grow and develop, usually within expected norms, providing they are nurtured and encouraged to do so. An understanding of human development, the theories of motor development and the factors which influence that development are vital for practitioners who work with children. This knowledge will assist you in your work as you will become more aware of the role of significant adults, such as parents and practitioners who work in Early Years and other settings, in supporting the physical and overall development of children. The recognition that each child lives within their own individual microsystem, with factors that are interdependent and influence each other resulting in a unique individual, is an important factor in being able to understand why it is so important to support individual children's needs.

A healthy child is the result of a complex interplay of many interrelated factors. An understanding of the consequences of some of those factors that prevent a child from achieving normal development will assist you in defining the steps you can take, as practitioners, should you find, or suspect, that children in your care are not developing in the way you would expect.

How to move on in your research

The Department for Education and Skills (2007), *The Early Years Foundation Stage.* www.des.gov.uk/foundation
The Department for Children, Schools and Families (DCSF) website provides up-to-date information on children's care and education. It is also useful for its recent reports on childcare facilities and publications such as *The Early Years Foundation Stage 2007.*

WHO (World Health Organization). Last accessed on 16 June 2008 at http://www.who.int/childgrowth/en/
The World Health Organization Child Growth Standards.

References

Abel, E. (1989), *Behavioral Teratogenesis and Behavioral Mutogenesis: A Primer in Abnormal Development.* Hingham: Kluwer Academic

Atkinson, J. (2000), *The Developing Visual Brain.* Oxford: Oxford University Press

Bee, H. (2000), *The Developing Child* (9th edition). Boston: Allyn and Bacon

Bronfenbrenner, U. (1979). *The Ecology of Human Development: Experiments by Nature and Design.* Cambridge, Massachusetts: Harvard University Press.

Bronfenbrenner, U. (1992). *Ecological Systems Theory*, as cited in, R. Vasta (ed.), Six Theories of Child Development. London: Jessica Kingsley.

Bukatko, D. and Daehler, M. (1998) (3rd edition), *Child Development: A Thematic Approach.* New York: Houghton Mifflin Company

Drachman, D. and Sokoloff, L. (1996), 'The role of movement in embryonic joint development'. *Developmental Biology*, 14, pp401–20

Gallahue, D. and Ozmun, J. (1998), *Understanding Motor Development.* Boston: McGraw Hill.

Gesell, A. (1928), *Infancy and Human Growth.* New York: Macmillan

Greenfield, S. (2000), *The Private Life of the Brain.* London: Penguin

Gould, S. (1992), 'Heterochroney', in Keller, E. and Lloyd, E. (eds), *Key Words in Evolutionary Biology* (pp158–65). Cambridge, MA: Harvard University Press

Hall, D.M.B., Hill, P. and Elliman, D. (1990), *The Child Surveillance Handbook.* Oxford: Radcliffe Medical Press

Hepper, P. (1991), 'An examination of foetal learning before and after birth'. *Irish Journal of Psychology*, 12, pp95–107

Hepper, P. (1992), 'Foetal psychology: An embryonic science', in J. Niehuis, *Foetal Behavior Development and Perinatal Aspects,* pp129–76. Oxford: Oxford University Press

Hepper, P. (1994), 'The beginnings of mind: evidence from the behavior of the foetus'. *Journal of Infant and Reproductive Psychology*, 12, pp143–54

Hepper, P. (2002), 'Prenatal development', in **Slater, A. and Lewis, M. (eds)**, *Introduction to Infant Development*. Oxford: Oxford University Press

Holt, K. (1991), *Child Development Diagnosis and Assessment*. Oxford: Butterworth Heinemann

Jones, K. and Smith, D. (1973), 'Recognition of the foetal alcohol syndrome in early infancy'. *Lancet*, 2, pp999–1001

Keogh, J. and Sugden, D. (1985), Movement Skill Development. New York: Macmillan

Lenz, W. and Knapp, K. (1962), 'Foetal malformations due to Thalidomide. *German Medical Monthly*, 7, p253

McAnarney, E. (1987), 'Young maternal age and adverse neonatal outcome'. *American Journal of Diseases of Children*, 141, pp1053–9

McBride, W. (1961), 'Thalidomide and congenital abnormalities'. *Lancet*, 2, p1358

McGraw, M. (1935), *Growth: A Study of Johnny and Jimmy*. New York: Appleton Century

McGraw, M. (1945), *Neuromuscular Maturation of the Human Infant*. New York: Haffner

Meggitt, C. (2007), *Child Development – Birth to 16 years: An illustrated Guide*. Oxford: Heinemann

Meggitt, C. and Sunderland, G. (2000), *Child Development: An Illustrated Guide*. Oxford: Heinemann

Moore, K. (1998), *The Developing Human*. Philadelphia: W. D. Saunders

Norbeck, J. and Tilden, V. (1983), 'Life stress, social support and emotional disequilibrium in complications of pregnancy. A prospective multivariate study'. *Journal of Health and Social Behavior*, 24, pp30–36

Pappalia, D. E. and Olds, S. W. (1990), (6th edition), *A Child's World: Infancy Through Adolescence*. New York: McGraw-Hill

Piaget, J. (1954), *The Construction of Reality and the Child*. New York: Basic Books

Sheridan, M. (1975), *From Birth to Five Years: Children's Developmental progress*. Windsor: NFER NELSON

Skoyles, J. R. and Sagan, D. (2002), *Up from Dragons: The Evolution of Human Intelligence*. New York: McGraw-Hill

Slater, A. and Lewis, M. (2002), *Introduction to Infant Development*. Oxford: Oxford University Press

Thelen, E. (1989), 'Self-organization in developmental processes. Can systems approaches work?', in **Gunnar, M. and Thelen, E. (eds)**, *Systems in Development: The Minnesota Symposia in Child Psychology*, Vol. 22, pp71–117. Hillsdale, NJ: Erlbaum

Thelen, E. and Smith, L. (1994), *A Dynamic Systems Approach to the Development of Cognition and Action*. Cambridge, MA: MIT Press

Waddington, C. (1971), 'Concepts of development', in **Tobach, E., Aronsen, L. and Shaw, E. (eds)**, *The Biopsychology of Development* (pp17–23). San Diego, CA: Academic Press

Wadha, P., Sandman, C., Porto, M., Dunkel-Schetter, C. and Garite, T. (1993), 'The association between prenatal stress and infant birth weight and gestational age at birth. A prospective investigation'. *American Journal of Obstetrics and Gynecology*, 169, pp858–65

Warkany, J. and Schraffenberger, E. (1947), 'Congenital malformations induced in rats by roentgen rays'. *American Journal of Roentgenology and Radium therapy*, 57, pp455–63

Useful websites

www.asbah.org
The official site of the Association for Spina Bifida and Hydrocephalus.

www.med.upenn.edu/meded/public/berp
This site from the University of Pennsylvania Health System gives a useful overview of foetal development.

www.pregnancyguideonline.com
An interesting and easy-to-read site providing information and advice about various aspects of pregnancy. Useful for parents and prospective parents.

www.qca.org.uk
This is the official site of the Qualifications and Curriculum Authority. It provides information relating to all aspects of curriculum.

www.norton.co.uk/gleitman/ch13/basis.htm
This refers to chapter 13 of the book *Psychology* (1999) (5th edition), by Henry Gleitman, Alan Fridland and Daniel Reisburg. This chapter discusses the physical basis of development and includes a definition of genotype and phenotype amongst other relevant definitions and theories.

www.Mostgene.org/gd/gdvol12h.htm
An American site about different aspects of genetics.

www.lifeclinic.com/focus/diabetes/pregnancy_main.asp
A useful site detailing information relating to diabetes and pregnancy.

www.expectantmothersguide.com/library/philadelphia/EPHnutrition.htm
Advice about maintaining good nutrition during pregnancy.

www.vrg.org/nutrition/veganpregnancy.htm
Detailed information about how to ensure that vegan mothers eat a healthy diet during pregnancy.

www.cleft.ie/noticeboard/archives/stress090900.htm
The Cleft Lip and Palate Association of Ireland website. This article refers to the link between severe stress in pregnancy and a child born with a cleft lip or palate.

5 Emotional and social well-being

Vivienne Walkup

This chapter aims to explore the emotional and social development of children and the role of the adult in this process. It considers the principles involved in providing an environment in which children may reach their potential and is, therefore, particularly relevant to those practitioners in Early Years settings who work with and seek to understand children.

The way that children develop emotionally and socially is of prime importance to an understanding of healthy development and learning. It is impossible to separate social and emotional development from other key aspects such as cognitive and physical development, as they are all integrated in the reality of the whole child. It is also difficult to observe these as accurately as other aspects, such as physical development. Therefore, while theories help to explain aspects of social and emotional development, it is important to challenge the assumptions they make and acknowledge the part played by interpretation, knowledge of the child and subjectivity. We will begin by looking at the psychodynamic theories of Freud and Erikson before moving to the development of emotions, attachments and emotional literacy.

The chapter starts by looking at psychodynamic theories of early emotional development and considers how these relate to attachment. Attachment formation is then examined and explored before moving on to a discussion of self-esteem. The issues involved in children making friends and how these relate to future interpersonal relationships are then discussed.

This chapter addresses the following areas:

➤ Psychodynamic theories of emotional and social development

➤ Attachment between infant and carer

➤ The development of emotional literacy

➤ Self-esteem

➤ Children making friends

By undertaking the suggested study within this chapter it is hoped that you will be able to:

1 make connections between early aspects of emotional development, attachment formation, self-esteem and making friends

2 understand significant concepts, processes and issues in the development of children's emotional and social development

3 understand the relevance of your knowledge of young children's emotional and social development in your work as a practitioner in an Early Years setting.

Psychodynamic theories of emotional and social development

These are based upon an understanding of development as an active process that is influenced by both inborn, biological drives (nature) and social and emotional experiences (nurture; see Chapter 4 for a discussion of the nature-nurture debate).

Both Sigmund Freud (1856–1939) and Erik Erikson (1902–1994) focused upon the development of personality. They considered that the personality developed as a result of psychological conflicts that the developing person must resolve as they occur in a series of stages.

Erikson, however, considered that development covered the lifespan, whereas Freud thought that personality was formed in essence before adulthood.

Freudian theory

This assumes that the individual's personality consists of the **id**, the **ego** and the **superego** (see Figure 5.1).

Freud suggested that development occurs through a series of **psychosexual** stages, involving conflicts between the id, ego and superego. At each stage, the focus

An individual's personality consists of the:	
Id	This is present at birth and contains the person's inborn biological needs and desires, seeking to maximise pleasure and minimise pain. So the newborn infant consists only of id as he or she seeks to have his or her needs for food, warmth and comfort met by crying.
Ego	This develops as the realistic part of the personality, which finds ways of meeting the needs of the id as well as dealing with external demands, such as those from parents and society. So the young child learns that smiling at mother is an effective way of gaining her attention and meeting his or her needs for food, warmth, comfort, and so on.
Superego	This is the moral and principled part of the personality, which acts as a sort of internalised parent. It consists of the conscience, which punishes unacceptable thoughts, feelings and actions with guilt, and the ego-ideal, which provides a sense of how we should behave.

Figure 5.1 Freudian theory of personality

Stage	Age (approx.)	Description
Oral	Birth to 1 year	The mouth is the focus of pleasure, stimulation and interaction (feeding and weaning involved).
Anal	1–3 years	The anus is the focus of stimulation (toilet-training focus).
Phallic	3–6 years	The genitals are the focus of stimulation (gender role and moral development central).
Latency	6–12 years	Period of little sexual activity (shift to physical and intellectual issues).
Genital	12 to adult	Genitals are the focus of stimulation (puberty and mature sexual relationships develop).

Figure 5.2 Freud's psychosexual stages of development

is on a different area of the body (see Figure 5.2).

Therefore, according to Freudian theory, development involves resolving these conflicts in a way that is sufficiently balanced for healthy development. If this does not occur, then a person can become **fixated** at a certain stage and **regress** (go back to an earlier stage) when in stressful situations.

Implications of Freud's theory for practitioners

Awareness of the need for balance at each stage suggests that the child should receive enough stimulation (id) but that the needs of the external world should be taken into account (ego), as well as expectations about the values attached. So a child who is allowed to constantly suck upon a dummy or other pacifier may become too dependent upon it and remain 'stuck' at this oral stage of development; but if he or she is completely deprived of the dummy in order to make him or her 'more grown up', the child may still remain fixated because of a constant desire to experience the pleasant stimulation he or she is being deprived of. Therefore, the practitioner might allow the dummy at certain times (such as before a nap) but not at others (such as at lunch or snack time) in order to provide a balanced amount of stimulation.

Erikson's psychosocial theory

This theory places more emphasis upon the social factors that the individual encounters, and proposes that there is a psychosocial crisis at each stage of development. Unlike Freud, Erikson does not stress the role of sexuality but focuses instead upon the emergence of a sense of identity (see Figure 5.3).

Erikson viewed social forces as an important element of development and considered psychosocial conflicts never to be fully resolved. Therefore, conflicts from earlier

Case Study 1

Freudian concepts

Tiffany is 3 years old and spends time at the local Children's Centre while her grandmother (her main caregiver) works. She usually wets herself several times during the three-hour session and sometimes soils herself unless she is allowed to cling to one of the caregivers throughout. Tiffany refuses to visit the toilet by herself and her grandmother usually shouts loudly at her when she collects her and finds that she has had to be given clean clothes to wear. She is adamant that Tiffany never 'has an accident' at home and is 'being a baby' to attract attention.

If we were to apply Freud's psychodynamic theory to this case study we would recognise that Tiffany is between the anal and phallic stages of psychosexual development. It seems that she regresses to the earlier stage when she is in an

unfamiliar environment which suggests that there are underlying conflicts which have not been resolved. Psychodynamic theory would suggest that she has received overly strict or extremely permissive toilet training. The practitioner working with Tiffany would need to strike a balance between allowing dependence and encouraging independence in terms of toilet training. Perhaps this would involve her close availability and accompanying Tiffany to the toilet when she first arrived then encouraging her to go alone, perhaps while the practitioner was standing at the door until she became more confident. The balance between supporting and encouraging Tiffany should contribute to her healthy development as she is currently fixated at this stage.

Stage	Age range (approx.)	Description
Trust versus mistrust	Birth to 1 year	Focus on oral sensory activity – development of trusting relationships (secure attachment).
Autonomy versus shame and doubt	1–3 years	Development of control over body (toilet training may result in shame if not handled sensitively).
Initiative versus guilt	3–6 years	Testing limits of discovery (becoming more assertive/aggressive).
Industry versus inferiority	6–12 years	Focus on competence and productivity (basic skills including school skills).
Identity versus role-confusion	12–19 years	Identity formation and self-concept (achieving adult identity).
Intimacy versus isolation	19–25 years	Intimate relationships and career (partners, marriage).
Generativity versus stagnation	25–50 years	Creative activity for future generations.
Ego integrity versus despair	50 and older	Belief in integrity of life (wisdom) (acceptance of self).

Figure 5.3 Erikson's psychosocial stages

stages may continue to affect later development if they have not been dealt with in a generally favourable way. For example, an infant may learn that adults are trustworthy most of the time but that they might sometimes fail to provide adequately for his or her needs.

Implications of Erikson's theory for practitioners

Understanding the importance of the demands that different contexts and cultures place upon a child at particular ages (such as toilet training and school-related skills) is key. So the child is striving for balance between the development of new abilities, leading to greater freedom and autonomy, and the caregiver is concerned with protecting the child from the dangers embedded in this new independence. Again, balance is the solution and the practitioner needs to gradually allow the control to move from him- or herself to the child. For example, a 2-and-a-half-year-old child (autonomy versus shame and doubt) who is keen to try to climb the play frame may

need to be supervised and supported initially, but as he or she gains expertise may be allowed to do this independently (with a soft surface beneath to ensure safety). This will ensure that the child moves towards a feeling of confidence in his or her own ability, rather than shame or guilt for falling off or failing to reach the top at the first attempt.

Emotional development

Parents have always claimed that they can read the emotions of their infants, but they have not always been in agreement, either with each other or professionals. One reason for this is that infants cannot use language, so conclusions have to be based upon facial expressions, physiological responses or cries. The ways in which these are interpreted depend upon the subjective response of the observer and what he or she actually knows about the child. For example, a baby's cry may be interpreted by:

➤ an older sibling as the baby wanting the soft toy that has fallen from the pram

Case Study 2

Erikson's theory

Jordan is a looked-after child who is currently placed with foster parents. He has recently started school and is in the Reception class at a large primary school. He has so far refused to attempt any drawing or writing despite encouragement from the teacher.

If we were to place Jordan within the psychosocial stages of development identified by Erikson, he would be in the *Initiative versus guilt* stage where he would be testing out his abilities and developing more assertiveness. Clearly this is not happening in terms of using drawing and writing materials which indicates that Jordan has not found a balance between feeling comfortable with using his *initiative* by trying out new activities and *guilty* because he might fail or seem inadequate. Perhaps his earlier unsettled home life has resulted in feelings of mistrust towards others (*Trust versus mistrust* stage) which means his later development is hampered. His teacher would, therefore, need to establish some trust in her relationship with Jordan before he is likely to try out any new behaviours. Perhaps she could enlist his help with some classroom activity such as putting out materials before lessons start in order to begin to build a relationship. Encouragement and recognition of his activities would be crucial.

> ➤ the father as a sign of being in need of attention
> ➤ the health visitor as the baby needing a nappy change
> ➤ the mother as a signal of hunger.

Innate or inborn emotions

Figure 5.4 lists the range of emotions associated with early childhood and the age at which they are usually experienced.

Despite difficulties of interpretation, however, there is evidence that infants are born with certain emotions already in place (Izard et al, 1995). These include interest, physical distress, disgust and surprise (in the form of the startle reflex). Soon after this the social smile appears, and by about 7 months old, infants exhibit joy, anger and fear. These latter are known as **primary emotions** because they appear in the first year of life and because there seems to be universal agreement about them. They are said to be innate, resulting from biological programming (Izard, 1994).

Secondary emotions

These appear in the second year (examples include guilt, envy, shame and pride) and require some sophisticated cognitive abilities involving self-awareness. For example, when a child feels ashamed because he or she has wet pants it means that he or she is able to distinguish between him- or herself and others.

Category	Age range	Type of emotion
Innate emotions	From birth	Interest, physical distress, pain, disgust and surprise
	Within first month	Sociability (smile)
Primary emotions	7 months to 12 months	Joy, anger, fear and sadness
Secondary emotions	Approximately 2 years	Guilt, envy, shame and pride

Figure 5.4 Early emotional development

Facial expressions

These are an important part of emotional expression and research has shown that infants have an early ability (at 2 or 3 months old) to differentiate between certain facial expressions (Nelson, 1987). After 6 months of age infants seem to understand the meaning behind the emotional expressions of others and by the age of one year they use **social referencing**; that is, they refer to the emotions of other people, communicated through facial expressions, vocal quality and gestures to help them make judgements about events and regulate their behaviour (Hornik and Gunnar, 1988).

Case Study 3

The visual cliff

1 A table was designed which looked as though there was a drop (by using chequered material and clear glass) to infants crawling over it.

2 An experiment carried out by Gibson and Walk (1960) to test infant depth perception found that most infants would risk crossing the 'visual cliff' if their mother (waiting on the other side) was smiling or looking happy and interested. However, if she looked frightened or angry very few infants would cross.

3 Interestingly, when the cliff was clearly safe nearly all of the infants would cross without looking at their mothers and, even when the mothers were signalling fear, the babies would ignore her and cross anyway.

It seems from this that infants are most likely to use social referencing when presented with an ambiguous situation.

When this is the case they will look for more information before making a decision about action. The visual cliff situation is one that is likely to be quite fear-provoking and so likely to induce this response. Other research into responses to strangers have produced similar findings (Feinman and Lewis, 1983).

This, of course, has much wider implications for personal development in infants and suggests that parents or carers (although mothers were used in this experiment, infants also use fathers and carers as social referents) influence the behaviour of the young more subtly and profoundly than might be assumed.

Adults also use social referencing and, as for infants, it is most apparent in ambiguous situations. For example, someone tells a joke that you are not sure about and you look at the reactions of others before deciding whether to laugh.

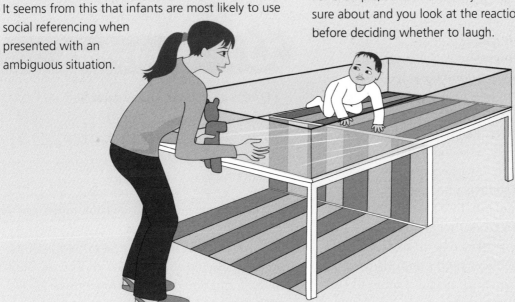

Early interactions can help to build attachment

Smiling

Smiling is an important social communicator, which appears as a voluntary response at about 3 weeks of age. This suggests that it is not entirely innate because it seems to develop from a non-discriminatory response (where a baby might smile at social and non-social stimuli alike) and towards a response attached to people. The smile is often reinforced by those around and becomes more frequent. So babies may start smiling because they are biologically programmed to do so, but it is the social response (for example, smiling back or talking to the baby) that makes it more likely that babies will repeat the smile.

Discussion point 1

Effects of smiling upon a carer

Describe the effects that a smiling baby might have upon a carer and how this might affect the way an infant is treated.

For comments on this discussion point, see page 125.

It seems then that these early interactions are mutually reinforcing and may be relevant to the formation of an emotional tie or **attachment** between infant and carer.

Attachment between infant and carer

Attachment, or emotional bonding, is usually formed between an infant and his or her carer during the first year of life and is seen by many as an important base for future relationships. Therefore, it is of major importance in the healthy social and emotional development of the child.

The most famous attachment theorist is **John Bowlby** (1907–1990), who argued that the need for attachment was an instinctive biological need and that mother-love in infancy and childhood was as important for mental health as are vitamins and protein for physical health (1951). Bowlby claimed that babies who were separated from their mothers before becoming securely attached would find it impossible to bond with others and in later life suffer ill-effects from this deprivation. Further, based upon his studies of delinquent boys in 1944, he suggested a link between maternal deprivation and juvenile crime.

The work of John Bowlby (1907–1990)

During his lifetime, Bowlby produced the following.

➤ *Forty-Four Juvenile Thieves, Their Characters and Home Lives* (1944) was based upon case-notes from his work at the London Child Guidance Clinic. The paper linked the affectionless nature of a significant minority of the children to their histories of maternal deprivation.

➤ He worked with James Robertson in a study of hospitalised children and produced a moving film in 1952 called *A Two Year Old Goes to Hospital*, which played a crucial role in the development of attachment theory and helped to lessen the negative effects of hospitalisation.

➤ *Maternal Care and Mental Health* (1952) was based on a report he carried out for the World Health Organization looking at the mental health of orphaned children placed in institutions in post-war Europe, which concluded that 'mother love' in infancy was vital for healthy social and emotional development.

➤ *The Nature of the Child's Tie to his Mother* (1957) drew upon ethological theory (that attachment is an essential aspect of human survival which evolved in order to ensure infant survival) and *Separation Anxiety* (1959) discussed the negative effects of separation from the attachment figure.

Considerations of Bowlby's work

Bowlby's work was very influential, not least because of the post-war social-economic climate. Women had been recruited into the workforce during the Second World War, as large numbers of men were serving in the armed forces and when the war ended many women were reluctant to give up the independence that working had given them. Consequently, there were not enough jobs for the returning men.

Bowlby's findings, in *Maternal Care and Mental Health*, that disrupted attachments were damaging to mental health, had the effect of sending many working women back into the home. This was convenient politically and meant that the economic status quo was maintained.

Methodological flaws

There were methodological flaws in Bowlby's work.

➤ Much of Bowlby's work was based upon research carried out on juvenile offenders. Since this group was not representative of the normal population, the findings cannot be reasonably generalised.

➤ The evidence gathered was retrospective, and much of it relied upon memory and accounts of the juveniles' early years. Retrospective data is notoriously unreliable and subjective.

Modifications of Bowlby's views

Bowlby himself modified his views during the course of his long working life and concluded that an attachment could be formed with any **primary caregiver**, not only the child's natural mother, as he had first proposed.

Attachment types

Mary Ainsworth worked with Bowlby at the Tavistock Clinic in London and suggested that attachment could be measured using a laboratory-based 'strange situation' test (Ainsworth and Wittig, 1969). This involved providing an unfamiliar but interesting environment where the child (usually approximately one year old) was motivated to explore but still needed to feel secure (an unfamiliar room with toys). An observer then recorded the child's responses to the departure and return of the mother. This research revealed significant differences between children, which Ainsworth categorised into three major **attachment types**. These are shown in Figure 5.5.below.

The importance of forming secure attachment

This has been indicated by many studies that have looked at connections between attachment type and later behaviour and development. These indicate that **securely attached children** are superior on a range of

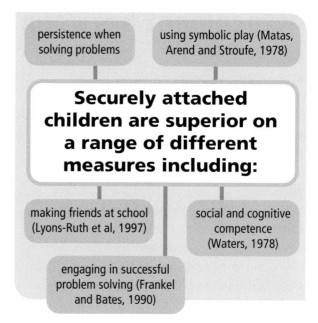

Figure 5.6 Some of the ways in which securely attached children perform better

different measures including those identified in Figure 5.6.

On the other hand, children classed as **insecurely attached** (anxious/avoidant or anxious/resistant) are:

➤ less effective when mixing with others

➤ succeed less when attempting to master challenging tasks

➤ have more behavioural problems (van den Boom, 1994).

Type of attachment	Child's behaviour
Anxious/avoidant	The child may not be distressed by the mother leaving and may avoid or turn away from her when she returns.
Securely attached	The child may be distressed by the mother's departure and easily comforted when she returns.
Anxious/resistant	The child may be extremely 'clingy' during the first few minutes and become very distressed when the mother leaves. When she returns the child will seek comfort at the same time as distancing him- or herself from the mother, for example by crying and reaching up to be held but trying to wriggle away when picked up.

Figure 5.5 Attachment types (Ainsworth, 1969)

Attachment and brain development

Increasingly, research (mainly from the USA) indicates that attachment may well be more than a means by which infants and young children develop emotional and social competence (Schore, 1996, 1997, 2001). Attachment also seems to be related to ways in which structures in the brain are organised and prepared. The human brain at birth is preparing for action, but takes a further three years to establish connections between neurons (nerve cells which transmit and receive information). These connections are formed when impulses are passed between neurons using axons to send these messages and dendrites to receive them. Synapses are then formed which become increasingly complex as the child develops rather like a tree growing more branches and twigs as it matures (see Figure 5.7). Between birth and three years of age the brain produces more synapses than it needs (around 15,000) even as an adult and a 'pruning' process occurs which means that only those neurons which are used will survive and become a permanent part of the brain (Bransford, Brown and Cocking, 2000).

It seems then that both innate, physiological factors (the result of nature) and experiential ones (the result of nurture) are involved in the development of the human brain. The brain cells form the framework (nature) but the connections made in childhood influence what happens to that framework (nurture).

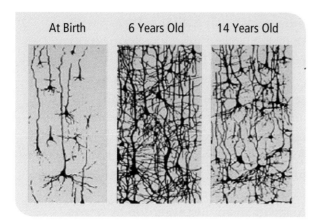

Figure 5.7 Development of the brain

This is relevant not only for the cognitive development of the child but also for its healthy social and emotional development. Ways in which the physical and emotional environment responds to the infant and toddler play a significant role in the creation and survival of neurons and synapses. The child's experiences are the stimulation which sparks the activity and create synapses. Therefore, it is important for caregivers to provide stimulating and responsive interactions with infants and young children in order to promote early brain development and support the child's future capacity to regulate emotions and recognise emotional states in others.

Case Study 4

Attachment formation

A 4-month-old baby, Lukas, is on a blanket on the floor of the living room as his main caregiver is cleaning the house, moving between the kitchen and the living room. When the caregiver walks in she talks to him, 'Hello there little boy, what are you doing down there? Are you kicking those legs?' She moves to him, bends down and tickles his tummy, watching his face for a smile. The baby looks at her and kicks his legs more energetically. 'My word, you are busy today, aren't you Lukas? You'll soon be running the marathon if you keep this up, won't you?' The caregiver picks up a nearby rattle and shakes it, holding it out for the baby to grasp but the sound of the rattle startles the infant and he begins to cry. The caregiver gently says, 'Oh dear, that frightened you, didn't it sweetheart?' as she picks him up for a comforting cuddle. She continues to rock him for a few minutes before putting him back onto the blanket with a soft toy to hold.

In the case study above the caregiver greets the baby enthusiastically after she returns to the room. She stimulates the infant's senses with her tickling and the rattle, encouraging Lukas's physical development by responding to his kicking and holding out the rattle for him to hold. When the sudden noise of the rattle frightens him the caregiver responds sensitively, giving meaning to his cries and providing physical comfort and affection to soothe him. These experiences help him to develop trust in the world and provide a basis for his healthy emotional development.

It can be seen that infants need sensitive, responsive care in order for the parts of their brains that regulate emotions to develop properly. A baby has limited ability to do this at birth and depends upon caregivers to help stimulate, calm when upset and keep from over-stimulation when playing. When this is managed effectively the infant develops the neurological and emotional foundations to allow these to develop gradually. However, there is evidence that children living in highly stressful situations such as overcrowded Romanian orphanages or abusive family settings experience a constantly stressed state which means that they are unable to effectively cope with emotional stress. When children are stressed, cortisol (a stress hormone) washes over the brain and causes some brain cells to die (National Scientific Council on the Developing Child, 2005). Whereas infants in secure attachment relationships seem to have a 'buffer' which protects them from raised levels of cortisol, children who have had little opportunity to develop secure attachments do not (Gunnar, 1998). These findings support earlier work (discussed below) which stress the importance of caregiver/child interactions.

A secure base

Ainsworth suggests that the primary carer needs to provide a **secure base** from which the child can explore the world. If the child develops a sense of trust in the caregiver, he or she is more likely to become independent earlier.

Maternal sensitivity seems to be a key factor here for the child's needs to be met. This includes attentiveness to the child, mutuality of interactions and the mother's ability to stimulate the child.

Mother-infant interaction

Brazleton, Tronick, Adamson et al (1975) and Brazleton and Cramer (1991) were interested in finding out about the causes of problematic relationships between infants and mothers. They investigated the very earliest interactions in a laboratory setting and found that there was a sort of harmonious 'dance' at times, which involved bursts of attention and then withdrawal. They identified a cycle of interactions, involving joint actions and mutual, continual influence. At times these were synchronised, but at others they were out of time.

Brazleton thought that these bursts of interactions related to the baby's biological need for arousal, which needs to be maintained at an optimal level. Arousal is based upon the need for humans to be stimulated in order to survive and develop. Arousal levels seem to vary between individuals and may be related to temperamental differences. When the baby looks away or fails to respond to the mother's conversation, this is a signal that no stimulation is needed or the infant wants to end the interaction.

Disrupting interactions

Murray and Trevarthen (1985) tested what would happen if mothers acted in unresponsive or disjointed ways with their babies and used a series of studies to do this.

In the first study a mother was asked to remain unresponsive – suddenly still, silent and with a 'frozen face' – in the middle of an exchange of expressions with her baby. A 2-month-old baby clearly signalled distress but was undisturbed by the mother talking to the experimenter. The infant then seemed to try to regain her attention by noises and gestures.

In the second study a delayed video replay situation was used. In this, the baby saw its mother playing with it on a television screen, acting in a happy, lively manner. However, this was not synchronised (except accidentally) with the actions of the infant. Again there were signs of distress but the baby was more withdrawn and protested less than in the 'frozen face' experiment.

In the third study a mother and baby interacted through a video link between two rooms. Here, a replay of the infant's part in a previous interaction was substituted (without the mother's knowledge). The mother still thought that she was taking part in a 'live' interaction with the baby, but in fact she was looking at an earlier interaction. This meant that there was activity on the part of the baby, but it was not synchronised with the mother's stimulation. The mother perceived the baby as being unhappy or perverse, even though it looked quite happy and lively. This is perhaps because she could not engage in a mutual interaction with the infant.

In the first study, the baby is obviously disturbed by the 'frozen face' of the mother but accepts the mother's distraction when talking to the experimenter. This suggests that the baby is used to seeing the mother in conversations with others and uses various means to regain her attention. The withdrawal of the baby in the second study suggests that the carer needs to be responsive, not just animated, in order for the baby to be happy. The third study shows the importance of the baby's responsiveness to the mother. If this is not happening, then it suggests that the mother will interpret the baby's actions negatively.

It seems then that these early interactions are relevant for the formation of emotional ties or attachments between infants and caregivers and, therefore, caregivers should be aware of the need for interactions involving sensitive responsiveness when working with infants and young children.

The factors that affect the parent-child relationship are shown in Figure 5.8.

Parent's emotional state	Mental disturbances in the mother or main caregiver may make the child less responsive and the attachment, therefore, less secure. For example, post-natal depression may result in the unresponsive 'frozen face', which Brazleton found related to infant distress. Mothers of anxious children are prone to insecurity, which affects their relationship with the child (Izard, Chishold and Baak, 1991).
Parental attachment status	The way that parents remember their own relationships with their parents seems to provide the basis for expectations about their own role. So, insecurely attached parents may find it more difficult to develop secure attachments with their own infants.
Attitudes and expectations	It seems that the more informed parents are, the more likely they are to do well with their infants. For example, a mother who expects her baby to let her sleep because she is tired is likely to be disappointed and develop negative feelings towards her baby. Help and support from others is also important.
Infant's abilities, temperament and gender	These may also be factors in attachment formation as certain characteristics can help or hinder attachment formation. For example, a responsive baby who smiles happily in response to the mother is likely to evoke more interactions and therefore foster attachment.

Figure 5.8 Factors affecting the parent-child relationship

The development of emotional literacy

So far we have looked at emotional development and the importance of early interactions in terms of attachment formation and healthy development. Currently there is an increased awareness that the emotional states of young children have a critical impact upon many aspects of their development including their self-esteem (more on this later in this chapter) and self-control. Terms such as 'emotional literacy' and 'emotional intelligence' are now included within educational and child developmental discourses so let us see how they might be important here. Emotional literacy relates to being able to manage yourself and your own emotions and to understand what other people are thinking and feeling (Gerry, 2000). As we have seen so far, if infants and young children generally receive a stimulating and responsive experience of the world they are likely to learn to identify emotion both in themselves and others. This ability to perceive and express feelings is one of the first, essential steps identified in the Mayer-Salovey model of emotional intelligence (Mayer and Salovey, 1997). Emotional intelligence involves skills and competencies which enable individuals to succeed in their lives at home and at work. For children it is now recognised that pupils' emotional states have a critical impact upon their learning and this is reflected within statutory provision. Emotional development is promoted within the Foundation Stage (for 3–5-year-old pupils) of the National Curriculum and personal, social and health education (PSHE) is included for those over the age of five (Bradley, 2003).

Case Study 5

Emotional literacy

During a free-play session at nursery, Redd is engrossed in creating a farm with building blocks. He needs a triangular brick to enable him to build a stable for the horse but cannot find it. As he unsuccessfully searches the room for this crucial piece he becomes increasingly impatient and starts shouting and disrupting the activities of the other children. Redd then sees that another boy, Eli, has the piece he wants and approaches him aggressively. Eli looks frightened as Redd shouts that he wants the brick and the practitioner, Baljit, approaches and stops Redd, just in time, from snatching it from Eli. At this point Redd launches into a full-scale tantrum which persists even when Baljit asks him to calm down.

The practitioner realised that Redd and some of his peers needed help to develop skills in labelling emotions in order for them to become more emotionally literate. She starts to make a conscious effort to label her feelings and those of the children during their time with her. She also encourages the other adults in the room to do the same. Baljit planned at least one song, game or story per session to introduce new, more complex feeling words. She also taught the children some strategies for regulating their own emotions such as taking deep breaths, relaxing their muscles and thinking of 'happy' places. When she spotted Redd or any of the other children becoming upset she would move towards them and ask what they were feeling, helping them to use some of the strategies for calming down and managing their emotions. Baljit was helping the children move into school with a good foundation in emotional literacy.

Separation anxiety is distressing for both parent and child

Stranger fear and separation anxiety

Babies usually begin to fear strangers at about the age of 6 months and this lasts until the child is about 2 years old. So the baby who happily held hands with strangers and delighted the bus with beaming smiles suddenly starts crying when unfamiliar people appear. Separation anxiety peaks between the ages of 12 and 16 months. It involves crying and displays of fear such as clinging and distress when the child's parent or caregiver is leaving.

Separation anxiety seems to be related to how well the child is prepared for the separation and to his or her past experiences of separation. There is less anxiety if the child is left with familiar people and it is reduced if siblings or favourite toys are present. While it is distressing to all those who witness a child clinging desperately to a parent's leg as he or she tries to leave, it is a clear sign that an attachment has formed and is therefore indicative of the child's ability to form other attachments. Obviously, this is relevant for those working with young children in order that they can anticipate this and minimise the distress involved.

Some of the ways in which you may help reduce separation anxiety in your work as a practitioner in an Early Years setting are identified in Figure 5.9.

Attachment and daycare

One of the areas of prime importance here is the question of attachment and daycare. Is Bowlby's original assertion that maternal deprivation and disrupted maternal attachment may have serious and long-lasting effects upon the child's later behaviour correct? Or are there other factors that may make this a more benign arrangement?

Perhaps we need to think back to Mary Ainsworth's findings about providing a **secure base**. Surely, if the child has this we can

A practitioner working in an Early Years setting should:	
welcome the child and recognise that parents are also undergoing a change in their contact with the child	Perhaps use a personal place label or poster.
encourage a slow transition from being at home to being in a new environment	If possible, allow the child to get to know you before being left in your care (perhaps by a home visit or having an 'open' policy for parents and children to visit before starting daycare). Arrange a gradual schedule, which builds up from perhaps one hour on the first day, then two hours on the second day, until the child is staying for a full day.
remind the child that the parent will return	Separation anxiety is often related to fear that the parent may not return, so it is important that the child knows what time the parent is returning. With an older child a clock can be used to indicate this, or some milestone such as 'after juice and biscuits' can be used.
use transitional objects	Items such as a favourite teddy or a blanket can help a child to feel secure because it connects them with the parent. Some children may find photographs or even an article with a familiar smell comforting.
talk with the parents about the child's particular needs	This often helps with anxiety, as does being ready to help to occupy the child when the parent is ready to leave.
warn the child that the main caregiver is about to leave.	This helps to prepare the child for the event. Discourage parents from leaving unnoticed, as this adds to the child's anxiety. Sometimes a routine for saying goodbye is helpful so that the child knows that they have three kisses or hugs before the parent leaves.

Figure 5.9 A practitioner's role in helping reduce anxiety separation

expect him or her to feel confident enough to explore and enjoy a stimulating environment without the fear and distress that might otherwise be the case?

In order to address these and other questions it is useful to examine cross-cultural studies that have looked at attachment. These should provide us with insights about what is 'instinctive' or biologically programmed behaviour and what is learned as the result of being reared in a particular environment (the nature-nurture debate again).

International cross-cultural studies and attachment

It seems that different cultures provide Ainsworth's secure base, but there are variations in the way this is implemented. Work by Liedloff (1986) found that all of the women in a community of South American people living in the Amazon rainforest provided security and continuity of care to the infants. Children were certain of comfort and support when it was needed, but there was no primary carer. A study by Troknick, Morelli and Winn (1987) showed that among the Congolese Efe or Pygmy (a people who are hunter-gatherers), infants are raised by multiple women during the first five months of life. Jackson (1993) argued that African-American infants do not exhibit an exclusive attachment, as most of those in the study were reared in two households consisting of approximately 15 people (both relatives and unrelated people).

The UK is increasingly mixed in terms of the cultures within it and many families may experience differences between their own ways of parenting and that of UK cultural norms. However, most research suggests that there are more differences within cultural norms than between them (Van Ijzendoorn and Kroonenberg, 1988).

Continuous care and security

The studies above suggest that attachment is not necessarily **monotropic** (a single attachment between infant and primary caregiver which ties them together, rather like an extension of the umbilical cord) but is much more flexible. It can include a number of people.

The implications for the professional care of children, then, are that these people can become part of the infant's attachment experience. Within a Western culture, many children are reared by mothers, fathers, siblings, grandparents and other family members, as well as receiving care from nursery staff and childminders. The important factors here are **continuous care** and **security**.

Working mothers and daycare

Many women still feel guilty about working when their children are small, even though they are often obliged or expected to do so. Perhaps we are still responding to Bowlby's ideas despite the fact that society has now changed significantly. Indeed, Bowlby's ideas have dominated childcare policy and issues for over 50 years (Holmes, 1993). However, there have been considerable changes in the composition of families and their dynamics and these continue. This means that many more children are experiencing exactly that which Bowlby warned against: separation, inconsistency, disruption and loss. There is much greater diversity in terms of family type than at the time when Bowlby first began publishing his work, and currently

single-parent and re-formed families are common. Therefore, many children entering daycare are not necessarily happy and secure, and this makes it particularly important that emotional security is provided within the context of care.

Generally the findings about **working mothers** or **primary caregivers** can be summed up as follows.

➤ Mothers who work are generally happier, leading to greater life satisfaction, as long as this is through choice rather than necessity (Parke and Buriel, 1998).

➤ Although working mothers have less time at home, they cope by focusing on essentials and becoming more efficient.

➤ Working mothers tend to emphasise independence, which may have positive effects upon children (particularly daughters).

➤ Children with working mothers tend to have better social skills, perhaps because they have been used to mixing with others from an earlier age.

Findings about daycare suggest that:

➤ most children are in fact cared for by relatives

➤ some children placed into daycare before one year of age exhibit anxious attachment patterns but most are securely attached

➤ poor quality or extensive daycare, combined with poor-quality care at home may lead to anxious attachments

➤ there are few differences between the attachment patterns of children entering daycare after the age of one year and those of children cared for at home

➤ there are positive associations between high-quality childcare and enhanced cognitive and social development especially for children from low income families (Lamb, 1998; NICHD, 2000).

Case Study 6

Making childcare arrangements

Jasmine is a single parent with a 3-year-old daughter, Sarah. When Sarah was a baby, Jasmine worked at a number of part-time jobs, while her mother helped out with childcare. However, Jasmine now has a good opportunity to take a job as a paramedic and the additional income will allow them to move to a safer neighbourhood with better schools and facilities. The new job would mean that Jasmine is at work all day and her mother (who is nearly 70) does not feel able to look after Sarah full time. Therefore, Jasmine has to look for childcare but feels guilty at the thought of leaving her daughter for long periods.

How would you advise Jasmine in this situation?

For comments on this case study, see page 124.

The 'key person' system

Many nurseries and childcare centres operate a 'key person' system in order to encourage a close relationship between each young child and an identified practitioner. This involves linking individual practitioners with individual children in terms of responsibility for their physical and emotional needs (such as changing them, talking with them and developing rituals), developing friendly relationships with parents or primary caregivers and keeping records of the child's progress. This is not meant to be *instead* of the attachment formed with their parent or main caregiver, but to build an *additional* supportive relationship to enable children to develop and feel secure. Elinor Goldschmied and Sonia Jackson commented that while there is currently no systematic research which compares the key worker system with others, feedback from childcare centres was generally positive (Goldschmied and Jackson, 2004). This system is embedded in the Early Years Foundation Stage (EYFS) curriculum which begins in England in 2008 to ensure that all pre-school children have a named practitioner who is responsible for their social and emotional well-being.

The key person system links with the need to manage **transitions** from one setting to another effectively for children as the case studies below illustrate.

Case Study 7

Managing transition

A large nursery school in the north of England recognised the need for young children to be supported in their transition from home to nursery and then from nursery to school through a transition programme. They arranged for a nursery teacher to liaise with parents/caregivers by visiting children in their home setting before they began nursery. The school held an information evening for new parents which provided information about the daily routines within the school and the expectations which would be placed upon the children and their main caregivers. Parents/caregivers were encouraged to be a key part in this gradual transition process (perhaps beginning with one morning per week then building up to every morning or the allocated time) by taking part in nursery activities. Initially they stayed with children for the first hour of each session, taking part in language games or other activities and the liaison teacher would be part of this as the key person.

This takes into account not only the challenge which transition involves for children but also for parents and main caregivers and is based upon notions and theories such as those discussed earlier in this chapter. If parents/main caregivers are comfortable and secure with the transition then this will be transmitted to the children who are also more likely to feel secure. When children were ready to progress to school then they were similarly supported with the school holding events such as parents' workshops which allowed children to work with their main caregivers within the school setting. These workshops included story writing sessions to encourage emergent literacy, story telling, arts activities and school outings.

Case Study 8

Cross-cultural issues

A primary school in the English midlands meets the needs of the different social and ethnic groups within the school in a number of ways. As well as managing transitions using some of the methods discussed in Case Study 7 the school gives equal status to the religious and cultural traditions of families represented in the school. Celebrations such as Eid, Diwali and Christmas are given equal status and are presented in such a way as to be inclusive of differing cultural traditions within as well as between religions and for those of no religion.

The school also holds an 'Arts Week' annually which invites all parents to contribute art work, music, dance and activities representing their own cultures and interests. Further, a small room with down lighting and no windows has been allocated to allow Muslim women to remove their veils when talking with female teachers. This is particularly valuable in order for them to be fully involved in information and reviews of their children's progress and also encourages trust and mutual respect in terms of acceptance of different cultural norms.

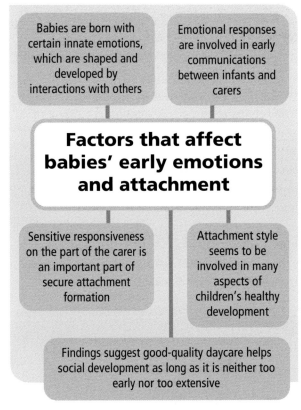

Figure 5.10 Summary of early emotions and attachments

Self–esteem

So far, we have looked at the early emotional development of young children and how this is part of their forming early relationships with others. This seems to form the basis upon which children develop autonomy or the ability to be independent. In other words, it provides them with the security that they are safe and cared for and that those who look after them are trustworthy. Because of this, they do not need to be anxious about the possibility of being abandoned and therefore begin to explore the world more independently, safe in the knowledge that their needs will be met on their return. This is clearly interwoven with another aspect of their social and emotional development: **self-esteem**. This is a central and critical aspect of psychological well-being, which has generated vast amounts of literature and research. In 1998 it was found that there were over 7,000 publications on the subject (Mruk, 1999), which gives an indication of the interest attached to this issue.

Self-esteem usually refers to the way we feel about ourselves. Coopersmith (1967:4) defines self-esteem as 'a personal judgement of worthiness, that is expressed in the attitudes the individual holds towards himself'. Clearly this relates to the development of a sense of self or **personal identity**. Assessing our self-esteem is something all of us continue to do throughout life and involves asking ourselves questions such as what sort of person we are and what we want to be like. When trying to answer these questions, we usually think about how we feel inside as well as the way that others behave towards us, as this tells us how they view us from the outside.

Activity 1

A short description of myself

Imagine you are asked to say what kind of person you are by someone you have never met. Write a short description to convey this to them (approximately 100 to 150 words).

For comments on this activity, see page 126.

Activity 2

Social categories

List the social categories which describe you, in terms of gender, position in family, age, marital status, nationality, religion, occupation, class etc.

Consider how each of these makes you similar to or different from most people that you know.

For comments on this activity see page 126.

Development of self-esteem

There is rapid development of aspects of self during the second and third years of life, and this happens in the context of social interactions and relationships.

Many researchers suggest that without these interactions, this sense of self cannot develop and this is borne out by studies of **feral children** (a term used to describe children who grow up in the wild or are raised in extreme isolation), who seem not to develop a sense of self.

Visual self-recognition

Around 2 years of age, most children display visual self-recognition, which means that they recognise themselves in a mirror or on a photograph. Researchers found that infants up to the age of 15 months did not touch their noses (which had been marked with red rouge without their knowledge) when placed before a mirror, but by the time they had reached 24 months, they did (Lewis and Brooks-Gunn, 1979).

Ability to describe physical self

Increasingly, children become able to describe themselves physically (beginning at about 19 months of age) and by the end of their second year are usually becoming more aware of adult expectations and standards.

Self-evaluation

There are also signs that children begin to **self-evaluate** (or make judgements about themselves or the things they do) towards the end of the second year and they may show satisfaction or pride about building a high tower with blocks or show frustration when they fail.

Activity 3

A young boy's self-description

Read this example of a young boy's self-description, which has been recorded and transcribed.

My name is Bobby and I am big. I can ride my bike now and be a fire-fighter (makes 'neenah' noise). My Emily is small and can't talk, but she makes a lot of noise. We have to turn the TV up so I can hear it. She goes shouting all the time. My hair is curly, look like this.

What would you guess to be Bobby's age and why?

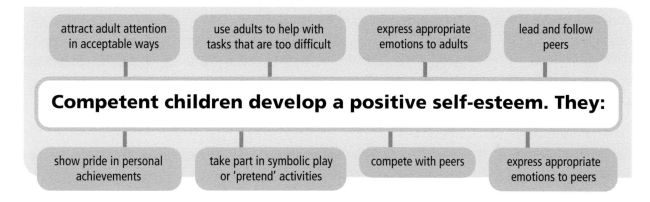

Figure 5.11 Behaviours exhibited by competent children (White, 1993)

For comments on this activity see page 127.

Competence and self-esteem

Research suggests that more competent children develop a more positive self-esteem as they gain confidence in their own abilities. This then has a snowball effect, allowing them to do more things, more competently, which, therefore, adds to their self-esteem.

This is apparent in the behaviours exhibited by competent children (see Figure 5.11).

Role of caregivers in promoting competence in a child

The influence of the parent/carer/child relationship is also seen to be important here. It seems that mothers of children with high levels of competence are more encouraging and supportive when their children wish to investigate and explore, providing a variety of stimulating toys and contexts within which this can take place. They are also more likely to use language and play in a manner that responds to the child's needs, interests and level of development. This sounds very similar to the earlier point about **sensitive responsiveness** and attachment formation, and it certainly seems as though this is the most important aspect of a healthy social and emotional development.

Measuring self-esteem

This is quite difficult, particularly in children, because self-esteem is not easy to define. It seems to relate to the picture a child has of him- or herself, which is drawn from two different areas.

➤ Knowing what he or she can do and valuing it.

➤ Comparing himself or herself with others.

Harter's (1983) Self-Perception Profile for Children identified five different domains. Children were either read a statement, or shown a picture showing a competent or less competent child, and asked to say which is most like them (see Figure 5.12).

Thus, a child can be assessed on these domains and the profile gives a much clearer and more in-depth picture of the child's general self-esteem. However, when trying to understand the way a child feels about himself, it is important to find out which issues matter most to him.

Domains of self-esteem	Questions relating to domains
Scholastic competence	How bright do you think you are? How well do you read? How well are you doing at school?
Athletic competence	How good are you at sports? Do you get picked to play? Do you like to try new games?
Social acceptance	How popular are you? Do others like you?
Behavioural conduct	Do you behave in the way that you should? Do adults and other children accept the way you behave?
Physical appearance	How much do you like the way you look? Do you think others like the way you look?

Figure 5.12 Harter's five domains of self-esteem (1983)

Discussion point 2

Assessing which factors are important to children

Read the attached self-descriptions and decide which factors seem most important to these children.

1 **Molly** (aged 5 years)
   I am Molly. I am the biggest girl in my class. I've got curly black hair and green bobbles. I like some girls, like Jenny and Kali, 'cos they play with me at playtime. I have a reading book, but it's only got pictures – I can't read letters yet. I help my mum at home with the pots and watching Daisy, my baby. My mum says she couldn't do without me. When it's story-time I sit quietly on the mat but Matthew's always getting told off.

2 **Suzy** (aged 7-and-a-half-years)
   My real name is Suzannah, but most people call me Suzy. My mum sometimes calls me Nanna 'cos when I was little I used to say 'Sunanna' 'cos I couldn't say Suzannah properly. I am quite small – I want to grow, but even though I eat lots of dinner I am still small. I am on the top table at school, but it is boring. My friend Joanna is always finished first and gets it all right. My brother Patrick is 12 and we are always falling out. It's not fair because he has a bigger bedroom than me and he never gets told off, even though he starts it. I like drawing and painting and my dad likes my pictures.

For comments on this discussion point see page 125.

The role of significant others

The significance of the development of positive self-esteem in children, combined with our understanding of how it develops, means that those working with children have an important part to play in its development.

Activity 4

Encouraging positive self-esteem

Read the following account and list ways in which you feel positive self-esteem is being encouraged or discouraged.

The children in Year 1 have recently visited a working farm and are being asked to talk about this during a class discussion.

Teacher: Who can tell me some of the animals we saw? Let's see – Marek.

Marek: Pigs and cows and sheeps and dogs.

Teacher: Very good, Marek, but don't shout. We do see dogs all the time though, don't we, and there is no such word as 'sheeps'. What about you, Katy, you're sitting nice and quietly. What did you see?

Katy: Some chickens and we seed an egg with a chick inside.

Teacher: Yes, we did, didn't we? And chick is the right name for a baby bird. How did you know there was a chick inside, Katy?

Katy: 'Cos the man shined a light and we seed it.

Teacher: Well done. I think you need a sticker for that. Now then, what did you see, Karendeep?

Karendeep: (mumbles) Don't know.

Teacher: I can't hear you if you mumble like that. Have you forgotten, perhaps, or don't know the word you want? *(Karendeep sits with head down and doesn't answer.)* Look, there are lots of people in this class with their hands up. They all want to tell me. I'll choose Justin.

Justin: Was a goat and it was eating a crisp bag and weeing (makes hissing noise) *(Class giggles.)*

Teacher: Don't be silly and rude, Justin. There were three goats actually, and they usually eat grass. What do goats eat, children?

Class: (obediently chant) Grass.

For comments on this activity see page 127.

Activity 5

Qualities that you value in yourself

1 List the qualities that you value in yourself.

2 Are these the ones that you tend to encourage in children?

For comments on this activity see page 127.

How to recognise high self-esteem in children

It is usually fairly clear which children have a positive sense of self-worth, as they tend to be proactive, cheerful and increasingly independent. You might see the behaviours shown in Figure 5.13 in these children.

How to recognise low self-esteem in children

These children usually seem to be lacking in self-worth and self-belief. Therefore, they generally seem to be unhappy, withdrawn and reluctant to engage actively with others.

They generally seem to be enthusiastic, communicative and motivated

When new topics or experiences are introduced they are keen to engage with them

They are happy to amuse themselves or play with others

Behaviours exhibited by children who have a positive sense of self-worth

They are ready to listen to adults and work within set boundaries

Their behaviour is generally good and they are able to exert increasing degrees of self-control as they develop

Within group situations they seem comfortable and able to make friends without difficulty

Figure 5.13 Recognising high self-esteem in children

They will sometimes voice their low self-esteem in terms of things they are being asked to do, such as:

➤ 'I'm rubbish at reading.'
➤ Everybody else can do maths but me.'

Children with low self-esteem view themselves and their future achievements negatively; for example, 'I know I'm gonna come last', or 'I can't do anything right'. This has the effect of actually causing the 'failure' to occur because they do not look at their achievements positively.

How to encourage positive self-esteem

Carl Rogers (1902–1987) was an American psychologist who took a humanistic approach to understanding human personality and behaviour. He suggested that if children are

Discussion point 3

Positive and negative self-esteem

Jack and Harry took part in the obstacle race on Sports Day. Jack came third and Harry came fourth. Here is how they reacted to this outcome:

Jack: I told you I was useless – I never win anything.

Harry: I got there before Billy and Jake – yes! Next year I'm gonna get third.

Discuss the role of positive and negative self-esteem here.

For comments on this discussion point see page 125.

to develop positive self-esteem, they need to have **unconditional positive regard** (UPR) from adults. This means that if the child is to develop his or her full potential, the right conditions are necessary to allow it to grow. This could be compared to planting a number of seeds in the garden, where you need to provide the right conditions for those seeds to develop into flourishing, healthy plants. Some of the seeds might not receive enough sunshine so do not grow as tall or strong as they might have, or they might have to stretch to reach the sun and, therefore, lean over in one direction but not grow in others. Some seeds might lack moisture and fail to thrive, others might be strangled by other stronger plants and not develop in the way they could have.

The important issue here from Rogers' humanistic viewpoint is that all these seeds have the potential to grow into healthy, beautiful plants, but they might not all develop or actualise this potential. Similarly, humans have this same potential, so it is important that the adults around children provide the opportunities for this to happen. UPR does not mean that we never discipline the child, or display anger, but rather that we allow the child to believe that he or she is a person who is valued but whose behaviour at any one time is not appropriate. For example, the child may be told not to pull the cat's tail because it is cruel to hurt the cat, rather than be told that he or she is a cruel person.

Activity 6

Acknowledging inappropriate behaviour

Change the following comments so that they do not label the child but rather acknowledge the inappropriate behaviour.

1 'Zane, you are a very naughty boy who is unable to sit still and listen on the mat.'

2 'There are ways of dealing with bad girls like you, Hayley Atkins – now stop poking your ruler in Chelsie's back.'

3 'Be quiet! You are the worst class I have ever had to deal with.'

For comments on this activity see page 128.

Self-fulfilling prophecy (Merton, 1957)

Labelling the whole child negatively tends to affect the way that the child sees himself or herself and the ways that others perceive him or her. So, if (in the activity above) others see Zane as a naughty boy because he has been labelled as such, then his behaviour is more likely to be viewed in these terms. For example, if Zane turns round to look at something when he should be listening, it will probably be seen that he is causing trouble by talking to those behind him. If, on the other hand, Chelsie (seen as a 'good girl') does the same, it might be assumed that someone is pulling her hair or causing her to be distracted. Zane then begins to carry with him this view of himself as naughty and this becomes part of his self-concept, resulting in low self-esteem. This has clear implications not only for children's personal development, but also for their learning experiences. It also relates back

to the earlier discussion of the categorical self, where we see children viewed in terms of being like or unlike those they interact with. So Zane is 'naughty', unlike most of the others in the class; it might also be that he is Asian or Afro-Caribbean. This also makes him different and it is likely that certain stereotypical behaviours may be attributed to him on the basis of this alone. It is important that those working with children are aware of their own preconceptions and attitudes towards gender, social class and race in order that they help, rather than hinder, the development of the children they work with.

Case Study 9

Self-esteem and self-fulfilling prophecy

Afshan, a 6-year-old girl, belongs to a Muslim family and wears a hijab or headscarf to school. Although there are other Muslim girls in the school who also wear hijabs, there are none in the lower part of the school. Afshan is often teased by her classmates, particularly the boys, who ask her whether she is bald underneath her scarf and tell her to take it off. Afshan lacks the confidence to stand up for herself and her religious beliefs and her self-esteem is very low. She never contributes in class and is often excluded in play sessions. Although her work is of an average standard she always cries when there are any negative comments on her work and says she is useless. This means that she is not improving and her teacher is becoming frustrated with her response.

It is likely that Afshan's low expectations of herself will lead to lack of progress and will become a self-fulfilling prophecy as her own beliefs affect both her own performance and her teacher's expectations. She is developing a low self-esteem which will impact negatively upon many aspects of her development. Afshan's teacher needs to check and operate the school's anti-bullying policy as the boys' behaviour is causing harm to Afshan. She also needs to ensure that she addresses issues such as different religious beliefs within the classroom and perhaps makes use of circle-time to raise Afshan's status within the class.

Carl Rogers and education

Although Rogers was best known as the founder of 'non-directive' or 'client-centred' therapy, he had much to contribute to education. Rogers stressed the importance of the self and believed that the interpersonal relationship between the teacher/caregiver and child was crucial to the experience of the learner. In his book *Freedom to Learn*, Rogers discusses the following qualities and attitudes necessary to facilitate learning.

Genuineness

The facilitator of learning needs to be self-aware, or 'real', in order to communicate effectively with the learner. Therefore, professionals working with children need to be in touch with their own feelings and attitudes, rather than present artificial or assumed ways of being.

For example, a teacher who is genuinely pleased with a child's behaviour or performance will be much more effective than one who says she is pleased but is in fact irritated because she feels that her view of the child as a troublemaker is being challenged.

Acceptance

Valuing the child as he or she is and accepting his or her thoughts, feelings and opinions is an important aspect of enabling learning to take place. This does not mean that learners are considered to be perfect at all times but that they are prized as individuals with the potential to develop in ways which are right for them.

Empathy

This involves the ability to understand the learner's experience from his or her point of view. Children, like adults, appreciate being listened to and being understood from their own point of view. This involves sensitivity on the part of the facilitator to how the experiences of learning feel to learners. Empathic understanding encourages independence on the part of learners because it allows them to develop confidence in their own reactions and ability to learn.

Discussion point 4

The practicality of Rogers' suggestions

How practical or possible are Rogers' suggestions? Consider each in turn and discuss with a colleague if possible.

For comments on this discussion point see page 125.

Children making friends

So far we have looked at the early emotional responses of infants and ways in which they develop as part of their early interactional processes. We have thought about how these relate to the formation of attachments with caregivers. We have further discussed the importance of attachment style and the development of positive self-esteem, particularly reflecting upon the role of caregivers and professionals in this. In moving on to another related aspect here, we consider the formation and importance of children's friendships. First, we need to be clear about:

➤ how children make friends

➤ what their friendships are like

➤ how these change as the child develops.

The development of friendships

In general, children become less self-focused, or egocentric (see Chapter 4), as well as less instrumental, or focused upon achieving a particular end for themselves, between birth and 6 years of age as they develop cognitively and acquire experience of social rules. Between the ages of 5 and 10 there is more cooperation involved in their friendships and the beginnings of a more in-depth appreciation of a friend's personal qualities (Bigelow, Tesson and Lewko 1996; see Figure 5.14).

Age range	Friendship patterns
Birth to 2 years	Respond to each other from a very early age, and most parents will find that very young children are fascinated by watching other children, particularly those who are a little older. However, it is not really until the second year of life that they begin to play socially.
2- to 3-year-olds	Generally begin to have playmates, usually children that they meet at nursery or play group, other family members or those nearby.

3- to 4-year-olds	Tend to see friends as those they happen to be in contact with or whose toys they like to play with.
	    For example, 'My friend is Christopher at nursery school and we play on the fire engines.'
	    'Grace is my friend – she has lots of Duplo.'

5- to 6-year-olds	Are still focused on themselves and their own needs, but they are beginning to understand that others may see things differently and have different needs. Friendship tends to be in short bursts and is based upon contact. For example, 'Ruth isn't my friend any more – she doesn't want to come round and play.' 'Mandeep is my friend 'cos he plays football when I want.'
7- to 9-year-olds	Begin to see friendships as personal and based on personality traits, which may mean that they like or dislike someone because of these. For example, 'A friend is someone you like and they like you too. They aren't nasty to you and they are kind if you fall over or get upset. I have been Germayne's friend all the time since we've been in Mrs MacMahon's class.'
10-year-olds	Are able to cooperate with their friends and take on their point of view. They might share feelings and be interested in their activities, even though they do not share them. They may exclude others from their friendships. There is an emergent independence as they begin to place more importance upon their friends and less upon their families.
11 plus	Have much more complex views of relationships and begin to appreciate them in more depth. For example, 'Pravin's a good kid, even though he doesn't like cricket. His family are quite religious, so he has to go to the temple and stuff – we've got different ideas, but we get on great. I tell him about how I'd like to be a rock guitarist and he doesn't make fun of me. We swap wrestling videos and talk about the moves they make and sometimes act them out. We don't hurt each other though, even though my mum says we sound as if we're coming through the ceiling.'

Figure 5.14 Children's changing friendship patterns

Gender differences

Research has established that boys and girls in the pre-adolescent years tend to have different expectations of friendship, with girls reporting higher levels of intimacy, trust and loyalty than do boys in same-sex best-friendships.

Why children's friendships are important

Humans are social beings and, therefore, their social interactions are an integral aspect of their development and well-being. Friendships are an important part of our sense of self-worth as they tell us things about ourselves. They allow us to have a sense of belonging and acceptance. Those children who are unpopular at school are more likely to have problems in later life such as alcoholism, depression, schizophrenia, delinquency, dishonourable discharge from the army and psychosis (Duck, 1991). Some children (one in ten) have a social learning deficiency, which means they do not know how to act in social situations. These children were found to have poor empathy skills and to behave in ways likely to alienate them from others, such as boasting, sulking, cheating and withdrawing from games when losing (Wear, 2000). Clearly then, some children find it difficult to make friends and it is necessary for those working with them to be aware of ways in which friendship-making might be facilitated.

Encouraging friendships

As an adult working with and caring for children, you provide a role model of how to behave and react. We looked earlier at the way very young children use social referencing in order to make decisions about ambiguous or novel situations, and this is particularly relevant where other children are concerned. You will be watched for your reactions to a child who is perhaps new to the group, or has failed to become an accepted member of it. Therefore, how you react matters and you need to find ways of working with all children.

Behaviourist approaches

Behaviourist approaches, which focus upon external influences on human behaviour, are useful in terms of understanding ways of helping children to form friendships.

Learning theory (Skinner, 1957)

This theory recognises the importance of rewarding or using **positive reinforcement** when the desired behaviour occurs, in order to increase the chances of it being repeated. So when the child is friendly or helpful towards others, this should be encouraged.

Social learning theory (Bandura, 1977)

This theory suggests that children learn not only from direct reinforcement, but also from observing and imitating the behaviour of significant adults. Therefore, they will learn from your behaviour towards others. So if you are sociable and friendly and you also reward this sort of behaviour in others, children are more likely to behave accordingly.

Discussion point 5

Encouraging sociable behaviour in children

Think of examples from your own experience where friendly or sociable behaviour in children could be encouraged.

For comments on this discussion point see page 126.

Skills used by children in forming friendships

Making friends is easier for some children than for others and seems to involve the skills identified in Figure 5.15.

Skills	Examples
Ice-breaking	The ability to be the first to make the approach and invite some interaction. For example, 'Hello, my name's Daniel. What are you called? Have you just come into this school?'
Maintaining contact	This can be done in a variety of ways, such as inviting the other child to play, carrying on talking and listening, and generally expressing interest. This is done sensitively by children who have good social skills and this is important, as it does not force contact where not wanted, for example feeling forced to hold hands or play something the child doesn't want to.
Managing conflict	Being assertive but not aggressive is an important social skill and allows conflict to be dealt with. For example, 'I was on this bike first – I don't want to get off just yet, so stop pulling it.'
Listening and acknowledging	Recognising that others may have feelings and taking this into account. This may involve negotiation. For example, 'If you wait for a bit, I'll let you have a go next. Don't cry.'

Figure 5.15 Skills used by children when making friends

Difficulties with friendships

Difficulties with friendships arise for less socially competent children, who may be aggressive, demanding, 'bossy', impatient, whining and inflexible. Therefore, there is a cycle of rejection because they have a lack of adaptive strategies at their disposal and they will tend to use less effective ones, such as: 'If you don't let me play I'll tell the dinner lady – so there – and you'll get told off.' It may also be that there are language differences, cultural barriers or special needs that are relevant here, and these may need additional consideration.

Parental involvement

Parents may become involved in helping children to make friends (see comments about reinforcement (learning theory) and modelling the desired behaviour (social learning theory) on page 118, which are relevant in this context too). However, there is also evidence that advice-giving and instruction by parents and caregivers can significantly increase the interactive competence of children (Russell and Finnie, 1990). It has also been found that suggestions of positive strategies and non-hostile attitudes resulted in better-liked, less aggressive children (Mize and Pettit, 1997). So parents might encourage children to listen and ask before joining in with other children playing, or offer something which might be used to play with, such as a skipping rope.

Since the evidence above suggests that it is possible to provide advice that can be absorbed on a cognitive level, professionals working with children need to be aware of this when planning tasks, activities and learning experiences.

Activity 7

Friendship building

1 Plan an activity for 5- to 8-year-olds that includes work on friendship building.

2 How might this fit into other areas of learning?

For comments about this activity see page 128.

Friendships as predictors of social adjustment

It has been suggested that children's friendships are not only relevant to their childhood but are also predictors of social adjustment in adulthood (Nangle and Erdley, 2001). They are seen as a kind of training ground for important adult relationships, including marriage. Parental influence is stressed, not only as role models, reinforcers and advisors but also as managers of their children's social interactions outside school or nursery. It seems that the children of those parents who provide opportunities for peer contact and participation in activities, as well as monitoring their interactions, are likely to be more socially adept (Hartup, 1979).

However, for those working with children this may not be an area over which it is possible to exert influence. It is thought important for professionals to be aware of those children who are not accepted by their peers and to implement ways of helping them to be so.

The information given in Figure 5.16 may be used to enhance children's social skills

The role of the practitioner in enhancing social skills	
Provide plenty of opportunities for play with other children	In order that they gain experience of interacting with their peers.
Play with the children yourself in a positive, equal way	Play as though you were another socially competent child, rather than controlling the activity. This might include responding to the child's ideas and responding, actively listening to them and contributing to the action of the play. This enables children to learn from the adult modelling socially competent behaviour as well as developing confidence in their own ability to play.
Talk about friendship, social relationships and values with the children	In order to communicate an interest in their well-being in this area, as well as providing them with a place to share information and experience. This adds to their ability to solve the problems they encounter in this area. (See the Circle Time below.)
Tackle difficulties from a problem-solving perspective rather than seeming to know all the answers	Help the child to consider a range of solutions and viewpoints and encourage positive strategies that are relevant to the situation. For example: **Alex:** Well, I could push him over if he gets in my way again. **Adult:** You could. What do you think he would do then? **Alex:** He might thump me back or tell the dinner-lady. **Adult:** What else could you try? **Alex:** I suppose I could ask him to move and say 'please'. **Adult:** That's a good idea. Try that next time.
Encourage resilience to setbacks and a constructive approach to future events	For example, 'I'll try to be careful not to knock the tower over next time.'
Intervene when necessary	But allow older pre-school children to work out their own solutions when possible.
Provide a positive attitude generally for getting along with others	So that the children are encouraged to behave in a friendly way.

Figure 5.16 Enhancing children's social skills

and therefore encourage friendship formation. Recently many schools have introduced schemes such as 'playground friends' or 'Buddies' which actively promote relationships between children and encourage children's awareness of the needs of others. The case study below provides an example of how this might work.

Circle Time

Circle Time was popularised by Jenny Mosley, and has its roots in social work and therapeutic approaches. Many schools across the UK now use Circle Time as a means of creating a positive environment and dealing with problems (See Figure 5.17).

An explanation of Circle Time	
Conditions	The children sit in a circle so that everyone can be clearly seen; they often hold something, such as a cuddly toy, to indicate who is speaking.
Role of teacher	The teacher sits with the children as part of the group and ensures that the rules are followed, emotions are protected and appropriate activities are prepared.
Rules	Only one person speaks at a time – the one holding the 'talking object'. If you do not want to speak you can say 'pass'. There are no 'put downs' of people.
Discussion and problem solving	After a warm up consisting perhaps of a pair-game of some kind, the focus can be decided by the teacher. This will depend upon the age, stage and immediate situation of the group. For example, at the start of the year Circle Time might focus upon getting to know each other. It might well be used for dealing with problems such as the child who is being socially excluded or bullied.

Figure 5.17 How to use Circle Time

Case Study 10

Playground friends

Ava is new to her primary school and so far has made no friends. She is a shy girl who has difficulties with clearly articulating words and her class teacher, after speaking with the head teacher and Ava's father (her main caregiver), has arranged an appointment with a speech therapist. In the playground Ava spends most of the time alone, usually looking through the windows at other classes or empty classrooms. Occasionally she tries to attach herself to a group of children but lacks the speech and social skills to be included by her peers in games. There are concerns that she is not 'settling' and Ava's father reports that he has difficulty getting her to school in the mornings.

Ava's school might benefit by introducing a 'playground friends' scheme to help children such as Ava to integrate with other children and make some friends. This often involves Y6 children who are either paired with Y1 children or who are available when younger children need company or support. They are usually identified by wearing a badge or a distinctive fleece to make them immediately visible in the playground. The older children usually have to apply to do this job and may receive some training in how to play with younger children and conflict resolution. If Ava had a 'pal' or 'buddy' it might well facilitate her making friends within her own peer group and increase her confidence both in and out of the classroom.

Case Study 11

Using Circle Time creatively

Nathan has become increasingly miserable since starting school. He is always alone at playtime and usually tries to force his way into games, which has made him even more unpopular. Most of the other children run away from him now when he approaches and have begun laughing at him and teasing him.

An attempt to solve the problem

Circle Time could be used creatively here in a variety of ways. The teacher could begin after a warm-up exercise by talking about the problem and then ask each child in turn to offer an idea about how to solve the problem. If the issues around 'who did what to whom' arise, then both sides must be heard before, perhaps, a discussion about what should have happened, or other things that could have been done. The teacher might use the discussion to put forward a few suggestions and ask the children to decide which is the best option for them.

Stories, poems and books are often a valuable resource since problems encountered in them can be used to stimulate related discussions.

For example, nursery children might look at a nursery rhyme such as 'Georgie Porgie' and the teacher could ask them questions about why the other children did not want to play with Georgie.

Georgie Porgie Pudding and Pie
Kissed the girls and made them cry.
When the boys came out to play, Georgie
Porgie ran away.

With older children the teacher could use books such as Berenstein Bears or Jacqueline Wilson stories, which deal with a wide range of real-world problems including bullying and friendship but within a fictitious framework.

In this way children can be helped with other real problems that they encounter.

Enabling environments

As we have seen in this chapter the environment within which a child develops has a significant impact upon the child's emotional and social well-being. As well as individual practitioners acquiring relevant knowledge and experience of ways in which they can facilitate this, there are a number of national and international initiatives which are currently working to encourage and support multi-professional working. For example, the National Children's Bureau in England and Northern Ireland (working in partnership with Children in Scotland and Children in Wales) launched the PCT Children's Network in 2003 to enable discussion between practitioners and raise the profile of health and well-being needs of children (see Chapter 15 for more on Children's Centres). Recent writers on child development suggest that children have the ability to overcome hardship as long as they have conditions which allow them to thrive. These include secure attachments to sensitive caregivers and good relationships with adults and peers (Aldegate et al, 2006). This, of course, is of great relevance to practitioners working with young children.

Conclusion

> Emotions are an important part of the infant's initial social and emotional development.

> Secure attachments are related to emotional development and seem important for healthy development in a variety of areas.

> Self-esteem is key to fulfilling potential.

> Friendships help to support children's personal development.

As you read the following, reflect upon the understanding of social and emotional development you have gained by reading this chapter.

Case Study 12

A review

Christopher was separated from his teenage mother, Joanne, at birth, as he was the underweight (just under 5lbs) half of twins. Although it was a full-term pregnancy and he was in good health, he was taken to a hospital 30 miles away, which had a Special Baby Unit. His twin sister, Paula, remained with her mother and was successfully breastfed. He was kept in this hospital for two weeks, where he was bottle-fed. During this time, it was possible for his mother to visit him only once.

When he was reunited with his mother and sister, his mother attempted to breastfeed him, but he was used to the bottle by this time and refused to feed from her.

Christopher was a noisy baby, with a loud, persistent cry. He was thin and bald, and wriggled when he was held, comparing unfavourably with his twin, who had black curls and dimples and was plump and contented. Joanne felt that Christopher had rejected her and became increasingly depressed by the way he stiffened his limbs when he was held and his refusal of breast milk. She confessed to a friend, 'Sometimes I feel like throwing him out of the window when he is screaming for food and kicking me away.' Because of the practicalities involved, the father usually fed Christopher, but he was at work for much of the time.

As the twins grew, Paula remained the 'easy' twin and Christopher the 'difficult' one. Joanne found it very difficult to cope with his behaviour, particularly when she became pregnant again when the twins were 8 months old.

When the twins started school, Paula settled in quickly, but Christopher cried most days and had to be dragged to school. This was distressing for all of them and resulted in considerable strain upon Joanne, particularly as Christopher would run to her but then refuse to have a cuddle when he came out of school. The other children at school began to pick on him and call him a baby, which made it even harder to get him there.

1 Were the twins born temperamentally different or was it their experiences that shaped their personal development? (See nature-nurture debate in Chapter 4.)

2 How might your understanding of early emotional development, attachment theory, self-esteem and friendship formation help to shed light upon the case study?

3 How might Christopher and Paula's teacher help him to settle in?

For comments on this case study see page 124.

Comments on case studies, activities and discussion points

Case Study 6 (page 108): Making childcare arrangements

1 Perhaps you might reassure Jasmine that at Sarah's age, there should be no ill-effects in disrupting the attachment, as long as this is currently a secure one. The evidence suggests, in fact, that it will help to improve the child's ability to interact with others.

2 The important things to look for are continuity (so that there is always someone reliable to care for Sarah) and security. It might be possible to arrange a gradual increase in the amount of time spent in day-care, as Jasmine's mother might be happy to share in this. This would allow Sarah to get used to the new situation in a more gentle way and, as long as she feels secure, she might soon enjoy the extra stimulation that it would bring.

Case Study 12 (page 123): A review

1 As these are fraternal or non-identical twins (dizygotic) they will be no more similar genetically than any brother or sister. Therefore, it is possible that there are some temperamental or dispositional differences to begin with. However, the twins experienced different early conditions (one with mother and breastfed, one away from mother and bottle-fed) and these may well have formed the foundation for later developments, which were then reinforced by social interactions.

2 There are a number of issues here and, of course, we can only make an informed guess about some relevant aspects. However, we might start by considering the early interactions between Christopher and Joanne. As she had not been able to have this baby close to her for two weeks, it made it more difficult for early interactions (sensitive responsiveness) to occur. Joanne was able to interact with her daughter, but Christopher had been kept in an incubator and, therefore, had little contact with a 'mother figure'. This, coupled with the rejection of the breast, encouraged Joanne to feel that her son did not want her and that she could not supply his needs adequately. Therefore, she saw his crying and stiffened limbs as a rejection of her as an inadequate mother, whereas Paula smiled happily and made her feel fulfilled as a mother. This could easily have led to the formation of an insecure attachment between Christopher and Joanne, whereas Paula seemed to have formed a secure attachment. Starting school highlighted this and Christopher's insecure attachment might be identified as anxious/ambivalent (running towards her but refusing to cuddle her). It also seems likely that his self-esteem will be low, as he is constantly compared unfavourably with his twin (whether overtly or covertly) and this continues at school, where the other children see Paula's behaviour as acceptable and Christopher's as unacceptable.

3 Circle Time as described on page 121 would be very useful here. The class could be invited to see the world through Christopher's eyes, in order that he and they understand some of the difficulties he faces. Rogers' person-centred approach has much to contribute here. Christopher needs to be accepted for himself and given unconditional positive regard in order to develop his potential. Perhaps it would be a good idea to have the twins in separate classes in order that they develop more as individuals, but this would have to be dealt with very sensitively.

Discussion Point 1 (page 98): The effects of smiling upon a carer

1   If the infant smiles at the carer this is likely to be interpreted as recognition of the carer and his or her caregiving abilities. It signals that all is well and that the baby is fine. This is likely to make the carer feel more confident in his or her own ability to do the job properly. Therefore, the carer will be more relaxed and responsive.

2   This leads to a mutual responsiveness or reciprocal interaction (Bell, 1979) as both parties are reassured by the responses of the other.

Discussion Point 2 (page 112): Assessing which factors are important to children

1   Molly talks about most aspects positively. She seems proud of the fact that she is the biggest and seems pleased with the way she looks (physical appearance). She seems to think that her behavioural conduct is important and feels that she behaves well, particularly compared with others. She also talks about her learning (scholastic competence) and friends (social competence). There is no mention of her athletic competence, however, suggesting that this is not important to her.

2   Suzy seems focused upon her size (physical appearance) and learning competence, again comparing herself with others. She also seems to find behavioural conduct important. There is a more negative feel to her description than Molly's.

3   Both of these descriptions include comparisons with others and it is clear that these comparisons impact upon the security of self-esteem. Suzy's self-esteem is perhaps less secure because she does not measure up in the ways she sees as important (being physically big and quick academically), perhaps because she compares herself with more competent or older others. However, she does recognise her artistic abilities (valued by her father). Harter stated that significant others have an influence upon the child's self-esteem. So for the school-aged child, not only is the parent or carer involved, but also siblings and peers as well as teachers.

Discussion Point 3 (page 114): Positive and negative self-esteem

1   Clearly Jack has low self-esteem because he sees third place as confirmation that he is a failure, whereas Harry's high self-esteem allows him to enjoy his achievement and view the future with enthusiasm and as a positive challenge.

2   So it is not necessarily the event in itself (because Jack actually achieved more) but the child's perception of it that contributes to self-worth.

Discussion Point 4 (page 116): The practicality of Rogers' suggestions

1   Rogers is often criticised for not taking on board a formal teaching context, where time constraints and class size may make it extremely difficult to adopt a person-centred perspective.

2   Self-knowledge on the part of the teacher may be achievable and is certainly desirable in order to enhance personal and professional effectiveness. However, you may have commented that we do not all undergo therapy and may be unaware of our own attitudes and predispositions.

   The important thing, perhaps, is to be open to the possibility of our own attitudes influencing the development of children and be ready to address these as they arise.

3   Accepting children as they are is obviously desirable, but it may be that you are constrained by the external demands of the school or educational policies such as SATS. This increases pressure, as there are expectations that children reach a certain standard. Perhaps, you might

value each child (UPR) but the system does not seem to.

4　Empathy involves being able to see the world through the eyes of each child. This is difficult when there are 30 children in the class, each with his or her own need for empathic understanding. Rogers worked with clients on a one-to-one basis which allowed for this to happen, but it is obviously much more difficult to achieve when working with groups.

Discussion Point 5 (page 118): Encouraging sociable behaviour in children

1　You may have thought about ways in which you have encouraged children to assist others when they have been struggling with something. For example, 'Billy, would you hold the door open for Jack, please? He's carrying the lunch boxes for us.'

2　Or you may have thought about occasions when a child has done something helpful without being asked. For example, 'How kind of you to pick up Jake's jacket off the floor. I'm sure he's very grateful.'

Activity 1 (page 110): A short description of myself

1　Your description will probably have included some of your characteristics, such as 'fairly confident' or 'shy'. You might have talked about your interests, such as 'I really enjoy working with children but find it very demanding.' Your account may have included the views of others; for example, 'People always think I am outgoing, but actually I am quite shy, particularly when I don't know people well.' You may also have reflected upon ways in which you would like to be different, such as 'I wish I was more assertive and often feel reluctant to say what I want.'

2　Although your account will obviously be different from this, the process you have gone through to write it will usually be similar.

That is, you will have thought about how you feel inside as well as how you feel about the comments that other people have made about you. You may have considered, perhaps, whether you feel differently on the inside from how you appear on the outside. Almost certainly, it will have involved your thinking about how you compare with others. Perhaps you thought of ways in which you might wish to be different, or maybe ways in which you are happy with yourself.

3　In carrying out this activity, your own description will have been built upon both internal and external information in the same way that children's pictures of themselves are built. It consists of some 'I' statements, known as the existential self (or the 'self as I' as William James called it), which is the first part of the self-concept to emerge.

4　Later, the categorical self (or self as 'me') emerges and this includes the social categories which describe a person, such as gender, age, ethnicity, size and relation to others.

Activity 2 (page 110): Social categories

1　Let us assume that your list looked something like this:
Woman, nursery worker, single, mother, northerner, Morris dancer, Buddhist.

2　Some of these descriptions might apply to people that you know/work with; for example, many of the people you know may be women, and it is women who predominantly staff nurseries. For a man working in a nursery, this would make him different from his colleagues.

3　Being a mother who is single may mean that you are unlike some of the people you know (who may be married or childless) and many people that you know may choose to jog or go to the gym rather than Morris dancing. Similarly, your friends and acquaintances may not be of the same (or any) religion. If you are working in London or Cornwall for example, your identity as a northerner (with possibly a different accent and culture) may make you different too.

4 Identifying yourself as different from most of the people you know may have negative effects, particularly if to do so is disadvantageous in some way; for example, if your northern accent is derided or looked down upon by those around you. This has implications for those living in different cultures and from different ethnic origins because it might well influence their sense of belonging (categorical self) and self-worth.

Activity 3 (page 110): A young boy's self-description

You might have reasoned something like this.

1 The child is showing that he has a sense of self – he describes himself physically ('I am big', 'My hair is curly') and is able to compare himself with Emily (who is small) so he must be more than 19 months old. Obviously his use of language would also indicate this.

2 He is able to reflect upon his abilities ('I can ride a bike now and be a fire-fighter') demonstrating that this is something he recognises as an achievement. So this means he is at least 2 years old. He also shows that he is taking on board the expectations about adult standards of behaviour (his sister is shouting all the time which affects TV viewing). This would indicate that he is at least almost three.

Activity 4 (page 113): Encouraging positive self-esteem

1 The teacher here is encouraging those aspects that she sees as important (such as the manner and content of what is said) but discouraging children who have other suggestions and information. This means that those whose perceptions and ways of communicating are different from hers are less likely to develop positive self-esteem within this class. There are important connections here then between the personality of the teacher and the way she responds to the individuals within her class.

2 You may have seen that Katy is being encouraged to develop positive self-esteem here and is being rewarded for her contribution to the discussion.

3 Marek, on the other hand, receives mixed messages here. He is told that his answer is 'very good' and indeed it contains relevant information, but attention is also drawn to what the teacher perceives as his mistakes. The overall effect may be to reduce his confidence in his ability to contribute (thereby decreasing his self-esteem) because he might get it wrong again.

4 Karendeep seems to have low self-esteem to start with and does not have the confidence to offer an answer, but this is likely to be lowered even more by the teacher's response and comparison with the other children. Her response may be partly due to the cultural differences between her and Karendeep, which she hints at with 'don't know the word'.

5 Justin is not encouraged here although his answer is a graphic one, which could have been built upon by the teacher. Like Marek, he is treated to critical comments, implying that he has contributed nothing of worth.

Activity 5 (page 113): Qualities that you value in yourself

1 Maybe one of the qualities that you value in yourself is politeness. It may follow that you value polite children more and, therefore, that you encourage their positive self-esteem. The teacher in the extract clearly valued 'sensible' behaviour and therefore discouraged those who were perhaps over-keen to contribute, reluctant to do so, or included 'silly' comments.

2 It is likely that your own experiences and sense of self-worth will influence ways in which you relate to the children you work with, so it is important that you are aware of this.

Activity 6 (page 115): Acknowledging inappropriate behaviour

1 This should involve pointing out that the behaviour is 'naughty' or undesirable because it is distracting to the others, or makes it difficult for the teacher to do her job, but it should not label Zane as naughty.
2 Hayley is being labelled as 'bad' here, rather than her behaviour – inflicting pain and distracting Chelsie.
3 The entire class is being labelled as the 'worst', rather than their noisy behaviour being dealt with.

Activity 7 (page 119): Friendship building

You could introduce friendship building using discussion or Circle Time sessions based around a particular question or problem. Keep things unthreatening by putting a number of relevant questions into a bowl and passing them round to be picked out. Role play would often follow naturally from these questions. For example:

'One of your friends is always left out of games in the playground. What do you think you should do?'

'Someone you know is very bad at sharing and always pushes in. What would you do?'

'Your friend is always getting into trouble by arguing. What do you think he or she could do about this?'

How to move on in your research

Dowling, M. (2005) (2nd edition), *Young Children's Personal, Social and Emotional Development*. London: Paul Chapman
A clear, informative and useful account of relevant theoretical accounts underpinned by examples and practical suggestions for those working with young children.

References

Ainsworth, M. and Wittig, B. (1969), 'Attachment and exploratory behaviour of one-year-olds in a strange situation', in Foss, B. (ed.), *Determinants of Infant Behaviour, Vol. 4, The Data* (pp839–78). Hillsdale, NJ: Erlbaum

Aldgate, J., Jones, D.P.H., Rose, W. & Jeffery, C. (2006) (eds.), *The Developing World of the Child*. London: Jessica Kingsley

Bandura, A. (1977), *Social Learning Theory*. Englewood Cliffs, NJ: Prentice-Hall

Bell, R. (1979), 'Parent, child and reciprocal influences'. *American Psychologist*, Vol. 34, pp821–7

Bigelow, B., Tesson, G. and Lewko, J. (1996), *Children's Rules of Friendship*. New York: Guilford

Bowlby, J. (1951), *Maternal Care and Mental Health*. Geneva: World Health Organization; London: Her Majesty's Stationery Office; New York: Columbia University Press

Bradley, P. (2003), 'Emotional intelligence'. *Report to Executive Member for Education and Lifelong Learning*. Available at www.portsmouth.gov.uk/media/ecll20040106r_item04.pdf

Bransford, J., Brown, A. and Cocking, R. (2000), *How People Learn: Brain, Mind, Experience and School*. Washington: National Academy Press.

Brazleton, T. and Cramer, B. (1991), *The Earliest Relationship: Parents, Infants and the Drama of Early Attachment*. London: Karnac Books

Brazleton, T., Tronick, E., Adamson, L., Als, H. and Wise, S. (1975), *Early Mother-Infant Reciprocity*, Ciba Foundation Symposium 33. Amsterdam: Elsevier

Coopersmith, S. (1967), *The Antecedents of Self-esteem*. San Francisco: Freeman

Davies, J. and Brember, I. (1995), 'Change in self-esteem between year 2 and year 6: A longitudinal study'. *Educational Psychology*, Vol. 15, No. 2, pp171–9

Dowling, M. (2000), *Young Children's Personal, Social and Emotional Development*. London: Paul Chapman

Duck, S. (1991), *Friends for Life*. Hemel Hempstead: Harvester-Wheatsheaf

Feinman, S. and Lewis, M. (1983), 'Social referencing at ten months: A second-order effect in infants' responses to strangers'. *Child Development*, Vol. 54, pp878–88

Frankel, K. and Bates, J. (1990), 'Mother-toddler problem solving: Antecedents in attachment, home behaviour and temperament'. *Child Development*, Vol. 61, pp810–20

Gerry, C. (2000), 'What is emotional literacy?' *Literacy Today*. September, 2000, Vol. 24. Available at http://www.literacytrust.org.uk/Pubs/gerry.html

Goldschmied, E. and Jackson, S. (2004) (2nd edition), *People Under Three*. London: Routledge.

Gunnar, M. (1998), 'Quality of care and the buffering of stress physiology: Its potential role in protecting the developing human brain'. *Newsletter of the Infant Mental Health Promotion Project*, 21, 4–7.

Harter, S. (1983), 'Developmental perspectives on the self-esteem', in Heatherington, M. (ed.), *Handbook of Child Psychology: Social and Personality Development, Vol. 4*. New York: Wiley

Hartup, W. (1979), 'The social worlds of childhood'. *American Psychologist*, Vol. 34, pp944–50

Heard, D. and Lake, B. (1997), *The Challenge of Attachment for Caregiving*. London and New York: Routledge

Holmes, J. (1993), *John Bowlby and Attachment Theory*. Routledge: London

Hornik, R. and Gunnar, M. (1988), 'A Descriptive analysis of infant social referencing'. *Child Development*, Vol. 59, pp626–35

Izard, C. (1994), 'Innate and universal facial expressions. Evidence from developmental and cross-cultural research'. *Psychological Bulletin*, Vol. 115, pp288–99

Izard, C., Fantauzzo, C., Castle, J., Haynes, O., Rayias, M. and Putnam, P. (1995), 'The ontogeny and significance of infants' facial expressions in the first nine months of life'. *Developmental Psychology*, Vol. 31, pp997–1013

Izard, C., Haynes, O., Chisholm, G. and Baak, K. (1991), 'Emotional determinants of infant-mother attachments.' *Child Development*, Vol. 62, pp906–17

Jackson, J. (1993), 'Multiple caregiving among African Americans and infant attachment: The need for an Emic approach'. *Human Development*, Vol. 36, pp87–102

Lamb, M. (1998), 'Nonparental child care: context, quality, correlates', in **Damon, W., Sigel, I.E. and Renninger K.A. (eds) (1998) (5th edition)**, *Handbook of Child Psychology: Vol. 4 Child Psychology in Practice* (pp73–134), New York: Wiley.

Lewis, M. and Brooks-Gunn, J. (1979), *Social Cognition and the Acquisition of Self.* New York: Plenum Press

Liedloff, J. (1986), *The Continuum Concept.* Harmondsworth: Penguin

Lyons-Ruth, K., Easterbrooks, M. and Cibelli, C. (1997), 'Infant attachment strategies: Infant mental lag and maternal depressive symptoms: Predictors of internalizing and externalizing problems at age 7'. *Developmental Psychology*, Vol. 33, pp681–92

Matas, L., Arend, R. and Stroufe, L. (1978), 'Continuity of adaptation in the second year: The relationship between quality of attachment and later competence'. *Child Development*, Vol. 49, pp547–56

Mayer, J. and Salovey, P. (1997), *Emotional Development and Emotional Intelligence: Educational Implications.* New York: Basic Books. Available at http://eqi.org/4bmodel.htm

Merton, R. (1957) (Revised edition), *Social Theory and Social Structure.* Glencoe: Free Press

Miell, D. and Dallos, R. (eds) (1996), *Social Interaction and Personal Relationships.* London: Sage/Open University

Mills, R. and Duck, S. (eds) (2000), *The Developmental Psychology of Personal Relationships.* Chichester: John Wiley

Mize, J. and Pettit, G. (1997), 'Mothers' social coaching, mother-child relationship style and children's peer competence: Is the medium the message?' *Child Development*, Vol. 68, pp312–32

Mosley, J. (1996), *Quality Circle Time in the Primary Classroom: Your Essential Guide to Enhancing Self-esteem, Self-discipline and Positive Relationships.* Wisbech: LDA

Mruk, C. (1999) (2nd edition), *Self-Esteem: Research, Theory and Practice.* London: Free Association Books

Murray, L. and Trevarthen, C. (1985), 'Emotional regulation of interactions between two-month-olds and their mothers', in **Field, T. and Fox, N. (eds)**, *Social Perception in Infants.* Norwood, NJ: Ablex

Nangle, D. and Erdley, C. (eds) (2001), *The Role of Friendship in Psychological Adjustment.* San Francisco: Jossey-Bass

National Scientific Council on the Developing Child (2005), 'Excessive stress disrupts the architecture of the developing brain.' *Working Paper No. 3.* Retrieved 11/07/07 from www.developingchild.net/pubs/wp/excessive_stress.pdf

Nelson, C. (1987), 'The recognition of facial expressions in the first two years of life: Mechanisms of development'. *Child Development*, Vol. 58, pp889–910

NICHD Early Child Care Research Network (2000), 'The relation of child care to cognitive and language development.' *Child Development,* Vol 71, pp960–980.

Roberts, R. (2002) (2nd edition), *Self-esteem and Early Learning.* London: Paul Chapman

Rogers, C. (1990), *The Carl Rogers Reader* (edited by Kirschenbaum and Henderson). London: Constable

Rogers, C. (1994) (3rd edition), *Freedom to Learn.* Upper Saddle River, NJ: Merrill

Rubin, Z. (1980), *Children's Friendships.* London: Fontana

Russell, A. and Finnie, V. (1990), 'Preschool children's social status and maternal instructions to assist group entry'. *Developmental Psychology*, Vol. 26, pp603–11

Schore A. (1996), *Affect Regulation and the Origin of the Self: The Neurobiology of Emotional Development.* Hillsdale, NJ: Earlbaum

Schore A. (1997), 'Early organization of the nonlinear right brain and development of a predisposition to psychiatric disorders'. *Development and Psychopathology*, Vol. 9, pp595-631.

Schore, A. (2001) 'The effects of a secure attachment relationship on right brain development, affect regulation and infant mental health'. *Infant Mental Health Journal*, Vol. 22, pp7–66.

Skinner, B. (1957), *Verbal Behaviour.* New York: Prentice Hall

Troknick, E., Morelli, G. and Winn, S. (1987), 'Multiple caregiving of Efe (Pygmy) infants'. *American Anthropologist*, Vol. 89 (1), pp96–106

Van den Boom, D. (1994), 'The influence of temperament and mothering on attachment and exploration: An experimental manipulation of sensitive responsiveness among lower-class mothers and irritable infants'. *Child Development*, Vol. 65, pp1457–78

Van IJzendoorn, M. and Kroonenberg, P. (1988), 'Cross-cultural patterns of attachment: A meta-analysis of the strange situation'. *Child Development*, Vol. 59, pp147–56.

Waters, E. (1978), 'The reliability and stability of individual differences in infant-mother interactions'. *Child Development*, Vol. 49, pp483–94

Wear, K. (2000), *Promoting Mental, Emotional and Social Health: A Whole School Approach.* London: Routledge

White, B. (1993), *The First Three Years of Life.* New York: Simon and Schuster

Useful websites

http://users.stargate.net/~cokids/Circle.html
This website provides a platform for teachers to share ideas about Circle Time as well as links to other sites.

www.antibullying.net
This website contains a bank of information on bullying and easy access to searching within it for particular issues and narrowing the search.

www.kinderstart.com/index.html
Go to this useful and comprehensive website for information and links – again you can search within it for particular areas, for example social and emotional development.

www.ican.org.uk/TalkingPoint/Themes/.aspx
Click on the 'Emotional Literacy' link for access to a range of resources and research related to emotional literacy.

6 Learning and cognitive development

Vivienne Walkup

This chapter aims to explore concepts of learning before moving on to examine theories of cognitive development and consider their relevance to early learning contexts. Its purpose is to encourage the development of students' critical thinking skills in considering how best to support children's cognitive development and learning.

Learning is a term used to describe a wide range of experiences and events. We begin with a brief discussion of learning and theories of learning before focusing upon cognitive approaches to learning. The term 'cognition' is generally used to refer to any intellectual process within the human experience and covers a wide range of related areas including attention, perception, memory, thinking and problem solving. It can be thought of as being about the way the 'cogs' within our brains work. There are whole sections of libraries devoted to various aspects of cognitive psychology for those with specialised interests, but the purpose of this chapter is to consider aspects that are important to those working with, and supporting, young children. So what follows contains a discussion of the three main theoretical views of cognitive development and a consideration of how these relate to our understanding of children.

This chapter addresses the following areas:

➤ Concepts of learning
➤ The work of Jean Piaget
➤ The relevance of Piaget's ideas to the care and education of young children
➤ The work of Lev Vygotsky
➤ The relevance of Vygotsky's ideas to the care and education of young children
➤ Information processing approaches to cognitive development
➤ Applying information processing principles in learning environments

By undertaking the suggested study within this chapter it is hoped that you will be able to:

1 recognise a range of different definitions and explanations of learning

2 critically assess the theories of Piaget, Vygotsky and the information processing approach to cognitive development

3 understand the relevance of the theories of Piaget, Vygotsky and the information processing approach to the care and education of young children

4 evaluate your own experiences of, and insights into, early cognitive development and learning in the light of this learning.

Concepts of learning

'Learning' is a word we all use frequently and often without really considering what it means. It is a word we use to describe a wide range of experiences and events. To illustrate this, consider Figure 6.1.

If you analyse each of the statements in Figure 6.1, you will find that we sometimes use the word 'learning' in the context of how we acquire skills; for example, learning to drive, walk or use a knife and fork. We also use the word 'learning' to describe how we acquire attitudes; for example, learning to enjoy books or appreciate the taste of olives. We use the word 'learning' in our development of social dispositions, including how we relate to other people. In short, 'learning' is a broad term that defines what happens to us in a range of circumstances and over an indefinite period. Children learn at home, in the playground, at school, in the streets; learning happens all the time.

Key learning theories

There are many formal theories of learning that address the question as to what learning

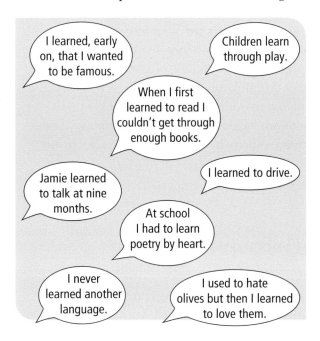

Figure 6.1 Some different meanings of 'learning'

involves; you may have studied these in your previous education or training. Behavioural learning theories, for example, assume that the outcome of learning is a change in behaviour and stress the importance of external events. For example, if a child has learned to read a word then her/his future behaviour will demonstrate the ability to do this. Behaviour management strategies (such as those suggested for use in classrooms by authors such as Bill Rogers and Sue Cowley) rely heavily upon this approach which includes assumptions about the reinforcement of desired and undesired behaviour. There are also many informal theories that practitioners come to through their involvement with children. In this sense, views of the ways in which children learn are the natural consequence of working with children; they arise from both practice and observation. Often ideas expressed in theory may be presented as something unique and different; however, newly presented ideas are often very similar to those that have gone before (see also Chapter 2, page 24). Some theoretical approaches look at the wider picture of how the individual learns within his/her culture and others look at processes within the individual.

Piaget and Vygotsky

Approaches to learning that acknowledge socio-cultural influences on children are generally built on the theories expounded by Piaget and, especially, Vygotsky which are included in this chapter. Planning for learning in accordance with these theories means that learning is seen to arise from the child's active participation in the learning process. Constructivist theory thus closely involves children in planning and constructing their own learning. Practitioners who adopt this approach will also acknowledge that children's learning is achieved via constructing and then building on increasingly more challenging tasks, thereby to develop and extend understanding. These ideas currently permeate the curriculum in the United Kingdom.

In addition, Vygotskian approaches emphasise the part played by the adult in helping children to remedy misconceptions about the world and make sense of their culture and environment.

Physiological aspects of learning

Approaches which focus upon the individual often take physiological processes into account. What is actually happening when we learn is that connections between cells in the brain are laid down and strengthened. Thus, 'learning' also has a very precise meaning in physiological terms. At birth, the human infant has all the brain cells needed for human development. In order for the human being to function, however, connections, or pathways, need to be formed between these cells. Learning during the first five years of life is more rapid than at any other time; thus the early years of life are crucial in terms of learning. Research has shown that these neural pathways are formed most effectively through experience. Each time a child encounters something new and interesting he or she explores the new object or situation and so connections between brain cells are laid down.

Learning styles

Children and adults, as individuals, learn in different ways; however, it is very useful to remind ourselves of the difficulties we may face when presented with new learning. People have different preferences of learning style. Children as well as adults will not learn effectively if they are expected to be passive recipients of a curriculum (David, Curtis and Siraj-Blatchford, 1992); most people prefer active approaches to learning.

You may have been presented with such a challenge when faced with a self-assembly flat-pack item of furniture: a group of adults presented with a 'flat-pack' kit to assemble will quickly demonstrate a very wide range of approaches. Some people will contemplate the diagrams and logically tackle the assembly in the correct sequence. Others may gather together the pieces and go straight into assembly. Most of us do not grasp things easily, particularly when mechanical or technological tasks are involved. Many if not most people need time to practise and make mistakes in order to consolidate their learning. Even when confident, we will often seek advice or reassurance that we are doing things correctly from another, more experienced person. When we have developed competence through trial and error, and by using skills in different contexts, we can approach these tasks in a more creative and playful way.

There may not be an exactly right way of tackling a problem and many methods may be equally effective in producing the desired result. As adults we often forget the importance of hands-on experience – solving problems by playing with materials or ideas, although we use this skill, or are forced to use it, at different points in our lives. Some may tackle this as a chore, others as a playful experience. If the latter approach is taken, learning may be not only more enjoyable but more effective and long-lasting.

The work of Jean Piaget (1886–1980)

Piaget is the best known and perhaps most influential of the cognitive theorists (Bjorklund, 2000) but he is also the most criticised. Just as with Freud, it is always easy to find lots of things he did that were methodologically flawed, but nevertheless we are left with interesting and valuable insights that add to our understanding of children.

Piaget, a Swiss biologist, first became interested in cognitive development as a result of his observations of molluscs existing in different environments. These caused him to ponder issues of flexibility and adaptation and he suggested that children's brains adapt to their environment through experience. He proposed that humans **construct** their own knowledge through their experiences of the world and that they learn by doing this rather than being told or given information. His work is therefore often referred to as a **cognitive constructivist** approach.

Summary of Piaget's theories of development

Piaget believed that:

➤ development proceeds through **maturation** and **adaptation**

➤ adaptation occurs because of **assimilation**, **accommodation**, and **equilibration**

➤ **schemas** allow knowledge to be shaped and stored

➤ **cognitive development** occurs in stages.

Figure 6.2 Flow diagram summarising Piaget's theory of cognitive development

Maturation refers to changes related to biological maturity over which the environment has little control. For example, a child's first teeth begin to develop around six months of age and there is little that can be done to change this. However, the quality of the child's teeth may be affected by environmental factors such as maternal diet or an excess of sugary drinks.

Adaptation describes ways in which the child is shaped by its environment in order to survive within it. For example, the child with poor teeth may learn to suck food thoroughly rather than biting it.

Assimilation is the term Piaget uses to explain the way that existing knowledge is used when we are confronted with problems we need to solve. For example, the child with poor teeth who has learned to suck biscuits will also suck an apple when first given one.

Accommodation is the process of changing what we already know to work in order to solve new tasks effectively. For example, the child finds that sucking the apple does not allow it to be eaten effectively and so begins to use his gums to break up the apple.

Equilibration is Piaget's term for the continual attempt at balance between **equilibrium** and **disequilibrium**. If new knowledge can be assimilated into our current knowledge easily, without having to change it, we are in a state of equilibrium. We feel steady and in control. However, if we have to accommodate our knowledge, we exist in a state of disequilibrium or unsteadiness until we have modified our cognitive structures. Thus, we strive for equilibrium but learning involves disequilibrium. For example, the child who finds that her apple does not respond to being sucked in the same way as the biscuit is concerted by this and may become distressed. She strives to find a way round this and eventually discovers that using her gums works. Therefore, the process of equilibration may not always be comfortable but results in more efficient means of understanding the environment.

Schemas or **schemata** are ways in which our knowledge is stored. They, like all cognitive structures, are abstract concepts and would not appear on a brain scan, but they are extremely useful ways of understanding the learning process. They are rather like mental files or folders stored on a computer. In them we keep everything that we know about particular aspects of the world, and when a new experience is encountered we open that particular folder in order to access the information contained within it. For example, the child's schema for eating now includes both sucking and using gums in order to eat food succesfully.

Case Study 1

Schema in action

A toddler sees a fire-engine for the first time and points excitedly at it. Her father says 'That's a fire-engine, Lara' and she repeats, 'fire-engine'. The next day when out with her childminder on the way to the park, Lara points to a bus and says, 'fire-engine'. Lara's childminder corrects her saying, 'No, Lara, that's a bus. We might go on a bus to town next week.' Lara seems a little confused. For the next week Lara constantly points to buses and names them but when she sees a lorry she says, 'Fire-engine'. Her big brother tells her that it is a lorry and that fire engines go, 'Nee-nah nee-nah' which makes Lara laugh. She then happily repeats, 'lorry'.

As we can see in the case study, Lara opens up her fire-engine schema (or mental file) for the first time when she sees the fire-engine and her father tells her the name for it which she repeats. When she uses this fire-engine schema again with her childminder this is an example of assimilation. However, this time it is incorrect because she is not looking at a fire-engine and her childminder tells her the correct name which is bus. Lara has to accommodate this new information into her fire-engine schema and learn to discriminate between the two. The feeling of confusion or being off balance is disequilibrium. Following this all goes well for a while until another new but similar object is encountered when Lara is with her brother. This time it is a lorry which again needs to be accommodated into her schema for fire-engine. When this has been done successfully Lara is again in a state of balance (equilibrium) about the world.

Activity 1

Schema for using a telephone

Think about your schema for using the telephone at home.

1 How do you modify it when using the phone at work?

2 Identify aspects of assimilation and accommodation.

3 How have equilibrium and disequilibrium been involved?

For comments on this activity see page 158.

Piaget believed that cognitive development occurred in stages that were related to the maturation of the child. Each of these stages involves a qualitative change that makes it different from the preceding one. The order in which these occur is fixed and applies to all children. It is not, therefore, possible to leave out or skip a stage. Each stage must be in place in order that the next can be laid upon it (see Figure 6.3).

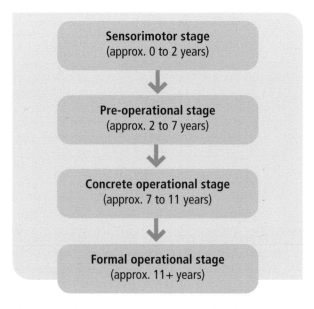

Figure 6.3 Piaget's stages of cognitive development

The sensorimotor stage

The sensorimotor stage sees the development of **object permanence**: the realisation that objects still exist even though they are not physically present. It begins to appear between 8 and 12 months. At this age, if an object is hidden under a cloth several times and the child grabs it, and then the object is transferred to another cloth in full view of the child, he or she will still look under the first cloth first because it was seen there most often. This is called the A not B error.

By the age of 18 months the child is able to **infer invisible displacement** (if an object is seen to be picked up, concealed in the hand, placed in the pocket, taken out and put in the drawer, the child will now look in the drawer even though he or she has not actually seen the object transferred) and develops complete object permanence.

It seems, then, that it is no longer the case that 'out of sight is out of mind' and carers will no longer be able to put things away in full view of the child and be confident that they will not be looked for there. Indeed, once children have grasped this concept, they may become very determined and use resources such as chairs and cushions to allow them to reach the confiscated objects.

The development of language and thought marks the end of this stage and children begin to engage in pretend play.

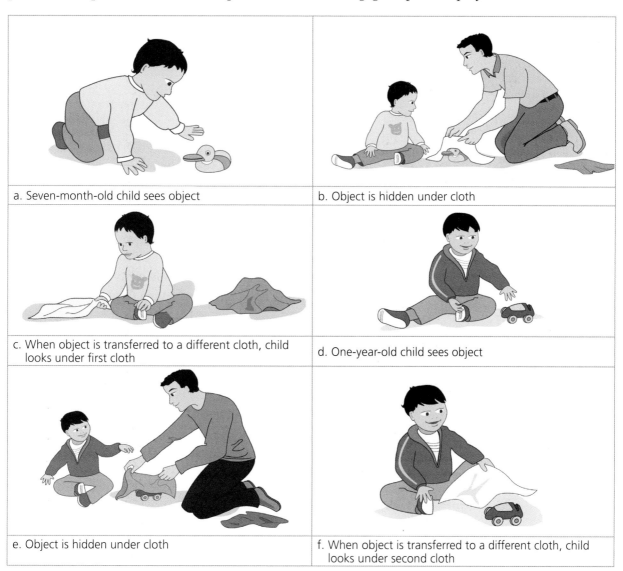

a. Seven-month-old child sees object	b. Object is hidden under cloth
c. When object is transferred to a different cloth, child looks under first cloth	d. One-year-old child sees object
e. Object is hidden under cloth	f. When object is transferred to a different cloth, child looks under second cloth

The development of object permanence

The pre-operational stage

At the pre-operational stage the child makes considerable headway in the use of symbols to represent aspects of his or her world. Rapid development in language, number, drawing and pretend play occurs as children learn to do this, although there are still some limitations.

There are two parts to this stage: the **pre-conceptual stage** and the **intuitive stage** (see Figure 6.4).

Egocentrism operates in the pre-operational child, who believes that his or her own view of the world is the one seen by others. For example, a child may assume that everyone can see what the teacher has written on the board because this is what the child can see. The child may be quite oblivious to the fact that he or she is blocking the view of others.

The concrete operational stage

At around 7 years of age, children begin to be able to use logical rules to deal with concrete problems. But Piaget would argue that they are still unable to solve abstract problems and that they do not consider all logically possible outcomes. Thinking is limited to real-world scenarios and their own past experiences.

The onset of **conservation** marks entry to this stage. This means understanding that quantities (such as mass, weight and volume) remain stable even though their appearance might change. So a child may no longer assume that pouring a bottle of lemonade into a tall glass makes it more or that a bigger parcel means a more expensive present. At this stage the child is capable of making decisions based upon all aspects of a situation, rather than just on one.

Stages in the pre-operational stage		
Stage	**Age range**	**Characteristics**
Pre-conceptual	2 to 4 years	This is characterised by **syncretic reasoning** (objects are classified according to limited and changing criteria) and **transductive reasoning** (relationships between objects tend to be based upon a single characteristic). For example, a boat may be used in water play one day because it floats on water and then put on the 'blue' table the next day because of its colour. **Animistic thinking** is common. Inanimate objects are believed to be alive particularly if they move, such as the sun and moon. For example, a child may believe that the moon follows him or her to light the way home.
Intuitive	4 to 7 years	This involves the reliance that children have upon what they sense to be true rather than on logic or reason. Children use their senses and imagination freely and may trust these more than the words used. Therefore, they may pay more attention to the apparent sense of what is being said rather than the actual language used. An example of this might be that when shown four toy cars put into three toy garages and asked whether all the garages have a car in them, children at this stage may answer 'no' because they can see that one car still remains. They have failed to 'disembed' the language from the visual sense of the scene and so respond to this rather than the explicit question.

Figure 6.4 Stages in the pre-operational stage

Piaget described this development as moving from **centration** (focusing upon the central aspects of a problem) to **decentration** (attending to the entire problem).

Centration applies to other everyday judgements, too, such as assuming that a friend's mother is older than your own because she is taller.

Class inclusion also appears during this stage and involves the understanding that a class must always be smaller than any more inclusive class that contains it. For example, when asked whether there are more sheep or animals on the farm table (which contains seven sheep, four cows and two pigs), a child becomes capable of answering 'animals'.

The formal operational stage

The formal operational stage (11+ years) is differentiated by the ability to think in abstract terms. This means that children are no longer limited to thinking about concrete objects but can include invention and fantasy unrelated to their previous experiences.

Hypothetico-deductive reasoning is the main factor here and involves being able to deal with possibilities, generate ideas and think in terms of symbols.

Children become capable of thinking scientifically and forming theoretical assumptions about the world, which can be tested and evaluated. For example, they are now able to play chess, begin to understand algebra and plan experiments in science.

Considerations of Piaget's work

Although Piaget's work has been heavily criticised, it is important to remember that there are also many strengths in his wide-ranging and comprehensive theory. Most significantly, it has succeeded in stimulating decades of research into children's cognitive development, and has provided scientific support for child-centred views of children's learning. Without Piaget's ideas we would lack a framework for understanding and interpreting some of the changes that occur.

Case Study 2

Conservation of quantity

Tarik, aged 5, and his 4-year-old sister, Adriana, have been given a bag of pennies collected by their aunt to share between them. They spend time at afterschool club counting these out carefully, 'one for you, one for me,' supervised by their play worker and at the end of it both are happy that they have an equal share of the pennies. They search for containers to keep these in safely so that they can take them home and put them in their money-boxes. Tarik finds an empty cardboard tube which had contained sweets and Adriana has hers wrapped in cooking foil. However, Adriana then begins to cry because Tarik has more pennies than her. When their play worker points out that they both had exactly the same amount she remains inconsolable and points at the tube standing on the table beside her tin-foil parcel saying, 'His is bigger than mine – he's got more now'.

Adriana is illustrating here that she is unable to conserve quantity – a characteristic described by Piaget as developing towards the end of the pre-operational stage. She believes that the cardboard tube containing Tarik's pennies has changed in quantity because it is in a taller container than hers. Even though she has seen the coins counted she is unable to grasp yet that because one container looks taller than the other it still holds the same quantity. Tarik is quiet throughout this either because he is developing this ability to conserve or because he thinks he might be gaining something.

Criticisms of Piaget's work

Generally these fall into three categories.

➤ Piaget underestimated the importance of previous knowledge to success in the tasks he set children.

➤ Piaget underestimated children's abilities because his tasks had methodological flaws.

➤ Piaget underestimated the role of culture.

The importance of knowledge

Gagné (1985) found that young children could acquire complex skills once the simpler skills required had been learnt, so children might well have failed some of Piaget's tasks because they just did not possess these prerequisite skills. For instance, young babies might not have demonstrated object permanence because they had not yet mastered the ability to coordinate hand-to-eye movements in order to reach towards the object that had been covered.

It could, therefore, also be argued that development is based upon learning new skills and is continuous not discontinuous as Piaget suggested.

Children's abilities

Piaget underestimated children's abilities because his tasks were methodologically flawed and failed to account for factors such as demands upon memory and physical ability, familiarity with the task and misleading questions.

Demands on memory and physical ability

These are involved in, for example, object permanence tasks, which relied upon infants being able to remember that the teddy was behind the screen and being able to reach out for the teddy at the same time. Young infants may not physically be able to do this. Baillargeon (1987) found that when the task is one that is based upon a visual rather than a reaching response, infants as young as 3 months of age demonstrate object permanence.

Familiarity with tasks

Piaget's tasks may have been too complex, abstract and unfamiliar to allow children to succeed. He suggested that they had an

---

The three mountains task

Children were asked to look at three mountains on a table. They were made of papier mâché and each of them was a different size and colour. Something was different on top of each of them: snow, a cross or a house.

A small doll was placed opposite the child, who was then asked which view the doll could see. The experimenter gave the child ten pictures taken from around the table and asked her to pick out the one that showed what the doll could see.

Piaget found that children younger than 7 or 8 years old were unable to do this correctly and usually picked out the view that they could see themselves.

The three mountains task

egocentric view of the world and were unable to decentre.

However, when children were presented with a task involving a boy hiding from a policeman, even 3-year-olds were able to say when the boy could be seen by the policeman, even though the viewpoint was different from their own (Hughes, 1975). It seems that tasks that are simpler and more meaningful allow children to show a higher level of competence.

Misleading questions

Donaldson (1978) suggested that children may be misled by, or not understand, the questions being asked. Perhaps being asked the same question twice led the children to expect the answer to be different. The reason for the changes also seems to be important and when children can make sense of these they are more likely to give the correct answer. When a 'naughty teddy', who was out to make mischief, was used to change things within conservation experiments, many young children were able to conserve. They recognised that changing one aspect of the situation (such as the appearance) did not necessarily mean that other aspects (such as quantity) had also changed (McGarrigle and Donaldson, 1974).

Conservation of liquids task

A child was shown two identical beakers, each containing the same amount of water. These were placed in front of the child, who was then asked whether the amount of water in both was the same. When the child was happy that this was the case (after perhaps adjusting small amounts) the experimenter poured the contents from one beaker into a taller, narrower one. The child was then asked whether there was now:

➤ more water in the new beaker
➤ more water in the original beaker
➤ less water in the new beaker
➤ the same amount in both beakers?

Piaget found that up to the age of 6 or 7, children said that there was now more water than before.

Child performing conservation of liquid task

The role of culture

Piaget's tasks were culturally biased because there are differences across cultures in terms of rates of development. Schooling and literacy, in particular, affect rates of cognitive development, and formal operational thinking is not universal.

Studies of illiterate adults in Liberia found that they had difficulty categorising geometric shapes (Irwin and McLaughlin, 1970). This should be an easy task, according to Piaget, as the skill is achieved during the concrete operational stage. However, these adults were able to sort different types of rice successfully. This suggests that their abilities are based on their experiences of learning rather than their maturational level of development. Schooling encourages problem solving that is abstract and decontextualised and for those who do not experience it there is no need for these types of skill to develop.

Activity 2

Adapting tasks

Suppose that you wanted to find out whether two new children in Foundation Stage had the ability to understand the conservation of liquids. How would you adapt Piaget's conservation of liquids task in order to avoid some of the methodological errors?

For comments on this activity see page 158.

The relevance of Piaget's ideas to the care and education of young children

Applying Piaget's ideas to the classroom, or Early Years learning environment, means that the role of the teacher is to provide an environment that is rich in stimulation for children to explore for themselves, in which they can actively construct their own knowledge (schemas) through their experiences (albeit constrained by social ideologies).

It is important to remember that the stages of development proposed by Piaget were general guidelines rather than labels for all children of the same age and that there may be long transition periods between stages. Therefore, it would be a mistake to take the view that knowing a child's age is a guarantee that we know how they think (Orlando and Machado, 1996).

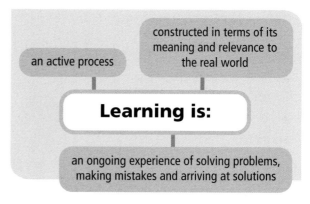

Figure 6.5 Key principles of Piaget's ideas

Learning environments	
Provide opportunities to construct knowledge through experience	Children need opportunities to construct their own knowledge through their own experiences, rather than being told about things by the teacher. There is less time spent upon teaching particular skills and more emphasis on making learning meaningful. For example, the children might operate a class bank or post office, rather than only doing skill-based numeracy exercises.
Use a particular topic or anchor	Learning and teaching should be centred around a particular topic or 'anchor', which may be a story, a video-clip or situation which is of interest to the children. This will include problems or issues for the children to engage with and resources that can be explored as children decide how to solve a problem. For example, an 'anchor' might be friendship, with the children engaging with problems such as which friends to invite for a sleepover and which not.
Relate something new to what is known	Teaching should involve relating something new to what is already known. Children are expected to learn to read and write in the same gradual way that they learn to talk, without much direct instruction. Learning rather than teaching is stressed and early writing might involve the child describing something familiar to the teacher (perhaps his or her house or neighbourhood) and the teacher writing this on the board or on a large piece of paper.
Use construction kits or toys	Construction kits or toys provide a means for exploration and learning about the properties of objects within a meaningful context. For example, a child may only be able to stick two pieces of Duplo together initially to represent a bus, but the bus has two pieces whereas a car has only one. Therefore, the child is building upon what he already knows (how to connect two pieces of Duplo) in order to solve the problem of representing the relationship of a larger object to a smaller one.

Figure 6.6 Providing different learning environments enhances the learning experience

The work of Lev Vygotsky (1896–1934)

Vygotsky was an important Russian theoretician who began as a schoolteacher of literature and moved on to become a psychology lecturer in a college of teacher education. Working with colleagues Luria and Leontiev, he created the Vygotskian approach. But Stalin banned his work, as it used some of the assumptions considered to be 'bourgeois pseudo-science'. After his early death from tuberculosis, colleagues and students kept his ideas alive, but it is only since the dissolution of the USSR that Vygotsky's work has become freely available and provoked wide interest.

Vygotsky's approach, like Piaget's, is a **constructivist** one as he sees children as actively constructing their understanding of the world. He drew attention to the external experiences of children, moving away from the Piagetian view of their internal development. His approach is often referred to as **social-cognitive** because it combines elements of cognitive theory (such as Piaget's ideas about children's minds developing through

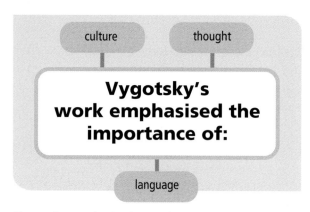

Figure 6.7 Emphasis of Vygotsky's work

interactions with the world) and social learning theory, which suggests that children learn by watching people model behaviours (Bandura and Walters, 1963). He thought that social interactions with more competent others allow the child to acquire the necessary 'tools' for thinking and learning and that language is one of the most important social tools for shaping the way we think (see Figure 6.7).

Culture

Vygotsky believed that unlearned abilities such as attention, perception and memory are built upon by the culture or context which the child is part of. Culture, he argued, is largely transmitted through language, which is invented by humans. 'Cultural tools' such as language and number systems have to be passed on from generation to generation, as they are complex.

Therefore, communication of these tools is an important part of cognitive development.

Vygotsky (1978) provides the example of pointing a finger. Initially, this behaviour begins as a meaningless grasping motion. However, as people react to the gesture, it becomes a movement that has meaning. In particular, the pointing gesture represents an interpersonal connection between individuals, which indicates that one is being singled out.

Language

Vygotsky argued that language begins as external speech in the context of social interactions, with **monologue**, or **overt inner speech**, and then **inner speech**, or **verbal thought**, developing later. This gives the child the power to reflect, makes thought possible and eventually controls behaviour. This development proceeds through three stages as shown in Figure 6.8.

Thought

Thought is therefore shaped by our first communications with others. Once these have been mastered, they become internalised and allow us to think. The language used is part of the culture that invented it and becomes an integral part of that thinking. So if our early carers speak to us in English or French, we learn not only to speak the language but to think in it.

Language development		
External speech	0–3 years	The child's use of language is in response to and directed towards the outside world. For example, a child asks for a drink and responds to a question about whether he wants orange or blackcurrant squash.
Egocentric speech (monologue/overt inner speech)	3–7 years	The child thinks aloud. For example, 'I'm putting teddy to bed now and he's going to go straight to sleep.'
Internal speech (inner speech/verbal thought)	7 years onwards	This involves a child thinking silently to him/herself. For example, reflecting upon the day's events at school and the need to take his or her PE kit the following day.

Figure 6.8 Vygotsky's theory of language development

Vygotsky suggested that when children are in a learning environment, they learn best when the material to be learnt is within their grasp but just beyond what they already know. He identified the importance of recognising, therefore, not only what a child knows but also what he or she is capable of understanding at any particular point. Vygotsky called this the **zone of proximal development**.

The zone of proximal development (ZPD)

This is the distance between the child's **actual** developmental level and his or her **potential** developmental level at any one point in time. Full development depends upon adult guidance or collaboration with more competent peers.

At each level or stage, individuals are ready to respond to a particular environment and the people in it, and an interaction occurs between their cognitive structures and the outside world. Therefore, different experiences and cultures shape a child's thinking processes.

Scaffolding

This is the framework which adults or more competent peers provide to enable a child to progress cognitively. (For example, a carer might help a toddler to manipulate shapes in order to post them into a shape-sorting box.) The term 'scaffolding' was introduced by Jerome Bruner, an American cognitive psychologist and educationalist in the 1950s, to describe young children's language acquisition but it is often used alongside Vygotsky's work which shares many similarities.

Scaffolding is most effective when it is within the ZPD but relates to an activity that the child has not yet achieved competence in. The idea is that the adult or peer provides assistance in the form of demonstrations, explanations, questions, corrections and other interactions to allow the child to move from the lower limit of what he or she knows to the upper limits of what he or she is capable of achieving.

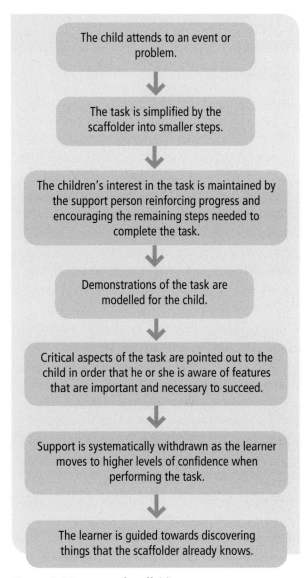

Figure 6.9 Features of scaffolding

For comments on this activity see page 158.

Investigations into scaffolding by parents (Pratt, Kerig, Cowan and Cowan, 1988) and

---

Activity 3

Using the concepts of scaffolding

How would you use the concepts of scaffolding to enable a 3-year-old child to construct a house with building blocks?

Case Study 3

Scaffolding of reading

Jesse is a 5-year-old boy who has recently started school. He enjoys looking at the pictures in the books and is beginning to read short words. The Teaching Assistant encourages this by sitting with him and reading her own book, ready to talk with him about his story or help him with longer words. Jesse follows the words with his finger and stops at the word 'supermarket', looking up at the Teaching Assistant for help. She looks over at him and says, 'That's a long word isn't it? What I always do with long words that I don't know is to break them up into smaller words. Shall we try that with this one?' When Jesse nods the Teaching Assistant covers up all but the first two letters of the word and asks, 'What do you think that says?' Jesse sounds out the letters, 'sss-uu' and the Teaching Assistant nods encouragingly and uncovers the next three letters. She looks at Jesse who sounds out these as well, 'p-e-rr' before she smiles and nods and uncovers the next three letters. 'M-a-r'. 'Yes now let's put those together and see what we've got so far', says the Teaching Assistant, and speaking slowly, matching her pace with his, she says. 'su-per-mar...' and Jesse jumps in excitedly with, 'Supermarket'. 'Yes, well done – we got there in the end didn't we – you are clever reading such a long word. I bet you could do some more now, couldn't you?' Jesse nods and continues with his book.

Jesse's Teaching Assistant has successfully scaffolded Jesse's reading of long words here. She provides him with assistance, questions, encouragement and a demonstration of how to read the word. This is within his zone of proximal development (ZPD) because he has started to read short words, but he has not yet mastered it. With her help in this way he begins to achieve this and is able to move forward on his own and practise the strategies he has now mastered. The Teaching Assistant's presence, as a co-reader, provides a positive role-model as well as support and help when he needs it.

older siblings/peers (Azmitia and Hesser, 1993) demonstrated the importance of **sensitive** scaffolding by a more competent other. When scaffolding was responsive to the child's ZPD and sensitive to their needs, the scaffolding was most successful.

There are obvious implications here for teaching and learning relationships, including awareness of what the child does know, recognition of effective strategies and finding appropriate ways of allowing him or her to learn more.

The relevance of Vygotsky's ideas to the care and education of young children

Vygotsky's ideas suggest that a child's learning development is affected by the culture, including the family environment, which they are part of. The child's experiences of care and education outside the home usually form part of this culture. Within these experiences:

➤ the curriculum should be designed to maximise interaction between learners and learning tasks. For example, children working together, or in groups, to measure their desk tops

➤ children should have opportunities to play, as this allows the developing skills of the child to be practised within safe contexts and provides opportunities to try out new skills and knowledge. For example, when children play at being shopkeeper and customer – developing an understanding of money and their language and social skills – nothing is actually at stake as it would be in a real situation

➤ since children can often perform tasks with appropriate help that they cannot do on their own, sensitive scaffolding (where the adult continually adjusts his or her help in response to the child's level of performance) is an effective aspect of teaching, for example reading

➤ assessment methods should take into account the child's current zone of proximal development. What children can do on their own is their actual developmental level and what they can do with help is their potential developmental level. Two children might have the same actual level but given appropriate adult help, one child might be able to solve many more problems than another. Therefore, assessments should take account of both actual and potential levels.

Experiment by Vygotsky (1986)

Two 8-year-olds of average ability were given problems that were a little too difficult for them to solve alone. They were then given help, in the form of hints and leading questions. With this help, Vygotsky found that one child was able to solve a problem designed for a 12-year-old and the other reached a 9-year-old's level.

This suggests that some children might not demonstrate their potential unless scaffolded appropriately. Well-designed instruction should be aimed at a level slightly ahead of what the child can do at the present time in order to draw it towards the next level of learning in the manner of a magnet. Therefore, it is important that the teacher is aware of each child's actual developmental level.

Activity 4

Using scaffolding at different levels

How might a teacher or facilitator provide scaffolding when teaching groups of Year 1 children to play snakes and ladders using a pair of dice?

For comments on this activity see page 159.

Criticisms of Vygotsky's theory

While there has been considerable research support for aspects of Vygotsky's theory, there have also been a number of criticisms (see Figure 6.10).

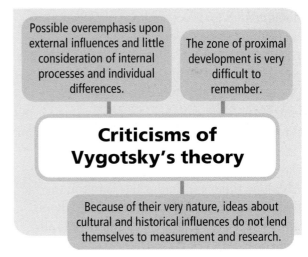

Figure 6.10 Criticism's of Vygotsky's theory

Activity 5

Experiences of scaffolding

Think of an example from your own experience of providing scaffolding to enable a child to achieve something he or she could not do without help. Was the scaffolding sensitive? How effective was it?

Piaget and Vygotsky – a summary

A summary of Piaget's and Vygotsky's ideas is shown in Figure 6.11.

Importance of the effects of cultural expectations and differences on children's learning

As discussed earlier, Vygotsky stressed the importance of the context in which learning takes place, seeing that as inseparable from the child's cognitive development. Let us look at some of the research findings about the effects of cultural expectations upon children's learning and see what might be concluded from these.

The effects of cultural differences on development have been researched and documented for a range of cognitive functions, including colour concepts (Moore et al, 2002) counting (Lefevre et al, 2002), number concepts (Ho and Fuson, 1998) and calendar calculations (Kelly et al, 1999). The following section summarises some of the research findings related to mathematics and attention regulation.

Mathematics

Although there are similarities between the mathematical knowledge of children growing up in extremely diverse cultures, there is also evidence that there are variations across cultural groups. These differences are often explained as *superficial* as in the following cases.

➤ Oksapmin children in Papua New Guinea use a number system based upon 27 parts of the body (Saxe, 1981) but the core principles (one object, one number word) are similar to Western systems.

➤ Brazilian children working in street markets use 'street' mathematics which share basic mathematics properties with 'school' mathematics (Nunes, 1995).

➤ Although the rate and nature of mathematical development may vary across cultures, there is universal similarity in terms of the sequence and basic principles (Klein and Starkey, 1988) as Piaget suggested.

However, those who take a Vygotskian approach suggest a more *culturally dependent* explanation of differences in mathematical knowledge. These relate to mathematical practices outside of school such as the way that cultures vary in the opportunities they provide for young children to develop their mathematical abilities as in the following examples.

➤ Korean children are not instructed in counting and money before entering schools because their culture discourages this (Song and Ginsburg, 1987).

➤ Many disadvantaged children have to work to exist so they develop the mathematical skills

Piaget	Vygotsky
Concluded that teaching a child something prevented him or her from learning it on his or her own.	Saw interactions between children and adults within a cultural context as the driving force in cognitive development.
Stressed the readiness idea: a child cannot achieve certain skills until ready to do so. His or her readiness depends upon his or her stage of development.	Thought that teachers needed to provide demonstrations, explanations and other forms of scaffolding to assist development.
	Emphasised the importance of assessing potential rather than actual abilities.
	Presented a strong argument for the use of challenging instructional materials and methods.

Figure 6.11 A summary of Piaget's and Vygotsky's ideas

they need for this. Children selling sweets in Brazil (Saxe, 1991) and working street markets in Nigeria (Oloko, 1993) with little or no schooling are able to calculate quickly and give correct change but they rarely use written numbers and calculations (Nunes et al, 1993).

➤ A study which compared Latino and Korean American children found that Korean American children were often questioned about the mathematics they were learning at school by their families but Latino American children were more likely to be asked about practical mathematics such as calculating money. These differences were reflected in their assessments of formal and informal mathematical knowledge (Guberman, 1994).

Cultural tools

Vygotsky suggested that cultural tools such as number systems allowed information to be passed from generation to generation. These vary across time and place and so may affect the development of children's cognitive development and mathematical understanding. For example, most European systems of number words are variable and irregular whereas in Asian languages they correspond to the written forms (16 is read as ten six and 58 as five ten eight). This seems to affect this aspect of development.

➤ Chinese children make fewer errors in saying number words up to 19 than English-speaking children in the USA (Song and Ginsburg, 1987).

➤ Chinese, Japanese and Korean children were more likely to apply the principles of tens and units successfully than French, Swedish and American children (Miura et al, 1994).

➤ English-speaking children are slower to use ten-structured concepts of numbers and more likely to use single unit concepts (Fuson et al, 1995).

It seems then that the language characteristics of number systems connect with young children's command of counting, understanding and calculation and may be a source of national differences in mathematical ability (Guberman, 2002).

Attention regulation

Cultural differences in directing young children's attention have been found between British and Chinese caregivers (Vigil, 2002). It seems that British caregivers are likely to follow the lead of infants (9–12 months old) and respond to their focus of attention whereas Chinese caregivers tended to direct the infant's attention. This may have implications for the development of vocabulary as there are differences in cultural communication styles.

Language production

Differences were found between the ways in which Italian and Canadian mothers respond to their children linguistically (Girolametto et al, 2003). Italian mothers spoke more often, more quickly and used a more varied vocabulary to their toddlers than Canadian mothers. However, Italian mothers responded to less of their children's utterances than the Canadian mothers did. The results from Girolametto et al's study found higher rates of language production in the Italian children even though there were similarities in the vocabulary size of both groups.

Thus it seems that although some evidence suggests that there are universal elements to children's cognitive development as can be seen in terms of similarities across cultures, there is also evidence of differences where social and cultural factors do impact.

Information processing approaches to cognitive development

Information processing approaches do not stem from a single theorist but are based on using the computer as an analogy for the human mind. This is seen as a useful way of understanding cognitive processes, as there are similarities such as encoding information, processing it and storing it for future use. Information processing theorists share the view that the mind, like a digital computer, is a system that uses symbols and works according to certain rules. The assumption is not that humans solve problems or 'think' in exactly the same way as computers but that they both solve complex problems by breaking them down into a series of simpler steps. If this is correct then we can study computers in order to gain insights into the working of the human mind and ways in which cognition develops.

Cognitive development

We might think of the 'hardware' of the human mind as the physical structure of the brain, including nerves and tissue, and the 'software' as the programmes or strategies we use to deal with the world. Therefore, we need to understand whether there are age-related changes in the basic system and its processing capacity (similar to Piaget's ideas of maturation) and/or to consider the learning needed in order to understand and use the programmes available.

Memory

This is an important part of the computer without which it would be simply a word-processor. Similarly, the human mind depends upon memory in order to learn and develop.

The dominant view of memory is based upon a model proposed by Atkinson and Shiffrin (1968). This is that memory is a theoretical structure and cannot be physically observed within the brain's structure. Three stages are involved in the processing and storage of memory (see Figure 6.12).

Stage 1

Sensory memory represents information in the environment that is experienced through the senses (sight, hearing, smell, taste, touch) and passed to the brain by electrical impulses. The brain then makes sense of these impulses, and in the process of transferring

Is a child's mind analogous with a computer?

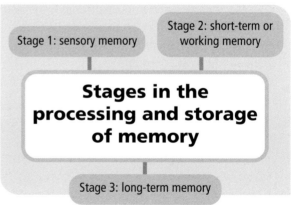

Figure 6.12 Stages in the processing and storage of memory

the messages from the senses to the brain a memory is formed. This takes a very short time (approximately half a second for visual information and about three seconds for auditory information).

Children, like adults, are surrounded by sensory stimulation when awake, but the amount of this that is processed is very small.

Activity 6

Awareness

Let your eyes focus upon an object within the room you are in. Now, without moving your eyes become aware of what you can see within your peripheral vision (out of the corners and tops and bottoms of your eyes). You will be aware that there is much more that you could be focusing upon which you are simply not aware of.

Similarly with sounds: if you stop and listen you will become aware of many different sounds in the room. Perhaps you can hear traffic outside, someone moving in another part of the building, your own breathing and so on.

Try this out with what you can feel without moving, or what you can taste or smell.

For comments on this activity see page 159.

Attention to the information is crucial then if the information is to pass to the next stage. This is most likely if the stimulus is interesting or relates to something familiar.

If attention is not paid then the information will simply be lost.

Stage 2

This is the **short-term** or **working memory (STM)** and represents what we are thinking about at the present moment. It is a critical part of the memory process because it allows us to process incoming information for storage and to retrieve memories we have already stored. It is, however, very brief (approximately 15

seconds) so if you are attending to the words you are currently reading, they are in your short-term memory but they may be lost (if I ask you to think about your date of birth, for example) and possibly need to be read again.

Short-term memory is also limited in terms of its capacity. Miller (1956) suggested that humans can hold 7 plus or minus 2 chunks of information in the short-term memory at any one time. So if you look up a telephone number (often 6 digits) in the directory you can remember it long enough to dial the number, but will probably have forgotten it by the time you get through. Perhaps this explains also the fact that many of us find it very difficult to remember mobile phone numbers (consisting of 10+ digits). These research findings became known as 'Miller's Magic Seven' as this seemed to be the average number of digits remembered.

Stage 3

This is long-term memory (LTM) and represents information stored for longer periods of time, perhaps for a lifetime. This forms the knowledge base of the human mind. It is a complex structure which seems to consist of different types of memories such as those given in Figure 6.13.

Long-term memory comprises:	
Episodic memory	This contains memories of past life events (such as your last birthday or your first day at school).
Procedural memory	This contains stored physical skills or behaviours (such as riding a bike or writing your name).
Semantic memory	This contains non-personal facts (for example, the capital of Australia or the name of the Prime Minister).

Figure 6.13 Constituents of long-term memory

Words that can be easily visualised are more likely to be remembered than abstract words. So if I read a list of words and ask you to remember as many as possible, you are more likely to remember words that you can 'picture' such as 'balloon', 'river' and 'kitchen' than those which you cannot, such as 'formation', 'reference' and 'summary'.

Retrieval of information from the LTM

This involves **cues**, which allows LTM to be accessed. For example, coming home from work and going upstairs to change may serve as a cue to remind you that you left your missing diary in the bedroom the night before, rather than in the other places you have searched for it.

The best retrieval cues are the same as those present when the information was first encountered or encoded. So being in your bedroom at the same time and in the same situation (or context) as the day before, served as powerful cues to retrieve the memory of putting your diary down there.

Recall and recognition

The difference between **recall** and **recognition** is a significant one, particularly when considering children's learning. Recall involves bringing to mind the information needed, whereas recognition involves being able to select the correct piece of information when presented with others. It might be that when you are spelling a difficult word aloud you need to write it down to see whether it 'looks right'. This allows you to recognise the correct spelling.

Forgetting

According to some theorists, forgetting does not involve actually losing something from our long-term memory. This can only occur if there is damage to the brain. If this is the case, then if we cannot remember something it is either because it was never encoded in the first place (perhaps because we were not attending to it) or because we can no longer retrieve it. So the phone number that we repeated just long enough to enable us to dial is forgotten because it was never transferred to our long-term memory. Probably you still have the first phone number you had when you were a child, stored somewhere in your LTM, but cannot retrieve it. This is probably because of **interference** (all the other phone numbers you have had to learn since then) but you might still recognise it if it was placed with others in a list.

Organisation

The way that material is **organised** affects retrieval. Miller's magic seven ignored the fact that we often arrange information to be remembered in different ways, in order to make it easier to remember. So you might remember your mobile number by **chunking** the digits together in twos or threes; for example, 0775860332 then becomes 077, 58, 60, 332. In this way, you are changing the number into four pieces of information rather than ten.

The development of memory

Changes in **processing capacity** may occur as children mature. Perhaps these relate to changes in the physical structure of the brain or increases in speed and efficiency.

Research continues into this area, and work such as that by Kail and Park (1994) supports the theory that there are changes in processing speed and that these are related to some kind of developmental change.

Strategies to aid memory

However, there are other aspects of memory development that occur as a result of children using strategies, or **mnemonics**, such as rhymes (Thirty days hath September, for example), to help them to remember.

The ability to use strategies such as **rehearsal** (repetition; for example, look/cover/write/check for spelling), **organisation** (structuring information), **retrieval** (using more explicit cues) and **elaboration** (using association to remember things) increases with age. Young children can be trained to use some of these, but they are less successful than older children, perhaps because of some of the factors outlined below.

Activity 7

Personal strategies that aid memory

Think of a strategy that you use to help you remember something in particular, such as your pin number or the colours in the spectrum. Were you taught this strategy, or did you develop it yourself?

For comments on this activity see page 159.

Encoding of information and knowledge base

Age differences in the ability to **encode** information mean that younger children have more limited vocabularies than older children and have a more limited **knowledge base** about specific events so they may fail to make connections between things in the way that older children do (Brainerd, Kingma and Howe, 1986). So if an adult is given a list of items from a shopping list to remember, he or she would probably sort them into categories such as fruit and vegetables, meat and fish, dairy products, and so on. However, if a 6-year-old is given a similar task he or she would probably not do this and would be unable to recall as many items. Even though 6-year-olds might be able to classify carrots as vegetables, they do not seem to make connections that identify carrots, potatoes, onions as the vegetables in the list.

Metamemory

Metamemory, or the ability to reflect upon the workings of one's own memory, increases with age. This involves knowing what you do know (such as your own phone number), what you might know (your previous phone number) and what you definitely do not know (the Prime Minister's telephone number).

This boy is learning to remember how letters are formed

Applying information processing principles in learning environments

Some theorists such as Robbie Case (1985) suggest that cognitive development is related to increases in the working memory, or STM, capacity. Case is often described as a neo-Piagetian because he combines aspects of Piaget's theory with information processing concepts. For example, he believes that children become quicker and more efficient at processing information and this allows them to progress to the next stage of development.

Siegler's (1996) model of strategy choice adds an evolutionary perspective to children's cognition, arguing that when faced with a problem, children try a variety of strategies to solve it. They will select these gradually on the basis of speed and accuracy. Which strategies are available at any one point will depend upon the age of the child and the strategies will develop from the simpler ones used by young children to the more sophisticated and complex ones used by older children. This suggests that all children will think differently even when dealing with the same task.

Examples of the means by which practitioners can support young children in learning environments are shown in Figure 6.14.

Applying information processing principles in learning environments	
Gain the learner's attention	This is important. You can do this by perhaps using cues to signal that you are ready to start. While engaged with the learner, keep his or her attention by perhaps moving around the room and varying pitch and speed of voice.
	Do not attempt to maintain children's attention for long periods, as their attention span is not extensive. Although there seem to be no definitive studies measuring attention span in children, it seems that 3 to 4 minutes per year of age is a rough guide. So, a 3-year-old might be expected to concentrate for about 9 minutes and a 5-year-old for about 15 minutes at a time. Obviously, this can vary, not only from child to child but also from activity to activity. Some children who are assumed to be suffering from Attention Deficit Hyperactivity Disorder (ADHD) are still able to pay attention for an extended period of time if the subject is interesting enough, for example their favourite television programme or video game. Similarly, toddlers may pay attention for longer periods when there are no distractions and the topic is interesting.
	A child's attention span develops in three stages.
	1 Young infants often stare at their mobiles for long periods of time and seem able to ignore other stimuli.
	2 At around 2 years of age toddlers' attention span changes rapidly and spontaneously from one object to another and they rarely play with one toy for an extended period of time.
	3 The school-aged child is able to concentrate for longer periods on a particular task and yet is able to shift this focus when necessary. This is known as selective attention and is required for the child to progress appropriately within educational establishments.

Relate back to things already known	In order to provide something to build upon, you might perhaps talk about the previous lesson on a topic or invite children to recall it as a group.
Pick out important points	By writing important points on the board or on handouts/transparencies, you are encouraging children to attend to these aspects. (This helps to overcome the limitations of sensory memory.)
Organise material	Ensure that material has a logical sequence and progresses from the easiest through to the most difficult.
Encourage categorisation (chunking) of material	Present information in categories. For example, you could present seven groups of seven, rather than 49 separate items. (This helps to overcome the limitations of short-term memory and the fact that only a limited number of chunks of information can be processed at any one time.)
Provide opportunities for both verbal and visual encoding	Although evidence is not conclusive that they are two different systems, it does seem that imaging can help memory.
Include opportunities for children to elaborate upon new information	Connect new information with something already known. This might include a discussion of similarities and differences.
Introduce children to the idea of using encoding when remembering things by devising mnemonics	For material that it is essential to memorise, have fun devising mnemonics with the class in order to encourage deep learning by meaningful association. For example, you could help to support the learning of difficult multiplication tables by associating 7 x 8 = 56 with the head teacher's age, or invite the children to find a personal connection such as father's age.
Include repetition	Include repetition within the teaching and learning situation in order to encourage transfer to LTM. Outline, perhaps, the contents of the session beforehand, then engage with children during the session and review at the end. By doing so, there is more chance that the learning will be processed. From time to time it would be useful to review previous learning.
Allow overlearning	This can be achieved through daily repetitions of important numerical facts, for example, or of games and quizzes involving knowledge of basic facts and information.
Arrange for a variety of practice opportunities	This helps the learner to generalise the information so that it can be used outside of the original context within which it was taught.
Help learners become autonomous	Assist children in choosing appropriate learning strategies such as making summaries or asking questions.

Figure 6.14 Supporting young children in learning environments

Case Study 8

Short-term and long-term memory

Irena is struggling to remember the points of the compass and is about to have a test at school. Her half-sister, who looks after Irena, finds her near to tears at breakfast and suggests that they can work out a way for Irena to remember this. With a flash of inspiration she jokes to her half-sister, 'Now cheer up because if you cry it will get into your breakfast and you should Never Eat Soggy Weetabix!' Irena is not impressed as she thinks her half-sister is not taking her problem seriously until it is pointed out to her that 'Never Eat Soggy Weetabix' has the same first letters as North, South, East and West, the points of the compass she cannot remember. Irena's half-sister suggests that if she thinks about her soggy Weetabix conversation she will be able to remember the compass points. It worked.

Irena's half-sister has used 'Never Eat Soggy Weetabix' as a mnemonic to help Irena remember the compass points. By connecting the information she needed to learn with something which was meaningful to her it meant that NESW was encoded in a way which was within her experience and accessible to her. This made it more likely for the information to be processed and transferred from her STM (short-term memory) to her LTM (long-term memory). The fact that the occasion was associated with emotion (Irena almost in tears followed by her half-sister's joke) and events in her own life also makes it more likely to be stored in her episodic memory (the part of LTM which stores personal events).

An evaluation of information processing approaches is given in Figure 6.15.

Evaluation of information processing approaches	
Major strength	A major strength is the way information processing approaches break cognition into separate elements so that each can be thoroughly examined. This can be very useful with conditions such as dyslexia because tests are used to establish the precise problem the child has with reading and then exercises and/or alternative strategies may be suggested to compensate for the deficit. It is also helpful for children and their families to understand precisely where the problem lies and therefore see it as a processing problem rather than a personal failing.
Criticisms	Information processing approaches are often criticised for their biased view of humans in that they take little account of their physical, social and emotional experiences. These are clearly integrated with their mental processes in the real world where, for example, a child's attention may be impossible to gain because he or she is frightened, hungry or angry.
Research findings	As yet, information processing lacks a cohesive theory which links the various approaches together; therefore the research findings lack a cohesive framework.

Figure 6.15 Evaluation of information processing approaches

For comments on this activity see page 159.

Conclusion

Piaget saw cognitive development as stemming mainly from the child. He stressed the 'readiness' idea, suggesting that a child cannot attain certain abilities until ready to do so. This depends upon the stage of development.

Vygotsky saw interactions between the child and adults/culture as the driving force of cognitive development, so adults need to provide explanations, examples, questions, clues, corrections, and so on, to scaffold/assist this development. Potential must be assessed

as well as actual abilities and therefore instructional materials and methods need to be challenging but within reach of the child.

Both Piaget and Vygotsky take a constructivist approach, viewing learning as an active process on the part of the learner.

Information processing approaches use the model of a computer to provide understanding of the way cognition works. Therefore, they stress the importance of processing and storing information.

Discussion point 1

Mikey

Mikey is a 7-year- old boy who has made little progress with reading since entering a mixed primary school at 4 years old. He also tends to be 'left out' in the playground and does not seem to have made friends.

1 If we took a Piagetian approach to understanding this boy's cognitive development, how would this help us to provide a suitable learning environment for him?

2 How would Vygotsky's ideas relate to Mikey? Outline ways in which his learning might be supported from this perspective.

3 Information processing approaches might provide other insights. Suggest ways in which they would explain Mikey's problems and how they might be applied in the learning situation.

For comments on this discussion point see page 159.

Comments on activities and discussion points

Activity 1 (page 136): Schema for using the telephone

1 It might be that to use your own telephone at home you pick up the receiver, wait for the dialling tone and then dial the number you require but when you do this at work this produces the unavailable tone.

2 This unsettles you, as you know this is the right number and you urgently need to contact this person (you are in a state of disequilibrium).

3 Perhaps you then try again (assimilation) even though it did not work the first time, to see what happens.

4 However, if this does not work, you may try pressing some of the other buttons to try to get a dialling tone.

5 Eventually, you discover that pressing the zero button on its own produces a dialling tone and you are then able to dial the number you wanted (accommodation).

6 Your schema for using a telephone now includes more information that may be used in future and you return to a more balanced state (equilibrium).

Activity 2 (page 142): Adapting tasks

1 Perhaps two new tubs of play dough could be used here as children are aware that these are equal and will not need to be asked. You might ask the children to take the play dough out and ask one child to roll theirs into a sausage shape and the other to make it into a ball. Ask the children whether they now both have the same amount of play dough.

2 The important thing here is that the children should not be asked twice whether the amounts are equal and that the problem is related to a meaningful situation – one that can be related to the real world which they are part of.

Activity 3 (page 145): Using the concepts of scaffolding

1 First the child must be interested in (attending to) the building blocks, perhaps spontaneously, or the practitioner may have drawn his or her attention to them. Alone, the child may be unable to work out how to make the blocks look like a house, so needs assistance.

2 The carer may suggest that the child makes a square/rectangular shape on the floor with the blocks and shows the child how to do this by starting off the rectangle (perhaps two adjoining sides) and encouraging the child to finish this off.

3 Next, the carer may carefully place a block on top of this bottom layer of blocks, perhaps exaggerating the care to be taken and talking through what he/she is doing before encouraging the child to join in.

4 The child may then choose some blocks and try to line them up on the bottom layer. The carer advises and encourages until the child succeeds.

5 The carer praises the child and gives encouragement to put some more in place.

6 The child does so, but knocks the blocks over in her/his haste and becomes frustrated.

7 The carer is cheerful but sympathetic, suggesting that they still have the bottom layer of blocks so could easily build again – perhaps a different coloured house or row this time. The child responds and works with the carer to rebuild. This time the second row is successfully placed and the

child is pleased, smiles and continues to add blocks.

8 The carer continues to give words of encouragement and is ready to help if the child gets stuck, but he or she is beginning to understand how this works and needs less assistance progressively until he or she is actually working alone.

Activity 4 (page 147): Using scaffolding at different levels

1 The teacher or facilitator will not need to provide much support or guidance to children who are already able to remember number combinations and perform mental arithmetic competently, as they will be able to add the numbers together and move the counter the correct number of places.

2 Children who are unable to do this could be prompted to count the numbers on the dice using simple addition techniques (such as counting all the spots individually and holding up their fingers to show how many spots there are). Modelling might be used to show the children how to do this slowly and methodically.

3 This support would be needed less as the children become more competent and take over the counting themselves. The facilitator has worked within the zone of proximal development to teach them something outside of it.

Activity 6 (page 151): Awareness

The important thing here is that you become aware that there is far more **sensory information** available than you are aware of at any one moment. What you are aware of depends upon what you are focusing upon or attending to at that moment. Without this, there will be no sensory memory or possibility of storage. Obviously it would be impossible to process all of the incoming information, so the brain attends to that which seems the most significant.

Activity 7 (page 153): Personal strategies that aid memory

You may have identified some very personal ways in which you use these strategies (or mnemonics) such as remembering your pin number in terms of someone's age or date of birth.

Activity 8 (page 157): Using principles of information processing

1 The attention of the class can be gained by the practitioner clapping, speaking more loudly or standing up, for example.

2 The teacher might then start by talking about where the children live and where the school is in relation to this. He or she might then move on to when their homes were built or who lived in them previously. The aim is to jog the children's memory about things they already know in order to build new information onto it.

3 Important facts could be written on the board or displayed on an OHT, perhaps including pictures, maps or diagrams as well as text. Children could be encouraged to discuss aspects of these facts, such as when their house was built and how this compares with the rest of the class.

4 Basic facts and information should be logically organised and 'chunked' where possible, for example types of houses, types of building materials, and local facilities, rather than just a flow of information. These facts could be repeated and the children encouraged to learn them, and a quiz held at the end of the topic.

5 Children could be helped to design a simple questionnaire for their parents, about their experiences of the area they live in.

Discussion Point 1 (page 157): Mikey

1 Piaget's approach would suggest that Mikey may still be in the pre-operational stage of

development and, therefore, has not yet learned to de-centre. This might account for his difficulties:

➤ with language (where the word might begin with the same letter/s but be different in other respects)

➤ and with other children (still egocentric).

The fact that most of his peers are already more competent might also suggest that Mikey's basic schemas for carrying out this operation (reading) are not yet adequate for dealing with this problems. So his understanding needs to be built up so that he is able to do this. Then assimilation and accommodation will allow him to expand his schemas. Perhaps he is currently dealing with his sense of disequilibrium by ignoring the problem because he does not have enough knowledge to build upon.

Providing situations in which Mikey encounters demonstrations of conservation would help him to acquire this ability, but they should be 'hands on' demonstrations and anchored in a topic that has real-world relevance.

2 Vygotsky's theory suggests that Mikey should be included in group work so that interaction between himself and other learners is encouraged (peer collaboration and scaffolding). Incidentally, although Vygotsky focused on cognitive development, becoming part of a group in the classroom would probably also help with Mikey's social interactions and this might encourage greater integration outside as well. Play might be used to allow him to safely rehearse his developing abilities, and sensitive scaffolding by teachers and other adults should be used to help him perform the tasks he is not currently able to.

Perhaps the teaching is not within Mikey's ZPD so he is not able to grasp it at present. Therefore, it is necessary to find out what he can do and what he might be capable of doing with support.

3 Information processing approaches would address Mikey's problem in a systematic way by assessing each of the areas, such as whether he is paying attention in the first place, and how well he is encoding the information. The National Literacy Strategy (introduced in 1998) encourages the use of 'phonics' which breaks down words into individual sounds (or phonemes) which is helpful for children who have difficulties with language (Parliamentary Office of Science and Technology, 2004). Perhaps it would also be useful to present pictorial and visual material alongside verbal information to allow for more opportunities for processing it in STM and transferring it to LTM. Mikey would be encouraged to connect the new information with what he already knows and to repeat the important points regularly. He would also be presented with well-organised teaching materials and allowed plenty of opportunities for practising new knowledge in different contexts. For example, if he learned to read new words these could be practised (rehearsed) in class activities such as post-office games. It is also likely that Mikey would be entered into a small group for teaching at a slower pace with more individual attention. If he still did not catch up then the SENCo (Special Educational Needs Coordinator) would probably be involved to design a suitable intervention. Mikey might also be recommended for assessment by an Educational Psychologist to test for possible dyslexia.

How to move on in your research

Bjorklund, J. (2005) (4th edition), *Children's Thinking: Cognitive Development and Individual Differences*. Belmont: Thomson/Wadsworth

A useful text which provides theoretical depth and relevant examples from a wide range of relevant research findings.

Cowan, N. (ed.) (1997), *The Development of Memory in Childhood*. Hove: Psychology Press

This book provides a comprehensive and readable account of all aspects of children's memory development.

Cunningham, P. (2006), 'Early Years teachers and the influence of Piaget: Evidence from oral history'. *Early Years: Journal of International Research and Develop*ment, 26, 1, pp5–16.

This research article explores ways that current Early Years teachers view the influence of Piaget.

References

Atkinson, R. and Shiffrin, R. (1968), 'Human memory: A proposed system and its control processes', in **Spence, K. and Spence, J. (eds)**, *The Psychology of Learning and Motivation: Advances in Research and Theory (Vol. 2)*. New York: Academic Press

Azmitia, M. and Hesser, J. (1993), 'Why siblings are important agents of cognitive development: A comparison of siblings and peers'. *Child Development*, 63(2), pp430–44

Baillargeon, R. (1987), 'Object permanence in very young infants'. *Developmental Psychology*, 23, pp655–64

Bandura, A. and Walters, R. (1963), *Social Learning and Personality Development*. New York: Holt, Rinehart and Winston

Bjorklund, D. (2000), *Children's Thinking: Developmental Function and Individual Differences*. Belmont: Wadsworth

Brainerd, C., Kingma, J. and Howe, M. (1986), 'Spread of encoding and the development of organisation in memory'. *Canadian Journal of Psychology*, 40, pp203–23

Case, R. (1985), *Intellectual Development: Birth to Adulthood*. New York: Academic Press

Donaldson, M. (1978), *Children's Minds*. London: Fontana

Fuson, K.C., Zecker, L.B., LoCicero, A.M. and Ron, P. (1995), 'El mercado in Latino primary classrooms: A fruitful narrative theme for the development of children's conceptual mathematics'. Paper presented at the annual meeting of American Educational Research Association, San Francisco.

Girolametto, S., Bonifacio, C., Visini, E., Weitzman, E., Zocconi, E. and Pearce, S. (2003), 'Mother-child interactions in Canada and Italy: Linguistic responsiveness to late-talking toddlers'. *International Journal of Early Years Education*, 11 (3), pp255–260.

Guberman, S.R. (1994), 'Mathematical activities of Latino and Korean American children outside school'. Paper presented at American Educational Research Association annual meeting, New Orleans, L.A.

Guberman, S. R. (1999), 'Cultural aspects of young children's mathematics knowledge'. in **Copley, J. V. (ed.)**, *Mathematics in the Early Years* (pp. 30–36). Reston, VA: National Council of Teachers of Mathematics. Available at http://spot.colorado.edu/~gubermas/NCTM_pap.htm (Viewed 15/04/07)

Ho, C.S-H and Fuson, K.C. (1998), 'Children's knowledge of teen quantities as tens and ones: Comparisons of Chinese, British and American kindergarteners'. *Journal of Educational Psychology*, 90 (3), pp536–44.

Hughes, M. (1975), 'Hiding from the policeman', in Donaldson, M. (1978), *Children's Minds*. London: Fontana

Irwin, M. and McLaughlin, K. (1970), 'Ability and preference in category sorting by mano schoolchildren and adults'. *Journal of Social Psychology*, 82, pp15–24

Kail, R. and Park, Y. (1994), 'Processing time, articulation time, and memory span'. *Journal of Experimental Child Psychology*, 57, pp281–91

Kelly, M.K. et al (1999), 'When days are numbered: Calendar structure and the development of calendar processing in English and Chinese'. *Journal of Experimental Child Psychology*, 73 (4), pp289–314.

Klein, A. and Starkey, P. (1988), 'Universals in the development of early arithmetic cognition'. *New Directions for Child Development*, 41, pp5–26.

Lefevre, J-A, Clarke, T. and Stringer, A.P. (2002), 'Influences of language and parental involvement on the development of counting skills: Comparisons of French and English speaking Canadian children'. *Early Child Development and Care*, 172 (3), pp283–300

McGarrigle, J. and Donaldson, M. (1974), 'Conservation accidents', *Cognition*, 3, pp341–50

Miller, G. (1956), 'The Magical Number Seven, plus or minus two: Some limits on our capacity for processing information'. *Psychological Review*, 63, pp81–97 [available online from Classics in the History of Psychology]

Miura, I.T., Okamoto, Y., Kim, C.C., Chang, C-M, Steere, M. and Fayol, M. (1994), 'Comparisons of children's cognitive representation of number : China, France, Japan, Korea, Sweden and the United States'. *International Journal of Behavioral Development*, 17, pp401–11.

Moore, C.C., Romney, A.K., and Hsia, T-L (2002), 'Cultural, gender and individual differences in perceptual and semantic structures of basic colors in Chinese and English'. *Journal of Cognition and Culture*, 2 (1), pp1–28.

Nunes, T. (1995), 'Cultural practices and the conceptions of individual differences: Theoretical and empirical considerations.' *New Directions in Child Development*, 67, pp91–103.

Nunes, T., Schliemann, A.D., and Carraher, D.W. (1993), *Street Mathematics and School Mathematics*. New York: Cambridge University Press.

Oloko, B.A. (1994), 'Children's street work in urban Nigeria: Dilemma of modernizing tradition,' in Greenfield, P.M. and Cocking, R.R. (eds), *Cross-cultural Roots of Minority Child Development* (pp197–224). Hillsdale, NJ: Erlbaum

Orlando L. and Machado, A. (1996), 'In defense of Piaget's theory: A reply to 10 common criticisms'. *Psychological Review*, 103, pp143–64.

Parliamentary Office of Science and Technology (POST) (2004), *Dyslexia and Dyscalculia*. July, 2004, Number 226, London: POST

Pratt, M., Kerig, P., Cowan, P. and Cowan, C. (1988), 'Mothers and fathers teaching 3-year-olds: Authoritative parenting and adult scaffolding of young children's learning.' *Developmental Psychology*, 24, 6, pp832–9

Saxe, G.B. (1981), 'Body parts as numerals: A developmental analysis of numeration among the Oksapin in Papua New Guinea'. *Journal of Educational Psychology*, 77, pp503–13.

Saxe, G.B. (1991), *Culture and Cognitive Development: Studies in Mathematical Understanding*. Hillsdale, NJ: Erlbaum

Siegler, R. (1996), *Emerging Minds: The Process of Children's Thinking*. New York: Oxford University Press

Song, M-J. and Ginsburg, H.P. (1987), 'The development of informal and formal mathematical thinking in Korean and US children'. *Child Development*, 58, pp1286–96

Spence, K. and Spence, J. (eds) (1968), *The Psychology of Learning and Motivation: Advances in Research and Theory (Vol. 2)*. New York: Academic Press

Vigil, D. (2002), 'Cultural variations in attention regulation: A comparative analysis of British and Chinese immigrant populations'. *International Journal of Language and Communication Disorders*, 37 (4) pp433–58.

Vygotsky, L. (1978), *Mind in Society*. Cambridge, MA: Harvard University Press

Vygotsky, L. (1986; original work published 1934), *Thought and Language* (A. Kozulin, trans.). Cambridge, MA: MIT Press

Useful websites

http://www.piaget.org
Visit the Jean Piaget Society website for a range of resources relevant to Piaget, Vygotsky and constructivism. Click on 'Web Links' and select from a list of topical pages.

http://chiron.valdosta.edu/whuitt/index.html
The Educational Psychology Interactive website provides useful resources and links including useful suggestions here about ways in which Piaget's ideas may be applied in the learning situation.

7 Communication and language development

Iain MacLeod-Brudenell

This chapter is designed to help you to consider a range of issues which affect children's development in communication. These include verbal and non-verbal communication and the use of language. It also encourages you to develop an understanding that verbal communication is only one of a range of means by which children communicate.

This chapter addresses the following areas:

➤ Introduction to the theory of language

➤ Language and communication

➤ Babies and language

➤ Development in language: the Early Years

➤ The role of parents

➤ Accent, dialect and grammar

➤ Bilingualism

By undertaking the suggested study within this chapter it is hoped that you will be able to:

1 question and reflect upon the development of children's language and communication skills

2 recognise the importance of observation in planning support for children's individual language and communication needs

3 reflect upon current methods and modify practice in the light of your new learning

4 make informed reflections upon recent issues in language and communication within your selected area of education and care provision.

The list of issues addressed is by no means exhaustive and provides starting points for reflection on theory and practice rather than detailed specific information, which may be readily accessed elsewhere.

Introduction to the theory of language

Most children use speech to:

➤ express ideas

➤ communicate needs

➤ convey desires

➤ give instructions.

Language is often regarded as being synonymous with the spoken word; but this is to deny the use of more visual forms of language such as signing.

How do children learn language?

We do not know exactly how children learn language. The development of language, how it is acquired, how it is used and how children learn language continues to be the focus of much research. Early attempts to explain children's acquisition of speech and of language focused largely on the role of imitation. It has been argued that this is the most natural way to view language development, as babies appear to have an innate ability to imitate sounds. The development from sounds and sound sequences towards language can be seen to be a logical progression as children experience wider opportunities to use language. Reward for correct imitation has figured prominently in the behaviourist approach (Pavlov and Skinner). The behaviourist approach in its most rigorous interpretation held the view that babies are equipped with biological reflexes and all that follows is learned. This extreme approach is now given little credibility but does form a basis for discussion.

In your previous study you will have had opportunities to consider the range of factors that influence children's development and you may be familiar with what is often called the 'nurture-nature debate'. This term is used to indicate two very different perspectives within the study of child development. Theories propose views regarding the effects of genetic inheritance (nature) or contextual factors (nurture) on various aspects of child development. Language development is no exception in this search for answers. You may find that your approach lies between the two views.

Biological, or innate, theory: Chomsky and Slobin

An interesting starting point for reflection would be to consider the biological, or innate, theory, initially proposed by Chomsky (1957) and to relate this to your own experience with children. This theory is based on the principle that the brain has an inbuilt facility for language and that human beings are genetically programmed to develop language. The theory sought to provide an explanation for the means by which a baby develops language skills. Chomsky's theory thus links language skills to the process of maturation. It emphasises the biological control of language development and dismisses contextual factors. However, Chomsky does indicate that in order to trigger this innate capacity for language, children need to hear language spoken. The importance of language as an activity is stressed, rather than the specific language spoken by those in contact with the child. Slobin, who extended Chomsky's approach, noted that babies and very young children respond to language sounds and sound sequences, which he termed operating principles. Research appears to go some way to support this view. Babies do initially respond to sound, tone, intonation and rhythm regardless of the language spoken. This would appear to be a logical answer to the question of how language develops; however, if we were pre-programmed to learn language then all children would learn language in the same way, regardless of the culture in which they were born. It appears that this is not the case.

Cognitive models: Vygotsky and Piaget

Biological models of language development stress the innate ability of children to acquire language; cognitive models focus more on the relationship between the development of children's thinking skills and language development. In Chapter 6, the thoughts of Vygotsky and Piaget on cognitive development are explained. Their cognitive-related models viewed the acquisition of language in the same way as the acquisition of other areas of knowledge. In terms of language, the approach taken by Piaget differs from Vygotsky in one essential aspect. Piaget considered language development to be primarily an egocentric activity and that the role of the adult was primarily to provide a challenging environment which would stimulate learning.

Heuristic play

There has been a resurgence of interest in Piaget's approach to the role of the adult in early language development, particularly in what has become popularly known as heuristic play.

Heuristic play involves babies and young children exploring a range of objects that will stimulate physical and cognitive development without adult intervention. Goldschmied and Jackson (1994:89) provided babies and children under the age of two with a range of everyday objects to explore, termed a 'treasure basket'. Observers noted that the language that emerged in these contexts was secondary and incidental to the activity; this supports Piaget's approach to language as being a means of children 'thinking out loud', rather than of communicating with others. Heuristic play does appear to encourage egocentric rather than social behaviour, although this does depend upon the context, the other experiences of the children and the nature of the objects that are presented for their exploration. In many ways, heuristic play presents Piaget's principles quite neatly. The emphasis in heuristic play is upon exploration. In heuristic play, by removing adult influence and interference from an activity, the child is provided with opportunities to become deeply immersed in an activity outside of a social framework. That is not to say that this form of play is not valuable. It most certainly is. Children who are offered this opportunity demonstrate deep and long periods of concentration, and are adept at making choices and decisions.

To Piaget, language was quite separate from actions that led to reasoning. Language is viewed as a system of symbols for representing the world. Piaget's approach would view talking to children in order to explain things before they were at an appropriate stage of understanding as futile. Critics of this approach consider that children's eagerness to communicate is given insufficient acknowledgement and that gauging the precise readiness of children to learn particular skills is beset with difficulty.

Language takes place within a social framework

Vygotsky's approach takes note of some of the issues raised by Piaget's concentration on the child as a lone individual learner. Vygotsky viewed language as taking place within a social framework and considered that the role of the adult was to actively stimulate in order to support and extend children's learning. Some of the observations made by Vygotsky can be viewed as common sense approaches, which are verified by any practitioner working with young children. To emphasise the part played by the social context of learning language, Vygotsky notes the part played by other and older children in modelling language in a child's development of language and communication skills.

Unlike Piaget, who separates the processes of speech and thought, Vygotsky sees them as being inextricably linked.

For young children, speech is used at first

to communicate, to make and share meanings. Later it becomes a tool of thought. By this, he meant that language itself could change the way in which children think and learn. A starting point for reflection on this key issue would be to consider your own view of the relationship between thought and language. Is it possible for young children to talk without thinking? Is it possible for them to think without talking? At first sight, this may appear easily answered, but if one considers children who cannot verbalise or make verbal communication the issue appears more clouded. Does speech have to be audible; can ideas and thoughts be spoken internally?

Inner speech is an essential link between language and thought

Vygotsky believed that in the earliest stages of speech, children talk aloud to themselves and practitioners who work with very young children will verify that this is often the case. Often this talk will involve descriptions of what they are doing. Vygotsky sees this inner speech as an essential link between language and thought in the young child. Inner speech becomes internalised as children become more aware of what they are thinking.

That both of these approaches to learning language are essential in the development of speech is not disputed; it is the degree to which context influences cognition that appears to be the primary focus of debate. It may be argued that heuristic play, 'inner speech' and social aspects of speech provide the basis for language development.

Adult scaffolding, learning and children's language: Bruner

One of the most influential theorists in the area of language development, Bruner focused his early research on the relationship between adult scaffolding, learning and children's language. You will recognise the influence of Bruner in much of the content of this chapter. Key aspects of Bruner's approach are located in the linkage between language and communication and the encouragement of children's understanding of how language works. The holistic approach to language includes visual cues, gestures and body language, turn-taking and the conventions of social use of language.

Activity 1

Language theory

1 Which aspects of this brief discussion of language theory do you find reflect your current perceptions of language development?

2 Which aspects reflect your experience with children?

3 Make notes of your thoughts and revisit these after reading the rest of the chapter to see if there has been any change in your understanding.

Playing with words

Bruner talks about children 'playing with words'. Between 2 and 3 years of age children may use the sound and the meaning of words in a playful way. They may take a familiar rhyme and extend the context of the rhyme whilst using the same format and the same metre.

Another example of playing with words will be familiar to those working with young children in nursery and school: children's jokes. Play with words can extend to early experiments with jokes even with children as young as 2 years of age.

Case Study 1

Children using the sound and meaning of words in a playful way

Henry (aged 2 years) took the following rhyme, which was taught to him by his grandfather, and changed the words to fit a wide range of situations:

'Sausage in the pan, sausage in the pan, sizzle, sizzle, sizzle, sizzle, sausage in the pan.'

When extended to bath time, this became:

'Henry in the bath, splishy splashy …'

And to his baby sister's sleeping time:

'Poppy in the bed …'

Following his experiments with changing words to make new rhymes, Henry began to use words with a similar sound but with a different meaning in a humorous way. For example, when Henry's grandmother dropped the gravy powder, she said, 'Oh no, granny dropped the gravy!' Henry responded with 'granny dropped the baby!' This became a joke between them that lasted for several weeks.

1 What does this form of playing with words demonstrate?

2 Note any similar examples of children playing with words – at any age. What conditions support this use of language?

Language and communication

Practitioners in early care and education settings know from their practice that there are increasing numbers of young children who do not have confidence in using language and have delayed development in language skills.

Delayed development in language skills

These children often display difficulty in communicating through language as they do not fully experience the sounds of spoken language. Conditions such as 'glue ear' or other illnesses that affect hearing, an absence of auditory response, are common in young children and this may impact on a child's confidence in speaking. Other physical factors may also impinge on confidence in speaking. There may be links between premature birth and a physical difference that causes delay in maturation and difficulty in communicating through speech. In some cases, young children may have temporary hearing loss. The stage of language development when this temporary setback occurs is crucial and the ability to communicate effectively in language may be hindered.

Communication at these points may rely more heavily on gesture to emphasise meaning. Crucially, the ability to communicate through gesture may also be insufficiently developed to compensate for oral language when temporary hearing loss occurs. Those children who have a longer term or a permanent hearing loss may find that spoken forms of language may prove to be a more difficult form of communication. However, when hearing impairment is diagnosed at an early stage and children are encouraged to use signing alongside speech, communication skills are allowed to develop more rapidly. The long-term effect of this is that these children have fewer problems in communication as they progress through school.

Non-verbal indicators of confidence

Young children whose speech is difficult to understand may have few problems at home where adult family members and other children are able to 'translate' their words. Problems arise when such children move to out-of-home settings, particularly where there is no support from speech therapists. After initial frustration at not being understood when speaking, children may rely more on gesture when trying to communicate. It is interesting to note that theories of language acquisition tend to focus on spoken language and largely ignore the part played within language development of the role of non-verbal indicators of confidence and, indeed, of body language and gesture. Children communicate their earliest needs through gesture, inflection and emphasis of sounds. As they become more skilled in articulating sounds and using words, gesture may be used less frequently. There appears to be a strong link between the modelling provided by adults and the use of gesture to accompany speech. Tone, volume and emphasis in speech patterns also appear to be acquired in children at an early age. Toddlers will often use the same intonations and phrases that have been modelled by an adult. Children born with a visual impairment will rely on auditory cues, intonation, and the stress placed on words.

Awareness of children's understanding

Children's readiness to speak may be indicated by a response to a thought expressed aloud by the adult.

Case Study 3

A child demonstrates understanding ahead of her speech

After a shopping trip, Courtney (13 months) was lifted from her pushchair and went into the kitchen.

'Oh dear, I've left the door open,' said her mother.

Courtney turned around, went back down the corridor and closed the door. This was the first time that her mother recognised that Courtney's understanding was far ahead of her speech.

Case Study 2

Responding to non-verbal indicators

For many years, a practitioner worked with children who were learning English as an additional language. During that time, he began to notice that there were non-verbal indicators of confidence that would help him to judge a child's readiness to speak on a one-to-one basis or in a small group activity. Children would demonstrate a readiness to use language before attempts were made to communicate verbally. This could be seen through their body language and the eye contact that was made during the often one-way conversations. The practitioner was able to respond to these triggers in order to encourage children to try out using words.

This knowledge helped him to plan activities that were most likely to make children feel comfortable enough to talk.

1 Note the ways in which a child demonstrates confidence through body language; for example through eye contact and the way in which the body is positioned in relation to you when the child responds to questions. Do you recognise any difference in the way the child responds when he or she knows the answer?

2 If you work with children with differing needs in their ability to communicate, note how they reveal confidence.

It has been shown that context is crucial in helping children to understand meaning. Very young children only need to recognise one or two words in context and they can grasp meaning.

Case Study 4

Joining in a conversation without using words

Flora (17 months) screamed when startled by a squirrel dashing past the window. For the rest of the morning, whenever she saw squirrels through the window she screamed and clung to her grandmother. When Flora's aunt came home, the grandmother began to recount what had happened; Flora pointed to the window and shrieked. They were in no doubt that Flora was joining in the conversation.

Adults go through similar stages of language acquisition when on holiday abroad. They will begin by picking out commonly used words in familiar contexts – the bar or restaurant – progressing to experimenting with one or two words and then, depending upon whether the response is positive or negative, attempt more complex sentences in a wider range of situations. Gesture may initially replace and later accompany such requests.

Case Study 5

Recognising different pronunciation

When George was 23 months old, he was able to discriminate between accents. His mother and grandmother both used a 'flat' 'a' in words such as 'bath' and 'grass'. George's father and grandfather both used a 'long' 'a'. Initially, George used a 'flat' 'a' when saying these words. He then switched to a 'long' 'a', as he began to be aware of his gender. He appeared to be using language to identify with males in the family. This continued for some weeks. He then used both forms of pronunciation and has finally settled with a 'flat' 'a'.

The recognition of different ways of saying words is not uncommon. Many children in this country learn more than one language. Some do so from birth, living in homes where more than one language is spoken.

In Case Study 5, George demonstrates another facet of learning a language: the role of gender in the ways in which words are pronounced. There may also be influences on children's attitudes to the use of language that are related to gender.

The ways we use words

We learn words and how to use them at the same time. Children not only learn a word but also any emphasis that may accompany the use of that word to convey subtle differences in meaning. The degree of urgency may be expressed through volume or tone; questioning may be indicated by intonation. Contextual factors are very important in this respect.

Family and cultural patterns of language are naturally acquired at the earliest stages of childhood. Familiarity with out-of-home experiences through contact with other children will not only extend the range of language, but also the use of gestures for communication. The expectations of adults in out-of-home settings for children to conform or adapt to speech conventions will also extend the range of language and communication skills. As adults, we adapt our style and forms of speech (we change the **register**) to match the context in which we use talk. The speech register used in a courtroom will be quite different to that in the pub. The use of register may be further illustrated by comparing the forms of language used during a wedding, where the formal legal or religious language will differ markedly from the family chatter at the end of the ceremony. Children will begin to recognise the changes in register adopted by adults in different settings if they are exposed to a variety of contexts in which they are used – and if adults are skilled in using them. It is not uncommon for children as young as 2 years of age to be able to recognise that adults switch registers in different settings. This may become increasingly obvious in their role play.

Case Study 6

Children match adults in body language, tone and intonation

Practitioners in a nursery were using face painting in a session designed to raise children's self-awareness. Children were asked to paint each other's faces and their language behaviour closely followed that used by staff when applying face paint to the children, including the use of body language, tone and intonation.

1 Have you noticed any similar instances of children copying adult language behaviour in your workplace setting?

2 Write your own account and make an analysis of the things that children are copying.

Body language

It will be seen from this discussion that communication is far wider in scope than spoken language, not just for children with physical differences that prevent spoken language, or conditions that may impede it, such as hearing impairment. Body language to emphasise communication may be formalised as signing, but it is more commonly used in our everyday efforts to communicate meaning to children as well as adults. The importance of body language in everyday communication is often not fully realised. Children are very aware of body language and often use it as a non-verbal cue for action or response. Confusion arises when the spoken language and the body language appear to give conflicting messages. As adults we can recognise this in some of our professional interactions with other adults. The experience may begin in early childhood, for example when an adult appears through their spoken language to be interested, while their body language gives the opposite impression.

Children appear to give messages conveyed by body language precedence over spoken language.

Use of gestures and cues

Language skills and communication skills are interdependent and not mutually exclusive. Sometimes gestures replace rather than emphasise the spoken word.

In their research on language use by toddlers, Acredolo and Goodwyn (1997) noted that gestures were used to replace words even where there was no direct association. Acredolo noted her daughter's use of blowing to represent fish. This gesture was based on Acredolo blowing her daughter's fish mobile (and was in contrast to the use by many toddlers of a popping, blowing bubbles movement of the mouth to represent fish). Gestures relate to experience and contexts and many different signs were uncovered in this research. A key aspect of the use of gestures is that adults recognise and respond to them. Without such recognition, the use of gesture would be abandoned. The use of gesture to replace words diminishes as toddlers become more confident in their use of speech.

Adults usually recognise cues from their children. This appears to help a toddler's language development, particularly when response to gesture is coupled with spoken language.

Signing

There is a current interest in the use of signing with babies to encourage communication and language as a search on internet sites will demonstrate. Some have been developed by enthusiasts (www.signingbabies.co.uk), others are based on research and tried methodology such as those of Joseph Gorman, for www.babysigners.co.uk, which is particularly well presented and has an extensive, if dated, bibliography. The Literary Trust (www.literarytrust.org.uk/talktoyourbaby/signing.html) provides a very thorough discussion of the issue and an extensive range of resources.

Signing is used extensively to support children with communication and language difficulties. The main signing systems follow the word order of spoken English and combine sign with the spoken word. These are:

➤ British Sign Language (BSL)

➤ Makaton

➤ Signalong

➤ Paget Gorman.

British Sign Language (BSL) is the language most commonly used by deaf people in Britain and Ireland (www.britishsignlanguage.com).

Makaton is widely used with young children in Early Years settings and uses some signs taken from BSL. Signing is used with spoken language at the same time as spoken language to provide additional clues to help children understand frequently used words. In essence it is a way of encouraging communication through the use of speech, gesture, facial expression, eye contact, body language, signs, symbols and words. Practitioners are becoming increasingly aware of Makaton and British Sign Language often as a result of professional necessity. The Makaton website (www.makaton.org) provides information about training workshops and distance learning courses for practitioners, and packs for parents.

The Signalong signing system also uses BSL signs and is often combined with Makaton by speech and language therapists (www.signalong.org.uk).

The Paget Gorman system also uses BSL signs and is primarily but not exclusively used to support children with specific speech and language impairment in some special schools and units. Unaltered BSL signs are used where possible using a system of hand shapes to represent a carefully regulated vocabulary (www.pgss.org).

Young children learn to decipher the nuances of messages conveyed through gesture. Such gestures are often culturally located: they may convey a different meaning from one cultural setting to another. Beckoning with the hand may indicate in one cultural sign language that the child should approach, but in another it may mean that the child should go back. The gap between children who do recognise cues and those who do not appears to widen at the age of 5 or 6. By the age of 6 most children will have knowledge of an extensive range of visual cues which accompany and enhance communication through speech; they may use many cues but also recognise many more. There are exceptions to this; children with autism may have more profound difficulties in learning to communicate and also in reading non-verbal cues, the gesture and body language that add subtlety to a request or instruction. Children who have an autistic spectrum disorder (ASD) also have great difficulty in recognising cues and responses from other children, and their apparent lack of interest can have a negative effect on friendship formation. Eye contact is usually maintained between children and practitioners when engaged in activities and it is usually only as children acquire more awareness of the social conventions of a cultural group that this contact diminishes. An exception to this generalisation will be recognised by those practitioners working with young children who have an ASD and who find making eye contact more problematic.

Producing speech

The act of speaking requires complex physical coordination. An inability to control a group of muscles can result in quite marked differences in pronunciation and clarity of speech. There are over 100 muscles within the mouth that are used during the act of speaking and so it is not surprising that even minor difficulties may emerge. You will become more aware of the difficulties faced by children with this problem if you concentrate on the movements of your own mouth when forming words. Speaking is like riding a bike, but more complex. We make automatic reactions without thinking of the number of distinct and separate tasks that are required. The range of physical tasks involved in speaking is often not fully realised; we take it for granted and expect others to manage in the same way. Children with physical disabilities can have a harder task to learn to speak when their disability directly affects their ability to form sounds through control of their mouth and tongue. It will also often mean that they will take longer to learn to talk. This may be because they find not only the control of tongue and mouth muscles difficult but also the interpretation and decoding of sounds. For some children with learning disabilities, the use of gesture or signing alongside speech will provide more ready access to communication and interaction with others.

Activity 2

Bodily contact

No discussion of gesture and body language in communication would be complete without raising the contentious issue of bodily contact. In recent years contact between practitioners and children has become culturally inappropriate.

1 Note occasions when touching is used to emphasise communication between adults.

2 Note occasions when touching is used to emphasise communication between an adult and child. In a setting where young children come from a range of cultural backgrounds it may be useful to discuss this aspect of communication with colleagues and parents.

Babies and language

Where does it all start? A child's interaction with language begins at birth. It may even be argued that it begins before birth as the baby is exposed in the womb to the sound of the mother's and others' voices.

Babies respond to the human face

Conversation could be said to start as soon as the baby responds to the mother's face. Research appears to indicate that most babies respond to the human face, and it would seem that there might be genetic reasons for this phenomenon. Those of us who have had regular contact with babies will recognise that babies' response to the human face is confirmed by everyday observation.

Close observation of the interactions between a mother and baby who bond well reveals another level of communication that is far subtler and is sensitive to the slightest signal.

Language that accompanies such interaction, sound and gesture, forms the basis for social interaction. The interaction between babies and adults has been likened to a form of conversation. This view is justified when one considers that a number of actions adopted by babies are present in conversational interactions of older children and adults. Babies are very aware of the non-verbal cues provided by adults through facial expression. They appear to control the pace of conversation by maintaining eye contact or by dropping their gaze. Either babies or adults may initiate the conversation; however, when babies react to the gaze of an adult and fail to receive a response they lapse into silence. Babies and toddlers need to be able to get adults' attention.

For further information on this fascinating aspect of communication, see Trevarthen and Murray (1993).

Adult-led conversation with babies will follow a pattern familiar to parents: initiating interaction through prompts, waiting for a response, allowing time for a response from the baby and then extending the interaction through eye contact or physical stimulation. Between 6 and 14 months of age most babies will produce a wide range of repeated and non-repeated sounds. These sounds and combinations of sounds will be used to represent familiar objects, animals and people. Sounds that are repeated will approximate ever more closely to accurate representation of recognisable words. The range of sounds and 'words' will be culturally located.

Use of songs, rhymes, facial and body gestures

Differences as well as similarities in approaching such conversations will be found in different cultural and social groups. Songs, rhymes, facial and body gestures are used in a variety of ways in different cultural groups, but are commonly used to build and reinforce bonding between the baby and primary caregivers. They may also be seen as a means of inducting babies into the distinct and particular traditions of the culture into which the child is born. Babies who have a rich and concentrated experience of focused speech appear to develop more rapidly in some aspects of their language. This is particularly noticeable in the range and use of communication gestures.

The key to providing an enabling environment is for adults to make opportunities for talk, to make time to talk with babies, not just to talk to them. Some adults find it difficult to talk with babies; they feel awkward or self-conscious. Playful use of sounds initiated by the baby may be a means of drawing in and involving the adult. The response is crucial. Without response the conversation will fail, as does any conversation. The type of response is equally, if not more, important. As babies explore their range of sounds, they will respond to adult interest. It is important for those working with babies to closely observe how babies develop their language and how body language and gesture are used to reinforce meaning. Observation of the relationship between spoken language and body language is crucial. It forms an essential aspect of communication throughout life. In your observations it would be useful to note if the words used by adults are supported or confirmed by their body language.

Activity 3

Recognising patterns in language and communication development

1   Do you recognise any patterns emerging in the way children acquire language and communication skills?

2   Are there times when children are particularly receptive to language?

3   Are there contexts or places that you have noted as being helpful in promoting development?

Using oral language to communicate

Speaking requires control of complex groups of muscles in the mouth. Physical differences that are present at birth may indicate the possibility of future problems with learning to talk. These physical differences may be recognised, or identified, at an early stage when feeding. Babies who have difficulty in sucking, for example, may have poor control over muscles in the mouth.

Every aspect of early childhood experience provides the potential for language development, whether this is communicating wants by speaking, signing to others or through internalised speech.

Parents, primary caregivers, family members, friends and other carers use oral language for communication. Children are surrounded by language being used by others and acquire language in a naturalistic way in all the activities they engage in at home. This applies to most children, whatever their backgrounds, cultures or languages. There are, however, exceptions to this. Some families and children with an auditory impairment or a physical or other difference that prevents oral communication will not use verbal language, either from necessity or from choice. Other forms of visual language and communication will be used to supplement or replace speech as a normal part of everyday life.

An indication of the development of children's skills in language is not just demonstrated by what they say, it is also visible in the cues they recognise and in responses that indicate their understanding of what adults say.

Activity 4

Reflection

1 Make brief observations of adults talking to children, in the workplace, in the home or outside.

2 Note any evidence of modelling: accent, gesture and body language.

3 Is there a connection between how much the child looks at the adult and the adult response?

4 How can this reflection help you in your planning?

Toddlers' first words

The first recognisable words emerge on average any time between the ages of 12 to 19 months. First words are drawn from their direct experience and there may be a gap between the first recognisable word and any repetition or utterance of other words. Often first words are unexpected.

Case Study 7

First words

Eleanor (15 months) is sitting in the back of the car with her brother Patrick (aged 4) and their grandmother. Patrick says he has been to the pub with his parents.

Granny asks, 'What did mummy drink?'
'Beer,' says Patrick.
'What did daddy drink?' asks Granny.
'Beer,' says Patrick.
'Did you have beer, too?' asks Granny.
'I had lemonade,' says Patrick.
'And what did Eleanor have?' asks Granny.
Before Patrick can respond, Eleanor says, 'Juice'. This is the first clear word she has spoken.

The first words used by children are usually used in a multi-purpose way (**holophrases**). Often at this early stage, the words will be used with a wide range of intonation to convey a variety of meanings. The same word may also be used to represent a range of things that have a common factor: 'juice' can mean any drink.

Case Study 8

Signing leads to improvement in speech

At 3 years of age, Asif was having difficulty with speech. He was monosyllabic and his vocabulary was very small. His words were indistinct and even family members found it difficult to understand him. Eventually, he began to have speech therapy and the therapist suggested using signing to communicate. His confidence in communicating grew through signing and led to improvements in speech.

Development in language: the Early Years

Parents and carers often use a modified form of language with babies and toddlers. Other older children often follow this modelling when speaking to younger siblings.

Babies seem to respond to language that is simple in structure, is expressive and uses repetitive phrases. Experiments have been conducted using this modified infant-directed speech in languages other than the home language, and babies have continued to respond positively. This would seem to indicate that at this early stage, tone, pitch and pattern in language are more important than the meaning of the words. Modified infant-directed speech is used in many cultures and appears to follow similar rules.

Physical and emotional support is important to language development

Infant-directed speech may improve a baby's language and communication skills as a result of the bonding relationship that is integral to the interactive communication process. Providing the optimum conditions for language development appears to be related to physical and emotional support. Research on mothers who experience depression has shown that although their children do learn to talk, the range and use of language is very restricted. Babies in this situation are often confined and given very little stimulus. Intervention strategies have been successful when mothers have been identified as having this problem and appropriate support has been available.

Showing and giving objects

Children of 18 to 20 months generally demonstrate an ever-increasing interest in showing and giving objects, initially real and then pretend. For example, some children may go through a phase of liking David Pelham's book *Sam's Pizza*; they may pretend to pick

out the 'disgusting' things which were added to the pizza – slugs, centipedes and so on – which they might then pretend to spit out. The part that the adult can play in extending the child's understanding and use of language on such occasions is extensive, and is crucial in opening up opportunities, not only for social interaction, but also for subject-located knowledge and understanding. Some of what an adult hears a child say may not be entirely accurate in terms of 'subject' knowledge; however, if the adult has been aware of the context of the child's learning experiences it may be possible to understand where these misconceptions or misunderstandings have come from.

There are some important questions to be asked here. For example, how can *Sam's Pizza* be used for extending scientific knowledge, for encouraging, teaching or finding out a child's understanding of differences between living things, or what can and can't be eaten, if we provide confusing information? Does the 'pretend eating' of objects confuse or reinforce children's understanding of inedible or unsafe things to eat? It is important to consider the types of language that could be encouraged and supported and how they are used.

Books are very useful starting points

Books can be very useful starting points at any age if the adult provides the scaffolding for language extension and modelling of reading behaviour. Pointing out familiar things in books encourages the child to respond, as any parent of a young child will know. Initially, this co-reading will be adult-led. The next stage will be triggered by responses from the child through their intervention: by making sounds, pointing and gesturing. The responsive adult will then extend the input to meet the child's requests and responses.

Young children soon acquire an enthusiasm for a particular book and for its detail. Sometimes this enthusiasm develops to the extent that the parent wishes the child would lose interest and move to another book! Such opportunities provide an ideal setting for language development, linking the everyday and familiar with the unfamiliar and unreal. Extending reading skills in this way may also be used to encourage rich descriptive use of language.

Usually, by the time children are approaching their second birthday, they are beginning to demonstrate their developmental stage of short-term memory through fetching and carrying. The stimulus presented to the child by the environment will be readily seen, not only in the range of objects, but also in the language that is used. The modelling provided by adults and older children may motivate extended use of language and gesture.

Case Study 9

Memory and communication

Kiran (18 months) occasionally went shopping with his grandmother. By the egg section was a button which, when pressed, produced farmyard noises, including a clucking sound.

Several weeks had passed since Kiran's last visit, but on entering the store Kiran bent his elbows and began to flap his arms up and down. This was his chicken gesture. It was some minutes before his grandmother realised that he was remembering the button that made farmyard noises.

Understanding the purposes and use of speech

For most children the first few months of their second year will be a period of rapid understanding of the purposes and use of speech. Between 18 months and 2 years of age most children will begin to use their first words. This age range is purely indicative of ages that events are likely to occur. Some children may speak at an earlier age, others much later. (Within this book any indication of the ages that events are likely to occur should be taken as a very broad indication of developmental norms.) Again, by this age children will begin to recognise and respond to their name. They also respond to requests related to giving and taking objects.

Toddlers will often structure short phrases from words that elide and combine. Examples of this would be 'heyare' and 'allgone'. The words most commonly used are, of course, those relating to giving and taking. Requests also feature as word combinations, which may be used in a range of situations, and for different purposes. Adults who care for, or work with, children of this age will recognise and respond to these context-related word phrases; to others they may make no sense. Clues to meaning are often provided by gestures as well as changes in tone and intonation in speech, which are modelled on those adults or other children with whom the children are in contact. Over a period of weeks or months, toddlers will respond and adapt to routines and recognise and use gesture and speech to match actions. Describing or commenting upon their own actions can be seen at this stage, especially in their self-directed play. A significant point to note is that toddlers appear to devise, or respond to, rules of language.

You may notice that some children in childcare settings will begin to discriminate between different registers of language. They may use different ways of speaking to adults and to other children or imitate adult speech patterns in some aspects of their role-play.

Children learn to speak more readily when they are involved in conversations. In this way, new words and phrases become part of the active vocabulary of young children. Where patterns of language experience are adult-directed and -dominated, children's language development will be impeded. A typical example of this approach is when children are sidelined by being talked to rather than encouraged to actively respond.

By the age of 3 and a half, many children will play with words, exploring differences in meaning, and ask questions in a more focused way. By this age, some children will be able to differentiate between alternative meanings for the same word, and jokes based on word play may emerge.

The interest shown in what young children do and the ways in which they express themselves are key aspects of the provision of scaffolding for language learning. Very young children are focused in the way that they perceive the world around them; they often have strong views, which need to be recognised, acknowledged and understood.

Physical interaction is supported by language

Much of the physical interaction that takes place between parents and primary caregivers and children is supported by language. The interchange of responses in interactions often becomes a complex turn-taking activity with the parent and child responding to each other. Language not only supports, but also extends, bonding and reinforcement of the social and emotional interactions. Bath time, bedtime, shopping and, even watching television with an adult who is attuned to their child's interests provide opportunities for extended and complex conversation. Language may be extended and supported in these familiar situations.

Case Study 10

Extending and supporting language through social and emotional interaction

Shareen enjoys bathing her daughter Aurely (age 4) while her mother looks after the other children. It is a time when Shareen and Aurely are able to spend some quiet, intimate, 'quality' time together. They talk about things that happen during the day.

At nursery, the practitioner notices that Aurely particularly enjoys opportunities to bath the dolls, shampoo their hair and talk to them. She becomes so engrossed in this activity that she is unaware of those around her. Observation of her behaviour led to the practitioner questioning her mother and the links between these activities were recognised.

The earliest experiences of language provide models for the use of language in communication. In these, and many other social contexts, this social function of turn taking will not be entirely possible for some children. Those children with an autistic spectrum disorder may already at 4 or 5 years of age have begun to display an inability to communicate in a conventional way. Their responses to cues from others either in speech or body language may be inappropriate to the context or be open to misinterpretation. This inability to communicate in a conventional way may increase as the child gets older.

Children still learn to talk regardless of their support at home. There are, of course, exceptions, but these are either due to physical differences that impede language development, or are extreme cases of language deprivation. Children who are completely deprived of human conversation, such as feral children, mimic and imitate the sounds they hear around them.

Lack of confidence in using language in pre-school settings

An increasing concern for many practitioners who work in pre-school settings is the number of children who on entry display very limited confidence in their use of language. Concerns for children who have had little stimulus may be addressed through language intervention strategies provided within settings, or by programmes provided by outside agencies. The provision of a home environment that is rich in opportunities for talk should not be confused with social class (see studies by Tizard and Hughes (1984) and Wells (1987)). Parents, whatever their socioeconomic background, can enable their children to acquire language skills which equip them well for pre-school and school through questioning, problem solving and conversation. The conditions that applied to this research in the 1980s have changed with the pattern of language use in homes, which have very different life styles than those that pertained nearly 20 years ago. Anecdotal evidence indicates that language use within the home and relationships between family members have more influence on children's capacity for language than socioeconomic background.

By 3 years of age most children are using language effectively to communicate their needs, and in ways that demonstrate much wider language skills.

Case Study 11

Language use within the home

Samantha is the youngest child in the family, with an age gap of 10 years between her and her 14-year-old brother. One day, while at nursery, Samantha in a very matter of fact manner stated that her mum was very upset with her brother because the police had been round to their house and that he was in trouble again and it was drugs. Although the subject matter was not what one might expect at nursery it did demonstrate the degree of expertise Samantha had with language.

Too few opportunities for one-to-one experience

McAuley and Jackson (1992) indicate that research shows there is a paucity of sustained conversation between any one individual child and an adult in nursery settings. Experience indicates that opportunities for this one-to-one experience are still difficult to achieve. Much of the language used in Early Years settings is instructional or organisational. The degree to which this occurs increases as the child gets older, when it is even less likely that time will be made available for one-to-one naturalistic conversations within school classrooms. Time constraints imposed by the demands of the curriculum are often presented as the prime reason for the lack of opportunity for quality conversation.

Careful planning can overcome this problem; focused conversation can be used within the delivery of the curriculum to enhance and consolidate learning. Children often find difficulty in responding to tasks when there are few opportunities for checking on, and confirming, the demands made on them by the practitioner. One-to-one conversations allow for matching tasks to a child's ability more readily and more accurately than relying solely upon group conversation, but both types need to be built into the planning cycle in order to test children's understanding and to counter any misunderstanding of concepts. No matter how carefully tasks are presented, some children will struggle with understanding new work within their existing conceptual framework. Children's misunderstandings often have a 'logical' basis, in that they use their existing knowledge to make sense of a situation to arrive at an answer, and children know only too well that an answer is always required when an adult asks a question. Conversation is an effective and possibly non-threatening means of eliciting answers to questions and gauging children's understanding of how they think about the world.

Talking to children about fire engines, trucks and ambulances, lifts, escalators and revolving doors, vacuum cleaners and DVD players can provide them with an amazing number of facts, with many of them being accurately – or partially accurately – understood!

Activity 7

Language specific to an area of knowledge

Collect some examples to demonstrate how children's questions indicate their growing awareness of language specific to an area of knowledge. You may, for example, look at children's understanding of science or technology in the home, in school or in the local environment.

Young children need to be encouraged to explore

There are many ways of encouraging children's exploration of science through language. Adults provide crucial role models and in order that we may effectively help children we need to be explorers with them (Siraj-Blatchford and MacLeod-Brudenell, 1999:14). If we, as practitioners, share children's pleasure in seeking answers to scientific or technological questions, wondering how and why things happen, we will provide models for further reflection.

Case Study 12

Answering children's questions

Holly (4 years, 6 months) loves eating mashed potatoes, but today she is eating crisps. 'What are crisps made from, Daddy?' she asks.

'They're made from potatoes,' he replies.

'Then how do they make them hard?' she asks.

Children see things in different ways to adults, not only from an intellectual viewpoint, but also by reason of their physical stature, from a different height. They notice things that may pass us by. Encouraging talk about everyday things – chairs, car door handles and soft drinks dispensers, for example – can be quite revealing. The detail that is noticed, which may be elicited with carefully supported questioning, often reveals knowledge of the intricacies of mechanisms and materials. Only adults who are sensitive to children's interests will draw out this detail in conversation.

The role of parents

You are probably familiar with the term 'parents are a child's first educators'. Parental influence can provide rich experience in social and emotional development. Indeed, the role parents or primary caregivers play in development of language is crucial. Negative parenting, or poor parenting skills, have a very negative effect on language development. Children who have not received encouragement to speak at home often lack spontaneity in using speech in their play both at home and in out-of-home settings. This can be rectified by providing opportunities for collaborative play, in which children and adults can demonstrate the use of words within an appropriate context.

Young children develop their innate capacity to learn to speak through their experience of language used by adults and other children. Exposure to language used readily and confidently by adults helps young children to understand words and link them to particular and specific contexts. Hearing words used in context also encourages imitation. A key aspect of play for some children is playing with words, revisiting contexts in which they have heard words used. The majority of children who suffer hearing impairment are born to hearing parents. The use of both spoken language and signing is very important for these children's competence and confidence in communication. Using and playing with words in play within everyday contexts is encouraged at as early a stage as possible.

Most parents know what their children are interested in and respond to these interests. It is not uncommon for a 4-year-old child to have a wide vocabulary related to an area of particular interest.

Children's vocabularies and special interests

In essence, the language users around children provide them with scaffolding for early learning (Bruner, 1983). This is addressed in further detail in Chapter 5.

Interactive speech cannot be replaced by simply hearing speech. Watching television is often denigrated as a negative activity for children, but there can be positive aspects to this experience if an adult sits with the child and talks through the experience, much as if they were reading a book together. This social activity could be extended to the use of a computer.

Case Study 13

Emily's dinosaurs

From the age of two, Emily has been interested in dinosaurs. This interest has developed over time to the present day (4 years, 9 months). Emily uses dinosaur names; recognises physical attributes; knows what they ate; knows they lived a very long time ago; knows about skin and links them with reptiles now; and knows about their skeletons. Emily says that she wants be an archaeologist when she grows up.

Case Study 14

Connor's cars

Connor, like many little boys, has an in-depth knowledge of vehicles. This began before he was 2 years old, with an interest in mini-cars. Now aged 3 years and 5 months, his knowledge is wide, and he recognises and names a huge number of cars. Recently, while a passenger in a car that was parked alongside a big green vehicle, he corrected an adult who said that he thought the vehicle was a bit like a Range Rover.

'No, it's not,' said Connor. 'It hasn't got a wheel on the back,' he added.

As he drove away, the adult checked and conceded that Connor was right.

Is Connor exceptional in his understanding or is it that he is able to express his thoughts well because he is highly competent in using spoken language to demonstrate his knowledge?

Case Study 15

Recognising language awareness

At nursery a practitioner chose *The Very Hungry Caterpillar* by Eric Carle to read to a group of children. A little boy became very excited and exclaimed that he had the video at home. He knew the words by heart and spoke them out loud, imitating the tone used by the narrator in the video, as the practitioner read the book. The next day, when he came to the nursery, he asked for the book and sat with the practitioner while they read it together. This event recurred on several days, until one day the practitioner suggested that he read the book to her. Not only did he do that, but he also gathered a little group of children and read to them, holding up the book to enable them to see the picture. The practitioner gave him a copy of the book to take home.

What aspects of language awareness are being demonstrated here?

Activity 8

Using a graphics package to aid language development

When Danny (aged 4) used to visit his grandparents for holidays, he regularly saw flooding en route to their home. Danny had problems with making his words understood and communicating his thoughts. He loved to use his grandfather's computer to draw. He became very adept at using the graphics package and would use the paint spray to make 'dark clouds'. Danny was able to use his painting as a means of prompting talking about his experiences as well as using his imagination. He was able to make up stories from his paintings, even though he had a very limited vocabulary.

1 How could this activity be replicated with children in out-of-home settings?

2 Tizard (1994) notes that extended conversations at home were often at relaxed times – over tea or during a one-to-one story time. Danny's experience illustrates this point. Similar conversations may only happen at Danny's nursery when an adult stays with him to talk through his explorations. Would Danny be able to work on a computer like this without adult help?

Scaffolding

Laura was interested – almost to the point of obsession – in cats. She was very shy and self-conscious and hid behind the persona of her cat. Her reception class teacher found the only way to involve her in classroom activities was through all things feline: drama and movement developed around cats, books and poems about cats and individual maths lessons – which cat is the odd one out?, draw three cats, and so on. As her confidence grew, she developed an interest in birds, but by this time she had begun to use the library to study her interest.

Young children often have very strong interests. How could you harness a child's interests through careful matching of their interest in your planning?

Activity 9

Scaffolding learning

1 How do you help to scaffold learning?

2 Do you recognise aspects of language support in this chapter's case studies that are reflected in your practice?

3 Which aspects of scaffolding do you find the most effective in your practice?

Accent, dialect and grammar

There are clear and definitive distinctions between accent, dialect and grammar and, at first sight, this appears to be quite a straightforward matter. There are, however, some issues pertaining to this area of study of which we should be aware and which are not generally discussed. For example, the accent we hear and use as children may determine the one we use for the rest of our life.

Earlier in the chapter, note was made of the relationship between manipulation of muscle groups, the tongue and making speech. Although this was in the context of children with physical differences or disability, the issue also has bearing on the development of speech for everyone.

Note how uncomfortable it feels when your mouth muscles are forced to make unfamiliar sounds. Try to concentrate on how your mouth and tongue move when pronouncing words in an unfamiliar way. You will become aware of the difficulties some children may have when trying to change their accent in order to 'fit in' when they move to another area.

The case study demonstrating George's awareness of different pronunciations illustrates a conscious effort to play with words (see page 170).

Standard English

There is an emphasis on the use of Standard English in school. Standard English is a dialect of English which has been selected for general public use throughout the country. It comprises conventions of grammar and spelling that are promoted as being the only acceptable form of language for public communication. Regional dialects are not supported as a means of public communication in this country.

Activity 10

Dialect

Dialect words may be in general use within a geographical location or be used by a particular age group. The following dialect words are used in parts of Nottingham:

➤ pawpaw: a sore or minor injury

➤ tab: ear

➤ cob: bread roll

➤ nobby greens: Brussels sprouts.

You will note that three of these words have different meanings in other language contexts:

➤ pawpaw: a fruit

➤ tab: a flap

➤ cob: a horse.

What dialect words do you encounter in Early Years settings?

Grammatical conventions

Young children quickly develop an awareness of the grammar, conventions of language and rules of speech used within their community. The forms of grammar used within a family as well as in the community may differ from those found in Standard English. Non-standard grammar and dialect may be acquired by children from their family and from people in the community. Tension frequently occurs when young children move to situations in which Standard English is required and they are expected to conform. It is not uncommon to find variations from Standard English grammar used widely within a community; for example, 'was' rather than 'were' as illustrated by 'we was going'.

As children become more confident in using grammatical conventions, they will adapt their own creative and non-standard variations to conform to their understanding of the rules! For example, 'I used to was.'

Children are generally adept at imitation and learn to switch between the types of language that are acceptable for use in different contexts. Usually, by the age of 5, children are beginning to be able to move between different registers of language use with confidence.

Bilingualism

Bilingual speakers have been present in England for many centuries, in fact for longer than England has been a nation. This fact is often neglected in current discussions on bilingualism, where the issue is often regarded as a fairly recent phenomenon. The use of a language other than English for everyday communication still appears to be regarded with varying degrees of indifference, antagonism or hostility. The recent history of bilingual education in England, therefore, is inextricably linked with attitudes to race and cultural difference.

Recent moves by the United Kingdom government to introduce tests in the English language for those seeking British citizenship have raised many issues relating to the role and place of languages other than English in British society. An acknowledgement that tests could be made in Welsh and Gaelic, as well as English, has indicated that these languages have equal status with English. This may be seen as a positive acknowledgement to speakers of these languages. Languages other than English have been used in religious contexts for many years as a means of maintaining religious or cultural identity.

The number of languages spoken in cities and larger towns has increased rapidly over the last decade due to the range of people seeking political asylum and more recently economic migrants. This has placed pressure on schools, nurseries, Children's Centres and other Early Years settings to respond to the communication needs of children who may be with them for an uncertain length of time. Supporting bilingualism is now a major issue in many schools in areas where economic migrants have settled on a temporary basis. The issue of support for children and families with a main language other than English has, for the first time in many rural areas, provided a challenge. Support for the specific geographical area provided by Sure Start and Education Authorities is the key to the solution. On a national level greater support is required, mainly through funding but also by recognising the difficulties when assessing and inspecting settings.

Other issues which relate to 'emergent' bilingual children are the difficulties associated with recognition of dyslexia and the identification and provision for children with other communication difficulties such as aphasia.

Using a range of languages in the home

Babies will learn the language of their primary caregiver and the acquisition of an additional language may occur in a number of ways. Children who are in daily, or regular, contact with a family member who speaks another language will acquire an understanding of, and varying degrees of competence in, communicating in that language. For children in bilingual families, there may be a range of scenarios of language use within the family as well as in their out-of-home experiences.

The following case study demonstrates the complexity of switching between languages that one child copes with on a regular basis.

The example focuses on western European languages but reflects the experiences of many, if not most, children who live in families that communicate through the means of different languages.

Case Study 17

Switching between languages

Gavin's mum was born of Italian parents in Wales. His father was born to Welsh-speaking parents. Gavin's mum and dad speak English to each other and their children. Gavin speaks English to his parents and siblings. He understands Italian and has learned Welsh at school and heard it spoken at his paternal grandparents'. This apparently complex linguistic context is found in very many homes in Britain.

Using a range of languages may be a necessity for some families, but in others it may be a matter of choice. Awareness of the benefits of the ability to communicate in more than one language may not emerge until families feel secure and confident within the wider community, or feel able to demonstrate pride in their ethnicity. If children are encouraged to learn two languages within a bilingual family, each language is often directed to different family members.

Case Study 18

Choosing to use a range of languages in the home

Alison is married to Juan, a Spanish speaker. Of their three children, the eldest, Jaime, speaks only English. Paul speaks English and understands some Spanish, and the youngest, Annabel, is bilingual.

Annabel experienced simultaneous learning of both languages as a young child.

Evidence indicates that bilingual children who learn two languages simultaneously may sometimes confuse languages. If there is a clear distinction as to which language is spoken to which individuals within the family, there are fewer opportunities for confusion.

The role of parents is crucial for the development of language. This may be seen even more keenly in those families that have the additional ability to use more than one language in everyday communication. Parents' perception of the importance of the home language is crucial. Without a positive understanding of the benefits that the use of this language provides for their children, opportunities for their children's language enhancement may be lost. The merits of bilingualism must also be recognised by those with whom children come into contact within their out-of-home experiences at school, pre-school or nursery (Karram, 2003).

Research appears to demonstrate that there are positive benefits for children who are bilingual: greater cognitive flexibility, problem-solving capacities and linguistic awareness (Hakuta and Pease-Alvarez, 1992).

Learning a second language in an out-of-home setting

Many children learn their second language when they move to an out-of-home setting: Children's Centre, nursery, pre-school or reception class settings or on entry to school. The existing language skills of the child should be acknowledged. Often children will already be confident users of their home language and be able to access a wide range of learning opportunities. Sometimes a child's lack of competence in spoken English is erroneously seen as an indication of a wider lack of understanding; children may choose not to speak!

Electronic communication

As reports tell us that children as young as 5 own mobile phones and the average age for getting a first mobile phone is now 8 years old (Derbyshire, 2005), it is important to consider electronic forms of communication. Despite health warnings about radiation from mobile phones and advice that under-8s should not use them, many children are being given phones for a range of reasons. Parents often agree for a child to have a phone as the benefits of being able to monitor the child's whereabouts may outweigh the cost and other concerns. However, there has been no definitive resolution to the health warnings and recently a report suggested bedtime use of a phone was unhealthy as the radiation from the handset can cause insomnia and headaches (Narain, 2008). Despite these concerns mobile use among young children is increasing with 9/10 owning a phone by the age of 12. Mobiles are central to children's social behaviour with 80 per cent of 11–17-year-olds claiming that mobiles give them a better social life and sense of belonging. Most young teens and pre-teens text rather than talk on the phone (Greek, 2006). This may relate to the cost of texting versus phoning or the fact that non-direct communication may feel 'safer' and less stressful. It may be that texting also controls the length of the communication and texts can be sent and read in the user's own timeframe.

Social networking sites have proliferated in recent years, many of them attracting young children and teenagers. Services and sites like MSN messenger, MySpace, ebuddy, bebo, Facebook, and YouTube are used to interact, make arrangements, chat and share music, video and images. The sites are used to alleviate boredom, to socialise and to provide an antidote to homework as many children multi-task on one or more social networking site while doing online homework projects. They are also sometimes used to sexually harass children with 4 per cent of 10–15-year-olds experiencing an 'unwanted sexual solicitation and 9 per cent reported being harassed while on a social networking site' (emaxhealth, 2007). However, although claims of online bullying are more common and in the UK a reported 22 per cent of children claim to have been the target (*Daily Telegraph*, 2008), the majority of children are not harassed.

Children and young teens may use social networking sites because their friends do and they may feel socially more acceptable if others interact with them. 'It's nice if someone leaves you a comment on bebo, it makes you feel popular' (Howell, 2008). Children may also talk to acquaintances on the sites more than they do in 'real life' and they may use the sites to get to know others better, sharing personal information and chatting. Sites are also used to create identity, with some sites offering the opportunity to present yourself as you wish, using pseudonyms and giving selected information about self (Howell, 2008). Children can create an ideal persona for themselves and also populate these sites with images of themselves, friends and their life. They may also have conversations that they would not feel comfortable having face-to-face, for example asking each other out or ending relationships. The downside of such sites is that they can become boring and repetitive and that they can be used to abuse other children, have disputes and arguments. Children may also accept communications from strangers, despite parental warnings, and put themselves at risk. One of the arguments about the use of these sites by children is the public nature of the communication on some of them and the risks children may take by sharing personal information. For adults, this may seem to militate against the privacy they assume in their own lives.

Concerns have focused around the possibility of online communication linking children to predatory adults and also in relation to whether children's face-to-face communication skills are eroded by electronic communication through the internet or by text. It is unclear whether this is actually the case, with counter-arguments that electronic communication can complement rather than replace face-to-face communication. There is a proliferation of internet sites dedicated to giving parents advice about controlling their children's use of these sites and about safe use. More research is needed to discover what the long-term implications of electronic communication may be on children's communication and language use, social behaviour and general well-being.

Conclusion

Communication is more than spoken language, in any of its forms. Interaction between people involves language, gesture and body language. Children's acquisition of communication skills is one of the most exciting developments of early childhood. Encouraging and influencing this development is potentially one of the most rewarding aspects of your professional role.

This development does not, of course, finish at the end of your course, the stage of education or in early childhood. You should make yourself aware of communication developments in later childhood. Aspects of communication development with older children have permeated early childhood; texting, email, the use of video cameras and video on mobile phones has brought a new range of communication skills to young children. Promoting confidence in using these channels and integrating them into everyday practice enriches and enhances children's experience of communication.

How to move on in your research

It is hoped that you will continue your reflection on the development of children's language and communication skills within your workplace setting and in conversations with the significant adults in the life of children with whom you work. It is also hoped that you will use the suggestions made in this chapter for further reading and as a basis for ongoing evaluation of your practice. Use the references provided below to follow up your particular interests. The suggested websites will provide accessible information at many levels, as a practitioner, for research and for updating practice.

References

Acredolo, L. and Goodwyn, S. (1997), *Baby Signs*. London: Hodder and Stoughton

Athey, C. (1990), *Extending Thought in Young Children: A Parent-Teacher Partnership*. London: Paul Chapman

Browne, A. (2001) (2nd edition), *Developing Language and Literacy*. London: Paul Chapman

Bruner, J. (1983), *In Search of Mind: Essays in Autobiography*. New York: HarperCollins

Carle, E. (1970), *The Very Hungry Caterpillar*. London: Puffin Books

Chomsky, N. (1957), *Syntactic Structures*. The Hague: Mouton

Cousins, J. (1999), *Listening to Four Year Olds*. London: National Early Years Network

Daily Telegraph (2008), 'Bullies "thrive on social networking sites"' *Online*. Last accessed on 4 March 2008 at URL: http://www.telegraph.co.uk/news/main.jhtml?xml=/news/2008/02/27/nbully127.xml

Derbyshire, D, (2005), 'Mobile phone fears for owners, aged five' *Telegraph Online* 12/09/2005. Last accessed on 4 March 2008 at URL: http://www.telegraph.co.uk/news/main.jhtml?xml=/news/2005/09/12/nmob12.xml

Donaldson, M. (1978), *Children's Minds*. London: Fontana

Emaxhealth (2008), 'Are social networking sites endangering young teens online?' Last accessed on 4 March 2008 at URL: http://www.emaxhealth.com/22/20708.html

Goldschmied, E. and Jackson, S. (1994), *People under Three*. London: Routledge

Greek, D. (2006), 'Mobile phones dominate young people's lives online'. Last accessed on 4 March 2008 at URL:http://www.computeractive.co.uk/computeractive/news/2164545/mobile-phone-survey

Grieve, R. and Hughes, M. (eds) (1990), *Understanding Children*. Oxford: Blackwell Publishers

Hakuta, K. and Pease-Alvarez, L. (1992), 'Enriching our views of bilingualism and bilingual education'. *Educational Researcher*, 21, pp4–6

Howell, A. (2008), 'Conversation with 16-year-old expert', unpublished

Karram, S. (2002), '"Auntie-ji, please come and join us for an hour": The role of the bilingual education assistant in working with parents with little confidence', in **Devereux, J. and Miller, L. (eds) (2002)**, *Working with Children in the Early Years*. London: David Fulton

Meadows, S. and Cashdan, A. (1988), *Helping Children Learn: Contributions to a Cognitive Curriculum*. London: David Fulton

Mukherji, P. and O'Dea, T. (2000), *Understanding Children's Language and Literacy*. Cheltenham: Stanley Thornes

Narain, J. (2008), 'Using a mobile phone before going to bed is bad for your health, says new study', *Daily Mail Online* 20/1/2008. Last accessed on 4 March 2008 at URL: http://www.dailymail.co.uk/pages/dmsearch/overture.html?in_page_id=711&in_overture_ua=cat&in_start_number=0&in_restriction=byline&in_query=jaya%20narain&in_name=on&in_order_by=relevance+date

Nutbrown, C. (1994), *Threads of Thinking: Young Children Learning and the Role of Early Education*. London: Paul Chapman

Pelham, D. (1996), *Sam's Pizza*. New York: Dutton Juvenile

Sutherland, P. (1992), *Cognitive Development Today: Piaget and his Critics*. London: Paul Chapman

Tizard, B. and Hughes, M. (1984), *Young Children Learning*. London: Fontana

Trevarthen, C. (1993), 'The function of emotions in early infant communication and development', in **Nadel, J. and Camaioni, L. (eds) (1993)**, *New Perspectives in Early Communicative Development*. London: Routledge

Whitehead, M. (1996), *The Development of Language and Literacy*. London: Hodder and Stoughton

Whitehead, M. (1999), *Supporting Language and Literacy Development in the Early Years*. Maidenhead: Open University Press

Vygotsky, L. (1978), *Mind and Society*. Cambridge, MA: Harvard University Press

Useful websites

www.literacytrust.org.uk
The Literacy Trust has a very useful website covering a very wide range of issues relating to communication. The Literacy Trust also has sections on children and TTYB and other interesting topics.

www.talktoyourbaby.org.uk

www.babysigners.co.uk.

www.signingbabies.co.uk
Based on research and tried methodology such as those of Joseph Gorman.

www.literacytrust.org.uk/talktoyourbaby/signing.html
An excellent site provided by the National Literacy Trust

www.makaton.org
A useful site for those interesting in signing. It provides links for training.

www.britishsignlanguage.com
Provides basic information and resources related to British Sign Language.

www.signalong.org.uk
The Signalong website provides detailed information about this approach to signing; book resources and training.

www.pgss.org
   The Paget Gorman website.

www.downsed.org/topics/language/
   This Down's syndrome site provides detailed
   information on language issues related to
   children with Down's syndrome as well as
   a useful list for further reading, training and
   research.

www.dsscotland.org.uk
   Another useful site for Down's syndrome.

www.surestart.gov.uk

www.tessla.org/project
   Teacher education for the support of second
   language acquisition. A useful site for those
   interested in bilingual issues.

www.scre.ac.uk/spotlight/spotlight6/
   The University of Glasgow site relating
   to Bilingual Primary school issues. Very
   interesting research reports.

www.ltsscotland.org.uk/earlyyears/
   Has very good sections devoted to
   supporting Early Years language
   development.

Playing

Elaine Hallet and Vicky Cortvriend with Caron Carter

In this chapter, play as an approach for children's learning and development is explored with a range of examples from practice. Play is embedded within the Early Years Foundation Stage curriculum through a play-based approach. The role of practitioners in extending, supporting and resourcing play within Early Years settings is discussed. The transition from playing at home to a more planned play environment within the Early Years setting is examined in detail, as is the role of parents in providing play experiences for babies and children from birth to three.

The Principles of Playwork which establish the professional and ethical framework for practice will be explored. Playwork theory is evolving and we will discuss the latest developments including the importance of play and playwork in children and young people's lives. Finally, additional contexts for play will be addressed such as extended school provision, hospital play and play therapy.

The chapter aims to provide examples from practice within a framework of recognising the value of play in children's and young people's holistic development.

This chapter addresses the following areas:

➤ What is play and why is it important?
➤ A children's right to play and providing a safe play environment
➤ Play as a way of learning
➤ Play within the Early Years and Foundation Stage curriculum
➤ Play, aged birth to three and the role of adults
➤ Play with parents
➤ Transition from playing at home to an Early Years setting
➤ Play and good health, including inclusive play, hospital play and play therapy

By undertaking the suggested study within this chapter it is hoped that you will be able to:

1 recognise the value of play as an holisitic approach to learning and development

2 understand the role of adults in providing, supporting and extending children and young people's play in the home, in the Early Years setting, in extended school provision and in play therapy to enable children with diverse needs to learn and develop

3 become familiar with a range of play environments and contexts

4 reflect upon your role as a practitioner in children and young people's play.

What is play and why is it important?

The importance of play was recognised in the new Children Act 2004 which sets out five key outcomes within the Every Child Matters framework.

➤ **Being healthy:** Play supports children's physical, mental and emotional health, growth and development.

➤ **Staying safe:** Through play, children are supported to explore physical and emotional risk and challenge safely.

➤ **Enjoying and achieving:** Play fosters children's self-esteem by extending their choice and control, and hence the satisfaction they gain from it.

➤ **Making a positive contribution:** Children's play is naturally participative and inclusive. It fosters a respect for others and offers opportunities for social interaction.

➤ **Economic well-being:** Through play, healthy, confident children and young adults will have a greater capacity to engage with life-long learning and development.

Reflect for a moment on how play in your setting can influence those outcomes.

There are various definitions of play and playing. One definition expressed in the Playwork Principles (commissioned by Play Wales; endorsed by Skills Active 2005, see below), is based on the five key outcomes described above that are found within the Every Child Matters framework.

All children and young people need to play. The impulse to play is innate. Play is a biological, psychological and social necessity and is fundamental to the healthy development and well-being of individuals and communities.

Play is a process that is freely chosen, personally directed and intrinsically motivated. That is, children and young people determine and control the content and intent of their play, by following their own instincts, ideas and interests, in their own way for their own reasons.

Bob Hughes and Frank King believe that play is a type of behaviour that is freely chosen, personally directed, and is intrinsically motivated. It actively engages the child. Jerome Bruner states that, 'The main characteristic of play – child or adult – is not its content, but its mode. Play is an approach to action, not a form of activity.' (Jerome Bruner, in Moyles (1989)).

Play can be also described as being fun or serious. Through play children explore social, material and imaginary worlds and their relationship with them, elaborating all the while a flexible range of responses to the challenges they encounter. By playing, children learn and develop as individuals, and as members of the community.

Play provides children with opportunities to enjoy freedom, and exercise choice and control over their actions; it offers children opportunities for testing boundaries and exploring risk; it offers a very wide range of physical, social and intellectual experiences. Over time it fosters children's independence and self-esteem. It develops children's respect for others and offers opportunities for social interaction; it also supports the child's well-being, healthy growth and development. Finally, it increases children's knowledge and understanding and promotes children's creativity and capacity to learn.

Children's right to play and providing a safe play environment

The following section provides the reader with an introduction to the field of playwork and children's right to play. A playwork setting is one that is underpinned by the Playwork Principles and therefore supports child-directed play. Current play theories are described, recognising their importance for playworkers and indeed all those working with children and young people. A playworker's primary focus regarding play is to support children's rights and their needs in relation to play, whereas Early Years workers utilise play as a medium for children's learning and development.

One of a playworker's inherent beliefs is that one of their roles is to support children and young people's natural play by creating spaces where play can occur naturally. The theory of **loose parts** developed by Simon Nicholson in 1971 and further developed by Fraser Brown in his theory of **combined flexibility** outlines the relevance of loose parts to the play experiences of the child. Nicholson and Brown both believed that in order to develop creativity, inventiveness, problem-solving skills and ultimately a positive self-esteem children need to be able to explore, interact with and have some degree of control over their world.

Children need an environment that will facilitate different types of play, for example object and mastery play. Therefore the play environment should contain a variety of loose materials which children can move around, play with and use to make different games and create dens.

The Playwork Principles also express the value of play and the role of adults in the facilitation of children's play.

The Playwork Principles

➤ All children and young people need to play. The impulse to play is innate. Play is a biological, psychological and social necessity, and is fundamental to the healthy development and well-being of individuals and communities.

➤ Play is a process that is freely chosen, personally directed and intrinsically motivated. That is, children and young people determine and control the content and intent of their play, by following their own instincts, ideas and interests, in their own way for their own reasons.

➤ The prime focus and essence of playwork is to support and facilitate the play process and this should inform the development of play policy, strategy, training and education.

➤ For playworkers, the play process takes precedence and playworkers act as advocates for play when engaging with adult-led agendas.

➤ The role of the playworker is to support all children and young people in the creation of a space in which they can play.

➤ The playworker's response to children and young people playing is based on a sound, up-to-date knowledge of the play process, and reflective practice.

➤ Playworkers recognise their own impact on the play space and also the impact of children and young people's play on the playworker.

➤ Playworkers choose an intervention style that enables children and young people to extend their play. All playworker intervention must balance risk with the developmental benefit and well-being of children.

The Playwork Principles include within them the ideals of relevant theories and are based on the recognition that children and young people's capacity for positive development will be enhanced if given access to the broadest range of environments and play opportunities.

It is important to recognise the importance of risk, challenge and stimulation in children's play, to recognise that children and young people will take risks in their play and free time. Children and young people should be able to experience and learn about risk and safety in their own way. Opportunities for playing should be challenging and free from unnecessary hazards, so that fear is understood and minimised.

Activity 1

Principles of play

Reflect upon your own play practice and setting.

1 Write an objective report about the children's play experiences within your setting.

2 Highlight the factors that demonstrate how you already incorporate the principles of play in your setting. Or reflect upon how in future you can begin to incorporate them.

One starting point would be to develop a Play Policy in order to raise the profile of play with parents and other users of the setting.

You could design one that reflects both the principles of play above and the United Nations Convention for the Rights of the Child, Article 31.

Parties recognise the right of the child to rest and leisure, to engage in play and recreational activities appropriate to the age of the child and to participate freely in cultural life and the arts.

Parties shall respect and promote the right of the child to participate fully in cultural and artistic life and shall encourage the provision of appropriate and equal opportunities for cultural, artistic, recreational and leisure activities.

Play theories

There are a range of diverse theories and approaches relating to children's play, the function of play and playwork. Some of these theories relate play to power and identity as in Sutton-Smith (1997), Sturrock and Else (1998), and Winnicott (1971). Sutton-Smith (2003) also relates play to the emotional health and well-being of children.

There are also those who see playwork as a technical skill, in which appropriate actions and behaviours for working with children can be 'learnt' and then applied in practice. The 'technical-rational' model, or didactic approach is goal driven, in which a 'professional posture is emerging, with reliance on "knowing" as being held by the adult to ward off the fear of not knowing' (Sturrock et al, (2004:33)).

Didactic approach

This approach to playwork rests on the belief that playworker interventions can help children to learn specific things. For example, that playing football helps children to develop physical skill, coordination and prowess, or playing in the home corner helps practise skills needed later in adult life. This approach also expects the playworker to intervene in situations where the child's behaviour is considered too risky or unacceptable in other ways, to teach children how to behave. This is an 'outcomes' approach, assuming that particular inputs (activities, guidance and teaching on the part of the playworker) leads to specific outcomes (developing skills and understanding, behaviour improvement, etc.). There are times when such an approach is appropriate, but this should not be the dominant position.

An alternative position to this, the ludocentric approach, situates playwork in quite a different arena (Sturrock et al, 2004).

When using a ludocentric approach the practitioner works with the play of children. Such a stance requires the playworker to develop reflective and reflexive practice, to appreciate their personal emotional responses to children's play, to work with uncertainty and creativity, to allow children choice.

Ludocentric approach

This approach recognises that play is a process by which children can gain an understanding of who they are and how they relate to their worlds. It recognises that play behaviour is not 'real' behaviour, and that the symbolic frame of playing allows for playing through issues that the child wishes to understand or come to terms with. Adult 'teaching' in this context reduces the benefit from the adaptive and symbolic process of playing when it is under the control of the child.

Play types

Different methods of playing are defined as **play types**. There are some 16 different play types that have been identified. These are descriptions of play that have been defined by various researchers such as Bruner, Jolly, Sylva, and Hughes among others. They serve to remind us of the nature of play, and indicate the importance and complexity of the focus of playwork.

Some of the different types of play are as follows.

➤ **Symbolic Play** – play which allows control, gradual exploration and increased understanding without the risk of being out of one's depth.

➤ **Rough and Tumble Play** – close encounter play which is less to do with fighting and more to do with touching, tickling, gauging relative strength, discovering physical flexibility and the exhilaration of display.

➤ **Socio-dramatic Play** – the enactment of real and potential experiences of an intense personal, social, domestic or interpersonal nature.

➤ **Social Play** – play during which the rules and criteria for social engagement and interaction can be revealed, explored and amended.

➤ **Creative Play** – play which allows a new response, the transformation of information, awareness of new connections, with an element of surprise.

➤ **Communication Play** – play using words, nuances or gestures, for example, mime, jokes, play acting, mickey-taking, singing, debate, poetry.

➤ **Dramatic Play** – play which dramatises events in which the child is not a direct participator.

➤ **Deep Play** – play which allows the child to encounter risky or even potentially life-threatening experiences, to develop survival skills and conquer fear.

➤ **Exploratory Play** – play to access factual information consisting of manipulative behaviours such as handling, throwing, banging or mouthing objects.

➤ **Fantasy Play** – play which rearranges the world in the child's way, a way which is unlikely to occur.

➤ **Imaginative Play** – play where the conventional rules, which govern the physical world, do not apply.

➤ **Locomotor Play** – movement in any or every direction for its own sake.

➤ **Mastery Play** – control of the physical and affective ingredients of the environments.

➤ **Object Play** – play which uses infinite and interesting sequences of hand–eye manipulations and movements.

➤ **Role Play** – play exploring ways of being, although not normally of an intense personal, social, domestic or interpersonal nature.

➤ **Recapitulative Play** – play that allows the child to explore ancestry, history, rituals, stories, rhymes, fire and darkness. Enables children to access play of earlier human evolutionary stages.

Taken from Hughes (2002)

Play as a way of learning

Play is a key approach in the Early Years for babies and young children's learning and development. A baby begins to engage with their environment soon after birth by using all five senses to interact with their new environment and to make meaning of it. Looking, seeing, touching, hearing and smelling become the baby's way of learning and finding out about the environment around them, the significant adults in it, and about themselves. As the baby grows and develops into a toddler and child, their physical activity increases and they explore their environment more through touching and feeling. The development of language helps children to express their feelings and knowledge about their world and make further meaning of it.

The value of play in children's learning and development has been recognised by research. The REPEY project (Siraj-Blatchford et al, 2002) showed that children who made the most progress had been offered play-based learning opportunities with curriculum, social and positive learning objectives and communication skills (Riley, 2007: xxv). The development of playwork and extended school provision has helped to promote play as an approach for learning and development with older children and young people. Case Study 1 shows how play was used by the teacher as an approach to learning and teaching for an older child to write a story. The activity started with the child's play interest.

Tina Bruce has written extensively about the important contribution play provides for young children's growth, development and learning. She describes play as 'a birth to death process' and states that 'play is for life'. Children whose play flows from birth onwards use their childhood as a lifelong resource, rather than 'something they grow out of and lose' (Bruce, in Abbott, Langston, 2005:130, 138). This play-based provision provides a firm foundation for children's holisitic development. Play provides a context for their physical, intellectual, social, linguistic and emotional learning and development.

Play is a complex process, and babies and children engage in it in different ways. Bruce (1991) developed twelve features of free-flow play, which identifies the different ways children play.

Using play to develop positive dispositions to learning

Wayne is an 8-year-old child who has difficulty in sitting down to produce a piece of writing of more than four lines. He begins to write and then will distract other children by throwing paper. He has to sit away from the class to complete his writing around a given topic.

The teacher noticed that when Wayne made Lego models he could concentrate for half an hour. The continual 'battle' to encourage Wayne to write in the same way as the rest of the class prompted the teacher to try another approach, through his play.

The next time for story writing, Wayne was asked to make a Lego model of his choice. After half an hour of concentrated thought and activity a Lego model of a garage with a moving car was produced by Wayne. The teacher then asked him to write a story about the car going to the garage. Wayne wrote a story of one-and a-half pages about how the man in the car broke down on a moorland road, a passing motorist was flagged down; he towed the man's car to the garage at the bottom of the hill. After a cup of tea in the garage his car was soon mended and he was on his way again.

Twelve features of play

1 In their play, children use first-hand experiences that they have in life.

2 Children make up rules as they play, and so keep control in their play.

3 Children symbolically represent as they play, making play props.

4 Children choose to play. They cannot be made to play.

5 Children rehearse possible futures in their role play.

6 Children pretend when they play.

7 Children sometimes play alone.

8 Children and/or adults play together, as companions, or cooperatively in pairs or groups.

9 Each player has a personal play agenda, although they may not be aware of this.

10 Children playing will be deeply involved and difficult to distract from their deep learning. Children at play wallow in their learning.

11 Children try out their most recent learning, skills and competencies when they play. They seem to celebrate what they know.

12 Children at play coordinate their ideas, feelings and make sense of relationships with their family, friends and culture. When play is coordinated it flows along in a sustained way. It is called free-flow play.

(Developed from Bruce 1991 in Abbott, Langston, 2005:132)

These twelve features continue to influence practitioners working with young children and families in the home and Early Years settings. You may like to reflect upon your own play provision using Bruce's features of play.

Activity 3

Using play to engage learners

1 Observe a child or a group of children you work with engaged in playing.

2 Identify one feature of play you observe the child/children engaged in.

3 Reflect upon how this feature helps the child or children's learning and development.

Play within the Early Years and Foundation Stage curriculum

Play as a way for children to learn is recognised in a pedagogy for the 'learning and development requirements' in the Statutory Framework for the Early Years Foundation Stage (DES 2007:11). The six areas of Personal, Social and Emotional Development; Communication, Language and Literacy; Problem Solving, Reasoning and Numeracy; Knowledge and Understanding of the World; Physical Development and Creative Development combine to support a rounded approach to child development. All areas must be delivered through purposeful play, with a balance of adult-led and child-initiated activities. Play underpins the delivery of the EYFS and childen must have opportunities to play indoors and outdoors.

Access to outdoor play provision for children has been an important development within the last few years. This has been influenced by Scandanavian provision in which children use the outside environment as an outdoor classroom to explore and play in the local area. Playing outdoors has developed from a tarmacked playground. Bilton in particular (1998) promoted outdoor play in the Early Years with ideas beyond the playground

apparatus for creating exciting outdoor play spaces for children to engage in.

➤ Sensory gardens
➤ Learning bays
➤ A gymnasium
➤ Quiet seating and areas
➤ Imaginative play resources
➤ Horticultural area
➤ Building, construction and material play area
➤ Environmental and science bay
➤ Play contexts, e.g. garage

(Bilton, 1998)

The following shows how a quiet area can be used to develop listening skills.

Case Study 2

Owler Brook Nursery Infant School, Sheffield
Beside the playground there is a windy path that leads to a Musical Toadstool.

Here the children can sit quietly underneath and by the push of a button can listen to nursery rhymes – and sing along if they wish.

Play, aged birth to three and the role of adults

The significance of the role of play in children's development is well established, based on research, the experience of practitioners, and the fact that children continue to play regardless of the current social and political status of play as a medium for learning and development. Theorists

such as Vygotsky and Bruner have embedded the social context of play in our concept and understanding of the role of adults in supporting development through play. The implementation of the Foundation Stage curriculum (2002) put play firmly back on the map for 3- to 5-year-olds in Early Years settings. This has now been superseded by the Early Years Foundation Stage 2007 which places even more influence and importance on the role of play as underpinning the delivery of all the curriculum. In this section, we will look at children's play and its role in development in the birth to three age group and the role of parents and other adults within this.

Play and development in young children

Tamis-Lemonda, Katz and Bornstein (2002:229) discuss the role of play in five areas of development. These are shown in Figure 8.1.

Psychological	Regulation of arousal, expressing emotions, resolution of conflicts
Mastery	Attention span and task-directed behaviour
Cognitive	Acquisition of information and skills, creative and divergent thinking, representational abilities
Social	Giving and receiving, taking account of others' thoughts and intentions in decision-making
Culture	Means of transmitting social roles and cultural values

Figure 8.1 The role of play in five areas of development (Tamis-Lemonda, Katz and Bornstein, 2002:229)

These five areas of development are crucial for a child to successfully access the community and curriculum of more formal educare settings. Tamis-Lemonda, Katz and Bornstein (2002) also suggest that an infant's development through play depends on a range of interactions with different types of others.

After the first year, play interactions with peers and siblings increase in prevalence and may be more intense and affectively charged than those with mother.

Tamis-Lemonda, Katz and Bornstein (2002:231)

The implication is that different aspects of young children's development are supported through play with different types of people. For example, play with parents tends to be about 'conventional object use and convergent thinking' (Tamis-Lemonda, Katz and Bornstein, 2002:234) based on conveying information about the real world, rather than fantasy or imaginative play, which is more likely to be found in play with siblings.

How do birth to 3-year-olds play?

It is generally agreed that children's play develops through stages that are loosely linked to the child's age and stage of development. Stages of play are far from rigid. Younger children will play at more advanced levels if they are with older children or adults; older children will return to previous stages of play if they are with younger children, or during times of stress, or just because they feel like it. Observe a family group of different-aged children and often they will cooperate in play across the stages. An older sister may play 'pretend play' using small world figures with a younger brother, and then help him to count or understand the rules of a board game. Piaget distinguished between 'practice play', 'symbolic play' and 'games with rules' as the stages of play young children go through. Developing the concept of stages further, Smilansky (1990) identified five basic forms of play, which are shown in Figure 8.2.

Children aged birth to three tend to be involved mainly in the first three categories of play, although many 3-year-olds will be learning about socio-dramatic play from siblings and other older children. Babies are most involved in functional or exploratory play, in which they develop manipulative skills and explore their environment through their senses. This may involve throwing, banging or chewing objects; manipulating objects to give a response, for example shaking a rattle. Effectively, children of this age play

Form of play	Examples
Functional or exploratory play	A baby chewing, throwing and shaking a rattle.
Constructive play	A baby or toddler building with plastic bricks; a 4-year-old making models with play dough.
Dramatic play	A 3-year-old pretending to parent a doll; a 4-year-old dressing up as Spiderman and acting in role.
Socio-dramatic play	A 5- and 6-year-old dressing up and acting out scenes from a favourite film; a group of 6- and 7-year-olds making up and putting on a play.
Games with rules	A group of 7- and 8-year-olds playing Tiggy-off-the-ground in the playground; a family group of children aged 5, 7 and 8 playing a board game.

Figure 8.2 Smilansky's five basic forms of play

largely as a medium of exploring their world and gaining knowledge and pleasure from it.

Goldschmied and Jackson (1994) discuss the concept of 'heuristic' play, suggesting that babies and young toddlers are absorbed in determining through experimentation what objects will 'do' or 'not do' through actions such as putting in and taking out (Holland, 1997).

Constructive play develops from earlier manipulation of objects and involves combining objects into structures, for example building with bricks. In dramatic play, the child is developing 'pretend play' by adopting roles and using objects or imagination to support this process. Curtis and O'Hagan (2003) suggest that pretend play starts as a solitary activity at about twelve months old and is played in parallel with other children at about two years old.

By the time the children are three or older they can engage in complicated dramatic play sequences, which become more and more involved with increasing age.

(Curtis and O'Hagan, 2003:119)

Babies playing

Initially, babies play as part of their early interactions with their carers. Everyday routines such as feeding, bathing, changing nappies are opportunities for play through interactions such as reciprocal noise-making, eye contact and facial expressions. This type of play starts from birth and develops rapidly.

Case Study 3

Babies' play in early interaction with carers

Jasmine is holding her 6-week-old baby son, Sol, on her lap in a café. She smiles at him and talks to him, while holding him to face her and making eye contact. He focuses on her face and follows the movements and sounds she makes with great attention. Jasmine makes nonsense sounds at him and when he responds with attention and movement of his arms and head, she makes more noises.

This reciprocal attention and giving of responses is central to play with very young babies and is an important part of the development of attachment between child and carer.

Babies play using all their senses of touch, sight, smell, hearing and taste. As they physically develop they begin to look at things as well as people, reaching out for objects to explore and manipulate. Babies will reach and try to grasp objects and also push, throw, roll, suck and bite anything that catches their interest. Repetition is important as the baby explores the properties of the object. As babies get older and physically more competent they require opportunities for physical play in order to slide, jump, ride, swing and climb supported by parents and interested adults (Goldschmied in Robinson 2003:114, 115).

Toddlers playing

Through play, toddlers rehearse roles, pretend and imagine using a range of play props such as dressing-up clothes, cardboard boxes, everyday and natural objects. Toddlers use symbols within their play, which helps them to pretend in play situations they have created, and to act out real-life behaviours in a safe environment.

Case Study 4

Acting out a significant life event

Sarah pushed a pram containing a soft toy cat with a blanket over the top for several days to and from the shops and to her grandmother's house. Her mother had recently had a baby and Sarah was acting out the significant life event of the arrival of her sister through this play scene.

Toddlers will increasingly play alongside, and in parallel with, others and will seek play with older children and adults. Tamis-Lemonda, Katz and Bornstein (2002) cite studies that support the view that different aspects of toddlers' development through play are influenced by who they play with, and that play with parents, siblings and peers is important to promote these different aspects of development. For example, language development is strongly associated with mothers who are verbally responsive in play (Tamis-Lemonda, Katz and Bornstein, 2002:237). By the age of two to three, toddlers are seeking play with a range of others and this supports aspects of their development differentially to play with parents.

All of the child's experiences are potentially material for use in play. The toddler may increasingly use language in play to develop the 'action' or play theme. Children's play experiences will be influenced by their access to playmates, parents, older or younger siblings or friends.

Case Study 5

The benefits of playing together

When Dan was aged 2-and-a-half, he wanted a farm in the garden. With the help of his 5-year-old sister, he built enclosures from a range of materials, including sticks, stones, pieces of cardboard, some plastic food storage boxes and huge quantities of sticky tape. He filled the farm with snails and slugs, woodlice and earthworms. His sister's involvement was vital to realising his play plans, as there were tasks within the play that were beyond Dan's capabilities at the time (catching woodlice, for example).

Play in the home for young children is often spontaneous rather than planned. It may involve the child alone or the child and others, and it fits into the pattern of the day. Spontaneous play may result from the child encountering potential play materials or seeking play opportunities with a play theme in mind.

Activity 4

The playgroup

It is morning at the playgroup and parents are mainly sitting chatting in pairs and small groups. The room is light and warm and toys and play resources are set out in different areas, including a table with paints, crayons, paper and collage materials. Outside, one adult supervises several children playing on a small slide or on tricycles and ride-on cars. Inside, Adam, eighteen months, is sitting on a blanket trying to get shapes into the shape sorter. He is watched by Emily, aged 2, who wants to intervene but is not sure how. Jasparl, aged 3, is sitting with a picture book looking at the pictures, although she would call this reading. She has the book the right way up and turns the pages one by one, looking at the left-hand page first. In a minute she will ask her father to read the words for her. Kyle, aged 2-and-a-half, is sitting with his mother's friend who is helping him to build a marble run. He watches her movements intently and then tries to put the connections together himself. When it is finished he repeatedly drops marbles into different openings in the run and watches them roll to the bottom. He is concentrating on the way in which the marbles emerge at different points, depending on where they are put in. In the home corner, Katie and Alisha, both 3 years of age, are 'making buns' using the play cooker and utensils and creating the action through shared language, until they squabble over who beats the mixture, at which point Katie's mother comes over and suggests that they have two bowls so they can both beat.

1 What sort of play is taking place here?
2 How might the play support the children's learning and development?
3 What role do the adults have in supporting the play?

The role of adults in play with babies and toddlers

Selleck (2001:81) discusses the knowledge we now have about young children's brain development and concludes that:

The main message from scientists seems to be that children need spontaneous playful interactions rather than any pre-planned or formal responses.

Selleck argues that young children are the 'creators of the curriculum' and the adult role is to observe and support that creativity. Vygotsky (1978) theorised that interaction with adults or peers at a higher stage of development than the child is central to children's learning development. Children can move from their actual level of development to the zone of potential development with adult support. Vygotsky argued that, in play, children demonstrated their skills at the highest level they could achieve at that point.

Wood, Bruner and Ross (1976) extended Vygotsky's ideas to introduce the concept of 'scaffolding' (see page 145). This theorised that adults can provide support in accordance with the child's level of development. This support can be removed gradually as the child accesses higher levels of ability and becomes more independent in play. Bruner also theorised that all play has rules and that children learn about the social and cultural norms of their society through acquisition of knowledge and understanding of these rules. Vygotsky and Bruner emphasise both child- and adult-initiated activities, with the adult taking a supportive role.

Facilitation and support

The adult's role in play should focus on facilitation and support of the child, rather than intervention to introduce adult themes into the play. This means that intervention should be considered and based on observation of the play to ensure that it is appropriate, sensitive and designed to extend the play successfully (Heaslip, 1991).

It is important that adults are willing to join in play, but that they should not expect special privileges within the play. Adults can make suggestions to extend or enhance the play but should not assume these will be adopted. They can also contribute to discussions on play themes, remembering that children often have agendas that may not be explicit to adults. Adults have a role in providing materials and a suitable environment for play, but children should have choices in this also. Children will choose their play materials to meet their own play agenda. These materials may not be 'toys' or objects that are designed specifically for play, but may be found objects, natural or manufactured materials, discarded items or household equipment.

Adult intervention in play, however, is not always child-centred. Lally (1989) found that adults generally believed that the activities they chose had a higher value than those chosen by the child, even where the adults were committed to the concept of play.

Play with parents

In this section we discuss the role of parents in play in the age group birth to three, and how this role differs between parents according to dominant cultural and child-rearing practices within the family. The impact on the child in terms of learning and development are discussed and, in the following section, related to the child's transition from home to Early Years setting and the wide range of diversity in developmental stage at this point. The term 'parents' will be used to refer to anyone with significant responsibility for a child.

The cultural context of play

Bruce (1991:82) describes children 'wallowing in play' and this is a fine example. First-hand experiences are crucial to free-flow play and allow children to wallow in ideas, feelings and relationships. In Case Study 6, the child's parent is supporting the play by joining in, sharing the moment and communicating his own pleasure in the activity. However, this child's experiences may not apply to all children. Different approaches to parenting and beliefs about play may influence the extent to which children have opportunity to 'wallow' in new experiences. This case study observation reflects another approach.

Case Study 6

Wallowing in play

Calvin, aged two, is observed walking through the park with his father when he sees a river of water running down the path from a recent cloudburst. He runs into the water, jumping, kicking and stamping, watching the silver spray patterns and experimenting with big and little jumps and kicks to see what the water does in response. His father watches and then joins in, creating even bigger splashes, to Calvin's delight. In the end they jump into the 'river' together holding hands, creating the biggest splash of all, whooping and yelling as they jump.

Ankle socks and red patent shoes

The toddler arrived at the playground with her mother, wearing a neat, pretty, pastel summer dress, white ankle socks and dark-red patent shoes. As she ran towards the slide, her mother anxiously warned her not to get dirty. As the girl came off the end of the slide, she twisted round and checked the back of her dress, and then ran to her mother in some distress to report that it had been stained. Tissues were produced, the stain dabbed, and the slide banned. The child got onto the pedal roundabout with other children, and they started to work together to create speed, calling out and urging each other on. Inevitably, the patent shoes dragged on the floor and, just as the children achieved their aim, the roundabout was stopped and the child removed to be scolded. By this time, all the other children and parents in the playground were anxious.

What parents know and understand about play

It is important to recognise that the knowledge and understanding that practitioners have about the role of play in development may not be shared by all parents. Parents may have diverse knowledge and understandings of play, and their personal experiences of play may also be very varied. Parents are often intuitive in their play with children, recognising that children enjoy and pass their time in play. However, not all adults value play in the same way, or recognise that promoting and supporting play is an important aspect of parenting.

Discussion point 1

Parents' reaction to play

Discuss the ways in which each parent's reaction to the play may impact on the child in Case Studies 6 and 7 above. What messages are the children getting about their play and how might this influence their future play?

A young child's family and community are significant in the type and quality of play experiences the child is provided with. The context in which children are brought up and the resources (personal, social and material) that a parent brings to the task of parenting will strongly influence the play that a child has access to. Different communities also have different expectations of children's play and may prioritise play differently. The cultural, linguistic, religious and social nature of a particular community will impact on how often children play, how this is valued by families, who children play with and where they play and what with. For example, in some communities, possibly those made up of British Asian families, older children may have responsibility for younger children and may play outside with babies and toddlers in tow. More affluent communities with bigger gardens and widely separated houses may see less play on the streets than estates with cul-de-sacs and speed bumps. Toys may be selected according to income, so, for example, a child of an affluent household may use computer games by the age of two, while another child may not have access to a computer, according to Sayeed and Guerin (2000:18).

Whiting and Whiting (1975) view play and culture as a two-way process. In their opinion play is affected by cultural influences and acts as an expression of culture.

Bruner argued that play reflects the cultural environment of the child and family and that children will play in ways that are determined by their cultural understandings. Tamis-Lemonda, Katz and Bornstein (2002:240) discuss the 'active socialisation' that takes place during role play and how this supports the acquisition of 'traditional thinking and behaviour'. Culturally specific play will influence what and how the child learns. In this way, play is an important factor in helping children learn in a culturally determined way. The cultural context, however, changes over time. For example, 'playing out' was common for toddlers as well as older children 30 or 40 years ago, but now it would be frowned on for such young children, and possibly for older children as well.

Differences in parental approaches to play are culturally determined. Studies showed that mothers in Mexico, Guatamala and Indonesia do not see value in, or the need for, play with their children, while middle-class American and Turkish parents actively play with their children (Tamis-Lemonda, Katz and Bornstein, 2002:240). The different content of role play between parents and children reflects and reinforces cultural values and influences different aspects of the child's development.

Case Study 9

Attachment and babies' development through play

Play was the focus of a series of group work sessions with young mothers in low-demand housing, all suffering from social isolation and depression, and all a cause for concern in terms of actual or potential abuse or neglect of their children. In discussing play with babies, some of the young mothers told the facilitators that they had no idea of how to play with a child who was not mobile and verbal. One mother said that she 'felt silly' talking to a baby who could not talk back. Another asked how a baby could play as 'she can't pick up toys, can she?' One woman queried the need for play with babies, as they 'just need feeding and changing and bathing until they walk'.

The facilitators introduced the concept of attachment to the mothers, and also the concept of children learning and developing through play. They demonstrated the ways in which babies could enjoy play, and the times when this could take place. Some of the mothers started to enjoy talking to their babies, blowing raspberries on them to make

Case Study 8

Analysis of play activity

Jake, aged 2-and-a-half, is sitting at the table with a pile of Duplo bricks. At the moment he is not building with these bricks by pressing them together as intended by the manufacturer, but instead he is trying to see how many he can balance, one on top of the other. After a while he introduces a colour pattern into the play, alternating red and yellow bricks and carefully putting aside blue bricks.

If we analyse this as a play activity, practitioners may see Jake's activities as experimental, as developing an understanding of the properties of the bricks, and as showing ability to recognise and make patterns, an important basis of mathematical understanding. However, an adult who lacks experience with young children may see that Jake is 'not using the bricks properly' because he is not putting them together.

them laugh, giving them objects to chew, throw and handle. Others found it hard to match their reactions to their babies and became frustrated when the child was unresponsive or cried. Many of the mothers continued to feel awkward and self-conscious in this 'playful' role for a long time.

For other parents, knowledge and understanding of children's needs may be more accessible and there may be positive social and economic circumstances to support time and energy for play. In the example of Jasmine and her baby given on page 200, Sol was responding to his mother's behaviour almost from birth. Within a short time he was tracking her movements with his eyes, intent on her face. When she talked to him and made noises, Sol's arms and legs would wave vigorously and he would bounce up and down in response to her voice and movements. When the interaction ceased, Sol's face would crumple and he would start to cry or he would turn his head looking for his mother's face. By the age of four months he was making noises in response to the sounds Jasmine made and this reciprocal noise-making took on the pattern of a conversation.

Parents may initiate play or support it as it develops. However, the involvement of parents in some form is an important factor in developing play for young children. According to Sayeed and Guerin's research (2000), parental involvement in play extends the length and enhances the quality of the child's play. They suggest that there is a continuum of involvement of parents in play from unaware parents who are not involved in play at one extreme, to very aware parents who have opted out of involvement to avoid interfering at the other extreme.

Within any culture these extremes can exist but a parent's/carer's clear understanding of his/her role and a reasonable level of involvement can enrich the child's play in any given context.

Sayeed and Guerin (2000:20)

During play with their parents, children absorb important information about the norms and values of their own culture and learn about culturally appropriate behaviour. First-hand experiences are significant in determining the play of younger children, and these are also culturally specific to families and communities. For example, cooking within one home may involve using the microwave to cook frozen food and serving it within a short space of time. In another household, the child may observe food being prepared in a much more lengthy and elaborate way. Children in some families may be taken on regular trips, holidays and days out, while others may be more home-based or use local facilities more often. The child's first-hand experiences are basic materials for role play and socio-dramatic play, providing a rich source of remembered images to be used by the child. Access to first-hand experiences can vary significantly, depending on a wide range of social, health, cultural and economic factors influencing family functioning. For example, a child raised in an affluent family with two working parents may have access to a wide range of play materials, but there may be limited interaction between the child and parents if work is demanding and involves long hours. Poverty can affect the experiences a child has, which may be limited by lack of access to affordable transport, few local facilities and no money for holidays or trips. Health problems may also affect the parent's ability to interact with a child.

Approaches to play within the family

The types of play materials and objects and beliefs about the best types of play are also subject to cultural and family differences. For example, gender-specific behaviours are culture bound and may vary from culture to culture. Parents exert a strong influence on their children's play behaviour and choice of toys in the Early Years, and for the youngest children these choices may be made largely by parents. Thompson found parents influenced children's choice of toys by comments like 'only sissies play with dolls', 'girls don't climb trees' and 'boys like guns' (1986:19). Walters (2002) found that girls played with a wider range of toys because fathers, in particular, were against boys playing with 'girlie' toys.

The availability and quality of play experiences for young children within the family therefore vary greatly, depending on many interrelated factors. The developmental outcomes for the child will depend on how play has been valued, supported and resourced within the home, as well as other factors affecting the child's ability to access play. These may include the child's level of ability, character and stage of development. Development will also depend on the cultural messages children learn through the types of play they have access to, and the involvement of parents within this.

Activity 5

Reflecting on home play

Reflecting on culturally specific and home play experiences can help practitioners to plan play and support children more effectively on entry to the Early Years setting. Recognising the wide range of experiences children have of play in the home, and the approaches to play children have already learned will help bridge the gap (where it exists) between home and Early Years setting.

1 What culturally specific and home play experiences have the babies or children you work with had?

2 Design a small questionnaire or interview to ask parents about play in the home.

3 How will this information help you in planning play experiences within your Early Years setting?

Transition from playing at home to an Early Years setting

In this section, we discuss the child's transition from the home to an Early Years setting, focusing on play within the curriculum and the challenges and expectations it creates for both children and practitioners. In addition, strategies for supporting a diverse range of young children in their transition to formal learning situations are considered.

Increasing numbers of children are entering Early Years settings at the age of three. The government agenda within the National Childcare Strategy, to extend early learning to all 3 and 4-year-olds, has produced many more places for children, although access to these remains highly variable, depending on geographical location and level of income (Pugh, 2001). Many parents seek places for

children in order to return to work and to ensure their children have access to pre-school social and educational experiences. Although play has come under attack in the past as a medium for learning and development, it is recognised today as being crucial to the delivery of the Early Years curriculum. Indeed the EYFS 2007 states 'Children must have opportunities to play indoors and outdoors.'

Play underpins all development and learning for children young and old. The majority of children given the opportunity will engage in spontaneous play, although some may require support. The EYFS defines the role of the practitioner as crucial in observing and reflecting on children's spontaneous play and then building on this by planning and resourcing a challenging environment which will support and extend specific areas of children's learning, and extend and develop children's language and communication in their play.

As children begin at an Early Years setting, they continue to need adults to help them to play, places to play and materials to play with. Their varied experiences of play within the family and other birth to three play environments need to be built upon and developed. The wide range of experiences that children have at 3 years of age is a challenge to Early Years settings and individual practitioners when planning the curriculum and developing relationships with each child. Children may find that their play and other experiences do not have much in common with events, activities and routines within the Early Years setting. They may find that they have little to build on or that expectations of them are hard to understand. Children may find that the experiences valued in their home and own culture are ignored or given little value within the Early Years setting.

The Curriculum Guidance for the Foundation Stage (2000:25) required a play-based curriculum of 'well-planned play' that is predominantly planned for children by practitioners. The role of the practitioner in children's play is defined to include:

➤ planning and resourcing a challenging environment
➤ supporting children's learning through planned play activity
➤ extending and supporting children's spontaneous play
➤ extending and developing children's language and communication in play.

The role of the practitioner is regarded as crucial in the Early Years Foundation Stage curriculum (2007:7) in observing, supporting and extending children's play 'in a secure but challenging environment with effective adult support' so that children can:

➤ explore, develop and represent learning experiences that help them make sense of the world
➤ practise and build up ideas, concepts and skills
➤ learn how to understand the need for rules
➤ take risks and make mistakes
➤ think creatively and imaginatively
➤ communicate with others as they investigate and solve problems.

Three-year-olds entering Early Years settings

The National Childcare Strategy, implemented in 1998, resulted in greater numbers of 3-year-olds in group care settings. The Children's Plan (published 2007) intends to extend the offer of up to 15 hours of free early education and childcare to 20,000 2-year-olds in the most disadvantaged communities over the next three years (by 2010) which will potentially create an even greater challenge for meeting the needs of these young children. The wide range of early experiences, languages, cultural behaviours and levels of development that Early Years settings may encounter with their youngest children require a well-planned and considered response in order to meet the diverse needs of the children in their care. When Early Years settings fail to acknowledge and respond adequately to this range of needs, children may suffer in terms of their emotional and social development, as well as their learning development. There is evidence that ability to successfully access the curriculum in an Early Years setting may have a strong positive influence on the child's long-term educational success. The reverse may also be true.

Parents may have complex feelings about their child going to an Early Years setting. These may focus on separation and loss of the special relationship, fear that the child

Learning delay

Lauren was 3-and-a-half when she started nursery school at a large inner city primary school in a socioeconomically deprived area that had a considerable number of children who did not speak English on entry. Lauren was fostered with a family in the area. She had few early first-hand experiences of her environment outside the home and her access to pre-school play had been limited by neglecting parents and an overburdened foster carer. When Lauren left the school just over a year later to live with her permanent family, the nursery teacher commented that 'she never spoke to anyone and she doesn't play with the others much.

I think she's shy and doesn't want to join in'. When she started in reception class at her new school a month later, Lauren was hysterically terrified of being left, cried every day, and could not play either by herself or with others. Despite the support of parents and the school, it took two years for Lauren to develop the confidence to make friends and join in with others. She continued to lack confidence in play and her development of play skills was slow. Lauren's learning delays persisted and her low self-esteem continued to influence all aspects of her development.

---

may 'change' in ways that the parent has little influence over, or that the child will be unhappy. The parents' reasons for sending their child to an Early Years setting may vary. Parents may find talking to professionals difficult or feel hostile to Early Years practitioners, because of their own experiences of education. They may not understand the expectations placed on them in terms of partnership and involvement and there may be resistance to this. Parents also have varied understanding of child development and children's needs and this may influence the extent to which they support current practices in childcare and education. Cultural factors may result in mothers, in particular, not being able to relate to, or communicate with, the staff in an Early Years setting. There may be language differences or perhaps cultural practices that, for example, do not allow women to be with men outside their family group. One school provided a room for Muslim women to unveil for special needs reviews and other purposes.

It is not uncommon for parents to question Early Years settings about the role of play

in the curriculum. The distinction between play and work may be made and there may be a lack of understanding of how children do their work through play. The role of play in development may be difficult to explain and practitioners need to be clear about their own position and the commitment of the Early Years setting to play. It is also important to recognise that planned activities chosen by adults may be described as play but not experienced as such by children.

Discussion point 2

Play and development

1 How do you establish a dialogue with parents in your Early Years setting about the importance of play in their child's learning and development?

2 How do you build upon the child's home play experiences?

3 How do you include parents in children's play in the Early Years setting?

Issues for children

These relate to the match between their experiences and the dominant cultural practices within the Early Years setting with reference to:

➤ languages spoken and conversational themes

➤ play themes, resources and expected experiences of play

➤ expectations of behaviour and responses to misbehaviour

➤ expectations of gender roles

➤ attitudes

➤ relationship development

➤ clothes, appearance, hygienic practices and attitudes towards these

➤ food and drink

➤ exposure to an understanding of popular culture.

For some children this list will also include the Early Years setting's response to developmental delays across the range of indicators including the impact of abuse and neglect on all aspects of the child's development.

Issues for parents

These include all the issues identified for children and also the parent's:

➤ own feelings about their parenting skills, abilities and the role of being a parent

➤ parenting style and child-rearing practices

➤ confidence in their ability to discuss their children's needs with professionals

➤ level of engagement with the parenting process

➤ attitudes towards and feelings about educational institutions and practitioners

➤ understanding of child development and their own child's needs.

➤ understanding of the place of play within the setting.

The parent's ability to effectively engage with the Early Years setting and form partnerships with practitioners will depend on the individual's socioeconomic, emotional and health status, among other factors.

Issues for practitioners and the Early Years setting

These include:

➤ acquiring knowledge and understanding of a range of different children's individual needs and the cultural and social underpinnings of these

➤ recognising the influence of the dominant culture within the Early Years setting on 'success' and 'failure' for some children

➤ developing skills to make relationships with a wide range of others

➤ planning the curriculum to meet the individual child's needs within a group context

➤ planning appropriate indoor and outdoor play experiences for each child

➤ understanding a range of strategies to engage parents and how to use these effectively

➤ acknowledging diversity in a positive and responsive way that does not patronise or stereotype

➤ becoming a reflective practitioner.

Practitioners also need to consider their own views about play and assumptions about the parenting role and their responses to a range of parental approaches. Approaches that are judgemental, negative and critical of parents and children or cultures different to their own can be damaging to relationships and limit the child's experience.

Case Study 11

Judgmental approach limits a child's experience

Di was cautioned by the police and her 3-year-old son was placed on the Child Protection Register after she admitted bruising his face. When she next went to nursery, although nothing was said about the incident directly to her, the reaction of the practitioners was sufficient to ensure that she withdrew her child and he no longer had a nursery place.

Making the transition work

Effective strategies for helping children to access the Early Years setting begin well before the first day of attendance. Practitioners need to have information about the child's needs and play experiences to date, and have time to reflect on what these needs mean when planning the curriculum. Practitioners may also need time to research into the specific needs of a child, where existing knowledge is limited.

Case Study 12

Baby with specific needs

A private day nursery agreed to offer a place to a 6-month-old baby with Down's syndrome. Few of the staff had worked with Down's babies and lacked knowledge about the child's possible needs or developmental pattern. The practitioner who became the baby's key worker went on a short course to widen her knowledge and also contacted other practitioners who had more experience in this area. She attended the child's review meeting, organised by social services, to find out about the range of support services offered to the child and family and to make links with other practitioners involved with them. She also made a home visit and spent time talking to the parent's about their hopes and fears for their child.

Reflective practice is central to the process of ensuring that differential needs are met successfully, and this needs to be promoted through both the individual practitioner's own development and through management strategies and ethos.

Practitioners who perceive themselves within a cycle of learning and development will be able to respond more effectively to diverse needs. Early Years settings need to regularly review their arrangements for the entry of young children in order to improve practice and meet a wider range of children's and parents' needs. Reflective practice is discussed in detail in Chapter 3.

Strategies to help children settle: pre-entry

The following are some suggestions about the sort of approaches that may work to help Early Years settings to meet children's needs before a child enters an Early Years setting. The list is not exclusive, and 'what works' will depend on:

> the experiences of the child

> the type of Early Years setting

> the cultural and socioeconomic context

> the skills and knowledge of individual practitioners

> the management ethos within the Early Years setting.

Strategies to forge a link between home and school need to be creative. For example, a nursery could take photos of the child playing with his or her favourite toy to display in the nursery, ready for the child's first day. A child could be encouraged to bring their favourite toy to play with on their first day. Play items of children's popular culture could be used in the setting, for example puppets of televison characters.

The aim of working with parents and children prior to entry is not just to assess the child and give information to the parent about play within the curriculum but also to establish a relationship with both parents and child and to set up a dialogue about the ways in which the child's needs can be met. Practitioners need to consider the use of interpersonal skills to engage with adults as well as the child, and to establish a positive relationship. This involves actively listening to the parent and establishing an understanding of the parent's approach, the child's early play experiences and ongoing factors influencing the child's development.

Strategies to help children settle: on entry

Factors to consider on entry to the Early Years setting may include:

➤ establishing a play-based curriculum that reflects the previous real-life and play experiences of all the children

➤ recognising the stages of play that different children are at and ensuring differential needs are met

➤ understanding the emotional and social developmental aspects of differential early experience and responding to these

➤ recognising and responding to language needs in all children, including those who have different types of English to the practitioners

➤ recognising that the use of controls may differ greatly in families depending on child-rearing practices and this may influence behaviour within the Early Years setting

➤ avoiding either assumptions or stereotypes about children's experiences and parenting.

Meeting the different needs of a group of children

The diverse nature of a group of children's experiences creates a challenge in itself. How do we meet the different needs of a group of children within a single curriculum structure? How can each child's unique early play experiences be reflected in the curriculum and built upon?

Case Study 13

Traveller children

Traveller children who attended nursery school during a winter layover found that staff did not understand their accent and that other children made fun of them and avoided their company when playing. The traveller children had a different understanding of play and had little experience of indoor play. Their behaviour was described as 'unruly'. The Traveller Support Worker was heavily involved in bridging the cultural, social and linguistic gap between these children and the rural school setting.

The type and size of the Early Years setting will influence the individual child's response and the extent to which individual needs can be met. For example, a childminder may have the flexibility to feed children at different times of the day and work with the child's natural patterns in terms of play, sleep, rest and nourishment. A group Early Years setting such as an independent day nursery may not have this flexibility because of staff shift patterns and the constraints of managing group care with a range of staff.

The factors shown in Figure 8.3 will also be significant in determining the young child's experience.

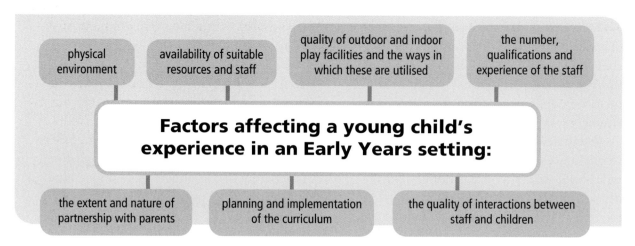

Figure 8.3 Factors that determine the child's experience in an Early Years setting

Play for all

A number of children are at a playgroup where parents bring their children and stay with them for the morning to enable both parents and children to socialise and play.

1 Fazan, 2-and-a-half years of age, leans against his mother's knee, staring at the other children playing. He has not moved to play or use toys or play materials. When the other children come near him he shrinks back further against his mother's knee. His mother has not spoken to anyone yet and she is the only British Asian parent there.

2 Jack, aged 2-and-three-quarters, is racing around in a play car. He comes only to play on the car, as there is no room for big toys in his home or garden. He has patiently queued for the car and will play on it for as long as possible. He does not play with other children.

3 Safura, nearly 3 years of age, and her friend who lives next door to her, Britney, aged 3, are playing in the home corner with the cooker, pretending to bake cakes for birthdays. They are partially playing alongside and partially playing cooperatively, using language to develop their play themes and ideas. They pretend to read a 'cook book' because this is what Britney's mother does at home. Declan, aged 2-and-three-quarters, is hovering close by and watching their play with great interest.

4 At the table, two other 3-year-olds are painting, gluing and talking about what they are doing with one of the volunteer workers.

In six months' time all these children will be in the same nursery school class.

The factors shown in Figure 8.3 are discussed in more detail in Chapter 11.

The challenge of meeting diverse play needs has to be met for all children in order to ensure that they can access a play-based curriculum successfully. If children are not able to extend and develop their learning through play, this may have an impact on their ability to tackle more structured learning activities at a later stage. In meeting their diverse needs, a range of play opportunities need to be provided, including socio-dramatic play, free flow, planned play, group and individual play activities.

Smilansky (1968) studied children in socio-dramatic play and concluded that it supported cognitive, social and emotional development. Children who were inexperienced, or unable to access socio-dramatic play, were supported by Play Trainers in order to help them learn to both plan and play in this way, and reflect on the play. This type of play became more common in these children after the play training. Practitioners need to be aware that some children will need support in learning to play in different ways. Ways in which play can be supported include those shown in Figure 8.4.

Individual children will need different levels of support to access play; therefore a broad range of play opportunities needs to be provided.

Figure 8.4 Strategies to support play

Activity 6

Providing support in an Early Years setting

Look back at Case Study 14. Fazan is on the waiting list for your nursery school and he will be offered a place to start two months after his third birthday. Fazan's first language is Punjabi and he lives with his mother, father and two older sisters, now 5 and 7 years old. Fazan's sisters had quite a lot of difficulty on entry to school because they did not attend nursery or pre-school and did not speak English very well. They are both settled into the school but still struggle with some aspects of the curriculum. Fazan's mother wants Fazan to have a better start to school, which is why she has joined the playgroup and put Fazan's name down for the nursery at his sister's school, where you work. However, she is worried that Fazan does not play or join in with the others at playgroup. Fazan's mother speaks some English and her husband is fluent, but he works long hours as a bus driver and is not around very much.

1   What sort of support could be offered to Fazan and his mother before he enters nursery?

2   What sort of support would help Fazan settle into nursery?

3   What strategies would you use to make a relationship with this family in order to better support all the children?

Play in other contexts

Play in extended and out-of-school provision

Extended schools provide a key way of delivering Every Child Matters outcomes. An extended school works with the local authority, local providers and other schools in the area to provide access to a core offer of integrated services; these typically would include supported study, sport and music clubs.

These will often be provided beyond the school day but not necessarily by teachers or on the school site. Ofsted will report during school inspections on how extended services are contributing to improved outcomes for children and young people.

In order to develop play within this arena it is necessary to work within the Extended School's agenda in partnership with schools in local areas in order to embrace the new Extended Schools legislation and recognise the strategic importance of school buildings in the community.

One way of achieving this would be for the local authority to liaise with the Head Teachers and the Governors of local schools. There may well be out-of-schools clubs already operating in some schools, however these are usually in the primary rather than secondary schools; figures quoted on the teachernet website state that 'There are currently over 7,000 (more than 1 in 4) schools providing access to the core offer of extended services' (press notice 19 September 2006).

Forest Schools

An evaluation of three Forest Schools by Forest Research and the New Economics Foundation found that play in a woodland environment increased children's knowledge and understanding of the natural environment and gave them the confidence 'to develop a responsible independence... and initiate their own play and learning' (Murray and O'Brien, 2005).

Forest Schools also increased children's language development and communication skills by facilitating spontaneous talk and the use of descriptive language through children's freedom to explore and play in the outdoors. The environment inspired children to learn through experimenting with language in imaginative play and encouraged children who had otherwise been reluctant to join in to increase their access to learning through discovery with their peers.

Activity 7

Play provision

Carry out some research in your local area to discover the extent of the out-of-school provision and whether there are any Forest Schools nearby.

Contact the organisations Groundwork UK and Play in Schools (their websites are listed at the end of this chapter) to gather information to enable you to put together a viable proposition as to how out-of-school provision could be of benefit to children.

Play and good health, including inclusive play, hospital play and play therapy

There is a growing body of evidence to illustrate the importance of play and play provision to children's mental and physical health. In the past two years this research has been taken seriously by the government in England. Consequently the need to provide for more and better play opportunities has begun to filter through into government policy.

In 2004 the Chief Medical Officer in England recommended that:

Children and young people should achieve a total of at least 60 minutes of at least moderate intensity physical activity each day. At least twice a week this should include activities to improve bone health, muscle strength, and flexibility.

Then in 2005 the Department of Health wrote:

Recent findings suggest that outdoor play makes a major contribution to children's overall level of physical activity, including playing in the street.

DCMS is currently considering how to take forward work on children's play. This work is in its early stages but will include the establishment of a cross-departmental group to devise a strategic approach to play policy.

Department of Health (2005a)

In 1999 the Mental Health Foundation recognised the importance of play to children's mental health and also as an effective way of giving them opportunities to practise making and consolidating friendships and dealing with conflict. These are basic skills needed in order to become 'emotionally literate', and to increase children's resilience to mental health problems (Mental Health Foundation, 1999b).

If we recognise the benefits of play for children and young people then we must also recognise that these benefits should be available for all children regardless of background, ethnicity, gender or ability. This is inclusive play. However, inclusive play is not just about inclusion. 'Equally important is the provision of high-quality play opportunities to children regardless of their needs and abilities. While children won't always be able to participate in all available activities, an inclusive project should offer all children a real choice of play activities.' (Ludvigsen, Creegan and Mills, 2005)

Activity 8

Inclusive play

Reflect upon your setting – does the level of activity that the children participate in meet government guidelines as stated above? Are you able to offer or provide inclusive play?

If the answer to the above is no, then consider how you could move forward and change for the better. If yes, is there room for improvements?

Hospital play

Play during a child's stay in hospital is not a new concept. Reports by Platt (1959), the World Organisation for Early Childhood Education (OMEP) (1966), the Department of Health and Social Security Expert Group on Play (1976), and the Department of Health (1991) all made clear recommendations that play should be provided in the hospital setting in order to maintain the emotional well-being of the child.

Many hospitals employ Play Specialists whose role is to use play in order to help the child adjust to the stay in hospital and the treatment he or she may be receiving. They can offer the child coping strategies for managing pain and invasive procedures and prepare the child and family for medical and surgical procedures.

It is far more than just a method of keeping the child amused. Other reasons for using play are: it can help to reduce developmental regression, promote confidence, self-esteem and independence. It may also be used to assist in the assessment and diagnosis of illness.

The skilful use of play by a trained professional can assist and hasten recovery and provide the child with a safe outlet to express his or her fears and fantasies. Through play, the child is given an opportunity to assimilate new experiences. For example, when having a blood test the child can be given an appropriate explanation using play and helped to understand why blood taken does not need to be replaced.

The use of focused and therapeutic play interventions assist the child and family to understand the illness, the treatment and the management of pain. (See the fact sheet 'Play in Hospital' Children's Play Information Service, National Children's Bureau 2006.1.)

Play therapy

There is only room here to briefly touch upon this complex and demanding discipline which is used by trained professionals when working with troubled children. The usual route into clinical practice is via an MA in Play Therapy which should prepare students for clinical practice within the public and private sector. On successful completion of the MA in Play Therapy students will be entitled to register as a full member of the British Association of Play Therapists (BAPT), the professional body. There are shorter courses available for people wishing to learn some of the skills for use in their Early Years or play practice.

Play therapy can be used in order to teach children essential social and personal skills using the medium of clay, paint, sand, water and other materials.

Conclusion

There are no easy answers to meeting diverse needs within any Early Years setting. Recognising that children differ greatly in their real-life and parenting experiences is an important starting point, as is absorbing the complex factors that influence the child's development to date. Responding to a range of needs means working hard at understanding and valuing what the child has done, rather than what the child has not yet achieved. Giving equal weight to different experiences and valuing cultural behaviour that is unlike your own requires the ability to learn, apply knowledge and reflect on one's own practice. Play is a medium through which children can express emotions and develop social skills, as well as learn. However, children may have very different experiences of play on entry to an Early Years or out-of-school setting and supporting the development of play behaviour is a crucial part of the practitioner's role in providing each child with a worthwhile experience.

Early Years practitioners and playworkers also have a role in promoting and supporting play between children and parents where this is limited or absent. Not all parents understand the role of a play-based curriculum and settings have a responsibility to explain this to them and to encourage play at home. Developing partnerships with parents is crucial to success in helping the development of play at home and in the setting. However, helping parents to understand the need for play with their children may lay the foundations of parent and child play throughout childhood.

How to move on in your research

Abbott, L. and Langston, A. (2005), *Birth to Three Matters*. London: Open University Press

This provides information about play with babies, toddlers and young children

Bilton, H. (2007), *Outdoor Play in the Early Years*. London: David Fulton

This provides a comprehensive view of outdoor play with lots of examples of activities and contexts to set up.

DES (2007), *Non-Statutory Framework for the Early Years Foundation Stage*. Nottingham: Crown Copyright

This provides guidance for providing a play-based curriculum.

Hospital Play Staff Education Trust
Administrator, HPSET
PO Box 30
Bramhall
Stockport
SK7 1FR
0161 439 5800
hpset@hpsetbates.freeserve.co.uk www.hpset.co.uk

National Association of Hospital Play Staff
Fladgate
Forty Green
Beaconsfield
Bucks
HP9 1XS
www.nahps.org.uk

Children's Play Information Service
National Children's Bureau
8 Wakley Street
London EC1V 7QE
Tel: 020 7843 6303
Fax: 020 7843 6007
Email: cpis@ncb.org.uk

The Children's Play Information Service produces factsheets and student reading lists on a variety of play topics, and can also provide customised reading lists in response to individual requests.
www.ncb.org.uk/library/cpis

This holds a large reference section and information service on children's play.
http://www.playtherapy.org.uk/

Play Therapy UK is an interesting website that provides details about play therapy and various accredited courses. It describes itself as 'The largest and most progressive organisation governing therapeutic play and play therapy in the United Kingdom. Helping the children. Supporting the practitioner.'

References

Abbott, L. and Langston, A. (2005), *Birth to Three Matters*. London: Open University Press

Aries, P. (1982), *Centuries of Childhood: A Social History of Family Life*. London: Cape and Sears

Bee, H. (2000) (9th edition), *The Developing Child'*. Boston, MA: Allyn and Bacon

Bilton, H. (2007), *Outdoor Play in the Early Years*. London: David Fulton

Brown, F. (ed.) (2003), *Playwork – Theory and Practice*. Buckingham: Open University Press

Bruce, T. (1991), *Time to Play in Early Childhood Education*. London: Hodder and Stoughton

Bruce, T. (1996), *Quality of Play in Early Childhood Education*. London: Hodder and Stoughton

Bruce, T. (2001), *Helping Young Children to Learn Through Play*. London: Hodder and Stoughton

Centre for Transport Studies (2004), *Making Children's Lives More Active*. London: UCL

Chief Medical Officer (2004), *At Least Five a Week: Evidence on the Impact of Physical Activity and its Relationship to Health*. London: DoH.

Cooper, P., Smith, C.J. and Upton, G. (1994), *Emotional and Behavioural Difficulties: Theory to Practice*. London: Routledge

David, T. (1996), 'Their right to play', in Nutbrown, C. (ed.), *Respectful Educators – Responsible Learners: Children's Rights and Early Education*. London: Paul Chapman

Dearden, C., Poursanidou, K. and Becker, S. (2004), *The External Evaluation of Nottingham City Children's Fund*. Loughborough: Loughborough University

Department for Education and Skills (2004), *Every Child Matters: Change for Children*. London: DfES Publications

Department of Health (2004a), *The Chief Medical Officer's Report, At Least Five Times a Week*. London: Department of Health

Department of Health (2004b), *Choosing Health: Making Healthy Choices Easier*. London: Department of Health

Department of Health (2005a), *Guidelines Choosing Activity – A Physical Activity Action Plan*. London: Department of Health

Department of Health (2005b), *Guidelines Choosing Activity – A Physical Activity Action Plan* 3/2005. London: Department of Health

DES (1990), *The Rumbold Report: Starting with Quality*. London: DES

DES (2007), *Statutory Framework for the Early Years Foundation Stage*. Nottingham: Crown Copyright

DES (2007), *Non-Statutory Framework for the Early Years Foundation Stage*. Nottingham: Crown Copyright

Else, P. and Sturrock, G. (1998), 'The playground as therapeutic space: Playwork as healing'. *The Colorado Paper.* Leigh-on-Sea: Ludemos Press

Frost, J.L., Wortham, S.C. and Reifel, S. (2005), *Play and Child Development*. New Jersey: Pearson.

Furedi, F. (2001), *Paranoid Parenting: Abandon Your Anxieties and be a Good Parent.* London: Penguin

Giddens, A. (1989), *Introduction to Sociology*. Cambridge: Polity Press

Goldschmied, E. and Jackson, S. (1997), *People Under 3: Young Children in Day Care.* London: Routledge

Groos, K. (1901), *The Play of Man.* New York: Appleton

Holloway, S. and Valentine, G. (2000), *Children's Geographies: Playing, Living, Learning.* London: Routledge

Hughes, B. (2001), *Evolutionary Playwork and Reflective Analytical Practice.* London: Routledge

Hughes, B. (2002) (2nd edition), *A Playworker's Taxonomy of Play Types.* London: Routledge

Hughes, B. *Play Types Speculations and Possibilities* London: Routledge

Hughes, B. (2002), 'The play types'. [Online]. Last accessed 19 March 2008 at: http://www.playwork.org.uk/Quanta/documents/6c%20The%20Taxonomy%20of%20%20Play%20Types.pdf

Hurst, V. and Joseph, J. (1998), *Supporting Early Learning: The Way Forward.* Maidenhead: Open University Press

Kindersley A. and Kindersley B. (1997), *Celebrations! (Children Just Like Me).* London: Dorling Kindersley

Ludvigsen, A., Creegan, C. and Mills, H. (2005), 'Let's play together: Play and inclusion', in *Evaluation of Better Play Round Three.* London: Barnardos. Retrieved from www.barnardos.org.uk/resources/research_and_publications

Messer, D. and Millar, S. (1999), *Exploring Developmental Psychology: From Infancy to Adolescence.* London: Hodder Arnold

Moyles, J. (ed.) (1994), *The Excellence of Play.* Maidenhead: Open University Press

Mental Health Foundation (1999a), *Bright Futures.* London: Mental Health Foundation

Mental Health Foundation (1999b), 'The big picture summary of the bright futures programme'. Retrieved from http://www.mentalhealth.org.uk

Murray, R. and O'Brien, L. (2005), *Such Enthusiasm – a Joy to See: An Evaluation of Forest Schools in England.* Forest Research and the New Economics Foundation

Nottingham Integrated Children's Services (2006), *Draft Nottingham City Children and Young People's Plan.* (23/1/06) Nottingham: Nottingham City Council

Nottingham Children's Fund (2005), *Nottingham Children's Fund Strategic Plan, 2005–2008.* Nottingham.

NPFA. Children's Play Council and PLAYLINK (2000), *Best Play: What Play Provision Should do for Children.* London: NPFA

Ofsted (2001), *Out of School Guidance to the National Standards.* London: HMSO

Ofsted (2005), *Managing Challenging Behaviour.* London: Ofsted

Opie, I. and Opie, P. (1969), *Children's Games in Street and Playground.* Oxford: Oxford University Press

Pellegrini, A.D. (1988), 'Elementary school children's rough and tumble play and social competence'. *Developmental Psychology,* 24, pp802–6

Piaget, J. (1951), *Play, Dreams and Imitation in Childhood.* New York: Norton

Pugh, G. et al (1994), *Confident Parents, Confident Children: Policy and Practice in Parent Education and Support.* London: National Children's Bureau

QCA (2000), *Curriculum Guidance for the Foundation Stage.* London: DfEE

Riley, J. (2007), *Learning in the Early Years.* London: Sage

Robinson, M. (2003), *From Birth to One: The Year of Opportunity.* Maidenhead: Open University Press

Rutherford, D. (1998), 'Children's relationships', in Taylor, J. and Woods, M. (eds), *Early Childhood Studies: An Holistic Introduction.* London: Hodder Arnold

SkillsActive (2005), *National Occupational Standards for Playwork, Levels 2, 3 and 4.* London: SkillsActive

Smilansky, S. (1968), *Effects of Sociodramatic Play on Disadvantaged Preschool Children.* New York: John Wiley

Smilansky, S. (1990), 'Sociodramatic play: Its relevance to behaviour and achievement in school', in Klugman, E. and Smilansky, S. (eds), *Children's Play and Learning: Perspectives and Policy Implications.* New York: Teachers' College Press

Smith, F. and Barker, J. (2000), 'Out of school, in school', in S.L. Holloway and G. Valentine (eds.), *Children's Geographies: Playing, Living, Learning.* London: Routledge

Sturrock, G., Russell, W. and Else, P. (2004), *Towards Ludogogy Parts l, ll and lll: The Art of Being and Becoming Through Play.* Leigh-on-Sea: Ludemos

Summerfield, C. and Babb, P. (2003), *Social Trends,* No. 33 National Statistics. London: HMSO

Sure Start (2003), *Birth to Three Matters.* London: DfEE/Sure Start

Sutton-Smith, B. (1997), *The Ambiguity of Play.* Cambridge, MA: Harvard University Press.

Sutton-Smith, B. (2003), 'Play as a parody of emotional vulnerability', in **J.L. Roopnarine (ed.)**

Sutton-Smith, B., Mechling, J., Johnson, T.W. and McMahon, F. (eds) (1999), *Children's Folklore: A Source Book.* Logan: Utah State University Press

Tamis-Lemonda, C., Katz, J. and Bornstein, M. (2002), 'Infant play: functions and partners', in **Slater, A. and Lewis, M. (eds)**, *Introduction to Infant Development.* Oxford: Oxford University Press

Thomas, G. and Thompson, G. (2004), *A Child's Place.* London: Demos

Thompson, J. (1986), *All Right for Some! The Problem of Sexism.* Cheltenham: Nelson Thornes

Thurtle, V. (1998), 'Child in society', in **Taylor, J. and Woods, M. (eds)**, *Early Childhood Studies: An Holistic Introduction.* London: Hodder Arnold

West, J. (1996), *Child-centred Play Therapy.* London: Hodder Arnold

Wilson, K., Kendrick, P. and Ryan, V. (1992), *Play Therapy: A Non-directive Approach for Children and Adolescents.* London: Bailliere Tindall

Winnicott, D.W. (1971), *Playing and Reality.* Harmondsworth: Penguin

Woods, M. (1998), 'Early childhood studies – first principles', in **Taylor, J. and Woods, M. (eds)**, *Early Childhood Studies: An Holistic Introduction.* London: Hodder Arnold

Vygotsky. L.S. (1978), *Mind in Society: the Development of Higher Psychological Processes.* Cambridge, MA: Harvard University Press

Useful websites

www.qca.org.uk
For information provided by the Qualifications and Curriculum Authority, follow the links to the Foundation Stage section. Includes downloads and curriculum guidance.

www.foundationstage.net
Discussion and advice on the Foundation Stage.

www.surestart.gov.uk
Covers all the aims and achievements of the government's SureStart programme.

www.parenting.org
Offers advice and answers questions about play.

www.bbc.co.uk/parenting/play
Play resources, toys and activities for parents to try with their children.

www.groundwork.org.uk
Groundwork UK is a federation of local trusts working with partners to improve the quality of the local environment, including play space in the community and in schools. Provides useful information about playing in extended schools provision.

www.ltl.org.uk
Learning Through Landscapes is a national charity which campaigns for children's right to good school grounds and helps schools to improve their school grounds.

9 Supporting children's healthy development

Vicky Cortvriend

This chapter is designed to encourage you to extend your knowledge about various aspects of childhood health.

What defines health? Good health can mean many different things – but to the majority of people it certainly means more than just the absence of disease. One of the first published definitions of health was that formulated in 1948 by the World Health Organization (WHO), which defined health as being 'a state of complete physical, mental and social well-being and not merely the absence of disease or infirmity.'

This belief that health encompasses more than the absence of disease was recognised by the government in the DfES publication *Practice Guidance for the Early Years Foundation Stage 2007* where it states 'Children's health is an integral part of their emotional, mental, social, environmental and spiritual well-being and is supported by attention to these aspects' (Principle into Practice 1.4, DfES 2007)

It is vital for practitioners working with children and young people to have an understanding of health and related issues because children develop in an holistic manner and their health can have a positive or negative effect on their overall development. Witness the DfES stance in the EYFS when they stress the importance of children developing an understanding of the importance of healthy eating and physical exercise, saying 'By the end of the EYFS children should recognise the importance of keeping healthy, and those things that contribute to this' (2007:15).

By undertaking the suggested study within this chapter it is hoped that you will be able to:

1 recognise the various factors that can affect the health of children, including poor nutrition, and know how to plan to minimise those factors

2 understand the role of the practitioner in promoting health, including mental health in children

3 plan and implement policies and procedures designed to ensure the safety of the children in your setting.

This chapter addresses the following areas:

➤ Factors affecting children's health

➤ Health promotion in context

➤ Preventing disease and promoting health

➤ Meeting children's nutritional needs

➤ Safety in the Early Years setting

Factors affecting children's health

If we accept that good health is not just the absence of illness, then it follows that there are many factors that can influence health. Hubley (1994) subdivides these factors into three main areas, as shown in Figure 9.1.

Factors influencing health	
Lifestyle and behaviour	Including health knowledge, customs, cultural beliefs and the influence of people in society (for example, peer groups).
Environment	Including housing, water supply, sanitation, hazardous waste, pollution, food production and climate.
Primary health care services	

Figure 9.1 Factors influencing health (Hubley, 1994)

Other factors, cited in the Black Report (1980) but not mentioned by Hubley, are **education**, **unemployment** and **poverty**. This report published the results of a research project that considered the health status of the different social classes found in Britain. The results demonstrated that social class and, by association, wealth had a definite impact on health. People in social class 1 had the best health status and those in class 5 the worst. There was a gradual decline of good health from class 1 through to class 5. A further disturbing point, which was highlighted, was that in cases of illness or disability those in the higher classes were significantly better off in terms of health than those in the lower classes. See Figure 9.2 for an explanation of social classes 1 to 5. The Registrar General's scale is an occupational scale ranking social class according to employment status and occupational skill.

Social class	Occupation
Class 1: Professional	Doctors, lawyers, architects
Class 2: Intermediate	Nurses, teachers, farmers, managers
Class 3: Skilled non-manual	Clerical, receptionists, sales assistants
Class 4: Semi-skilled manual	Postal workers, bar workers, agricultural workers
Class 5: Unskilled manual	Road sweepers, refuse collectors, labourers

Figure 9.2 The Registrar General's scale of social class

This scale, although quoted in the Black Report, was largely replaced in the 1990s by the Standard Occupational Classification, which contains a wider range of occupational groups. There are nine major groups as shown in Figure 9.3.

Class	Occupations
Class 1	Managers and administrators
Class 2	Professional
Class 3	Associate professional and technical
Class 4	Clerical and secretarial
Class 5	Craft and related
Class 6	Personal and protective services
Class 7	Sales
Class 8	Plant and machine operatives
Class 9	Other occupations

Figure 9.3 The Standard Occupational Classification (Browne, 1998)

In 1998, Sir Donald Acheson published a report commissioned by the government on health inequalities. This demonstrated that the health gap is in fact widening between the professional or rich people and the unskilled or poor. The report highlighted a range of areas where these inequalities could be targeted. These included increasing benefits for women of childbearing age, expectant mothers, young children and older people, as well as providing more funding for schools in deprived areas, better nutrition and health promotion in schools. Another proposal was to restrict smoking in public places, ban tobacco advertising, increase the price of tobacco and prescribing nicotine replacement therapy on the NHS.

In October 2006 the then Public Health Minister Caroline Flint outlined the government's radical new approach to improving health and tackling health inequalities as she unveiled the most comprehensive picture ever of the state of the nation's health.

The Health Profile of England shows the full scale of public health improvements over recent years and highlights the problems we continue to face. *Health Challenge England – Next Steps for Choosing Health* sets out public health achievements since 2004 and the next stage of that particular programme of action.

Key findings documented in the Health Profile include:

➤ life expectancy is increasing across the board
➤ the quality of housing stock is better
➤ more children have been lifted out of poverty
➤ mortality rates under 75 years from cancer and circulatory diseases have fallen year on year since the mid-1990s
➤ the gap between the most disadvantaged areas and the national average has narrowed.

However, the profile also shows that there remains a consistent north/south divide with people in the north of England experiencing poorer health than those in the south and that life expectancy is one year shorter for women and two years shorter for men in the north compared to the south.

Lifestyle and behaviour

Ignorance about the causative factors of some health problems is a very real threat to good health. This ignorance is reflected in the way that we live our lives. Children learn by example and cannot be expected to always know what constitutes a healthy lifestyle or what might be dangerous. The EYFS 2007 charges practitioners to provide time to support children's understanding of how exercise, eating, sleeping and hygiene promote good health.

Examples of harmful situations could include:

➤ eating or drinking poisonous substances, for example berries, medicines, cleaning fluids
➤ crossing the road dangerously
➤ not being aware of 'stranger danger'.

In older children and young people harmful situations or behaviour could include:

➤ smoking
➤ alcohol consumption
➤ sexual encounters.

Examples of ways in which children and young people may maintain and improve their health include:

➤ knowing how to clean their teeth correctly
➤ understanding the need to wash their hands after using the toilet
➤ taking sufficient exercise
➤ eating healthily.
➤ understanding how to practise safe sex
➤ understanding the potential harmful effects of smoking and alcohol.

Practitioners in Early Years and other settings have a responsibility to the children in their care to educate them in age-appropriate ways about how to protect themselves and to teach healthy living practices. They have a further responsibility to protect children while they are in their care. This means meeting their individual health needs and ensuring their safety while in the setting.

Our customs and cultural beliefs prescribe the way in which we live our lives; they influence our diet, our social habits, our dress, the way we exercise and our belief in medical practices. In turn, the adults of any culture influence the children. For example, many Jehovah's Witnesses do not accept any form of human tissue as a medical treatment. This includes blood transfusions. As a practitioner in an Early Years settings, you should have an awareness and understanding of the cultural background of the children in your care, again so that you can plan how best to meet their individual needs.

Environment

This discussion of how the environment affects health looks at the impact of poverty, poor housing and pollution.

Poverty

Childhood is a critical and vulnerable stage when health inequalities can have lasting effects throughout life and into other generations. Poverty is generally regarded as the most important determinant of health and also one of the most difficult areas in which to achieve change. The worst health is found amongst social groups with the lowest income or in areas with the highest deprivation. Causes of poverty are manifold and include:

➤ unemployment

➤ poor qualifications or lack of them

➤ ill-health (mental, or physical)

➤ disability and reliance on the state

➤ addictions

➤ crime.

Lone-parent families are most at risk of living in or falling into poverty.

The possible outcomes for children born into poverty are shown in Figure 9.4.

The NHS plans to reduce inequalities in health, recognising that one-third of children under the age of four live in poverty in Britain today. A Children's Fund was initiated in 2001, to be implemented over three years to address some of these inequalities.

The National Service Framework (NSF) for Children, Young People and Maternity Services, was published on 15 September 2004; it is to be implemented over 10 years by NHS trusts and local authorities although the timing and planning of the framework are to be left to local discretion.

The NSF will play a key role in helping us achieve better health and life chances for children and young people. Children and their families will receive integrated health, social care and education services, that are prompt, convenient, and responsive. These will often be provided from one place such as Children's Centres or extended schools.

Charles Clarke, Minister for Health (2004)

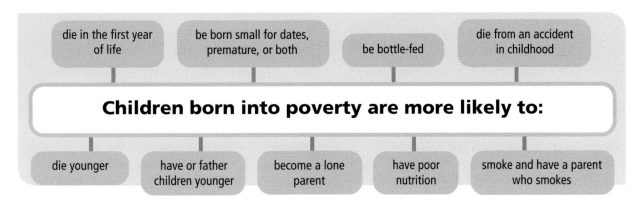

Figure 9.4 Possible outcomes for children born into poverty (Source: www.esbhhealth.nhs.uk/publications/public-health/inequalities.asp)

This National Service Framework sets out our vision to improve the health and well-being of all our children, young people and their families. Its aim is to improve their lives in three main ways: by actively promoting good health, by ensuring that care is centred on the child's needs, and by improving the experiences and satisfaction of mothers, children, and young people with their health services. At its heart is a fundamental change in the way that we think, with services being designed and delivered not around organisations or professionals, but around the real needs of children and their families.

Professor Al Aynsley-Green, National Director for Children's Services (Department of Health Children's Charter for Health and Social Care 2004)

Housing

Access to affordable and good quality housing is an important factor in determining health status. Poor housing conditions include overcrowding, damp, cold and infestations of pests. These all have a negative effect on children's health, leading to recurrent or chronic illness and in some cases hospitalisation. Conditions identified by the Health of Londoners Project 1998 that were directly linked to the quality of housing are shown in Figure 9.5.

Poor housing is often associated with poverty and a variety of other social factors, including poor educational qualifications and unemployment.

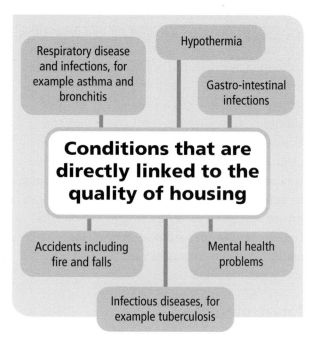

Figure 9.5 Conditions linked to quality of housing (The Health of Londoners Project, 1998)

Access to primary health care services

Access to primary health care services should be the right of every person and child in Britain today, particularly in the light of the NHS plan to reduce health inequalities for people living in Britain. If everyone had equal access, all children would be able to take part in screening programmes (if their parent/carer so wished), which would reduce the incidence of childhood morbidity and mortality (the incidence of childhood disease and death). Unfortunately, there are many groups of children who do not have easy access to primary health care clinics. These include children of travelling families, illegal immigrants and itinerants (children whose parents do not have any fixed abode). These children may not attend any childcare setting (where they would have their basic health care needs met), despite the fact that the government provides five free childcare sessions per week in a recognised setting for children between 3 and 5 years of age. At age 5 they are eligible for school.

Health promotion in context

In 1978, the WHO and the United Nations Children's Fund (UNICEF) sponsored a conference at Alma-Ata in the then Soviet Union that was attended by representatives from 134 countries. A resolution was passed – 'Health for all by the year 2000'. A declaration of intent was drafted, which was designed to provide guidelines for the establishment of a primary health care service in any country. This conference was considered to be the official introduction to the concept of primary health care worldwide. However, even the United Kingdom, a wealthy developed country, has still not achieved that resolution. In fact, the health of children in some areas of the country is still very poor with a higher chronic disease and mortality rate. This was a fact recognised by the government in 2004 when the Health Development Agency produced *Promoting Healthier Communities and Narrowing Health Inequalities*, a self-assessment tool designed for local authorities, to be used from 2005. One of the four main themes of the promotion is to support families, mothers and children.

Health in childhood determines health throughout life and into the next generation. The period between birth and 5–6 years of age is critical. Ill-health or harmful lifestyle choices in childhood can lead to ill-health throughout life, which creates health, financial and social burdens for countries today and tomorrow.

Despite overall improvement, children's health in Europe shows large differences according to age, gender, geographical location and socioeconomic position, both within and between countries. Social inequalities are increasing in all countries, but particularly in the eastern half of Europe.

The inequalities in children's health are unacceptably large, and overwhelmingly affect the countries, societies, communities, families and children with the fewest resources to cope with them. Even in more affluent countries, the poorer members of society carry a disproportionate share of the disease burden.

The European Health Report (2005)

Activity 2

What does feeling healthy mean to you?

Take a moment to consider your own state of health. Do you consider yourself to be healthy at present? Remember that health is not just a matter of physical fitness. Write down what makes you feel healthy, under the following headings: physical, emotional, psychological, social and spiritual.
For example:
I feel healthy when:
Physical: I am not feeling ill.
Emotional: I feel relaxed.
Psychological: I don't feel down.
Social: I have time to go out at least once a week with my husband.
Spiritual: I feel at peace with my soul.

Now write down what makes you feel unhealthy.
For example:
I feel unhealthy when:
Physical: I have a cold, or I can't run for 5 miles without stopping because I have become unfit.
Emotional: I am under pressure from work, family and my pets.
Psychological: It is dark and wet outside, which makes me feel depressed.
Social: I am too busy even to chat to my husband and children.
Spiritual: I feel I have neglected my soul.

Clearly, feeling healthy or unhealthy is unique to each individual. This applies equally to the children we work with, so it is very important that we understand all the different components that influence a person's health. This will enable us to provide a balanced setting considering all the above in which to care for the children. It is also important to be able to recognise when children are in danger of becoming ill and be aware of the importance of early detection and liaison with parents, carers and other professionals. There are steps you can take to help children feel better and become healthier again. This is vital for all children whatever their level of need, including those who may have a chronic illness, physical, learning or mental health need.

Health promotion initiatives

The concept of primary health care that was introduced at Alma-Ata in 1978 resulted in the governments of different countries introducing various health promotion initiatives, designed to improve the general health of their population. The initiatives differed depending upon the specific health needs of each country. In some developing countries, such as South Africa, people living in remote rural areas had little or no access to health care, so one of their first initiatives was to set up community health centres, staffed by nurses and utilising mobile health clinics. The United Kingdom already had some health promotion programmes in place such as immunisation schedules and screening programmes for babies and young children. The present Labour government has recognised the importance and need to provide comprehensive initiatives to promote good health in children.

National Healthy School Standard

It is important and necessary for different national and local departments to work together to provide resources and information. The National Healthy School Standard (NHSS) is a joint initiative between the

Department for Education and Skills and the the Department of Health. Their remit is to support the development of healthy schools in England through local education and health partnerships. Standards have been written to guide these partnerships in developing local schools programmes. A copy of this guidance can be found on the Health Development Agency website (see Useful websites at the end of this chapter). The agency provides interactive websites aimed specifically at young people from the ages of 5 to 14. These sites cover health topics relevant for the specific age group that they are targeting; they are updated on a regular basis.

Welltown, for example, (last updated 22 October 2004) is aimed at Key Stage 1 pupils aged 5 to 7 years old. Children are encouraged by the use of symbols and words to visit the different areas and discover ways of keeping themselves and their friends healthy and safe. There is a link for parents and practitioners in Early Years settings that explains the philosophy of the site and how the activities link in with the National Curriculum. This site would be useful for practitioners to either download information to use with the children during health promotion activities, or for the children to have access to during free-play time.

There are similar websites for older children. These are:

➤ Galaxy-H for Key Stage 2 (7–11 years)
➤ Lifebytes for Key Stage 3 (11–14 years)
➤ Mind Body & Soul for Key Stage 4 (14–16 years).

In September 2004 a healthy school blueprint was unveiled that provides resources for schools to use to encourage children to live healthier lifestyles.

Sure Start

Sure Start advertises itself as 'the government programme to deliver the best start in life for every child'. It is designed to 'bring together, early education, childcare, health and family support'.

The government's £452 million Sure Start initiative, which began in 2000, aims to improve the life chances of children under four years of age in areas of need in England, by improving access to health, family and education services. Again this is encouraging partnerships and joint initiatives to develop projects that will build on existing good practice and link with other government initiatives. Targets included:

➤ a 5 per cent reduction in the proportion of low birth-weight babies by 2001

➤ a 10 per cent reduction in the number of children aged under one admitted to hospital emergency departments with severe injuries, gastroenteritis, or respiratory infections.

Local programmes work with parents and parents-to-be to improve children's life chances through better access to family support, advice on nurturing, health services and early learning.

Local authorities have now been given more responsibility for providing reliable and consistent services for families and children with the publication of the 10 Year Strategy for Childcare, 2004, followed by the Childcare Act 2006, and the Children's Plan 2007/8. As part of the Childcare Act 2006, local authorities have a duty to provide information, advice and training, free of charge to providers via the Sure Start website.

In 2007, Together for Children, a new consortium, was formed to work with the DfES in order to help local authorities develop Sure Start Children's Centres.

New initiatives and updates are being published almost monthly and it is important to remain up to date with the latest information. The Sure Start website is a good place to start.

Preventing disease and promoting health

There are three distinct parts to preventing disease and promoting health. These are primary prevention, secondary prevention and tertiary prevention.

Health education is part of the cycle of maintaining good health. Caring for an ill child is another part of the cycle, as is maintaining children's safety. Supporting children who have been ill or children who have a disability or chronic illness are equally important. These different parts of the health cycle have been defined as health promotion, disease prevention, and rehabilitation.

Figure 9.6 illustrates how each area, although a distinct area in its own right, interlinks with the others.

Primary prevention	Prevention of illness before it occurs	Primary health clinics, home, Early Years settings
Secondary prevention	Treatment Prevention of complications	Primary health care clinics, home, hospitals
Tertiary prevention	Supporting children in their recovery Enabling children with a disability or chronic condition to maximise their potential	Primary health care clinics, home, Early Years settings, hospitals and outpatient specialist settings

Figure 9.6 The links between primary, secondary and tertiary protection

Disease can occur at any time during the cycle; for example, it is not uncommon for a child suffering from a common cold to then catch an ear infection at the same time. This is because the cold virus has compromised his or her immune system and enabled the bacteria to take hold, causing the ear infection. Similarly, a child undergoing treatment with antibiotics for a throat infection may catch chicken pox. Chicken pox is caused by the herpes virus, which does not respond to antibiotics. This explains why the promotion of health must be ongoing whether the child is in a state of good health or not. Children who have a chronic condition such as asthma or diabetes, or children who have a special need, are also prone to catching infections. All practitioners should have detailed knowledge of the needs of the individual children in their care so they can make sure they meet their primary, secondary and tertiary health needs. An ongoing health promotion programme within the setting should ensure that this happens.

Activity 3

Health profiles

1 Compile a health profile for the children in your setting detailing their individual health needs.

2 Design a health promotion programme for your setting that aims to meet those needs. Remember all of the children's health needs should be met – physical, emotional, psychological, social and spiritual.

You can get some ideas from the Directgov website on health promotion for children.

Primary prevention

Primary prevention aimed at reducing the incidence of disease in a population is an important step in disease control. The government initiatives designed to improve children's nutrition, encourage exercise and reduce poverty will all result in improving children's health and, therefore, their resistance to disease. Conditions such as rickets, anaemia, gastroenteritis, malnutrition and pneumonia are all linked to poverty, poor diet and poor living conditions. Eating disorders, obesity, alcohol and substance abuse which are on the increase in children and young people, are other conditions linked to the modern lifestyle as well as to peer pressure and the media.

One proven method of reducing the incidence of disease in the population is to develop an effective immunisation schedule so that babies and children are protected from some potentially dangerous diseases such as measles, diphtheria, polio, tuberculosis, meningitis, mumps and tetanus.

Immunising children against disease gives them the best chance of developing immunity against specific diseases in a safe and effective manner. Babies are not immunised until they are 2 months old because they still have antibodies in their systems from their mother prior to this, which can stop the vaccines from working. Some vaccines such as the pertussis (whooping cough) are better given at the recommended times to prevent adverse reactions.

The present UK guidelines for immunising children are given below.

Babies up to 15 months

➤ Polio – by injection at 2, 3 and 4 months of age.

➤ Diphtheria, tetanus, pertussis (whooping cough) and hib (DTP-Hib) – one injection at 2, 3 and 4 months of age.

➤ Meningitis C – one injection at 2, 3 and 4 months of age.

➤ First dose of measles, mumps and rubella (MMR) – one injection shortly after the first birthday.

This recommended schedule for childhood immunisations gives children the best chance of developing immunity and minimises their risk of catching the diseases. In addition, some babies in high-risk groups are given a BCG immunisation for protection against tuberculosis shortly after they are born. Higher-risk infants may also receive immunisation against hepatitis B.

Children aged 3–5 years

➤ Polio – one injection.

➤ Diphtheria, tetanus and acellular pertussis (DTaP) – one injection.

➤ Second dose of measles, mumps and rubella (MMR) – one injection.

Children aged 6–14 years

➤ BCG (against tuberculosis) – immunity test (Mantoux test) then one injection for those categorised as high risk.

Young people aged 13–18 years

➤ Tetanus and low dose diphtheria (Td) – one injection.

➤ Polio – one injection.

Notes

➤ This schedule is considered the ideal.

➤ The gap between the vaccinations is to ensure that each dose has time to work.

➤ If a vaccine is missed it does not mean that the whole schedule has to be started from the beginning; it can continue, after a break, until all vaccinations have been given.

Other immunisations such as flu jabs and pneumococcal vaccines are recommended for certain children who are considered to be high risk. These tend to be children who suffer from a chronic condition such as diabetes, kidney disease, or heart problems.

Safety of vaccines

As a result of negative press coverage, many parents have become concerned about the safety of vaccines and the MMR vaccine in particular. Practitioners in Early Years settings should be aware of the various issues in order to be able to give parents facts rather than opinions. It is important, however, not to influence parents' decisions but to provide them with information to enable them to make an informed choice.

MMR: the facts

The following issues often give cause for concern.

➤ A possible link between MMR vaccination and autism in children.

➤ A possible link between bowel disease and MMR vaccination.

➤ Articles published about case histories, linking children who have developed autism after having the MMR vaccine.

The measles, mumps and rubella vaccine (MMR):

➤ contains three separate vaccines in one injection

➤ is given twice, firstly shortly after the child reaches one year old, and once more while the child is aged between 3 and 5 years. The second vaccination protects any child who did not respond to the first injection

➤ was introduced into the UK in 1988, and since that time, according to Department of Health statistics, the number of children catching these diseases has dropped significantly

➤ causes some children to suffer side-effects from the immunisation; these are usually mild and may include a raised temperature, swelling of the glands and a rash

➤ about 1 in 100,000 immunisations results in a severe allergic reaction. Health professionals administering the immunisations are trained to respond to such incidents and if treated quickly the child should recover fully.

The suggestions of MMR's risks followed research headed by Dr Andrew Wakefield at the Royal Free Hospital London. Two reports, one in March 1998, which reviewed the evidence from the Royal Free team, and one in June 1999, which evaluated over 100 children's records, concluded that the information available did not support the suggested causal associations. The first report did not find evidence to link MMR vaccination and bowel disease or autism, and the second one reported that the information available did not give cause for concern about the safety of MMR or MR (measles and rubella) vaccines. Further reports have been published by the Department of Health, reviewing the evidence on MMR safety and identified the arguments about why separate vaccines are not considered an alternative to MMR. They asserted that there is no good scientific evidence to support a link between MMR vaccine and autism or inflammatory bowel disease. They state that there is considerable evidence on the safety of the MMR vaccine and that giving separate vaccines would be a backward step in protecting children from infectious disease. They concluded by acknowledging that the final decision had to rest with the parents, but health professionals should have no hesitation in recommending its use.

In the light of this controversy, the World Health Organization (WHO) in January 2001 issued a report that came out strongly in support of the MMR vaccine.

Various studies quoted by the Department of Health demonstrate that although there was an increase in the diagnosis of autism between 1988 and 1999, there was no change in the proportion of children who had been vaccinated with MMR. In February 2004, the editor of *The Lancet*, in which Dr Wakefield's study had been published, stated that the original research had been flawed by a conflict of interest, because Dr Wakefield had been conducting research on behalf of parents hoping to take legal action.

Research into the MMR is ongoing and all details are published on the MMR facts website.

Proposed new immunisations, 2007
Chickenpox immunisations

There is a debate amongst the medical profession as to whether the government should introduce an immunisation programme for all children against the chickenpox virus. Chickenpox affects around 200,000 children a year but only around 100 are admitted to hospital with complications following an attack of the virus. The joint committee of vaccination and immunisation is to examine the new research carried out by Bristol University and published in November 2007.

However, not all doctors are convinced that the move would be a positve one. Dr Richard Halvorsen, author of *The Truth about Vaccines* (2007), believes that before a decision is made to introduce a new vaccine for all children a much stronger case must be made. Chickenpox in children is an illness that causes most children a few days of discomfort and it is rare for a child to suffer a serious complication.

Shingles, however, is caused by the same virus and is much more serious than chickenpox; it is usually picked up by adults (who can also catch chickenpox). One of the concerns raised in relation to vaccinating children against chickenpox is that it will increase the incidence of chickenpox and shingles in adults who are much more likely to suffer severe side-effects, particularly older adults.

Some countries do vaccinate against chickenpox although Germany is the only country in Europe that currently vaccinates. Studies from Japan where the vaccine has been used for 20 years and America where it has been used for 10 years have shown it to be safe.

Human Papilloma Virus (HPV)

The Department of Health has agreed, in principle, to accept advice that HPV vaccines should be introduced routinely for girls aged around 12–13 years, subject to independent peer review of the cost benefit analysis.

Human Papilloma Viruses cause 99 per cent of invasive cervical cancer. The vaccine protects against the viruses responsible for about 70 per cent of cases. Routine vaccination of girls could start as early as autumn 2008 but details of the programme will not be published until details have been finalised with the NHS on how to implement the programme.

Cervical cancer is the second most common cancer of women worldwide. In the UK alone, the lifetime risk of developing cervical cancer is one in 116.

It is great news that vaccines have been developed that protect women against this form of cancer and I am delighted to announce that we intend, in principle, to introduce an HPV vaccine into the national immunisation programme.

The benefits of introducing this vaccine will be felt by women and their families for generations to come. In England, 2,221 new cases of invasive cervical cancer were diagnosed in 2004 alone. In addition around 200,000 women in England are identified through the cervical screening programme (smear tests) as having a pre-cancerous change.

The highly successful and comprehensive cervical screening programme (smear tests) will continue after an HPV vaccine has been introduced. This is because of the gap between the age of vaccination and age of first screening. Also, screening will be required as the vaccine does not protect against all HPV types that may cause cervical cancer.

Public Health Minister Caroline Flint, June 2007

As this is still only a principle and has not yet been implemented it is suggested that the reader keeps abreast of the latest developments by reading the updates on the Directgov website.

Activity 4

Increasing vaccinations

Should we add more vaccinations to the 17 already received by most children by the age of 18?

Carry out your own research into vaccinations including the potential risk to all children if people decide not to have their children vaccinated. For instance, there is a fear that measles cases could rise to the highest number in 10 years as a direct consequence of people not having their children vaccinated. As measles can cause meningitis, pneumonia, liver damage and other problems this could be considered a cause for concern.

Screening

Screening is another method of reducing the incidence of disease in children and young people and of reaching an early diagnosis. It helps to minimise complications and manage the disease effectively. Screening means checking babies and children for potential problems rather than waiting for symptoms to appear. Antenatal screening takes place for all pregnant women. If problems are picked up in good time, then the condition can be managed, or even prevented, depending upon the condition or illness. Screening covers a wide variety of conditions including those illustrated in Figure 9.7.

Midwives, health visitors, school nurses and medical practitioners are all skilled in screening techniques for diseases or abnormalities relevant to the age of the children they work with. An example of a screening tool commonly used by health visitors, the personal child health record, is described in Chapter 4, page 70.

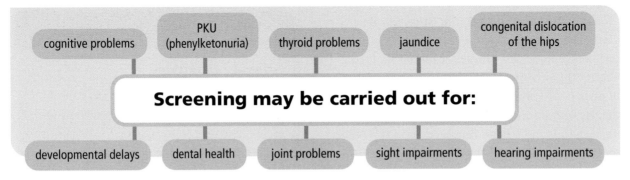

Screening may be carried out for:

- cognitive problems
- PKU (phenylketonuria)
- thyroid problems
- jaundice
- congenital dislocation of the hips
- developmental delays
- dental health
- joint problems
- sight impairments
- hearing impairments

Figure 9.7 Health screening

The World Health Organization (WHO) has published growth reference data for children from birth to 19 years old. The data for birth to 5 years was published in 2006 (see Chapter 3) and was updated in 2007 to include the older age ranges. It covers BMI for age, height for age and weight for age.

Antenatal screening

Standards to support the screening programme in pregnancy currently in place in the UK were published in August 2003.

It involves regular check-ups that will probably include:

➤ blood pressure checks

➤ weight

➤ palpating (feeling) the abdomen (to check the baby's size and position)

➤ listening to the baby's heartbeat

➤ checking urine for infections and blood sugar problems

➤ checking the prospective mother's general well-being

➤ blood tests.

Tests may include:

➤ identifying blood group and type

➤ HBV testing (HBV causes hepatitis B)

➤ testing for conditions such as syphilis, anaemia or the sickle cell trait

➤ testing for immunity to rubella (German measles)

➤ HIV testing

➤ Down's syndrome.

The mother may have one or more scans before 20 weeks and possibly an amniocentesis, depending upon her individual needs.

Practitioners in Early Years and other play settings should be aware of the various screening techniques used, the diseases, or conditions, that can be picked up by screening, and the age at which these procedures take place.

The National Screening Committee makes recommendations on screening that local health authorities act upon. The Child Health Screening Subgroup advises this committee on the implementation, development, review, modification and where necessary the cessation of UK childhood screening programmes.

In 1996 a report was published on the Third Joint Working Party on Child Health Surveillance. This report, by D. M. Hall, suggested that local authorities implement a programme of regular screening of children, aimed at detecting problems in children and using these opportunities to promote health. A typical programme would include a check:

➤ within 24 hours of birth, by a paediatrician

➤ at 8 weeks, by a GP and health visitor

➤ at 7 to 9 months, by a health visitor

➤ at 20 to 24 months, by a health visitor

➤ at 3 to 4 years, by a health visitor.

Details of the minimum assessment programme are shown in Figure 9.8.

Timing of test	Details of screening
8 weeks	Weight Length Head circumference Heart and femoral pulses Hips Testes in males Eyes, e.g. following and fixation/red reflex Head control Behaviour, e.g. smiling Congenital abnormalities, e.g. cleft palates
7–9 months	Distraction test for hearing (currently being phased out, to be replaced by universal neonatal hearing screening) Vision, e.g. squint Hips Testes Motor development Head circumference Social behaviour
20–24 months	Parental concerns relating to: • vision, hearing or behaviour • motor development • speech • head circumference • hand/eye coordination.
3–4 years	Height Weight Motor development Parental concerns relating to vision, hearing or behaviour

Figure 9.8 Minimum assessment programme

Activity 5

Screening

Choose one of the conditions mentioned that children can be screened for.

1 Research the screening techniques used to detect any abnormalities in that area.

2 Design a chart that you could display in your setting that would inform and educate parents about that particular screening routine.

Health education

Health education occurs throughout the primary, secondary and tertiary phases, but is mainly linked with primary prevention.

The DfES considers health education to be an integral part of the EYFS, challenging practitioners to 'maintain children's healthy interest in their own bodies, their own well-being and food preferences, while helping them to understand why some choices are healthier than others' (EYFS, 2007).

The healthy living initiative was launched in March 2007 by the government in order to help families lead healthier lives. Families with children under the age of 11 years have been identified of being in particular need of support. Potential barriers for parents and carers are:

➤ limited parental awareness of weight status and associated health risks

➤ parental beliefs that a healthy lifestyle is too challenging

➤ pressures on parents which undermine healthy food choices

➤ a perception that there are limited opportunities for active lifestyles.

The first part of the initiative is aimed at healthy eating, with Top Tips for Top Mums, an extension of the 5 A Day campaign. This encourages parents across the country to share tips and ideas with each other on how they get their children to eat more fruit and vegetables. A host of practical tips have been posted on website www.5aday.nhs.uk to help parents improve their children's diets and share their own experiences.

The initiatives are designed to give parents the support and tools they need to recognise when their children are overweight and to tackle the problem. Building on existing programmes the initiatives will be rolled out throughout the year and into 2008 by the government and its partners. See pages 240–249 for more in-depth information relating to healthy eating.

The directgovKids website has been developed as part of the health promotion initiative. It is an interactive website that provides activities and ideas to help support the teaching of healthy living initiatives, including healthy eating, keeping fit and staying safe.

Mental and emotional health

Children and adolescents can experience emotions, thoughts and behaviours that are painful, disruptive and disabling. Often these are part of the normal developmental phase that the child or young person is going through, such as the 'temper tantrums' of a 2-year-old struggling with independence, or a 12-year-old at the start of adolescence. However, when these behaviours become extreme or last longer than one would expect they may be indicative of an underlying mental health disorder. The most common mental health problems seen in children and young people are anxiety disorders, depression and other mood disorders, hyperactivity, behavioural and cognitive disorders. They appear in families of all cultural and economic groups. As in adulthood, there is no single reason a child or adolescent develops a mental disorder. However, recognised risk factors include:

➤ prenatal exposure to malnutrition, infections or substances

➤ perinatal trauma

➤ physical illness or injury to the brain

➤ inherited genetic vulnerability

➤ disaffected families, school, and community environments

➤ exposure to traumatic events.

Some of the common signs you might observe that may indicate a child is troubled are:

➤ becoming disruptive in class or nursery

➤ getting fussy about food or cleanliness, or developing eating problems

➤ becoming sad and depressed

➤ trying to harm themselves

➤ having trouble making friends, or finding relationships at home difficult

➤ becoming fearful and resentful

➤ getting into fights and becoming aggressive.

Parents or carers may complain that their child or young person is not sleeping, having nightmares, or wetting the bed again after being dry at night.

The policy relating to children and young people's mental health differs across the UK. Following devolution there are different policy agendas in England, Scotland, Wales and Northern Ireland.

In England, the Children's National Service Framework (NSF) 2004 consists of 11 standards. Children's mental health is included across all standards but standard 9 focuses on Child and Adolescent Mental Health Services (CAMHS). 'All children and young people, from birth to their eighteenth birthday, who have mental health problems and disorders, have access to timely, integrated, high quality, multidisciplinary mental health services to ensure effective assessment, treatment and support, for them and their families.'

The Care Services Improvement Partnership (CSIP) have various initiatives linked to and helping services to implement Every Child Matters, the Children Act 2004 and parts of the National Service Framework (NSF) for children, young people and maternity services. The initiative concerned with children and young people's mental health and well-being is the Children, Young People and Families programme.

For Northern Ireland policy, see Children in Northern Ireland, at http://www.ci-ni.org.

Scotland published a framework in 2005 specifically focusing on children's mental health. Headsup Scotland and Well Scotland provide details of the policy.

Wales set out a Welsh policy document in 2001 describing how CAMHS would be managed in Wales. In 2006 the National Service Framework (NSF) was issued for children, young people and maternity services in Wales which includes child and adolescent mental health.

In England the CAMHS is structured into a four-tier model. It is envisaged that most children and young people will be treated/managed within the first two tiers although it is recognised that it is not possible to be rigid about this and the reality is that some children will move up and down the tiers or indeed be managed by practitioners in all four tiers at the same time.

Tier 1

CAMHS at this level are provided by practitioners who are not mental health specialists working in universal services; this includes GPs, health visitors, school nurses, teachers, social workers, youth justice workers, voluntary agencies.

Practitioners will be able to offer general advice and treatment for less severe problems, contribute towards mental health promotion, identify problems early in their development, and refer to more specialist services.

Tier 2

Practitioners at this level tend to be CAMHS specialists working in community and primary care settings in a uni-disciplinary way (although many will also work as part of Tier 3 services).

For example, this can include primary mental health workers, psychologists and counsellors working in GP practices, paediatric clinics, schools and youth services.

Practitioners offer consultation to families and other practitioners, outreach to identify severe or complex needs which require more specialist interventions, assessment (which may lead to treatment at a different tier), and training to practitioners at Tier 1.

Tier 3

This is usually a multi-disciplinary team or service working in a community mental health clinic or child psychiatry outpatient service, providing a specialised service for children and young people with more severe, complex and persistent disorders. Team members are likely to include child and adolescent psychiatrists, social workers, clinical psychologists, community psychiatric nurses, child psychotherapists, occupational therapists, art, music and drama therapists.

Tier 4

These are essential tertiary level services for children and young people with the most serious problems, such as day units, highly specialised outpatient teams and in-patient units. These can include secure forensic adolescent units, eating disorders units, specialist neuro-psychiatric teams, and other specialist teams (for children who have been sexually abused, for example), usually serving more than one district or region.

Practitioners working in CAMHS will be employed by a range of agencies. Many (but not all) of those working at Tier 1, for example, will be employed directly by the PCT or the local authority. CAMHS specialists working at Tier 2 are less likely to be working for the PCT (although some of them might be), and more likely to be working for another NHS trust (or the local authorities in the case of educational psychologists).

Most practitioners working in the more specialised services at Tiers 3 and 4 will usually be working for other types of NHS trust (such as mental health trusts, acute trusts or care trusts, for example).

As practitioners working with children and young people in a range of care, Early Years and play settings you will in all probability be involved mainly with Tier 1 practice if a child or young person in your setting requires support for a mental health or emotional problem.

Promoting mental and emotional health in Early Years and play settings

Children and young people change rapidly and develop all the time. In addition, they have to learn to cope with many different situations and unfamiliar challenges, as well as with stresses that may be going on in their daily lives. It is not surprising that most children will feel sad, anxious, angry or upset from time to time. One of the most important ways that practitioners can support the children in their care is to have the time to listen to them and provide appropriate responses that will differ from child to child according to their particular needs. Building up warm caring relationships with the children so that they develop a sense of trust is important, as is acting as a good role model. It is vital that practitioners build up constructive relationships with parents and carers so that they can discuss children's needs and share observations with them because sometimes children manage reasonably well in one area of their life for a time, but not in others. For example, they may show odd moods or behaviour at school, but not at home, or vice versa. Should any behaviour that is a cause for concern continue then professional advice should be sought.

Bullying is a common cause of emotional stress in children and in some cases can lead to a child becoming distressed, physically ill or developing a phobia about attending the setting. Emotional abuse of children, which would include discrimination of any kind, can induce fear and undermine self-confidence, again possibly leading to mental health problems for the child. Preventing bullying and discrimination in your setting is therefore an important part of promoting and safeguarding the mental and emotional health of children.

The requirements stated in the EYFS 2007 in relation to children's personal social and emotional development are 'that children must be provided with experiences and support which will help them to develop a positive sense of themselves and of others; respect for others; social skills; and a positive disposition to learn. Providers must ensure support for children's emotional well-being to help them know themselves and what they can do.'

Activity 6

Promoting emotional, moral, social and spiritual development

Plan a series of activities that are aimed at building up children's self-confidence, and promote their emotional, moral, social and spiritual development.

Use the Practice Guidance for the EYFS for children aged 0 to 5 years.

The Kidscape website has some excellent ideas for professionals to use with children of all ages.

Secondary prevention

Secondary prevention of disease is concerned with early detection and prompt treatment to minimise complications and shorten the duration of the disease. Screening plays an important part in secondary prevention as well as in primary prevention. For example, in a child with suspected hearing loss, using the otoacoustic emission screening will determine the level of impairment, which can then be treated or managed. In order for the correct treatment to be prescribed it is important for infants and young children to be taken to a doctor at the first signs of illness.

Health promotion and education are also important during illness. Parents and childcare workers need to be aware of the importance of diet, rest and gentle exercise in the treatment and management of disease. A strong immune system helps to fight illness and will also help the child to recover quickly.

Tertiary prevention

This is when a diagnosis has been made and the child has a condition or impairment that is either long term or permanent. Tertiary prevention is aimed at ensuring the child continues to develop and be as healthy as his or her condition allows. The intention is to minimise the impact of an established clinical disease. It often requires specialist input and services to reduce disabilities and assist the child in living his own individual life. For practitioners working in Early Years settings it may mean adapting the premises in order to enable a child who uses a wheelchair to attend the setting. Specialist equipment such as walking aids, eating utensils, speaking books and sensory toys should be provided in order to include children with special needs in the daily routine of the setting. It is essential that practitioners are aware of the particular needs of each child who attends their setting in order to plan effectively for their needs. This includes knowing how to give any medication that a child may be prescribed (with parental consent); children with asthma, epilepsy and diabetes may well require medication on a regular basis during the day.

Health promotion in Early Years and play settings

Educating children about their own body and how to take care of it is part of both the Early Years Foundation Stage curriculum and the National Curriculum. The 'Keep Children Safe' (2003) document is concerned with all aspects of child safety, not only abuse. Practitioners in Early Years settings, therefore, have a responsibility towards the children in their care. Health promotion topics and activities should be a routine and regular part of the daily curriculum.

At the end of the EYFS children should 'show some understanding that good practices with regard to exercising, eating, sleeping, and hygiene can contribute to good health' (EYFS, 2007:99).

Practitioners in Early Years and other settings are in a unique position because there are a number of ways in which they can practise health promotion in their setting. Some examples are shown in Figure 9.9.

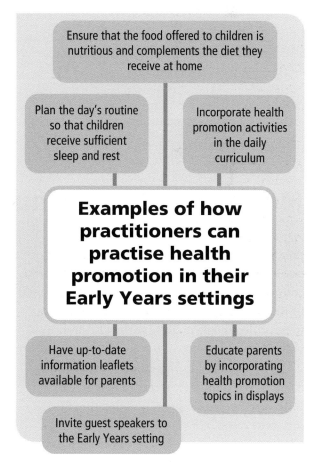

Figure 9.9 How practitioners can practise health promotion

Health promotion

1   What health promotion topics would you choose as being suitable for a group of 4-year-old children? (Or choose the age of the children you work with.) What sort of activities would you do?

2   Use the curriculum/practice/standards for the Early Years Foundation Stage/Key Stage 1 or 2 and the websites described above and at the end of the chapter to devise a short-term and medium-term plan that would be appropriate for the children in your setting.

3   Explain how you would adapt any activities to ensure that all children could take part (Inclusive practice).

4   How would you involve parents in the programme?
    Examples could include:

   ➤   healthy eating: introducing different fruits to the children, or different vegetables.

Include foods from other countries, for example guavas, yams, okra, Sharon fruit

➤   hygiene, for example why we need to wash our hands. Introduce the idea of germs

➤   keeping teeth clean, inviting a dental hygienist to visit the nursery or setting

➤   exercise is fun. Plan an indoor and outdoor sports day with games and sports that everyone can join in with

➤   road safety. Invite your local traffic officers, or road safety team to pay you a visit.

Involve parents by giving them a complete programme of the activities you have planned. Invite comments and suggestions. Invite any who may be able, to join you and their children in taking part in the activities.

Meeting children's nutritional needs

As a practitioner in an Early Years setting you need to have an understanding about what the components of a healthy diet are, and you need to work in partnership with the parents/carers to provide a healthy diet for the children in your care.

Healthy eating is absolutely vital for all-round development and physical growth. Individual children grow and develop at different rates. There are charts designed to provide standardised norms of development to help guide parents, carers and health professionals (see Chapter 4).

By carrying out detailed observations on children and comparing the results with the expected norms you can decide if a child falls within the expected norms for his or her height and age.

Healthy eating for children of all ages has been recognised as a key factor for promoting good health. The EYFS suggests that mealtimes should be treated as an opportunity to promote children's social development, while enjoying food and highlighting the importance of making healthy choices.

Food classification

Food is classified by organising it into groups according to type. There are five separate groups, as shown in Figure 9.10.

Classification	Foods
Group 1	Cereals, potatoes, yams, couscous, rice, polenta, pasta
Group 2	Vegetables, fruit
Group 3	Milk (cow, goat, ewe, buffalo), dairy products such as cheese, yoghurt, fromage frais
Group 4	Meat and alternatives, for example soya, some beans and pulses
Group 5	Sugars, fats

Figure 9.10 Food groups

All food contains some nutrients (nutrients are collections of the components that occur in food). The important point is to get the balance right, to provide the required mixture of essential nutrients that will enable the body to grow, repair damage and fight infections. We need to take in sufficient nutrients to support a healthy energetic lifestyle. The seven essential nutrients are:

➤ carbohydrates
➤ water
➤ protein
➤ vitamins
➤ fats
➤ minerals
➤ fibre.

Carbohydrates

These are found in Group 1. They are our single most important source of energy.

A deficiency in carbohydrates results in thinness, failure to thrive and an inability to maintain body temperature.

Protein

This is found in Groups 2, 3 and 4. It is required for growth and to build and repair all the cells that make up the human body.

Proteins do not all have the same nutritional value so it is important that childcare workers know which foods provide the best quality protein. These are known as complete proteins or high biological value (HBV).

Protein deficiency results in a condition known as **kwashiorkor**. Children with kwashiorkor do not initially always appear undernourished, because they are not thin. They have swollen bellies and a distinctive orange tint to their hair.

Fats

These are found in Group 5. Fats provide more concentrated energy than either carbohydrates or proteins. The body requires energy for all its functions including organ functioning, growth, repair and movement. The body also uses fat to protect internal organs; it cushions delicate structures and forms a layer of insulation beneath the skin. Excess fat is stored in the body as adipose or fatty tissue.

Fatty acids play a part in regulating blood pressure and assists in the maintenance of the body's immune system. Recent research also indicates that they may help to reduce the incidence of strokes/heart attacks due to blood clots.

Fats containing a majority of saturated fatty acids tend to be solid at room temperature, while unsaturated are liquid. The exceptions are margarine spreads that can be up to 75 per cent unsaturated, and palm and coconut oils, which are liquid, but contain a high proportion of saturated fat.

Fibre (cellulose or roughage)	Foods
Type 1 Insoluble dietary fibre (IDF)	For example, bran, found in some breakfast cereals. IDF is indigestible by humans but is necessary to provide bulk to help the digestive system in the formation of stools to remove waste products from the body. It also helps us to chew our food properly and gives us a full, satisfied feeling following a meal. However, it provides little or no energy, nor any other nutrients for the body to use. Raw bran should never be given to children under 5 as it can cause bloating and wind, and can affect the absorption of other important nutrients.
Type 2 Soluble dietary fibre (SDF)	This is digested and absorbed in the intestine or gut. As well as providing similar functions to IDF, it also helps to control blood sugar levels and lower cholesterol levels. Soluble fibre is found in fresh fruit and vegetables, pulses and cereals. It is also found in some dried fruit such as raisins, sultanas, dates, apricots and prunes. It is a source of energy and provides other nutrients, particularly vitamins and minerals.

Figure 9.11 Fibre

Fibre (cellulose or roughage)

This is found in Groups 1 and 2 and is a form of carbohydrate. There are two types of fibre: Type 1 and Type 2 as shown in Figure 9.11.

Minerals

These are found mainly in Groups 3 and 4.

A calcium deficiency can result in rickets and fluoride deficiency in tooth decay (but too much fluoride results in mottling of the tooth enamel). Iron deficiency causes anaemia.

Vitamins

These are found mainly in Group 2. But yeast, meat and fish are important sources of the B group vitamins, whereas vitamins D and A are found in oily fish.

Thirteen vitamins have been identified as essential to health and for fighting infections caused by bacteria and other microorganisms. They are required in very small quantities compared with some others. Vitamins are either soluble in water or in fat.

A deficiency in vitamin A will result in skin problems and problems with vision. Vitamins B2, B6 and B12 are necessary for the circulatory system and a deficiency can result

in anaemia. A deficiency of vitamin C can result in a depleted immune system, leading to slow healing of wounds and infections.

Water

This is found in Groups 1 and 2. Water makes up about two-thirds of our body weight.

Water is required for:

➤ the formation of cells and tissues, lymph, blood and all body fluids

➤ transport of oxygen, carbon dioxide, nutrients and enzymes around the body

➤ the excretion of waste products

➤ helping to regulate the temperature.

Children who are ill and running a fever can become dehydrated very quickly and will require extra water and other fluids.

The body cannot store water and is constantly losing it through respiration, sweat, urine and stools. Therefore, it needs to be replaced regularly. Adults need at least 2 litres of water daily and children's requirements vary according to their age and weight. Should the children be very active or the weather hot then they will need to increase their intake.

Water is found in many foods, for example

juicy fruit and vegetables, but the best source is water from the tap or bottled water.

Special requirements

Practitioners in Early Years settings need to take into account the particular needs of the children in their care when planning how best to cater for their daily nutritional requirements. Some examples of children who may have particular dietary requirements are children:

➤ following vegetarian or vegan diets

➤ following coeliac diets

➤ with food intolerances or allergies

➤ with a disability

➤ whose culture or religion determines what foods they may eat.

Vegetarian and vegan diets

A strict vegetarian will not eat any fish, meat products or poultry. A vegan does not eat any animal, dairy, fish or fowl products at all. Some people are part-vegetarian in that they don't eat red meat, but are happy to eat fish and sometimes poultry. It is important to determine exactly what the children in your care are allowed to eat and ensure this is recorded.

It is possible that without careful planning a child who is following a vegetarian or vegan diet could become deficient in one or more nutrients, particularly iron and protein. A balanced nutritional diet can be provided that will ensure that the full range of amino acids is eaten, by including foods from each of the four main food groups on a daily basis – and always combining foods from Group 1 (grains: carbohydrates) and Group 2 (pulses, nuts and seeds: proteins) in a single meal. Figure 9.12 shows an example of a day's menu suitable for a 3-year-old vegetarian child.

Meal	Suggested menu
Breakfast	Fresh orange juice diluted with water Cornflakes and milk Brown toast, with some low-fat spread and honey or jam
Mid-morning snack	Milk to drink Oatcake with low-fat spread
Lunch	Water to drink Potato curry with rice, dhal, chapatti and an orange
Mid-afternoon snack	Milk to drink Apple Breadsticks and cheese
Tea	Orange juice diluted with water Pizza with tomato, apple and fruit yoghurt to follow

Figure 9.12 An example of a day's menu for a 3-year-old vegetarian child

Food intolerances and allergies

The distinction between food intolerances and allergies is highlighted in Figure 9.13.

True food allergies only affect about 5–8 per cent of young children under the age of 3 and

Distinction between food intolerances and allergies		
Food intolerance	Causes an unpleasant reaction to the ingestion of a particular food. Intolerances can cause diarrhoea, vomiting and skin rashes.	It is not life threatening and may disappear or appear at different times of life. Because the reaction does not involve the immune system it is not considered an allergy.
Food allergy	The ingestion of a particular food causes an immune reaction and can result in anaphylactic shock.	Can be life threatening.

Figure 9.13 Food intolerances and allergies

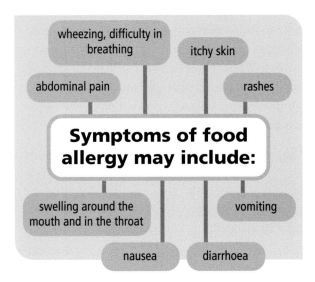

wheezing, difficulty in breathing

itchy skin

abdominal pain

rashes

Symptoms of food allergy may include:

swelling around the mouth and in the throat

vomiting

nausea

diarrhoea

Figure 9.14 Symptoms of food allergy

about 2 per cent of older children. Most children will grow out of their allergy by the time they are 3 years old. However, if a child has had a severe allergic reaction under the age of 3 it is very important to refer to the doctor before reintroducing the same food later on. Among adults, about 1 per cent suffer from an allergy to a particular food. Symptoms of a food allergy can include those identified in Figure 9.14.

Symptoms of food allergy can occur within minutes of ingesting the food but may take a few hours to appear.

The most common foods that cause food allergies in children are peanuts, tree nuts (for example, walnuts or pecans), fish, shellfish, eggs (particularly egg whites), milk, soy and wheat.

It is important to remember that just because a child has eaten a food and not had a reaction it is not true that he or she is definitely not allergic to that food. Children can develop allergic reactions to foods that they have happily eaten in the past. This is because it may take some time for the immune system to build up a reaction to a food.

A doctor can carry out skin tests or blood tests if you suspect a food allergy. If the child is found to be allergic to a particular food then he or she may be issued with an EpiPen (epinephrine auto injection device) and should wear a medic alert bracelet to warn people of his or her allergy.

It is vital that there is always a member of staff on duty who is capable of giving an EpiPen injection.

A food diary is a good method of recording what the child eats over a period of time and may assist in making a diagnosis of food allergy. Practitioners and parents should record whatever the child eats, the symptoms he or she develops and when they develop, to enable them to share this with the child's GP or paediatrician.

Children who have physical or learning difficulties

Eating independently requires physical coordination, social skills and cognitive ability. Where one or more of these areas is challenged then the child may have difficulty in eating and, therefore, requires help in order to have a balanced diet. This cannot be achieved in isolation so the practitioner in an Early Years setting needs to work in conjunction with the child's parents and other professionals such as a dietician, paediatrician and health visitor.

A portage programme may be planned to suit the child's individual needs. Portage originated in America in the 1960s and arrived in England in the 1970s. It consists of developmental tasks and skills put together in an individual programme worked out to meet the needs of the child. It aims to support the children in a way that builds upon the child's strengths. The specially trained portage worker works with the child, parents and other helpers in the home and the setting to support the child in achieving the tasks.

Note: A portage programme does not necessarily have to do with nutrition per se. It could be for developmental delay, either physical or cognitive. However, whatever the need, it will have an effect on the child's ability to receive a balanced diet, which is why a portage programme should help meet the child's nutritional needs.

There is a National Portage Association (NPA) which operates at national and regional level throughout the UK supporting individual members and registered services.

Figure 9.15 illustrates a portage record chart.

Note: Any portage service registered with the National Portage Association should be offering support based on the following characteristics.

➤ Assisting the development of play, communication, relationships and learning for very young children within the family.

➤ Assisting the child and family's participation and inclusion in the community in their own right.

➤ Working together with parents within the family with them taking the leading role in the partnership that is established.

➤ Helping parents identify what is important to them and their child and plan goals for learning and participation.

➤ Responding flexibly to the needs of the child and family when providing support.

➤ Portage home visitors accessing support through regular team meetings, on behalf of the family they work with.

National Portage Association Information Leaflet

Age level	Card	Skill/behaviour	Entry skill/ behaviour	Date achieved	Comments
0 to 1	1	Sucks and swallows liquid			
	2	Eats liquefied food when fed			
	3	Eats strained food when fed			
	4	Eats mashed food when fed			
	5	Eats semi-solid food when fed			
	6	Feeds self with finger foods			
	7	With help, takes spoon filled with food to mouth			
1 to 2	8	Uses spoon independently			
2 to 3	9	Feeds self from spoon and cup			
	10	Begins to use fork to feed self			
	11	Uses fork and spoon independently			

Figure 9.15 Example of portage record chart

In September 2002 the SEN and Disability Act access rights came into force. The legislation, for the first time, gives disabled pupils and students wide-ranging rights within the mainstream education system. It affects LEAs, schools, Early Years, as well as youth services and further and higher education. Educational institutions are under a duty not to treat disabled people less favourably and to make certain types of reasonable adjustment to ensure disabled pupils and students are not at a substantial disadvantage.

Portage is one method of supporting inclusive practice. For younger children there is a portage home visiting programme as part of the Sure Start programme. The extent of this provision in England in 2005 was that there were 152 NPA registered portage services in England in 2004/5 with a total of 1194 portage home visitors providing support for 5,370 families through home visits and other related activities. (NPA report Nov 2005). Tameside is one local authority that has a thriving portage service.

The last figures published in 2005 show that portage was found to be available to less than 8 per cent of children under 3 who are estimated to be eligible and there has been little increase in the number of portage services and children supported since a previous survey in 1992/3 (Kiernan 1993).

Multicultural and religious aspects

Practitioners in Early Years settings must respect the culture and beliefs of the children in their care. The following recommendations and menus give the key points and ideas for meals, in relation to the main cultures found in society. This is a very broad outline; there is a wide range of diverse cultures and beliefs in society and it is of the utmost importance that each child's beliefs are upheld and that the Early Years setting provides a balanced diet in accordance with what the child is allowed to eat. Practitioners have a responsibility to liaise with the child's parents to ensure that they are fully aware of any dietary restrictions and that the setting complies with the parents' wishes. This information should be shared with the rest of the team and the cook so that no mistakes are made. The information should also be recorded on the child's records. Examples of the dietary requirements of some religious faiths are shown in Figure 9.16. Obviously, these may vary from person to person.

An example of a suitable menu for children with special dietary requirements is shown in Figure 9.17.

Activity 9

Portage programmes

1 Research portage programmes in local Early Years settings and local paediatric units or child health clinics. Describe different uses for portage citing examples from your research.

2 List the advantages of such a programme for
   – the child
   – the parent
   – the childcare worker.

3 Devise a portage programme for a child in your setting who you consider would benefit from such input.

Religion	Dietary requirements of adherents
Hinduism and Sikhism	Strict followers do not eat eggs, meat, fish and some fats.
Islam	Do eat meat, except for pork, but it must be Halal.
Rastafarianism	Some are vegan.
Jainism	Do have restrictions on some vegetable dishes.
Buddhism	Do not eat meat or poultry, but some eat fish except for shellfish. Also do not eat butter, ghee or lard.
Judaism	Do not eat meat with milk or cheese products. The meat eaten must be Kosher. Only fish with fins and scales is eaten; pork, shellfish and lard are not eaten. Separate utensils are used for meat and dairy products.

Figure 9.16 Religion and diet

Menu for a 4-year-old child in a daycare setting	
Mid-morning snack	Milk, scone and margarine
Lunch	Baked sweet potato, rice and peas, spinach Pineapple to follow
Mid-afternoon snack	Milk, banana, plain popcorn
Tea	Orange juice diluted with water Pasta, cheese sauce and sweetcorn Mandarin orange to follow
Drinks offered with meals or when thirsty could be water, milk, goat or soya milk, diluted fresh fruit juice.	

Figure 9.17 A menu for children with special dietary requirements

Children have different nutritional requirements according to their age, gender, and also differing needs. The Caroline Walker Trust (dedicated to the improvement of public health through good food) in 1998 commissioned an expert working group to research nutritional guidelines for practitioners in Early Years settings working with children under the age of 5 years. This report, *Eating Well for Under-Fives in Child Care*, explains why nutritional guidelines are required and describes how practitioners can ensure the children in their care have a healthy diet.

Offer alternative lunchtime options such as vegetable and chicken curry, shepherd's pie, lamb stew, fish fingers and other home-cooked main meals. Puddings such as fresh fruit crumbles and pies, rice pudding and fresh fruit jellies are all nutritious options.

A useful reminder that provides a nutritional daily guide for Early Years practitioners, and which can be adapted for educating children of appropriate age, is the Food is Fun pyramid on page 248.

Food is fun
Healthy eating helps you
work, rest and play

3 servings

2 servings

2 servings

2 servings

6 servings

The Food is Fun pyramid helps children and parents to understand how to ensure a balanced diet

Meeting all children's dietary needs

Imagine that you are the manager of a busy private day nursery. Children arrive from 7 am and some don't leave until 6 pm. An important part of your role is to ensure that the nutritional needs of all the children in your care are met. You have received application forms from four new families requesting full daycare for their children. Their ages range from 1 year to 4 years. The 1-year-old has a diagnosed milk and egg allergy, while the other three are all members of the Hindu faith, one being a strict Hindu. Their parents have requested a meeting to discuss their individual dietary needs.

1 How will you ensure you meet these children's needs as well as the other children in the setting?

2 What precautions should you take for the child with allergies?

3 Plan a menu for a week that will meet all their nutritional needs and that you could share with the parents to allay any fears they may have.

Common childhood illnesses

Illness in infants and young children is inevitable. There is a school of thought that we are becoming so overprotective and 'over hygienic' that our babies and young children are not being allowed to come into contact with dirt and germs that would help them to build up a strong immune system. There may be some merit in this argument and apart from helping to build a strong and effective immune system, playing in dirt and mud is good fun! See Figure 9.18 for some details of chronic and acute illnesses in children.

Children should not be in an Early Years setting if they are unwell, but sometimes a child may run a slight temperature when teething, or when suffering from a slight cold. If after three days there is no improvement then the child should be cared for at home and medical attention sought. In the majority of cases there will be no lasting after-effects.

General signs and symptoms of illness

Practitioners in Early Years settings need to know the general signs and symptoms of illness in children and, in particular, any

Childhood illnesses		
Chronic	Juvenile arthritis, epilepsy, progeria, cystic fibrosis	Long-term illnesses or conditions that can be terminal.
Acute	Measles, mumps, chickenpox, flu, gastroenteritis	Last for only a short time. While the child is incubating the illness, he or she may be lethargic, fractious, clingy and have little appetite. During this period, the parent may remark that the child is 'off colour' or 'sickening for something.'

Figure 9.18 Chronic and acute illnesses in children

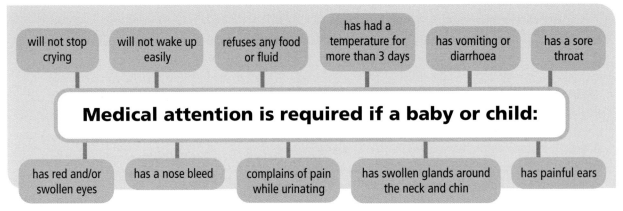

Figure 9.19 Symptoms in a baby or child that require you to seek medical attention

danger signs that would require immediate medical attention. The practitioner needs to use common sense when dealing with sick children in his or her care.

➤ There should be a set of policies and procedures in place to cover such issues as a child being taken ill while at the setting, the giving of medicine and first aid.

➤ There should be regular in-service training for staff to update them on any changes to the policies.

➤ There should be a room, or quiet place, where children can rest until a parent or carer can collect them.

➤ It is important to keep children warm (not hot) and dry, and give plenty of fluids, especially if they have sickness and diarrhoea.

➤ They should be kept amused and distracted with stories and quiet activities.

➤ They should not be left on their own.

➤ A record should be kept of when the child began to feel ill, or when the Early Years practitioner first became worried. Any signs and symptoms, (including behavioural changes), what food or fluid was taken by the child and whether the child vomited, had diarrhoea or urinated, should be carefully recorded. These notes should be entered in the child's records and shared with the parent or doctor. Medical attention is required if a baby or child has any of the symptoms shown in Figure 9.19.

Should the child have any of the symptoms shown in Figure 9.20 then a doctor should be called immediately.

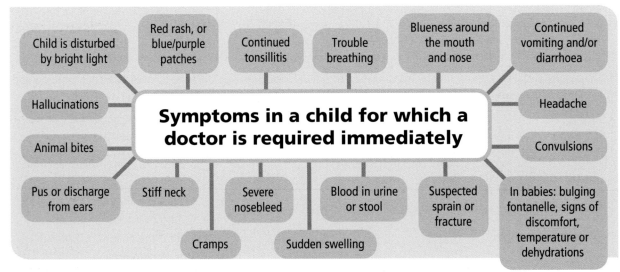

Figure 9.20 Symptoms requiring immediate medical attention for a child

In addition if you are at all worried about the health of a child or baby in your care then you need to seek medical advice and inform the parents or carer.

Fevers, febrile convulsions/fits

The normal body temperature is between 36°C and 36.8°C (97.7°F and 99.1°F). A fever or high temperature is the body's defence mechanism against infection. The body tries to kill the organism causing the infection or illness by creating heat. Children's temperatures can rise and fall very quickly because their temperature control in the brain is not yet fully developed. They can also suffer from convulsions or fits caused by this sudden change in temperature. One in 20 children can be affected between the ages of 1 and 4 years of age. But children as young as 6 months can suffer from febrile convulsions, as can children as old as 5 years.

If a child has a high temperature they need more fluid than usual, rest and sleep. Parents should seek advice from a doctor or pharmacist regarding the best medication to use and the correct dosage. Practitioners in Early Years settings should follow the policy regarding the giving of medicines in their setting. This should explain the procedure to be followed when a child requires medication.

Notifiable diseases

There are some diseases that are designated as notifiable. This means that it is a statutory requirement under the Public Health (Control of Disease) Act 1984 and in the Public Health (Infectious Diseases) Regulations 1988 for doctors to notify a 'Proper Officer' of the local authority, usually the Consultant in Communicable Disease Control of cases of certain infectious diseases. Should any of the children in your care develop symptoms of any of these diseases then you must inform a doctor and the parents immediately. Practitioners in Early Years settings should develop a procedure to explain how to manage this eventuality. The procedure should cover exclusion from the nursery and state how long the child should be excluded for. The procedure could be included in a general illness procedure, covering all instances when a child should be sent home, seen by a doctor, or excluded until the infection is clear. Alternatively, there could be a separate procedure or appendix to cover notifiable diseases. These procedures should be part of the setting's health and safety policy.

Notifiable diseases in England and Wales

- Acute encephalitis
- Acute poliomyelitis
- Anthrax
- Cholera
- Diphtheria
- Dysentery (amoebicor bacillary)
- Food poisoning
- Leprosy
- Leptospirosis
- Malaria
- Measles
- Meningitis
- Meningococcal septicemia (without meningitis)
- Mumps
- Ophthalmia neonatorum
- Paratyphoid fever
- Plague
- Rabies
- Relapsing fever
- Rubella
- Scarlet fever
- Smallpox
- Tetanus
- Tuberculosis
- Typhoid fever
- Typhus
- Viral haemorrhagic fever
- Viral hepatitis
- Whooping cough
- Yellow fever

Although AIDS is not a notifiable disease, certain powers can be applied to people with AIDS under regulations issued in 1985. Doctors are urged to report HIV infections and AIDS cases to the voluntary confidential surveillance schemes at CDSC (Communicable Disease Surveillance Centre).

Infection from animals

Playing with and owning pets is, on the whole, a positive experience for children. Hamsters, mice, chipmunks and chinchillas are small and

Illness	Cause	Symptoms	Prevention
Toxocariasis	Roundworm in dog and cat faeces	Allergic symptoms (rarely) blindness	Ensure play areas are clean Ensure children wash their hands after touching dogs or cats
Ringworm	A fungal infection of the skin caught from infected children, cats or dogs	Round, red itchy area	Treat with prescribed cream Do not allow child to touch infected areas
Fleabites	Fleas are usually found on cats or dogs	Small, round, red lumps	Cream, prescribed by GP or pharmacist

Figure 9.21 Some illnesses that can be caught from animals

easy to care for within an Early Years setting. Looking after them is a good way of teaching children about responsibility for animals. Maintaining hygiene and preventing infection is largely a matter of good sense and may be achieved by observing the following.

➤ Ensure that the children do not go near the animals on their own.

➤ Ensure children wash their hands after touching animals.

➤ Ensure that a child with an allergy to pet fur does not go too near to the cage.

➤ Don't allow pets to lick the children.

➤ Ensure faeces are cleared away immediately.

➤ As cats and dogs could foul the outside areas of the setting, take care not to allow children to play outside until the area has been thoroughly checked and cleaned.

➤ Always act in accordance with parents' wishes in all matters including playing with animals.

Figure 9.21 shows some illnesses that can be caught from animals.

Safety in the Early Years setting

Keeping children safe

Keeping Children Safe (2003) and the Green Paper *Every Child Matters* (2003) set out the government's proposals for reforming the delivery of services for children, young people and families. Children and young people, when consulted during this inquiry, considered that being healthy and staying safe were among the five outcomes that mattered most to them. Professionals in Early Years settings can, through planning for children's effective care and education, help them to achieve those two outcomes. This will then support children in enabling them to fulfil their potential. The Children Act 2004 part 2 section 11 provides

the legal underpinning for the Every Child Matters document in relation to 'arrangements to safeguard and promote welfare'.

The Childcare Act 2006 (previously the Childcare Bill) guarantees accessible, high quality childcare and other services for children under five and gives parents greater choice in balancing work and family. It places responsibility for childcare provision with local authorities and is mentioned here because keeping children safe within childcare provision is part of maintaining good health. (See Chapter 13 for more information pertaining to the Childcare Act 2006 and the Children Act 2004.)

National standards for childcare

The Health and Safety at Work Act 1974 is still the main piece of legislation giving general guidance about health and safety. The Management of Health and Safety at Work Regulations 1992 (the Management Regulations) generally make more explicit what employers are required to do to manage health and safety under the Health and Safety at Work Act. Like the Act, they apply to every work activity.

Several regulations have been passed since the introduction of the Act, designed to bring the United Kingdom into line with European laws. These are:

➤ the Control of Substances Hazardous to Health Regulations1994 (COSHH)

➤ the Health and Safety (First Aid) Regulations 1981

➤ Reporting of Injuries, Disease and Dangerous Occurrences Regulations 1995 (RIDDOR)

➤ the Regulatory Reform (Fire Safety) Order 2005

➤ the Food Handling Regulations 1995.

The National Standards for Child Care 2001 and the Practice Guidance for the Early Years Foundation Stage 2007 explain in detail what Early Years settings need to do in order to comply with the above regulations, and to ensure good practice and quality care.

The Office For Standards in Education (Ofsted) and the Department for Education and Skills (DfES) have produced publications that explain the National Standards that providers of childcare and education should aim to achieve. There are different publications for different childcare settings; they include full daycare, out-of-school care, sessional care, crèches and child minders.

Ofsted expects providers to demonstrate how they achieve each of the standards and the guides have been produced in order to help them do this.

Chapter 2 of the new Children's Plan 2007 is titled 'Safe and Sound' and describes the government's commitment to safeguarding the young and vulnerable.

Keeping children and young people safe from harm must be the priority and responsibility of us all. However, children need also to be able to learn, have new experiences and enjoy their childhoods, so we will help families strike the right balance between keeping children safe and allowing them the freedom they need. So we will:

- *publish Dr Tanya Byron's review on the potential risks to children from exposure to harmful or inappropriate content on the internet and in video games [now published]*
- *commission an independent assessment of the impact of the commercial world on children's well-being*
- *fund a new home safety equipment scheme to prevent the accidents which happen to young children in the home*
- *encourage local authorities to create 20mph zones, where appropriate, because they can reduce child pedestrian deaths by 70 per cent*
- *strengthen the complaints procedure for parents whose children experience bullying.*

Government also has a responsibility to put in place the right frameworks and systems for safeguarding children and young people, working in partnership with key national and local organisations and so we will:

- *publish the Staying Safe Action Plan in early 2008, responding to the Staying Safe consultation*
- *ensure that schools and local authorities take a proportionate approach to health and safety to allow children to take risks.*

Children's Plan (2007)

A health and safety policy should include the various procedures necessary to ensure that the health and safety needs of all children in the setting are met. The relevant standards in relation to health and safety in the setting, which can be used to help formulate some policies and procedures, are discussed below.

Safety

The standards suggest carrying out a risk assessment in order to identify hazards inside and outside the Early Years setting. Security is an important factor today, not just ensuring that the children remain on the premises, but also keeping unwanted people out. Are outside areas secure? What is the general security of the building like? Other points to consider under safety include questions about potentially hazardous areas. Are there any:

- poisonous plants or bulbs on the premises
- hazardous shrubs or trees
- water features
- outdoor play areas?

Fire safety

A statement of the procedures to be followed in the event of fire must be kept. It would also be a good idea to have an evacuation procedure that could be followed in the event of a terrorist attack or other disaster.

Health

This standard covers hygiene practices, aimed at reducing the spread of infection and maintaining the cleanliness of the premises. Smoking, animals in the setting, sandpits, food handling and medicine are all included. Procedures should be in place to inform staff on how to manage and work with those issues. The standards state that non-prescription medication may be administered to children in daycare, but only with the prior written consent of the parent and only when there is a health reason to do so. Blanket consent should not be given by the parent to cover all non-prescription medicine.

This standard also covers first aid in the setting, and sick children. In this section it mentions the care of the sick child while awaiting collection and contingency arrangements that should be in place if the parents cannot be contacted, or cannot collect a sick child. The setting's procedures should state when to seek medical advice and what to do in the case of infectious, notifiable and communicable diseases. The Children Act regulations state that you must notify Ofsted of any infectious disease that a qualified medical person considers notifiable.

Activity 11

Risk assessment

1 With regard to the above information relating to illness and safety, carry out a risk assessment of your setting. Then design a set of procedures to minimise or remove those risks.

2 Describe how you would ensure the safety of the children and staff once they were in the setting.

3 Did you include procedures to cover both the sick child and excluding a child from the setting: when ill, or if suffering from a notifiable disease? Did you cover accident procedure, giving of medicine, animal care, evacuation procedures, record of visitors, procedures for the safe collection and arrival of children and outings?

4 The following are all effective methods of improving security and ensuring the safety of children and staff: monitoring access to the Early Years setting, use of a visitor's book, seeking advice from a crime prevention officer, making arrangements for answering the door, the use of security systems (including locks, alarms, intercoms and cameras), up-to-date CRB checks on all people who work in the Early Years setting (including parents and students).

Accidents

Childhood injury has overtaken infectious disease as the main source of death in young children in the United Kingdom. Road accidents, or transport-related deaths, are the commonest cause of accidental death at all ages, apart from in the 0–4 age group where the commonest cause is drowning, choking or suffocation. As with infectious disease, poverty is a major contributing factor in childhood injury. The cost of childhood injury is high: road accidents and accidents in the home are estimated to cost the community in Britain alone over £10,000 million each year.

Accidental and other violent deaths in childhood by age group, England and Wales, registered deaths, 2004

External causes of morbidity and mortality	Under 1	1–4	5–9	10–14	Total
All accidents	28	67	32	103	230
Pedestrians	-	9	9	34	52
All other transport accidents	4	10	9	38	61
Falls	-	7	1	3	11
Drowning/choking/suffocation	20	22	5	17	64
Exposure to smoke, fire and flames	-	13	6	4	23
Poisoning	-	2	-	3	5
Other	4	4	2	4	14
Intentional self-harm	-	-	-	5	5
Assault	1	9	3	3	16
Event of undetermined intent	9	5	6	15	35

Source: Mortality Statistics Cause DH2 no.31, Review of the Registrar General on deaths by cause, sex and age, in England and Wales, 2004. Office of National Statistics.

Figure 9.22 Accidental and other violent deaths in childhood by age group, England and Wales, 2004

Accidental and other violent deaths in childhood by age group, Scotland, 2004

External causes of morbidity and mortality	Under 1	1–4	5–9	10–14	Total
All accidents	2	5	11	9	27
Pedestrians	-	-	6	2	8
All other transport accidents	-	2	1	2	5
Falls	-	1	1	1	3
Drowning/choking/suffocation	1	2	2	2	7
Exposure to smoke, fire and flames	1	-	1	1	3
Poisoning	-	-	-	-	-
Other	-	-	-	1	1
Intentional self-harm	-	-	-	2	2
Assault	2	-	1	-	3
Event of undetermined intent	-	-	-	-	-

Source: 'Scotland's Population - the Registrar General's Annual review of Demographic Trends'. Vital Events Reference Tables. Table 6.4 Deaths, by sex, age and cause, Scotland, 2004.

Figure 9.23 Accidental and other violent deaths in childhood by age group, Scotland 2004

Accidental and other violent deaths in childhood by age group, Northern Ireland, 2004					
External causes of morbidity and mortality	Under 1	1–4	5–9	10–14	Total
All accidents	4	6	4	4	18
Pedestrians	-	2	2	-	4
All other transport accidents	3	1	1	3	8
Falls	-	-	-	1	1
Drowning/chocking/suffocation	-	1	-	-	1
Exposure to smoke, fire and flames	-	-	-	-	-
Poisoning	-	-	-	-	-
Other	1	2	1	-	4
Intentional self-harm	-	-	-	-	-
Assault	-	-	-	-	-
Event of undetermined intent	-	-	-	-	-

Source: The Registrar General Northern Ireland Annual Report 2004. Table 6.4 Deaths, by sex, age and cause, 2004.

Figure 9.24 Accidental and other violent deaths in childhood by age group, Northern Ireland, 2004

Practitioners in Early Years settings have a responsibility to the children in their care, as part of the ongoing health promotion programme, to educate them in all aspects of safety, including road safety.

Road safety

Educating children about road safety should begin at an early age. Every local authority employs a Road Safety Officer who is always happy to visit childcare settings with new ideas about teaching children about road safety.

Activity 12

Road safety

Contact your local Road Safety Officer to find out what is on offer in your area. Invite him or her to your setting to share new ideas with you.

The Green Cross Code is still an effective way of teaching young children about road safety. You should ensure everyone practises it when they take children out of the Early Years setting for walks or outings.

1 Find a safe place to cross with a clear view in both directions.

2 Stand on the pavement facing the road.

3 Look right, then left, then right again.

4 Listen carefully.

5 Wait until you cannot see or hear any traffic coming.

6 Walk swiftly across the road. Do not run.

7 Keep looking and listening while crossing the road.

Accidents in the setting

Accidents in the home and Early Years settings happen very easily and are often directly linked to the child's stage of development. Accidents, however, do happen despite your best efforts.

Activity 13

Assessing children's safety

1 Refer back to the chapters on development. Make developmental notes on three different ages of children, linking these to the age range found in your setting or place of work.

2 Carry out a situational analysis of your workplace and perhaps your home, (particularly if you are a childminder). Highlight any areas of concern in relation to children's safety, in the light of your knowledge about their holistic development.

3 Using your analysis, design new procedures to ensure the children's safety when playing with toys and equipment inside and outside the setting. You may need to design a different set of procedures for the different age groups of children who attend the setting.

For example, if you research the holistic development of 2-year-olds you will find that they are curious and impulsive; they want to explore independently and easily become frustrated. At this age they can run and enjoy climbing. They can easily walk up and down the stairs. Therefore, when you carry out your situational analysis you will be checking for such things as safety gates on stairs, space to run safely, soft and safe surfaces under playground equipment and large equipment that allows them to climb in safety. You will also check that the equipment is in good condition and carries the British Kite mark for safety.

Making your Early Years setting and home as safe as possible is an important factor in reducing the possibility of an accident, but it cannot be stressed strongly enough that the most important factor in reducing the incidence of accidents is adult supervision. The EYFS 2007 states 'there must be at least two adults on duty in a setting at any time when children are present'.

This is one reason why the government, in the Children Act 1989 set down minimum requirements for the ratio of adults to children in childcare settings. This has been reinforced with the introduction of the EYFS Practice Guidance 2007 Appendix 2 which includes the qualifications members of staff must hold.

Children aged under two in any Early Years group setting

➤ There must be at least one member of staff for every three children; at least one member of staff must hold a full and relevant level 3 (as defined by CWDC), and have suitable experience of working with children under two.

➤ At least half of all other staff must hold a full and relevant level 2 (as defined by CWDC).

➤ At least half the staff must have received specific training in the care of babies.

➤ The member of staff in charge of the babies' room must have suitable experience of working with children under two years.

Children aged two in any Early Years group setting

➤ There must be at least one member of staff for every four children.

➤ At least one member of staff must hold a full and relevant level 3 (as defined by CWDC).

➤ At least half of all other staff must hold a full and relevant level 2 (as defined by CWDC).

Children aged three and over in any registered Early Years provision

Between the hours of 8 am and 4 pm, where a person with Qualified Teacher Status, Early Years Professional Status or another suitable level 6 qualification (which is full and relevant, and defined by CWDC) is working directly with the children, the following requirements apply.

➤ There must be at least one member of staff for every 13 children.

➤ At least one other member of staff must hold a full and relevant level 3 (as defined by CWDC).

At any time outside the hours of 8 am and 4 pm, or between the hours of 8 am and 4 pm but where a person with Qualified Teacher Status, Early Years Professional Status or another suitable level 6 qualification (which is full and relevant, and defined by CWDC) is not working directly with the children, the following requirements apply.

➤ There must be at least one member of staff for every eight children.

➤ At least one member of staff must hold a full and relevant level 3 (as defined by CWDC).

➤ At least half of all other staff must hold a full and relevant level 2 (as defined by CWDC).

Children aged three and over in independent schools

Where a person with Qualified Teacher Status, Early Years Professional Status or another suitable level 6 qualification (which is full and relevant, and defined by CWDC) is working directly with the children, the following requirements apply.

➤ There must be at least one member of staff for every 13 children.

➤ At least one other member of staff must hold a full and relevant level 3 (as defined by CWDC).

Where a person with Qualified Teacher Status, Early Years Professional Status or another suitable level 6 qualification is not working directly with the children, the following requirements apply.

➤ There must be at least one member of staff for every eight children.

➤ At least one member of staff must hold a full and relevant level 3 (as defined by CWDC).

➤ At least half of all other staff must hold a full and relevant level 2 (as defined by CWDC).

Children aged three and over in maintained nursery schools and nursery classes in maintained schools

➤ There must be at least one member of staff for every 13 children.

➤ At least one member of staff must be a school teacher as defined by Section 122 of the Education Act 2002 and the Education (School Teachers' Qualifications) (England) Regulations 2003.

➤ At least one other member of staff must hold a full and relevant level 2 (as defined by CWDC).

Children aged four and over in reception classes in maintained schools

Reception classes in maintained schools are subject to infant class size legislation. The School Standards and Framework Act (as amended by the Education Act 2002) limits the size of infant classes to 30 pupils per school teacher. 'School teachers' do not include teaching assistants, higher level teaching assistants or other support staff. Consequently, a school must employ sufficient school teachers to enable it to teach its infant classes in groups of no more than 30 per school teacher. (EYFS 2007, Appendix 2 pp49–50)

Childminder ratios and qualifications are also laid out in the guidance.

First aid

Accidents will happen however vigilant you are and however safe you make your Early Years setting. It is the responsibility of the manager of Early Years settings to ensure that there is a qualified first aider, skilled in resuscitation techniques, on every shift. However, it is advisable for all practitioners to obtain a recognised qualification in first aid. This should be updated every three years. There should be an accident and emergency procedure to be followed that states:

- what to do in accidents or emergencies
- who the first aiders are
- where the first aid box is (which needs checking, replenishing and signing for weekly, and/or following use)
- who to contact in the case of an accident or emergency
- how to record the incident.

Should any accident occur in your setting, no matter how minor, then it should be recorded and the child's parents notified.

Alternative therapies

Today more people are becoming aware that there are alternatives to conventional medicine, not only for themselves but also for their children. It is important as a practitioner in an Early Years setting for you to have some knowledge if not about the efficacy of various therapies then at least where to obtain relevant information, as you may well be asked for an opinion on such matters. Alternative therapies most often used effectively with children include homeopathy, massage (in particular baby massage), cranial head massage and aromatherapy.

Activity 14

Alternative therapies

Choose a common childhood condition, for example asthma, or one perhaps that a child in your Early Years setting suffers from. Research the alternative therapies that could possibly be used for this condition and describe the rationale behind them.

If each member of your group chooses a different condition then you could share your findings and increase your knowledge.

Note: it is important you do not try to influence the parents or carers in their choice of treatment. Rather, you should increase your own knowledge so you can give objective factual information, if asked.

Conclusion

The purpose of this chapter has been to encourage you to think about different aspects relating to the health of children and also your own health. Some areas have been covered very briefly and you are urged to do your own more in-depth research into those areas that interest you. There are many texts and websites covering health and illnesses that you can refer to. The internet is a useful source of valuable information. Health promotion activities and initiatives are constantly being updated as research continues to grow and develop. As a practitioner in an Early Years setting you have a duty to stay informed about new research related to health, and review your own practice and the policies and procedures of your Early Years setting accordingly.

How to move on in your research

The following websites are updated regularly and provide important information relating to the health of children and young people.

www.hda-online.org.uk
  The Health Development Agency website, which contains details of the National Healthy Schools Standard, for reducing health inequalities and promoting social inclusion.

www.directgov.uk
  The public services website that lists all public services including child and young people health topics.

http://www.surestart.gov.uk/magazine/
  Sure Start is a quarterly magazine for everyone who works with children and families. Featuring good practice, innovation and different views from right across the sector.

http://www.ofsted.gov.uk
  This official website has publications, updated news and reports relating to its inspections of all types of settings that care for/educate children and young people.
  CAS (The Department of Child and Adolescent Health and Development). The World Health Organization website responsible for interventions concerning the health, growth and development outcomes for children and young people from birth to 19 years of age. Accessed through Ofsted website.
  CAMHS (Child and Adolescent Mental Health Services) has a wealth of information including an interactive website 'Meet Jess'. Jess follows the experiences of a service user experiencing mental health issues and the mental health system for the first time. It follows Jess's journey providing useful information and advice on the way. Accessed through Ofsted website.

http://youngminds.org.uk
  Young Minds parents' information service provides confidential advice for any adult concerned about the mental health or emotional well-being of a child or young person. It is a national charity committed to improving the mental health of all children and young people.

www.portage.org.uk/
  A home-visiting educational service for pre-school children with additional support or special needs.

References

Acheson, D. (1998), *The Acheson Report: Independent Inquiry into Inequalities in Health.* London: HMSO

Caroline Walker Trust (1998), *Eating Well for Under-5s in Child Care.* London: The Caroline Walker Trust

Childs, C. (2001), *Food and Nutrition in the Early Years.* London: Hodder Arnold.

Department of Health (1989), *The Children Act 1989 Guidance and Regulations.* London: HMSO

Department of Health (2003), *Every Child Matters.* London: HMSO

Department of Health (2003), *Keeping Children Safe.* London: HMSO

DfES (2001), *Full Day Care: National Standards for Under 8s Day Care and Childminding.* Nottingham: Sure Start/DfES

DfES/DfWP (2003), *Birth to Three Matters.* London: Sure Start/DfES

DfEs (2007), *Statutory Framework for the Early Years Foundation Stage. Setting the Standards for Learning, Development and Care for Children from Birth to Five.* Nottingham: DfES

DHSS (1980), *Inequalities in Health. Report of a Research-Working Group to the DHSS (the Black Report).* London: HMSO

Disability Information Trust (2001), *Children with Disabilities.* Oxford: Disability Information Trust

Fullick, A. (1998), *Human Health and Disease.* Oxford: Heinemann

Hall, D. and Elliman, D. (2003), (4th edition), *Health for All Children.* Oxford: Oxford University Press

Halvorsen, R. (2007), *The Truth About Vaccines.* London: Gibson Square Books

Hubley, J. (1993), *Communicating Health.* Oxford: Macmillan Education Ltd

Keene, A. (1999), *Child Health: Care of the Child in Health and Illness.* Cheltenham: Stanley Thornes.

McCormick, A. (1993), 'Communicable disease report'. *British Journal of Nursing*, vol. 8, issue 14, 22 July 1999, pp943–47.

Meggitt, C. (2001), *Baby and Child Health.* Oxford: Heinemann

Meguid, N.A. and Ismail, S. (2002), 'Early intervention in Down's syndrome: The effect of antioxidants'. *Journal of Intellectual Disability Research*

Paterson, G. (1999), *First Aid for Children Fast.* London: Dorling Kindersley

Roberts, I., Norton, R., Taua, B. (1996), 'Child pedestrian injury rates: The importance of exposure to risk relating to socio-economic and ethnic differences in Auckland, New Zealand'. *Journal of Epidemiology and Community Health* 50, pp162–165

Spencer, N. (2000) (2nd edition), *Poverty and Child Health.* Abingdon: Radcliffe Medical Press

Stordy, B.J. (1994), 'Is it appropriate to apply adult healthy eating guidelines to babies and young children in the growing cycle?'. London: National Dairy Council Conference

Thompson, J. (1997), *Nutritional Requirements of Infants and Young Children.* Oxford: Blackwell Science

Varma, V. (ed.) (1992), *The Secret life of Vulnerable Children.* London: Routledge

World Health Organization (1978), 'Report on the International Conference on Primary Health Care, Alma-Ata, USSR, 6–12 Sept 1978'. *Health for All Series* (1). Geneva: WHO

World Health Organization (1999), 'International consultation on environmental tobacco smoke (ETS) and child health'. Geneva: WHO

Useful websites

http://society.guardian.co.uk/publichealth/story/0,11098,941030,00.html
Report from *The Guardian* newspaper's website about the rise in children's consumption of ready meals.

www.keepkidshealthy.com
This website has useful tips and up-to-date information relating to children's health.

http://www.mmrthefacts.nhs.uk/
This website has been put together to answer any questions you might have about MMR. You can look for information and resources in the MMR library, ask their expert panel a question, and read up on the latest news stories relating to MMR.

www.netdoctor.co.uk
Net Doctor is a constantly updated website produced by doctors in the UK to answer queries relating to health, including treatment of illnesses. Follow the links to find information specific to children.

www.sids.org.uk
Contains the latest research findings on Sudden Infant Death syndrome.

www.welltown.gov.uk
Welltown is an excellent website produced by the government, which contains health promotion activities for adults to carry out with children. It can also be accessed by children, who can try the interactive activities.

www.galaxy-h.gov.uk
Galaxy-H for Key Stage 2 (7–11 years)

www.lifebytes.gov.uk
Lifebytes for Key Stage 3 (11–14 years)

www.mindbodysoul.gov.uk
Mind Body & Soul for Key Stage 4 (14–16 years)
There is a leaflet available which explains the Wired for Health series of sites. If you would like a copy of this leaflet you can email wfh@hda-online.org.uk.

www.tameside.gov.uk/portage
Local authority that runs a successful portage scheme.

http://www.euro.who.int/hfadb
European health for all database [online database]. Copenhagen, WHO Regional Office for Europe, 2005.

Children's Environment and Health Action Plan for Europe. Copenhagen, WHO Regional Office for Europe, 2004 (http://www.euro.who.int/document/e83338.pdf).

Coleman, R.J. (2002), *Reducing Social Inequalities in Health Among Children and Young People.* Brussels, European Commission (http://europa.eu.int/comm/dgs/health_consumer/library/speeches/speech156_en.pdf).

Convention on the Rights of the Child. Geneva, Office of the United Nations High Commissioner for Human Rights, 1989 (http://www.unhchr.ch/html/menu3/b/k2crc.htm).

Rigby, M. and Köhler, L. (2000), *Child Health Indicators of Life and Development (CHILD): Report to the European Commission.* Keele, Centre for Health Planning and Management, 2000 (http://www.europa.eu.int/comm/health/ph/programmes/monitor/fp_monitoring_2000_frep_08_en.pdf).

www.direct.gov.uk
'Cervical cancer vaccine will be introduced'. Published: Wednesday, 20 June 2007, Directgov.uk

UNICEF Innocenti Research Centre. *Child Poverty in Rich Countries 2005.* Florence, United Nations Children's Fund (Report Card No. 6; http://www.unicef-icdc.org/publications/pdf/repcard6e.pdf).

Wagstaff A et al (2004), 'Child health: Reaching the poor'. *American Journal of Public Health*, 94(5), pp726–36 (http://www.ajph.org/cgi/content/full/94/5/726)

The World Health Report 2005 – Make Every Mother and Child Count. Geneva, World Health Organization, 2005 (http://www.who.int/whr/2005/en).

www.hda.nhs.uk
Promoting Healthier Communities a self-assessment tool.

Useful contact numbers

Parentline Plus helpline on 0808 800 2222 provides help and information for anyone caring for children.

ChildLine on 0800 1111 offers help to young people in trouble or danger.

10

Parenting and parent partnership

Janet Kay

In this chapter, the key themes are the differential developmental experiences babies and young children have within a range of family types and contexts, and the impact these experiences have on the individual child's learning and development. The role of parents in promoting their young children's holistic development will be explored along with the role of practitioners in supporting parents in their complex task, by developing effective parent partnership strategies.

Differences in the ways in which children are reared are discussed, and the implications of these for children's access to developmental opportunities in Early Years settings are appraised with reference to the wide range of cultural, environmental and parenting experiences.

The chapter also examines how Early Years settings can respond to the wide range of children's needs and stages of development they encounter, and the ways in which parents and children can be effectively supported, within the legislative and policy context. This includes discussion on how practitioners can support families effectively through multi-interdisciplinary and/or multi-agency working.

This chapter addresses the following areas:

➤ The family and context of parenting

➤ Parenting styles and child-rearing

➤ Partnership with parents and the Early Years setting

➤ The value of partnership to children, parents and practitioners

➤ The policy framework for partnership with parents

➤ What partnership means and types of partnership

➤ Factors supporting the development of effective partnerships

➤ Factor that may inhibit the development of effective partnerships

➤ What really works to develop partnership with parents?

By undertaking the suggested study within this chapter it is hoped that you will be able to:

1 recognise how parents and the family context influence children's early development

2 identify the impact of different early experiences and their role in children's effective access to Early Years settings

3 evaluate the ways in which practitioners/ settings can support the diverse needs of parents and children by developing partnerships with parents and working effectively with other professionals.

The family and context of parenting

It is critical to understand the role of parenting in children's development if we are to understand the skills, abilities, knowledge and understanding of the environment that individual young children bring with them into Early Years settings. Acknowledging that parents are children's first educators is a starting point, but parents also influence many other aspects of their children's development, and all of these developmental aspects contribute to the child's ability to access learning situations outside the home. Child-rearing styles and approaches to parenting vary considerably and children will, through both genetic factors and their early experiences, vary significantly in their stages of development when they enter Early Years settings. Children will have reached different stages in their aptitudes and skills; their speech and language; physical development and ability; social skills and emotional maturity; and comprehension of their environment. Some children may have more extreme developmental delays, while others may need to acquire a second language in order to access the Early Years curriculum. These variations pose a significant challenge to practitioners in all Early Years settings.

The variety and range of these early experiences will differ according to the child's parenting, the culture, language and situation of the family, family type and any significant events affecting a family. As such, each child's experience is unique, and this presents every Early Years setting with the challenge of both acknowledging the validity and equal importance of each child's unique experiences, and ensuring that play and activities are relevant to them all.

Meeting this challenge requires settings to understand and respond to parents' needs and to make effective partnerships with parents, recognising their diversity and acknowledging the complexity and difficulties many parents experience in raising their children. All practitioners in Early Years settings will be familiar with the concept of 'partnership with parents' and the need for practitioners and parents to work together to support children's developmental progress. Every major legislative or policy document currently influencing, or guiding, practice contains reference to 'partnership' and the importance of ensuring that parents are informed about and involved in strategies and approaches to the care and education of their child. However, for some parents, partnership is a gateway to providing additional support where parents are struggling to meet the needs of their children. Within the current policy context, all agencies, professionals and practitioners are required to ensure that parents have access to the support they need to parent effectively. In order to provide this, practitioners in Early Years settings need to be able to offer support through the setting and also to work with other children's services professionals to ensure additional support is accessed as required.

This section discusses the notion of a 'family' and its changing composition, in addition to considering families as systems.

Defining the family?

In British culture, children are usually raised within families, but in the early 21st century asking the question 'What is a family?' poses some difficulties. For a start, we may have difficulty defining 'family', as diversification over the last 30 years or more has led to a much broader range of family types than were previously common. For example, families may consist of children and parents who are biologically connected; those who are connected by sharing parents but not all sharing genes (stepfamilies); those who are legally family but not all biologically connected (adoptive families, children born through donor eggs or sperm). Families may have one parent, two parents of different sexes, or two parents of the same sex; children may be in families where parenting is done by aunts, uncles, grandparents, foster carers or older siblings. A child may have two biological parents and one or more step-parents who may or may not also be legal parents and this may change throughout the child's early life.

Expansion in the range and complexity of family types has rendered most traditional definitions of the family redundant. As such, the family may be more fruitfully thought of as a social construct, in that defining a family realistically may be dependent on self-definition. For example, 'we are a family because we think of ourselves as a family'. This type of definition gets us away from the idea of listing characteristics of families in order to define them, and acknowledges that families are very diverse in both structure and functions.

Legally, a parent is someone who has 'parental responsibility' for a child as defined in the Children Act 1989. Parental responsibility means that the parent has the right to be involved in all major decisions about the child including education, religion, medical treatment and where the child lives. It also confers responsibility for the child's welfare and upbringing on the parent. Parental responsibility is automatically conferred on birth mothers and fathers who are married to birth mothers. Since 2003, unmarried fathers have parental responsibility if they and the birth mother register the birth together. Otherwise, unmarried fathers have to sign a legal agreement with the mother or go to court and have parental responsibility conferred on them through a court order. Other parental figures such as step-parents do not automatically have parental responsibility but can obtain it:

➤ by being appointed as a guardian to care for the child if those with parental responsibility for the child have died

➤ by obtaining a residence order from the court which requires that the child lives with that person

➤ by becoming the child's special guardian

➤ by adopting the child.

Children's Legal Centre (2007)

If those with existing parental responsibility agree, a step-parent can make a legal agreement and gain parental responsibility for a child in addition (not instead of) those who already have it. For example, a child may have a mother, father and stepfather who all have parental responsibility for her.

Changing family types

Family types are not only increasing but are also now less stable, with increases in the rates of divorce and remarriage or cohabitation leading to a shifting pattern of lone parent and 'blended' families (Thurtle, 1998). Over the last 30 years there has been a decrease in the number of couple-headed families, corresponding to the increase in lone-parent-headed families. At present there are 1.8 million lone-parent-headed families in the UK, with 3 million dependent children. Black and ethnic minority children are more likely to be in lone-parent families as they make up 12 per cent of lone-parents although only 7.9 per cent of the population (ESCR, 2007). Ninety per cent of all lone-parent families are headed by a female.

However, although lone-parent families are a fast-growing category of family type, the majority of lone parents re-enter marriage or cohabitation, often with partners who have children of their own. The average length of time a lone-parent family remains as such is five years (ESCR, 2007). Seventy-seven per cent of children still live in households headed by a couple, of which 66 per cent are married. Some of these households are stepfamilies, which constitute about 10 per cent of all families. Stepfamilies are defined as 'couple families with stepchildren or with step and natural children to both parents' (National Statistics

Online, 2007). In 2001, there were 0.7 million stepfamilies in the UK of which 0.4 million are married couples and 0.3 million cohabiting and of which 80 per cent were headed by a birth mother and stepfather.

These statistics cannot really reflect the changing patterns of family type that many children experience. However, falling marriage rates and increased numbers of children conceived outside marriage (over 50 per cent in 2000) confirm the possibility that many children do not spend their whole childhood with two married biological parents. This is supported by the fact that two-fifths of all marriages are remarriages (Summerfield and Babb, 2003). It can be concluded that many children are raised in a range of family types within their childhood; for example, when families separate, operate as lone-parent families, and then become part of 'blended' or 'reconstituted' families.

A small percentage of children are raised within the care of local authority social care services. Many of these children will experience more than one change of family, with some experiencing three or more foster care placements, as well as parenting within their family of origin. Some children who enter the care system will be placed in adoptive families and lose their legal ties with their birth families, although, increasingly, some adopted children are maintaining contact with birth family members throughout their childhood. Greater numbers of children are being raised in lesbian and gay households by parents who may or may not be related to them biologically. The advent of scientific and technological developments in the fields of fertility and conception have also influenced the ways in which parenting can be achieved. Increasing numbers of children are born into families through fertility treatments which may mean no biological connection to one or both parents. Biological links are part of what may constitute the relationship between parent and child but this is not universal and many children are raised for at least part of their childhood by parents with whom they have no biological connection.

The 'family' is a much more fluid and diverse structure than it has ever been and this has implications for children and for practice in settings. For example, practitioners need to be aware that a child may live with some carers who have no parental responsibility but who care for the child on a daily basis; or that some carers with parental responsibility for the child may rarely be seen. They need to be aware that the parents of some children in foster care may still retain parental responsibility, but where a Care Order is in place this is shared with the local authority, who have the power to make decisions about the child. Practitioners also need to be aware that changing family structures means that children's family circumstances should never be assumed but should always be treated with sensitivity. Not every child has happy early memories of both parents or wants to discuss an absent father or a current step-parent with practitioners. For some children, changes in family situations may mean the loss of contact with grandparents and other relatives, which may feel bewildering and sad for the child.

Activity 1

Who has parental responsibility?

Draw up a checklist of issues that need to be considered about parental responsibility and family issues. What sort of issues need to be considered to ensure the welfare and safety of all children in the setting and the development of positive relationships with all parents and carers?

Families as systems

Understanding the impact of the family and parenting on children's development is a key element of recognising and responding to children's diverse needs in a setting. Practitioners all have their own first-hand experience of family life, but acknowledging that there are many different approaches to raising children and factors that underpin these approaches is an important step in being able to work effectively with parents and children.

The relationships within families and their impact on children's development are not easy to understand. Families can be analysed as a series of separate one-to-one relationships or as more complex systems reflecting the interplay of relationships between all family members and the reactions and adjustments they make in their dealings with each other. In studying the role of parenting in the development of children in the Early Years, it is important to recognise this complex interplay within families. Children are no longer viewed as 'lumps of clay' to be moulded and socialised by others, but as active participants in determining the parenting styles within their families (Bee, 2006; Messer and Millar,1999).

Practical experience tells us that events affecting one member of a family will affect the family as a whole. Examining patterns of influence within families can give us an insight into how different child-rearing styles develop and the impact that various approaches to parenting can have on young children's development. Events affecting one family member can affect all family members in different ways, creating 'feedback loops' where the impact of the change passes back and forth between different family members in a complicated pattern.

Environmental influences on the child and family

As well as viewing the family as a system in itself, it is also important to recognise that families are influenced in their behaviour by environmental factors, which may affect family functioning directly or indirectly. These factors could include the social and work situation of the parents, the support systems that adults and children have access to, and the stresses on the family, which may include economic status, housing situation and health status. Bronfenbrenner's ecological approach (1979) is a useful model with which to explore family systems. This model reflects the 'complex, interactive and interdependent nature

Case Study 1

Family systems in practice

The serious illness of a parent can produce anxiety and distress in both the parent's partner and the children. The illness of one parent combined with the anxiety of the other parent could make the children feel insecure and anxious. At a time like this, the children may receive less attention and less parental focus. This may add to the children's feelings of insecurity and anxiety. The children may seek to redress the balance and gain parental attention through demanding behaviour, 'clinginess' and openly expressed distress. In dealing with this, the parents might not have the time and energy to focus on child-centred approaches in their response and may be more abrupt and less sensitive in their responses than usual, adding to the children's feelings of anxiety and insecurity. The parents may become more anxious, guilty and less able to cope as they perceive themselves as parenting less well and not meeting their children's needs, while they may also become angry as they see the children as misbehaving and causing stress at an already stressful time.

Think of a family you know that has recently been subject to change, for example in employment patterns, addition of new members or bereavement. Consider how the change has affected all parts of the family and how 'feedback loops' may have developed as outlined in the example above.

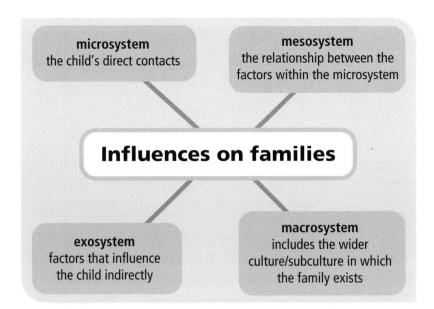

Figure 10.1 Bronfenbrenner's ecological approach

of environmental influences on a child' (Woods, 1998). Bronfenbrenner described the influences on families as:

➤ **microsystem:** the child's direct contacts; mainly family, Early Years setting, school

➤ **mesosystem:** the relationship between the factors within the microsystem, for example parents' relationship with practitioners in the Early Years setting

➤ **exosystem:** factors that influence the child indirectly; for example, parent's work, social contacts, income, local environment

➤ **macrosystem:** includes the wider culture/ subculture in which the family exists; for example, social Early Years setting, cultural Early Years setting, political context.

Case Study 2

The impact of change on a family

When 4-year-old Jasmine's parents separated, she was very upset that her father moved out of the marital home. The house was then sold and Jasmine moved to a flat with her mother, Alexa. This meant changing to a new nursery and separation from friends and neighbours. Alexa started to have financial problems and became less tolerant and more short-tempered with Jasmine, often crying, shouting and making negative comments about Jasmine's father. Jasmine started to bed-wet, found it difficult to mix with other children at nursery and had angry outbursts at home and in the Early Years setting. Her mother

found this behaviour very difficult to cope with on top of her other concerns, and she frequently shouted at Jasmine, locked herself in the bathroom and cried for long periods.

Measuring the impact of change on a family

1 What are the environmental influences on this family and how are they affecting Alexa's parenting?

2 What impact are the environmental influences having on Jasmine and how might they affect her development in the short- and long-term?

As Pugh (1994) argues, parenting cannot be seen in isolation from the social context within which it takes place, and work and unemployment, health, poverty and housing are all significant in determining the child's experience directly or through other family members. Parenting styles are influenced by many factors but environmental factors are important in this. One of the key factors is poverty, which can have widespread and pernicious negative effects on children directly, such as the child's access to learning and leisure, safe housing and neighbourhoods, good quality diet, play space and Early Years provision. Poverty can also have a negative effect on children through the impact living in poverty has on parental ability to cope and to parent effectively. At the time of writing, 30 per cent of children in the UK live in poverty (3.8 million children) (End Child Poverty, 2007).

Activity 2

Researching the impact of poverty on families

Using the End Child Poverty and Child Poverty Action Group websites (see the end of this chapter for URLs), do some research into the impact of poverty on children's lives and parents' ability to parent effectively. Share your findings with your study group, mentor or supervisor. Some questions that may help to think about this topic are as follows.

1   How does poverty impact on parent's lives, for example health, stress, housing, employment and relationships?

2   What factors contribute to poverty in a family?

3   How might poverty impact on a child's ability to access learning and development opportunities in an Early Years setting? For example early first-hand experiences; social skills, early learning in the home?

4   What factors influencing parents or characteristics of a family may help to offset the negative impact of poverty?

Parenting styles and child–rearing

In this section, the extent to which parents can influence children's development and the evidence to support the view that different approaches to parenting have different developmental outcomes for the child will be explored. Basically, does it really matter what parents do in terms of outcomes for a child's individual development? In discussing this, it is important to recognise that there is no one single concept of 'childhood'. Both 'childhood' and 'child-rearing practices' vary between different cultures and over time, depending on dominant social and cultural norms and values (Woods, 1998). The history of childhood reveals a range of different approaches to child-rearing that reflect the economic and social conditions of different classes at different times and in different cultural contexts (Aries, 1982). As such, it is important to remember that child-rearing is a changing concept which is dependent on the social circumstances of the time.

Models of parenting styles

Models of parenting styles are used to analyse the relationship between parental behaviour and developmental outcomes for the child. However, as discussed briefly above, parents do not just pluck a parenting style from nowhere. Parenting approaches tend to be shaped by a range of social, cultural and personal factors and experiences that combine to determine how an individual perceives and implements the task of parenting. Belsky's (1984) model of parental functioning identifies three main influences on the quality of parenting.

These factors and the interplay between them will influence the parenting approach used by an individual. The factors that have shaped an individual's experiences and lifestyle will also shape their approach to parenting. For example, the parent's own parenting experience is significant as is the level of security and standard of care the parent received as a child. Success or failure in school and beyond, access to interesting, stimulating work and a decent income may be important in shaping the individual's ability to cope as a parent. The ability to make and sustain good relationships with partners, friends and family will impact on the parent's ability to create and draw on supportive social networks. The individual's psychological and emotional maturity and stability will be key factors in their ability to parent demanding young children effectively.

The interactions between these factors are also determinants of how a person will parent. For example, a parent who has experienced poor attachment and lack of support in his or her own childhood may find it more difficult to sustain relationships with partners or friends. This will have an impact on the social support he or she receives while parenting, which may in turn make the parenting task more stressful. However, the other significant factor is the child's own characteristics which will influence the response of the parent and the parenting style used.

Cleaver, Unell and Aldgate (1999) identified several factors that commonly had a negative influence on parenting. These include: the incidence of domestic violence in the household; a parent's mental health problems; and drug and alcohol abuse. These factors are key indicators that the children in the household may be 'children in need'. This concept is discussed more fully in Chapter 14. However, a 'child in need' is one who is deemed to need support services in order to maximise his or her developmental opportunities.

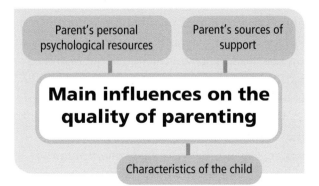

Figure 10.2 Main influences on the quality of parenting (Belsky, 1984)

Activity 4

Influences on parenting style

With reference to the three influences on parental functioning discussed in Figure 10.2, analyse your own parenting or that of someone you know well in terms of these influences. Note the interrelationships between the factors, and the impact on parenting style. Remember to maintain sensitivity and confidentiality when completing this exercise.

Baumrind developed a model of parenting styles that was adapted by Maccoby and Martin (1983) to establish a four-fold classification based on how demanding or undemanding parents are about a child's behaviour and how responsive or unresponsive the parents are to the child's needs (see Figure 10.3).

	Responsive	Unresponsive
Demanding	Authoritative	Authoritarian
Undemanding	Permissive	Uninvolved

Figure 10.3 Parenting styles (Maccoby and Martin, 1983)

Maccoby and Martin classified the following parenting styles.

➤ **Permissive parents** value the child's freedom of expression, provide few and inconsistent controls and accept lower standards of cognitive and behavioural performance from the child.

➤ **Authoritarian parents** are more likely to be colder, more controlling and punitive, showing lower levels of affection towards the child. They are more likely to make strict rules without explanations for these, and to demand high levels of performance and achievement. Authoritarian parents are more likely to use harsher punishments and physical punishment in particular.

➤ **Authoritative parents** set high standards for behaviour and self-reliance, encouraging independence and providing controls; they reason and explain, and are committed to all areas of the child's development.

➤ **Uninvolved** or neglecting parents are 'psychologically' unavailable to their children, displaying little warmth and providing few controls. They are usually unresponsive to the child's needs and not always able to recognise these. At the extreme, neglecting parents may not meet their children's physiological or emotional needs.

Parenting style and implications for child development

Authoritative parenting styles have been shown to have the best indicators for the child's development. Authoritative parents tend to provide children with: clear, firm behavioural boundaries; explanations for rules and disciplinary measures; good communication; and warmth and responsiveness. Such children are regarded positively, given praise and affection and expected to behave maturely. Children raised in families where an authoritative parenting style predominates are likely to be more confident and independent, to socialise more effectively with peers and to conform more readily to controls and disciplinary measures. They are likely to be less anxious and to achieve better in school. The long-term outcomes for such children in terms of success in education and beyond are better overall than for children raised in families where the other parenting styles predominate.

Children raised in authoritarian households are more likely to be less happy, more anxious and withdrawn, and possibly more hostile and aggressive with peers. They do not necessarily do less well in school than children raised in authoritative households but they may well be less emotionally capable in their relationships.

Children raised in permissive households may be less able to regulate their own responses and therefore have poorer impulse control. This may affect social relationships and the ability to get on with peers. They may have less persistence at tasks and be more likely to give up, which may have a negative impact on learning.

Children raised in neglecting families may be insecurely attached, may do less well at school and be more likely to be socially isolated. They may not be able to make good relationships, and may struggle with aspects of maturity and independence.

However, it is important to remember that:
➤ most parents use a range of styles at different times and stages of the child's development
➤ the child is not passive in this relationship and will influence the parenting style.

Limitations of parenting models

Models of parenting are limited in that none of them really reflects what actually goes on in families. Maccoby and Martin's (1983) classification has been criticised for reflecting the parenting of white families rather than those from a range of cultural groups. However, the classification does give us a starting point from which to analyse the impact of parenting behaviour on the child's development.

The extent to which parents can influence their child's development is disputed. Scarr (1992) referred to twin and adoption studies, which apparently demonstrated that family environment has little influence on the child's development. Scarr concluded that genetic factors are primary in determining the child's development and that parenting, beyond the minimum requirements, has little influence. The factors that determine how an individual behaves as a parent are too many and complex to claim a cause-and-effect relationship between parenting style and child development. However, evidence shows that certain characteristics associated with authoritative parenting styles are positive in their influences on the child's development (Bee, 2006). These are:
➤ **warmth** – families in which affection and praise are openly and frequently expressed are linked with good attachment, and cognitive and social development for children

➤ **responsiveness** – parents who are sensitive to their children's needs are likely to have children who do well in cognitive, social and language development and who have secure attachments
➤ **control** – consistency of rules and high expectations of mature behaviour are linked with confident, competent children with good self-esteem and social skills
➤ **communication** – quality of communication depends on parents talking to, and listening to, their children. Children have a role in family decision-making and can disagree with parents, who expect to have to explain things to their children.

There are a number of studies that demonstrate the impact of lack of warmth and harsher use of discipline with young children. In a study commissioned by the Department of Health (1995) into the long-term effects of child abuse, the impact of low warmth/high criticism parenting was determined to have a much longer-lasting and significant negative impact on the child's developmental outcomes than inflicted physical injuries. A study of 2-year-olds showed that harsh discipline has a negative effect on young children's behaviour, but that where warmth is shown by parents the effects of the harsh discipline are modified. However, in low warmth parenting the effects of harsh discipline on the child's behaviour are exacerbated (Zona, Saudino and Gagne, 2007). The NICHD longitudinal study of 1,000 children showed that the single most significant parental behaviour influencing children's cognitive development is the demonstration of warmth (NICHD, 2001).

It is also important to remember that siblings, grandparents and other close relatives and friends may all have their own influence on a child's development. There have been far fewer studies about the impact of behaviour of other relatives on young children, but there is evidence that, for many children, relationships develop early on with a range of significant others and not just parents.

Partnership with parents and the Early Years setting

Children's early experiences are diverse for a myriad of reasons, some of which have been discussed above. Parenting style, economic circumstances and other environmental factors all have an influence on the child's development, as does the child's own character and developing personality. Other factors which affect the child's early experiences are ethnicity, culture and the community in which the child is raised. The presence or absence of a disability is significant as this may impact directly on the child's ability to access first-hand experiences and learning opportunities including social experiences. However, the presence of a child with disability may also impact on the family in other ways, for example on the family income. The majority of families with a disabled child are less well off than other similar families as the child's care needs may impact on the parents' ability to earn.

As such, within any setting there will be a wide range of needs to meet and significant differences between children in terms of their ability to access the learning and developmental opportunities within the setting. Some of these issues are discussed in more detail in the next section. One of the key factors that will support the development of all children in the setting is the extent to which parents are involved in their child's care and education outside the home and the extent to which settings can support the needs of parents in their parenting task. The arrangements, policies and practices which result in effective communication and liaison with parents are generally referred to as parent partnership.

Why have partnership with parents?

The value of the concept of partnership with parents is based on the belief that good working relationships, clear and reciprocal communication, and common goals between parents and professionals are crucial to the successful delivery of effective services to children.

Common sense and, for many practitioners, real-life experience tell us that 'working together' will reduce the incidences of confusion, misunderstanding and hostility between parents and practitioners that can adversely influence effective work with the child. Common sense also tells us that effective partnerships between home and setting will mean that all the adults working with a child will have a good understanding of the child's needs and how these can be best met at home and in the Early Years setting. Yet many questions about both the principle and practice of partnership with parents need to be critically considered in order to ensure that the factors determining effective partnership are genuinely understood.

Wolfendale (2000:3) acknowledges that the value of partnership with parents has been recognised since it was stated in the Plowden Report (1967) that 'by involving the parents, the children may be helped' and the fact that many settings now routinely work closely with parents. However, 'a number of schools have maintained a rather suspicious not to say distanced view of the benefits of closer working relationships and still regard too much parental presence within schools as an intrusion'.

More recently, parent partnership has become a key theme within policy-driving developments in Early Years practice. Parent partnership is central to the philosophy and strategic approach underpinning the Every Child Matters agenda. The most recent developments in provision such as Children's Centres and extended schools have parent partnership firmly at the heart of their approach. However, despite the universal belief that parent partnership is a 'good thing' and should be part of the work of every setting, there is a significant gap in putting this policy effectively into practice in all settings, often based on a lack of common understandings of what parent partnership is and how it can be achieved.

Achieving partnerships

There is no simple formula for either achieving effective partnerships or for ensuring that all parents are involved. However, there are some key points to consider. These are illustrated in Figure 10.4.

One of the first issues to explore is where the common ground between parents and practitioners exists. What sort of areas should be the focus of partnership? Should this include all aspects of the child's care and education, or should it be limited to areas directly related to the services provided by the Early Years setting?

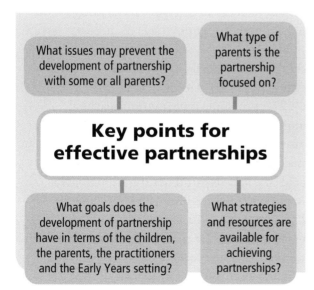

Figure 10.4 Achieving effective partnerships: some key points

Case Study 3

Parent partnership in practice

Some schools have rules that prevent children from bringing sweets and chocolate bars to school for lunch or snacks. These rules relate directly to an area that may be considered by some to be firmly in the parent's domain – the child's diet and eating habits. Is this an area over which schools should have jurisdiction? Or should they leave this to parents, and concentrate on teaching and learning? Some would argue that parents have a right to feed their children as they like. Others would argue that children's diet affects their overall health and well-being and, as such, has an influence on their ability to learn across the whole curriculum and to access good quality care. Currently, the Healthy Schools agenda supports intervention in this particular area of child development. However, the introduction of healthy schools meals has not been universally applauded by parents and the number of children taking school meals has gone down.

Healthier school meals

Look at some of the media reports about the introduction of healthier schools meals.

1 Why do you think some parents have resisted this development?

2 What should settings do to get parents 'on board' with developments such as healthy eating?

It is likely that the issues about young children that practitioners will share with parents will be mainly in the areas of:

➤ learning development

➤ emotional and social development

➤ Special Educational Needs (SEN) or disabilities that impact on learning development

➤ support for parents in the parenting task

➤ socioeconomic disadvantage that impacts on parenting and the child's development.

However, other areas of partnership with parents that may be of concern to some settings or services may be:

➤ parent education and training

➤ parent input into managing/running/decision-making in the service or Early Years setting

➤ parents developing community-based services to meet their own needs.

The value of partnership to children, parents and practitioners

The rationale for developing and sustaining partnerships with parents is based on the belief that, for a variety of reasons, promoting partnerships with parents in the Early Years will lead to positive outcomes for children, families, practitioners and settings, and communities and society as a whole. In this section, we examine the evidence that supports these beliefs, which underpin the commitment of resources to developing and promoting partnership with parents across a diverse range of approaches, settings and projects.

The value of partnership with parents

It is clear that the ability of parents to engage in activities that support the development of partnership is a strong indicator of success. Families, however, are diverse in their composition, their stability, their effectiveness in parenting their children, and their flexibility in responding to change. The traditional view, that parents from economically successful middle-class homes are likely to be more successful in engaging with partnerships in the Early Years than families from lower socioeconomic groups, needs to be challenged as a stereotype which

may hinder the progress of partnership. But how do we measure the contributions of families to the effectiveness of Early Years education and care? With reference to the role of parents in school, Bastiani (2000:20) argues that the effectiveness of the contribution of the family is very difficult to assess because it is underplayed or ignored; takes place outside the setting and is most significant in the years before the child enters a setting; and has a much wider and longer-term impact than the setting does. Bastiani argues that a family's contribution to school success is largely hidden, and that measuring it is hampered by the fluid nature of family life and wide variations in family types and behaviour.

The problems with measuring the contribution of parent partnership to success are compounded by the diverse ways in which partnership is perceived and implemented. Is a setting successful if compliant parents agree to support their children in ways suggested by the practitioners and sanctioned by the establishment? Or can success be more easily measured when parents have a significant influence on the core functions of the setting, such as in some pre-schools that are largely staffed by parent volunteers?

Figure 10.5 Factors influencing the success of partnerships

The extent to which partnership with parents is successful depends on a complex range of issues relating to the family, community, establishment, the current climate in Early Years and many other factors (see Figure 10.5.).

Despite the variable nature of partnership and the evidence that many Early Years settings lack true involvement in and commitment to genuine partnership, Bastiani (2000:21) found a very positive picture in a survey of 11 schools:

A majority of the parents and the other main carers in the 11 schools provide regular encouragement and practical support for their children's school learning, are actively engaged as a family in a wide range of 'educational' activities, both in the home and throughout the wider community, and are involved in a range of opportunities that relate to their own learning and development.

It is probably unnecessary to emphasise to practitioners that developing partnerships with parents requires the commitment of time, resources and energy, and must be based on a firm belief in the benefits of partnership to those involved. Although practitioners are urged to focus their resources on building partnerships with parents, it is not always easy to evaluate the benefits to key individuals. How do we measure, for example, the extent to which partnership

helps children's development and learning? Bastiani (2000) suggests a 'What works?' or 'Stakeholder model' for evaluating the contribution of partnership with parents to school effectiveness. This approach is based on a belief that any evaluation must take into account the views of all involved, and draw on evidence from a wide range of sources, charting the perspectives of parents, children and teachers, rather than be based on more limited formal evidence such as Ofsted reports and the extent to which targets have been reached. Evaluation within this model is 'formative and developmental' and 'a continuous task', rather than a periodic snapshot of progress. It is focused on development and using what we know to make further progress and better outcomes.

In order to be effective, this approach to evaluating parent partnership needs to be part of the daily agenda within the Early Years setting, supported by clearly stated policies and plans for action and based on an action research type of approach, where evidence is used to plan the next stages of improvement. Although this model is developed with reference to schools, the principles of the approach have meaning for many Early Years settings. The main benefits of this type of approach are:

➤ ensuring that the effectiveness of partnership is measured from the perspective of all 'stakeholders' – parents, children and practitioners

➤ an ongoing developmental approach within which evidence is translated into action for change

➤ ensuring that there are clear plans and strategies for the development of parent partnership which are embedded in the business of the setting.

How do we know what works and why it works? Evaluating the benefits of different approaches to parent partnership within an Early Years setting can present a challenge to practitioners. Many approaches that are successful work in a complex range of interrelated ways.

Strategies to develop relationships between setting and parents

At one school, parents are invited every year to a week of art activities involving nursery, infants and juniors. The children work on related themes across the classes, and parents are encouraged to work with their children on tasks and projects. At the end of the week, the whole school presents the work in visual images and group performances. The benefits are enormous, involving:

➤ parents gaining a better understanding of what happens in school

➤ parents sharing and developing their own skills

➤ parents having the opportunity to talk to teachers and share ideas and information about their child

➤ children being able to show parents their skills and abilities and share the development of these

➤ children having pride in their own achievements and the achievements of their parents

➤ teachers having the support of other adults to provide a very broad curriculum involving ambitious and complex tasks

➤ teachers having the opportunity to share ideas and information with parents

➤ everybody having fun!

The event is evaluated through many methods involving feedback from the children as individuals, and through school council; feedback from parents as individuals and through governors and the parents' group; and the teachers' views and perspectives.

Think about what sort of strategies you use in your workplace to support the development of parent partnership. How do you evaluate the effectiveness of these? What other ways could you evaluate your approaches to parent partnership?

Draper and Duffy (2006) analysed parent partnership in terms of its value to children, parents and practitioners.

The value to children

Children benefit from better working relationships between practitioners and the closer involvement of their parents with the Early Years setting on a number of interrelated fronts. Perhaps the key benefit to young children is continuity, as defined by Draper and Duffy (2006). See Figure 10.6.

Children also learn and develop better in an environment where there are good relationships between the adults around them, based on mutual respect.

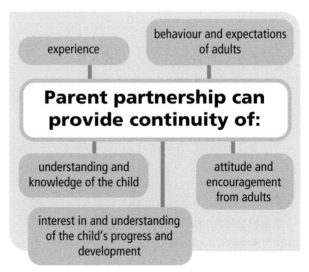

Figure 10.6 Parent partnerships can provide continuity (Draper and Duffy, 2006)

Developing relationships with child and parent

When Davey first went to Cherubs Nursery, he was just 3 years old and developmentally delayed for his age. He received a great deal of support and warmth from one of the nursery staff, who was sensitive to his fears and concerns and who recognised that he became tired and a little anxious towards the end of the afternoon. She would make sure that he had quiet activities when he was tired and during the sing-song, which ended the day, he would often sit next to her for moral and physical support.

Davey's father was relieved to see him gain confidence and start to enjoy the nursery, and he recognised and acknowledged the role of the practitioner in this.

Sharing their ideas and concerns about Davey helped both the father and practitioner to recognise each other's roles and to develop a respect for each other's views and opinions. When Davey's learning difficulties became more apparent and a more structured response was required to meet his needs, the adults in his life had an excellent basis on which to build a closer partnership in order to meet these needs.

The key factors which supported parent partnership at the nursery in Case Study 5 were a key worker system which meant the parent had a focus for any concerns or discussion and staff availability at the beginning and end of the day. The nursery provided a welcoming environment for parents giving them chance to ask questions and discuss their child and giving feedback on the child's progress and activities in the setting.

An analysis of the benefits to children in the Cherubs Nursery is shown in Figure 10.7.

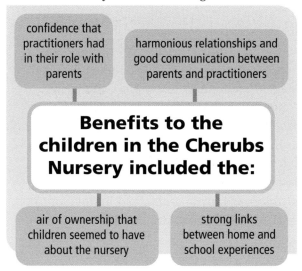

Figure 10.7 Analysis of the benefits to children in the Cherubs Nursery

The value to parents

Parenting is a complex and demanding task and one which some parents struggle to fulfil effectively as discussed in more detail earlier in this chapter. Most parents need support, advice and help with parenting at some stage. Many parents have support networks which help them through difficult times and provide childcare, support, advice and someone to share difficult times with. However, other parents are more socially isolated and less able to access support networks. They may have poorer relationships and fewer resources and their difficulties may be more significant and ongoing. Whatever the problems parents experience, whether minor, temporary or more severe, all parents will benefit from good relationships with their child's Early Years setting.

The benefits of parent partnership to parents depend on the roles and attitude of practitioners. A goal of many Early Years settings is to encourage parents to feel more confident about their role and to understand that role more fully. Parents need to feel welcome and to be acknowledged as the most important people in their children's lives. Practitioners need to share, rather than display their expertise, and to recognise that some parents may be daunted by their professionalism, training and qualifications.

The benefits of parent partnership to parents can be summarised as:

➤ support in the parenting role

➤ sharing ideas and expertise in supporting the child's development

➤ reflective and balanced feedback about the child's progress

➤ encouragement and help with the aspects of support for the child's development

➤ understanding the Early Years curriculum and approach to care and education within the setting

➤ opportunities for self-development/professional development

➤ access to a varied range of support services if required.

The value to practitioners

The benefits of parent partnership for practitioners are well documented, and focus on improving knowledge in order to better meet the educational and care needs of the children they are involved with. However, not all practitioners feel sure about the benefits of partnership with parents. It may be that their training has helped them to develop skills with children, but less so with adults. Some practitioners may feel uncertain about the prospect of sharing their expertise or lack confidence in explaining the basis and rationale of their approach to childcare and education in the Early Years. Others may feel that parenting and professional work in the Early Years are separate issues and should remain so. It may be that some practitioners feel that they are not equipped to work with parents who come from diverse cultural and linguistic backgrounds. However, those who

are enthusiastic about and involved in actively developing parent partnerships will be aware of the benefits.

The benefits of parent partnership to practitioners and settings can be summarised as:

➤ learning more about the individual needs of the children in their care

➤ contextualising the support of individual children within the child's cultural, religious and linguistic background through gaining more knowledge of these

➤ understanding more about the child's early experience and making links between home experiences and those in the setting

➤ learning from parents about how best to support their children's development and meet their needs

➤ learning about the challenges parents face and the range of services available to support parents

➤ learning how to support parents in their role.

Not all parents find it easy to relate to practitioners. The parents who drop off their children as quickly as possible and pick them up in a hurry, without pause for a chat, may not be indifferent to the children's experiences in the Early Years setting or lacking in concern about how they are behaving, progressing, settling in or achieving. They may simply feel they do not have the experience, the language or the confidence to talk about their children's progress and achievement, activities and developmental stage. Parents may not share a common language with practitioners; they may come from very different socio-cultural backgrounds and have very different views on children's education and care. Practitioners can gain a great deal for themselves, the parents and the children if they take the lead in developing good relationships with all parents.

The policy framework for partnership with parents

The concept of parent partnership has been rooted in all major policy and legislative developments for some time. The Rumbold Report (1990) emphasised the need to work with parents in education settings and the Children Act 1989 was significant in establishing the principle that parents should be seen as partners in the care and welfare of their children, even during legal proceedings resulting from child protection concerns. The Act established that parents should be kept informed about issues affecting their children and should have information and their views ascertained about any decisions about their child. Subsequent legislation and policy has reflected this view but Bastiani (2000) points out that there are many different ways of interpreting parent partnership, not all of which are common to parents and setting.

The current policy agenda for children's services is dominated by the Every Child Matters: Change for Children programme, a wide-ranging strategy to support significant changes in children's service planning and delivery which all practitioners are familiar with. In line with trends over the last 20 years a key statement is that 'Parents, carers and families are the most important influence on outcomes for children and young people.' Partnership with parents and support for parents are key principles of all aspects of the strategy and a key aim is to ensure that these principles are embedded in all service delivery across the range of children's services. The main goals are as follows.

> Good quality universal support, in the form of information, advice and signposting to other services, is available to all parents. It is important that support can be accessed in places where, and ways in which, parents and carers feel comfortable, such as Early Years settings, schools,

primary healthcare services, and through childcare information services, telephone helplines and the web.

> More specialised targeted support is available at the local level to meet the needs of families and communities facing additional difficulties. Types of support offered could include structured parenting education groups, couple support, home visiting and employment or training advice.

> All settings actively seek to engage parents in children and young people's education, helping parents to understand what they can do at home to work with the setting.

> Children's centres and extended schools develop a coherent set of services both to support parents and to involve them properly at all stages of a child's learning and development.

Every Child Matters: Change for Children (2007)

There is a wide range of materials on the Every Child Matters website to support practitioners in developing skills and understanding of the issues involved and strategies which can be used to promote parent partnership and readers are strongly recommended to explore these. In 2007, the National Academy for Parenting Practitioners was established to support the training and development of practitioners working with parents. Information about this is also available on the website listed at the end of this chapter.

The SEN Code of Practice (DfES, 2001)

The SEN Code of Practice (DfES, 2001) emphasises the areas shown in Figure 10.8 for working with parents.

The Code of Practice guidance emphasises that parents should be listened to and supported in dealing with the complex systems available to support children with SEN. The

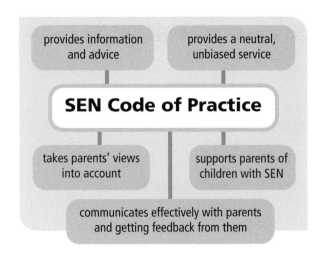

Figure 10.8 Emphasis of the 'SEN Toolkit'

focus of partnership is on ensuring that parents have good quality information about their child's needs and how these can be assessed and met. Involving parents in their child's assessment and support is considered crucial to ensuring success in promoting the child's global development. Roffey (1999) argues that there has been less support for and involvement with parents at the earlier stages of the Code of Practice, but that independent support for parents and the dissemination of good practice have been introduced to address this. Each Children's Services Authority has to provide a Parent Partnership service to support parents in their dealings with the setting or school around any aspect of their child's SEN but in particular through the statementing process.

Diverse socio-cultural contexts of parenting

One of the problematical issues with the concept of partnership with parents is that parents are sometimes presented as an homogenous group, although, as all practitioners are very aware, parents vary greatly. Partnership with parents is often presented as a concept relating equally to all parents, but evidence shows that there are differences in the extent to which parents become involved in partnerships with Early Years settings. Research findings suggest that women are much more involved in their children's care and education than men and that levels of involvement with school are also determined by race, culture and class (Vincent, 1996). These findings raise a number of questions.

> Why are some parents more likely to be involved in partnership than others?

> How does this impact on the children involved?

> What strategies can be used to involve a wider range of parents in partnership?

It is commonly accepted that parents have the most significant role to play in their children's early learning. Parents teach their children about the world around them, providing experiences, information and explanations as part of the day-to-day interaction between themselves and their child. The range of these experiences, the ways in which the child perceives his or her environment, and the type of cultural values and norms the child absorbs will vary significantly between families, as will the languages used within the home and the quality and quantity of communication between family members.

The type of learning children access within the family is linked to the social and cultural context within which the family exists. Barratt-Pugh (2000) illustrates this point in discussion of the complex and variable ways in which children develop literacy. She argues that children develop literacies according to the socio-cultural context of their family life. However, for some children, the literacies they learn in the home have less value than others when they access more formal learning situations. She states that:

This puts some children at a disadvantage as soon as they enter formal learning contexts, where their knowledge and experiences of literacy are not recognised or built on.

Barratt-Pugh (2000:4)

While children and families have a very wide range of understandings about what literacy is, there is evidence that 'the sorts of literacy practices carried out across educational settings appear to be quite similar' (Barratt-Pugh, 2000:20). The implications for children's learning in Early Years settings is determined by the ways in which some children's types of literacies are valued more than others within the setting because they more closely match the setting's own literacies, resulting in advantage to certain children over others. Drury (2000:86) also points out that we must be careful to note the discontinuities between home and setting as well as the continuities, and she gives an example about how easy it is to make assumptions about a child's home learning experiences.

In terms of partnerships with parents in developing children's early learning there are some significant considerations to be drawn from these observations. Parents who have socio-cultural roots in common with practitioners, and who support their children's learning in ways which correlate with those within the Early Years setting, may be more likely to enter into partnerships with the Early Years setting than parents who may have other socio-cultural backgrounds and different types of learning in the home.

The result may be that some parents develop close bonds with the Early Years setting, matching the learning styles found there and providing their children with closely connected home/setting experiences; others, however, may connect less readily with the Early Years setting and the children may experience dislocation between what they learn at home and in the Early Years setting. This may impact on the child's confidence and enthusiasm for learning, and may result in the child being less likely to take advantage of learning opportunities.

Inequalities in access to partnerships

A significant issue for those who are responsible for developing and maintaining partnerships with parents is to acknowledge and address the inequalities in access to such partnerships. Within this there are a number of issues to consider:

➤ the ways in which partnerships are developed and whether they focus on and are accessible to all types of parents represented in the Early Years setting

➤ the social, cultural, psychological and practical barriers parents face in becoming more involved

➤ the power differentials between practitioners and parents, and how these may impact on access to partnership.

Activity 5

Developing strategies to engage all parents

Consider your own Early Years setting and how parent partnership is planned and encouraged. Observe the type of parents who are closely involved with the Early Years setting, and those who are not.

1 Why do you think some parents are not involved?

2 Are there any links between the reasons for some parents not being involved and the ways in which parent partnership is promoted within the Early Years setting?

3 What could be done to encourage different types of parents into partnership with the Early Years setting?

There are other considerations about the role of parents in partnership. It is important to recognise that the majority of parents will support their children's education and care at home and in an Early Years setting. For some children, however, the support may be minimal or their learning in the home may result in negative outcomes for the child. Not all of the learning that children have in the home is positive in terms of their experiences

Making relationships with hostile parents

Sam, 4, started in nursery after his mother received a caution for assaulting him and bruising his face. The family social worker encouraged Sam's mother to take him to nursery because he had global developmental delays. His attendance was erratic, because his mother did not prioritise nursery and efforts to encourage her to become more consistent usually resulted in longer absences. Sam hardly spoke, did not get involved in activities and had occasional angry and aggressive outbursts. At home there was very little communication and day-to-day life was chaotic with no routines or plans. The children were disciplined with slaps and loud angry outbursts. They were given instructions, but there were few conversations. The family had no friends and no contact with other family members or neighbours.

Sam's mother had a fear of, and became angry with, anyone she believed to be an authority figure and Sam reflected her negative stance in his behaviour and attitude in nursery. He was at best uncommunicative with staff and other children, and at worst hostile and aggressive. In Sam's case, his learning in the home had resulted in patterns of behaviour that inhibited his development. He had learned not to talk; he had learned to treat others with suspicion, hostility and anger; he had learned to be withdrawn and to avoid involvement with others; and he had learned that, if others did things that he did not like, the response was to attack them verbally and physically.

Sam's learning in the home reflected the norms within his household, based on his mother's own negative experiences of the wider world and the ways these had shaped her beliefs, her behaviour and the development of her personality. In nursery, he was confused and unhappy because different ways of behaving were expected of him and he had little experience of these.

---

in the outside world. Some children may learn attitudes, behaviours and concepts of the world around them which are likely to impede learning and development in an Early Years setting. Children who:

➤ are abused and neglected
➤ are in families where domestic violence dominates patterns of behaviour within the home
➤ live in social and cultural isolation through extreme poverty
➤ live with parents who are limited by drug or alcohol abuse

may not only receive little support at home for their learning and development, but may learn behaviours that make their access to learning in a setting problematical.

Case Study 6 above highlights one of the major issues in partnership with parents. Despite the well-documented benefits of partnership to children, parents and practitioners, how do we engage parents in partnership where they are unwilling to be involved or are hostile to the concept of partnership?

Activity 6

Parents and partnership

With reference to Activity 5, consider the parents in your service or Early Years setting who are not involved to any great extent in partnership.

1 Can you find links between the behaviour, learning development and general progress of the child, and the parent's approach to the setting?

2 What sort of strategies could you use to work more closely with the parents and convince them of the benefits of partnership?

Remember to consider issues of confidentiality when discussing or writing about parents and sensitive issues.

The key issue to consider is not what 'parents' in general need in order to become more involved in partnership, but what the parents of the children you work with need in order to become involved. Practitioners must develop knowledge and understanding of the range of cultural, linguistic, economic and social contexts in which the parents they work with live and raise their children. This knowledge is crucial to developing strategies to involve more parents in partnership and it is unique to each Early Years setting or service. How this knowledge and understanding can be translated into positive action for developing inclusive partnerships will be explored later in the chapter. The next section analyses the various meanings of partnership with parents.

What partnership means and types of partnership

The term 'partnership with parents' is somewhat glibly used to describe a whole range of ways in which parents and practitioners work together. However, 'partnership' can mean lots of different types of 'working together' arrangements depending on a number of factors. One of these factors is the extent to which parents and practitioners are equal in the partnership. Vincent (2000) developed her model of parental involvement with educational establishments with reference to what she describes as 'subject positions'. She refers to the 'parent as supporter/learner' position as the partnership between parents and teachers, but argues that:

such 'partnerships', with the connotations of equality inherent in the term, are often legitimating devices used by schools to encourage parental support for their aims and objectives.

Vincent (2000:5)

The view that partnerships between settings and parents are not equal, in that the goals of the partnership are determined by the setting and not the parents, is widespread. The role of parents in relationship to the Early Years setting can seem to be to conform to expectations of the practitioners and to perform functions suggested by the Early Years setting.

The ways in which partnerships with parents are developed within an Early Years setting and the perceptions that both parents and practitioners have about the purposes and goals of the partnership are crucial in determining the success of the partnership for all involved. As such, it is important to ensure that partnerships are based on a sense of participation by all involved, rather than dominated entirely by the perceptions of the Early Years setting and those who work in it. Yet to what extent does this seem practical or desirable? Parents may want very different things from partnership to those that are on offer.

The role of partnership must be based on areas of work where partnership is both possible and desirable. The key issue is how to establish genuine opportunities for communication between parents and practitioners and a clear concept of the areas in which partnership can be effectively developed.

Are parents equal in partnership with settings?

1 With reference to your own work setting or service, consider the ways in which parents are involved in the work of the setting, or supporting their children's learning at home, or any other relevant function. Who determines the following?

➤ Areas in which parents are involved, for example supporting literacy at home.

➤ Ways in which that involvement is expressed, for example reading to the child.

➤ Extent and level of the involvement, for example reading with children in class.

2 Try and evaluate the extent to which parents determine what parent partnership is about within the setting and discuss with a mentor or colleague to find out their views.

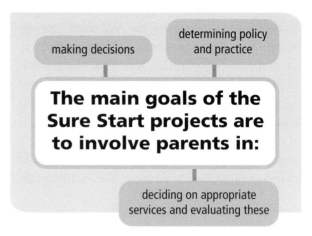

Figure 10.9 Main goals of the Sure Start projects

This poses the question about what evidence there is for partnerships with parents, within which parents have genuine power to determine the extent, goals and purposes of the partnership; and how the partnership is established, maintained and evaluated.

One of the key issues here is the extent to which parents have a sense of empowerment that will support them working in equal partnership with professionals, especially parents who have negative views of learning formed through their own experiences and family background. An example of the importance of supporting parents to choose to take a greater role in partnership was enshrined in the principles and goals of the Sure Start Local Programmes (SSLPs), which functioned partly to empower parents to become involved in community-based projects supporting families and children in the Early

Years. The main goals of the SSLPs are shown in Figure 10.9. The National Evaluation of Sure Start (NESS, 2007) confirmed that there has been a considerable level of achievement of the goals of SSLPs in respect of parent partnership. However, despite this progress, NESS also reported that many SSLPs had not managed to engage those parents who most needed support in their communities.

This concept of practitioners supporting and empowering parents to participate more fully in decision-making, policy development and practice is not new. However, it is not universally applied in Early Years contexts, and in many 'partnerships with parents' there remains room to develop the parent's role to one that involves higher levels of responsibility and equality with practitioners.

Types of partnerships with parents

Partnerships with parents appear in many different guises, many reflecting the specific purposes for which the partnership has been developed. For example, in a reception class, partnership with parents may focus on helping children to settle into school, developing children's learning skills, and sharing information about a child's needs and how these can be met. The level of the parent's involvement depends on the child's needs and the parent's efforts tend to focus on their own child. The goals of partnership are general, but may become more specific if the child has any particular or special needs.

There are two dimensions on which types of partnerships with parents can be explored:

➤ the purposes for which partnership with parents is promoted

➤ the extent to which parents are involved in aspects of the service.

In other words, we can explore different aspects of the concept of partnership with parents by evaluating the range of partnership types and the extent of parental involvement in the partnership. For example, Willey (2000:1) discusses the ways in which parents used to be involved in nursery education at her child's school. The children were left at the school gates and collected from the playground. Contact with teachers was restricted to assemblies and parents' evenings. A few parents were invited to help with practical tasks. The purpose of this type of partnership with parents seemed to be based on parents having limited and formally presented information about their children's progress and achievements. The extent of the partnership was limited.

Approaches to developing partnership with parents fall into a number of different categories as shown in Figure 10.10.

Universal approaches	Potentially involve all parents and children, for example parents' evenings, open days.
Targeted approaches	Focus on particular parents and children, for example parent partnership approaches within the SEN Code of Practice, literacy summer schools.
Community-based approaches	Focus on socially and economically disadvantaged geographical areas, for example Sure Start Children's Centres.

Figure 10.10 Different approaches to partnership with parents

Partnership with parents can also be categorised by the level of involvement of the parents and the extent of equality in the relationship between practitioners and parents.

Epstein and Saunders (2002) devised a model of different types of parent partnership reflecting the extent to which the partnership is equal between the setting and the parents.

➤ **Protective model** – the setting tends to avoid making demands on parents or asking for their involvement.

➤ **School-to-home transmission model** – communication tends to be one-way and reflect the requirements of the setting for parents to support their work with children, for example giving information, asking parents to read to children. Parents are fairly passive in this model.

➤ **Curriculum enrichment model** – parents are seen as support for the teaching and learning processes, for example going on trips, reading with children in school, sharing skills such as cooking and sewing.

➤ **Partnership model** – parents are seen as 'stakeholders' involved in all aspects of planning and delivering the curriculum and developing the setting's ethos and policies.

Activity 8

Types of partnership with parents

Consider the types of partnership with parents in which you are involved in your service or setting.

1 What determines the type of partnership?

2 Which types of partnerships are most effective in involving a diverse range of parents?

3 What other types of partnership would benefit 'stakeholders' in your service or setting?

Factors supporting the development of effective partnerships

The factors that may support the development of a partnership are, to some extent, contextual. The types of approaches and strategies that may work in one situation may be ineffective in another, depending on various factors, as illustrated in Figure 10.11. A key question at this point could be to determine who is responsible for ensuring the development of effective partnerships? This is a complex question, relating to the power differentials between parents and practitioners and the barriers to both practitioners and parents getting involved in genuine partnership.

The legal and policy framework seems to suggest that the bulk of the motivation for partnership comes from practitioners as part of their professional responsibilities to the children in their care. This view may be supported by the fact that often the agenda for partnership is presented as one that originates from the Early Years setting or service and is supported by documentation outlining goals and objectives for the service and how they can be achieved more effectively through partnership. This type of approach seems to be based on an underpinning belief that parents are more passive in developing partnerships and more compliant in determining the goals of partnership than the Early Years setting or services. However, parents may have their own goals and motivations for involving, or not involving, themselves in partnerships, based on a number of complex and interrelated factors, including:

> the parent's own social, cultural and learning experience of education as a child and adult

> the family's relationship with agencies, professionals and authority

> the parent's views on the value and place of Early Years care and education

> the parent's views on the deficits or problems they perceive in the Early Years setting and how this impacts on themselves and their children

> the parent's own agenda for their own child

> the family's cultural, social, religious and linguistic background and how this shapes their approach to their children's education and care.

These factors will influence the willingness and ability of parents to involve themselves in partnership with Early Years settings and services, and the goals that parents may have for such partnerships.

Clearly, what needs to be acknowledged is that:

> parents will have their own agendas for partnership

> these agendas will differ between parents and may be different to the goals of the Early Years setting

> not all parents will initially have a positive view of partnership

> parents will have different levels of motivation, ability and skills to get involved in partnership

> these factors will be unique to each Early Years setting or situation.

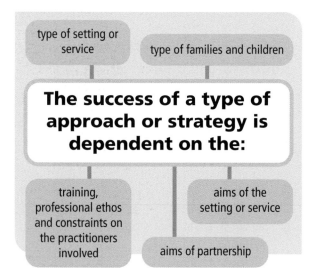

Figure 10.11 Factors determining the success of an approach or strategy in specific Early Years settings

Case Study 7

Meeting diverse needs

Consider three different families whose children are going to nursery school for the first time. The children are all aged 3-and-a-half.

Shirley and Danny

Shirley is desperate for Danny to start nursery. He is extremely lively and demanding and, since his father left two years ago, Shirley has received little help with him. Sometimes she becomes very tired or angry with Danny and she feels that she never has a moment to herself. Shirley believes Danny may be bright, but she does not know much about helping him to learn, although she reads him stories sometimes. She does not play with him much, as she finds it boring and she does not see the point. Shirley did not enjoy her own school years and left with few qualifications. She had a job in a sandwich shop but has not worked since she became pregnant with Danny. It does not occur to Shirley that she will have a relationship with the reception teacher unless Danny is naughty at school.

Alex, Mary and Rose

Alex and Mary sent their other two children to nursery school and feel that it supported their early learning development and helped them to do well in school. They are very keen on learning in the home and have a wide range of educational toys and books for the children to use. They both spend time reading with Rose and helping the older children with maths and other homework. Alex and Mary have considered private schools but they believe in state education and want their children to benefit from and do well in school. However, they are concerned about class sizes and the amount of individual time children receive in classes of 30. They also feel that standards in schools may be slipping and are determined that this will not affect Rose's education as they believe she is a gifted child.

Shiraz, Safina and Jamal

Shiraz works long hours and is often away from home so Safina has the main responsibility for Jamal, their only child. Safina, who came from Pakistan shortly before Jamal's birth, has little contact with English speakers in her community and does not speak much English although she would like to learn. She is worried that Jamal will be unhappy in school because of language problems. Safina is also worried that the school has no non-white teachers or Punjabi speakers. She wonders how Jamal will be supported and helped in a largely white school and whether he will be bullied.

Differences between families

1 With reference to each of these families, try and think about:

   ➤ the parent's agenda

   ➤ strategies to meet this agenda through partnership

   ➤ the approaches that may work to help the parent become involved in partnership

   ➤ what issues, if any, may arise to cause tension between the school and parents.

2 Look at the differences between the families in the case study in terms of their needs, how they can be met, and the problems in achieving this. Try the exercise with reference to different types of families you are involved with.

Building partnerships

In order to build genuine and effective partnerships, practitioners need to consider the following in relation to their own Early Years setting or service.

➤ The diverse needs of parents.

➤ A range of different approaches to involve parents.

➤ The fact that some parents will initially be more responsive than others.

➤ The fact that some parents may be negative about or even hostile to the concept of partnership.

➤ That achieving partnership requires planning, short- and long-term goals and a range of strategies to meet diverse needs.

Draper and Duffy (2006) suggest that successful partnerships need to be based on sharing information, sharing decision-making, sharing responsibility and accountability.

Activity 9

Developing partnership with parents in your setting

Building partnerships with parents takes time and cannot be achieved overnight. In order to ensure partnerships have a secure basis, they need to be rooted in the day-to-day activities of the setting or services, and not a series of isolated events to involve parents on a temporary basis. They also need to involve all types of parents, not just those willing and able to join in the activities of the setting. Practitioners need to be committed to the concept and practice of partnership.

Using the list above, consider how these factors are addressed in your workplace on a day-to-day setting. Share your views with a mentor or colleague and discuss their views also.

Skills for building partnerships

A key factor in effective partnership is the extent to which genuine participative communication takes place between parents and practitioners. Fisher (2002) discusses the need to have 'conversations with parents' in order to learn more about the child as a learner.

A good case for home visiting is made when teachers recount what they have learnt from seeing the child in the surroundings of their own home, and how relationships change when parents meet teachers on their own territory.

Fisher (2002:22)

It may be difficult to have conversations with some parents who may avoid engaging with you or the Early Years setting as a whole. These parents are often described as 'hard to reach' but this label may belie the fact that the setting's strategies for building parent partnership may simply not be suited to engaging some parents. There are, however, some approaches that should support the efforts of settings to build relationships with all parents. These are outlined in Figure 10.12.

Communicate regularly	Ensure that regular communication is part of the work of the Early Years setting or service, for example written communication, phone calls, informal discussion.
Actively seek out 'hard to reach' parents	Seek out 'hard to reach' parents and encourage them to share information with you about their child.
Give regular feedback about child	Give regular feedback on the child's progress and achievement as well as more formal methods of conveying information to parents: for example, conversations at the beginning and end of the day, feedback on the child's work and progress.
Recognise parents' reasons for avoidance	Recognise that parents may avoid involvement for many and varied reasons.
Seek parents' views and opinions	Ask parents for views and opinions, and ask for advice about their child.
Plan	Make plans and strategies with parents for dealing with issues about their child.

Figure 10.12 Strategies to support the engagement of all parents in partnership with the setting

Case Study 8

Developing skills in engaging parents

Harriet entered reception class in a primary school when she was nearly 5 years old. Although her general development did not give cause for concern, the nursery she attended had noted that her social development was delayed and that she had difficulty relating to other children and joining in. She did not seem able to make friends easily or feel confident with others. She had some skills in dealing with other children on a one-to-one basis, but these disappeared when with a group. Harriet spent many of her breaks alone or with the lunchtime supervisor.

Harriet's teacher waited in the playground and spoke to Harriet's mother when she collected her. The teacher commented on Harriet's achievements and good progress with reading. She also commented on how helpful Harriet was in the class and the good standards of work she produced. She then commented that she was a little bit concerned that Harriet was shy with other children and found it hard to join in. Harriet's mother agreed that Harriet had always found it difficult to make friends. The teacher asked if Harriet's mother could come into school so they could make plans together to help Harriet gain confidence with others. She implied that the mother's knowledge and expertise on her own child would be invaluable in helping devise a successful strategy. She also suggested several different times in order to find one to suit the mother. The mother agreed and the meeting took place.

Analysis of skills used by teacher in Case Study 8

The teacher in Case Study 8 was using her communication skills to:

➤ engage the mother with the concerns she had

➤ help the mother feel that she had much to offer in seeking a solution to her child's difficulties

➤ help the mother feel that she was not being critical but wanted to support the child

➤ develop a sense of partnership between the two of them.

Good communication is a key to effective partnership. The attributes of good communicators are shown in Figure 10.13.

Figure 10.13 Attributes of good communicators

Factors that may inhibit the development of effective partnerships

Parents

Parents have diverse motivations, agendas, and skills to bring to partnership with Early Years settings. Some will want to have a high level of involvement; others may appear to want to have no involvement at all. Some may want to be involved but do not know how to engage; others may be hostile, even aggressive in their relationship with practitioners.

Figure 10.14 illustrates those factors that may influence parents' contributions to partnership.

Practitioners

The factors that influence the extent to which practitioners are committed to developing partnerships with parents are shown in Figure 10.15.

Early years settings

Practitioners bring their own contributions to the development of partnership, but a key factor will be the level of commitment the work setting or organisation has to partnership and the management ethos in respect of the 'genuineness' of a partnership approach. Factors that may influence the organisational approach are shown in Figure 10.16.

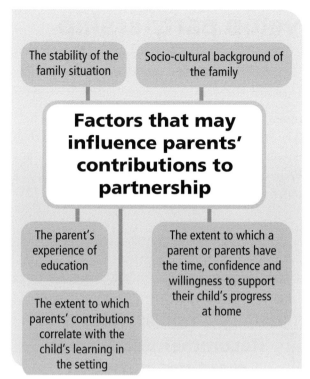

Figure 10.14 Factors that may influence parents' involvement with partnership

Figure 10.15 Factors that influence practitioner commitment to developing partnership with parents

Figure 10.16 Factors influencing the organisational approach to partnership

What really works to develop partnership with parents?

In this final section we discuss strategies and approaches that work to develop partnership and ways of overcoming the inhibiting factors listed above. The strategies suggested are those that have been successful. However, Willey (2000:94) points out that 'There is no single model for working with parents that would meet the needs of every setting'.

Fisher (2002) suggests that parents should be given invitations to join in activities or use resources in the Early Years setting before the child starts there. She argues that such informal contacts are valuable in engaging parents as well as more formal contact. It is important to consider the extent to which parents may need support to become involved and what help they may need to access facilities. This could include:

➤ asking an experienced parent to 'befriend' a parent who lacks confidence

➤ showing parents around to familiarise them with the facilities

➤ checking that invitations are given in a medium that is understandable to the recipient.

Practitioners may need to befriend, encourage and support parents to cross the threshold into the setting.

Home visiting, usually prior to entry or at crucial stages, is a key determinant in establishing good relationships with parents and developing understanding of the child's needs (Fisher, 2002; Draper and Duffy, 2006). Practitioners can also gain an insight into how literacy is developed in the home so that they can build effectively on the child's previous experience (Campbell, 2000). In order to ensure that home visiting contributes to the development of partnership, practitioners need training in working with parents and families, organisations need to commit resources to home visiting and there needs to be a strong ethos supporting home visiting that is enshrined in policy within the organisation. Willey (2000:96) suggests a range of 'formal' meetings as essential contact (see Figure 10.17).

Figure 10.17 Formal meetings suggested as essential contact (Willey, 2000:96)

Settling-in period

Draper and Duffy (2006) emphasise the settling-in period as a key period for developing effective relationships with parents. Parents and children should both be given the chance to get used to the Early Years setting before the child stays alone. Some of the methods that may be used to achieve this are shown in Figure 10.18.

Practitioners need to be responsive to, and patient with, parents' concerns about leaving their child. They need to recognise that parents have a range of feelings at this stage and that separation can be easy or painful. They need to be sure that they listen to concerns and not assume they know what these are.

Figure 10.18 Some ways of familiarising parents and children with the Early Years setting

Communication between parents and practitioners

Opportunities for communication between parents and practitioners are crucial. Trying to catch busy practitioners before and after nursery or school, being told you can just have a few minutes of their time, not being able to contact key people by phone – all these barriers to communication are very frustrating for parents who may be anxious about their child. Communication should include those elements shown below in Figure 10.19.

Practitioners need to be skilled in communication at a range of levels and audiences. They should be aware that some parents may need different communication approaches to others, and have the interpersonal skills to judge this successfully. There should be strategies within the Early Years setting to support communication with parents who do not have English as a first language and parents who have other communication difficulties, and there should be policy and resources to support these strategies. Written communications should be considered in terms of the audience and be appropriate to that audience.

Commitment to specific goals

Parents and practitioners need to have a common understanding of and commitment to specific goals in respect of each child's learning and development. Parents' views should be sought and incorporated in the practitioner's understanding of the child's needs. Use should be made of home-setting diaries, initial information-gathering about the child, and opportunities to meet to keep this understanding current. Willey (2000:94) describes the use of a nursery diary in which practitioners and parents record children's work, photos, observations and comments as an important tool for communication.

Practitioners should be aware of parents' aspirations for their child, their concerns and hopes. Records should be up to date, confidential and used as a working tool to aid the practitioner's work.

Communication between practitioners and parents should include:	
Informal and formal meetings	Opportunities for parents to meet with practitioners formally and informally to discuss aspects of their child's learning and development.
Methods of conveying information about the child	Methods of ensuring information about the child is conveyed between parents and practitioners on a regular basis.
Forums for parents' views	Forums for parents' views on aspects of the setting or service to be aired.
Regularly updated information about the Early Years setting	Regular information about events, developments and items of interest to be conveyed from the Early Years setting to parents.

Figure 10.19 Range of communication between practitioners and parents

Parents should be made to feel part of the community of the Early Years setting. They should be welcomed at arrival and departure times; given verbal and written information; and involved in key events within the setting. Parents should be included in delivering the curriculum. Practitioners need to find out about parents' skills and utilise these where possible. They should pay particular attention to those parents who are not involved and communicate less with the Early Years setting. Stereotypes about the sort of experiences and skills parents can offer should be avoided (let the white British parents make curry with the children for a change, for example).

Parents should have access to information about the Early Years setting and the community. They should also have access to information about other services available, which they may want to use. Practitioners need to be knowledgeable about the range of services available to young children in their community and share this information.

Seek parents' views

Parents need to have opportunities to make suggestions; give feedback; make complaints and offer views and opinions. This entitlement should be part of policy and supported by a strong management and organisational ethos of listening and responding to feedback. Where possible, parents should be represented on the management of the service or Early Years setting.

Within the Early Years setting or service there should be policies, strategies and ongoing discussion about the best ways of reaching those parents who are less likely to get involved. Parents should be asked for their help and ideas. Schemes such as befriending, 'father's days' and other strategies targeting specific groups should be tried and assessed for their impact. There should be an ongoing and dynamic debate within the Early Years setting about what parents want and how best to get them involved.

Conclusion

The concept of partnership with parents is often presented simply and with the underlying assumption that developing relationships will benefit the children and the Early Years setting. Yet parents can gain enormously from being involved in their children's learning: developing new skills and using existing ones to support others; learning about child development; having opportunities to discuss hopes and fears and show pride in their child.

Developing partnerships is complex and messy, involving a large quantity of imagination and determination in order to reach the diverse range of parents with whom each Early Years setting is involved. The key elements are a strongly supportive ethos,

ongoing discussion and feedback on strategies adopted and practitioners who have the knowledge, commitment and skills to work effectively in this area.

How to move on in your research

Bee, H. (2006) (11th edition), *The Developing Child*. Boston, MA: Allyn and Bacon
Chapter 13 in this book gives a clear and easy to assimilate outline of theories and studies of parenting styles and the links between these and children's developmental outcomes.

Cleaver, H., Unel, I. and Aldgate, A. (1999), *Children's Needs – Parenting Capacity: The Impact of Parental Mental Illness, Problem Alcohol and Drug Use, and Domestic Violence on Children's Development.* London: Stationery Office

This is widely recognised as a key text on the relationship between particular environmental and individual issues and the capacity to parent children safely and effectively.

Draper, L. and Duffy, B. (2006), 'Working with parents', in **Pugh, G. and Duffy, B. (eds) (3rd edition)**, *Contemporary Issues in the Early Years.* London: Paul Chapman

This chapter discusses key aspects of working with parents and gives practical advice and information on how to engage parents with the setting.

References

Aries, P. (1982), *Centuries of Childhood: A Social History of Family Life.* London: Cape and Sears

Baldock, P. (2001), *Regulating Early Years Services.* London: David Fulton

Barratt-Pugh, C. and Rohl, M. (2000), *Literacy Learning in the Early Years.* Maidenhead: Open University Press

Bastiani, J. (2000), '"I know it works! … Actually proving it is the problem!" Examining the contribution of parents to pupil progress and school effectiveness', in **Wolfendale, S. and Bastiani, J. (eds)**, *The Contribution of Parents to School Effectiveness.* London: David Fulton

Bronfenbrenner, U. (1979), *The Ecology of Human Development.* Cambridge MA: Harvard University Press

Campbell, R. (2000), 'Literacy learning at home and at school', in **Drury, R., Miller, L. and Campbell, R.,** *Looking at Early Years Education and Care.* London: David Fulton

Children Act (1989), London: HMSO

Children's Legal Centre (2007), *Parental Responsibility.* Accessed online in August 2007 at http://www.childrenslegalcentre.com/Templates/Topic.asp?NodeID=89632

Drury, R. (2000), 'Bilingual children in the pre-school years: Different experiences of early learning', in **Drury, R., Miller, L. and Campbell, R.,** *Looking at Early Years Education and Care.* London: David Fulton

End Child Poverty (2007), Key Facts. Accessed online in August 2007 at http://www.endchildpoverty.org.uk/key-facts.html

Epstein, J. and Saunders, M. (2002), 'Family, school and community partnerships', in **Borstein, M. (ed.) (2nd edition)**, *Handbook of Parenting Vol.5 Practical Issues in Parenting.* London: Erlbaum

ESCR (2007) Welfare and Single Parenthood in UK – Lone Parents in the *UK Factsheet.* Accessed online August 2007 at http://www.esrc.ac.uk/ESRCInfoCentre/facts/UK/index40.aspx?ComponentId=12614&SourcePageId=18133

Every Child Matters: Change for Children (2007). Online, last accessed December 2007 at www.everychildmatters.gov.uk

Fisher, J. (2002) (2nd edition), *Starting from the Child.* Maidenhead: Open University Press

Messer, D. and Millar, S. (1999), *Exploring Developmental Psychology: From Infancy to Adolescence.* London: Hodder Arnold

National Statistics Online (2007) Stepfamilies. Accessed online in August 2007 at http://www.statistics.gov.uk/CCI/nugget. asp?ID=1164

NICHD Early Child Care Research Network (2001), 'Nonmaternal care and family factors in early development: An overview of the NICHD study of early child care.' *Applied Developmental Psychology*, 22, pp457–92.

Plowden Report (1967), *Children and their Primary Schools. A Report of the Central Advisory Council for Education (England).* London: HMSO

Pugh, G. et al (1994), *Confident Parents, Confident Children: Policy and Practice in Parent Education and Support.* London: National Children's Bureau

Pugh, G. (2006), 'A policy for early childhood services?', in **Pugh, G. and Duffy, B. (eds) (3rd edition)**, *Contemporary Issues in the Early Years.* London: Paul Chapman

Roffey, S. (1999), *Special Needs in the Early Years.* London: David Fulton

Rumbold Report (1990), *Starting with Quality.* DES London: HMSO

Rutherford, D. (1998), 'Children's relationships', in **Taylor, J. and Woods, M. (eds)**, *Early Childhood Studies: An Holistic Introduction.* London: Hodder Arnold

Shah, M. (2001), *Working with Parents.* Oxford: Heinemann

Summerfield, C. and Babb, P. (2003), *Social Trends,* No. 33 National Statistics. London: HMSO

Thurtle, V. (1998), 'Child in society', in **Taylor, J. and Woods, M. (eds)**, *Early Childhood Studies: An Holistic Introduction.* London: Hodder Arnold

Vincent, C. (2000), *Including Parents? – Education, Citizenship and Parental Agency.* Maidenhead: Open University Press

Willey, C. (2000), 'Working with parents in Early Years' settings', in **Drury, R., Miller, L. and Campbell, R.**, *Looking at Early Years Education and Care.* London: David Fulton

Wolfendale, S. (2000), 'Effective schools for the future: Incorporating the parental and family dimension', in **Wolfendale, S. and Bastiani, J. (eds)**, *The Contribution of Parents to School Effectiveness.* London: David Fulton

Woods, M. (1998), 'Early childhood studies – First principles', in **Taylor, J. and Woods, M. (eds)**, *Early Childhood Studies: An Holistic Introduction.* London: Hodder Arnold

Zona, K.P., Saudino, K.S. and Gagne, J.R. (2007), *Harsh Parental Discipline and Child Externalizing Problems in Early Toddlerhood: The Moderating Effects of Parental Warmth.* Accessed online in August 2007 at http://www.bu.edu/psych/labs/ kateSRCD2007.doc

Useful websites

www.cpag.org.uk

www.endchildpoverty.org.uk

www.everychildmatters.gov.uk/parents

11 Developing strategies for supporting learning: Early Years Foundation Stage and Key Stage One

Melanie Henshaw

This chapter will explore in more detail what learning in the Early Years should look like and how adults support children both in the Early Years and in their transition to KS1.

To a great extent children's learning today is driven by an outcome-based curriculum. Over a decade ago, the Rumbold Report (DES 1990) investigated the quality of education for children under five, identifying the tension between process- and outcome-based learning. The report concluded that how children were being encouraged to learn was of equal importance to what they were learning.

By undertaking the suggested study within this chapter it is hoped that you will be able to:

1 plan to meet the individual needs of the children and match this to the appropriate framework or curriculum

2 effectively adapt your teaching strategies to meet the individual needs of children

3 reflect on practice and adapt your practice to facilitate learning.

This chapter addresses the following areas:

➤ The National Curriculum

➤ The Foundation Stage: an Early Years curriculum

➤ The Early Years Foundation Stage (EYFS)

➤ Primary Framework for literacy and mathematics

➤ The role of the adult – pedagogy

➤ Planning for learning

➤ Extending children's existing learning – developing thinking skills

➤ Learning styles

➤ The role of observations in planning and assessment

➤ Creating a thinking and problem-solving environment

The National Curriculum

The National Curriculum was introduced in 1988 as part of the Education Reform Act; an Early Years curriculum was later established in England via the Desirable Learning Outcomes (DLOs), (SCAA, 1996). The planning and implementation of the DLO was largely influenced by the National Curriculum. This influence was not entirely beneficial, resulting in a high-content, goal-centred and adult-led curriculum rather than a curriculum that was process and child-led. It became apparent that a curriculum intended for 5–7-year-olds was not appropriate for 3–5-year-olds. It would have been more appropriate for the National Curriculum to have emerged from the principles of the Early Years curriculum. Prior to the introduction of the DLOs in England (SCAA, 1996) there was no uniform approach to the Early Years curriculum; local education authorities (LEAs), individual nurseries and schools had generally developed their own curriculum.

The National Curriculum sets out the stages and core subjects taught to children aged 5 to 16. This is a mandatory requirement for **maintained** or **state** schools. Following a number of revisions and changes in emphasis upon curriculum areas, a 'slimmed down' version of the curriculum is now in place for schools in England. The development of literacy and numeracy skills in the Early Years is now a priority, and the methods prescribed within the Literacy and Numeracy Strategies provide a template for curriculum delivery. As a result, in English schools the original emphasis on a broad and balanced curriculum providing opportunities for creative thinking and a holistic approach to curriculum delivery has been overtaken by a narrow skills-based curriculum. The National Curriculum is in danger of having three core subjects, English, Mathematics and science, with other subjects such as history, music etc. becoming specialist programmes.

In 2007 the new secondary National Curriculum was launched. The new programmes of study have been designed to change the focus within the curriculum for post-14 pupils. This change aims to give teachers a less prescriptive, more flexible framework for teaching, creating more scope to tailor the curriculum to meet the needs of each individual student. Further information is available online (see the list of useful websites at the end of this chapter). Possibly in time this creative approach will filter down through the rest of the National Curriculum and offer a more creative approach to teaching and learning, putting learning into context. An example of a successful creative curriculum is that used in the Reggio Emilia region of Italy. The children lead a process-based curriculum rather than a content-based curriculum (as in the UK), in which adults support and extend children's learning through careful observation, documentation and dialogue with children and their significant adults.

The National Curriculum across the United Kingdom

The curriculum in Scotland has always been distinctly different and has provided guidance for teachers rather than prescriptive targets. The 5–14 years curriculum is divided into five broad curricular areas: language, mathematics, environmental studies, expressive arts and religious and moral education. For each curricular area there are broad attainment outcomes, each with a number of strands or aspects of learning that pupil's experience. This offers teachers the flexibility to adapt the curriculum and teaching strategies as required.

Primary schools in Wales must, by law, teach the basic curriculum and the National Curriculum. The six years of the primary phase are divided into two key stages. The basic curriculum consists of religious education

(RE) and personal and social education (PSE). Primary schools are also required to have a policy on sex education.

Ireland has a centrally devised curriculum. However, there is a strong emphasis on individual school and classroom planning. At school level, the particular character and location of the school makes a vital contribution to shaping the curriculum in classrooms. Adaptation of the curriculum to suit the individual school is achieved through the preparation and continuous updating of a school plan. The schools select textbooks and classroom resources to support the implementation of the curriculum as opposed to the Department for Children, Schools and Families or the National Council for Curriculum and Assessment.

Further information on the different curriculums is available online – see the list of useful websites at the end of this chapter.

The Foundation Stage: an Early Years curriculum

In September 2000 the Foundation Stage was introduced as a phase of education for children aged 3–5. The **Curriculum Guidance for the Foundation Stage** (DfES/QCA, 2000) set out six areas of learning which formed the basis of the Foundation Stage curriculum. The Education Act 2002 extended the National Curriculum to include the Foundation Stage, making the six areas of learning a statutory element within the Early Years in March 2002. This was the first time that educating children of this age had been recognised as a distinct and separate phase of learning within the maintained, state sector. The 'Stepping Stones', which form an integral part of this educational programme, feed into the National Curriculum Key Stage 1 programme but allow for development at a pace appropriate to the needs of the individual child. The Foundation Stage approach recognises that learning occurs constantly, whether intentional or incidental.

The Curriculum Guidance provided a structure for the education of children. This structured approach however has not proven successful in the Early Years. The Curriculum Guidance 'is to be replaced with a framework, whereby the focus has moved more towards the environment and naturally occurring experiences'. The language of quality is hopefully to be redirected towards the process of learning. The Foundation Stage Curriculum Guidance will therefore be abolished in September 2008.

Limitations of the Foundation Stage

There are various drawbacks arising from the approach outlined in the Foundation Stage curriculum.

➤ Difficulties have arisen for some Early Years settings with a long-established curriculum that differs from that promoted by the current government. For example, some Foundation Stage practitioners follow methods supported by organisations such as the Pre-School Learning Alliance, Montessori or Steiner; others may have implemented methods used within a maintained school to which their nursery class is attached. Early Years settings that subscribe to these philosophical traditions need to achieve a compromise with the government-driven curriculum in order to receive funding.

➤ In a bid to produce a planning cycle that provided evidence for Office for Standards in Education (Ofsted) many practitioners spent large amounts of time away from the children, or with the children but preoccupied completing planning sheets.

➤ The Effective Provision of Pre-School Education (EPPE), a longitudinal study of children's development between the ages of 3 and 7 years, highlighted the complexities of this document and the general lack of understanding amongst practitioners, implying that to fully understand the documents practitioners need to be trained to degree level.

The Foundation Stage Profile

The Education Act 2002 also established a single national assessment system for the Foundation Stage. The Foundation Stage Profile was introduced in 2002–3. The Profile has thirteen summary scales covering the six areas of learning, which must be completed for each child by the end of his or her time in the Foundation Stage.

The Profile summarises children's achievements and is based upon teachers' on-going assessments through day-to-day learning and teaching, as well as the information provided by practitioners in previous settings and by parents/carers. However, in practice the information sharing between pre-schools and schools leaves a lot to be desired. It is designed to be completed gradually as children progress through the reception year. Nursery practitioners can also contribute to the Profile by recording any of the scale points that children achieve before moving into reception. Both reception and nursery practitioners should use the Profile as the most effective way of monitoring children's progress and sharing assessments. The Profile remains in place from September 2008, despite the fact that Ofsted suggests the new national assessment wastes teachers' time, stating that it is too complicated for parents and does not prepare children for Year 1. Ofsted further suggests that teachers have to give children extra tests because the assessment does not provide the information they need. Although the Foundation Stage Profile was introduced as a replacement for baseline assessment, Ofsted claims it does not provide the same information.

Birth to Three Matters

In 2003, Sure Start published *Birth to Three Matters*, a framework for learning to support practitioners working with babies and young children. Its aims were to raise the quality of learning and development opportunities for babies and children from birth to three years and to provide training and professional development for practitioners to implement curricula frameworks. The opportunities for learning identified within the framework formed the basis of an holistic approach for very young children, and focused on caring for children as individuals. However, it is important to note that the Birth to Three Matters Framework was not intended to be a curriculum for the under threes, rather it was a supportive framework for practitioners to obtain guidance. The Framework was not focused on individual areas of development: it started from **the child.** It identifies four **Aspects**, which identify the skills of babies and young children and the links between growth learning and development and how the environment impacts on these.

These four Aspects are:
➤ A Strong Child
➤ A Skilful Communicator
➤ A Competent Learner
➤ A Healthy Child

Each Aspect is divided further into **Components**. The main problem arising from this was that practitioners trained in birth to three found it difficult to transfer to the Foundation Stage and vice versa. It led to two distinctly different planning systems and the Birth to Three assessments were difficult to transfer over to the six areas of learning.

The Early Years Foundation Stage (EYFS)

The government announced, in 2005, that the Early Years Foundation Stage was to replace the Birth to Three Matters Framework (Sure Start 2003, 2005), the Curriculum Guidance for the Foundation Stage (QCA/DfEE 2000) and the National Standards for Under 8s Day Care and Childminding (DfES 2003). This single framework received legal force through the Childcare Act 2006 and was released in 2007, becoming a statutory document in 2008. From September 2008 all Early Years providers who register with Ofsted will have a duty to comply with this single document. The Early Years Foundation Stage is a major part of the government's Ten Year Strategy for Childcare, Choice for Parents. The key principles of this strategy are to provide parents with a range of affordable quality childcare options that are flexible and available in all areas.

The Early Years Foundation Stage separates the Early Years from the National Curriculum and applies to children from birth to five. It is believed that this separation will develop a framework that integrates education and care. There is still no compulsion for children to attend pre-school in England and the statutory school starting age remains the term following the child's fifth birthday. However, the number of children attending pre-school is increasing. The Office for National Statistics published figures in April 2007 suggesting that the number of 3- and 4-year-olds enrolled in schools in the UK have tripled from 21 per cent in 1970/71 to 64 per cent in 2005/06.

The word 'curriculum' has been removed and replaced with 'framework', recognising that it is offering a support system as opposed to a teaching agenda; this embraces the principles of Birth to Three Matters which placed a greater emphasis on care and routine. Many practitioners expected the EYFS to be split into components similar to those of the Birth to Three Matters Framework and were surprised that the six areas of learning had been maintained. These learning outcomes and assessment requirements carried over from the Curriculum Guidance remain indicative of a teaching and learning environment which in turn leaves it open to being labelled as a curriculum.

The term 'guidance' has been replaced with 'statutory' – this now means that settings who previously were not in receipt of government funding and as such did not have to show regard for the previous guidance documents, will now have to comply with the care, learning and development aspects of the document. This will include Early Years settings affiliated to international educational bodies such as Montessori or Waldorf/Steiner. It is believed, however, that these settings are able to comply with the EYFS as it does not prescribe teaching methods; it simply identifies the learning goals for children to work towards. Individual settings have the flexibility to decide how they work towards those early learning goals.

The major change is that while the age range of Early Years previously referred to birth to eight, the EYFS recognises that the care and education of children over the age of five is significantly different from that of children under five. There is a worry here however that as children start school at five the transition from a play-based framework to a subject-driven curriculum will be difficult. The trend within school nurseries has been to offer a watered-down version of the National Curriculum to Foundation Stage children in preparation for school. However, this document will release school nursery settings from the constraints of the National Curriculum and re-emphasises the importance of play, care and routine.

The aims of the Early Years Foundation Stage (EYFS)

The EYFS aims to ensure that children from birth to five have access to consistently high quality Early Years care, learning and development regardless of the setting they attend or the area in which they live. The guiding principle of this document is to help children achieve the five Every Child Matters outcomes.

➤ Staying safe.

➤ Enjoying and achieving.

➤ Making a positive contribution.

➤ Achieving economic well-being.

➤ Being healthy.

They EYFS aims to achieve this by setting the standards for care, learning and development, ensuring that all children regardless of ethnicity, culture or religion, home language, family background, learning difficulties or disabilities, gender or ability, make progress and no child is left behind. The set of standards within this document aims to improve quality and consistency within the Early Years sector, and provide a single benchmark for inspection and regulation. There have in the past been inconsistencies with the inspection process,

where schools were subjected to a lengthy inspection process and the private sector only one day. By standardising the Early Years sector the document suggests that all settings are to be equal in terms of delivering the Early Years Foundation Stage. By complying with these standards it is suggested that settings will reflect the personal experiences that many parents provide for their children within the home environment. In essence the document is trying to encourage all settings to be more like home and less like a school classroom, focusing on children's individualised learning needs based on their interests and having regard for their culture.

Learning and development requirements of the EYFS

This mandatory section of the EYFS sets out the learning and development requirements that by law all Early Years' providers must deliver. The six areas of learning now apply to children from birth.

➤ Personal, social and emotional development

➤ Communication, language and literacy

➤ Problem solving, reasoning and numeracy

➤ Knowledge and understanding of the world

➤ Physical development

➤ Creative development

The document acknowledges that learning and development is an holistic process and clearly states that:

None of these areas of Learning and Development can be delivered in isolation from the others. They are equally important and depend on each other to support a rounded approach to child development.

(DfES, 2007: 11)

However, in order to assess children against the many individual stepping stones there is a danger that these will be reproduced as a tick list assessment chart. This could lead to activities being carried out with children in order to tick a box and return to the adult-led days of the DLOs. Many practitioners believe that the birth to three aspects and components would have been more appropriate than the subject specific learning goals of the Curriculum Guidance. However, this would not have allowed the Primary Framework for literacy and mathematics to be incorporated, and although the principles of the EYFS suggest development is holistic, this drive to focus on literacy and maths is slowly filtering into the Early Years. On the whole the guidance contained within the EYFS offers practitioners of all levels advice about caring for and extending the learning of young children and should prove to be an extremely valuable resource.

Activity 2

Curriculum perspectives

Choose an alternative curriculum approach. This may include:

➤ Steiner

➤ Montessori

➤ Reggio Emilia

➤ Froebel

➤ Isaacs.

How does it differ from the EYFS? In what ways is it similar? How can they adapt their philosophies to ensure they are complying with the EYFS? What would prevent them from making these changes?

Look closely at your practice. How are you going to change your practice when this document becomes statutory in 2008?

Points to consider

There are those, such as Dahlberg et al (2007) and Wilson (2003), who question the universal application of standards or development targets, suggesting that in a diverse society children should be considered in the context of their own community and not be accountable to the standards of other communities. The EYFS implies that all children during their first five years of life, within which times there are vast individual differences, will require the same skills and knowledge in preparation for school, while at the same time advocating that children are individuals requiring individual learning strategies. At the end of the EYFS they will be compared against the same set of goals.

It could be argued that the prescriptive nature of the EYFS will deter practitioners from adapting their practice to meet the cultural needs of their children, attempting to drive them towards the learning goals regardless. For example, children attending a setting of predominantly middle-class children in the south of England would be assessed against the same learning goals as children attending a setting with high levels of special educational needs (SEN) or English as an additional language. This does not embrace diversity.

There is also a danger that, as children are assessed against the learning goals, quality will be misrepresented as the largest number of learning goals obtained, and produce nursery league tables as it has in schools. Quality childcare is not an end product, it is a process. Quality is very subjective, however – it has to be about children leaving nursery with the personal, social and emotional skills that give them confidence to explore, to problem solve, to question and most importantly to want to learn. This can be achieved through the EYFS as long as practitioners do not see this document as a new and revolutionary approach to childcare, requiring them to change everything. Have confidence in your practice and view this document as support and guidance for those moments where you think 'how can I do that?' and do not get bogged down with the quantity of information on the CD. Use it as an encyclopaedia to answer those questions.

Individual learning strategy

Read the case studies below and, considering the application of universal standards, discuss with other colleagues the following:

1 How would the needs of each child differ? Identify what each child might need to take them forward.

2 What are the skills that each child needs to cope with their environment?

3 How you would assess the two children?

Case Study 1

Assessment

Sarah is 18 months old. Her mother is homeless and currently living in a local bed and breakfast. Sarah attends nursery five mornings a week; she is very tearful and has to be taken from her mother crying each morning. Sarah sits alone watching the other children; she will not play with any toys, she only moves when her key worker carries her. Other than crying Sarah makes no attempt to communicate her needs. Sarah has been at the nursery now for two months and there have been no significant changes.

Chloe is 18 months old. Her parents are both doctors and Chloe attends nursery five full days a week. Chloe is a confident child and plays alongside other children. Chloe leaves her parents in the morning and cries for about five minutes before going to play with the toys. Chloe is able to make her needs known to her key worker but her dummy is hindering her progress. Chloe has been at the nursery for three months and is becoming more settled.

The Early Years curriculum across the United Kingdom

In Wales the Early Years curriculum has seven principles of foundation learning.

➤ Personal and social development and well-being

➤ Language, literacy and communication skills

➤ Mathematical development

➤ Bilingual and multicultural understanding

➤ Knowledge and understanding of the world

➤ Physical development

➤ Creative development

Emphasis has been placed on developing children's knowledge, skills and understanding through experiential learning, learning by doing and by solving real-life problems both inside and outdoors.

The government attaches great importance to developing Welsh language provision for the Early Years. This explains the bilingual and multicultural learning goal. It is important that the curriculum fosters an understanding of diversity from an early age. Just as there are in England, there are changes being made to the education system in Wales. There does not appear to be any official guidance on caring for children under three currently.

Scotland separates birth to three as does England. However, the Scottish curriculum is undergoing a national review with the aim of developing a streamlined curriculum for 3–18-year-olds and implementing new approaches to assessment. In Scotland the Birth to Three Guidance is based on three key features through which it suggests that effective support and learning opportunities for very young children can be developed through:

➤ relationships

➤ responsive care

➤ respect.

The curriculum framework for 3–5-year-olds refers to planned learning experiences based on different key aspects of children's development and learning. There are five areas of learning.

➤ Emotional, personal and social development
➤ Communication and language
➤ Knowledge and understanding of the world
➤ Expressive and aesthetic development
➤ Physical development and movement.

As with the UK the Republic of Ireland is also reviewing policies. The Centre for Early Childhood Development and Education (CECDE) launched *Síolta*, the National Quality Framework for Early Childhood Education in 2006, and is set to launch the Framework for Early Years. The framework will begin with a set of broad principles which highlight how children learn and develop in their Early Years. Using the four themes of:

➤ well-being
➤ identity and belonging
➤ communicating
➤ exploring and thinking

the framework will focus on developing children's dispositions and skills, nurturing attitudes and values, and building knowledge of their world.

➤ Skills like walking, climbing, cutting, writing.
➤ Dispositions like curiosity, concentration, resilience.
➤ Attitudes and values like respect for others, positive attitudes to learning and to life.

➤ Understanding/knowledge like developing a sense of colour and shape, place, learning that words have meaning, how things work.

The framework will also give suggestions for how adults can develop their practice. These are presented in guidelines on:

➤ interacting with children
➤ developing partnerships with parents and families
➤ using play to support learning and development
➤ assessing children's progress and planning for the next steps in learning.

Activity 4

International curriculum perspectives

Look in detail at the Early Years Foundation Stage document and compare it to an Early Years framework from another country.

1 Compare the principles that underpin each document.

2 Look at the different learning outcomes. Consider why they are different.

3 Look at the different age ranges. How are the learning and teaching strategies differentiated?

4 Do the frameworks or curricula take into account the culture?

5 Which of the two frameworks truly embrace diversity?

6 Does it positively promote an inclusive Early Years system?

Primary Framework for literacy and mathematics

The Primary Framework for literacy and mathematics utilises the existing materials introduced with the National Literacy Strategy in 1998 and the Numeracy Strategy in 1999. The revision, however, contains improvements to make it easier for teachers and practitioners to plan lessons, monitor pupils' progress and keep an overview of learning from Foundation Stage through to Year 6. The renewal of the Primary Framework for literacy and mathematics provides those involved with teaching children aged from 3 to 11 the opportunity to continue the progress made in raising standards by embedding the principles of both *Every Child Matters: Change for Children* (2004) and *Excellence and Enjoyment: Learning and Teaching in the Primary Years* (Ref: 0518-2004) into practice. This framework links the Foundation Stage to the National Curriculum in literacy and mathematics, despite the fact that mathematics as a learning goal has been replaced with reasoning and problem solving in the EYFS. This area of learning is embedded in the mathematics section of the Framework to maintain continuity once the EYFS is implemented. It involves children building an understanding of problem solving, reasoning and numeracy in a broad range of contexts in which they can explore, enjoy, learn, practise and talk about their developing understanding. Mathematical development depends on becoming confident and competent in learning and using key skills.

The aim of the Primary Framework for literacy and mathematics is to support and increase all children's access to excellent teaching, leading to exciting and successful learning. There is a shared determination between the Primary National Strategy, schools, settings and local authorities (LAs)

that all children are appropriately supported to make the progress of which they are capable.

Children deserve:

➤ to be set appropriate learning challenges

➤ to be taught well and be given the opportunity to learn in ways that maximise their chances of success

➤ to have adults working with them to tackle the specific barriers to progress they face.

The Primary Framework for literacy and mathematics is designed to help practitioners, teachers, schools and settings achieve this ambition.

Some of the key changes

Some of the main differences between the National Literacy Strategy in 1998 and the Numeracy Strategy in 1999 and the Primary Framework for literacy and mathematics are:

➤ the interactive nature of the framework and the electronic versions now available

➤ the Early Years integration – for the first time, teachers and practitioners will receive the same information whether they access Foundation Stage guidance through the Primary Framework or the EYFS

➤ the Framework now provides a clearer set of outcomes organised into twelve strands of learning in literacy and seven in mathematics.

There are two concerns, the first being that if subjects are prioritised there is the danger that in removing them from context children will be driven away from them as opposed to excelling in them. This in turn devalues other subjects such as creativity. In Sweden it is accepted that children have the right to play and explore before they start school; they do not learn to read until they are six and then by ten they lead the literacy tables. This is achieved by using the Early Years to foster a love of learning, consequently by the age of six they want to read. The second concern is that children are being returned to the carpet for 'quality' phonics and adult-directed activities. Young children need to be active and learn through exploration, not by being confined to a carpet square.

The curricula and frameworks that advise the United Kingdom focus on the knowledge and skills that children are required to learn at a given age. There is a real danger that this focus on knowledge and timescales prevents children and adults developing that thirst for knowledge that drives their exploration. While there are many who see a framework for Early Years as recognition of its importance, the universal application of documents that focus on typical development becomes exclusive as opposed to inclusive. Nursery care should – in that it is locally controlled – be more able to embrace diversity and establish milestones that celebrate individual achievements. Practitioners should see this document as a resource that will inform practice and take into account their locality and the individual needs of the children in their care. Holding children up to a set of culturally influenced norms contradicts the claim that children are individual and fails to embrace diversity and inclusion.

So, by all means let there be frameworks of normalisation, if these are wanted. But equally let us not fool ourselves about what they are or what they can do. Let us recognise their limitations and dangers, their assumptions and values. Let them not be at the expense of ignoring other ways of thinking about making sense of early childhood institutions and the work that they do.

Dahlberg et al (2007)

What is learning

If we are to interpret and deliver the various frameworks and curricula in a way that children will learn and develop new skills, we need to understand how to facilitate learning and enhance this process. It is widely acknowledged that we never stop learning, yet it is very hard to identify exactly what is meant by learning. Many suggest that learning is the acquisition of knowledge or skills. In the Early Years this is achieved by providing experiences or activities that engage and challenge children's thinking.

Activity 5

Learning skills and knowledge

Imagine an alien has landed in your kitchen. They have no knowledge of Earth but they can read. They have asked for food. You will need to give written instructions as to how to make beans on toast. Break down this process and provide them with written instructions. Start right from the beginning by describing the equipment they will need.

1 Once you have done this look at your instructions, how much will the alien have learned?

2 Break this learning down into knowledge acquisition and new skills.

3 Think back to the last time you had to learn something new, for example learning to drive. List all of the emotions you experienced during this process.

Attached to learning there are many emotions, fear, excitement, apprehension, frustration to name but a few. As adult learners we find these hard to deal with so imagine how these complicate the learning of young children who have not yet learnt how to control or understand many of these feelings.

Delivering or teaching the curriculum

With the introduction of the EYFS in 2008 children of all ages will have a framework for learning, or a curriculum of some description.

Although there are slight variations that enable countries in the UK to take ownership and embed their culture into the documents on the whole they are all very similar. They provide practitioners with an agenda for learning. Contained within these documents are the skills and knowledge that adults have decided all children will require to become 'useful' adults. However, transition between the age groups is not as smooth as it could be. During the Early Years children learn in context. It is well known that children of this age need to see a purpose for their learning. They make choices and are free to explore creatively. As children enter the National Curriculum this is often lost and the focus is driven by the knowledge required for SATs. The revised post-14 curriculum now returns to the Early Years ethos that learning in context is more likely to engage learners. This is to be achieved through hands-on work experience, allowing learners to see how the skills and knowledge they acquire are transferred to real-life situations. The QCA is now reviewing how the National Curriculum is being delivered, advocating that the National Curriculum should in fact be taught and not delivered.

QCA has developed a curriculum big picture to reinforce the concept of curriculum as the entire planned learning experience of a young person. This would include the lessons that they have during the school day, but also recognises how much young people learn from the routines, the events, the extended school day and activities that take place out of school. These are as much a part of the curriculum as the lessons.

The aim here is to balance the skills and knowledge transfer that has become the focus of the National Curriculum with attitudes and attributes. This should provide a single principle of contextual learning which links the EYFS, the National Curriculum and the post-14 sector; this in turn should not only aid transition but empower teachers to regain control over their teaching and reintroduce the creative teaching that has fallen by the wayside.

Activity 6

Who is the teacher?

1 Make a list of all the things you have taught today – it would be helpful to define exactly what you think teaching is.

2 Make a list of all the things the children have learnt today – it would be a help to define learning before you start.

3 Examine the two lists. What have the children learnt from:
   ➤ you
   ➤ their peers
   ➤ their parents
   ➤ their environment?

Personalised learning – taking into account children's interests

Put simply, personalised learning and teaching means taking a highly structured and responsive approach to each child's and young person's learning, in order that all are able to progress, achieve and participate. It means strengthening the link between learning and teaching by engaging pupils – and their parents – as partners in learning.

The overarching aim of the EYFS is to develop teaching and learning strategies that are individual to the needs of each child. These strategies require us to demonstrate how we are taking into account the child's needs when planning activities and to ensure that the activities are suitably challenging. It involves practitioners finding out about the child's interests and using these to tailor their planning. Many practitioners have a very good knowledge of the children in their care and although they have till now not recorded this information they naturally tailor their behaviour and teaching strategies for each child. The key worker system, whereby one practitioner has overall responsibility for forming partnerships with parents and the care of individual children, lends itself to personalised learning. To ensure personalised learning is effective, practitioners need to identify the preferred learning style of each child, how they learn best, a clear ongoing assessment strategy that demonstrates what children can do and what practitioners can do to challenge and extend this. Many settings pondering how they can evidence personalised learning have taken to putting initials on plans and how each activity will be adapted and extended for each child. This may be successful in small settings but in large settings with children attending random sessions there is a danger that we shall not see the plans for the initials. Personalised learning can be evidenced by demonstrating a good planning structure combined with good assessment procedures and knowledge of the children in your care. If you are about to change everything for the EYFS, brush up on change management procedures and ask yourself if you really do need to change so completely.

The role of the adult – pedagogy

Whether as a practitioner you agree that pre-defined learning goals are appropriate for children from one to five or not, from 2008 this will be out of your control. How the EYFS is interpreted and used to inform teaching and learning strategies should remain under the control of individual settings and practitioners. How we view the Early Years will influence the strategies we use. By adopting learning and teaching strategies that focus mainly on the transmission of skills and knowledge, the environments will tend to be adult led with a didactic approach to teaching. This method is often adopted by those who see the Early Years as preparation for school. A strategy that more embraces the philosophy that the Early Years should be embraced and accepted as a crucial learning period in its own right is more likely to adopt learning strategies that embed the acquisition of knowledge and skills into meaningful context; secure in the knowledge that as children explore and investigate their environment, their creativity and problem-solving skills allow them to take control of their own learning, uncovering knowledge.

Many practitioners shy away from the term 'teaching' in the Early Years, claiming that the didactic connections between teaching and learning are too formal to apply to the play-based creative exploration carried out by children in the Early Years. They see themselves more as facilitators of learning. The art of combining the curriculum with teaching and learning strategies is increasingly referred to as pedagogy. The term pedagogy has many definitions; however, one of the definitions that more suits Early Years places the child at the centre of the learning process. This approach appears to more readily define the interactive nature of early learning.

Siraj-Blatchford et al (2002), through the Researching Effective Pedagogy project, identified three major approaches to early education.

➤ The teacher-directed, programmed learning approach.

➤ An open framework approach where children are provided with 'free' access to a range of instructive learning environments in which adults support children's learning.

➤ A child-centred approach where the adult's aim is to provide a stimulating yet open-ended environment for children to play within.

They concluded that the most effective pedagogy combines teacher-directed activities with child-initiated activities supported by adults.

The adult's role is not only to provide an environment that facilitates learning, but also to act as a role model for learning, entering into a learning partnership with children. Adults who demonstrate they are still learners themselves will help children to appreciate that learning is a life-long process. Early learning is not simply to transmit knowledge, it is to provide the skills required to find knowledge and to foster an enjoyment for learning. Children enter the learning environment with their own cultural knowledge from which the adults caring for them can also learn, demonstrating a genuine interest in children's lives, interests and abilities in order to engage and challenge them.

Planning for learning

Practitioners or potential practitioners in childcare and education need to have a clear grasp of why we are planning for learning and, more importantly, who we are planning for. The role of the practitioner in both supporting and extending children's learning is a complex one. We will not provide a range of experiences for learning that are well matched to the individual needs of the child unless we make the effort to understand how children learn (see Chapter 6). Skilled practitioners should ensure that planning:

➤ interprets the curriculum or framework – in a culturally appropriate way

➤ is grounded in the natural qualities which children possess – their capacity to learn and their individual needs.

It is important to remember that planning for learning does not mean controlling the environment in order to meet our learning intentions or to tick off an assessment box, learning belongs to the child. If we take control children become reliant on the adult, which in turn hinders their creativity and ability to develop essential problem-solving and thinking skills. There is much talk currently about adults having the confidence to allow children to manage risks – adults also have to stand back and allow children to manage their learning. Children need to be challenged for learning to take place. If nothing is new or challenging, nothing changes and therefore no progress is made.

Planning for learning

The primary purpose of planning is to meet the learning needs of children and embedded within the EYFS there is great emphasis on meeting children's individual needs. The key to planning an environment that facilitates learning is listening to what children are saying and watching what they are doing. This enables practitioners to identify the strategies that will take children forward in their learning. Some ways in which this may be achieved are to:

➤ be aware of children's existing skills in order to extend their learning

➤ work collaboratively with other professionals in the setting to ensure consistency in approach to avoid confusion for children

➤ consider time factors: children need different periods in which to learn, and learn at different rates; activities and extension activities should reflect these needs. It is important when planning to include periods when children are able to explore ideas, develop skills and solve problems

➤ plan for extending learning and the careful introduction of a new aspect: the bridge between this new aspect should be carefully considered so that it extends learning in measured steps. The gap between the existing knowledge and the new learning must be carefully matched in small steps and short-term achievable goals

➤ plan for the role of the practitioner – how will she or he support learning?

➤ extend learning and develop learning experiences and opportunities through talking, open-ended questioning and listening. How will these provide resources for learning?

➤ keep the focus on what children can do and not what they have yet to achieve

➤ build on the interests of the child – talk to parents and children, ask them what they like best.

It may be useful to consider the following factors:

Where does learning take place?	How may the context in which learning takes place affect a child's ability to learn? Should planning take account of where learning takes place, for example indoors, outside, in a quiet area, as a collaborative activity?
Does the way in which we learn affect our ability to learn?	Do individual children have different preferred methods of learning? Can these be included in the way that we present new learning opportunities? Individual learners may have different interests and dispositions that affect the way they learn. (The term 'disposition' is here used to explain the way in which children approach learning, particularly in their openness of response to learning opportunities.)
How do we learn from others?	For many children, learning opportunities are enhanced through interaction with others, both experienced children and adults. How can planning take account of this? Learning may be promoted through language and imitation, replication and modelling. We copy and imitate to acquire skills in making best use of tools to achieve a purpose, for example writing, drawing, spreading and fastening. Imitation is particularly important for children's acquisition of skills in using materials and tools. We also learn to use equipment in particular ways, for example holding a pencil for purposes of writing may differ between cultures.

Figure 11.1 There are many factors that can influence learning; an awareness of these factors can help practitioners plan more appropriately

Planning principles of the Early Years Foundation Stage

Within the EYFS, the developmental stages noted in development matters identify the knowledge, skills, understanding and attitudes that children need to achieve the early learning goals. These goals should not be transferred into a checklist and are not sequential. Whilst they refer to an age range, all children are individual and it should be remembered that this is only guidance.

The looking, listening and noting section offers practitioners examples of the kinds of reactions and behaviours to observe; these observations then inform the planning. Take care not to look specifically for certain behaviours – part of the joy of observing is about being surprised; if we only look for one thing we miss a thousand other things.

These three elements combine to provide practitioners with a view of where the children are, where they need to go next, and how best to support them in this learning journey. This is achieved in an holistic manner through planned, purposeful play, with a balance of adult-led and child-initiated activities.

The ongoing cycle of development awareness (Development matters), observation and assessment (Look, listen and note), planning and resourcing, and learning and teaching (Effective practice) enables practitioners to provide opportunities for all children to play, learn and succeed in an atmosphere of care and of feeling valued.

Assessment for learning means:

➤ observations – sharing observations with the child

➤ photographs of the children in action

➤ discussing children's work with them

➤ talking with children and their parents about what the children enjoy doing and what they find difficult

➤ planning, that includes the views of children and their parents.

Good planning is the key to effective learning. It enables practitioners to develop a knowledge and understanding of how individual children learn and progress. It also provides opportunities for practitioners to reflect and talk about how to sustain a successful learning environment. Wherever possible if a child attends more than one setting then a collaborative approach should be adopted. However, my research tells me that many settings consider their planning system as the unique selling point for their setting and are reluctant to share this with the 'competition'.

Recognising assumptions

Knowledge of the child's skills will provide evidence on which to base planning. This knowledge base will differ – a practitioner's views may be influenced by his or her training, values and experience. In addition, the practitioner's understanding of and relationship to the expectations of society will influence the behaviour he or she looks for and encourages. Thus, people working with young children in different types of setting may have different expectations of children. In planning a curriculum it is therefore valuable to reflect upon where and how your views have originated and accept that while these may differ from those of the parents of the children you work with, you should not be judgemental by allowing your views to influence your expectations of children.

An effective long-term plan for the Early Years Foundation Stage is likely to include:

➤ an indication of when you plan to teach aspects/areas of learning

➤ an indication of how regularly and frequently you plan to teach aspects/areas of learning

➤ an indication of how you will link aspects/areas of learning in a relevant and interesting way for children, that is, via special events and activities that provide a meaningful context and enhance learning, for example a visit to a city farm, a cultural or religious festival.

Activity 8

Reflective practice

Planning the curriculum is a complex process. The following activity will help you to reflect upon your own understanding of planning as well as your involvement in it. Write down your responses to the questions below. When you have finished, make recommendations for improvement based upon your personal reflection.

1 What type of planning is used?

2 How are you involved in the planning process?

3 Is the planning amended and adapted as it is being implemented?

4 Who sees the planning?

5 How is planning monitored to ascertain implementation?

6 How is assessment integrated into planning?

7 How is planning part of your setting's policy and approach to learning?

8 How are parents involved in the planning process?

9 How are governors involved in the planning process?

10 How are children involved in the planning process?

To make sure that your planning is balanced check that:

➤ you have included all aspects of learning

➤ there is a balance between and within the six areas of learning

➤ there are sufficient opportunities for children to revisit all aspects of learning regularly and frequently.

Extending children's existing learning – developing thinking skills

For learning to take place it must challenge children's thinking. This is achieved by:

➤ using real-life and imaginary situations

➤ utilising spontaneous and planned play

➤ asking open-ended questions

➤ investigating and exploring the environment

➤ having the opportunity to discuss and share events and life experiences

➤ supporting when necessary with sensitive intervention to extend learning.

Learning environments and teaching strategies must be challenging, enjoyable and develop creative and imaginative thinking. It is important to remember when trying to extend children's learning in specific areas that children's learning is holistic and should avoid the constraints of subject boundaries. Learning builds on existing knowledge using the children's interests to motivate and inspire them to learn. Children will all have their own individual experiences, learning therefore should be tailored to their individual experiences and needs.

Before a child enters nursery, he or she will already have begun to learn through an informal, often unplanned curriculum based on events and happenings within his or her home, family, local community and local environment. This is provided by interaction with significant adults and the environment and culture in which the child lives. Each child acquires knowledge, skills and understanding through this learning process. It is important that nursery and pre-school settings build upon the learning and experiences that a child has had in their home and local environment. The practitioner who provides the first experiences of out-of-home education will build on this past experience. Recognising, valuing and extending what children already know and can do is crucial in order to extend their learning and development.

Learning through interaction

Babies learn from their interactions with people and their immediate environment. Most babies learn a great deal very rapidly about the world that surrounds them; this is acknowledged in *Birth to Three Matters* (DfES, 2002). Planning for working with very young children builds on these skills, and this theme is set to continue within the EYFS.

Planning for these first out-of-home learning experiences requires that children have a wide range of learning opportunities. They need to be actively and physically engaged in meaningful and purposeful activities. These should be intellectually stimulating and involve first-hand exploratory and imaginative experiences that fully develop the use of their senses. Learning experiences should be matched to the child's level of ability and concentration, building on his or her home experience.

For some children, their home experience will not have provided opportunity for practising social skills; for others, early pre-school experience will offer opportunities to refine their existing social skills. Planning should include opportunities that will enable children to be nurtured and supported in their efforts to become confident and independent learners. Interested and informed practitioners can plan for and provide opportunities for

children to solve their own problems, and talk about and share these experiences.

Figure 11.2 considers the learning styles of three- and four-year-old children, and the implications of this for planning.

Equality and diversity issues

Children today are growing up in a multicultural environment; this diverse society should be reflected in the Early Years setting. Children need to see their families represented to help develop their sense of identity, self-worth and self-esteem. Such representations also include, but are not limited to, disability, gender, religion and age. As practitioners, our aim is to enhance children's learning and development. This is achieved through education. We cannot assume that children 'just know'; they need to learn about other cultures to understand them and develop a respect for them. Such learning should be appropriately matched to the child's stage of development, and the activities we present to children must be relevant to their needs, and children should embrace diversity and difference. It is therefore essential within our planning to take account of a child's home life, culture and religious belief and build this information into everyday situations; diversity and difference does not belong in a separate resource box, it should be embedded into the planning structure. Research by the Commission for Racial Equality (CRE), which has examined Ofsted inspection reports, reveals that the reports contain little reference to cultural diversity. Clearly this is an area of utmost importance and the absence of this aspect when planning teaching and learning is a concern.

You must promote positive attitudes to diversity and difference within all children. In doing this you will help them to learn to value different aspects of their own and other people's lives.

EYFS (2007) p6

How three- and four-year-old children learn	Implications for planning
They are active learners and like hands-on activities	Vary activities and have plenty of different resources, experience and contexts. Introduce new equipment gradually and over a period of time. Consolidate skills by offering opportunities to practise use and evaluate skills in different contexts.
They are keen to use all their senses	Provide a range of sensory experiences to support their exploration.
They are often very 'physical' learners	Provide staged but physically challenging opportunities. Use outdoor opportunities to build confidence in using and developing physical skills.
They have a short span of attention	Do not use the same form of learning activity – provide a variety of experiences.
They experiment with materials in different ways	Find new ways of using resources. Help children to make connections between their home and pre-school experiences. Provide adults to interact with them.
They are social beings	Plan for opportunities to practise and refine their social skills within other activities. Encourage focused conversation – allow children to talk about their experiences.

Figure 11.2 Understanding how three- and four-year-old children learn and the implications for planning

Practitioners will be called to question their values and beliefs and ensure they do not allow these to have a negative influence on the children. The term 'politically correct' is often used when practitioners are advised against singing 'baa baa black sheep' or referring to the blackboard. However, the language we use in front of and to children is not about being politically correct, it is about developing a language structure that demonstrates respect for all. The term 'spastic' or 'handicapped' has been replaced with the phrase 'person with a disability', recognising that they are a person first. Often we use inappropriate language with the best intentions or through lack of thought, for example we relay information to each other such as 'all the SENs are to go with Mr Jones today'. We are language role models and children soon pick up our bad habits.

We shall only know that we fully embrace diversity and difference when we do not have to plan for it simply because it is the way of life.

Special educational needs (SENs)

Children have differing needs at particular points within their stages of development; for some children developmental differences will necessitate specific and highly structured provision. The Special Needs Code of Practice (DfEE, 2001:32–37) provides detailed advice for appropriate planning to meet the individual learning needs of such children. For some children, a specific need may be of a temporary nature.

The personalised learning philosophy, which advocates the need to identify children's individual needs, currently filtering into Early

Years, is by no means a new or revolutionary concept. It has in fact been the philosophy of special education for many years. Identifying a child's individual needs early enables SEN children to acquire the skills to be educated alongside their peers, and remove barriers to learning. The key principle is that all children can learn and the adult's role is to find out how each child learns best. To some extent these principles are now being transferred to all Early Years settings with the introduction of the EYFS. The EYFS acknowledges that all children have individual learning needs that are unique and as such require a learning environment representative of the child's needs and interests. While the EYFS contains goals based on culturally biased developmental norms which do not fully embrace inclusion, this shared belief that all children require individual strategies could indicate a step towards removing labels such as SEN. It can not be disputed that children are individuals and as such no two children are the same; unfortunately this statement is used widely and by many professionals to explain the deviation from developmental norms. SEN children are often categorised according to their disability, as wheelchair users or blind children, for example, which in fact strips them of their individuality. If all children are educated according to their individual needs then maybe children will no longer require segregated education establishments.

There are many positive elements of the EYFS. Nevertheless in terms of SEN and diversity this document lacks commitment. On the one hand it talks about equality of opportunity and difference in the form of individual needs and yet it presents a uniform set of goals and concludes with a uniform assessment profile; this is setting children with atypical development to fail. These stepping stones and goals are born of the dominant culture and often do not transfer equitably. Can all children be held up against the same set of goals and if so how accurate are the results? While the profile is to inform transition,

these results will emphasise difference and could destroy parents' belief in their children's ability to achieve. Assessment should focus on achievement and not conformity; personalised learning plans demand personalised transition reports that focus on the individual learning journey.

Activity 9

Why do we all have to do this?

All children will be expected to sit on the carpet for a 'plenary', a task that a child with attention deficit hyperactivity disorder (ADHD) would find very difficult.

Monitor your day and write down every thing that you ask all of the children to do.

Look at this list and ask yourself the following.

➤ Did they all need to do this?

➤ Was this for the benefit of the child or the adult?

➤ Was there another way of doing this that would give the child the choice?

➤ Did any child rebel and refuse to comply?

➤ Are children trained to do this, i.e. sit down for the story or do they want to hear the story?

The learning frameworks and curricula are currently developed for the majority and differentiated for the minority; a curriculum that embraces inclusion and celebrates diversity and difference should be differentiated for all children according to their individual needs. Differentiation refers to how the curriculum and teaching strategies are adjusted to meet the individual learning needs of children. This differentiation should relate to the pace at which children learn or the depth of the learning, while focusing on what children can do and building on this as opposed to being driven towards what they cannot do. This requires practitioners with a secure knowledge of child development and an educational environment that trusts practitioners and enables them to have a flexible approach to the curriculum.

Differentiation may include the following.

➤ Altering group sizes.
➤ Flexible time allocation to activities – allowing children time to think.
➤ Adapting buildings and play areas.
➤ More in-depth planning.
➤ Combining a variety of learning strategies.
➤ Simplifying things while ensuring they are challenging.
➤ Presenting information in smaller parts.
➤ Breaking down tasks into smaller steps.
➤ Using picture cues to enable children to make choices.
➤ Providing activities to meet the child's interests and preferred learning style or pattern of behaviour.
➤ Providing additional support from a practitioner or specialist.
➤ Sensitively choosing when to intervene, to provide further resources, or challenge the child's thinking.
➤ Making suggestions to move the play forward.
➤ Modelling, demonstrating and supporting the child by example.
➤ Using indoor and outdoor space.

➤ Allowing children time with an adult for reviewing their activities during the session.
➤ Writing clear plans that include the learning objectives and experiences planned for individual children that build on the child's strengths and developmental stage.

These strategies are currently embedded into good quality Early Years practice, finding out how children learn best and facilitating this.

Planning for children with special educational needs and disabilities

Planning for inclusion is important. All children have a right to have access to an appropriate curriculum, however learning may be different through approach but it should aim to achieve the same goal.

Planning for all children, but particularly those with special education needs, requires a good understanding of children's learning styles. Geoff Read (Tilstone et al 1998: 128–36) discusses, in detail, how inclusion can be promoted though learning styles.

Understanding teaching and learning styles remains a major key in the development of inclusive learning, and it is essential for teachers to move beyond a general acceptance of this principle and consider its practical applications.

Tilstone et al (1998:128)

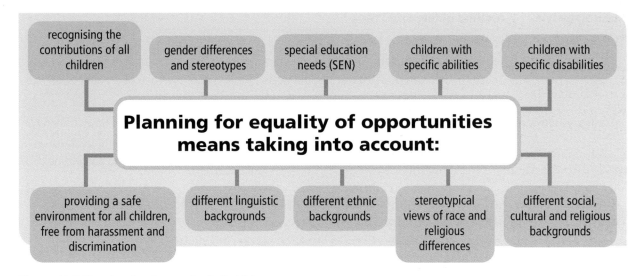

Figure 11.3 Planning for the needs of all children

Learning styles

Children and adults learn in different ways. However, it is very useful to remind ourselves of the difficulties we may face when presented with new learning. People have different preferences of learning style. Children as well as adults will not learn effectively if they are expected to be passive recipients of a curriculum (David, Curtis and Siraj-Blatchford, 1992); most people prefer active approaches to learning.

You may have been presented with such a challenge when faced with a self-assembly flat-pack item of furniture. A group of adults presented with a 'flat-pack' kit to assemble will quickly demonstrate a very wide range of approaches. Some people will contemplate the diagrams and logically tackle the assembly in the correct sequence. Others may gather together the pieces and go straight into assembly. Most of us do not grasp things easily, particularly when mechanical or technological tasks are involved. Many if not most people need time to practise and make mistakes in order to consolidate their learning. Even when confident, we will often seek advice or reassurance that we are doing things correctly from another, more experienced person. When we have developed competence through trial and error, and by using skills in different contexts, we can approach these tasks in a more creative and possibly playful way.

There may not be an exactly right way of tackling a problem and many methods may be equally effective in producing the desired result. As adults we often forget the importance of hands-on experience – solving problems by playing with materials or ideas, although we use this skill, or are forced to use it, at different points in our lives. Some may tackle this as a chore, others as a playful experience. If the latter approach is taken, learning may be not only more enjoyable but more effective and long-lasting.

There are three main learning styles: **visual** (reading or seeing), **auditory** (listening and speaking), and **tactile/ kinaesthetic** (doing). How much children remember and their level of involvement in the learning is reliant upon how well practitioners have catered for their preferred learning style. However, children often learn through a combination of the three.

Learning style	Method of learning
Visual learner	Prefers visual information, in picture or diagram format. Children like props, video, television. Children learn better in a quiet environment, and often dislike group work. These children can be artistic or doodle while listening and have pen and paper at all times.
Auditory learner	Prefers spoken information. Children will enjoy group times such as circle time. Children will enjoy stories from audio tapes. They remember by talking out loud, and need to have things explained verbally. They may talk to themselves while learning something new.
Kinaesthetic learner	Prefers 'hands on learning', like to try things out for themselves. Children learn by watching and doing and are keen to do what is being talked about. When talking they may use hand gestures. Children like to be moving around while listening or talking. They like to touch and feel things in order to learn about them.

Figure 11.4 Knowing a child's learning style can accelerate their learning as they access activities that best fit your preferred style

Activity 10

Meeting the needs of individual children

Have a look around your setting and using the information above identify activities and toys that best facilitate learning for the individual learning styles.

Observe the children in your group: try to identify their preferred learning style, observe the activities they choose to play with.

Is there a connection between a child's learning style and the activities they freely choose to play with?

Honey and Mumford (1986) suggests four learning styles, as shown in Figure 11.5.

Activists	Prefer to learn by doing as opposed to reading or listening.
Reflectors	Stand back and observe, they collect as much information as possible before they take on a task.
Theorists	Question and assess how new information fits with existing information.
Pragmatist	Look for new ideas and new ways of doing things.

Figure 11.5 Many find these four headings easier to associate with children and find them easier to assess a child's learning style

Pritchard (2005) offers an overview of learning theories and learning styles, also looking at brain-based learning and how to relate theory to practice.

Recognising opportunities for learning

Practitioners will acquire skills in recognising opportunities for learning that relate to specific experiences. For example, when regularly observing an activity where children explore floating and sinking using the water tray, the practitioner will note patterns of behaviour. Children will respond in particular ways, similar questions will be asked and similar discoveries made. Capturing young children's imagination provides a starting point, and an incentive and impetus for an interest in learning. As practitioners become more familiar with the curriculum and, through their observations of individual children, concerning how children respond to planned experiences, they will be able to match activities to children's capabilities. When activities are planned on the basis of what has been observed, the appropriateness and match of learning goals to children's needs will be secure.

Making judgements

One of the key skills of an effective practitioner is helping children to make connections between areas of learning. In order to do this, the practitioner must be confident in making judgements that identify connections in their planning. Providing 'match' and extension of the learning will only occur when there is a sound grasp of the curriculum or framework for learning and the opportunities for the child to support experience of one area of learning with another.

Modelling

Modelling by an adult is often incorporated into planning as a means of encouraging a child's participation in an activity. Modelling may be seen simply as a 'show and copy' approach; however, this fails to recognise the immense potential of modelling. The adult's role is not simply as a director of learning or a role model; rather, for effective learning, modelling should be considered and carefully constructed. The balance between observation, intervention, direction and stimulation is thus crucial, as is effective conversation with the child.

Supporting children's learning

Look at the following list and reflect on how you achieve these goals.

1   Help children to build on existing knowledge.

2   Provide opportunities for children to concentrate on an activity.

3   Provide opportunities for extending thinking.

4   Become involved in what children are doing but do not 'take over'.

5   Observe and provide appropriate intervention/extension when required.

Activity 11

Observing children's activities

1   Undertake an observation of an activity in your workplace, for example children playing with malleable materials.

2   Make a reflective evaluation of this activity.

➤ Look at the roles played by children and adults. How do they interact?

➤ Who has control of the learning experience? The child or the practitioner?

➤ What evidence do you have to support your view?

➤ Do the children extend or determine the outcome of the activity in any way?

➤ Does the practitioner extend or determine the outcome of the activity in any way?

The role of observations in planning and assessment

Observations form an integral part of planning and assessment. Although this chapter does not discuss assessment, it is important to acknowledge its integral role in the planning process.

Having conversations with children and observing them in action acknowledges the competences with which children come to school, not only at the beginning but throughout their school careers. Observations and conversations are tools for assessment that recognise children's individual competences as the baseline against which their future learning needs should be identified.

Fisher (2002:37)

Practitioners who have a grounding in understanding child development and who can relate theory to practice are better equipped to observe children and to act on these observations in their planning.

Creating a thinking and problem-solving environment

Increasingly within the Early Years the importance of the process of teaching and learning is being given equal weighting to what children are learning. The philosophy here is that knowing facts and skills is meaningless if children do not know how to acquire them for themselves, raising the importance of thinking skills and problem-solving skills.

Wilson (2000) suggests that 'thinking skills' are ways of looking at the problem.

- *Thinking = the process of cognition, knowing, remembering, perceiving and attending.*

- *Skills = the acts of collecting and sorting information; analysing, drawing conclusions, brainstorming, problem solving, evaluating options, planning, monitoring, decision making and reflecting.*

Providing experiences in problem solving will help children develop curiosity, patience, flexibility, concentration and understanding of cause and effect. They have a focus for their learning and gain confidence in their ability to reach a solution. All children can discover things for themselves; the key to developing this discovery into problem solving is in allowing them to explore for themselves. By not rushing in and 'helping' young children who are facing problems, young children develop confidence and increase their thinking abilities.

The environment

In order to learn, children must be motivated. How the environment is set up will play a crucial part in their motivation. The environment should foster motivation as shown in Figure 11.6.

Setting up the room to maximise learning potential

The amount of space available will vary according to the type of setting; invariably there will never be enough space so the space available must be fully utilised. To maximise the space available consider how you could reorganise it to provide space which works for you. Often in the Early Years we hoard things that we think may come in handy and before we know it our shelves and cupboards are cluttered and untidy. This restricts the movement of the children and their access to resources. The resources on offer should be high quality and open-ended to encourage thinking skills, a challenge and investigation. Resources do not have to be expensive; often it is the simplest of things that offer learning potential.

Children should have the freedom to choose their resources and to return them to their rightful place; resources and equipment should be presented in a way which not only enables children to access them but to

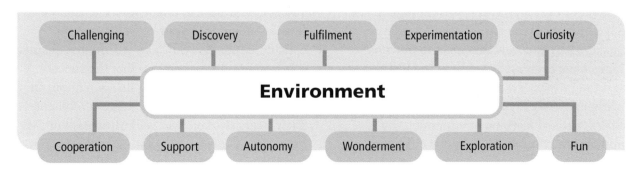

Figure 11.6 The environment we provide for children should motivate them to want to find out more

Children should be able to access all areas of their environment and the resources within it

take pride in their environment, and become independent learners. Consider zoning your room so that you can easily identify the potential for learning that each zone offers. Do not be afraid to change the room around, or encourage children to design their own room; however, take care if you have children with a visual impairment.

Conclusion

This chapter has discussed the historical context of the Early Years curriculum and the development of the Early Years Foundation Stage (2007) and how this links to practice. Links have been made between the EYFS and the Primary Framework for literacy and mathematics, and strategies for supporting a personalised learning environment. By undertaking the activities in this chapter you should be able to reflect on current practice and consider how to effectively incorporate this document into your setting. Having considered the EYFS briefly within this chapter it is important to remember that the success of this document lies not in its content but in its implementation. As possible or practising Early Years workers you will ultimately decide for yourself how best to do this.

How to move on in your research

Miller, L. and Devereux, J. (2004), *Supporting Children's Learning in the Early Years.* London: David Fulton

    This book will develop your knowledge, understanding and skills for working with young children and your understanding of the Early Years curriculum.

Porter, L. (2002), *Educating Young Children with Special Needs.* London: Paul Chapman

    This book will help you to recognise when young children have atypical needs and help you to provide individualised and relevant learning programmes for them. While its title specifies special needs, much of this information will help you to consider the individualised learning of all children.

Pritchard, A. (2006), *Ways of Learning.* Oxford: David Fulton

    This book will enable you to develop learning situations and make best use of your planning and teaching in order to create better opportunities for effective and lasting learning.

References

Dahlberg, G., Moss, P. and Pence, A. (2007), *Beyond Quality in Early Childhood Education and Care.* Oxford: Routledge

DES (1990), *Starting with Quality in the Rumbold Report.* London: HMSO

DfEE/QCA (1999), *The National Curriculum: Handbook for Primary Teachers in England.* London: DFEE

DfEE (2000), *Curriculum Guidance for the Foundation Stage.* London: QCA/DfEE, HMSO

DfES Siraj-Blatchford, I., Sylva, K., Muttock, S., Gilden, R. and Bell, D. (2002), *Researching Effective Pedagogy in the Early Years.* http://www.dfes.gov.uk/research/data/uploadfiles/RR356.pdf

DfES (2003), *National Standards for Under 8s Day Care and Childminding.* London: HMSO

DfES/QCA (2000), *Curriculum Guidance for the Foundation Stage.* London: HMSO

DfES/QCA (2007), *Early Years Foundation Stage.* London: HMSO

Fisher, J. (2002) (2nd edition), *Starting from the child.* Buckingham: Open University Press

Honey, P., and Mumford, A. (1992, 1986), *The Manual of Learning Styles.* Maidenhead: Peter Honey

Jones, L., Holmes, R. and Powell, J. (2005), *Early Childhood Studies.* Maidenhead: Open University Press

Learning and Teaching Scotland (2005), *Lets Talk Pedagogy: Towards a Shared Understanding for Early Years Education in Scotland.* http://www.ltscotland.org.uk/earlyyears/images/talkpedagogy_tcm4-193218.pdf

Miller, L. and Devereux, J. (2004), *Supporting Children's Learning in the Early Years.* London: David Fulton

Porter, L. (2002), *Educating Young Children with Special Needs.* London: Paul Chapman

Pritchard, A. (2006), *Ways of Learning.* Oxford: David Fulton

Schools Curriculum and Assessment Authority (1996), *Nursery Education: Desirable Learning Outcomes for Children's Learning.*

Sure Start (2003), *Birth to Three Matters: A Framework to Support Children in their Earliest Years.* London: DfES

Tilstone, C., Florian, L. and Rose, R. (1998), *Promoting Inclusive Practice.* London: Routledge Falmer

Wilson, V. (2000), *Education Forum on Teaching Thinking Skills* http://www.scotland.gov.uk/library3/education/ftts.pdf

Wilson, R. (2003) (2nd edition), *Special Educational Needs in the Early Years.* London: Routledge Falmer

Useful websites

http://curriculum.qca.org.uk
Post-14 Curriculum

www.ltscotland.org.uk
Scottish Curriculum 5–14

www.ncca.ie
Primary Schools Ireland

http://old.accac.org.uk/eng/content.php?cID=5
Primary Schools Wales

http://accac.org.uk
Early Years Wales

http://www.siolta.ie/ and http://www.ncca.ie
Early Years Ireland

http://www.everychildmatters.gov.uk
Every Child Matters

www.standards.dcsf.gov.uk
The Primary Framework for literacy and mathematics

www.qca.org.uk
The bigger picture

www.standards.dfes.gov.uk/personalisedlearning
Personalised Learning

12 Observation

Vicky Cortvriend and
Iain MacLeod-Brudenell

This chapter is designed to encourage you to extend your skills in the complex process of observing children. It will help you to develop skills in reflection on the purposes and practice of observation as a pedagogic process. In addition, it will enable you to achieve the analytical and reflective skills required for work at degree level.

Typically, students who undertake a Foundation Degree are aspiring to achieve a greater depth of understanding and knowledge about children, and will have completed training in undertaking observations of children in childcare or playwork courses in further education. Such observations will usually have focused on sequential recordings of the developmental progress of an individual child. Those students who have progressed to work in early years or playwork settings – pre-schools, out of school clubs, nursery or school classrooms – may well be using their skills in a range of ways. Classroom teaching assistants may, for example, be required to monitor children's cognitive development or to record specific educational targets. Practitioners working with children under 3 years of age will be using the observational skills acquired in their course of further education to observe, record, monitor and assess children's emotional, social and physical development, as well as their levels of understanding. Practitioners working in playwork will use their reflective skills to observe children's play in order to identify play needs and preferences.

Observation of children should be used to inform and strengthen our support for all aspects of child development in every context. The skill of a practitioner in any setting is in recognising and acting upon all aspects of children's developmental progress through a holistic and integrated approach.

This chapter will provide you with suggestions for developing observational skills. It is hoped that by using the approaches suggested you will be sufficiently encouraged to undertake further reading.

This chapter addresses the following areas:

➤ The reason and purpose of observations

➤ Children's developmental, play and learning requirements

➤ Developing your skills in using observations and understanding the different techniques

➤ Making informed reflections upon your own

By undertaking the suggested study within this chapter it is hoped that you will be able to:

1 reflect on the purposes of observation

2 link children's developmental, play and educational needs more closely to your planning

3 use observation skills more effectively as a tool and choose a technique to suit your purpose

4 reflect upon your own practice.

The reason and purpose of observations

Observation is often introduced to students new to Early Years and playwork studies as a means of eliciting information about a child. This is a useful starting point; general unfocused observations provide opportunities for seeing how children interact in different contexts and react to different stimuli. Focused observations encourage the observer, for example, to look at a specific behaviour and to note conditions or factors which relate to actions during the space of the observation.

Why observe?

In some childcare courses at level 2 and level 3, students are required to follow formal patterns of observation; these are often referred to as observation methods or techniques. However, students are often not sure about:

➤ how they can use their observations

➤ what to do with the data

➤ why they are required to carry out so many observations on the children in their care.

It is important that students understand the rationale behind observing children and young people, so that they observe with enthusiasm and rigour.

Observational methods or techniques are of little value in themselves; they are often simply a descriptive record of what the observer sees. A primary purpose of observation is to record in order to inform our response to the needs of children. Observation is therefore more than looking and seeing – it is a means of recording linked to considered reflection and analysis. Sound reflection on the observations we make not only enhances professional practice, but also aids our understanding of children.

Observations must be undertaken in as objective a way as possible. It may be difficult to make a completely objective observation of children with whom we are familiar. It is essential that value judgements

do not influence the accuracy of description in our observation. However, the crucial value of the observation lies in how the complex data contained in such description is evaluated; that is, how we unravel and interpret the findings. This is because the key to developing our understanding of children is in the interpretation of what we see. Interpretation involves careful consideration of all of the detail recorded in an observation, with an informed eye for detail and a wide understanding of the purposes of the activity or events observed. Analysis of the information, the data, draws on our understandings of the child, the area of development we are considering (for example, the 'norm' levels of capability), the response offered by the child to particular stimuli, or the development stage achieved by the child compared with other children in similar cultural contexts.

It is clear that observations on children and the conclusions that practitioners in Early Years settings draw from them are among the most important and rewarding aspects of their work. The knowledge of the child that practitioners gain from their observations should underpin all the work they do with children. This knowledge can then be shared with the parents or main carer as part of working in partnership with them in order to ensure continuity of care for the children. The information may also be shared with other professionals, for example child psychologist, social worker, health visitor, on a need-to-know basis to ensure the best possible care and education for each individual child.

The principal reasons for observation are to:

➤ determine how the baby/child is developing, and further develop your own understanding of a child's development; the observation may be recorded on their personal child health record. These individual records usually contain pictures of 'milestones' alongside which the parent or health visitor can record when the baby/child first achieved each one

➤ share information with parents or main carer

➤ enable the practitioner in any setting where children or young people are cared for to plan effectively for their needs

➤ share informed, accurate and objective information with other professionals on a need-to-know basis.

The EYFS refers to observations using the heading 'Look Listen and Note' and as well as the reasons stated above includes carrying out observations in order to 'get to know a child better and develop positive relationships with children and their parents' (2007:11).

Observation has far more potential value to practitioners than simply recording actions in order to see how well the child is progressing, or to plan effectively to meet their needs. Observational records are useful data by which to measure and monitor our own effectiveness in predicting progress, and as a means of assessing our skills in making accurate and useful observations. Analysis of our observations can be very revealing. Reflection on our assumptions and predictions can raise doubts in our ability to make valid interpretations. What must be remembered is that not only are children and young people's behavioural patterns difficult to predict, but also our behaviour as observers can be subject to mood, time and other conditions.

Recording and interpretation

Observation is a diagnostic tool, confirming capability or progress at a point in time. It is a means of unobtrusively collecting potentially rich information about children's development. Most children will usually be observed in naturalistic conditions, at play either inside or outside, although there will be occasions where children are more formally assessed, using observations in contrived and regulated situations. An example of this is when carrying out baseline assessments in reception class. The data from either of these situations may be used to obtain factual information, often recording physical development or a child's capability to perform an action. Or, an observation may focus on providing data for interpretation, on unravelling factors, and providing evidence for analysis. This is likely to be related to observation of emotional, social or cognitive development.

All observations must be recorded, and then evaluated using recognised milestones, goals or recognised theories (see Figure 12.1).

The EYFS expects practitioners to accurately complete each child's EYFS profile and other data returns. Observing the children you work with will provide much of this data.

Milestones of development	
The Stycar Sequences	Described by Mary Sheridan in the 1950s and demonstrated very clearly by Meggit and Sunderland (2001). These milestones of development are to be found in the majority of childcare textbooks.
The goals described in the Curriculum Guidance for the Foundation Stage	Can be used as an extra source of information when the child reaches the age of 3. Published by the Department for Education and Employment in May 2000.
The works of theorists such as Piaget, Erikson, Chomsky and Kohlberg	These theories are described in detail in Chapters 6 and 7.
The National Curriculum Key Stages 1 and 2	Can be used once the child reaches the ages of 6 and 7.

Figure 12.1 Recognised milestones of development

Observations may present the unexpected, that is, information that had not been predicted, and such data will inform our understanding of the observed child. As practitioners we may be unaware of subtle changes in children's development. We all recognise that there will be times when we are required to observe the changing patterns of behaviour of a child, or the way in which he or she relates to other people, both children and adults. Observation can provide the opportunity to note and record these changes. We could say that this data is the best means to record our sensitivity to the variations and changes that occur in children over a period of time. It provides evidence of our professional approach to assessment, showing that we know the children in our care.

This important aspect of observation is often undervalued in an assessment process where recording targets is the primary purpose. As practitioners, we should approach undertaking observations with a fresh enquiring mind, rather than seeing the activity simply as a required task. We need to remember that periods of stress and pressure may impact on our ability to make objective judgements.

It is useful to retain observations, not to simply discard them after they have served an immediate use. This data can be used to monitor progress and to provide evidence of development.

Research

The use of observation as a research tool in early childhood studies is invaluable and central to our personal understanding of children as well as for our own professional development. Young children may not be able to convey verbally what they are thinking. The key to unlocking our understanding of young children's development is through careful reflection on the observations we make.

Observation may be used in conjunction with other methods and approaches such as interviews or questionnaires in more formalised research projects (see Chapter 16).

Planning

A further important use of observations is their use in planning the curriculum for the setting. When planning, in the short, medium or long term, it is essential to be able to demonstrate how you are meeting the children's individual needs. The theorists Vygotsky and Bruner both expounded the belief that children will develop to their full potential only with the assistance of adults or more experienced peers (Vygotsky's Zone of Proximal Development and Bruner's Scaffolding theory – see Chapter 6). Using the detailed evaluation from each observation it should be possible to plan or moderate activities so that each child benefits according to his or her own unique needs. Differentiation is a key word that practitioners in Early Years settings need to keep in the forefront of their mind when planning the curriculum. The judicious use of observations will provide you with the information needed to enable you to plan for individual children's needs by either moderating, or extending, planned activities. Some children may benefit from an individual learning programme, which could be devised using the information gleaned from the evaluations. Following the activity, observations will then tell you if your adaptations were successful. This differentiation ensures the practitioner is committed to equality of opportunity as he or she is meeting the needs of all the children in the setting.

The Statutory Framework for the Early Years Foundation Stage states quite clearly that 'Enabling Environments (one of the four complementary themes of the EYFS principles) plays a key role in supporting and extending children's development and learning. The commitments are focused around observation, assessment and planning: to provide support for every child' (DfES, 2007:9).

Sharing information

Confidentiality must be foremost in the practitioner's mind when deciding who needs to know about specific observations. There may be times when he or she will be required to write reports on the children in the Early Years setting. These may be routine reports to share with parents or main carers, or reports to be sent to other professionals such as educational psychologists, pediatricians, speech therapists and social workers. Reports might also be sent to a child's new setting. It is of vital importance that these reports are accurate and only contain relevant objective information.

Demonstrating professional responsibility and integrity is essential when building and maintaining a partnership with parents. The EYFS 2007 Principles into Practice states the importance of working with parents as partners respecting diversity, communications and learning together.

Reflection

Reflection can change our practice for the better. When reflecting on our own practice, records of observations provide the data by which we may measure and monitor our own effectiveness as practitioners. Such reflection cannot only provide opportunities for self-assessment but also help to set targets for professional development. The EYFS recognises the importance of continuing professional development and that in order to raise the quality of provision it is necessary for staff to gain higher qualifications. It is important to assess personal skills in an objective and honest way. The use of accurate observations is a useful tool in helping to assess these skills. Careful analysis of professional observations can reveal aspects of practice that may otherwise go unnoticed. It is not uncommon for practitioners to undertake observational tasks as part of regular routine without fully realising the detailed knowledge that is brought to these activities. Reflection and justification of the assumptions we may make in our judgements on children may promote a reassessment of the validity of some of the ways in which observation is tackled.

Action research

One method of continuing development is by using action research, which is carried out in the workplace in order to reflect upon and inform practice. Observations that include details of a practitioner's own practice in an Early Years setting, or that of other practitioners, can be a very useful tool. They can assist you to become aware of yourself as a practitioner and can be used as part of the cycle of enquiry, helping you to reflect upon, and then plan, how to modify your practice. Finally, they can be used to compare your previous practice with your present practice.

Ethics in observation

Observation is usually associated with recording what is seen for a variety of purposes and for different professionals concerned with children. Increasingly, they are also used as evidence for inspection purposes. As with all records, there are issues relating to ethics in terms of objectivity of the observer, storage of the data, accessibility, and the purposes to which the data is applied.

As a student and a practitioner you must consider two contexts for your own observational records: your university or college, and your workplace. An ethics checklist is shown in Figure 12.2.

Maintain anonymity

It is essential that you maintain the anonymity of those you observe and the contexts in which they are observed. The identity of those observed and the setting in which the observation takes place may be recognised by people reading your notes. It is therefore important that you neither identify the children you observe, nor the Early Years setting in which the observations took place. You can refer to the Early Years setting by describing it as a nursery setting, or a school, or a playgroup. Refer to the child purely in factual terms, for example 'a female child aged 3 years 5 months'.

Ethics checklist

Before the observation

Permission

Obtain permission from supervisor or setting. ☐

Obtain permission from parents of child. ☐

After the observation

Anonymity

Change all names of children. ☐

Change all names of place. ☐

Change all names of staff. ☐

Objectivity

Check that all statements are accurate and
not discriminatory. ☐

Check that all statements are supported
by evidence. ☐

Confidentiality

Ensure records are kept in a secure place. ☐

Figure 12.2 An ethics checklist

Obtain permission

When planning to do an observation in a setting, you will need to obtain permission from the supervisor and from the child's parents or carers; if the child is old enough to have an understanding of what you are doing then you should ask the child as well. It is preferable to obtain the permission from the parents or carers in writing. Various techniques suitable for carrying out observations are described on page 336, but it is important to maintain a professional attitude and carry out observations in a discreet manner at a time that does not disrupt the routine. Sharing of information should be discreet and limited to your supervisor at the setting, the child's parents or carers and your college tutor, unless otherwise directed.

Bias

Another ethical consideration relates to bias. We all bring a personal bias to bear on our observations and the reflection and analysis of the data derived from such observations. We must be aware of our own personal values, particularly where they may compromise our impartiality as neutral observers. Initially, we may be unaware of bias and for some practitioners this continues to be an issue.

Children's developmental, play and learning requirements

Observations are the key to helping adults develop an understanding of a child's development and plan their support for children's ongoing development and needs. So where does this process begin? Different professionals carry out observations on babies and children throughout their early years. Health care observations of babies and young children

take place before birth, directly after birth and through the early years of a child's life.

Pre-birth medical observations

Probably the very first pre-birth medical observation for most babies is an ultrasound scan, carried out at around 12 to 18 weeks of pregnancy to determine:

- position of foetus
- size of foetus
- normality of development
- number of foetuses
- the probable delivery date

and to detect any problems with the foetus, placenta, uterus or cord. This screening observation is carried out by a suitably qualified health professional and measures the foetus's long bones, circumference of skull and pelvic girdle. It checks the spine, internal organs and the primitive heart and blood supply.

The results of the scan are recorded on the mother's chart and it is common practice that she is given the opportunity to obtain a copy of the scan picture. Even at this early stage, before the foetus could be deemed viable, the professional is beginning to develop a partnership with the prospective parent. This partnership is necessary so that both can work together to ensure the best possible care for the baby.

Post-birth medical observations

The next series of observations (unless any problems were detected on the first scan, in which case the foetus would be monitored and observed closely throughout the pregnancy) take place directly after the birth. The midwife, paediatrician, obstetrician or doctor will carry out a full head-to-toe check on the baby, including observing its reflexes and recording its Apgar rating. The results of these observations are again recorded and shared with the parents. The mother is given a Personal Child Health Record book in which health care professionals record the results of all the developmental and health checks and observations they carry out on the child. (For examples of child health surveillance, see Chapter 4.)

Should any deviation from the norm be noted then the health care professional may refer the child to a specialist.

Children's health observations

During the first year of the child's life the health visitor may if the parent wishes monitor the child's development and health. This is done in the child's home and at the local clinic and recorded on the child's personal child health record.

Screening tests can be carried out to determine if there are any problems relating to hearing, sight, growth or developmental skills. The child will in all probability undergo an immunisation programme to protect him or her against some childhood diseases.

Childhood observations

Once the child attends a playgroup, or other Early Years setting, then the observations that health care workers can continue to record (usually until the child reaches the age of five years), if the parent or carer chooses, will be augmented by the observations that the staff in the setting carry out. These regular observations will continue throughout the child's life, becoming less frequent towards the end of primary education, dependent of course on the child's particular needs. The observations that practitioners in Early Years settings carry out will measure the child's holistic development and will be used in the planning of activities aimed at consolidating and extending each area of development. They will also use their observations to plan appropriate play and learning experiences based on the child's interests and needs. The observations that playworkers carry out may focus more on the child's play and the adult interventions that take place. They will be used to identify play needs, inform staff, discuss the needs of the children in relation to the environment or identify what extra resources, for example loose parts, are required to enhance play.

Developing your skills in using observations and understanding the different techniques

This section discusses the range of techniques that you may choose to use when conducting your observations.

Skills and abilities required for observation

Observation requires a disciplined approach. This disciplined and systematic approach can be acquired through practice. There is a danger that established practitioners may undervalue the importance of observation as a means of professional understanding and development because they are so familiar with the activity within the workplace. However, for work at university level, more is required than a disciplined approach; the ability to record accurately is of equal importance. The process of observation if done well is not easy; it requires concentration, an open mind and an ability to make skilled and informed analysis based not only on practice, but also on reading and discussion. A skilled observer who is also a reflective practitioner has an understanding of the advantages and disadvantages of a range of techniques, and can apply an appropriate method to a specific need then use the data for focused reflective analysis.

Means of recording

The ways in which you will record your observations will differ according to the method you use. It is certain, however, that as a practitioner you will not often be able to take time out to make lengthy observations – so how do you manage the process?

If a 'key worker' system operates in your Early Years setting (that is, one practitioner has responsibility for a particular group of children), you may have the responsibility for observing the children in your group only. But in practice it is highly likely that children will not be restricted in their movements and you may be required to make informal observations of other children as well. It is common for a practitioner to observe not only the children in his or her group but others who happen to be in proximity but are not part of the key group. In settings that use the key worker approach, the organisation of reporting and recording of observation is usually undertaken as a group activity.

There is no 'right' way, but some ways are more efficient than others.

Case Study 1

Recording techniques

In one nursery school, each of the eight staff has a group of children for whom they are responsible. During the week staff are expected to undertake observations, which are usually recorded on clipboards in their areas or in their diaries. At the end of each session, staff talk about anything particular that they have noticed and these are recorded in the main log. This is useful as children do wander between the two rooms and sometimes another key worker will notice something that is important and which can be followed up. On Fridays, staff write up notes about each child.

Case Study 2

Taking turns

At a second nursery school, staff take turns for a week and observe the children in different areas of the pre-school. Observational notes are recorded in notebooks. Because staff do not have time to make the long observations they were trained to do, they jot down the things they think are important. They talk about the children at lunch time and home time and share their observations. This ensures that they all see the overall picture of the children in different activities and get to know them better. Staff have also started to share these observations in their daily dairies, which they write for parents.

Case Study 3

Compiling an observation file

At a playsetting, staff agree in a team meeting what to observe during the following week and everyone contributes to building up an observation file which can be used to inform practice and form the basis for useful discussion. Examples of topics might be play cues and returns, play frames, staff interventions, play types, moods and emotions expressed during play, spaces used or created by the children.

Activity 1

Personal needs analysis

Considering the above case studies and thinking about your own particular setting, it would be a good idea to complete a personal needs analysis before beginning your own observation portfolio. Make a personal analysis of your own needs in relation to observation.

➤ List your skills.
➤ List your development needs.
➤ How can you address these needs?
➤ Make a plan of action.

The format shown below may be helpful for you when carrying out this activity.

Date	Skills I currently have	Development needs	Actions to take

Monitor this plan of action – place dates next to the action when you have started and then note when you have developed skills in the area.

Participatory observation

Participatory observation occurs when you are observing children whilst engaged in an activity with them, or involved in part of your daily routine of caring for and educating the children in your care.

Parents or carers watch and note the actions, reactions and responses of the children in their care. They observe, note and often comment on their children. It would be highly unlikely that such observations would be recorded. This is, however, valuable information.

Practitioners in Early Years settings and some teachers may write a diary of observed details relating to a child in their care. This is often to inform parents or carers of their child's daily activity. Most people who work with young children use participatory observation as part of their everyday practice. It is an almost instinctive part of caring for children.

But this does not always lead to written entries in the child's record. Participant observation may initially seem difficult to manage, in that notes must be made either at points during work with the children, or immediately afterwards if the knowledge and evidence is not to be lost. Often practitioners think that they will remember something and will be able to note it down later. Given the pace at which events can develop in the nursery, play setting or classroom however, these observations can easily be lost or inaccurately remembered.

Observations made in this way may often be incidental and unplanned, but they can, like planned observations, be incorporated into the general system of observations, which add to the developing picture of a child.

The habit of recording observations almost automatically comes with practice and notes often become shorter but more telling in their content as your experience increases. One teacher in the PROCESS Research Project (Stierer et al, 1993) said that as she became more experienced at observing she wrote less but it told her more!

Hints for recording observations

➤ Place sticky notes, clipboards with paper or notepads strategically around the room. This will help provide both the incentive and the means with which to record the incident, briefly, as it happens.

➤ Ensure that you always carry a notepad with you, from place to place.

➤ Notepads often become the focus for children's attention too, with them leaving messages and writing their own 'notes' down.

Non-participatory observation

Non-participatory observation means that the observer stays outside the activity in order to concentrate on the child or aspect being watched. If a single child is the focus it allows the observer to watch that child both as an individual and in the context of an activity. Similarly, a focus on an aspect of provision, or on a particular activity, allows the observer to concentrate on that aspect of the nursery alone, without having to watch for anything else.

If the observation is to be non-participatory, children need to know which adults are available for help while that person is busy observing. One teacher in the PROCESS project (Stierer et al, 1993) wore a hat when observing, and the children knew that they had to go to the other adults while this hat was being worn. Where to sit while observing in this way is also important, but becomes less of an issue as children become used to seeing adults watch them. Sitting too near or far from an activity may affect the quality of what is seen or heard by the observer. What is most important is that where an adult sits does not have a limiting effect on the children's activity.

Understand the purpose of the technique you are using

Health professionals and practitioners in Early Years settings often use different names for the same technique. This is not important; but it is essential that you are clear about the purpose of the technique.

In selecting a method of observation to apply to a particular situation you will focus on choosing a technique that will best serve your purpose, matching the appropriate technique to the aim of the observation. You may choose to use a number of different and complementary techniques to provide the information required to test for accuracy of your findings.

Confirming your conclusion may lead naturally to more rigorous forms of observation as research. Your ideas and hunches may be formulated as a hypothesis – your theory. You can test your hypothesis by collecting observations and examining them. For example, by using sociometric observation (see page 342) of a child you may identify a particular friendship, which encourages sustained concentration on a particular task or activity. Focused tracking observation (see below) or duration recording (see page 342) in this area would highlight any other factors that contribute to sustained concentration. By using these techniques, you will gather specific data which can help you to predict behaviour, support learning, and ultimately to test and verify the accuracy with which you can predict the child's behaviour. Hypothesis testing in this way will provide very good experience for using observation as a research tool.

Tracking

This method of observing a child is usually non-participative and involves having a floor map of the setting with the various activities marked on it. A child is then tracked during the course of a morning or afternoon session in order to observe:

➤ concentration levels

➤ social interactions

➤ interest and play preferences

➤ behaviour.

The time spent at each activity is recorded, and the sequence of activities. Other relevant information may also be recorded.

Case Study 4

Observing behaviour – tracking

Joe, age 4, is due to start reception class in September. He has problems socialising with peers and concentrating on activities. The educational psychologist is working with him and the staff of the nursery to help to prepare him for the transition to Key Stage 1. He is going through the statementing process in order that he can obtain the necessary support at school.

This observation tracks Joe's choices of activity throughout a morning session with a view to evaluating his level of concentration for particular activities and his behaviour exhibited.

continued ▶

The observation		
Time (am)	Activity	Joe's behaviour
9.10	Group Time	Joe sitting quietly listening; suddenly he knelt up, pointed to a picture on the wall and shouted, 'What they doing?'. He then began to move to the front of the group, pushing through the other children.
9.20	Free Play	Joe leapt to his feet and dashed over to the sand tray, where three children were playing. He began to frantically gather wet sand, piling it up at the side of the tray. Picking up a bulldozer, he started to use it to push the sand back and forth so that some fell onto the floor. During this time, he carried on a conversation with a practitioner.
9.25	Speech Therapist	The speech therapist came over to the sand tray and asked Joe if he would like to come and have a chat with her. Joe began jumping up and down, shouting, 'Look at my yellow shoes'. Then he took her hand and said, 'Yes'.
10.14		Joe arrived back in the playroom, holding the speech therapist's hand. Letting go of her hand, he looked around the room.
10.15		Joe rushed over to the sand again; there were already four children playing there. 'How many children are allowed at the sand tray, Joe?' a practitioner asked him. 'No, no, no,' he shouted. 'Joe, would you like to come and paint?' she then asked. He turned and ran to the aprons, asking 'Can I paint, can I paint?'. He painted quietly for 5 minutes, lips pursed, gazing intently at his work.
10.21		After hanging up his apron, he dashed back to the sand and began grabbing fistfuls of wet sand, throwing it into the sink. 'Joe, please don't do that,' the practitioner said, taking him by the hand and leading him to the play dough table. 'No, no, no,' he shouted, struggling in her grasp.
10.22		Joe cuddled a teddy and sat close to the practitioner, listening to the story and looking at the illustrations.
10.30	Snack Time	Joe picked up his milk carton and threw it over the table.

Joe did not move quietly around the room; he rushed everywhere, unless an adult held his hand. He was aware of the rules of the setting as demonstrated by his shouting 'no' when the carer asked how many children were allowed at the sand tray. He was aware that he had to wait for one child to leave before he could join in the activity, but he did not want to. He seemed to behave in a way designed to attract adult attention by messing in the sand tray, throwing sand around, and finally spilling his milk over the table. When he gained the attention he then wanted adult touch, holding the adult's hand or cuddling up beside her, clutching a teddy. He was in fact capable of maintaining concentration during an activity as shown when painting; however, this lasted only 5 minutes. During the entire observation there was no interaction with his peers.

Range or norms of development

Joe is almost 5 years old. At this age, according to the expected range or 'norms' of development, he 'should be able to understand the needs of others and be able to share and take turns'.

He should enjoy being with other children, show some sensitivity and be developing a sense of humour (Meggit, 2007). At the age of 4, he should enjoy companionship with other children and adults. He may have bouts of quarrelsome behaviour as well as close cooperation. At the age of 5, he should pick his friends and play companionably, understanding rules and find them acceptable. He should want to please, cooperate and help (Holt, 1991). Holt also writes that much of the period between 1 and 5 years of age is spent exploring and moving through stages of transition, which is often a cause of rebellion, but most of these problems are usually resolved as children approach 5 years of age. By the end of the EYFS 'children should maintain attention,concentrate and sit quietly when appropriate' (DfEs 2007:12).

It is clear that Joe is still expressing rebellious feelings and has not yet reached the developmental norms, or the early learning goals, in relation to the personal, emotional and social development that would be expected of a 4-year-old child.

This observation was one of a series on Joe. It is not possible to build up an accurate picture of a child based on one observation, as so many different factors can influence the findings.

Diet, illness, allergies, emotional distress, personal likes and dislikes, and even mood and temperament are significant in this context.

This observation and evaluation was shared with Joe's parents, the educational psychologist and his teacher to be. The purpose was to continue to build up a picture of Joe in order to plan for his particular individual needs.

Free description (longer than 5 minutes) or snapshot (less than 5 minutes)

There will be many opportunities for teachers and other adults to observe children while they are working alongside them. This is not quite the same as a participatory observation. By supporting a child in a task, or facilitating their activity, the adult is able to observe and, if appropriate, to record what the child says and what the child does as evidence of their growing conceptual awareness or skill development. They can also observe how the child approaches tasks, what strategies they use for solving problems, their persistence and motivation and their attitudes in general. This can then be recorded using the free description technique, which involves recording the event as it happened over a period of perhaps 10 or 20 minutes. If the event lasted for less than 5 minutes it is known as a snapshot observation.

Frequency sampling

Frequency sampling is a way of tracking incidences of particular aspects of behaviour

---

Activity 2

Tracking

As part of your usual assessment routine you may use tracking as an observation tool.

1 Carry out a tracking observation on one of the children in your setting, and then list the advantages of tracking.

2 Every form of observation has disadvantages as well as advantages. List any disadvantages of tracking which may occur in your setting. How could these be addressed?

in a child or group of children. In this, the observer identifies a feature of behaviour and notes whenever this occurs. For example, a child may appear always to play alone in the nursery. Observations would focus on whether or not this was indeed the case, and would include:

➤ looking at whether he or she approached another child, children or adults

➤ whether he or she initiated any interaction

➤ how any interaction was initiated

➤ where in the nursery this occurred.

As its name suggests, frequency sampling can be useful in giving an accurate picture of the frequency of aspects of behaviour, and can be used to monitor both progress and concerns.

Time sampling

Time sampling is similar to frequency sampling except that the observer records behaviour over a set period of time, typically recording behaviour, social interactions and language over a two-minute period every 10 minutes for a total period of one hour. It involves, therefore, observing children at the end of a predetermined period and recording exactly what is happening.

The recording format in this case would be a chart, as shown in Figure 12.3.

Yule (1987) suggests that precise timing is needed in order to avoid biased results. He gives the example of a nurse on a busy ward who is observing a patient every 5 minutes to see whether he or she is rocking or is engaged in some other self-stimulatory behaviour: 'Unless the nurse does look at exactly the end of the five minute interval, then she may find herself remembering to record only when she sees the patient engaged in the undesirable activity' (Yule, 1987:19–20). In this case, the technique was useful in revealing whether the behaviour was as problematic as was first thought. If the nurse recorded that the patient was rocking on the hour, six or seven consecutive times, she would need to investigate the problem further. If, however, the rocking only occurred once during the six or seven occasions on which she recorded, perhaps it was not such a problem after all! Repeated (compared with random) observations will reveal the extent to which the behaviour is consistent.

Wragg (1994) uses time sampling (which he refers to as 'static sampling') rather differently in that observers build up a series of snapshots of a situation at regular intervals. Using the technique in this way, it is possible to take a small number of children and to build up a comprehensive picture of their activities over a period of time.

Time sampling chart				
	identifies			identifies

Figure 12.3 Format for a time sampling chart

Event recording and diary observations

This method is often used to record a sequence of events and its frequency and occurrence. It may be used to track the number of times an action occurs within a given time. Typically, it will be used as a means of recording the effectiveness of an intervention programme for modifying a child's behaviour.

It can be used to provide data for an identified problem where there is a need to record the frequency of a particular response given by a child or group of children. Event recording is a useful method for observing a child's emotional development as you can record responses to a range of different events over a period of one or two days. Any longer and the type of observation becomes a diary observation. This is essentially the same as an event sample but is longitudinal, carried out over a period of time.

An extension to event recording is referred to by Wragg (1994) as a 'critical event approach', in which the observer looks for specific instances of classroom behaviour that are judged to be illuminative of some aspect of the teacher's style or strategies. This might be an element of class management, for example, perhaps a rule being established, observed or broken, something which reflects interpersonal relationships or some other indicative event.

Recording can be carried out on an adapted ABC chart, which can then be discussed with the children in order to obtain their perceptions. (A means Antecedents of the behaviour, B is the Behaviour itself and C is the context in which the behaviour took place.)

Although event recording is an appropriate observational technique for a wide range of behaviours, it has obvious limitations. Hall, Hawkins and Axelrod in Weinberg and Wood (1975) emphasise that it is most appropriate for responses of a short duration, which can be readily divided into single units. They give examples of its use in measuring the frequency of a shy pupil speaking, or an aggressive student making positive (rather than negative) comments, but they stress that the technique can have limitations when a behaviour cannot be defined precisely.

Tick list or check list

This is a simple method of recording whether or not a child is capable of achieving specific age-related tasks. The observer designs a chart using either norms of development (see Chapter 4) or Foundation Stage Goals or Key Stage 1 attainment targets, depending upon the child's age; he or she then observes during set activities whether or not the child can achieve the task with or without assistance, or cannot manage it at all.

Child A: 3 years old Physical development			
Skill	Can do	Can't do	Requires assistance
Build a tower of nine bricks			
Cut paper with scissors			
Thread large beads onto a thread			
Jump from a low step			
Climb upstairs with one foot on each step			

Figure 12.4 Example of a tick list to record a child's physical development

The professional in an Early Years setting can then use this information to plan appropriate activities to extend the child's development, and inform other interested professionals of the child's ability. The information can also be used to write a factual report for parents. It can be recorded in a form like that shown in Figure 12.4.

Duration observation

Duration observation is a way of accurately tracking how long children spend at particular activities or using certain equipment. It may seem sometimes as though a child or group of children spend all of their time in the construction area or riding the bikes: duration observation is a good way of establishing just how much time they do spend in these areas, and can help to ensure that the observations we record are accurate. 'Kuldip spends all of his time on the bikes' may, in reality, be that Kuldip chooses the bikes first, generally spends half an hour on them and then moves on to other activities.

Sociometric observation

This is usually used when observing children to research their friendship groups and integration into groups. The findings may be demonstrated using a pie chart or graph.

One method of observing friendship groups is to ask a group of children who their friends are, write that in a table (Figure 12.5) and then compare it with a timed observation (Figure 12.6) to see who they play with.

Over a period of an hour:

➤ Dan plays alone, with Fazan and once in the large group

➤ Kuldip and Kyle play with everyone

➤ Paige plays alone, with Kuldip and with Kyle, Kuldip and Fazan

➤ Fazan prefers small groups of 2 or 3 and once in the large group.

This type of observation might be carried out over a period of time and used if a practitioner had concerns about a child that did not seem to be mixing socially. A parent or carer might voice concerns about their child and this type of observation could be used to either allay their concerns or if found to be factual to design a plan for the child to encourage them to mix.

The EYFS states that children of this age 'form good relationships with adults and peers'. It suggests providing activities that involve turn taking and sharing (EYFS 2007).

Kuldip	Dan	Kyle	Fazan	Paige
Paige	Fazan	Kuldip	Dan	Kuldip
Kyle		Dan	Kyle	Kyle
		Paige	Paige	
		Fazan		

Figure 12.5 Table of friendship groups (Children of 40–60 months old)

10am	10.15	10.30	10.45	11am
Ku + Ky + Fa. Dan alone Paige alone	Ku + P + KY Fa + D	Fa + D + Ky Ku + P	D + Fa P + Ky + Ku	Dan alone P + Ky + Ku + Fa

Figure 12.6 Timed observation of the children playing outside

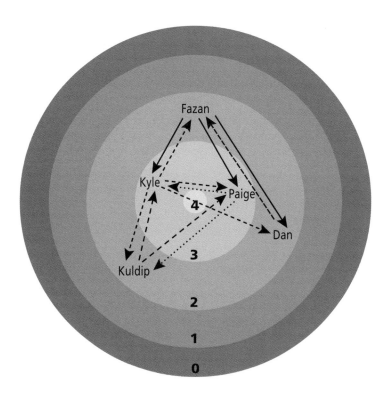

The central circle would be for children chosen 4 times.
The next circle is for those chosen 3 times (Kyle and Paige).
The next circle is for those chosen 2 times (Fazan, Dan and Kuldip).

Note: For a large group you might have the inner circle representing children chosen between say 10 and 20 times, the next circle 5–9 choices and an outside circle 1–4. If children are not chosen at all then they would be outside the circle completely.

Figure 12.7 The spiral graph method

Another method would be to use a spiral graph such as the one in Figure 12.7.

1   Begin as above with a chart (Figure 12.5).

2   Make a large diagram of concentric rings so that it looks like an archery target. Have one more ring than the greatest number of times any child was chosen. Start outside the last ring and number the spaces from the outside towards the inside starting with zero.

3   Write each child's name inside the ring space corresponding to the number of times she/he was chosen.

4   Draw arrows from each child to the child selected by them.

5   Survey the diagram to assess popularity and interaction preferences. This information should remain confidential.

This method of using a spiral or graph is often used by playworkers to observe either play types, loose parts used, or choice of games played by one or other gender or by both equally.

Making informed reflections upon your own role

This section discusses how to use observations to reflect upon and develop your own practice. In addition it considers both the short- and long-term management of any observations carried out.

Using observations to reflect upon and develop your own practice

A vital skill to develop when writing up observations is how to evaluate or analyse the observation and then decide what to do next. (Refer to the case study of a tracking observation on Joe on page 337.) The evaluation depends upon the aim of the observation. If the observation took place in order to determine if the child was developing according to expected norms in development, then the evaluation would compare the skills observed with those described in developmental charts. (See chapters 4, 6 and 7 for developmental ranges or norms.) If the observation was made to determine if the behaviour exhibited by the child is socially acceptable for his age, then the evaluation would focus on acceptable behaviour, comparing the child's behaviour with the expected behaviour for that age. Observations may also be carried out to determine if a child is settling into the setting, or socialising with peers. If so, the analysis or evaluation would focus on that aspect of the child's behaviour. We are analysing what we know about that particular child, and also what we know about how young children learn. So we use what we see and hear as the information we record and then interpret this in light of our knowledge. Close observation allows us to make guesses about what children already know and about what their current interests are. We make our guesses in the light of what we already know to help us plan what we will offer next to take learning forward.

Recommendations that are related to the aims of the observation

Once you have determined, by analysing the observation, whether the child is developing according to expected norms or not, you can make informed recommendations, again related to the aim of the observation. Typically, these recommendations would be:

➤ activities to consolidate or extend the child's skills
➤ identify play needs and play preferences
➤ a plan to manage the child's behaviour
➤ plans to inform parents and/or other professionals about the child's progress
➤ a referral to other professionals for a second opinion.

Observing children and evaluating the findings in this manner inform practice by enabling the practitioner in an Early Years setting to plan effectively for individual children's needs and then, by carrying out further observations, determine whether or not the plans have been successful. By using the observations to reflect upon your own practice (see chapters 3, 9 and 11) or to carry out your own action research (Chapter 16) you are able to constantly be aware of your effectiveness as a practitioner in a setting and to modify your practice accordingly.

What to do with your observations

The first and most obvious thing you do with your observations is to use them to plan what to offer next. In this way, you are basing your planned programme on the interests and needs of the children as you have observed them. So observation informs planning. Planning based on the observed interests and needs of individual children ensures that the programme provided offers genuine equality of access and opportunity to all children.

Once you have used your observations to plan what to offer next, you can also think about how to use them to build a record of the child's progress over time. Inevitably, if all members of staff are keeping notes on what they notice, you will gather a veritable mountain of paper over the days and weeks. It is here that you need to use your judgement about what is significant. Each key worker could be responsible for collecting together the bits of paper relating to his or her key children, then sift through them, extracting what is significant and discarding the rest. There is absolutely no point in keeping every observation note made. You need to track each child's progress and the best way of doing this is to chart leaps in learning.

In addition, each key worker needs to ensure that he or she has observation notes covering all aspects of the curriculum. When you have been worried about a child's emotional development it is natural that your observation notes will reflect this. But the child's overall development needs to be charted and you need to ensure that you have noticed something about the child's learning across the curriculum.

Your skills in using observation as a reflection on your practice and the practice of others may lead to situations in which you may feel uncomfortable. In Early Years practice the tensions between curriculum demands and the needs of individual children may sometimes appear to be at odds. Criticism of established as well as more recent patterns of teaching and learning strategies or comments about what should be happening in classrooms may not be pleasant to hear.

Management and storage of observations

As the notes and paperwork accumulate it is important to have some way of managing the volume, both in the short and long term. These pieces of paper initially provide support and information for the planning of future work with the children: they have a formative purpose. They are also needed for formative, and then summative, report writing, when statements are made about the child's progress, often for communication to others, in particular to parents or carers, and other practitioners.

Develop a manageable filing system

In the long term, developing a manageable form of filing system for the observations is important if all of these observations are to be useful, and are not to be lost. A pocket file for each child, ring binders and a section in a filing cabinet are all possibilities, but solutions will be individual, dependent upon available space and storage facilities and the time to support them. Keeping these samples of evidence is, however, very important both in order to inform planning, and for when it comes to the summative stage(s) in a child's time in the

nursery or class. They give insights into the child that can inform the understanding of parents, head teachers, inspectors, educational psychologists and other agencies, and provide evidence that can support statements made of the child's competence, in a wide range of contexts and areas of experience.

Short-term management

The short-term management of observations includes the sharing of these with other staff at the end of day or at team meetings so that everyone is aware of the successes, efforts and concerns about individuals, areas and resources. Gaps in professionals' knowledge about particular children can be identified, and plans can be made to fill these gaps.

Sharing observations with parents/carers

How these observations and records are shared with parents and carers is an important aspect to consider, and ways of doing so need to be developed. Not all parents are able to collect their children at the end of a day or session. This does not, of course, mean they are not interested in their child or do not care about supporting them. In order for all parents to have the opportunity to share such observations on a regular basis, the setting may have to examine ways of making time available for practitioners to do so – time which may involve extra resourcing, and therefore have staffing implications. Having another adult come in to take a story session at the end of the morning or afternoon for half-an-hour a week, or putting groups of children together for a period at the end of the day, may free up some time, but a range of options need to be considered if as many parents as possible are to have the opportunity to participate. Bartholomew and Bruce (1993) describe how parents who cannot come in actually contribute observations to the records via a parent observation sheet, which feeds in to the nursery's records. Recording in a home and setting diary is another idea that different settings use.

At summative stages, at the end of the school year, not all of the observations themselves will go forward to the next teacher or setting. They do, however, form the basis for formal records and report writing. Evidence for the statements you make will be drawn from the observational records. The summative statement or report then goes forward, the observations that fed it are stored or discarded, and the process begins again with the next intake.

Involving parents

Although a cliché, it is true to say that parents know more about their own child than anyone else. Workers and teachers do get to know children well, but their knowledge of the child is limited. The person who sees the child in every situation at every time of the day and year is the parent.

Parents send young children to a nursery, crèche or playgroup for many reasons:

➤ they feel their children will benefit from contact with other children

➤ they want their children to have a head start in the education stakes

➤ they need to work or study.

But all parents want the best for their children and all parents deserve to be kept informed about their children's progress.

In the Italian nurseries, (see Chapter 11, page 300) a great deal of work goes into keeping parents informed about their children's progress. Each child has a plastic wallet up on the wall and staff put brief comments into this about what the child has done that day. This makes parents of very young children feel involved in their children's progress – they don't miss their child's first step or first word. Furthermore, they will notice changes in their child's behaviour and learning at home and can add these to the child's profile.

Involving parents in this process is sometimes difficult and always requires that workers be sensitive and supportive in their approach. Most nurseries and playgroups collect information from parents when the child starts in the nursery. This will often include practical details, but some nurseries now invite parents to say something about their child's interests, fears, passions, likes and dislikes. This gives practitioners a starting point on which to base their assessment of progress. All children starting in the nursery or playgroup arrive with a history. You can only assess progress against a starting point.

Many nurseries and playgroups now invite parents to become involved in contributing to the child's profile. Parents are invited to read through the profile and add their comments. You will, of course, need to think carefully about how you can manage this.

Activity 3

Self-analysis

1 What aspects of observation do you enjoy most?

2 Which aspects of observational research have been of most professional interest to you?

3 Indicate how data gathered in an observation has influenced your understanding of a child.

4 Have your views been changed purely as a result of this observation or have other things influenced you? For example, has your response to the child changed because you have focused more on the child as an individual?

5 Have your perceptions changed because you have talked to others?

6 Is all this evidence reliable?

Conclusion

Observation provides the only true test of the quality of the practitioner's work and offers the most reliable information about each child's progress. Using it turns the practitioner into a learner and often brings about a transformation of perspective, since the open-minded stance necessary makes practitioners question previously held assumptions and rethink their practice.

How to move on in your research

Riddall Leach, S. (2005), *How to Observe Children*. Oxford: Heinemann

> This book provides further information on observing children.

References

Bartholomew, L. and Bruce, T. (1993), *Getting to Know You: A Guide to Record Keeping in Early Childhood Education and Care*. London: Hodder & Stoughton

Cockburn, A. D. (2001), *Teaching Children 3–11: A Student's Guide*. London: Paul Chapman

DfEs (2007), *Statutory Framework for the Early Years Foundation Stage. Setting the Standards for Learning, Development and Care for Children from Birth to Five*. Nottingham: DfES

Fisher, J. (2002), *Starting from the Child*. Maidenhead: Open University Press

Harding, J. and Smith-Meldon, L. (2000), *How to Make Observations and Assessments*. London: Hodder and Stoughton

Hobart, C. and Frankel, J. (1999), *A Practical Guide to Child Observation*. Cheltenham: Stanley Thornes

Laishley, J. (1999), *Working with Young Children*. London: Hodder and Stoughton

MacNaughton, G., Rolfe, S. and Siraj-Blatchford, I. (2001), *Doing Early Childhood Research: Theory and Practice*. Maidenhead: Open University Press

Meggitt, C. (2007), *Child Development, Birth to 16 years: An illustrated guide*. Oxford: Heinemann

Meggitt, C. and Sunderland, G. (2000), *Child Development: An Illustrated Guide*. Oxford: Heinemann

QCA (2000), 'Curriculum Guidance for the Foundation Stage'. London: QCA

Stierer, B., Devereux, J., Gifford, S., Laycock, L. and Yerbury, J. (1993), *Profiling, Recording and Observing: A Resource Pack for the Early Years*. London: Routledge

Taylor, J. and Woods, M. (1998), *Early Childhood Studies: An Holistic Introduction*. London: Arnold

Wragg, E. (1994), *An Introduction to Classroom Observation*. London: Routledge

Weinberg, R. and Wood, R. (1975), *Observation of Teachers in Mainstream and Special Education Settings*. Reston VA: Council for Exceptional Children

Yule, W. and Carr, J. (1987), *Behavioural Modification for People with Mental Handicaps 2nd edition*. London: Croom Helm

13

Evaluating Early Years policy and legislation

Janet Kay and
Iain MacLeod-Brudenell with Candida Brudenell

In this chapter, a range of legislation affecting the Early Years in England will be analysed in terms of how it influences and shapes services to children and families, and how legislative change impacts on content and delivery of Early Years services. The legislative framework comprises laws influencing Early Years services, and relevant policies, guidelines and regulations. The ways in which the legislative framework not only shapes, but is also shaped by, practice and by theoretical and empirical developments will be explored as will the role of the practitioner within this developmental process. Key considerations for practitioners working within the legislative framework will be discussed, in terms of strategies for achieving and maintaining high standards of services for young children. The ways in which legislation changes and develops over time will be discussed.

Although space restricts discussion of legislation to that affecting provision in England you are encouraged to compare and contrast this with legislation affecting the Early Years in Wales, Scotland, Northern Ireland and the Republic of Ireland.

The expectations placed on Early Years practitioners are not immovable, they are not 'set in stone'. The focus of legislation changes with time and in response to events in the wider world and, more particularly, to the way government policy interprets and responds to social need. The ways in which legislation changes and develops practice over time thus raises topical and critical discussion. These 'critical issues' will often emerge when they challenge personal, cultural or ethical values in the interpretation of 'quality' and effectiveness

of provision of education and care of young children. Each policy development will raise critical issues discussion and some of these will be discussed within the chapter.

The concept of raising quality in Early Years services is inextricably bound up with beliefs about what quality entails. Developing an understanding of debates about what constitutes quality in early childhood is a crucial part of self-development towards becoming a reflective practitioner. Examination of critical issues encourages reflection on your own personal experiences and values. The quality of experience offered to children is often a direct result of the practitioner's awareness of these issues.

This chapter addresses the following areas:

> Setting the context for discussing policy and legislation
> Role of legislation in developing quality services in the Early Years
> Current policy issues
> The Every Child Matters policy strategy
> The Children Act 2004
> Change for children
> Health policy
> The Childcare Act 2006
> Early Years education and childcare policy and legislation
> Special educational needs and additional support needs
> Children's Centres inspection and regulation

By undertaking the suggested study within this chapter it is hoped that you will be able to:

1 understand that legislation shapes practice and that practice influences legislation

2 consider, within the legislative framework, factors which ensure quality of Early Years services

3 understand the distinction between legislation and policy and how policy is developed

4 identify those aspects of legislation and policy which influence practice in your setting

5 reflect upon the principles attached to policy with reference to the needs of society and individuals

6 critically evaluate the issues of quality which apply to policy in practice.

Setting the context for discussing policy and legislation

Legislation affecting early childhood is, in the simplest terms, the product of government activity and is designed to control and shape expectations and behaviour within Early Years service development and delivery. But legislation is influenced by changes in beliefs and understandings about the best approaches to Early Years services. These understandings may be part of wider social policy developments affecting a broader range of the population. For example, social policy developments around social inclusion have not only impacted significantly on Early Years policy, but have also introduced measures to support parents returning to work or study and a raft of retraining and upskilling measures to improve an individual's employment chances. It is important to recognise that Early Years policy may be part of a wider mandate and therefore may be designed to achieve goals that are not all directly related to children's well-being. Legislation and policy are also shaped by the work of practitioners and their understandings of that work, research findings in the field, and events that have highlighted flaws in existing legislative structures.

Factors contributing to developments in policy and legislation are given in Figure 13.1.

Legislation can be seen as a social construct, in that it is a product of a particular set of social and cultural conditions and, therefore, will differ between diverse social and cultural settings, and will change over time as societies develop. The key importance for practitioners in recognising legislation and policy as social constructs lies in their understanding of legislation, not as an immutable force developed outside the Early Years context, but as changeable, subject to many forces, and developing in line with particular sets of beliefs and opinions within the field. This means that we can disagree with the principles and theories underpinning legislation and we can believe that a different approach may be better. It also means that policy and legislation will develop and change over time as social opinion and beliefs about what children's needs are and how to meet these move on.

As practitioners, possibly as researchers, we may have the opportunity to contribute to changes in beliefs about principles and practices, enshrined in policy and legislation, as

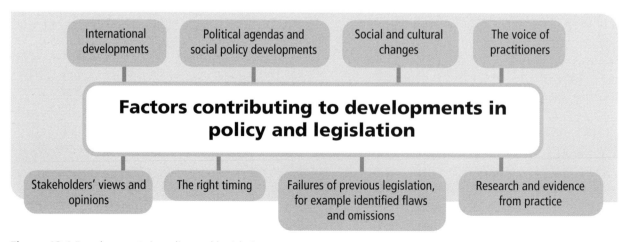

Figure 13.1 Developments in policy and legislation

do other stakeholders. This means we may work sometimes within legislative frameworks that do not necessarily entirely support our own views on 'best practice'. It is important for practitioners to recognise that they can contribute to the debate on legislative change and that legislation is a product of human activity and therefore may be flawed. For example, the debate about whether children in the UK start their formal schooling at too young an age continues to be a contended area of Early Years policy.

At present, key influences on policy are: the government mandate to reduce social exclusion and family poverty by a raft of measures which support parents returning to work and provide children and families with a range of Early Years services to improve their health and welfare; educational attainment; and economic security in the present and future. It is important for practitioners, researchers and others to critically examine such policy in terms of its effectiveness in supporting children in their early childhood and also to determine whether policy outcomes are all positive for children. Policy outcomes are often complex, can be unpredictable and may be negative at times. For example, the extended school agenda may provide new childcare opportunities for working parents, improving their chances of employment and reducing family poverty. However, it may also mean that children of 4 and 5 years old are in school from 8 am to 6 pm, which many may feel is too long for children of this age.

Background

Historically, services supporting children and families have developed separately, creating a situation that began to be described as 'fragmentation' in the 1990s. The key mainstream services for young children – education, health and social care services – developed from different historical beginnings into separate services with differently trained and qualified professionals within them. These services were governed differently and

managed differently, had different goals and aims for the children they provided services for, and even different understandings of children and childhood.

Health services for children developed within generic health services for all patients, and health service governance and boundaries developed differently to those of local authorities. Education and social care services both came under local authority provision but whereas education was a separate service for children, children's social care services were until recently part of larger social services departments catering for whole populations. Many of these did have nursery provision to offer, but social services day nurseries became a service to children in need and not to the general population. As such, places were offered to children where perceived deficits in parenting made institutional care seem more desirable than home care. Daycare was not supported through policy as meeting the needs of the majority of children as discussed further below.

The development of Early Years services for children was dominated by a split between education services provided mainly by the statutory sector and childcare services provided mainly by the independent and voluntary sectors. Although nursery classes and nursery schools offered places to some 3- and 4-year-old children these were far from universal and many children did not get a place in nursery. Nursery education places were free for half-day places, but working or studying parents had difficulty using these unless they had a childminder or relative who could care for the child for the rest of the day. This situation arose from the policy that nursery places should be offered to support children's educational development, and not to provide a service to working parents. This policy was rooted in the belief that children should be primarily cared for at home by their mothers, supported by attachment theories developed by John Bowlby and others from the 1950s onwards. As such, the state did not have a remit to provide daycare for working parents until relatively recently.

The failure of mainstream services to provide effective childcare services to children in their Early Years and their families resulted in the expansion of private and voluntary sector childcare provision from the 1960s onwards. Playgroups (pre-schools) developed in communities to offer children a chance to play, socialise and learn and private day nurseries and childminders filled the gaps for working or studying parents who could afford them. However, these services offered childcare and not education and for many families childcare services remained complex, confusing and unaffordable. Parents often had to make complicated arrangements for children in order to ensure they were cared for while they worked. Many relied on extended family members for care and others had arrangements that relied on more than one carer for the child each day. Not all children had access to childcare or education places and although playgroups sometimes filled the gap, provision was not universal. These problems were much more severe for children with disabilities, children in poorer areas and many rural children.

In addition, there was no real link between welfare services for young children and childcare services for the same young children (Cameron, 2003).

It was within this historical context that the New Labour government came to power in 1997, heralding policy development in children's services generally, and Early Years services specifically, at a rate and level unprecedented in previous years.

National Childcare Strategy, 1998

This umbrella strategy was launched in 1998, not long after New Labour came to power in 1997. Key drivers for change in Early Years services were the interlinked policies to reduce child poverty, help parents to return to work, and improve educational outcomes for children

Activity 1

Changing Early Years provision
In the early 1990s …

Leon is 4. He has just got a place in a nursery class at a school nearby. His name has been on the waiting list for nearly a year. Before this, Leon went to playgroup two mornings a week with his mother. Leon has two-and-a-half hours at nursery in the afternoons. His mother has started a job and so in the mornings Leon goes to a childminder. The childminder also picks Leon up from nursery at 3.20 and cares for him until his mother gets back from work.

Maisie is 3. Both her parents work and Maisie goes to a private day nursery. The family finds this a big expense but both parents are concerned that working part-time or taking time off from work will affect their careers negatively. There is a nursery school near the family home, which may have a place for Maisie eventually. Her parents would like her to attend the school because they want her to have a good educational start before formal schooling begins and this is not offered in the day nursery. However, they are worried about moving her and what they would do with her after the morning session finishes, as there are few childminders in the area they live in and no family available to collect and care for Maisie from 11.30 am onwards.

Do you think the situation for these two families has changed since the 1990s and if so, what changes have taken place and why?

through better quality, more accessible early education. As such, the strategy focused on increasing places for 3- and 4-year-olds, setting targets for all children of this age group to have a place in an Early Years setting eventually. The push to get all pre-school 3- and 4-year-old children into an Early Years setting was supported by the change in policy earlier on that allowed non-maintained sector services to apply for nursery grants and offer free early education places to 3- and 4-year-olds. Children placed with private day nurseries, pre-schools and some childminders could now access their free half-day nursery provision within these settings. In this way the strategy started to tackle the long-term split between Early Years education services and childcare services. However, this process was hampered by years of underfunding and the previous lack of an over-arching policy, which had promoted the ad hoc growth of services and no coherent development strategy for Early Years services. The result was a postcode lottery for service provision, with many socio-economically deprived areas particularly under-provided for. In addition, the ability or lack of ability to pay for services was significant in terms of access. Children in inner cities and some rural children were the most likely not to have access to pre-school provision.

Another key issue was that quality (like access) was very variable with significant differences in standards between different sectors and types of setting. The Children Act 1989 had introduced an under-8s inspection regime for all daycare settings, but in the meanwhile, nursery classes were inspected by Ofsted. Quality was also affected by the levels of qualified and trained staff in the setting, with large proportions of unqualified staff in the Early Years sector. In order to meet the needs of the developing sector, the National Childcare Strategy also focused on funding and developing training opportunities for existing and future Early Years practitioners as part of a drive to raise standards in the sector through workforce development. The quest

for improved quality was also supported by the introduction of the Desirable Outcomes for nursery-aged children, which eventually became the Early Learning Goals within the Foundation Stage of the National Curriculum.

The National Childcare Strategy was delivered through Early Years Development and Childcare Partnerships (EYDCPs), which were significant in establishing a more coordinated planning approach to Early Years service development and delivery across the various sectors within local authority areas. However, these partnerships were not always successful in engaging all sectors and were often dominated by local authorities at the expense of the less well-resourced private and voluntary sector providers.

Sure Start Local Programmes (SSLPs)

The introduction of SSLPs in the late 1990s was a significant development in the drive towards more integrated service planning and delivery. The programmes offered a range of services to children under 4 and their families, including maternity services to support healthy pregnancies, childcare, adult education, parenting education and support and health visiting services. SSLPs were unique to their area, but most offered a comprehensive range of services to children and families, including strategies to engage a wider range of parents, for example to encourage more fathers to become involved. The programmes were based in socio-economically deprived areas and sought to work with or incorporate existing Early Years/family support provision. The SSLPs were based on the Head Start programmes in the USA which supported the view that early intervention in health, education and parenting ability would produce better developmental outcomes for children and higher levels of educational achievement.

SSLPs were evaluated through the National Evaluation of Sure Start (NESS). They found that SSLPs generally worked well to engage parents and that some parents were involved in decision-making within the programmes through their role on the SSLP management boards. However, in general, NESS found that SSLPs were less successful in engaging a broad range of agencies involved with young children and families and that some programmes had limited involvement with other local initiatives. In addition, SSLPs were found to have generally failed to work with the most deprived children and families who needed their services most. SSLPs were also criticised for creating areas without such programmes, many of which had children and families who would have benefited from Early Years services but who were not living in an SSLP catchment area.

Despite these limitations on their success, SSLPs were significant in changing the ethos of Early Years services provision by virtue of building parent partnership and multi-agency/multi-disciplinary approaches into their core principles. Most SSLP teams were multi-disciplinary, giving staff experience of working together across professional boundaries, and giving managers opportunity to develop skills in leading multi-professional teams.

From about 2004 onwards, the majority of SSLPs have been transforming into Children's Centres in line with current policy agendas.

Critical issues

We have tried to emphasise that policy is a social construct and also that policy may be controversial in terms of underpinning values, content, implementation and outcomes. As such, policy developments raise what we refer to as critical issues. The term 'critical issues' is used to indicate areas of discussion that are topical and contested, are subject to debate, within the area of early childhood. Critical issues are:

➤ live and contentious, and have an impact upon the quality of experiences for young children and their families

➤ become the subject of debate because they are the source of tension between the values and expectations of different groups.

Occasionally a particular critical issue arises in response to an incident or event, which demonstrates a failing in the system to provide adequate and appropriate services for children. Other critical issues arise from ongoing debates about the principles and values underpinning approaches to Early Years services.

If this chapter had been written ten or more years ago the range of critical issues would have been different. The contents may have included such burning issues as the introduction of a standard curriculum for the pre-fives, baseline assessment or subject emphasis within the National Curriculum, funding of pre-school places for 4-year-olds and the emerging emphasis upon skills in numeracy and literacy. These issues were very contentious at that time and in most cases they still have relevance today. They may be less critical because events have changed practice in the area of early childhood education and care. Some areas remain topical but the emphasis has changed. Perhaps, for example, we would still question the appropriateness of a standardised curriculum for 3- and 4-year-olds (see Chapter 11), but now this would be from the standpoint of experience of delivery and inspection of this provision.

It is clear then that critical issues change in emphasis over time, but often remain 'live', with new areas of concern and questions and debates to be considered in respect of any particular issue. Another example is the legal care of young children 'looked after' by local authorities. One of the key critical issues in the past was about permanence and the extent to which efforts should be made to rehabilitate children to their birth families before making decisions about a child's long-term care. This issue is still of great importance, but a more current key issue in this field is the educational, health and welfare outcomes for children 'looked after' and the impact of failures to ensure these are positive on the child's long-term life chances. Critical issues are those that impact on children, families and professionals within the field at a particular point in time.

To summarise, it is important to recognise that the nature of critical issues is that they will change in both the priority given to them at different times and in different places and also in the emphasis placed upon them for political and economic purposes.

Recognising the existence of critical issues and determining what creates contentious debates in the Early Years field is crucial to your personal and professional development. Understanding the ways in which particular issues become topical and contested is part of your development towards becoming a reflective practitioner.

Quality issues

At the heart of any discussions of critical issues is the debate about quality. Quality of experience and outcomes for children is the overriding issue and is central to all of the themes discussed in this chapter. However, notions of quality in Early Years services change over time, with developments in our understanding of children's needs and how best to meet them. In order to take part in debates about critical issues, practitioners need to have a concept of quality and how it can be achieved. One of the reasons why topics become 'issues' is because changes in views on quality in the Early Years alter our perceptions of existing services and practices. For example, in the past the growing dissatisfaction with separate care and education services in the UK developed from perceptions that quality in Early Years services was very variable; there was lack of equity in provision for different children depending on family income and location, and the child's cultural background; ability and social class. In addition, there was a confusion of different provision, which was fragmented and often failed to meet the real needs of children and their families.

Stakeholders in critical issues

'Stakeholder' is a term used to identify those who have an interest in the quality and effectiveness of the provision, but also may wish to actively influence decision-making. Stakeholders may be passive, in that they have a role to play but may not exercise their right to be involved, or they may be active. Some stakeholders may have the public ear or eye, such as the media, politicians and professional bodies but some less prominent individuals and groups may be influential at other levels.

Stakeholders have different levels of influence on the development of specific critical issues, depending on the issue itself and the various roles of those involved. Some stakeholders have consistently more or less influence than others. For example, the inclusion of children as potential stakeholders in the planning and delivery of Early Years services is relatively recent in comparison to the more established role of other stakeholders.

Stakeholders appear in all walks of life, for example shareholders in the financial world and users of the health services. The role of the community as stakeholders in the local provision of education and care is self-evident. Faith and community groups may be the most obvious groups of people with a strong interest in shaping the educational experiences of young children in a community. Businesses, emergency services, and social services may be less obvious but are of equal importance.

Activity 2

Stakeholders in Early Years services

The structure of the education system in the UK has changed considerably over recent years, reflecting successive governments' aims to improve quality, increase diversity and make institutions more accountable to students, parents, employers and taxpayers.

List all those people, agencies and organisations you consider to be stakeholders in the care and education of young children. Discuss your list with a colleague or mentor and ask if they have other ideas.

The influence of the media as stakeholders

When reading this chapter, you are encouraged to consider some of the underlying factors that may influence your perceptions of a particular issue. For example, awareness of a critical issue may emerge in the workplace, but the way in which the issue is presented in the media may be at odds with your personal experience. The approach taken by different sections of the media may be expressing a particular standpoint, which some may consider biased. Contradictory viewpoints may be expressed within and through the media.

The media are some of the stakeholders in Early Years policy and legislation and, as such, may represent viewpoints of individual commentators, editors and different shades of political and public opinion.

Activity 3

Using the media to analyse issues

Consideration of your personal experience and the values that underpin your opinions may help you to identify factors that influence parental involvement in Early Years services. You may be aided in this venture by making a point of using the media to support your analysis of issues. In consideration of a particular critical issue currently under debate, read newspapers and watch television reports, consult local and national press and relevant websites. Most importantly be aware of bias. This will raise your awareness of critical issues currently appearing in the media and identify some of the underlying factors that may influence your personal stance on the issue.

The role of government

It is useful to reflect upon how national policy influencing Early Years is decided and by whom. Who are the national stakeholders in care and education in the Early Years?

Political agendas can be determined from a variety of sources. For example, examination of relevant documentation will indicate how the expectations of political opinion are represented in the curriculum guidelines, in terms of both the content and delivery of the curriculum. Other sources are government papers, local authority guidelines, legislation and discussions on legislation. Many early childhood organisations monitor government policy closely and publish commentaries on developments (see websites listed at the end of the chapter). Policies affecting early childhood may well be part of wider agendas. For example, many policies currently affecting early childhood are part of the government's wider agenda on social exclusion and raising skills and educational standards within the workforce. The focus of government policy can be found in both the type of critical issue prominent at the time and the type of developments made within a particular critical issue. Governments do not operate in a vacuum. They are influenced by wider public and political opinion, research, and developments in other countries.

Values and perceptions

Values underpin all aspects of our work with children and families: personal values and beliefs; the values generally agreed upon within the communities in which we work; and the values that are promoted by our elected representatives in parliament. The term 'values' is open to wide interpretation and so it is important to consider and clarify our understanding of the term. Consider the range of values: these may include social, cultural, moral, ethical, religious and political values, but you may well think of others. How do these affect work with young children? For example, you may wish to consider what the effect of a strongly held religious belief may be on the ways in which a practitioner works with children.

This remains a critical issue for many practitioners. For those practitioners who hold atheist or humanist beliefs, this may influence their participation in quasi-religious practice such as 'broadly Christian' school assemblies. Observant practitioners of a faith who wish to demonstrate their belief through their work may find similar conflicts of interest.

Values affect our perception of critical issues. They are at the root of agreement or disagreement about fundamental issues in our professional role. Values are different from opinion or preference and in this respect we must be vigilant to separate our personal from our professional views. Particular values underpin policy and legislation relating to young children at any one point in time. However, dominant sets of values and beliefs change over time within particular social and cultural contexts. One of the key driving forces for changes in legislation and policy is the need for this framework to continue to reflect the dominant values and beliefs in the field at the time.

Values also differ between social and cultural contexts. For example, values are visible in the curriculum offered to children and the quality of experience provided by staff delivering that curriculum. A comparison of the curriculum offered in England with Scotland or another European country quickly reveals differences as well as similarities in values through the selection of curriculum areas, the curriculum content and the means of teaching. The differences between the curriculum offered in different countries is also an expression of the differences within societies. Values are at the heart of our work with young children. Reflective evaluation of personal values will often lead to analysis of practice in order to develop and improve professional competence. (See Chapter 3 for further discussion on reflective practice.)

Role of legislation in developing quality services in the Early Years

In this section, the development of legislation will be examined in terms of the processes through which legislation is formed and the significance of underlying values and principles in shaping legislation. The section will focus on the example of the Children Act 1989 to 'unpick' the complex influences on legislative development and to explore the value of legislation in improving the quality standards of Early Years services.

There are a number of factors that need to be considered when discussing the role of legislation in developing quality services in the Early Years. These include:

➤ that legislation has a purpose/purposes
➤ the extent of the effectiveness of legislation and policy in shaping and supporting quality services in the Early Years
➤ recognition that legislation is not 'set in concrete' but subject to change and development

- understanding of the processes by which legislative change is driven

- the social, cultural and political basis of legislation.

These factors will be explored further through the example of the Children Act 1989.

The Children Act 1989 – a case study of the development of legislation

The Children Act 1989, implemented in 1991, embodies both public and private aspects of legal proceedings related to children. It brought together a range of already existing legislation under one Act, and introduced some new measures.

The Children Act 1989 provides:

- for the protection of children from abuse

- for the welfare of 'children in need'

- measures to ensure the welfare of children in private proceedings such as divorce.

It is based on a set of underlying principles that changed the ways in which children and their families were viewed within legal proceedings, some of which were drawn from concepts of children's rights.

Influences on the development of the Act

The Children Act 1989 was one of the most significant pieces of legislation determining the protection of children and the promotion of their welfare for many years. However, the Act did not come about through a single process or factor. Instead, many different influences shaped the legislation, both in terms of timing and content.

These are given in Figure 13.2.

The development of the Children Act 1989 was influenced by a variety of factors which converged at a particular point in time to shape the legislation. As Figure 13.2 shows these influences were rooted in both concerns within

Some influences on the development of the Children Act 1989	
Children in Care report, 1984	Recommending a review of the law which it described as 'at best, complex and confused, and at worst, contradictory' (DoH, 2001:5).
White Paper 'The Law on Child Care and Family Services', 1987	Outlining the principles on which new legislation should be based.
Failures in practice	Including the conclusions of the child death inquiries during the 1990s in respect of: • Tyra Henry • Jasmine Beckford • Kimberley Carlile.
The inquiry into the Cleveland child sexual abuse crisis, 1987, during which more than 100 children were removed into care within the space of a few months	Practitioners' concerns included: • gaps in provision, for example no order to enforce assessment of children • a 'back door' into care, through which children who had been in voluntary care for 6 months could be made subject of a Care Order without a court hearing • the increasing and inappropriate use of wardship by local authorities • inadequate emergency protection provisions for children.
The United Nations Convention on the Rights of the Child. which came into force in 1989	This strongly influenced the underlying principles of the Children Act 1989, in terms of children's rights issues.

Figure 13.2 Development of the Children Act 1989

government about the need to clarify and consolidate welfare legislation for children and in lessons from failures in practice. Some of the problems identified in practice prior to the Children Act 1989 included:

➤ poor information sharing between agencies, which often contributed to faulty judgements being made about the welfare of children
➤ children being removed from parents on inadequate evidence of abuse
➤ focus on working with parents, rather than children, contrasted with lack of genuine partnership with parents in decision-making processes
➤ lack of effective permanency planning for children in care, resulting in children drifting in and out of care or lacking a stable permanent home.

These factors prompted the need for legislative change. However, the concurrent development of the UNCRC was influential also, particularly in shaping the values and principles underpinning the Act.

Key issues in determining the principles underpinning the Act

One of the key issues in child welfare legislation is the balance between the role of the state and the role of the family in supporting children's growth and development. The extent to which different states intervene in the role of the family in nurturing and raising their children varies, but the Children Act Now: Messages from Research (DoH, 2001), an evidence-based review of the Children Act 1989, points out three common factors.

The first of these relates to the role of a state in nurturing children and promoting their best interests.

The principles of the 1989 UN Convention on the Rights of the Child, for example, support the view that concerted attention should be given by families and the State to various aspects of children's lives, including education, care, recreation, culture and health, and children's social behaviour.

DoH (2001:3)

The second theme relates to children's rights as citizens, embodying their rights to be party to decision-making about themselves and to have their wishes and feelings taken into account.

The third theme relates to protecting children from harm. The role of the state within this process is determined by where the boundaries are placed between the responsibilities of the family and the duty of the state to intervene. This boundary is variable between different cultures and countries, and where this boundary is placed will influence the type of services delivered to children and families and the ways in which they are delivered.

The principles on which the Children Act 1989 rests are rooted in attempts to balance the privacy of the family with the obligations of the state to both support children's welfare and protect them from harm, while respecting and promoting the rights of both children and families.

Underlying principles

The Act introduced a range of new principles on which the spirit of the law rests. The underpinning ethos behind these principles is the belief that the concerns of children and their families should be located much more firmly at the heart of legal procedures affecting them. The paternalistic approach, which had dominated proceedings until that point, had resulted in many families being 'acted upon' rather than 'worked with'. Research findings, particularly about the outcomes for children subject to welfare legislative proceedings, had led to a widely held belief that improvements in the quality of welfare services for children could only be achieved through a different emphasis on their rights within procedures.

Organisations such as the Family Welfare Association had spent several years lobbying for parent's and children's rights to be more central to proceedings, and they had highlighted flaws in practice where children and families did not have a say in the decision-making processes about them. For example, many children who came into the care system did not have continuing contact with their families and other significant individuals. There was a lack of consistency in practice around ensuring contact between children and families, and the onus was often on families to ensure that contact took place, despite a range of practical and psychological barriers. Failure to ensure contact was maintained often opened the door to permanent separation of children from their families. The impact on children growing up in care with no knowledge of, or contact with, birth families was often very negative. A sense of dislocation and lack of sense of self, low self-esteem and poor levels of confidence were common among children who had lost contact with their birth families and/ or had little or no knowledge about their own origins and early lives or the processes that had brought them into the care system.

Influenced by the United Nations Convention on the Rights of the Child, the Children Act 1989 sought to improve and balance the rights of both the child and family within child welfare law by introducing the following underpinning principles.

Children are better off with their families

This principle underpins the whole of the Children Act 1989 and influences the ways in which the Act was constructed and implemented. It clarified the goals of welfare work with children and families and changed practice to some extent, in that the central goal of work with children and families became to support and maintain family functioning wherever this is possible. The exception to this is in cases where the child cannot be safeguarded effectively within the family. This principle militated against poor practice where children were removed into care for trivial reasons because of concerns about their general welfare, often resulting in long-term or permanent separation from families of origin. Resources had to be focused on maintaining

families where unmet needs made this difficult without service provision.

Avoiding delay

Delay in the progress of court proceedings had come to be seen as harmful to the child's welfare. For some children, childhood meant long periods of uncertainty about the future and a sense of impermanence in their living situation. Were they going home, or being adopted, or returning to live with their families of origin? For some children, there were long delays in determining these issues, while their childhood passed by. The Children Act 1989 introduced the 'no delay' principle to ensure that children's futures were settled much more quickly than previously.

The non-interventionist principle

This principle was based on the belief that a court should only make decisions in respect of a child if this step is best for the child. Legal intervention came to be viewed as a last resort in efforts to resolve public or private disputes about a child's welfare. In terms of both the child and family's best interests, legal action should be minimised and only used if all other avenues have been explored unsuccessfully. In addition, if a court is presented with a request for legal action in respect of a child, it has to determine whether making an Order is in the best interests of the child. Otherwise the court should do nothing.

The non-interventionist principle means that those responsible for children's welfare must make every effort to resolve welfare issues in respect of a child without recourse to the law. The intervention of the courts is considered to be heavy-handed and inflexible compared to a voluntary arrangement between those involved with a child, which can be reached amicably. This also applies to children in private proceedings, such as divorce, where Orders are now only made in respect of contact between non-resident parents and children if no agreement can be reached.

This principle facilitated some important changes in practice. For example, when a child is considered to be in 'acute physical danger' and therefore immediately 'at risk', it is the responsibility of social care workers to secure the child's safety as soon as possible. However, within a non-interventionist approach, this no longer means an immediate recourse to legal action. Before considering legal steps, the Children Act 1989 demands that social care workers must explore alternative methods of ensuring the child's safety. Effectively, this principle supports the rights of families to privacy from state intervention, except where it is imperative in order to protect the child from harm.

The feelings and wishes of the child

The Act introduced an explicit requirement that the wishes and feelings of the child should be elicited and taken into consideration in proceedings related to him. Although good practice had, for many years previously, demanded that the child should be consulted before decisions were made about his future, the lack of emphasis on this requirement and variations in practice meant that this did not always happen effectively.

Underpinning this principle is the recognition that the child's best interests may not be represented by either the local authority or by his parents.

The extent to which a child's wishes and feelings are considered depends on the child's age and level of understanding. These are critical factors in determining the weight that is placed on the child's view and feelings. Younger children may have very limited influence on outcomes affecting them because they are not considered to have sufficiently developed understanding about the issues under consideration. Similarly, the court cannot allow children to act against their own best interests. If the child's wishes and feelings contradict his or her best interests, the child's best interests remain paramount. For example,

a child may want to live with a particular parent, but if that parent is unable to care safely for the child, then the child's wishes will be denied. This principle reflects the increased emphasis on the rights of children within legal proceedings.

Parental responsibility

The concept of parental responsibility replaced the notion of parental rights within the Children Act 1989. The concept of parental rights was seen as outmoded, representing a view of children as the property of their parents that was out of step with the children's rights ethos shaping the principles underpinning the Children Act 1989. The notion of parental responsibility was intended to emphasise the view that parents should have responsibilities to their children rather than rights over them. Similarly, the extent to which parents can legally lose their parental responsibility for a child was curtailed. Under the Children Act 1989, parental responsibility is retained by the parent through all childcare procedures unless the child is adopted. Sharing of parental responsibility between individuals and between individuals and the local authority was introduced to ensure that children retained contacts with all significant others, whether they were in the care of the local authority or not.

It was thought by some that the Children Act 1989 had not gone far enough in establishing and securing parental responsibility for unmarried fathers. However, the automatic retention of parental responsibility by both parties after divorce is seen as a positive move in efforts to retain links between children and their fathers after family breakdown. Similarly, retention of parental responsibility when children are subject to a Care Order was seen as a positive step in encouraging parents to maintain contact and possibly to eventually resume the care of their children. This principle attempts to support both increased rights for children in relation to their parents, and the maintenance of parental responsibility as a link between parent and child as a goal for legal proceedings where at all possible.

Partnership with parents

The Children Act 1989 was built on the premise that parents and children needed to have their rights much more clearly recognised within the legislative process. As such, local authorities have a general duty to ensure that parents are party to legal processes involving their children. This duty raises a number of difficult questions about how practitioners can remain in partnership with parents when involved in actions that may be seen as adversarial by those parents. The obligation to discuss options with parents and to ensure that they have all relevant information about the social services' views and actions may be difficult to fulfil when serious child abuse has taken place. The principle was introduced partly to reduce this adversarial element to the relationship between social services and parents, but the involuntary removal of children from the care of their parents very often raises extremely strong feelings, making dialogue with parents difficult and sometimes even risky. Despite this, practitioners involved with children and families retain this duty and the onus is on service providers to ensure that it is fulfilled.

In terms of services to children in need and their families, there is an emphasis on partnership with parents to provide appropriate services to support the family where unmet need threatens family functioning or stability. Initially, the concept of a 'child in need' was interpreted solely at local authority level, producing a wide range of different service levels depending on location. To remedy this disparity, the Framework for Assessment of Children in Need and their Families (DoH, 2000) was introduced as a national tool for assessing need. It ensures that:

➤ families receive equitable access to services with clearer boundaries for when service provision should be triggered

➤ all the child and family's needs are identified and responded to through a comprehensive assessment process

➤ family strengths should be identified and worked with

➤ services provided should be acceptable and seen as helpful by children and parents

➤ resources should be used wisely by ensuring services are appropriate, effective and targeted on identified need.

Shaping services through legislation

The Children Act 1989 shaped welfare services to children and families by emphasising the key role of social care services in child protection work. Although there is a strong emphasis on joint agency and multi-disciplinary responses to child abuse both at strategic planning and individual case level, the fact that ultimately legal responsibility lay with social care services has meant that they continued to dominate the child protection process, with ramifications for the perceived roles of other agencies and professionals. Although social care services had regular contact with families in need and families where abuse has already been identified, other agencies were much more likely to have contact with children where abuse might be ongoing but not yet identified. In addition, as family support services developed in a range of agencies including health, education and voluntary sector organisations, there was a split in the delivery of services to children that left child protection services isolated from other provision.

Health visitors, Early Years practitioners and teachers had a key role in initial identification and response to child abuse and monitoring of children where abuse had taken place. Yet expertise in these areas continued to be located largely within social care services, ensuring that child protection work took place outside the provision of mainstream services to children. Although health and education are specified as having a duty to being involved in child protection within the legislation, their role was minor compared to social care services and professionals in these agencies were much less likely to have had relevant training and staff development. This was significant in terms of the balance of roles within multi-disciplinary child protection teams. For example, there is evidence that, despite the emphasis on 'working together', in fact other agencies dropped out of the multi-disciplinary core groups designed to implement child protection plans soon after the initial investigation.

Efforts to ensure that services were effectively integrated and that a multi-disciplinary approach was maintained were promoted through the DoH guidelines Working Together to Safeguard Children (DoH, 1999; 2006), which outlined the roles of all practitioners working with children in the child protection process. The requirements of these guidelines, which all establishments and workers with children should comply with, are given in Figure 13.3.

Despite this, there were considerable failures to establish effective partnerships between all relevant agencies, as exemplified by the Laming Report into the death of Victoria Climbie (DoH, 2003).

Summary

The underlying principles of the Act reflect concerns with child welfare, children's rights and the protection of children from harm. The principles support a particular approach based on partnership between agencies and between agencies, children and families. The rights of both children and parents were enhanced within the Act through the application of the principles discussed above. However, in some areas problems persisted in applying these principles effectively. Failures or limitation of the effectiveness of inter-agency partnerships continued to be at the root of many criticisms of child welfare in the UK after the Children Act 1989 was implemented in 1991 and eventually this failure led to further developments in policy and legislation (see current policy discussed below).

Activity 5

Considering the effectiveness of the Children Act 1989

This examination of the Children Act 1989 tries to show the complex influences on policy development and the importance of the principles underpinning legislation in shaping services. However, it also shows that legislation may only partially achieve its aims and that failures in some areas of effectiveness may then lead to further legislative and policy development.

Look back at the list of factors that need to be considered when discussing the role of legislation in developing quality services in the Early Years on pages 357–8 and comment on each of these in terms of the Children Act 1989.

Figure 13.3 Requirements of Working Together to Safeguard Children (DoH, 1999)

Current policy issues

More recent policy affecting services for young children has been driven by a particular set of principles and goals introduced by New Labour from 1997 onwards. These relate to improving the quality of children's services to achieve an interrelated set of policy objectives, which include:

➤ reducing child and family poverty
➤ reducing social exclusion, youth crime and anti-social behaviour
➤ supporting parents returning to work or retraining
➤ increasing daycare and out-of-school care capacity
➤ improving educational attainment
➤ improving the well-being of all children
➤ supporting parenting.

Joined-up services

One of the key principles underpinning children's services at present is the concept of joined-up services, building on the multi-agency approach promoted by the Children Act 1989 to suggest a multi-layered range of types of cooperative working. This principle is based on the belief that more integration between agencies and professionals in planning and delivery will produce better, more effective services. This principle has been reflected in policy changes at every level. Within central government, traditional splits between government bodies have been subject to change to improve joined-up policy development. In addition, the New Labour focus on Early Years services was reflected in changes in central government bodies after the 1997 election. One of the earlier changes was placing the responsibility for Early Years services within education instead of health within central government, in 1998, closely followed by transferring the inspection role for daycare services from local authorities to Ofsted in 2000, establishing the lead role of education in Early Years services. In 2002, the DfES established the Sure Start Unit, giving Early Years policy a lead body within central government and emphasising the focus on integration of services. A Minister for Children was established in 2003 within the Children, Young People and Family Directorate in the DfES. However, the bulk of joined-up service development has come about through the development and implementation of the Every Child Matters policy strategy currently dominating policy developments across services for children and families.

The Every Child Matters policy strategy

Factors influencing policy change

The Laming Report (2003) into the death of Victoria Climbie at the hands of her carers highlighted serious flaws in the ways in which agencies worked together to support vulnerable children. Particularly, the report stated that poor communication and information sharing between agencies were key factors in the failure to protect Victoria. Despite the Children Act 1989 provisions, child protection strategies and services mainly stayed within the remit of social services and the levels of communication and cooperation between these and other services in health and education particularly continued to be variable and in some areas ineffective in terms of protecting children. Laming made a number of recommendations, some of which were enshrined in the *Every Child Matters* (ECM) Green Paper (DfES, 2003). The Green Paper and the subsequent passing of the Children Act 2004 precipitated wide-ranging changes to the structure and delivery of services to children and their families, based on key underpinning principles, which included:

➤ services should be outcome focused rather than service-led

➤ multi-professional working and inter-agency cooperation are at the heart of effective service delivery

➤ parent partnership and children's participation in service planning and delivery are crucial elements in developing effective services

➤ services to vulnerable children need to be embedded in universal services to all children.

Changes suggested in the Green Paper focused on four areas:

➤ supporting parents and carers

➤ early intervention and effective protection

➤ accountability

➤ integration of services workforce reforms.

The main developments proposed were:

➤ creating Children's Centres in the 20 per cent most deprived wards

➤ promoting full-service extended schools

➤ funding to increase out-of-school activities

➤ funding to extend Child and Adolescent Mental Health Services (CAMHS)

➤ extending speech therapy services

➤ tackling homelessness

➤ reforming the youth justice system.

The Green Paper was the most radical change to policy affecting children's services in a long time, introducing or consolidating a range of principles in service planning and delivery which affected all agencies and professionals across the sectors.

The timing and content of the Green Paper (DfES, 2003) were influenced by:

➤ the political agenda around social inclusion for all children

➤ the recommendation of the Laming Report (2003) into the death of Victoria Climbie

➤ perceptions of flaws in existing arrangements to ensure inter-agency cooperation and communication.

The Green Paper was published for consultation and rapidly following on from this the Children Bill was published to encompass the parts of the strategy needing legislation to implement and also *Every Child Matters: the Next Steps*. In 2004 *Every Child Matters: Change for Children* was published and is accessible online (see links at the end of this chapter).

Key developments within the strategy
Outcomes base
One of the main features of the ECM: Change for Children strategy is to bring about a cultural change by emphasising an outcomes-based approach to services for children and their families as opposed to a service/professional-led approach. This change was underpinned by the principle of placing child and family at the heart of service planning and delivery. The ECM strategy focuses on five outcomes, which are the basis of service planning and delivery to all children of all ages. They are:

➤ Be healthy

➤ Stay safe

➤ Enjoy and achieve

➤ Make a positive contribution

➤ Achieve economic well-being.

The policy strategy emphasises that in order for all children to achieve these outcomes, there needs to be additional support for particular vulnerable groups, including looked after children and children with disabilities and learning difficulties. The outcomes now form the basis of target setting, planning, evaluation and inspection for children's services.

Developing joined-up services

On publication, it was clear that ECM (DfES, 2003) indicated that to some extent attempts to develop partnership between agencies were to be superseded by policies to integrate some services to children. The proposals within ECM were aimed at placing child protection within the context of other services to children and families, rather than as an additional (and sometimes unwelcome) duty for the majority of practitioners. The subsequent integration of education and children's social care services within local authorities and the grouping of a wider range of children's services within Children's Trusts was intended to achieve a much higher level of cooperation between services than existed previously. The current policy and practice is complex with a range of types of cooperative arrangements between agencies as well as integrated services and practice. Some of these are discussed further below.

Parent and child involvement

The ECM strategy is also based on a stronger commitment to hearing the voice of children and families in service delivery and planning than was evident previously. Strategies for including parents in planning and delivery of services have drawn on the lessons from Sure Start which have emphasised the need for a multi-layered approach including formal and informal opportunities to seek parents' views (NESS, 2007). These can include seeking parents to be involved in forums or as representatives in development groups, but also using informal processes, particularly where parents are reluctant to engage. Support for parents is outlined in the policy statement Every Parent Matters (2007).

Similarly, child involvement is promoted through a range of strategies including school councils and youth forums. In Early Years,

strategies such as the Mosaic approach have been used successfully to get feedback from young children in nurseries (Clark and Moss, 2001).

Embedding services for vulnerable children in universal services

The key elements in achieving better services for vulnerable children have been to ensure that service provision is better coordinated and planned between agencies and professionals to ensure that vulnerable children receive timely and effective services. Divisions between services and failure to share information or cooperate effectively have been cited as the cause of failure to deliver safeguarding services, but are also significant for looked after children, children with disabilities and other vulnerable groups. The ECM agenda has promoted a rapid increase in joining-up services at all levels to ensure vulnerable children's welfare and needs are better met.

In order to put these principles into practice the following actions were proposed and subsequently implemented.

➤ Removing barriers to information sharing between services by creating an electronic database through which agencies can share information about children.

➤ Developing a Common Assessment Framework to ensure speedier and more efficient assessment processes and introducing a lead professional responsible for coordinating and monitoring service delivery where more than one professional is involved.

➤ Developing extended school provision and Children's Centres as delivery points for a wide range of services to improve the speed and efficiency of the response to identified need.

The following areas of change required legislation in the form of the Children Act 2004 to implement.

➤ Integrating education and children's social services and establishing the post of Director of Children's Services to lead the new Children's Services Authorities.

- Development of joint working arrangements to promote integrated service development and to include children's health services and other agencies.
- Establishment of a lead council member for children in each authority.
- Replacing Area Child Protection Committees with more accountable Local Safeguarding Children Boards.
- Appointing a Minister for Young People, Children and Families.

- Appointing a national Children's Commissioner for England (this post was already established in Wales and Scotland).
- Workforce reform including a common qualifications framework and training routes for those working with children and a Children's Workforce Unit in the DfES.
- Creating an integrated inspection regime covering a wide range of children's services headed by Ofsted.

The Children Act 2004

The Children Act 2004 provided the legislative basis for the ECM developments listed above. The Act was necessary because these developments required changes in local and central government structures and processes. The Act was controversial during its passage through Parliament due to several factors.

- An anti-smacking clause raised strong reactions within both the pro-smacking and anti-smacking lobbies, leading to a compromise clause that allows parents to smack their children unless a mark is left. This was considered unsatisfactory by anti-smacking organisations such as the umbrella organisation Children are Unbeatable which continues to lobby for a smacking ban (2007).
- The Children's Commissioner role was seen as weak (compared to the same role in Wales and Scotland) and lacking the power to determine change effectively. Although Children's Trusts were not named in the Act as such, they were strongly promoted as the best structure for developing integrated service planning and delivery. This was seen by some as lack of flexibility as it was felt that this model may not work in all authorities.
- The dominant role of local authorities within the policy and legislation was seen as possibly

marginalising health and other agencies, and also private, voluntary and independent organisations.
- The ethical and safety issues around data-sharing through electronic means were also discussed, highlighting concerns about the safety of data held electronically and issues in respect of children's rights to privacy.

These issues continue to be debated to a greater or lesser extent.

Activity 6

Ongoing concerns

Using internet sources look at one or more of the following and make notes on the extent to which concerns in this area have continued or been resolved.

1 The effectiveness of the Children's Commissioner role.

2 The adequacy of legislation to prevent children being beaten.

3 The safety and appropriateness of electronic databases for information sharing about individual children.

Change for children

In the next sections, some of the main changes brought about by ECM and the Children Act 2004 will be discussed.

Children's Trusts

Amongst other developments, ECM heralded a much more direct and determined policy strategy in terms of integrated service planning and delivery for children and families. This was evident in changes to structures and strategies at all levels of service planning and delivery for children and families. The key approach to developing more effective joint working within local authorities was the development of Children's Trusts in the majority of areas. Children's Trusts are local multi-agency organisations which include children's social care services, education services, health services and other agencies such as Connexions, youth services, probation and so on. Although Children's Trusts have different remits and structures within different authorities, they share the aim of promoting integrated working through joint planning and the development of integrated services for children at all levels. These include the following.

➤ **Inter-agency governance** – within local authorities, education and children's social services have been joined into Children's Service Authorities (CSAs) which replace the LEAs and hive-off children's social care services from adult social care services. CSAs have a remit to work closely with other child and family services providers such as health services, police and Early Years providers from the private, independent and voluntary sectors (PVI).

➤ **Integrated strategies** – local authorities now have a remit to produce a single Children and Young People's Plan reflecting a joint assessment of local needs and a joint approach between children's services to meet these needs, based on agreed targets related to the five outcomes for children. Inspection of children's services are now done through Joint Area Reviews (JARs) which combine inspection processed for all services to children.

➤ **Integrated processes** – these include the introduction of the Common Assessment Framework, an assessment tool available to all practitioners and professionals working in the range of children's services, designed to provide a universal initial assessment for child and family needs to reduce the number of assessments children are subject to and to minimise the waiting time while referrals between agencies take place. Information sharing through electronic databases has also been introduced at local and national levels.

➤ **Integrated frontline delivery** – there have been a number of strategies to promote integrated delivery of services. These include:
  ➤ co-located service delivery through Children's Centres and extended schools
  ➤ introduction of a common core of knowledge and skills for all members of the children's workforce
  ➤ development of multi-disciplinary teams in a range of children's services
  ➤ introduction of the lead professional role to coordinate multi-disciplinary teams working with a child and family.

Evaluations of Children's Trusts found the following.
➤ Timescales for developing trusts needed to be realistic.
➤ New ways of working together need time to develop and inter-agency training needs developing and funding.
➤ The size and range of the change agenda set out through ECM: Change for Children is daunting for all involved and this size has implications for the rate of change.
➤ Pooling funds between agencies remains difficult in some areas.

> Lack of shared boundaries can be a complication.

Involving all partners in multi-agency work continues to be a challenge with PCTs and GPs the main 'missing' partners.

There is still work to do to convince all involved of the benefits of integrated working and to find measures to provide evidence that this approach is more effective than single-agency approaches.

UEA (2007)

Common Assessment Framework (CAF) and lead professionals

The CAF is a standardised approach to conducting an assessment of a child's additional needs and deciding how those needs should be met. It can be used by practitioners across children's services in England.

ECM (2008a)

The implementation of CAF has been slow but generally seen as effective, according to the evaluation by Brandon, et al in 2006. However, the report found that CAF was not always fully understood and that it was sometimes used as just a method of referring to other agencies, rather than the beginnings of the assessment process. Practitioners generally found CAF time-consuming, adding to their workload and creating some anxieties. Some concerns were expressed about how to complete CAF forms and about the need to involve parents, with different levels of understanding between professional groups on the role of holistic assessments and how to implement these. The lead professional role also created some anxiety, leading to the authors suggesting that ongoing multi-agency training was needed to ensure CAF and the lead professional were fully understood and to foster new working practices to improve the effectiveness of these approaches. They suggested that not enough managers undertook CAF training and that there needed to be a strong top-down lead to ensure CAF is implemented effectively, including ongoing awareness raising and multi-agency training (Brandon et al, 2006).

Information sharing

One of Laming's recommendations was to investigate whether a national database with information about all children was possible, in order to facilitate improved information-sharing between practitioners and professionals involved with the same child and family (2003). Trailblazer authorities involved in developing local databases were established and evaluated in terms of their contribution to development of the national database called ContactPoint, which is rolling out through late 2008-9, linking up existing local databases. The data held on ContactPoint is limited by the Children Act 2004 (ECM, 2008b).

ContactPoint will only hold the following basic information for all children in England (up until their 18th birthday):

> name, address, gender, date of birth and a unique identifying number

> name and contact details for a child's parent or carer

> contact details for services working with a child: as a minimum, educational setting (e.g. school) and GP practice, but also other services where appropriate.

A means will be used to indicate whether a practitioner is a lead professional and if they have undertaken an assessment under the Common Assessment Framework.

The lessons from the trailblazers seemed to imply improved services; speedier and more effective interventions; and reduced time spent by practitioners trying to discover which other agencies and professionals are involved with a child and family (DfES, 2005). These findings and a study to examine the safety of the systems in terms of security and confidentiality may have gone some way to allaying initial concerns about the proposed systems which included possible invasions of children's privacy and breaches of confidentiality. However, concerns also included the cost and technical difficulties associated with a database on this scale; the fears of practitioners on security issues; the extent to which it is acceptable for governments to have this degree of information on children; and concerns as to whether the data included could identify children as problematical and therefore label them early in life. It remains to be seen whether all these concerns are addressed through the implementation of ContactPoint.

Activity 7

Is ContactPoint seen as safe?

Check out the ECM website to follow the implementation of ContactPoint and further evaluation of its safety and effectiveness. Share what you find with colleagues or a mentor.

Local Safeguarding Children Boards (LSCBs)

LSCBs replaced the Area Child Protection Committees (ACPCs) previously responsible for planning and management of child protection services local authorities, because ACPCs had no legal basis to ensure they achieved their role effectively. LSCBs are responsible for developing multi-agency strategies safeguarding and promoting the welfare of children and implementing these.

Although there has been little controversy over the change from ACPCs to LCSBs, the safeguarding remit for LSCBs is much wider than the child protection role the ACPCs had. Ryan (2006) suggests that the wider remit of safeguarding may pose challenges as other aspects of safeguarding, such as safety and bullying, may be swamped by the child protection remit. Ryan also suggests that LSCBs will need to have a much more significant role with adult services and parenting support as safeguarding may well be best achieved by helping parents to protect their children more effectively.

Extended schools

Extended schools are schools that offer additional services including daycare, out-of-school activities, weekend and holiday clubs, and other agency services available on school premises. Extended school provision is not new, with many schools having offered a range of activities to support children for a long time and with some health and welfare benefits such as free school meals and health checks having been offered for over a century. However, it is planned that by 2010, every school will offer access to a core of extended services and schools will be judged on this in their Ofsted inspections.

In primary schools the 'core offer' includes:

➤ childcare from 8 am to 6 pm all year round

➤ a range of additional activities to support study and enrich the curriculum, through for example after-school clubs

➤ support for parents including parenting classes and family learning

➤ swift and easy referral and access to other child and family services, for example speech therapy, child and adolescent mental health services

➤ community access to facilities for ICT, sports and arts.

The pathfinder evaluation of extended schools found that schools were more skilled at developing activities to support improvements in pupil achievement than in developing community aspects (Cummins, Todd and Dyson, 2004). A TDA report found that only 23 per cent of schools were involved in supporting parents and developing community use (Rowntree, 2006). This may relate to schools being initially more familiar with curriculum-enrichment activities for pupils than they were with providing parent support or developing community involvement. Current reports suggest a successful learning and development process has improved all aspects of extended school provision (DCSF, 2007a). Ofsted reported that extended school provision was promoting multi-agency work and was effective in terms of ECM outcomes (2006a). Small improvements in achievement have also been recorded in some schools and improvements for the most disadvantaged children were also noted.

The implementation of extended school services has involved structural and cultural change for schools and introduced new demands in terms of working with parents, partner agencies and the wider community. Ofsted (2006a) reported that heads had their own developmental needs, to work as part of multi-agency teams, and that they could suffer overload if trying to manage extended schools services. However, in many schools, the role of coordinating extended school provision has been placed with a coordinator to prevent overload of the head, while much of the delivery is done by external partners and service deliverers, teaching assistants and other support workers (DCSF, 2007a).

Funding has been an issue with concerns that start-up funding may establish services that parents may not be able to pay for in the long run. Funding for disadvantaged families to access extended school services is promised for 2011.

Ongoing issues for extended schools include: the need to develop capacity to meet the needs of parents and communities and to develop effective partnerships in these areas; to ensure the core business of schools is not affected by additional provision through increased workloads for heads and staff; to build up relationships with other agencies and organisations and develop multi-agency approaches; and to monitor and evaluate the success of the extended schools services developed.

Health policy

Recent health policy influencing the development of children's services is based on a range of principles that support an holistic view of health and a multi-agency approach to achieving better health for children. They include recognition of:

➤ the importance of health to the success of all other initiatives for children

➤ educational achievement will be better if children are healthy

➤ many patterns of health are established in childhood

➤ lifelong health depends on a good early start

➤ inequalities in health persist.

Current policy also acknowledges that children's health is influenced by social and environmental issues, as well as the presence or absence of disease. Persistent inequalities in health have been a major influence on policy development. In 1980, the publication of the Black Report highlighted the impact of social and economic inequalities on health chances. In 1997, the Acheson Report was commissioned to update the Black Report and evidence of ongoing and persistent inequalities affecting health chances was found. Health was found to be affected by social class, ethnicity, gender, geographical location and age. Since the Acheson Report, reducing the impact of health inequalities has been a key goal of policy as enshrined in the programme for action 'Tackling Health Inequalities' published in 2003. Initiatives such as Sure Start focused on reducing smoking in pregnancy, encouraging breastfeeding and improving maternal and neo-natal care. Key aspects of health inequalities, such as poverty, have been recognised through the introduction of tax credits to support some poorer families financially.

The way services are delivered is also the subject of policy change. It is now recognised that health promotion and support for health issues is the remit of all practitioners working with young children and not just the preserve of health professionals. New ways of working in partnership between agencies have facilitated developments. For example, Children's Trusts have paved the way for joint commissioning of services for children between local authorities and primary care trusts.

This section outlines some of the key health policy influencing services for children at present.

National Service Framework for Children, Young People and Maternity Services

The overall aim of the NSF for Children, Young People and Maternity Services published in 2004 is to stimulate and sustain improvements in children's health. It is a 10-year strategy to improve and sustain improvements in children's health and well-being. The NSF sets out 11 standards for high quality services and improved outcomes for children. These are made up of three parts – standards for universal services, standards for children with particular needs (and their parents), and standards for maternity services. The government expects the relevant services to have met the standards set out in the NSF by 2014, and progress to be monitored by the recently established Child Health and Wellbeing Board.

The NSF refers to a need for integrated provision to children, young people up to the age of 19 and their families across three core services: health, education and social care. The framework sets standards for health and social care and the interface between these and education services. This emphasis on multi-agency working is highlighted by the Department of Health report 'Children's health, our future: A review of progress' against the National Service Framework for Children, Young People and Maternity Services 2004.

The standards set out in the National Service Framework for Children, Young People and Maternity Services stress the importance of partnership working and the need to tailor services to the requirements of children and young people, as well as involving service users and their families and carers fully in decisions about how and where they are treated. They provide a focus for all health and other organisations providing services for children as they work to achieve these goals and improve clinical outcomes and experiences of care for children and young people.

Shribman (2007:4)

The implementation of the NSF is assisted by a number of supporting documents, including a range of exemplars which outline care pathways and core skills needed by staff to deliver effective services. The NSF delivery is closely aligned to the Every Child Matters – Change for Children framework for delivery of services to children.

Partway into the 10-year plan there is cautious agreement that progress is being made to improve children's health services and to promote a multi-agency approach. However, traditional NHS structures and practices need to be revolutionised in order for targets to be reached and it is acknowledged that this is a major change to achieve successfully (Shribman, 2007).

Choosing Health: Making Healthy Choices Easier

The Choosing Health White Paper is a public health policy statement and an integral part of the NSF. It sets out a raft of measures to improve the public's health, including children's health. The overall aim for children is to improve their physical and mental health and to reduce health inequalities. It also embeds improvements for children's health in those for adults, emphasising that lifestyle choices and habits are formed early in life and as such the focus on children's health is an investment for adult health. It includes a target of 75 per cent of schools to achieve healthy school status by 2009, and two key measures aimed at tackling childhood obesity, which are a ban on junk food advertising and coding food to enable easy identification of healthy foods. There is a national target to stop obesity among children under 11 from increasing year on year by 2011. The paper also includes measures to increase the number of school nurses and make one available to each cluster of schools. In terms of children's health, aims are to:

➤ improve information about healthy choices to children and families
➤ coordinate services better
➤ promote a whole school approach to health including support for sports and other physical activity.

Healthy schools

The Healthy Schools programme has been established since 1999 as a joint initiative of the Department of Health and the Department for Children, Schools and Families. The programme has been established in at least 90 per cent of schools and aims to:

➤ improve children and young people's health
➤ reduce health inequalities
➤ raise children's academic achievement
➤ reduce social exclusion
➤ improve joint working between health and education.

The whole school approach aims to incorporate healthy lifestyles and choices into all aspects of the school day including getting to school, the content and delivery of the curriculum, daily activities, sports and PE. In addition, the Healthy Schools initiative has demonstrated that interagency cooperation in improving services for children can be achieved. There are four criteria for a healthy school:

➤ healthy eating
➤ physical activity
➤ PSHE
➤ emotional health and well-being.

DCSF (2007b)

Although the Healthy Schools initiative has been welcomed there is some evidence that there has been a failure to establish effective partnerships with parents and children to implement aspects of change. This has been most publicly demonstrated by the mixed reception to changes in school meals, aimed at improving the quality of the food, which was shown to be generally very poor in a TV series by the celebrity chef Jamie Oliver. Branigan (2007) reported that the introduction of healthier school meals led to a significant reduction in children taking these by 2007 (424,000 children across primary and secondary). At the time of reporting two-thirds of secondary school children did not eat school meals. Primary school figures are better, possibly because parents have more control over children's eating choices at this age. However, this outcome was a reminder that lifestyle changes are not easily made and the importance of making sure that parents and children are convinced of the need for change and by the means of achieving change.

Activity 8

Health settings

Write a short account of the steps you are taking to improve children's health in your setting.

1 Are there plans for change across the whole range of activities in the setting?

2 What steps have you taken to share your aims with parents and children and how successful have you been in convincing them to be involved?

3 What other measures could be considered to improve children's health?

4 What other steps could you take to bring children and parents 'on board' with your plans?

Share your ideas with a mentor or colleague.

Government Comprehensive Spending Review 2007

The 2007 Comprehensive Spending Review established a Public Service agreement (among others) which focuses on children and young people's health and well-being over the next year, focusing on 'prevention, early intervention and enabling children, young people and their families to make healthy choices'. Indicators include:

➤ increasing breastfeeding at 6 to 8 weeks

➤ promoting the take-up of school lunches

➤ reducing childhood obesity

➤ improving emotional health and well-being, and child and adolescent mental health services (CAMHS)

➤ improving services for disabled children (see below).

ECM (2007c)

Aiming High for Disabled Children: Better Support for Families (2007)

This policy document sets out plans to improve services for children with disabilities in three areas:

➤ access and empowerment

➤ timely, responsive services

➤ targeting support at critical projects.

Overall aims include improving outcomes for disabled children and reducing inequalities between disabled and other children. Key aspects are to include parents and children in service planning and development and to continue to devolve budgets to families. More information and consultation about services and a focus on early intervention are also in the plans. In addition, PCTs and local authorities are provided with an audit framework to support their efforts to assess the needs of disabled children and their families. Financial commitments to implementing this programme include finance for developing improved access to childcare for disabled

children. The recently established Child Health and Wellbeing Board, a joint DoH and DCSF body, has been established to monitor the progress and implementation of the children's NSF and public service agreements in relation to children's health. Introducing this board has been significant in highlighting the focus on children's health improvements in current government policy.

The Family Nurse Partnership

This recent initiative is currently being piloted to assess effectiveness in the UK. It is based on a US model which determines that pregnancy and the first years of life are crucial to development and that successful attachment is vital to cognitive development. The model also incorporates the view that pregnancy and infancy are times when young deprived parents, who may not ordinarily access services, may be open to the involvement and support of health professionals.

The approach is to provide intensive home visiting support from a trained nurse or midwife to young parents having their first child, where risks have been identified. The visiting will take place throughout pregnancy and until the child is 2 years old.

Research evidence has shown that the service has been successful in the US.

Three trials in the US in 1977, 1987 and 1994 have produced strong evidence consistently showing the scheme led to improved prenatal health of mother and baby, fewer childhood injuries, fewer subsequent pregnancies and longer breaks between births, increased maternal employment and greater readiness for school. Researchers returned to children in the first trial when they reached 15 and found a 48% reduction in child abuse and neglect, a 59% reduction in arrests and a 90% cut in numbers receiving supervision orders.

Ward (2007)

Possible drawbacks may include the reduction in health professionals available for other sectors of the community and the labelling of children as potentially 'criminal' later in life (Ward, 2007).

Child Health Promotion Programme

The Child Health Promotion Programme was published as a document in its own right in April 2008, giving detailed guidance on its implementation and with the particular intent to raise the profile of the CHPP. The CHPP offers a structure to promote the health and well-being of individual children. It has replaced child surveillance as a method of monitoring children's healthy development, putting into place a system of care that encompasses:

➤ assessment of child and family needs

➤ health promotion

➤ childhood screening

➤ immunisation

➤ early intervention to address identified needs.

The CHPP is an integral part of the NSF and links to the ECM early intervention strategy to ensure a rapid recognition of and response to children's health and development issues. It is aimed at meeting targets to improve children's communication, social and emotional development, so that by 2008, 50 per cent of all children reach a good level of development by the end of the Foundation Stage. It is also intended that the CHPP will help achieve the target to reduce health inequalities and also to reduce child obesity. Other intended outcomes are:

➤ achievement for children of the best possible levels of physical and emotional well-being

➤ support for children, young people and families to enable them to make healthy lifestyle choices

➤ integrated services which provide effective checks and more targeted support for children and young people.

The CHPP represents a shift away from a narrow focus on health screening and developmental reviews to a more broad-based programme of support that helps to address the wider determinants of healthy development and to reduce health inequalities. Responsibility for delivery is multi-agency, including practitioners from education, health, social care, Early Years and other relevant agencies. It is aimed at pregnant women and children and is evidence-based. Priority areas include healthy eating, physical activity, and child safety.

The CHPP includes formal assessment from pre-birth to age 5 years and ongoing support at school, which includes:

➤ access to a school nurse

➤ referral to specialists as required

➤ nursing care in school for children with medical needs who require this.

Formal assessment includes screening, immunisation and assessment across the whole range of developmental indicators. At age 4–5 this links to the teacher assessment of the child's development for the Foundation Stage Profile.

Children's mental health

Young children's mental health promotion has become a key feature of modernised service planning and provision based on a growing understanding that mental health problems can be rooted in the experiences of early childhood. However, despite the fact that 20 to 30 per cent of children experience mental health problems and 10 to 20 per cent have diagnosable mental illness, there has been a chronic lack of funding and development in children's mental health services and little research to support this.

The review in 1995 and subsequent reviews, research and mapping showed that specialist CAMHS were generally in short supply: there was uneven distribution of services, long waiting lists and poor communication between specialist services and other children and family services. The specialist services rarely worked with children under five or with young people over 16 and there was low engagement of children from black and minority ethnic groups.

Most crucially, the referral mechanisms and the clinic based approach of specialist services meant they were not meeting the needs of some of the children and families who needed them most: 'hard to reach' families, disabled children, children at risk of exclusion from school, looked after children and young offenders.

Ryan (2007)

The Children's NSF found that there was a need for better access to mental health services for all children and funding has been made available to make year-on-year improvements to Child and Adolescent Mental Health Services (CAMHS) as part of the NSF standard 9 targets and the public service agreement target to:

Improve life outcomes of children with mental health problems, by ensuring that all patients who need them have access to comprehensive children and adolescents mental health services.

Updates on progress have indicated that specialist CAMHS services are still limited in some areas, but the newer concept of comprehensive CAMHS (all services contributing towards children's mental health) is growing, with an emphasis on the role of Early Years settings and schools in terms of basic support for healthy emotional and psychological development. Key factors are prevention of mental ill-health and early intervention to support children who are showing signs of mental health problems. The role of settings includes supporting all children's mental health through positive behaviour management; anti-bullying strategies and good use of teaching assistants and learning mentors to support children individually. Parent partnership and a good understanding of the needs of specific groups of children who may be more vulnerable to mental health problems (children with disabilities, looked after and adopted children, abused children) are also key aspects of the role of schools and settings in this area.

Activity 9

Children's mental health

1 Using Appleby, L., Shribman, S. and Eisenstadt, N. (2006) and Ryan, M. (2007), make notes on key developments in children's mental health services in recent years and the progress towards meeting targets to improve mental health services to all children. URLs for these documents are available at the end of this chapter.

2 Assess your setting in terms of the support for children's health, emotional and psychological development across a broad range of indicators. What are you doing well? What could be improved? Share your findings with a mentor or colleague.

Health policy for children's services has developed massively in recent years, reflecting a range of concerns about lifestyles and choices and the need for preventative approaches to child and adult health and well-being. The policy discussed here is only a brief synopsis of the raft of policy goals and targets for children's health services and implementation plans to achieve these. Many more guidelines and policy documents can be found on the Department of Health and Every Child Matters websites. The challenge is no longer focused on recognising what needs to be achieved but on implementing this challenging array of policies and supporting the changes in structures and cultures at service delivery level to achieve this. Key elements are supporting change within NHS services and continuing to develop effective partnerships between key agencies delivering services.

The Childcare Act 2006

The Government's Ten Year Childcare Strategy, *Choice for Parents, the Best Start for Children,* was published in December 2004. It was a significant move forward in the development of childcare provision and came along with substantial financial investment from the Government. Its key themes, which have since been legislated for within the Childcare Act 2006, were:

➤ **choice and flexibility** – this related to achieving greater choice for parents in how they balanced their work commitments and family life. It included reference to enhanced parental leave and easy access to Sure Start Children's Centres

➤ **availability** – this gave commitment to achieving flexible childcare for all families with children aged up to 14 who needed it, plus 15 hours a week free early education for all 3- and 4-year-olds for 38 weeks a year, with 20 hours as a longer-term goal

➤ **quality** – this aspired to high quality provision delivered by a skilled Early Years and childcare workforce. A strengthened qualification and career structure within fully daycare settings was set out and the requirement that all settings become professionally led

➤ **affordability** – the creation of the tax credit system to support parents' ability to pay for childcare appropriate to their needs.

The Childcare Act is the first ever piece of legislation that specifically covers the Early Years. Its name is somewhat misleading as it encompasses key areas regarding early education, childcare, Children's Centres and information for children, young people and parents. It brings together a range of regulations covering the following areas:

➤ Duties on local authorities (England and Wales in separate sections)

➤ Regulation and Inspection (England)

➤ General Provisions.

Key aspects

➤ **Sections 1–5** place on local authorities, JobCentrePlus and the NHS the duty to work together to improve the ECM outcomes for children, in particular by reducing inequalities. This underpins the Sure Start approach to delivery of services and encompasses legislation to secure a Children's Centre for every community.

➤ **Sections 6, 8–11 and 13** require local authorities to ensure there is sufficient childcare available to meet local needs and in particular that it needs to be affordable and meet the needs of children with disabilities. Section 7 re-enacts the requirement for local authorities to ensure that there is free provision for 3- and 4-year-olds where parents want it.

➤ **Section 12** requires local authorities to extend information and advice services to parents.

➤ **Sections 39–48** bring in the Early Years Foundation Stage which combines the existing Birth to Three Matters, Foundation Stage and the national standards for daycare and childminding.

➤ **Sections 31–38 and 49–98** bring together a simpler and reformed inspection regime that encompasses measures to reduce the level of bureaucracy and ensure better outcomes are achieved for children.

➤ **Sections 99–101** give local authorities powers in relation to the collection and holding of data to enable them to meet the duties of the Act.

Such wide-ranging requirements may appear complex and removed from the practitioner's day-to-day responsibility, however this legislation moulds all Early Years practice in England.

Early Years education and childcare policy and legislation

Practitioners often deal with education legislation on a 'need-to-know' basis, rather than considering how and why these requirements are made. As a practitioner you may be familiar with the requirements of the curriculum in theory and in practice, and yet you may not have considered how legislation influences what you do with children in the setting. The term 'practitioner' is used to refer to anyone working in a paid or unpaid capacity with babies and young children. The term does have formal recognition and there are specific responsibilities that accompany this role. The term 'practitioner' is specifically used within Early Years settings, as it can be used in a wide range of contexts and be used to describe people with varied training and areas of professional responsibility. It may in different circumstances include, for example, qualified nursery nurses, voluntary workers and teachers. The term 'practitioner' relating to legislation for the Foundation Stage means any person who teaches the Foundation Stage in a Foundation Stage setting. New legislation in education often reflects political response to change in social and cultural conditions. Factors that contribute to such developments in education policy and legislation include those given in Figure 13.4.

All legislation relates very closely to social and cultural contexts, and legislation for educational practice reflects social context, cultural needs and aspirations and will also differ between countries. Legislation for education broadly relates to three key aspects:

➤ the curriculum, that is, the framework of learning experience
➤ the regulation of where this experience is located
➤ the regulation of those who work with and teach children.

The curriculum

Practitioners should have an informed understanding of legislation relating to the curriculum and to its implementation. The difficulty for some practitioners in education, particularly those working in the Foundation Stage, is that the curriculum has been subjected to frequent change. Reflective practitioners will be aware of changes in legislation not simply by response to directives but through questioning for meaning and purpose, reading media reports and critically analysing government documentation.

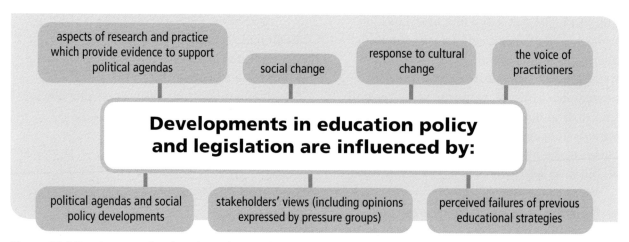

Figure 13.4 Developments in education policy and legislation

Making comparisons

Foundation Degree and other Early Years degree students, particularly those working in Early Years settings that receive government funding, will be familiar with the curriculum requirements of the country in which they work. As students of early childhood it is useful to compare and contrast the curriculum, which they support in their workplace, with those of our nearest neighbours. There is much to be learnt from such comparison. Differences in approaches to learning and teaching methods, which at first appear sharp in contrast, may diminish after studied comparison. The structure of the education system in the United Kingdom has changed considerably over recent years. The introduction of national assemblies has provided greater autonomy in many areas of policy making, including education. Educational policy is determined by the departments of education for each of the four countries which comprise the United Kingdom and there are four distinct national systems of education.

The policies that determine the curriculum and funding for education in Scotland, England, Wales and Northern Ireland reflect the philosophical approaches to education of the different nations. The curriculum for Wales was, for example, until the establishment of the Welsh Assembly, similar in content to that of England. Recent developments in Welsh educational circles have encouraged greater response to local need and indeed to the philosophy of education. Divergence of approaches to testing of young children between Wales and England has emerged as a fundamental difference in philosophy between the two countries. Philosophical differences have been present between the Scottish and English approaches to curriculum from the outset. Scotland, unlike England, does not have a legally prescribed national curriculum but provides guidelines for teachers.

Activity 10

Using government and other websites

There is an expectation of students on a degree course of study that they will consult web-based resources. Much of the legislative material we describe within this chapter is accessible through government websites, such as the Office of Public Sector Information website (www.opsi.gov.uk/legislation), although much of this is in more formal language than that which we have used. Another relevant site for legislation is http://www.uk-legislation.hmso.gov.uk. Special interest groups, particularly those related to children's special needs, often have sections of their websites dedicated to interpretation of legislation, for example www.autism.org.uk or www.rnib.org.uk. In order to help you to extend your understanding of curriculum provision in the United Kingdom and to develop your skills in ICT, it is suggested that you access and compare the curriculum approaches demonstrated on government websites given at the end of this chapter.

Political intervention

The substantial and frequent change that has taken place in the National Curriculum in the last 15 years is not discussed here, but it is sufficient to say that change is neither always negative, nor is it always positive. Mistakes have been made and acknowledged and no doubt there will be further development and change to curriculum content to reflect government policy. Political intervention is the driver of curriculum change in England. Educational development strategy is not considered in isolation, it is closely connected to ideas and initiatives in other aspects of social policy. This is clearly seen in the links between the introduction of literacy and numeracy strategies in schools and adult and family literacy and numeracy initiatives.

As a practitioner, you will already be conversant with a framework for learning, either the Foundation Stage curriculum or the National Curriculum. You may well have followed the practice of many others by focusing solely on the teaching content when reading the documentation for the curriculum; this is a mistake. It is important to read the introductory section of key documents as this provides the reader with the intended rationale as well as instruction for the means of delivery of the curriculum. The National Curriculum is provided as a means by which all children in maintained schools may be taught a prescribed range of subjects through a broad and balanced curriculum. The literacy and numeracy strategies and more recently prescribed methods of teaching reading may be regarded as factors in breaching the last requirement, as their introduction has resulted in a reduction of the time available for the effective experience of other curriculum areas.

Reflecting the needs and values of society

The curriculum should reflect the needs of society and legislation relating to equality and non-discriminatory practice applies to all school settings. Careful and considered planning for the delivery of the National Curriculum is essential in order to achieve equity of experience for all children. Breadth applies to the relevance of the curriculum for children regardless of culture, gender, religion or physical difference. All children are entitled to have equal access to the curriculum. The learning experiences we offer children reflect the values of society and these values are present within statutory documentation. Party political views and values on education issues are often ephemeral and subject to change, sometimes this is very rapid change. The values of the present government are clearly demonstrated in legislation and in their commitment indicated in political manifestos. However, priorities are flexible and

within socio-political agendas some aspects of education fare better than others. As a reflective practitioner it should be an aim to consider an issue from a range of viewpoints. Legislative issues are as suitable for scrutiny as any other issue.

Activity 11

The National Curriculum

Select a National Curriculum foundation subject: Physical Education, Geography, History, Design & Technology, Music, or Art.

1 Provide your own rationale for children studying this curriculum area.

2 Why study it?

3 What does it mean to young children?

4 Why is it a life skill?

Consider how your values mirror or differ from those expressed in the National Curriculum. You could compare your responses with those outlined in the draft for the new curriculum proposals for Scotland which can be found at http://www.curriculumforexcellencescotland.gov.uk. You will also find a range of questions and pointers for reflection on professional practice in the Development Lines section on this website.

Consideration of the purposes of the curriculum will not only provide you with a sense of real purpose in working with children in this area but also help you to understand the purpose for the inclusion of the subject in the legislative curriculum framework. As you begin to undertake web-based research of the curricula developed in other countries you will notice that areas of learning within a curriculum will vary in scope, approach and importance. The English National Curriculum contains subjects that are not present in exactly the same form in the curricula of other countries. National Curriculum Key Stage 1 documents provide statutory curriculum detail for the teaching of 5-, 6- and 7-year-old children. The content of this curriculum builds on the traditions of existing early childhood curricula, which were current in England at the time of writing the first statutory orders in 1988. Nowhere was this more clearly seen than in the curriculum for Design and Technology in the first Statutory Orders (DfES, 1988).

The link between planning, identifying a need for making something, making and evaluating an object was present in best practice in many Early Years settings. This approach to best practice was promoted by support with curriculum guidance materials;

an idea promoted in Foundation Stage documentation (DfEE/QCA, 2000). The Design and Technology example is particularly apt, as it is an area that does not appear as a distinct curriculum area in many other national curricula. Britain is a world leader in technological innovation and it may be judged appropriate that this subject appears in the curriculum from its earliest stage. The design technology area of learning experience has changed many times over the last 19 years, but in essence it still helps teachers to provide children with opportunities to develop their thinking skills as well as their abilities to control and manipulate materials.

Special educational needs and additional support needs

A child with special educational needs (SEN), or additional support needs (ASN) in Scotland, may have one or a range of specific needs. He or she may have significantly greater difficulty in learning than the majority of children of their age and cannot make full use of the educational opportunities provided for children of their age.

A child with SEN or ASN is entitled to receive full-time education that is appropriate to their needs. This would normally be provided in a mainstream school. Extra help would be provided (known as school action in England and Wales), may include extra help from an adult, access through different methods of teaching and use of specific or adapted equipment. If this is not sufficient to meet the child's needs the school will consult parents and arrange a statutory local authority assessment (LA). Following statutory assessment by the LA a Statement of Special Educational Need for the child will be made.

This will recommend the best way to meet the child's needs. The school will then work with the LA to respond to these needs. In Scotland the Education Authority will produce a coordinated support plan for any child with additional support needs.

The SEN Code of Practice aims to support schools and local authorities in interpreting those aspects of the1996 Education Act, the 2001 Special Educational Needs and Disability Act and Regulations arising from these Acts, which relate to the support of children with special educational needs.

The Code of Practice was introduced in 1994 and National Standards for Special Educational Needs Coordinators was introduced in 1998 (guidance was provided in the Teacher Training Agency booklet National Standards for Special Educational Needs Coordinators).

Guidance on the implementation of the Code of Practice was provided at its

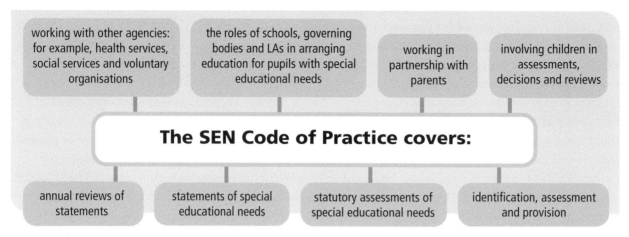

Figure 13.5 The SEN Code of Practice in outline

introduction and this has been further strengthened with training for practitioners and by web-based resources. Revisions were made to this document in 2001, which came into force in January 2002. These revisions have been informed by a number of research projects and papers undertaken by Ofsted: Ofsted (1996), 'The Implementation of the Code of Practice for Pupils with Special Educational Needs', Ofsted (1997), 'The SEN Code of Practice: Two years on' and Ofsted (1999), 'The SEN Code of Practice: Three years on'. Further Ofsted reports (2004) and 'Removing barriers: A report on developing good practice for children with special needs in Early Years childcare and education in the private and voluntary sectors' (2005). In these surveys the voice of practitioners is evident and this is reflected in the revisions introduced in 2001.

The Special Educational Needs Code of Practice 2001 provides guidance for educational settings, schools and local authorities. The Code does not have the force of law, but it is a requirement that 'notice' must be taken. Figure 13.5 illustrates what the SEN Code of Practice covers.

The underpinning principles of the SEN Code of Practice are given in Figure 13.6.

Legislation translated into local authority policy documentation, together with processes for its monitoring, is clearly seen in the area of special needs. Special educational needs policy documents are readily available for scrutiny on the internet. Local authorities publish their response to SEN legislation by means of a strategy document, available through the internet, which will include actions required by legislation, performance indicators and key local targets. All documents which relate to special educational needs, both national legislation and local response, are

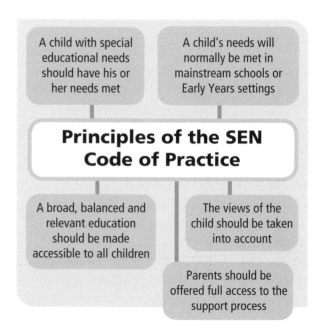

Figure 13.6 Underpinning principles of the SEN Code of Practice

available electronically. This means that you are able to see how legislation is translated into local policy and this can be measured against your experience in the workplace.

Activity 12

Researching SEN policy

Access your LA policy for special educational needs by typing 'Special Educational Needs (SEN) Strategy' and the name of your LA into your search engine. This will provide information about legislation and policy delivery in your area. Further scrutiny of policy into practice can be obtained through searching Ofsted reports on an individual setting.

The parliamentary website www.parliament.uk records responses to questions from Members of Parliament to government ministers on educational matters. Using these sources can provide an insight into 'official' interpretation of the effectiveness of special educational needs provision.

Activity 13

Researching the Parent Partnership Service

Local Authorities now have to provide information and advice to all parents of children with special educational needs. This information and advice is available through the Parent Partnership Service.

Contact your local PPS to find what types of support are offered. Find out about: The Schools Admissions Code of Practice (2002) and the Code of Practice (Schools), which covers the disability discrimination aspects of the new Special Educational Needs and Disability Act. Information is available on the Department for Education and Skills website.

Activity 14

SEN interview research

Interview a parent or carer of a child who has special or specific need to elicit how provision works in practice. Match this against the outcomes of the previous task.

Guidance for local authorities in the area of special educational needs is provided by many stakeholder groups with a particular remit or interest in a particular need or in partnership with government departments. An example of this is the Department for Education and Skills and the Royal National Institute for Deaf People (2003) document *Developing Early Intervention/Support for Deaf Children and Their Families.* It contains guidance for local education authorities and considers the implications of very early identification of deafness through newborn hearing screening, for services for families with deaf children.

The guidance offers advice on:
➤ appropriate aims for education service provision to families
➤ partnership with parents
➤ multi-agency working
➤ developing professional knowledge and experience
➤ evaluating the effectiveness of services provided
➤ the necessary professional competencies to achieve the desired standards.

The definition of special needs and disabilities used in the Sure Start Guidance (2002) indicates that children who have special needs are those experiencing delays, in one or more of the areas of cognitive development, physical development, communication development, social or emotional development or have a condition which has a high probability of resulting in developmental delay.

Ofsted has measured effectiveness of practice in a report *Removing Barriers: A 'Can-do' Attitude* (2005), available online. The report particularly focused on the response to the application of the Disability Discrimination Act (DDA) 1995. The DDA is an important piece of legislation in terms of the provision of equitable experience for children but has only applied to the provision of childcare since it came into force in 1996; at that time education provision was exempt. The Special Educational Needs and Disability Act 2001 brought in further changes to both the special educational needs legislation and to the DDA. These changes extended the coverage of the DDA to include education and associated services. Since September 2002 therefore it has been unlawful to discriminate against disabled children in the provision of any service. The DDA has been implemented incrementally. From October 2004, providers of any goods or services (including childcare) are expected to make reasonable adjustments to the physical environment in order to improve accessibility for disabled people. Revisions to the DDA in 2005 placed a duty on all childcare and education providers who receive public sector funding and statutory services to ensure equality of access.

Activity 15

Researching equality and human rights

The Equality and Human Rights Commission website provides access to a wide range of information about the legislation which affects Early Years provision, providers and employees. Look at the range of obligations and rights which are applicable to you in your workplace situation.

Children's Centres

The Sure Start Local Programme initiative saw 524 programmes set up across the country,

initially in the 20 per cent most deprived electoral wards. The impetus behind the development of these programmes was the government's aim to reduce child poverty. The original proposal was for programmes to be funded for ten years. The development of the Every Child Matters agenda following the Laming Inquiry led to the national roll out of the Sure Start Local Programme model as Sure Start Children's Centres. By 2010 there will be 3,500 Children's Centres in the country, predominantly focused in the 30 per cent most deprived 'Super Output Areas' in the country, but with services available to all families with a child under the age of five.

In the context of the Ten Year Childcare Strategy, a predominant strand of the role of Sure Start Local Programmes was to deliver affordable and accessible childcare and early education. This strand became part of the Core Offer of services that have to be delivered from a Children's Centre in order for 'designation' status to be achieved.

The Core Offer for Sure Start Children's Centres encompasses the following.

> **Integrated childcare and early education** – this is not always on the site of the Children's Centre itself but it is a requirement that every Children's Centre has qualified teacher input to work across the settings within a Children's Centre area.

> **Child and family health services** – in the main this is midwifery and health visitor services.

> **Family support** – with a particular emphasis on support for teenage parents and families who might have particular needs.

> **Information and advice** – this includes access to information from JobCentre Plus in relation to accessing employment and training.

In line with the Sure Start Local Programme model, a typical Children's Centre will serve an area with approximately 800 children under the age of five. A Children's Centre team will encompass a range of professionals from different backgrounds working together to deliver services. The activities within a building itself will only be part of the range of services offered and the partnership with parents and other stakeholders in an area remain as important in Children's Centres as they were within the Sure Start Local Programme model.

In the early years of Sure Start Local Programmes there was significant debate as to the value of the services and questions were raised about the impact they were having. National evaluation is now beginning to show that there is some positive impact from what was always designed as a long-term programme to radically change the way services are delivered to families and improve outcomes for future generations by intervening early.

The National Evaluation of Sure Start research team's report 'The Impact of Sure Start Local Programmes on Three-year-olds and Their Families' (2008) found that children living in a Sure Start Children's Centre area were more likely to have had childhood immunisations; were less likely to have suffered accidental injuries in the home; had parents with less negative approaches to parenting and had higher levels of independence and self-regulation than children in similar areas that did not have a Sure Start Children's Centre.

It is clear however that there are other factors, such as wider changes in the delivery of services, that may also be impacting on these outcomes and that it will take years for the true picture to emerge as to the success of early intervention through Sure Start Children's Centres.

Children's Centres inspection and regulation

In the Sure Start Children's Centres Planning and Performance Management Guidance (DfES, 2006) a framework for inspection and regulation for Children's Centres was introduced. The key role of Children's Centres within the context of the Childcare Act 2006 is in respect of reducing inequalities and narrowing the gap in achievement. In 2010 Children's Centres become a statutory universal service and as such their performance is likely to be inspected. The process for inspection will mirror that used in the school and childcare inspection regime. A Self Evaluation Form (SEF) will be completed by each Centre and an annual performance review will take place between the local authority and individual Centres. The SEF form will cover the five outcome areas of Every Child Matters. Additionally, the individual performance of the Centre against national and local performance indicators will be established.

National performance indicators for Children's Centres include:

➤ reduction of obesity levels measured at the end of the Foundation Stage

➤ improvement of levels of breastfeeding initiation

➤ improvement of children achieving the level good in CLL and PSED at the end of the Foundation Stage

➤ reduction of smoking during pregnancy

➤ increase in the percentage of mothers aged 16–19 accessing employment, education or training.

Under the provisions of the Childcare Act 2006, anomalies and inconsistencies that have arisen through the development of integrated services that blur the boundaries between early education and daycare will be dealt with through a new legal framework for integrated early education and childcare for 0–5s provision. This is being introduced in 2008. This initial framework deals with the quality of a childcare setting within a Children's Centre rather than with the wider delivery of services within the Children's Centres 'Core Offer' of health, family support, information and advice, alongside early education and childcare.

In terms of inspection Ofsted will carry out assessments of the quality of the childcare setting within a Children's Centre. Where a Children's Centre is integrated or co-located on a school site the integrated daycare and early education will normally take place at the same time as a school inspection although two separate reports will be issued. This inspection regime will not specifically judge around the wider performance of the other services delivered as part of the 'Core Offer' of services within the Children's Centre. However, they might comment on these other services in terms of how they contribute to the children's well-being. Additionally, there is scope for inspectors to comment on the leadership and management within the Centre.

Policy into practice

A number of government-sponsored projects target specific areas for development of practice. The Effective Provision of Pre-School Education (EPPE) project and the more recently reported Early Learning Partnerships Project (ELPP) are examples.

EPPE project

This large-scale longitudinal project follows the progress and development of 3,000 pre-school children in order to help to identify the aspects of pre-school provision which have a positive impact on their attainment and so provide guidance on practice.

The Early Learning Partnerships Project (ELPP)

This has targeted 'hard to reach'/vulnerable parents of children aged 1–3 identified as being

Activity 16

The aims of the EPPE project

➤ To produce a detailed description of the 'career paths' of a large sample of children and their families between entry into pre-school education and completion (or near completion) of Key Stage 1.

➤ To compare and contrast the developmental progress of 3,000+ children from a wide range of social and cultural backgrounds who have differing pre-school experiences including early entry to reception from home.

➤ To separate out the effects of pre-school experience from the effects of education in the period between reception and Year 2.

➤ To establish whether some pre-school centres are more effective than others in promoting children's cognitive and social/emotional development during the pre-school years (ages 3–5) and the beginning of primary education (5–7 years).

➤ To discover the individual characteristics (structural and process) of pre-school education in those Centres found to be most effective.

➤ To investigate differences in the progress of different groups of children, for example second language learners of English, children from disadvantaged backgrounds and both genders.

➤ To investigate the medium-term effects of pre-school education on educational performance at Key Stage 1 in a way which will allow the possibility of longitudinal follow-up at later ages.

➤ To establish long-term effects, if any.

➤ To relate the use of pre-school provision to parental labour market participation.

What do you understand these aims to mean? Re-write them in a format that would be accessible to a wider range of readers.

at risk of learning delay, the purpose being to aid early learning support for families and thereby improve children's 'readiness to learn at school'. This has been achieved through the use of a range of approaches to encourage the targeted parent groups to become more involved in activities that support the early learning of their children. Identifying parents who would need such support has been achieved through referral by health visitors, Sure Start Children's Centres and other Early Years settings and self-referrals. A second strand of the project has been to implement training courses to extend the skills of practitioners in order to encourage parents to support their children's early learning.

Examples of projects working with parents include Sure Start Children's Centres and home visiting schemes. The focus of the projects is encouragement of parents to engage with their children's learning through everyday situations.

Information about the training for practitioners in helping them to reach vulnerable parents is available online.

Conclusion

The role of policy and legislation is significant in determining the type and range of services available for children and their families at any particular time, within the cultural context. Practitioners need to be aware not only of the provisions within current legislation shaping their roles and responsibilities, but also of the principles that underpin that legislation and give it a meaningful context. These principles are not static but subject to development through complex processes influenced by a wide range of factors including political objectives, lessons from practice and research, and the dominant cultural norms. Stakeholders within the Early Years are part of these influences and play a role in shaping policy and practice. Practitioners in Early Years settings need to be aware of developments that may lead to changes in policy and legislation and the ways in which policy and legislation shape services and determine their objectives.

Legislation, therefore, needs to be considered within the cultural and policy context and not as an isolated phenomenon. It is not unusual, for example, for problems to be identified in legislation when it is put into operation. Often issues and difficulties that may not have been foreseen emerge in the light of practice. Practitioners in Early Years settings are required to work within the current policy and legislative framework, but this requirement should be fulfilled alongside a critical appraisal of that framework and an understanding of the processes by which it may be changed.

How to move on in your research

http://live.ofsted.gov.uk/gettingonwell/
annexes/annexe.htm

Greater emphasis is now being placed on self-evaluation and personal reflection than was previously the case. An excellent self-evaluation exercise is presented on the Ofsted site. Annex E presents a wide range of questions to aid reflection on practice and it would be helpful to use this either during your work placement for personal target setting, or as a means of identifying strengths or areas for development in practice-related coursework.

Health policy

http://www.opsi.gov.uk/Acts/acts1989/Ukpga_
19890041_en_1.htm

National Service Framework.

http://www.everychildmatters.gov.uk

All documents relating to the Every Child Matters (ECM) agenda can be found here. The site is an extensive, multi-layered site covering a wide range of issues and topics relating to ECM strategy and delivery.

http://www.dh.gov.uk/prod_consum_dh/
idcplg?IdcService=GET_FILE&dID=153913&
Rendition=Web

This outlines support to implement the Children's NSF within the ECM strategy.

Shribman, S. (2006), 'Children's health, our future: A review of progress against the National Service Framework for Children, Young People and Maternity Services 2004'.

This is a report on progress towards meeting the objectives of the Children's NSF.

http://www.dhgov.uk/publications April 2008
Shribman, S. and Billingham, K., *Best Practice Guidance*

Special Educational Needs

www.earlysupport.org.uk

This site provides a range of useful links to support children with disabilities.

Research developments

http://www.ioe.ac.uk/schools/ecpe/eppe/eppe/
eppeintro.htm
http://www.ioe.ac.uk/schools/ecpe/eppe/

These sites link to recent research reports.

References

Appleby L., Shribman, S. and Eisenstadt, N. (2006), *Report on the Implementation of Standard 9 of the National Service Framework for Children, Young People and Maternity Services.* London: DH Online. Last accessed on 26 February 2008 at http://www.teachernet.gov.uk/wholeschool/sen/ypmentalhealth/cyppublications/

Brandon, M., Howe, A., Dagley, V., Salter, C. and Warren, C. (2006), 'What appears to be helping or hindering practitioners in implementing the common assessment framework and lead professional working?', *Child Abuse Review*, 15, pp396–413

Branigan, T. (2007), 'Schoolchildren spurn Jamie Oliver lunches', *Guardian Online.* Last accessed on 26 February 2008 at http://www.guardian.co.uk/uk/2007/sep/04/politics.schoolmeals

Cameron, C. (2003), 'An historical perspective on changing child care policy', in **Brannen, J. and Moss, P. (eds)**, *Rethinking Children's Care.* Buckingham: Open University Press

Clark, A. and Moss, P. (2001), *Listening to Young Children: The Mosaic Approach*. London: National Children's Bureau for the Joseph Rowntree Foundation

Cummings, C., Todd, L. and Dyson, A. (2004), *Evaluation of the Extended Schools Pathfinder Projects*. London: Department for Education and Skills. Last accessed 16 February 2008 at http://www.dfes.gov.uk/research/data/uploadfiles/RR530.pdf

Department for Children, Schools and Families (DCSF) (2007a), *Extended Schools – Building on Experience*. Last accessed on 27 February 2008 http://www.everychildmatters.gov.uk/_files/41989AB45948163B6B7CD07D5D2D1C72.pdf

Department for Children, Schools and Families (DCSF) (2007b), *National Healthy Schools Programme*. Last accessed 19 February 2008 at http://www.healthyschools.gov.uk/

Department for Education and Skills and the Royal National Institute for Deaf People (2003), *Developing Early Intervention/Support for Deaf Children and Their Families*. Nottingham: DfES Annesley

DfEE (1994), *Code of Practice. On the Identification and Assessment of Special Educational Needs*. London: HMSO

DfEE/QCA (2000), *Curriculum Guidance for the Foundation Stage*. London: HMSO

DfES/QCA (2001), *Planning for Learning in the Foundation Stage*. London: HMSO

DfES/QCA (2003), *Foundation Stage Profile*. London: HMSO

Department for Education and Skills (DfES) (2005), *Learning from Information Sharing and Assessment Trailblazers*. Last accessed on 28 February 2008 at http://www.everychildmatters.gov.uk/_files/5E8CB225811E2C2A02D8E3CA93D5AA81.PDF

Department for Education and Skills (DfES) (2005), *Implementing the DDA: Improving Access: Early Years accessibility planning guidance*. London: DfES/Sure Start

Department for Education and Skills (DfES) (2007), *Every Parent Matters*. Last accessed on 1 March 2008 at http://www.teachernet.gov.uk/_doc/11184/6937_DFES_Every_Parent_Matters_FINAL_PDF_as_published_130307.pdf

Department of Health (DH) (1998), *Independent Inquiry into Inequalities in Health Report (the Acheson Report)*. London: HMSO

Department of Health (DH) (1999; 2006), *Working Together to Safeguard Children*. London: HMSO

Department of Health (DH) (2000), *Framework for Assessment of Children in Need and their Families*. London: HMSO

Department of Health (DH) (2001), *The Children Act Now: Messages from Research*. London: HMSO

Department of Health (DH) (2003), *Every Child Matters Green Paper*. London: HMSO

Department of Health (DH) (2004), *Choosing Health: Making Healthy Choices Easier*. Last accessed 26 February 2008 at http://www.dh.gov.uk/en/Publicationsandstatistics/Publications/PublicationsPolicyAndGuidance/Browsable/DH_4097491

Department of Health and Social Security (1980), *Inequalities in Health (the Black Report)*. Last accessed 3 March 2008 at http://www.sochealth.co.uk/history/black.htm

Every Child Matters (2004), *Every Child Matters: Change for Children*. Last accessed on 1 March 2008 at www.everychildmatters.gov.uk

Every Child Matters (2008a), *Common Assessment Framework*. Last accessed 29 February 2008 at http://www.everychildmatters.gov.uk/deliveringservices/caf/

Every Child Matters (2008b), *Contact Point*. Last accessed 29 February 2008 at http://www.everychildmatters.gov.uk/deliveringservices/contactpoint/about/

Every Child Matters (2008c), *Children and Young People's Health*. Last accessed on 1 March 2008 at http://www.everychildmatters.gov.uk/health/ 'Early Years – the first national picture' (Ofsted 2003).

Education (National Curriculum) (Foundation Stage Profile Assessment Arrangements) (England) Order 2003 (Statutory Instrument 2003 No.1327).

Education (National Curriculum) (Foundation Stage Early Learning Goals) (England) Order 2003 (Statutory Instrument 2003 No.391)

Education Act (1988)

HM Treasury/DCSF (2007), *Aiming High for Disabled Children: Better Support for Families*. Last accessed 26 February 2008 at http://www.hm-treasury.gov.uk/media/C/2/cyp_disabledchildren180507.pdf

Laming, Lord (2003), *The Victoria Climbie Inquiry: Report on an Inquiry by Lord Laming* (The Laming Report). London: HMSO

National Curriculum for England and Wales (1988)

National Evaluation of Sure Start (NESS) (2007) Online. Last accessed on 3 March 2008 at http://www.ness.bbk.ac.uk/

Office for Public Service Information (OPSI) (2007), *The Children Act 1989*. Last accessed on 1 March 2008 at http://www.opsi.gov.uk/Acts/acts1989/Ukpga_19890041_en_1.htm

Office for Public Service Information (OPSI) (2007), *The Children Act 2004*. Last accessed on 1 March 2008 at http://www.opsi.gov.uk/acts/acts2004/ukpga_20040031_en_1

Ofsted (1995), *Handbook for Inspecting Primary and Nursery Schools*. London: HMSO

Ofsted (2005), *Removing Barriers: A 'Can-Do' Attitude*. Available on www.ofsted.gov.uk.

Ofsted (2006a), *Extended Services in Schools and Children's Centres, Report 2609*. Accessed at www.ofsted.gov.uk/assets/Internet_Content/Publications_Team/File_attachments/extended2609.pdf

Pinney, A. (2007), 'A better start: Children and families with special needs and disabilities', in *Sure Start Local Programmes*. Annesley: DfES

Rowntree, N. (2006), 'Education news: Extended schools – Support for parents causing concern'. *Children Now*, 8 November 2006. Last accessed on 1 March 2008 at http://www.childrennow.co.uk/news/index.cfm?fuseaction=details&UID=ec1c2ebd-af87-4118-be1c-59f291defcf7

Ryan, M. (2006), 'Safeguarding (Champion for Children Research Briefing for Councillors)'. *Research in Practice*, October 2006. Last accessed on 3 March 2008 at http://www.rip.org.uk/publications/documents/champions_docs/champions7.pdf

Ryan, M. (2007), 'Promoting mental health across children's services', in *Research in Practice Champions for Children* Report. Last accessed on 3 March at http://www.rip.org.uk/publications/documents/champions_docs/champions9.pdf
School Standards and Framework Act (1998)

Shribman, S. (2007), *Children's Health, Our Future – A Review of Progress Against the National Service Framework for Children, Young People and Maternity Services 2004.* London: Department of Health. Last accessed on 1 March 2008 at http://www.dh.gov.uk/en/Publicationsandstatistics/Publications/PublicationsPolicyAndGuidance/DH_080379
Tax Credits Act (2002)

University of East Anglia (UEA) (2007), 'Children's Trust Pathfinders: Innovative partnerships for improving the well-being of children and young people'. *National Evaluation of Children's Trust Pathfinders Final Report*, March 2007. Last accessed 1 March 2008 at http://www.everychildmatters.gov.uk/_files/B8FD7B0E555C71497035139DFCA270DF.pdf

Ward, L. (2007), 'Q and A nurse family partnership programme', *Guardian Online.* Last accessed on 1 March 2008 at http://www.guardian.co.uk/world/2007/may/16/qanda.children

Useful websites

www.childrenareunbeatable.org.uk
Children are Unbeatable

www.opsi.gov.uk/legislation
Office of Public Sector Information website

www.autism.org.uk and www.rnib.org.uk
Examples of special interest groups, particularly those related to children's special needs, which often have sections of their websites dedicated to interpretation of legislation.

http://www.curriculumforexcellencescotland.gov.uk
Contains the new curriculum proposals for Scotland. You will also find a range of questions and pointers for reflection on professional practice in the Development Lines section on this website.

http://www.ncaction.org.uk/subjects/design/index.htm

http://www.parliament.uk/publications/index.cfm
The parliamentary website responses to questions from Members of Parliament to government ministers on educational matters.

http://www.equalityhumanrights.com
The Equality and Human Rights Commission website which provides access to a wide range of information about the legislation which affects Early Years provision, providers and employees.

http://www.familyandparenting.org/ELPP
Examples of projects working with parents, including Sure Start Children's Centres and home visiting schemes.

http://www.peal.org.uk/
Information about the training for practitioners in helping them to reach vulnerable parents.

14 Safeguarding children

Janet Kay

This chapter covers issues relating to the safety and welfare of children in their Early Years, exploring the broad concept of safeguarding and its relationship to child protection and child and family support. The role of practitioners in Early Years settings in respect of safeguarding is discussed in terms of the rights of young children and our responsibilities towards them. The role of the legislative framework and procedural guidelines in shaping a practitioner's duties and responsibilities is critically examined in the context of multi-agency child protection procedures. Ways in which safeguarding can be integrated into the role of the practitioner or organisation are discussed, as are supporting children's rights to 'be safe' through implementing strategies to raise standards in this area within Early Years settings.

By undertaking the suggested study within this chapter it is hoped that you will be able to:

1 recognise the significance of effective safeguarding in supporting children's rights to well-being and safety

2 recognise the significance of supporting children's rights in child protection and other safeguarding processes

3 understand the legal and policy framework and current practice issues for safeguarding children

4 recognise the role of settings and practitioners in safeguarding children within a multi-agency policy and practice context.

This chapter addresses the following areas:

➤ Defining safeguarding and child protection

➤ The policy context for current approaches to safeguarding

➤ Children's rights and safeguarding

➤ Safeguarding and Early Years settings

➤ Concepts of child abuse

➤ Defining child abuse

➤ Recognising indicators of child abuse and the impact of abuse on the child

➤ Responding to disclosure

➤ Common Assessment Framework (CAF)

➤ Procedural framework

➤ Principles of working to safeguard children and promote their welfare

➤ Responding to suspected child abuse

➤ The role of the practitioner in child protection enquiries

➤ The Child Protection Case Conference

➤ The legal and procedural framework

➤ Multi-professional approaches to child protection

➤ The Framework for Assessment of Children in Need and their Families

➤ Failures in child protection

➤ Best practice in safeguarding children in Early Years settings

Defining safeguarding and child protection

Safeguarding is a concept relating to ensuring children are not abused or subject to harm. One of the five outcomes of the Every Child Matters strategy 'be safe' focuses on ensuring children are kept safe from harm. However, safeguarding is a broader concept than child protection as it encompasses safety from other forms of harm than child abuse and it has become the responsibility of all practitioners and professionals working in children's services, rather than mainly the remit of children's social care services. The Children Act 2004 places a statutory duty on agencies and individuals to ensure that children are safeguarded and that steps are taken to support their welfare.

Safeguarding can be defined as 'Keeping children safe from harm, such as illness, abuse or injury' (Children's Rights Director, 2004).

The key concepts of child protection and safeguarding are closely related and can easily be confused. Child protection is the range of activities that take place when child abuse or neglect is suspected and/or identified in respect of a particular child or children. However, safeguarding refers not just to the prevention of harm to children. It is also about actively promoting the well-being of children and taking steps to prevent harm to all children.

As such, safeguarding involves:

➤ protection from abuse or neglect (child protection)

➤ prevention of harm

➤ action to promote children's welfare.

Although child protection is a significant aspect of safeguarding, ideally the activities of promoting well-being and preventing harm should reduce the need for child protection procedures to be instigated. As such, the current practice and guidelines place a clearer emphasis on preventing child abuse and neglect than was previously the case.

The current key guidance to practitioners and settings (Working Together to Safeguard Children, 2006) gives the following definitions of safeguarding and child protection.

1.18 Safeguarding and promoting the welfare of children is defined for the purposes of this guidance as:

* protecting children from maltreatment

* preventing impairment of children's health or development

* ensuring that children are growing up in circumstances consistent with the provision of safe and effective care

* and undertaking that role so as to enable those children to have optimum life chances and to enter adulthood successfully.

1.20 Child protection is a part of safeguarding and promoting welfare. This refers to the activity that is undertaken to protect specific children who are suffering, or are at risk of suffering significant harm.

1.21 Effective child protection is essential as part of wider work to safeguard and promote the welfare of children. However, all agencies and individuals should aim proactively to safeguard and promote the welfare of children so that the need for action to protect children from harm is reduced.

HM Government (2006:34–36)

The policy context for current approaches to safeguarding

The emphasis on multi-disciplinary and multi-agency working continues to be a key aspect of safeguarding. This is not a new aspect related to the introduction of the concept of safeguarding, but a principle that has been in place within child protection guidelines and practice for some time. However, recent policy and practice have been strongly influenced by the perceived failures of agencies and professionals to work together effectively to protect children, documented in a long series of child death inquiry reports over more than 30 years that highlight this failure, culminating in the Laming Report (2003) into Victoria Climbie's death in 2000. Current policy reflects clearer structures and strategies to support the existing commitment to multi-agency and multi-professional approaches to safeguarding since the advent of the Every Child Matters strategy in 2003 and the Children Act 2004.

Despite recent policy developments, many practitioners continue to find this area of work one of the most stressful they are involved in, particularly in relation to the demands of child protection procedures. Child protection is one of the key roles of any practitioner working with children whatever their professional status, discipline or job. It is also one of the most closely regulated systems within which practitioners in Early Years settings operate, with a raft of legislative and policy requirements, procedures and guidelines to know, understand and implement.

Extreme cases, where children have died, where gross abuse and neglect have not been recognised early enough, or responses have been inadequate, have led to a child protection system which has been procedurally and legalistically driven.

Baldwin (2000:5)

Yet levels of child protection training remain a problem within many organisations, and many practitioners do not feel equipped for the demands of the child protection role. Widespread media coverage of key cases in the last 20 years has supported the notion that it is both easy to 'get it wrong' and disastrous when this happens. The sheer level of responsibility the child protection system places on individual practitioners is daunting to many, and fears about making errors of judgement in this area of work are rife. The safeguarding agenda has placed an even higher level of responsibility on individual practitioners and settings to both ensure they are able to protect children from abuse and also to prevent harm and promote children's welfare. However, ensuring children's safety and well-being is a key element in supporting children's rights.

Children's rights and safeguarding

The notion of children's rights has been enshrined for some years in the 1989 UN Convention on the Rights of the Child which supports the concept, amongst others, of children having the right to be protected from abuse (Article 19). The concept of children's rights has become part of theory and practice in the Early Years, and the principles of the Children Act 1989 and other significant legislation and policy reflect these ideas.

However, children also have a right to be heard in any decision-making process about their individual circumstances and living situations and as such it is extremely important that all aspects of safeguarding are considered in terms of this right. In the past there has been a heavy emphasis on protecting children, possibly at the expense of their own wishes and feelings. As such, some aspects of protection were seen as possibly harmful, for example where it failed to consult a child about contact with significant others. As Howitt's research (1992) established:

'once started, the child protection process can acquire such powerful momentum of its own that it can sometimes operate against the child's best interests.

Pettican (1998:194)

The concept of safeguarding is wider than that of child protection and encompasses the view that children should not just be supported and protected when abuse has happened, but that active efforts should be made to prevent harm and promote well-being. Exploring safeguarding through the concept of children's rights allows us an alternative view of how best to ensure children are safe and of the role of the practitioner in Early Years settings. Rather than regarding this aspect of the work as a rare (hopefully) and unwanted part of the job, building the concept of safeguarding into the day-to-day work of the setting, and the regular duties of practitioners, can improve standards in this area and support a clearer understanding of how children can best be protected from abuse.

One of the key issues to consider when discussing safeguarding is the conflict between private and public aspects of child abuse, between the role of the state and the role of the family (Pettican, 1998). Inherent in British culture is the belief that the family is a private entity with rights to conduct family life without state intervention and to raise children in accordance with the parent's beliefs and wishes. Child protection work, in particular, often involves a breach of this privacy, invading the lives of adults and children alike. The notion that children's rights may only be protected at the expense of the family's rights to privacy can be a difficult concept for practitioners and organisations to negotiate (Hodgson, 1999). For example, making a decision about whether to instigate child protection procedures may feel like a Catch-22 situation. If you intervene, the child and family's rights to privacy may be destroyed and they may suffer considerably through a child abuse enquiry. If you do not refer the case, the child may continue to suffer abuse.

Another key issue to consider is the complex nature of the influences in every child's life. Safeguarding focuses on key issues influencing a child's well-being. However, as Baldwin (2000) points out, every child is uniquely influenced by (at the very least):

➤ his or her own personal characteristics
➤ family relationships
➤ environment
➤ socioeconomic circumstances
➤ local and wider cultural context.

Practitioners need to be acutely aware of the range of factors and influences in every child's life and the complex interrelations between these, or as Baldwin (2000:2) states 'the feelings, thoughts, lived experience of individual children' when acting to safeguard.

Effective safeguarding should support the rights of the child to protection from harm but should also ensure that the child's views and feelings are heard in the process. Parents' rights are also important and they should be consulted, informed and included in all decision-making processes about their child in order to preserve significant relationships and maximise the possibilities of children remaining within their birth families safely.

Safeguarding and Early Years settings

Ofsted report on their findings in respect of young children's welfare and development, according to the extent to which settings achieve the five outcomes for children. In 2005–6 Ofsted found that of 25,000 childcare settings, 97 per cent were at least satisfactory in their safeguarding of children and 3 per cent were inadequate. However, half the inspection reports included recommendations to improve safeguarding in the setting and the reports identified 1,500 complaints about safeguarding including:

➤ concerns or allegations about mistreatment not being reported to social care services or Ofsted

➤ a person living or working on daycare premises or living in a childminder's house being not suitable to have unsupervised access to children

➤ a child being smacked or mistreated

➤ poor behaviour management, leading to mistreatment of a child

➤ provider not assessing and dealing with risks.

Hocking (2006)

The 2007 report found similar results but also commented that many settings had improved in response to recommendations in their previous inspection report. However, the number of outstanding settings remains very small and there is, according to Ofsted, still room for improvement, especially in respect of ensuring all adults in contact with the children are safe and ensuring that concerns about any child were always reported (Ofsted, 2007).

Concepts of child abuse

The Children Act 1989 makes it clear that to be legally considered as abuse, behaviour must result in 'significant harm' to the child's health and development. Therefore, child abuse may appear to be quite a narrow concept, excluding many cases where there is genuine concern for the child's welfare. However, one of the key tenets of children's rights is that children should be raised in their own families where possible. To achieve this, it is important to ensure that the law does not allow professionals to intervene on a statutory basis because of poor standards of parenting alone. However, in respect of children who are not abused, but where there are deficits in the child's circumstances that may impair the child's health and development, support is also required to ensure the child reaches his full potential.

The Children Act 1989 introduced a demarcation between children who are abused and those who are 'in need' to clarify this distinction and to ensure all children received the support they needed. Children in need are defined in the Working Together guidance as follows.

Children in need
1.22 *Children who are defined as being 'in need', under s17 of the Children Act 1989, are those whose vulnerability is such that they are unlikely to reach or maintain a satisfactory level of health or development, or their health and development will be significantly impaired, without the provision of services (s17(10) of the Children Act 1989), plus those who are disabled. The critical factors to be taken into account in deciding whether a child is in need under the Children Act 1989 are:*
- *what will happen to a child's health or development without services being provided;* and
- *the likely effect the services will have on the child's standard of health and development.*

Local Authorities have a duty to safeguard and promote the welfare of children in need.

HM Government (2006:36)

Gibbons et al (1995) argue that child abuse 'is a socially constructed phenomenon which reflects values and opinions of a particular culture at a particular time'. The sorts of behaviours that are deemed to be abusive to children have changed over time and differ between cultures. This does not mean that the behaviours are different, but that our view of whether they are abusive or not abusive has changed (Munro, 2002:58). For example, it would now be generally considered to be emotionally abusive to a child to lock him or her in a dark cupboard for any period of time, but in the past this was a common punishment. In addition, certain behaviours towards children that can be or are harmful to their welfare and development may not be defined as abusive. For example, regularly smoking in the same room as a child may be strongly disapproved of by many but would not at this moment in time be described as abusive (although this may change in the future as smoking becomes less acceptable as a social habit especially since the 2007 ban on smoking in public places).

Levels of child abuse are measured statistically based on data drawn from children's social care services across England and Wales. These statistics reflect the number of children who are subject to a Child Protection Plan across the country. These are agreed when there has been a child protection inquiry leading to a child protection case conference which has then decided that a Child Protection Plan is needed to prevent further harm to the child. The figures reflect only the cases which have attracted official attention and been drawn into the child protection system. It is widely understood that these figures do not represent anywhere near all of the children who suffer 'significant harm' from the actions or omissions of their parents or carers. In March 2007, there were 27,900 children subject to a Child Protection Plan in England. Forty-four per cent of children were deemed to have been neglected; 23 per cent emotionally abused; 15 per cent physically abused; and 18 per cent sexually abused (DCSF, 2007).

Perhaps the most significant gap in our understanding of child abuse is the child's view of what is abusive. MacLeod (2000:131) in discussion on the influential compilation of research findings in the field of child abuse, *Child Protection: Messages from Research* (DoH, 1995), points out that 'there was no discussion about how children might define abuse. The question was not even posed.' There is very little research to help us understand the child's view of what is abusive or how children assimilate the experience of being categorised as abused. This is particularly true of children in their Early Years.

Defining child abuse

There have been many definitions of child abuse over time, but the definitions currently used are those set out within the Working Together to Safeguard Children (DCSF, 2006) guidelines. These definitions are used as a guideline to remind practitioners of what may be the full range of abusive behaviours and to clarify some particular questions about what is and is not abusive. However, definitions may only cover certain specific behaviours and it is important to recognise that they have limitations.

Child abuse is currently defined within four categories: physical, sexual, emotional and neglect. These categories are useful tools for analysis, but do not reflect the real lives of children who may experience a range of different abuses over time. Definitions can also fail to clarify the extent to which an event has to take place in order to be abusive or whether the age of the child makes a difference to the nature of the behaviour. For example, shaking a baby to only a moderate degree may result in serious and possibly fatal injuries. Shaking an 8-year-old to the same degree may be undesirable but not injurious or abusive.

Recognising indicators of child abuse and the impact of abuse on the child

Recognising abuse is not usually about identifying single indicators against a checklist of possible signs and symptoms. Evidence of abuse is often gathered over time and from different sources. This evidence may include observations of the appearance and behaviour of the child, linked to knowledge of the family situation, and observations of the interactions between the child and parent. It may include records of conversations and the concerns of other practitioners or parents, or professionals from other agencies. Evidence should relate to aspects of the child's welfare and development that are being affected by the suspected abuse and any indicators of abuse that have been identified. Some points to consider when gathering evidence are shown in Figure 14.1.

Effective recognition of child abuse depends on your ability:

➤ to believe abuse takes place

➤ to believe that many different types of parents are involved in abuse

➤ to accept that it is your responsibility to respond to evidence of any such abuse

➤ to observe and accurately record events, conversations and behaviour.

The need for practitioners working in the child protection system to develop child observation skills and knowledge of child development has been highlighted by Rouse and Vincenti (1994:68). They argue that recognition of child abuse should be factually based, drawing conclusions from observations of children's appearance and behaviour. In this way,

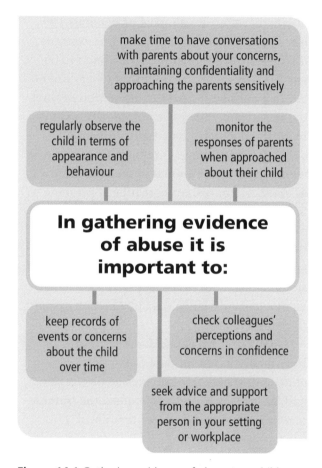

Figure 14.1 Gathering evidence of abuse to a child

recognition of abuse should be more clearly based on 'hard evidence' and the problems of opinion, hearsay, prejudicial judgments and skewed perceptions can be avoided.

The use of observation to identify indicators of abuse means that judgments are soundly based and robust. It is significant that of all professionals working with children, practitioners in Early Years settings are probably the best trained and most able to use observation effectively in this way.

It is particularly important when discussing the recognition of indicators of abuse to consider the needs of children with disabilities, children with communication difficulties, and children who do not have English as a first language. The indicators may be more difficult to recognise and confirm with some children and there may be barriers to believing that all types of children can be abused (Kennedy, 2000).

There are a number of factors which can make it difficult to develop and exercise skills in observation and identification of indicators of abuse:

➤ lack of time with individual children in large groups or classes
➤ the demands of the curriculum
➤ recording and other paperwork
➤ rising numbers of children with special needs
➤ poor standards of training in child protection
➤ lack of clear policy guidelines within some Early Years settings or workplaces.

These factors may act as real deterrents to practitioners involving themselves in child protection work. However, as discussed above, children have a right to be protected from abuse and the Children Acts 1989 and 2004 and the guidelines Working Together to Safeguard Children (HM Government, 2006) place the responsibility for upholding this right firmly on the shoulders of Early Years practitioners along with a wide range of other practitioners and agencies.

Physical abuse

Physical abuse may involve hitting, shaking, throwing, poisoning, burning or scalding, drowning, suffocating, or otherwise causing physical harm to a child. Physical harm may also be caused when a parent or carer fabricates the symptoms of, or deliberately induces, illness in a child.

HM Government (2006:39)

Physical abuse may be one of the better understood types of abuse of children, but recognising physical abuse and defining it are complex. One of the main issues is the relationship between corporal punishment and physical abuse in some cultures. Debates about physical abuse are dominated by what is or is not 'normal and lawful' chastisement of a child (Pettican, 1998). In Britain there is a long-held cultural belief in the use of smacking to punish children or control their behaviour, supported by the existence of a strong pro-smacking lobby. Smacking remains a common experience for young children in this society, despite long-term campaigning by many children's organisations, including Children are Unbeatable, an umbrella organisation representing over 300 children's organisations in the anti-smacking lobby. The Children Act 2004 disappointed many such organisations by failing to outlaw smacking and retaining the defence of 'reasonable punishment' except in cases where there is 'visible or provable' injury to the child. Children are Unbeatable argue that the current law allows common assault on children to be justified as 'reasonable punishment' and that this both infringes children's human rights and is inequitable in terms of rights accorded to adults (Children are Unbeatable, 2007).

Practitioners often report problems of assessing the extent to which children have to be harmed by their parent or carer in order to be deemed abused. There is no doubt that a significant proportion of physical abuse arises from over-chastisement and that this can escalate to dangerous levels of assault in some cases. The legal view that physical abuse must result in a bruise, mark or other injury ('visible and provable injury', Children Act, 2004) in order to be seen as abusive gives practitioners some guidelines as to what is currently considered the benchmark between punishment and abuse.

Another problem with recognising physical abuse is the difficulty in determining the difference between accidental and inflicted injuries. Guidelines can give some help with this, but there are a number of pitfalls in following these faithfully. Children do have injuries that may be unlikely to have been caused accidentally, but in fact are. They may have other injuries where the explanation is likely and the story acceptable. Recent cases such as Victoria Climbie and Lauren Wright have highlighted the plausibility of some physically abusive carers. In both cases, injuries were not identified as abuse because the carer asserted that they had been caused accidentally, and this was believed.

How can we recognise physical abuse?

Practitioners have a responsibility to ensure that their assessments of whether a child has been abused or not are made in the context of their knowledge and understanding of the child and family. One of the difficulties that arises when child protection work is not a regular part of the work of the practitioner or Early Years setting is that judgements can be made out of context. For example, the appearance of a bruise on a child may result in a child protection response where there have been no other concerns or injuries to the child. Guidelines have to be followed in the light of what is already known and understood about the child and family.

One of the major pitfalls practitioners face when assessing whether abuse has taken place or not is the belief system they have about particular types of families or individuals. These stereotypes about the likely behaviour of particular types of people can predispose practitioners to assume that certain parents could abuse or others will not. Stereotypes of parents often arise from the degree of social and cultural congruence between the parent and the practitioner. In other words, we are less likely to believe that individuals who are socially and culturally similar to us would abuse. Practitioners have a responsibility to ensure that they are aware of how such stereotypes may affect their work.

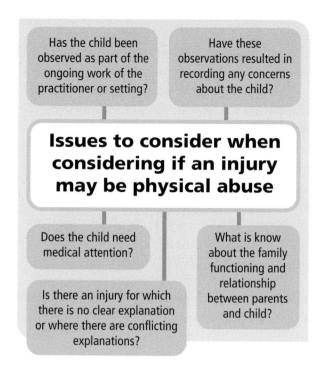

Figure 14.2 Physical abuse and making an abuse referral

In considering whether an abuse referral should be made for physical abuse, it is important to ensure that the points shown in Figure 14.2 have been addressed.

The impact of physical abuse on the child

For some children, physical abuse results in death or permanent injury. Every year about 80 children die at the hands of their parents or carers.

The most common causes of death are head injuries and internal injuries. For example, Lauren Wright died when her digestive system collapsed after a beating. For other children, the long-term impact of physical abuse is less to do with injuries and more to do with the emotional impact of being abused. The long-term outcomes for physically abused children may be linked more to the 'harshly punitive, less reliable and less warmly involved style of parenting' associated with physical abuse, than with the direct impact of the physical abuse on the child's development (Gibbons et al, 1995).

Suspected physical abuse

Ben, aged 4 years, attended a family centre day nursery as part of a family support package; this had been designed to help his single-parent mother, Brenda, to improve her parenting skills and to support Ben's delayed speech and learning development. Brenda attended parenting classes but often went out to have a cigarette or chatted to other mothers in the centre instead. She sometimes smelled of alcohol when she arrived in the mornings and slurred her words, talked very loudly or became verbally abusive with staff and other parents. Sam, Ben's key worker, noticed that on several occasions over a period of time Ben was very distressed on entry to nursery and that he would remain withdrawn and easily upset all day. Sam recorded these observations and the fact that Ben's mother was often abrupt with him, handled him roughly and made disparaging remarks about him to the staff.

One day, Sam noticed bruises on Ben's thigh and buttocks when helping him in the toilet. He asked Brenda how Ben might have got the bruises. She became angry and told him to mind his own business and that she did not know how the bruises had happened. However, later she came back and gave a long explanation about how Ben had fallen off his skateboard and bumped his bottom. Brenda kept telling Ben that he must tell the truth about what had happened, insisting that her version was the truth. When Ben looked bewildered and said he had not got a skateboard, Brenda shouted at him.

1 Using the list in Figure 14.2, write down the points you believe should be considered within this case study.

2 Do you think a child protection response should be made? Give your reasons.

Emotional abuse

Emotional abuse is the persistent emotional maltreatment of a child such as to cause severe and persistent adverse effects on the child's emotional development. It may involve conveying to children that they are worthless or unloved, inadequate, or valued only insofar as they meet the needs of another person. It may feature age or developmentally inappropriate expectations being imposed on children. These may include interactions that are beyond the child's developmental capability, as well as overprotection and limitation of exploration and learning, or preventing the child participating in normal social interaction. It may involve seeing or hearing the ill-treatment of another. It may involve serious bullying, causing children frequently to feel frightened or in danger, or the exploitation or corruption of children. Some level of emotional abuse is involved in all types of maltreatment of a child, though it may occur alone.

HM Government (2006:39)

Emotional harm to young children can be analysed in two categories: emotional abuse and emotional neglect. It is important to remember that, although emotional abuse involves active behaviour on the part of the parent and emotional neglect involves passive behaviour, the child must be deemed to have suffered 'significant harm' in order to be considered abused. Emotional neglect is categorised as an aspect of neglect and is discussed in more detail in the section on neglect below.

Emotional abuse is usually ongoing over a period of time, tending to involve a range of behaviours from the parents that are 'low on warmth and high on criticism' (Pettican, 1998; DoH, 1995; Kay, 2003). Parental behaviour may include indifference to the child's needs; rejection of the child; verbal assaults on the child's self-esteem (scapegoating, blaming or constant criticism); or a refusal to accept the child as he or she is. The parent may be unattached to the child and/or hostile and rejecting. Emotional abuse may appear alone or as part of other types of abuse.

Emotional abuse is an assault on the child's emotional and psychological welfare. It may involve:

➤ targeting the child for ridicule and verbal abuse

➤ frightening or terrorising the child on a regular basis

➤ preventing the child from making friends and taking part in the normal activities a young child may be involved in

➤ making the child take on responsibilities beyond her years and then punishing the child for failing

➤ shaming the child

➤ treating the child as unwanted and unloved

➤ forcing the child to perform tasks for food and comfort.

For example, in one case, a 5-year-old boy was forced to sleep on the floor, told every day that he wasn't wanted or loved, refused food if he misbehaved, and never touched or picked up by his mother. His two sisters were treated as loved and cherished children. The boy became very distressed, wetting and soiling himself at school and ripping wallpaper and setting it on fire at home.

Emotional abuse is often a feature of other forms of abuse. For example, sexually abused children may be emotionally damaged because they are treated as valuable and lovable only in so far as they gratify adult sexual needs, rather than for themselves. It is also now acknowledged that children who witness domestic abuse, even when not physically harmed themselves, will be emotionally harmed by seeing others assaulted, particularly when this is a parent or other significant person.

How do we recognise emotional abuse?

Recognising emotional abuse involves observing and monitoring the child's behaviour. Emotionally abused children are usually very low in self-esteem. They may lack confidence to tackle their tasks in the Early Years setting and may respond emotionally under pressure. They may seek inappropriately close relationships with staff or draw attention to themselves through unwanted behaviour. Alternatively, the child may be withdrawn and sad, unable to join in and be socially isolated. Emotionally abused children may demonstrate neurotic behaviour at times, such as pulling out their own hair or self-harming. They may have bursts of anger or distress or complete withdrawal. On the other hand, the child may be over-compliant and try too hard to please.

Emotional abuse of a child needs to be monitored over time in order to demonstrate that there is 'significant harm' to the child's health and development. The effects of emotional abuse are found in the child's developmental rates, including physical growth, speech and cognitive development and social skills development. Close observation and careful recording are needed to ensure that there is an ongoing record of concerns about the child's development. Measures to ensure that the child is properly monitored should include a multi-agency response involving health professionals who can monitor growth and weight, and the child's attainment of developmental milestones. Issues to consider when monitoring a child to check for emotional abuse are shown in Figure 14.3.

The impact of emotional abuse on the child

Emotional abuse may occur alone or as part of a more complex abusive situation. For example, the relationship between sexual and emotional abuse is well-documented. Emotional abuse is present in most cases of abuse and can have the most significant effects

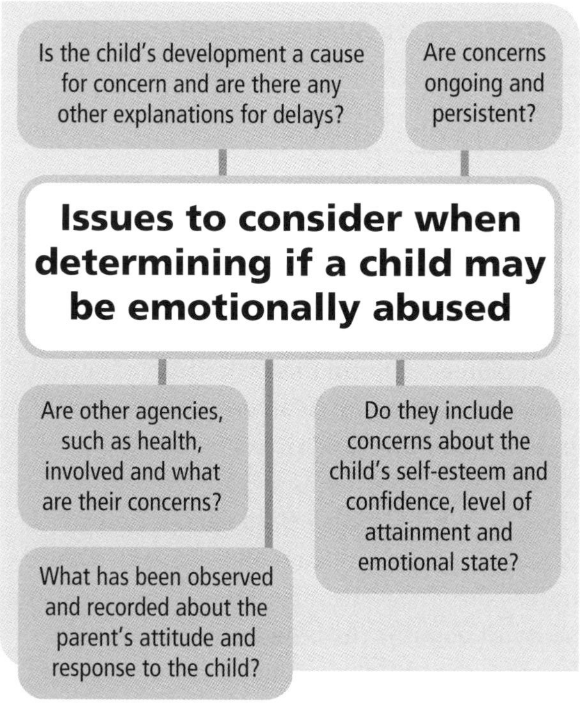

Figure 14.3 Recognising emotional abuse

The flowchart contains the following boxes:

- Is the child's development a cause for concern and are there any other explanations for delays?
- Are concerns ongoing and persistent?

Issues to consider when determining if a child may be emotionally abused

- Are other agencies, such as health, involved and what are their concerns?
- Do they include concerns about the child's self-esteem and confidence, level of attainment and emotional state?
- What has been observed and recorded about the parent's attitude and response to the child?

on the child. Long-term outcomes of emotional abuse can be amongst the most significant for children's long-term life-chances and well-being (Parton, 1996). They may include:

➤ lack of achievement in school

➤ failure to develop supportive relationships

➤ drug and alcohol abuse

➤ chronic low self-esteem and lack of confidence

➤ self-harming and possibly even suicide.

Case Study 2

Suspected emotional abuse

Adam, aged 3 years, has just started at nursery school. He has very limited speech and a chronic inability to concentrate. He tends to sit in a slumped position, staring into space unless directly addressed by a staff member. He does not make eye contact and has not attempted to join in activities with either adults or other children. Adam is thin and small and unkempt in appearance. When his mother collects him from nursery she likes to talk to the staff. She does not speak directly to Adam and she tends to put him into his coat hurriedly, without looking at him or responding to his struggles. She does not make eye contact with him and is apparently unresponsive to him at all levels.

The school nurse has contacted the health visitor with the mother's permission and the health visitor reports delays in Adam's speech, weight, height and cognitive development that have no explanation in terms of illness or disability.

1 What steps might you take in response to any concerns about Adam?

2 Who might be involved?

Sexual abuse

Sexual abuse involves forcing or enticing a child or young person to take part in sexual activities, including prostitution, whether or not the child is aware of what is happening. The activities may involve physical contact, including penetrative (e.g. rape, buggery or oral sex) or non-penetrative acts. They may include non-contact activities, such as involving children in looking at, or in the production of, sexual online images, watching sexual activities, or encouraging children to behave in sexually inappropriate ways.

HM Government (2006:39)

The extent and nature of the sexual abuse of children was little understood before the 1980s, when it became apparent through the work of a range of professionals in the field that sexual abuse of children was much more common and widespread than previously believed. The secret and taboo nature of child sexual abuse within the family meant that many cases never came to light prior to this, and worse still many others were dismissed or not responded to by the professionals involved. Many sexually abused children never received the support and help they needed to help them with the trauma they suffered, and grew to adulthood without sharing their secret.

Sexual abuse within the family is more common than stranger abuse

Now it is widely recognised that sexual abuse within the family is common in comparison with stranger abuse, with the majority of children, both boys and girls, abused by close male relatives. The debate about child sexual abuse over the last two decades has erased some of the taboos surrounding this type of abuse and raised awareness among professionals and public alike. However, child sexual abuse remains a secret act, often only known to the child and the abuser. Successful prosecutions of perpetrators continue at a low rate, and many cases are suspected but not proven. A number of widely reported cases in the 1990s highlighted the dangers of child sexual abuse within institutional settings, particularly those which were meant to provide a safe and secure environment for children who have already suffered from abuse.

Sexual abuse of children can take many forms, including using pornography to stimulate children sexually, abuse by groups of adults, and involving children in the making of pornographic material for distribution to others. Sexual abuse can involve coercion, violent attack, threats and intimidation. It can also occur within an apparently loving relationship where the child is gradually introduced to sexual activity through a series of small steps, progressing towards penetrative sex. This is sometimes described as 'grooming'.

Recent developments include an increased recognition of the role of children in abusing other children, particularly within the family. An NSPCC survey (NSPCC, November 2000) found a much greater prevalence of sibling abuse than has been previously recognised. The child abused was usually a sister or stepsister, the abuser usually a brother or stepbrother. Brothers were found to be responsible for more than one-third of sexual abuse committed by relatives (reported in the *Independent on Sunday*, 19/11/2000).

How do we recognise child sexual abuse?

Recognising child sexual abuse can be difficult unless the child 'discloses' the abuse by telling an adult about it. Although this can and does happen, the child may find it difficult to talk to others about the sexual abuse if it has been accompanied by threats of violence or separation from non-abusing family members, or if the child has developed a sense of shame about the abuse.

Many children who are sexually abused will show signs of emotional abuse. The child may perceive himself or herself as worthless and unlovable, valuable only in terms of the extent to which he or she can satisfy adult sexual needs. The impact of the emotionally abusive aspects of the sexual abuse may last longer and have more negative implications for the child than any physical consequences.

Depending on the type and severity of the sexual abuse, not all children will show physical symptoms. However, for some children the physical consequences can be very severe, in terms of diseases such as hepatitis, HIV, gonorrhoea and syphilis, and physical damage to the reproductive organs. One of the common indicators of child sexual abuse is inappropriate sexual knowledge and behaviour in the child. This goes far beyond the normal curiosity and experimentation that every child involves himself or herself in during different stages of sexual development.

Case Study 3

Suspected sexual abuse

James, 6, had developed some problems in school over a period of several months. These involved aggressive behaviour with peers, sexually explicit comments to adults and children, poor performance, lack of concentration and weeping fits if tackled about his behaviour. His teacher was deeply concerned that James had made comments about her breasts, and, as she put it, 'leered at me'. Attempts to discuss these issues with the parents had met with complete denial and a fear that James had been severely punished at home for attracting attention by his behaviour in school. James began to linger in the classroom at breaks and avoid other children. The local children's social care services contacted the school to ask for information about James when an older sister who had just left home came to their office and alleged that an uncle was abusing all the children in the family.

1   Discuss with a mentor or colleague how James could be supported through the ensuing investigation.

2   What sort of issues may arise for James' teacher in offering this support and how could they be dealt with?

It may involve:
➤ persistently introducing sexual themes into conversation, play and art work
➤ sexual attacks or sexually coercive play with other children
➤ sexualised behaviour with adults.

Other indicators that should not be ignored are related to the child's sense of self and self-esteem, any self-harming behaviour and social isolation. Sexually abused children often carry a burden of secrets that make the day-to-day sharing of friendship difficult to sustain. These children are emotionally distressed, isolated, feel different to other children and often blame themselves for the abuse.

The impact of sexual abuse on the child

Sexual abuse of young children may lead to physical harm including sexually transmitted diseases and physical damage. However, often (but not always) this type of harm is short term. The long-term effects can be severe and relate to the emotional damage that is common in sexual abuse. These effects can include low self-esteem, failure in education, difficulties in making relationships, abusive relationships, self-harming, drug and alcohol abuse and even suicide.

Neglect

Neglect is the persistent failure to meet a child's basic physical and/or psychological needs, likely to result in the serious impairment of the child's health or development.

Neglect may occur during pregnancy as a result of maternal substance abuse. Once a child is born, neglect may involve a parent or carer failing to:

* *provide adequate food, clothing and shelter (including exclusion from home or abandonment)*
* *protect a child from physical and emotional harm or danger*
* *ensure adequate supervision (including the use of inadequate caregivers)*
* *ensure access to appropriate medical care or treatment.*

It may also include neglect of, or unresponsiveness to, a child's basic emotional needs.

HM Government (2006:38)

The debate about neglect used to relate to the dividing line between low standards of care related to poverty and social deprivation and the wilful neglect of children by their carers. However, this debate has moved on in response to the development of clearer legislative and procedural foundations for our understanding of abuse. To be categorised as abusive, neglect must result in 'significant harm' to the child's welfare and development and must involve a substantial failure to meet the child's basic needs.

Maccoby and Martin (1983) included neglect as a category in their classification of parenting styles, arguing that neglect occurs where the child's needs have low priority within the family and, therefore, there is little or no attempt to meet them to any acceptable extent. Their model of neglecting parents suggested that they are both low on warmth towards the child and poor on communication within the family, and also that they have low expectations of the child and poor controls over the child's behaviour. Neglect is not, therefore, just about food, warmth and shelter. It is also about the failure to give children appropriate guidance and support, discipline and controls. Children who are neglected may receive little instruction about behaviour and social presentation and, as such, may be socially isolated not only because they are poorly dressed or smelly, but also because they do not know how to behave in ways that are acceptable to others. Similarly, they may have little support for their educational progress or for their efforts to develop friendships.

Emotional neglect

Emotional neglect is sometimes used to describe the passive process of ignoring or failing to respond to the child's emotional needs, and is linked to parenting by those who have severe unmet needs of their own (Iwaniec, 1995). Emotional neglect involves the failure of parents to meet the child's need for love, security, positive regard, warmth, praise and a sense of 'belonging' in their family and the wider world. Emotional neglect may be associated with a failure to respond to even the child's most basic needs or with a parent who is 'psychologically unavailable' to the child; in other words, a parent who is unresponsive to the child's needs because he or she does

not recognise these. An emotionally neglected child may have insecure attachments within the family, and as a result may suffer from poor self-esteem, delays in development and difficulties in social relationships. Emotional neglect may be accompanied by other sorts of neglect, such as failure to meet the child's basic physical needs on a consistent basis, and failure to ensure the child is safe and secure through proper supervision.

How do we recognise neglect?

The impact of neglect is not usually instantaneous, but develops over time and is evident in a range of aspects of the child's growth and development. Neglect can have a cumulative impact on the child's development. For example, failure to provide for basic physical needs, such as clean clothes, baths and teeth-cleaning, may lead to increased social isolation and subsequent low self-esteem, impacting on social, emotional and cognitive development. Neglect can be identified through indicators such as the child's appearance and behaviour, and also observation of the parent's behaviour and attitude towards the child. Neglecting parents tend to be disinterested in or unconcerned about their children's physical and psychological state. The cues that tend to elicit a response in a non-neglecting parent may have little impact on a neglecting parent. For example, crying, screaming, evidence of illness or distress in the child may not seem to gain the expected response. In a recent child abuse case in which a young child died after drinking his mother's methadone, it was reported that she took him on a shopping trip to town despite the fact that he was showing serious symptoms of illness. The mother then left the child with a friend so she could smoke heroin, although by this time he was dying.

Other indicators of neglect are found in the results of assessments of the child's developmental and educational progress. A neglected child may fail to thrive in terms of physical development and this will be reflected in height and weight charts for children under the age of 5 years, where no other cause of delays in physical development are identified. Neglected children often struggle educationally, lacking a strong basis of early learning and home support for education on which to build. Parents are unlikely to engage significantly with practitioners unless it is to access support for themselves. With reference to the discussion above, the child's social relationships may be poor, and the child may be socially rejected. This may be due to a lack of appropriate social knowledge, lack of self-control or disturbances in the child's behaviour.

Recognising neglect involves careful observation and recording of incidents, events about the child, the child's appearance and behaviour and the parent/child relationship over time. However, neglect is the most common form of abuse recorded and it is increasingly identified as highly damaging to children's long-term prospects. The issues shown in Figure 14.4 need to be considered.

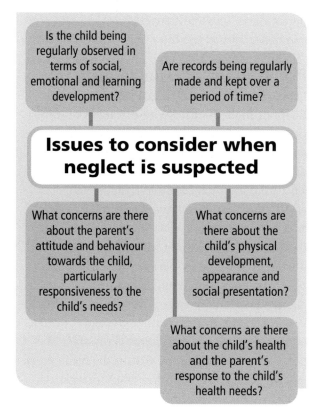

Figure 14.4 Recognising neglect

Case Study 4

Suspected neglect

Jessica, aged 5, entered school after a short period in a family centre day care unit. She was extremely shy, saying very little to anyone and avoiding eye contact when spoken to by adults. Jessica was a thin child, poorly dressed in ill-fitting clothes that were not suitable for the weather conditions. She had difficulty sitting still in class and often got up and wandered around. Some of the other children started to avoid sitting near Jessica in the classroom and she was usually alone at breaks. The teacher suggested that some children could try and get Jessica to join in, but they complained that she smelled and that she did not know how to play their games.

The teacher asked Jessica a few questions, as she often smelled strongly of urine. It became clear that Jessica did not use toilet paper after urinating and that as a result she was extremely sore in the genital area. The teacher spoke to the mother about this, suggesting a visit to the doctor was required, but received little response. The mother took no action, although Jessica was obviously in discomfort, and she began to avoid the teacher at the end of school, waiting outside the playground. Jessica's attendance became erratic and she was often absent without explanation. It also became obvious that she did not read or play at home, and the contents of her reading folder grew as unread letters from school to home gathered in it.

1 Plan a strategy that the teacher could use to engage this parent with the school and within which concerns could be raised effectively.

2 Discuss the proposed strategy with a colleague or mentor.

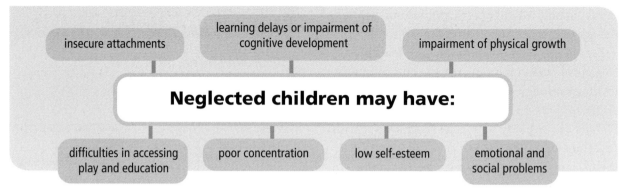

Figure 14.5 Long-term effects of neglect

The impact of neglect on the child

There is evidence that the long-term effects of severe neglect may be extremely serious. See Figure 14.5.

The life chances of the child may be permanently impaired if the neglect is serious and long term.

Responding to disclosure

Some child abuse is made apparent or is confirmed by a disclosure from the child. Disclosure simply means that the child tells an adult or another child what has been happening to him and this includes evidence of abuse or neglect. For example, a child, when asked about a nasty bruise, may tell a teacher or practitioner in an Early Years setting that a parent has inflicted it. Disclosure is most common where there is physical or sexual abuse. Children may disclose in a range of contexts including public settings. Young children's disclosures may be unclear if they do not have the language skills to explain what is happening to them and it is possible not to recognise such a disclosure for what it is. The question of whether a disclosure is genuine or not has long been considered a difficult area of judgement. However, evidence shows that younger children are unlikely to fabricate disclosures and that all such events should be taken seriously. Other factors to consider are whether the child's story remains consistent through retelling, and whether there

are other concerns that support suspicions of abuse. However in a small number of cases, particularly those of sexual abuse, disclosure can come 'out of the blue' with no forewarning.

Practitioner's responsibility in responding to disclosure

Responding to a child who discloses requires patience, sensitivity and a calm and structured approach. Children may be significantly affected if a disclosure is handled poorly. Children are most likely to disclose to those adults they like and have warm relationships and regular contact with. The child has placed trust in the individual to whom he or she discloses and it is important that this trust is not broken, as discussed below.

Disclosure may have a different meaning to the child than to the adults involved. For the adults, disclosure often heralds the start of a child protection inquiry within the framework of procedures. The child is often unaware of what may happen after disclosure. He or she may simply want to tell a trusted adult about what is happening to make him or her so unhappy and for that adult to stop the events that are causing the unhappiness.

As a practitioner you need to consider the following if a disclosure is made to you.

➤ Privacy and a quiet place for the child to talk.

➤ Using active listening skills to promote the disclosure without asking questions.

➤ The role of the person who comforts and supports the child and the limitations of this role, for example not being able to keep this to yourself; knowing the inquiry will be painful for the child.

➤ Accurate and objective recording of the conversation, that is, facts only and no speculation, opinion or assumptions.

➤ Evidence of other indicators of abuse that may support the child's disclosure, for example previous enquiries, observations of the child's relationship with parents, behaviour, attitude and ability to engage with the setting.

➤ The setting's policy on how to handle a disclosure from the practical point of view.

Case Study 5

Responding to disclosure

Karen, aged 6 years, asked her teacher if she could stay in at break, as she wanted to help clear up after art. The teacher had been concerned about how quiet Karen had been in the last few weeks and agreed to the plan. Karen said nothing for 15 minutes, and as the other children started to flock back through the door, she urgently whispered 'Dave touches me on my front bottom and I don't like it...'. The teacher turned the first child round and told her to go to the office and ask another adult to come immediately. She took Karen into the corridor, explaining that she wanted to listen to what she had to say but she needed to sort the other children out first. She then asked the returning children to sit down quietly. When the head teacher arrived she explained that she needed to talk to Karen urgently and asked him to cover the class for 10 minutes. The teacher took Karen into the cooking room and listened to what she had to say. A teaching assistant stayed with Karen doing quiet reading while the teacher and head discussed the situation and contacted social care services for advice.

1 What would you do in the same situation and how would you deal with the practicalities in your setting?

2 What are Karen's needs in this situation and how can they best be met?

Common Assessment Framework (CAF)

All practitioners and professionals working with children can complete a common assessment at any time for a child they work with. CAF was introduced to provide practitioners with children with an assessment tool that any 'frontline' worker can use, in order to ensure children with immediate needs did not wait for referral to another agency for assessment. The aim is to ensure assessment is timely and holistic and that children with a range of needs do not have repeat referrals to and assessments by a number of agencies, which could cause unacceptable delays to the child's chance of receiving services. CAF is normally completed in agreement with the parents and child (if old enough to understand the issues), but may be completed without their cooperation as long as this is made clear in the form. The assessment is holistic, identifying both the positive aspects of a child's circumstances, welfare and development and the areas of unmet need. The practitioner completing the CAF will use the outcomes to identify where her own service can meet the child's needs better and where referral to another agency is required to ensure the child's needs are met.

Guidelines suggest that CAF is used when:
- you are concerned about how well a child (or unborn baby) or young person is progressing. You might be concerned about their health, welfare, behaviour, progress in learning or any other aspect of their well-being
- the needs are unclear, or broader than your service can address

- a common assessment would help identify the needs, and/or get other services to help meet them.

DfES (2007:2)

The CAF is based on the same areas of assessment as the Framework for Assessment of Children and Need and their Families (2000) which is the assessment tool used mainly by social care staff to identify unmet need and services for children in need, including children at risk of significant harm, which is discussed in more detail later in this chapter. The three areas are:
- child's development
- parenting capacity
- family and environmental issues.

It is possible that while completing a CAF in respect of a child and family, evidence that the child may be requiring children in need services or child protection services may come to light. The practitioner must be aware of this possibility and be prepared to contact children's social care services to discuss their concerns or make a referral.

Procedural framework

Responses to suspected child abuse need to take place within the procedural framework supporting the child protection process. These procedures are defined at central and local government levels, and at the level of a particular service, agency and/or setting. The Children Acts 1989 and 2004 set out the statutory basis for protecting children as discussed below and key documents such as Working Together to Safeguard Children (HM Government, 2006) outline the responsibilities of different agencies and individuals in safeguarding children from abuse.

Local Safeguarding Children's Boards

The Local Safeguarding Children's Board

(LSCB), a statutory multi-agency body in every local authority, has the responsibility 'to coordinate local work to safeguard and promote the welfare of children' (HM Government, 2006:76) and ensure the agencies involved work together to achieve this. The membership of the boards is defined in section 13(3) of the Children Act 2004 and includes:
- health agencies
- local authorities
- police
- Youth Offending Teams (YOTs)
- Connexions.

In order to achieve their objectives LSCBs are involved in promoting effective safeguarding through:

- training
- safe recruitment of staff
- dealing with allegations
- planning
- communicating the need for effective safeguarding
- monitoring the effectiveness of local arrangements and procedures.

While LSCBs have a remit to promote the welfare of children within a wider safeguarding role, their core business is child protection. The boards are responsible for developing local procedures to safeguard children and also protocols and guidelines to ensure this work is done effectively.

Schools

Schools have a responsibility to create safe learning environments for children, including child protection procedures, health and safety arrangements, bullying strategies and security in the school. The key roles of schools in child protection is to be aware of all children's state of well-being and any concerns about a child or children's welfare and to refer these concerns to (usually) children's social care services. Schools are not expected to investigate possible child abuse but they are required to assist assessment processes, and contribute to developing and implementing Child Protection Plans. All schools are required to have a designated senior teacher who takes responsibility for coordinating and promoting safeguarding policy and practice in the school.

Early Years settings

All childcare settings have a responsibility to recognise and respond to any concerns about children's well-being and to have procedures in place in line with LSCB procedures to ensure staff know what to do in suspected cases of abuse. Like schools, a designated member of staff must be responsible for taking a lead in safeguarding issues. Early Years settings also have a wider remit to promote safeguarding for all children, which will be discussed later in this chapter.

Practitioners involved with children are encouraged to recognise that their role in child protection is not voluntary, but part of their more general roles and responsibilities. Within the procedural guidelines there is a strong theme of supporting parents and children through the child protection process and ensuring that they are kept informed and consulted at all stages.

Principles of working to safeguard children and promote their welfare

There are a number of principles underpinning work with children which are developed to try and ensure a robust and effective service to children and families. They state that safeguarding should be:
- child-centred
- rooted in child development
- focused on outcomes for children
- holistic in approach

- ensuring equality of opportunity
- involving of children and families
- building on strengths as well as identifying difficulties
- multi- and inter-agency in approach
- a continuing process, not an event
- providing and reviewing services
- informed by evidence.

Responding to suspected child abuse

Initial responses to suspected abuse

The decision to refer suspected abuse to children's social care services is never taken lightly. There is evidence that teachers struggle to know when the right time to make a referral has arrived and what the thresholds for referral are. For many practitioners, such referrals involve a weighty responsibility and a number of concerns. These may include concerns that:

➤ the inquiry may harm the child's emotional well-being

➤ the parents may become angry and/or distressed and cease to work with the setting or become hostile

➤ the child may be withdrawn from the setting

➤ the child may be removed from home unnecessarily

➤ the basis of the referral may be mistaken.

Why refer?

Referring suspected abuse is not an individual choice in theory. Practitioners are encouraged to consider their role in relation to that of colleagues and professionals from other agencies, and to act within prescriptive procedures. Perceptions that practitioners may hold about making a referral to child protection agencies are shown in Figure 14.6.

The decision to refer abuse to a child protection agency needs to be objective and with the child's best interests in mind. Factors influencing this decision must be weighed and considered in the light of the primary goal, which is to promote the child's welfare. In order to ensure this goal remains primary, other factors need to be evaluated in terms of their validity, and perceptions need to be considered in terms of their objectivity. For example, a belief that particular parents could not be involved in abuse of their children needs to be considered objectively. Why do we

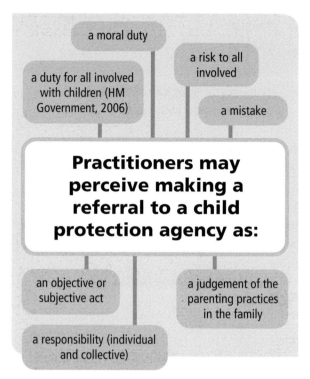

Figure 14.6 Perceptions of practitioners when making a referral to a child protection agency

believe this? What evidence do we base this belief on?

> ## Activity 1
>
> **Why not report abuse?**
>
> 1 List any reasons why a practitioner may not wish to refer suspected abuse of a child.
>
> 2 Note down the possible consequences of not referring suspected child abuse.

Making a child protection referral

The practitioner should first discuss concerns about the child with the appropriate person. In schools, this will be the designated teacher. In other Early Years settings, this will be a designated member of staff who may be the manager. In some cases, it is appropriate to contact children's social care services and ask for advice on how to proceed. It is possible that after taking advice:

➤ a referral may be made to children's social care services

➤ children's social care services may decide to act on the information given to them.

Not all types of abuse require the same response. See Figure 14.7 for information about the options available.

Responding to abuse	
Child protection referral	If there is evidence of physical or sexual abuse then a referral to social services should be made promptly.
Single-agency response	If there are concerns about neglect or emotional abuse you may agree to monitor the situation and work with the parents on your concerns.
Multi-agency response	You may agree to work with other agencies or professionals working with the family to provide support, for example health visitors, social services.

Figure 14.7 Making an appropriate response to abuse

The circumstances in which a referral to children's social care services should always be made are where:

➤ the child makes an allegation of abuse

➤ there are physical injuries which are cause for concern

➤ there are concerns about sexual abuse

➤ there are concerns about emotional abuse or neglect and the situation has deteriorated to the extent that the child may be suffering significant harm

➤ a child is being refused vital medical treatment

➤ there is a credible allegation from a member of the public

➤ the child is in contact with an individual who may put them at risk

➤ there are further concerns about a child who is already subject to a Child Protection Plan.

Referrals can be made in one of two ways, as shown in Figure 14.8. Either way it is important to record your concerns as soon as possible.

A child protection referral	
Make the referral	*Either* by completing an inter-agency referral form for reporting suspected child abuse to social services *or* by making a telephone referral first in situations where there appears to be some urgency.
The report should include:	Basic details about the child, for example name, age, address, class, any special needs or particular issues affecting the child including any communication difficulties the child may have. Details of your concerns, including dates, and any discussion you have had with the child and parents about these concerns. Details of any discussions you have had with other staff about your concerns. The level of your concern and extent of risk you believe the child to be in.

Figure 14.8 Making a child protection referral

It is important to ensure that reporting is factual, based on observation and evidence, rather than opinion, hearsay or speculation. This means that practitioners need to attend closely to the language used in their reports and to ensure that they are objective and not subjective in tone and content.

Working with parents

In order to ensure that parents' rights are maintained in this situation, parents need to be:

➤ informed that a referral to children's social care services is to be made and why (unless informing the parents could put the child at risk of acute physical harm)

➤ kept informed of the progress of the child protection process

➤ supported to remain as involved as possible in the process and any decision-making within that

➤ supported to continue to care for their child wherever possible.

Parents differ in their responses to child protection inquiries, but many will feel angry, threatened, frightened or distressed by the process. This may mean that they behave in ways that are hard to manage and may feel very disturbing to practitioners. Factors that may help to support parents and reduce the possibility of conflict are shown in Figure 14.9.

Working with the child

Referring a child, whether the child has disclosed or you have collected information about indicators of abuse, can feel like a betrayal of the relationship you have. Part of

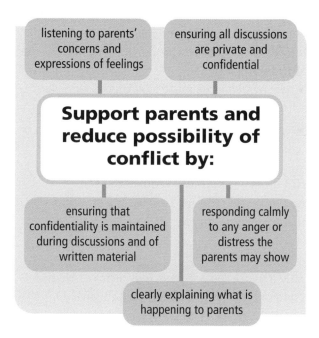

Figure 14.9 Factors that may help to support parents and reduce the possibility of conflict

this feeling can come from the knowledge that you have about the possible consequences of a child protection inquiry, and the recognition that the child's wishes in the situation may not be complied with. Evidence shows that many abused children do not want separation from their abusing parent, but that they want the abuse stopped. Young children in particular many have difficulty in understanding that this may not be possible in all cases.

Case Study 6

Children's rights in safeguarding

Hayley, aged 4 years, has been in nursery for about three months and you are her key worker. Today your manager was contacted by children's social care services, who want information about Hayley, and to interview her with her mother's permission about allegations of sexual abuse made by Hayley's older sister to a teacher in school. The social care worker intends to see Hayley after nursery finishes and asks if she can speak to her at the nursery

as the alleged abuser, a friend of the mother's, is a lodger in the home. The mother arrives at the end of nursery absolutely distraught, crying and incoherent.

1 Make notes on what both Hayley and her mother's rights are in this situation.

2 Discuss what could be done to support both Hayley and her mother in this situation and what issues need to be borne in mind.

The skills and abilities required for working with children in a child protection inquiry include:

➤ good listening skills – the child's concerns may not be what you assume they are

➤ ability to offer emotional and practical support

➤ trustworthiness

➤ time and energy

➤ ability to focus on the child when under pressure to ensure procedures are being followed correctly

➤ ability to recognise and focus on the child's needs where others' needs and wishes are strongly competing.

Staff development and training issues

There are a number of issues arising from the role of the practitioner in an Early Years setting in child protection in terms of staff development and training that, as a practitioner, you may wish to consider. They are:

➤ the need for practitioners to develop child observation skills and knowledge of child development (Rouse and Vincenti, 1994:68 Figure 5.1)

➤ developing skills in providing emotional support for children

➤ inclusive practice which takes into account each child's unique character, needs and circumstances

➤ training to support multi-disciplinary and inter-agency approaches (Kay, 2003; HM Government, 2006; Rouse and Vincenti, 1994).

The child protection inquiry

The majority of reports of suspected child abuse go to children's social care services which are located within Children's Services Authorities in local authorities. However, in situations where it is clear that the child has been harmed by someone outside the family it may be appropriate to refer to the police, who have specialist Child Protection Units to deal with such cases.

Local authorities have a duty to investigate any allegations of child abuse. The main purposes of any such investigation are to:

➤ establish the facts and make a record of them

➤ assess the risk to the child as a basis for taking action to protect him or her

➤ assess the extent to which the child's needs are being met within the family.

Since 2000, assessment of the child and family, which is a central part of any investigation, is achieved through the Framework for Assessment of Children in Need and their Families (DoH, 2000), which is a detailed assessment tool used to establish what the child's needs are and the extent to which they are being met within the family and wider environment (see page 424 for a full discussion).

Action following a child protection referral

The child and family are initially assessed within the Framework for Assessment by an experienced child protection social care worker, within seven days from referral. This assessment covers the needs of the child, the extent to which parents can meet these needs, and the family and environmental factors that support or hinder this process. The initial assessment will conclude whether:

➤ immediate action, possibly legal measures, should be taken to protect the child

➤ a child protection inquiry should be instigated

➤ the child and his or her family should be referred for family support services as a 'child in need'

➤ no further action should be taken.

A child abuse enquiry will be instigated if there is evidence that the child is suffering or likely to suffer significant harm related to the care he or she is receiving. This involves a core assessment within the Framework for Assessment. This establishes a range of factors, as shown in Figure 14.10.

Assessment is achieved through interviews

with family members and key professionals mainly, and examination of any relevant records. However, if it is considered that there is a high level of risk of 'acute physical harm' to the child, the social care worker may:

➤ try and persuade the suspected abuser to leave the household or make other arrangements to safeguard the child in the short term

➤ apply for an Emergency Protection Order (EPO)

➤ apply for a Child Assessment Order, if the parents refuse access to the child for medical or other assessment (see section on the legal and procedural framework page 418, below).

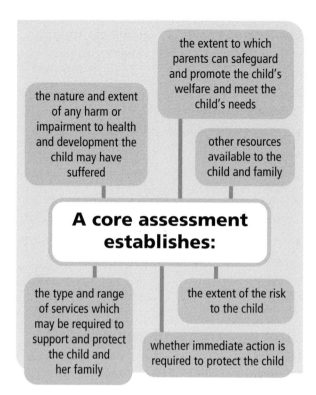

Figure 14.10 A core assessment

The role of the practitioner in child protection enquiries

The roles of all professionals are outlined in the Working Together to Safeguard Children (HM Government, 2006) guidelines and it is important that you are fully aware of your responsibilities. Knowing what is expected of you as a practitioner in an Early Years setting is a significant step in working towards supporting the child in this situation. Perhaps one of the child's most essential rights is to have competent and well-prepared adults working with him or her within the child protection process. You should have the knowledge and ability to:

➤ recognise indicators of possible abuse

➤ make considered decisions about referring children to social services where abuse is suspected

➤ ensure all communication with children and parents is sensitive and involves active listening

➤ report accurately, based on observation

➤ inform the investigating social care worker of any special needs or communication difficulties the child may have

➤ give information to any social care worker involved in a section 47 inquiry

➤ support the child in the setting and be aware of the stress the inquiry may place on the child and his family

➤ maintain confidentiality of speech and written records.

The Child Protection Case Conference

The Child Protection Case Conference is a meeting between children's social care services and other professionals who are involved with the child and family, and also usually involving parents. The aim of the conference is to pool information about the child and family in relation to child protection concerns. The meeting may include professionals from health, education and voluntary organisations.

Child Protection Case Conferences:

➤ pool information about the child and discuss any concerns about him or her
➤ assess the level of risk to the child and any other children in the household
➤ establish significant influences on the family functioning
➤ determine whether the child will need a child protection plan to safeguard him or her in the future
➤ decide on a key worker for the child if a child protection plan is agreed
➤ make arrangements to review the plan at regular intervals.

Child protection case conference recommendations

The Child Protection Case Conference also makes a series of recommendations designed to support and promote the child's welfare and the parents' ability to parent safely and effectively. These recommendations are incorporated in a child protection plan, which sets out goals for involved agencies on how they can contribute to safeguarding and promoting the child's welfare. The plan may include legal action to protect the child, such as care proceedings to make the child the subject of a Care Order or Supervision Order. This may involve, in a small number of cases, removal of the child into local authority care on a short- or long-term basis. The child protection plan is subject to regular review, usually biannually or more frequently, and is monitored by the key worker.

Core groups

The core group is made up of professionals with direct responsibility for the child and family. They monitor and discuss the progress of the child protection plan in between case conferences. You may be involved in the core group for a particular child in your care. However, research evidence shows that core groups often fade away after the initial case conference, leaving children's social care services to monitor and implement the child protection plan alone. Clearly, this is not in line with current guidelines and policy and continuing efforts to strengthen multi-agency approaches to child protection are taking place, within the Every Child Matters: Change for Children strategy.

The role of practitioners in the Child Protection Case Conference

Early Years practitioners involved in child abuse cases may be asked to attend the case conference and contribute their knowledge of the child and family to the proceedings. Normally, a report is written based on the records kept within the Early Years setting or workplace. Your knowledge and experience of the child and family is crucial to ensuring that a clear picture of the child's welfare and situation is established. You may also be asked to be part of the core group, as discussed above, and to take on responsibilities within the child protection plan. In order to support the child and parents within this process, the following needs to be considered:

➤ factual verbal and written reporting based on observations
➤ objective, not subjective, views and opinions
➤ consideration of what your Early Years setting or organisation can offer to support the child and family in order to meet the child's needs.

Objective views and opinions are factual and based on observation and actual knowledge rather than speculation, hearsay or assumptions. For example, we could describe a child as 'really battered, covered in bruises and obviously been beaten' or we could say 'the child had a number of bruises on her upper arms and shoulders that appeared to be of different ages: some purple, some green and yellow'.

The child protection plan

The core group develops the child protection plan in response to recommendations made by the case conference. Targets are set to ensure the child's safety, to promote the child's welfare and to support the family to parent more safely and effectively. The plan will also determine the roles and responsibilities of different professionals and agencies in meeting these targets.

In Early Years settings the practitioner's roles and responsibilities may include those identified in Figure 14.11.

Figure 14.11 The child protection plan: practitioner's role in meeting targets

---

Case Study 7

The practitioner's role in implementing the child protection plan

Harry, aged 4 years, has been placed by social care services for part of the day with a childminder after he was found to be neglected by his parents. The childminder is expected to monitor Harry's health and welfare as part of the child protection plan.

1 Describe which aspects of Harry's development the childminder could be expected to monitor.

2 How might she go about this?

3 Which areas of Harry's development would the childminder not be monitoring?

The legal and procedural framework

The legal and procedural framework for child protection processes in England and Wales determines the responses that are available to professionals when faced with suspected child abuse. Knowledge and understanding of the legal and procedural process can help practitioners in Early Years settings to perform their roles more effectively. This knowledge includes:

➤ the rights of the child and parents within the legislative and policy framework

➤ the roles and responsibilities of different professionals involved in protecting children

➤ the role of legal intervention in protecting children

➤ the limits and boundaries of legal intervention.

The Children Act 1989

The Children Act 1989 is based on a number of key principles that underpin the ethos in which child protection work should take place. The key principles of the Children Act 1989 are:

➤ the child's welfare is paramount

➤ delay in legal processes is prejudicial to the child's welfare and should be avoided

➤ courts should only make orders where it is better for the child to do so than not (the non-interventionist principle)

➤ decisions should be made in partnership between professionals from different agencies, and families

➤ the child's views and opinions should be considered (but cannot override the need for the child's welfare to be paramount)

➤ parental responsibility is retained by parents throughout, even if the child is in care (it is transferred only through the making of an adoption order).

Essentially these principles support a child-centred approach, based on partnership between parents and professionals, and between professionals. They underline the belief that legislative action is a last resort when acting to protect children.

Under section 47 of the Act, local authorities have a duty to:

➤ investigate suspected child abuse cases

➤ take steps to ensure the child's welfare is safeguarded.

Although many cases are investigated under section 47, only a small proportion of these result in legal action. Procedural guidelines support the non-interventionist principle, in that steps have to be taken to try and safeguard the child without resorting to the law. Legal action can be traumatic for the child and family and may result in the child being separated from her caregivers. It is in the child's best interests to avoid legal intervention unless this is the only way to protect the child. For example, if the child can remain with a non-abusive parent within his or her own home, with siblings, school and friends, then the impact of abuse will be lessened. If the child is removed from home through the legal process, this means disruption to family and other relationships, education and care arrangements, and loss of familiar environments, routines and people.

'Significant harm'

In order for legal steps to be taken, the child must be deemed to be suffering or likely to suffer significant harm for such intervention to take place. 'Harm' is defined as 'ill-treatment or the impairment of health and development' (section 31, Children Act 1989).

'Development' refers to all aspects of the child's physical, emotional and social development and learning development. There must be evidence that the quality of care the child is receiving will result in or has resulted in 'significant harm' to the child. Evidence of 'significant harm' will be gathered in a child protection investigation from the observations of practitioners, medical evidence, educational and psychological assessments and the child's story. Such evidence may include charting of physical injuries or impairments to growth and development.

Court orders

Court orders will only be granted if it is in a child's best interests for the court to make the order. Normally court orders are applied for by local authorities, but the police and NSPCC have authority to apply for orders also. The evidence that is presented to the court can be drawn from a range of sources, so it is important to ensure that all relevant records are kept.

Emergency Protection Order

An EPO is used to remove the child to, or keep the child in, a safe place in cases where the child is considered to be in 'acute physical danger'. It is used where:

- delay could be extremely harmful to the child, and immediate action to protect the child needs to be taken
- when a child protection investigation is taking place and access to the child is being 'unreasonably refused'; for example, the parents consistently refuse to allow the social worker to see or speak to the child.

The person applying for the EPO must ensure that no alternative arrangements can be made to safeguard the child, such as:
- parents agree for the child to be accommodated (cared for by the local authority on a voluntary basis)
- parents agree that the child can be placed with a suitable relative or other person
- the person suspected of abuse agrees to leave the household for the time being.

EPOs are short term, lasting eight days initially, with provision for a seven-day extension. The options available to the child after this time are shown in Figure 14.12.

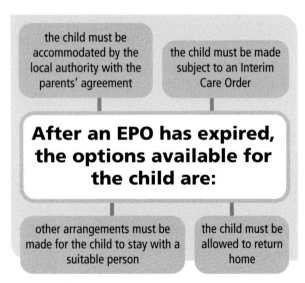

Figure 14.12 Options for the child after expiry of an EPO

Child Assessment Order

The CAO allows the local authority to gain access to a child for medical or other types of assessments. Criteria for successfully applying for a CAO include proving:

- that the child may suffer or be likely to suffer from significant harm, and
- that an assessment is necessary to determine this, and
- that an assessment is unlikely to take place without the CAO.

A CAO lasts for seven days and requires the parents to make the child available for specific assessments, which could include stays away from home. Assessment is interpreted very broadly and can include physical and mental health assessments; psychological assessments; and educational assessments.

In order to ensure that children have some control in this situation, children who have 'sufficient understanding to make an informed decision' can refuse an assessment. However, this tends to apply to children over the age of 10 years at least.

Care Orders

A Care Order made in respect of any child results in that child being placed in the care of the local authority, although the parents continue to share parental responsibility. The conditions under which a Care Order is made are shown in Figure 14.13.

For a Care Order to be made:	
a child must be shown to be suffering from or likely to suffer from significant harm	due to the standard of care he or she receives *or* because the child is beyond parental control.

Figure 14.13 Requirements for a Care Order

The child is 'looked after' by the local authority until the Care Order expires (when the child is 18) or is revoked, usually through application by the parents.

The court can make an Interim Care Order for eight weeks to give the local authority time to make a full case; for example, where an

EPO has previously been made and it is not considered safe for the child to go back to his or her parents' care. Care Orders are not made lightly, as they involve the long-term removal of the child from the parent's care. As such, alternative solutions to protecting the child are sought, such as the removal of the abuser from the home or for the child to live with other caretakers. While the Care Order is in place, the local authority has to promote contact between the child and her significant others, except where there is considerable risk, in which case an application can be made to deny contact with named individuals.

The majority of children under 12 years old in local authority care are placed with foster carers, but chronic shortages of the full range of foster placements in many areas mean that policies supporting placements which reflect the child's religious, linguistic and cultural background cannot always be complied with. Children may be placed in short-term or inappropriate placements, and many children experience multiple placements. A small number of children under the age of 12 may still spend periods of time in residential care, although local authorities usually have policies to place children under 12 years in foster care.

Supervision Orders

Supervision Orders can be made for a period of from one to three years. The local authority monitors and supports the child and family where a Supervision Order is in place. The usual reason for a Supervision Order is when there are concerns about the child's welfare and regular monitoring needs to be enforced. The child is usually supervised by a social worker, who is charged with advising, assisting and befriending him or her and ensuring the parents cooperate with the supervisory process.

Accommodated children

Accommodated children are 'looked after' by the local authority with their parents'

agreement. The majority of children under 12 years of age will be accommodated with foster carers. The parents can reclaim their child at any time, as there is no legal transfer of parental responsibility. Accommodation can be a long- or short-term arrangement and can sometimes be arranged as an alternative to a Care Order.

The role of the practitioner in legal proceedings

The role of the practitioner in an Early Years setting is often limited in terms of direct involvement in legal proceedings. Giving information during investigations and at Child Protection Case Conferences; monitoring and supporting the child and family; and providing support services to the family may be the extent of your involvement. However, perhaps the most significant role you can take is that of providing continuity of care and support for the child during what is often a very difficult time. Parents need to be supported also, and their needs considered within the process. Practitioners in Early Years settings need to recognise that their role in supporting the child can be central in helping the child come to terms with some difficult changes in his or her life.

Working Together to Safeguard Children

These government guidelines provide every relevant children's practitioner or professional with information about their role in child protection. The guidelines also include definitions of abuse and information about the indicators of abuse. They are based on research that has been carried out to establish 'best practice' in protecting children and supporting children and families in the child protection process. The role of the LSCBs is outlined (as discussed above). Practitioners reading the guidelines will find that there are sections relevant to their own role.

Activity 2

Guidelines to the practitioner's role

Read sections 5.3 and 5.4 in Working Together to Safeguard Children 2006 (URL is at the end of this chapter) to determine the significance of these points in more detail.

Multi–professional approaches to child protection

Some of the reasons why professionals need to work together in child protection are:

➤ lessons from child death inquiry reports about failures in inter-agency communication (Reder et al, 1993; Laming, 2003)

➤ to prevent social disadvantage and exclusion through support for children and families

➤ to reduce incidents of abuse and the costs of these

➤ to maximise resource use by avoiding duplication of services.

Working together in conjunction with other agencies is clearly an important principle of successful child protection work. Agencies and professionals need to share information,

work together to protect children and support families, in order to improve parenting to a safe standard. While children's social care services take a lead in child protection work, the legislation and guidelines emphasise that other agencies such as health and education have a duty to cooperate and provide support for the process by providing information and services, as required. All practitioners involved with children have a role. However, inter-agency cooperation is not always easy to achieve. There are a number of problems in developing a multi-agency approach, as shown in Figure 14.14 (see also Chapter 15 Leading and working in multi-professional teams).

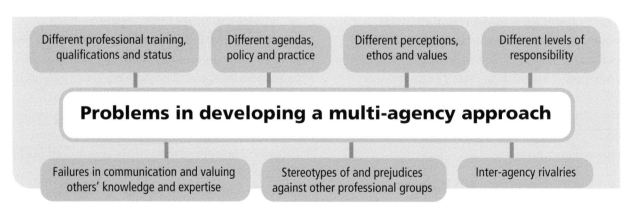

Figure 14.14 Factors that contribute to problems with a multi-agency approach (Hallett and Birchall, 1995, in DoH, 1995; Kay, 2000; Doh, 1999)

The Children Act 2004

The Children Act 2004 made inter-agency co-operation to support the well-being of children a duty for a number of relevant organisations, including local authorities, health services, education services and police amongst others. In order to achieve this the Act established LSCBs to replace the non-statutory Area Child Protection Committees, and also established a Director of Children's Services in every local authority to lead combined education and children's social care services. In addition, every local council must have a lead member for children to raise the profile of children in local authority business and every local authority has to produce a single Children and Young People's Plan to streamline the multi-agency planning process for improving children's welfare and attainment.

See also Chapter 13 Evaluating Early Years policy and legislation for more on the Children Act 2004.

Information sharing

The Children Act 2004 also established the legal basis for information sharing in every local authority and between local authorities. Information about the child and about which agencies are involved with him/her can be accessed by designated staff in all children's services through local databases linked by the national Information Sharing Index. The information shared is restricted to basic details about the child, contact details of practitioners/agencies involved and an indication of whether a CAF had been completed in respect of the child. However, despite these limitations on data held there have been concerns that the databases may harm children's welfare by:

➤ 'losing' child abuse cases among the many other children involved

➤ sidelining parents' and children's views and involvement

➤ labelling children as potentially 'criminal' at an early age

➤ intruding on family privacy, invading children's rights and contravening basic human rights.

FIPR (2006)

The Framework for Assessment of Children in Need and their Families

The Framework for Assessment is a tool for assessing all 'children in need' including cases where abuse is suspected. An initial assessment within the framework will establish if there are child protection issues to consider or if children and families only need to receive services for 'children in need' under section 17 of the Children Act 1989. Assessment takes place around three broad areas:

➤ the child's developmental needs

➤ parenting capacity

➤ family and environmental issues.

Children's social care services are responsible for undertaking assessments, but other agencies are required to offer information, expertise and support towards the assessment of and provision of services to the child and family. Early Years settings and organisations may be involved in assessment of:

➤ the child's educational achievements and ability

➤ the child's behaviour, and any difficulties in the setting

➤ the child's ability to access the curriculum

➤ the parent/child relationship

➤ the parent's ability and willingness to support the child.

These contributions can be significant in ensuring that children and families are comprehensively assessed and a clear picture of the full range of their needs and areas of strength is gathered.

Failures in child protection

Failures in child protection tend to only be widely discussed when there are tragedies associated with a breakdown in the child protection system, such as the death of children like Victoria Climbie. However, failure in child protection can lead to misery for the child and family through lack of provision of services to prevent abuse and support the family. Failures in child protection are complex and involve many interrelated factors. These can include:

➤ failure to recognise the indicators of abuse or respond to disclosure

➤ failure to refer suspected abuse

➤ incomplete investigation/no investigation/poor assessment of risk

➤ lack of necessary information at the child protection case conference

➤ poor or incomplete recommendations

➤ inadequate child protection plan

➤ the child protection plan is not implemented or is only partially implemented

➤ liaison between key professionals fails or is unclear.

There are a number of reasons for failures in child protection; these are shown in Figure 14.15.

The investigation of abuse and action taken by professionals may also have negative aspects in relation to the child and family. This may be due to:

➤ failure to keep parents and children informed

➤ separation of the child from significant others

➤ failure to focus on the child and family's needs within the enquiry

➤ disruptions to the child's routines, care and education.

Figure 14.15 Some reasons for failures in child protection

Case Study 8

Negative aspects of safeguarding

Annie, 6 years, and her younger brother and sister lived with both their parents, who have severely neglected them from birth. Yesterday, children's social care services removed Annie and her siblings from their parents' care and placed them in foster homes on the other side of the city. Unfortunately, Annie's baby brother has gone to a different foster home because Annie's foster carer could only cope with two children. Annie has looked after her brother from birth and she loves him very much.

Consider how Annie must be feeling today.

What losses has she suffered? How do you think an adult could help Annie to understand what has happened? What steps need to be taken to help her cope?

In the next section the role of Early Years settings and organisations in developing high standards in safeguarding will be discussed, and the requirements of a supportive environment to promote the welfare and safety of all children will be outlined.

Best practice in safeguarding children in Early Years settings

Developing a safe environment for all children

A safeguarding setting does not just react to individual cases of abuse that may arise, but creates an environment in which children's needs come first and where children are supported to develop confidence and high self-esteem. It is an environment in which children's emotional and physcial security is promoted, achieved through working with children directly and also though developing supportive relationships with parents. It is also an environment in which observation is used to monitor the well-being of children as well as their educational progress.

In a safeguarding setting the care of children is seen in terms of emotional and psychological care as well as meeting children's physical needs. In a safe environment children are:

➤ valued in all aspects of their selves and their achievements, including their religious, cultural and linguistic background

➤ given genuine and considered praise and rewards for achievement

➤ supported to behave appropriately

➤ encouraged to respect themselves and others

- protected from all forms of bullying including verbal assaults

- encouraged to try new activities, make mistakes and experiment.

66 Discussion point 2

Promoting a safeguarding environment in your Early Years setting

In discussion with a colleague or mentor, make some suggestions for your Early Years setting about how a safeguarding environment could be promoted further.

These could include how children from diverse backgrounds are best supported; how the self-esteem of all children can be supported; how mutual respect is developed. Remember the role of practitioners as models of behaviour and ways in which all staff can be involved.

An Ofsted report into safeguarding in Early Years settings in 2005–6 found that in the best settings:

They take all reasonable steps to minimise the risk of harm, and they are fully prepared to identify any concerns about a child's welfare and to respond and report them appropriately. Adults view the protection of children as of supreme importance. They would not hesitate to take the difficult step of acting on a concern; they know when and how to seek advice, and they report concerns competently to the appropriate people and authorities.

Ofsted (2006)

Other aspects of safeguarding that need to be considered should be part of the setting's policies that include:

- ensuring all staff are suitable to work with children by making sure CRB checks are done and references are checked

- having rigorous procedures to ensure children are only collected by adults with parental responsibility or their authorised delegates

- behaviour management policies that support children's development and self-esteem and a developmental approach to improving behaviour

- strictly upheld confidentiality policies that support the rights of the child and parents to privacy in terms of personal information unless this is incompatible with safeguarding effectively

- parent partnership policies that promote partnership with all parents and carers.

Allegations against staff

On occasion allegations of child abuse are made against staff in Early Years settings although this is relatively rare compared to schools. However, all allegations need to be dealt with as follows:

Figure 14.16 The role of Early Years settings in child protection work

- the designated staff member investigates the allegation

- usually parents should be informed but the designated staff member may seek advice about this if there are concerns about possible repercussions

- a referral needs to be made to the police/social care servcies for a child abuse inquiry to take place

- normally staff members are suspended during the investigation

- false allegations can be very distressing to staff and the setting as a whole and it is important that accused staff seek support through their management system and trade union during the process.

Supporting children who have been abused

Abused children may feel angry and bewildered, confused and scared, guilty about the impact of their abuse on the family, sad and unloved. Those who are separated from their parents may be in despair and unable to understand the outcomes of the abuse enquiry. Stopping the abuse may seem a simple solution to the child's problems, but the process of doing this may result in further pain. Butler and Williamson (1999:12) conclude that to work effectively with children who have been abused 'it is vitally necessary to establish what children themselves see as the primary causes of pain, distress and fear'.

Some children may receive therapeutic support, such as play therapy or counselling, in the aftermath of abuse, but this is not always available or relevant for all children. A child's response to abuse will depend on:

- the extent, severity and type of abuse
- the child's relationships with the abuser and other carers
- the support the child has
- the child's personality and personal characteristics.

Other factors may affect the child's response to abuse differently. Children who are disabled

may 'have to work through the dual oppression of disablism and abuse' (Kennedy, 2000). Lees (1999:79) suggests that 'the inability of disabled children to communicate experiences is one of the factors that make them, as a group, more vulnerable to abuse'.

It is characteristic of abused children that they will suffer learning delays, social withdrawal or isolation, behavioural problems and low self-esteem.

Practitioners have a responsibility to support children during the aftermath of abuse on a number of fronts. These include:

- maintaining a supportive and caring relationship with the child
- using routine, daily activities and familiar events to 'normalise' the child's days
- helping the child with difficult and painful feelings
- supporting the child's behaviour
- helping the child to maintain friendships and other social relationships
- supporting the child's self-esteem and confidence
- helping the child to continue learning
- getting specialist support for children with disabilities/communication difficulties.

In order to support the child, there needs to be a clear understanding between practitioners, parents or carers and other professionals involved as to what the child's needs are and how best to meet them. Some of the ways in which the child could be supported in an Early Years setting are shown in Figure 14.17.

Activity 4

Supporting an abused child

Refer back to Case Study 3 on page 405 and answer the following questions.

1 How would you respond to James' behaviour?

2 What strategies would you use to help him behave more acceptably?

3 What other needs does James have and how else could you support him?

Figure 14.17 Examples of how a child could be supported in an Early Years setting

Supporting children who have been abused requires a range of interpersonal skills in order to ensure that the child is benefited by the relationship with the adults who care for him or her. Shemmings (1999) suggests that in order to make effective helping relationships with children, the six qualities and skills identified in Figure 14.18 are required.

Improving skills to work with emotionally damaged children is a crucial part of an Early Years practitioner's own self-development and learning.

Figure 14.18 Qualities and skills required for effective helping relationships with children

Conclusion

The role of practitioners in Early Years settings in safeguarding children and contributing to the child protection process is extremely important in terms of the outcomes for the child and family. Upholding the rights of the child through good practice, positive relationships with other professionals, and strategies to support the child and family is part of the development of a safeguarding setting. Recognising that safeguarding (including child protection) is ongoing within the setting and not just related to individual cases is an important part of this process. Knowledge of legislation and procedures can give practitioners confidence to work well in this area and to apply their understanding of the child and family within the safeguarding process. Keeping the child and his or her needs at the centre of safeguarding strategies and practice at all times ensures that good practice is developed and the child is safeguarded in the setting as well as within the family situation.

How to move on in your research

Beckett, C. (2007), *Child Protection – An Introduction*. London: Sage
An excellent introduction to issues and procedures.

Lindon, J. (2003) (2nd edition), *Child Protection 2nd ed.* London: Hodder Arnold
A good introductory text focusing on child protection in Early Years contexts.

Munro, E. (2002), *Effective Child Protection*. London: Sage
A useful text exploring professional roles in child protection in terms of effective practice.

References

Baginsky, M. (2000), *Child Protection and Education*. London: NSPCC

Baldwin, N. (2000), 'Protecting children: Protecting their rights?', Chapter 1 in Baldwin, N. (ed.), *Protecting Children: Promoting their Rights*. London: Whiting and Birch

Butler, I. and Williamson, H. (1999), 'Children's views of their involvement', Chapter 2 in Shemmings, D. (ed.), *Involving Children in Family Support and Child Protection*. London: HMSO
Children Act 1989. London: HMSO
Children Act, 2004. London: HMSO

Children are Unbeatable (2007), *Children Are Unbeatable! Alliance – News*. Last accessed on 5 Nov 2007 at http://www. childrenareunbeatable.org.uk/#review

Children's Rights Director (2004), *Safe from Harm: Children's Views Report*. Commission for Social Care Inspection

DCSF (2007), *Referrals, Assessments and Children and Young People who are the Subject of a Child Protection Plan or are on Child Protection Registers* (year ending 31 March 2007, England). Online. Last accessed on 4 November 2007 at http://www.dfes. gov.uk/rsgateway/DB/SFR/s000742/SFR28-CPR30607comment.doc

DfES (2007), *CAF Quick Guide*. Online. Last accessed on 11 November 2007 at http:// www.dfes.gov.uk/commoncore/docs/ CAFQuickGuide.doc

DoH (1995), *Child Protection: Messages from Research*. London: HMSO

DoH (2000), *Framework for Assessment of Children in Need and their Families*. London: HMSO

Gibbons, J. et al (1995), *Development after Physical Abuse in Early Childhood: A Follow-up Study of Children on Child Protection Registers*. London: HMSO

HM Government (2006), *Working Together to Safeguard Children*. London: HMSO

Hobbs, C. (1994), 'Key issues in diagnosis and response in child abuse', Chapter 1 in Pugh, G. and Hollows, A. (eds), *Child Protection in Early Childhood Services*. London: National Children's Bureau

Hodgson, D. (1999), 'Children's rights', in Shemmings, D. (ed.), *Involving Children in Family Support and Child Protection*. London: HMSO.

Howitt, D. (1992), *Child Abuse Errors – When Good Intentions Go Wrong*. Hemel Hempstead: Harvester Wheatsheaf

Iwaniec, D. (1995), *The Emotionally Abused and Neglected Child*. Chichester: Wiley

Kay, J. (2003) (2nd edition), *Protecting Children*. London: Continuum

Kay, J. (2000), 'Working together: The role of schools in child protection', in *ChildRight*, October 2000

Kennedy, M. (2000), 'The abuse of disabled children', in **Baldwin, N. (ed.)**, *Protecting Children: Promoting their Rights*. London: Whiting and Birch

Lees, J. (1999), 'Children with communication difficulties', in **Shemmings, D. (ed.)**, *Involving Children in Family Support and Child Protection*. London: HMSO

MacLeod, M. (2000), 'What do children need by way of child protection? Who is to decide?', Chapter 10 in **Baldwin, N. (ed.)**, *Protecting Children: Promoting their Rights*. London: Whiting and Birch

Munro, E. (2002), *Effective Child Protection*. London: Sage

NSPCC (November 2000), 'Child maltreatment in the United Kingdom', reported in the *Independent on Sunday* 19/11/2000.

Parton, N. (1996), 'Child protection, family support and social work'. *Child and Family Social Work*, 1, pp3–11.

Pettican, K. (1998), 'Child protection, welfare and the law', Chapter 10 in **Taylor, J. and Woods, M. (eds)**, *Early Childhood Studies*. London: Arnold

Reder, P., Duncan, S. and Gray, M. (1993), *Beyond Blame – Child Abuse Tragedies Revisited*. London: Routledge

Rouse, D. and Vincenti, O. (1994), 'Observation assessment and support: The contribution of Early Years workers', in **Pugh, G. and Hollows, A. (eds)**, *Child Protection in Early Childhood Services*. London: National Children's Bureau

Shemmings, D. (1999), 'The importance of relationships', in **Shemmings, D. (ed.)**, *Involving Children in Family Support and Child Protection*. London: HMSO

Victoria Climbie Inquiry (2003), *Report of an Inquiry by Lord Laming*, (January 2003). Last accessed 12 February 2008 at http://www.victoria-climbie-inquiry.org.uk/finreport/finreport.htm

Waterhouse, L. (ed.) (1993), *Child Abuse and Child Abusers*. London: Jessica Kingsley

Useful websites

http://www.everychildmatters.gov.uk/strategy/guidance/
Children Act 2004 Guidance

http://www.everychildmatters.gov.uk/socialcare/safeguarding/
Every Child Matters – Safeguarding Children

www.nspcc.org.uk/
NSPCC

http://www.victoria-climbie-inquiry.org.uk/finreport/finreport.htmictoria
Victoria Climbie Inquiry/Laming Report 2003

http://www.everychildmatters.gov.uk/_files/AE53C8F9D7AEB1B23E403514A6C1B17D.pdf
Working Together to Safeguard Children, 2006

15 Leading and working in multi-professional teams

Janet Kay

This chapter focuses on developing and leading multi-professional teams in Early Years contexts. Different types of multi-professional teams are considered and the difficulties these teams can face, and strategies for resolving these difficulties, are discussed. Aspects of leadership in multi-professional Early Years contexts are explored and the support available for leaders in these contexts outlined.

By undertaking the suggested study within this chapter it is hoped that you will be able to:

1 understand the need for 'joined-up' working

2 understand the challenges facing multi-professional team development

3 know strategies to promote the development of multi-professional teams

4 support the development of multi-professional teams as a leader

5 know about the available support for multi-professional teams and leadership in Early Years contexts.

This chapter addresses the following areas:

➤ Current structures and settings for multi-professional teams

➤ Advantages and challenges of multi-professional teamwork

➤ Developing effective multi-professional teams

➤ Leadership and management of multi-professional teams

➤ Support for developing multi-professional leadership capacity

Current structures and settings for multi-professional teams

In recent years there have been significant developments to address perceived fragmentation of services for children, in order to improve the quality of these services and to amend some of the issues arising from the historically separate development of services such as health, social care services and education. Brown and White (2006:6) state that since New Labour came to power in 1997:

there has been a wealth of initiatives aimed at encouraging more collaboration between different agencies and professionals, improving joint working and achieving more effective partnership working to deliver more seamless, joined-up services for the public.

The fragmented development of children's services is seen to have created a situation where services are less responsive and where child and family needs can sometimes not be met as they fall into the gaps between separate agencies' ability and willingness to deliver services. The most extreme examples of this are the deaths of children at the hands of their parents/carers, where the inability of services to work effectively together has been cited as a major factor in failing to prevent this. As a result, the Every Child Matters (ECM) strategy has integrated working at the heart of its policy and practice, developing new ways of working and new services in which multi-disciplinary teams are crucial.

However, developing effective multi-professional teams is not easy, as the long history of separate development, professional differences and many other factors has created barriers to effective 'joined-up' working. Leading multi-professional teams is a particular challenge as leaders often come from a single disciplinary background and have to understand the needs of and respond to the requirements of a diverse team. However, the policy drivers are clear that integrated approaches to service planning and delivery are the way forward and developing skills for multi-professional team leadership is important for any Early Years practitioner. The policy context behind multi-professional approaches to working in children's services is discussed in more detail in Chapter 13.

Multi-professional teams have been developing across children's services for some time now resulting in a proliferation of different types of teams and contexts in which Early Years practitioners may be involved in 'joined-up' working. In this section the different contexts for and types of multi-professional teams in Early Years services will be discussed. Early years practitioners may find themselves working in a range of multi-professional teams at any one time or over time. The context and type of team may affect team functioning and effectiveness and the quality of experience of team members. However, the field of multi-professional working is dogged by a confusion of terminology which may leave the reader very confused as a wide range of terms are used interchangeably or sometimes to mean different things. In the next section, the terms used in this chapter will be defined and different ways of classifying joint working will be discussed.

Types of multi-professional teams

There are a number of different structures for joint working, which can be defined in different ways. The ECM (2007) website suggests two main types of multi-professional team, differentiated by whether the team is a permanent or more ad hoc structure and whether the team members relate mainly to the multi-professional team or whether their main identity is with their home agency.

1 **Multi-agency teams** – these are teams that are made up of members of the children's workforce drawn from a range of different disciplines and agencies who meet for specific reasons either regularly or on an ad hoc basis. The team members continue to be employed by their home agency and to identify with the goals and purposes of that agency. However, they participate in joint working with other professionals through the multi-agency team and have joint goals and aims within that team's remit and functioning. They are less likely to be co-located than multi-disciplinary teams.

Child Protection Case Conference

The case conference membership is drawn from practitioners and professionals working with a child(ren) and family and takes place when it is considered that child abuse has taken place. The conference is usually arranged by children's social services and will typically include some of the following staff.

➤ Child Protection Case Conference chair
➤ Social care worker/team manager (possibly for each child involved)
➤ Early Years practitioner/manager and/or school teacher/head/learning mentor
➤ Health visitor/manager
➤ Family support worker
➤ Paediatrician
➤ Probation officer.

The conference meets and agrees a child protection plan, which may involve actions by some or all of the members of the conference, for example monitoring the child's nursery attendance. The conference will continue to meet at regular intervals to review and revise the plan and to monitor the child(ren)'s well-being until it is agreed this is no longer necessary.

2 **Multi-disciplinary teams** – these are teams where the team relationship is permanent and members are recruited or seconded to the team rather than still attached to another agency. These teams are typically made up of a range of professionals and practitioners from different disciplinary backgrounds. Although employed by the multi-disciplinary team, members may still have links to a home agency for supervisory support or because they have access to training or management support from that agency. There may be a mixture of permanent and seconded staff on this type of team. These teams are more likely to be co-located than multi-agency teams but it is also possible that some team members may not be co-located.

Children's Centre team

The team in the Children's Centre is made up of a manager who is from a primary teaching background, a deputy who is a speech therapist who is seconded to the team from the health service, a social care worker who is employed by the Children's Centre, but who has supervision from a social work manager, a number of Early Years practitioners, some of whom work for the Centre in a variety of roles including family support and some who work for the private daycare providers who run the Children's Centre daycare provision.

Other types of multi-professional teams

Obviously there are other types of multi-professional teams that combine aspects of the two models discussed above and there are teams that may have a larger balance of particular types of practitioners or professionals than others.

However, Brown and White (2006:9) draw on a range of sources to suggest a continuum of types of service delivery structures with autonomous (single agency/professional) working on one extreme and fully-integrated (multi-professional services 'synthesised and co-ordinated') working at the other. The authors suggest that coordinated services are somewhere in between these two extremes.

Brown and White (2006:9) drawing on the work of Atkinson et al (2005) also suggest other models of working together including:

> strategic level working where joint planning and decision-making takes place

> placement schemes where posts cross the organisational divide such as social workers working in primary care divisions

> centre-based service delivery where professionals from different agencies work together in the one site although not necessarily in an integrated manner

> coordinated service delivery where there is a co-ordinator to pull together different services

> multi-agency teams where professionals from different agencies work together on a day-to-day basis as a team

> case management models where a key person has responsibility for ensuring a coordinated service to families.

Frost (2005) characterised partnership working between agencies as a continuum rather than using a model of distinct types of joined-up working. He suggests this continuum would include:

> **co-operation** – agencies are working together but remain separate bodies

> **collaboration** – agencies work and plan jointly and have common goals to provide a comprehensive service

> **coordination** – goals are 'shared and agreed' and agencies work closely together in a 'systematic' way

> **integration** – elements of agencies join into a single organisation.

Cited in Anning et al (2006:6)

The main message is that there is a wide range of different approaches to joint working in children's services. In this chapter, multi-

professional working will be used as a generic term for arrangements for joint working between agencies; multi-agency working will be used to denote agencies working together as in the first definition above; and integrated working will suggest that agencies are 'synthesised and coordinated' at all levels of planning and delivery.

Activity 1

Types and roles

Make a list of all the multi-professional teams you are involved in and have been involved in during your working life. Using one or more of the models above answer the following questions.

1 What type of teams are they?

2 What are your roles in the different teams?

Contexts for multi-professional teams

The ECM website identifies integrated services as a way of delivering a range of different services from a single source and as a context for multi-professional teams (ECM, 2007b). Integrated services that have been recently developed in line with the ECM agenda are Children's Centres and extended schools. These act as centres (or hubs) for the provision of a range of services to children and families, minimising the difficulties they may face in accessing services and providing for rapid referral between services. The ethos is to provide services to meet the child and family's holistic needs from a 'one-stop shop'. Children's Centres and schools are the obvious bases for integrated service provision as they have contact with the largest numbers of children and families. However, multi-professional teams in both these contexts can be complex. It may be that there is a core team of permanent employees who work in the setting and other more peripheral staff who work for home agencies but deliver services from the setting, who together constitute a multi-agency team. The core team may be a multi-disciplinary team in itself and may include recruited and seconded staff.

For an **extended school team**, the core team is made up of school staff, including teachers, teaching assistants, learning mentors and administrative and support staff. However, the team also includes speech therapists and physiotherapists who work part-time in the school but are employed by their home agency. There is also a family support worker who is seconded to the school and an adult education coordinator shared between this and another school, and a number of adult education workers who work part-time in the school.

There are many other contexts for multi-professional working, located in services for children in need; children with disabilities; and children with specific medical conditions amongst others. Early Years practitioners may work in a range of roles in multi-professional teams of different types and in different contexts across their working life. It is important that you ensure that you have the skills and ability to work effectively in a range of types of teams and the flexibility to belong to more than one team at a time.

The next section discusses the advantages and challenges of multi-professional working to help you consider the reasons why working in multi-professional teams is a key characteristic of Early Years service delivery and the difficulties you may face in working in this way.

Advantages and challenges of multi-professional teamwork

Measuring and defining the advantages

The key question is why work in multi-professional rather than single-agency teams? It is clear that effective multi-professional teamwork can be complex and difficult to achieve and that there are considerable barriers to establishing multi-professional teams and supporting their development.

There is a range of evidence drawn from a number of evaluations and research projects around multi-professional services which have been cited to support the view that joint working is more effective and a better use of resources than single-agency work.

Benefits of multi-agency working

Read the section on the ECM website that outlines some of the evidence that supports multi-agency approaches. The URL is listed at the end of this chapter.

One of the key areas of evidence has been the outcomes of child death inquiry reports which have documented failure to share information and coordinate services effectively as a key factor in child deaths for over 30 years. This 'negative evidence' suggests that if poor communication and coordination of services are factors in failure to prevent child deaths then better 'working together' will reduce the risks to children. This view is supported by Laming's (2003) report into the circumstances surrounding the death of Victoria Climbie. However, Brown and White (2006) comment on the difficulties of establishing robust evidence to link particular ways of working with improved outcomes and suggest that as joined-up working becomes the norm, there needs to be models and frameworks for evaluating these approaches that provide this evidence. They acknowledge that to achieve effective service delivery through multi-professional approaches, there are usually a range of barriers which need to be overcome. As it is agreed that multi-professional working requires time, effort and resources to achieve they argue that:

setting up and making partnerships work requires significant investment in time and resources and needs to be justified in terms of the benefits such partnerships deliver.

Brown and White (2006:13)

However, measuring outcomes and identifying success factors for multi-professional working can be difficult, because it is sometimes not clear what is expected in terms of better outcomes (What are we measuring?) or how all improvements can be measured (How do we measure?). For example, not all improvements may be numerically quantifiable, but may still be very significant. Brown and White (2006) also found that some research focused mostly on the processes and not the outcomes of joint working so that it was unclear whether the outcomes were enhanced by multi-professional approaches or not. They also argued that some of the financial benefits of integrated working are hard to measure as the costs of setting up integrated working and the benefits of improved outcomes may be difficult to measure and there is no control group to judge what would have happened differently if integrated work had not been introduced. In addition, ascribing improved outcomes to the introduction of integrated working can be difficult as there are a multiplicity of variables at work. Sloper (2004) suggested that there is little evidence as yet about the effectiveness of inter-agency work in terms of outcomes for children and cost-effectiveness.

Another factor is identifying at what stage outcomes can be measured. One study cited by Brown and White (2006) particularly highlighted the timescales needed for the benefits of multi-professional work to be apparent. Webb and Vuillamy (2004) found that inter-agency work to reduce permanent exclusions from school did not show positive results until after the first year of the project. This is significant in our understanding of multi-professional working and the expectations we can have of working in this way.

Despite these reservations and the need for continuing efforts to establish a robust evidence base for joint working, there is a strong and general belief that joint working will be more effective than single-agency working in meeting young children's needs. Halsey et al (2006) found that multi-professional working in Behaviour and Education Support teams (BESTs) not only benefited children and parents by providing a more responsive, holistic service to children and parents, but that staff working within the team also learned new ways of working and a better understanding of each other's roles. Brown and White (2006) and ECM (2007c) both cite Atkinson et al's (2002) findings which outline the benefits of multi-agency working. ECM (2007c) summarise these as:

➤ access to services not previously available, and a wider range of services

➤ easier or quicker access to services or expertise

➤ improved educational attainment and better engagement in education

➤ early identification and intervention

➤ better support for parents

➤ children's needs addressed more appropriately

➤ better quality services

➤ reduced need for more specialist services.

Sloper (2004) found that coordination of services where a multiplicity of agencies are involved benefited families through better access, less stress and more positive relationships with service providers. Fitzgerald and Kay (2008:5) summarised some of the more general benefits of 'working together' as follows.

➤ A streamlined process to record family details.

➤ A reduction in the number of practitioners that work with each family.

- Opportunities for practitioners to work in partnership to ensure an efficient response to the individual needs of each family.

- A more efficient approach to meeting with the family to support initial assessment and provide ongoing support.

- The potential to share information in a more coherent and efficient way.

- A coordinated response from practitioners that ensures that the information and support given to each family is consistent and supportive.

- The opportunity to share workload and avoid duplicating assessments, visits and support.

- The opportunity for practitioners from different professional backgrounds to work together and learn from each other.

- Additional opportunities for practitioners to develop skills to offer holistic support to families.

The implications of these findings are that families, children and professionals can all benefit from multi-professional working. However, it is also recognised that establishing and maintaining joint-working arrangements can be very costly in terms of time and energy and may not always be experienced as positive by stakeholders involved. It should not be assumed that multi-professional working will always be the most effective way of planning and delivering services to children, without robust evidence to support this view. The next section looks at the challenges of joint working and how some of these have been met.

Challenges to effective joint working

Organisational and professional cultures

Organisational and professional differences in service goals, understandings of children and families and professional purposes are frequently cited as a possible barrier to integrated working is the difference in organisational cultures between partner agencies and professionals. These differences may be evident in the following range of areas.

- Jargon, terminology or 'language' used to describe and discuss aspects of the organisation's work can differ significantly between professionals creating barriers to effective communication. Aubrey (2007:99) found that the majority of staff in her study felt the need for a 'common language across professional groups' although concerns were expressed about the difficulties of achieving this. In addition, the study found that many of the staff involved felt this 'language' should be one that service users could also understand.

- Traditional suspicions or even hostilities between groups of professionals based on stereotypes of other's roles and behaviour. These may be deep-rooted and based on the long-term separation of agencies in terms of service planning and delivery.

- Hierarchical issues between professionals, in which some professionals assume precedence in terms of their professional views, opinions and judgments to the detriment of other team members.

- The aims and purposes of the service and those working within it, for example the aim of education services is to improve all children's educational attainments. The aim of health professionals with young children is to support healthy physical and psychological development. Professional goals may not only differ, but may at times conflict. Although there is now a single Children and Young Person's Plan in each local authority, agencies may have different views and approaches to achieving these and priorities may still vary between agencies.

- There may be lack of clarity of roles and responsibilities in multi-professional working which may cause anxiety and stress among those professionals who are unclear about their role or who fear that they will lose their specialist contribution or who do not know what the boundaries of their role are; for example some staff are struggling with the responsibility of completing Common Assessments as assessment may not have been a regular part of their role previously.

Structural issues

Some of the difficulties faced in establishing effective multi-professional working are rooted in the structures and arrangements established to support that working. If the basic structures do not promote effective multi-professional working then even professionals willing to work in that way may have difficulties in overcoming these barriers. Structural issues can include the following.

➤ Issues about the location of team members and the co-terminosity of geographically based services, for example where some team members may work in different geographical areas to others; where some or all team members may not be based together; where some team members may have to work with more than one multi-professional team because of mismatched boundaries; where some team members stay on familiar home 'turf' whereas others have to uproot.

➤ The nature and composition of the multi-professional team and the professional backgrounds of the staff in the team. Large, complex teams may pose a challenge in terms of the lines of accountability and clarity of roles and responsibilities of each professional.

➤ Difficulties in sharing budgets effectively because of ring-fencing, other financial commitments or lack of funds, for example multi-agency training groups reported difficulties in budget-sharing because of the cost of single-agency training commitments; voluntary and community groups may struggle to be involved because of poorer, more unstable funding.

➤ Lack of time and commitment to supporting and training groups to work together in multi-professional teams, for example the assumption identified in some areas that new types of working groups can 'just get on with it', rather than be involved in committed, sustained multi-professional team building.

➤ Differing levels of commitment to joined-up services from different agencies, for example some agencies may have more status and ability to fight to maintain single-agency services than others.

➤ Variations in pay and conditions between agencies that may impact on the individual worker's experience; for example some workers being seconded to multi-professional teams to avoid loss of pay and conditions, which may raise issues of conflicting commitments; a split in managerial and supervisory responsibility for some workers; hostilities between staff who perceive themselves doing a similar role but for inferior pay and conditions.

➤ Staff development opportunities, training and qualifications. These may vary substantially between staff in a multi-professional team with funding available for some and not others and different qualification and progression structures for different professionals. Team members may be concerned that being seconded to a multi-professional team away from their home agency may negatively impact on their promotion chances within the home agency hierarchies.

➤ Leadership and management of multi-professional teams can be problematic as the manager will not share a professional background with all team members (this aspect is discussed in more depth below).

➤ Timescales which have forced a pace of change that may not be easily sustainable and which may have resulted in compromised structures and lack of genuine evaluation of progress.

➤ Conflicting demands of the multi-professional team and home agency that may affect some staff. This may be in terms of time commitments; values; goals and objectives of the service; or ways of working with children and families. Aubrey (2007) suggested that differences in focus on preventative versus crisis intervention work could be an area of difference between agencies.

The difficulties of establishing effective multi-professional working are well documented because they continue to be a cause for concern. However, it is important to remember that in many cases, multi-professional working is relatively new compared to decades of single-agency service planning and delivery. The Sure Start evaluation emphasised that it takes time to establish different ways of working and that embedding new cultures and approaches cannot be achieved overnight. Aubrey's (2007) study of four integrated centres confirmed that staff felt time to establish services was 'essential'.

Much of the available information focuses on the difficulties experienced by multi-professional teams in establishing effective working arrangements rather than the barriers multi-professional teams may pose for service users. It is possible that multi-professional work may, in some circumstances, detract from effective service delivery because of the time and effort such teams may need to put into coordinating different professional needs and views. There may also be more elaborate funding arrangements associated with multi-professional working which may require more time to manage, and in situations where staff time is split between home agency and multi-professional team there may be additional stresses to deal with.

In the next sections, strategies to establish effective multi-professional teams and the required skills and attributes for leadership in this context will be discussed.

Developing effective multi–professional teams

Simply bringing a group of professionals from different agencies together and calling them a 'team' will not guarantee integrated working.
Rushmore and Pallis (2002) as cited in Brown and White (2006:19–20)

Contextual issues

There are a number of issues that need to be considered, in order to understand the aspects of teamwork under discussion. First of all, there is a wide range of literature on teamwork in the range of children's services developed in all of the relevant disciplines. This literature focuses on the required personal attributes, skills and behaviour of team members and leaders in order to achieve effective teamwork. The terminology and focus differs between disciplines. There is also a significant body of generic leadership and management literature, which explores organisational issues for effective leadership and management, theoretical issues and skills and attributes for leadership. In more recent years there has been a newer body of team and leadership literature in the Early Years, drawing to some extent on the established theories and research but also building a new body of knowledge and understanding about leadership in Early Years contexts. However, this body of literature is still relatively new and research into the role of Early Years practitioners in multi-professional teams is still relatively limited.

It is also important to remember that multi-professional teams involving Early Years practitioners may include both Early Years professionals and children's workforce professionals from across the field. In this section, it will be assumed that Early Years practitioners are involved in multi-professional teams which include a wide range of children's services professionals.

Key success factors

It is becoming clearer that there is no one formula for establishing and supporting multi-professional teams and that there are many strategies for achieving effective joined-up working. However, Brown and White (2006) draw on a range of evidence to summarise some of the key success factors. These include:

- clarity of aims and objectives that are understood by all parties
- clearly identified roles and responsibilities
- commitment from both senior management and frontline staff
- strong leadership
- good systems of communication and information sharing (Sloper, 2004)
- structures for joint planning
- joint training in new ways of working (Sloper, 2004)
- appropriate support for staff
- recruitment of the right people with the right skills
- shared resources
- robust monitoring and evaluation of integrated working
- organisations that support teamwork, flexibility, open flows of communication and promote a shared vision are better able to delivery positive outcomes for clients and provide more integrated services.

Adapted from Brown and White (2006:19)

They also go on to suggest that there must be support from the organisations involved at both strategic and operational levels in order to ensure the success of joint working. Moran et al (2007) state that effectiveness of multi-agency teams also depends on clear protocols and methods for reviewing these; informal as well as formal communication between team members; financial support for the team and agreed timetabling for developments in the service.

Activity 2

Effectiveness

Look back at Activity 1 and in respect of at least one of the teams you identified, use the checklist of key success factors above to consider how effective the team is in respect of these.

Chandler (2006:135–136) also points out that the initial guidance for children's centres (DfES, 2003:11) emphasised that perceptions of the multi-professional team were significant aspects also. The guidance suggests that it is important that users of the service perceive 'cohesive and comprehensive services' and that the team members also perceive themselves as having 'a shared identity, purpose and common working practices' with the team as a whole.

Reflecting on the list of key success factors, it is clear that there are a number of important linked strategies to ensure these are in place.

1 A good communication system within the team and wider organisation to both disseminate information about the aims and objectives of the service and the focus of the current tasks at hand, and also to clarify the underpinning ethos and principles guiding service planning and delivery and the individual team members' roles and responsibilities. These things also need to be made transparent to service users as well.

2 Clear processes and structures to support effective, shared planning, delivery and evaluation of progress towards service objectives, including joint training of staff from different disciplines, individual support for staff, a good standard of induction of new staff and a transparent management structure.

3 Support for multi-professional team development through knowledgeable and experienced leadership and the commitment of the wider organisation.

4 Considered recruitment processes that ensure that the right staff from the right backgrounds are incorporated in the team, bearing in mind that what constitutes the 'right' person will vary between teams and at different times.

Developing these linked strategies for building effective multi-professional teams may be more difficult in some contexts than others. For example, factors that hinder these processes may include:

➤ where team membership is determined externally and unwilling members are co-opted into multi-professional teams

➤ where teams are established through complex negotiations within which some potential groups are more powerful and able to opt out than others, resulting in team membership that is unbalanced or skewed in terms of professions represented

➤ where there is weak, inexperienced or unwilling leadership and/or lack of genuine commitment to team-building processes

➤ where the immediate demands of or stresses on the team preclude a chance to build the team before trying to meet aims and objectives

➤ where there are structural issues such as problems with team location, lack of time together, poor communication and unclear processes which prevent team members from truly understanding their own and others' roles and responsibilities.

There is often no easy remedy for these problems and one of the key factors in building effective multi-professional teams – time – may be the most elusive factor of all.

Characteristics of effective multi-professional team members

As with all types of teams, it is the quality of the mix and blend of team members that ensures the success or not of the team. Multi-professional team members need to have some specific characteristics to contribute well to complex and sometimes stressful team-building processes.

Values

Chandler suggests that staff working in multi-disciplinary teams bring three dimensions to the multi-professional team.

1 Their personal life history and what has motivated them to work in their chosen profession.

2 Their professional background, training and experience.

3 The agency in which they work and what the beliefs, values, aims and objectives of the agency are.

Chandler (2006:142)

These dimensions are important because they may determine the ability of the team member to engage effectively with multi-professional team processes. These dimensions will have had a strong influence on the value-base the individual has developed in terms of their work with children and families. It may be that this value-base differs at times to the values central to the multi-professional team and this can be problematical.

Activity 3

Development of your beliefs and values

Using Chandler's three dimensions mentioned above as a guide, note down the influences on the development of your beliefs and values about the work you do with children and families.

1 What factors/events were significant in the development of your beliefs and values?

2 Are these beliefs and values in line with the central ethos of the team(s) you work in now or are there differences?

3 Share your findings with a colleague in your team and seek his/her views.

It may be helpful to do this activity as a timeline starting with the first things you can remember about wanting to work with children.

As such, Chandler (2006) suggests that it is the degree of commonality between the team members in terms of their values and beliefs that is an important success factor for multi-professional teams. Shared beliefs and values will contribute to cohesive team thinking and behaviour.

Flexibility

Working in multi-disciplinary teams requires developing different ideas and understandings of colleagues from other disciplinary backgrounds, concepts of children and childhood and approaches to work. In addition, multi-professional teamworkers need to be able to learn about and understand aspects of children's needs and how these are met from the perspective of other professional roles while at the same time maintaining their own specialist knowledge, experience and role. Aubrey (2007:102) found that while 'The vast majority recognised the need to go beyond existing roles to work in new ways,' this was an ongoing challenge to staff in integrated centres and was difficult to achieve.

Flexibility is a key characteristic of successful multi-professional team members because working in such teams requires the ability to absorb and make sense of new knowledge and come to new understandings and to recognise one's own role within these. Team members also need to be flexible because they will need to learn new professional jargon and 'languages' and to accommodate the different ways of working with, thinking and discussing children and families within their team. However, flexibility does not mean abandoning one's own views and beliefs about children and families. It means maintaining these but being willing to learn from and share knowledge and understandings with others, hopefully coming to new shared approaches encompassing the different ethos' and viewpoints represented.

Reflective practitioners – professional confidence and competence

Multi-disciplinary teams need to be made up of well-qualified and trained professionals and practitioners who have the experience and skills to become part of a new learning community through reflection, sharing and co-creating new meanings to their understandings of the work they are doing with their co-members. Many multi-professional teams are still breaking new ground in their approaches to meeting the needs of children and families. Time to reflect on how this is best achieved and on the work that is being done is an important part of ensuring multi-professional teams deliver better quality services as expected. Team members need to be individuals who see their own learning processes as ongoing and who are comfortable being part of and contributing to a learning community. They need to be confident and competent professionals in their own right, but also have the ability and willingness to continue to learn within and beyond their own discipline.

Skills for teamwork

In addition to specific attributes for multi-professional teamwork, all team members need generic skills for teamwork which may include:

➤ good communication skills, especially listening skills

➤ positive approaches to sharing and resolving different viewpoints and beliefs

➤ a constructive, problem-solving approach to achieving work goals

➤ a strong commitment to other team members, a supportive collegial approach and empathy, tact and warmth towards others.

Leadership and management of multi-professional teams

The importance of effective leadership cannot be overstated, and yet the number of texts on leadership in the Early Years has only really grown significantly in the last decade (see the end of the chapter for further reading). Theorising Early Years leadership through a range of models can support a deeper understanding of how leadership in Early Years contexts is developing. However, Aubrey (2007) identifies a lack of research into Early Years leadership as a significant issue in learning more about effective practice in this area. In addition, the range of types of Early Years settings in which multi-professional work is taking place means that a single concept of leadership may not suffice. Leaders of multi-professional teams in Early Years settings may be working in Children's Centres, extended school provision, independent nurseries, pre-schools and a range of other contexts. Moreover, Early Years practitioners may have leadership responsibilities on a range of other multi-professional teams including 'teams around the child' where children have special needs or disabilities and child protection conferences.

Leadership and management are not necessarily the same thing in Early Years contexts. Many Early Years practitioners have leadership responsibilities without holding management posts. As such, leadership is no longer just the province of managers, but is a set of skills and behaviours that most Early Years practitioners need to develop. In the current climate leaders need to be able to support teams through periods of uncertainty and change and to develop new processes and services to meet the 'joined-up' agenda at the same time. This is a significant challenge for the Early Years workforce, in which a focus on leadership skills is relatively recent. One of the key issues is what sort of concepts underpin leadership in the Early Years and whether the existing body of literature is sufficient to support the development of a theory base for this area.

The contribution of leadership theories

Many of the theories used to discuss leadership in the Early Years have been drawn or adapted from leadership theory developed in management in other contexts. However, Rodd cites Kagan (1994) in suggesting that most existing theories generally do not provide an adequate model for Early Years leadership.

These approaches ignore important features of early childhood settings, which are the emergence of the multiple, shared and joint forms of leadership conventionally preferred by women; the need for intimacy, flexibility and individualisation of organisational strategies and processes; and an ethos of collaboration and collective success for all.

Rodd (2006:10)

Newer thinking suggests that there are unique characteristics of Early Years leaders that shape the leadership role, not the least of these being that the vast majority of leaders in Early Years settings are female. Savage and Leeson (2007) summarise the main types of leadership and management models as those relating to:

➤ **the personal characteristics of the leader (traits)** – implies that there are a set of characteristics which a leader requires and the possession of these would make an individual fit to be a leader

➤ **behavioural or leadership style theories** – leaders differ according to their actions and behaviour in their role, usually in terms of the extent to which they dominate or work with the team

➤ **contextual theories** – the style of leadership used needs to be relevant to the context of the leadership role and leaders need to be able to adapt to different styles as the context changes

➤ **transactional and transformational theories** – 'getting things done' and 'visionary leadership' both of which have a place in current leadership contexts.

Adapted from Savage and Leeson (2007:148–51)

Savage and Leeson (2007:151) suggest that transformational leadership is the most relevant model in Early Years contexts as it is 'about empowering people to learn and seek change and improvement, not about controlling them'. Rodd (2006) also suggests that concepts of participatory or shared leadership are significant in the Early Years context as is the idea of transformational leadership. These models suggest a leadership style in Early Years contexts that is participatory, in which the leader works cooperatively with the team rather than exerts control over them and in which the leader seeks to support and empower team members to effectively fulfil their roles, rather than 'manage' them to do this. However, it is important to remember that in multi-professional teams there may be team members who have come from different professional backgrounds and who may be more used to and comfortable with different leadership styles and approaches than those prevalent in Early Years contexts. This creates a significant challenge to leaders in Early Years multi-professional teams, exemplified by the need to synthesise leadership approaches drawn from both Early Years and multi-professional models.

The leadership role

Leaders in this context need to consider a range of aspects in order to effectively fulfil their role.

1   Determine the structure of the team, and the roles and responsibilities of each member of the team. This may include determining the lines of accountability and supervision, the management structure and possibly identifying different types of membership within the team.

2   Clarifying the team goals/tasks/objectives and ensuring these are fully understood by the whole team.

3   Building the team in terms of supporting the development of a team identity and common ethos, a common understanding of the team's purposes and goals and effective working practices to ensure the team functions well to achieve their goals, including a communication strategy.

4   Ensuring individuals within the team are supported in their roles and are integrated into the team.

5   Ensuring that other stakeholders (children, parents, wider agencies) understand the team membership, goals and purposes and that the team establish effective communication with other stakeholders.

In the next sections these aspects will be examined in more detail. However, it is important to note that leading change has not been included as a specific role and that it is assumed that change is central to the Early Years leadership task and that all the other aspects of leadership rest on the principle that change will be taking place. The traditional concept of managing change can suggest that this is a discrete task that is performed resulting in a new status quo being established until the next change comes along. However, it is more realistic in the current climate to accept that all leadership in Early Years contexts is focused on change.

The team structure

Leaders need to have a clear understanding of who is in the team and who is not, who is within their line management responsibility and who is managed elsewhere, who is a core member of the team and who is peripheral (as in only part of the team for part of the time)

and who is supervised by other professionals because of their specific roles. This may sound complex and often is. One of the stressors for multi-professional teams is that the answers to these questions may not initially be clear to either the leader or the team members. Anning et al (2006) suggest that many staff on multi-professional teams are temporary, seconded or only work part-time on that team as agencies limit the funding they are prepared to commit. In this situation, staff may see themselves as peripheral or they may be only partially committed to the team goals and objectives. Aubrey (2007:97) found that there was significant concerns about the 'tensions and problems' caused by staff being managed by their home agency among respondents in her study of integrated centres.

As such, leaders need to consider who is actually the leader and who are the team. Ovretveit (1993) suggested five different types of multi-professional teams.

1 **Fully managed team** – the team leader leads and manages all the team

2 **The coordinated team** – the team leader manages most of the team but some of the team are supervised by others in their specialist roles, for example a Children's Centre where social workers and health visitors retain supervisory links with their home agencies to support their specialist roles.

3 **The core and extended team** – the core team is managed by the team leader and other peripheral members are part of the team for some of the time but are managed within their own agency, for example an extended school where the school-based team are led by the head but other staff such as speech therapists work on the team for part of their time but are managed and supervised within their home agency.

4 **The joint accountability team** – the team members share tasks out between them including leadership but each

member is accountable to their home agency, for example the Child Protection Case Conference where the members take responsibility for different aspects of safeguarding the child but remain managed by their home agency.

5 **The network association** – different professional working together but not formally designated as a team and all accountable to their home agency, for example the 'team around the child' with complex disabilities.

Adapted from Ovretveit (1993) cited in Anning et al (2006:27)

This model is useful in helping us recognise that leadership of multi-professional teams is very variable in context and that these types of teams can be complex. In some of these types of teams individual workers may be managed by one leader, supervised within their home agency and accountable to more than one team.

Leadership task

The team leader has responsibility for seeking answers to these questions and for trying to clarify these for team members to reduce this stress.

Activity 4

Team diagrams

1 Think about a multi-professional team you are part of.

2 Draw a diagram to represent the management structures, lines of accountability and support structures for each team member.

Are these simple or are these complex? Are there some lines that you are uncertain about? Share this diagram with another team member or manager and seek clarification if required.

The team purpose

Multi-professional teams are often brought together for specific reasons to achieve particular goals and objectives. However, differences in the team members' professional training and backgrounds may lead them to interpret these goals in different ways and this may lead to confusion or even conflict between team members as to what the priorities are. Anning et al (2006:97) suggest that ideological differences between team members in multi-professional teams can result in different understandings of what the issues are for children and families and what approaches should be used to support them. The authors go on to state:

the important point is that these different professional voices have a right to be heard within multi-professional teamwork. In fact the central argument for joined-up working is that the multiple perspectives enrich the treatments offered to clients.

Leadership task

The team leader needs to share their own view of the team goals and objectives widely within the team. The leader also needs to provide opportunities for team members to share their own views on this within the team and to start to modify and clarify goals through a process of reflection and discussion. It is important that professional differences are recognised and acknowledged in this process and that team members have time and opportunity to air these and start to seek common ground.

Team building

Team building is an ongoing process, and is a strong determinant in the extent to which teams can work effectively together. Team building involves dedicated time for team members to share ideas and concepts about their aims and goals, and the processes by which they will reach these. There also need to be clear lines of communication between team members and between team members and

the leader. Team building and communication strategies could include:

➤ regular formal and informal meetings with opportunity for team members to reflect on the goals and tasks of the team and how best to achieve these

➤ joint training in respect of specific aspects of the team objectives and strategies to meet these

➤ written communications including briefings, newsletters, announcements

➤ relationship building activities such as social events, team rituals around birthdays or other significant times, away days

➤ acceptance of conflict as a normal part of team behaviour, but also strategies to ensure that this is not personalised and is resolved

➤ positive feedback on all team members from the leader

➤ working processes that support individual team members and create opportunities for team members to work together.

Leadership task

The team leader needs to be able to manage the team functions and tasks to make space for team building as a priority. This needs to take place on a regular basis and to involve all team members. It needs to focus on building knowledge of each others' roles and approaches to children and families and to developing and maintaining positive and respectful relationships between team members.

Supporting individual team members

Moving into multi-professional teams can be disorientating and team members may suffer a sense of loss over their previous working situation (Anning et al, 2006). Team leaders need to be sensitive to this aspect of their leadership role and ensure that team members have a sense of their place in the team and a clear understanding of their own roles and responsibilities in the processes to achieve team goals and objectives. Staff who are only committed to the multi-professional team for part of their working time may have particular difficulties conceptualising their own and others' roles in the team or feeling part of the team. Aubrey (2007:97) found that 'Staff not being clear about their roles was considered a concern', in her study of four integrated centres.

Leadership task

Establishing strategies to support individual team members, clarify their roles and ensure that they have 'membership' of the team and are committed to the team's goals and objectives. These strategies need to include formal meetings such as supervision and appraisal and informal meetings to establish rapport and share concerns and successes. Individual staff may also need support to determine how they can contribute to team functioning and any barriers there may be to achieving this. Leaders can be challenged by insufficient knowledge of other professional backgrounds and agendas in supporting team members from different disciplines to their own.

Communicating with other stakeholders

One of the issues that has arisen from multi-professional working arrangements is the need to explain and clarify what this means to other stakeholders, including children, parents and other agencies and professionals. There may be a tendency for multi-professional teams to become inward-looking as they seek to develop their team and overcome barriers to this process. However, working with other agencies, parents and communities continues to be a significant part of the task of teams in Early Years contexts. As such, multi-professional team leaders need to ensure that the structure, purposes and goals of the team are communicated effectively to other stakeholders including parents and children. Effective engagement of parents and children means involving them in decision-making processes, consulting them and seeking and acting on feedback about the processes and outcomes of service delivery. In terms of other stakeholders and the external 'world', Rodd (2006) suggests that leaders have a responsibility to represent both their team and children in general in broader contexts than their immediate work setting. Traditionally, Early Years leaders have had a low profile and possibly lacked confidence in developing their ability to influence policy and determine the goals and objectives of Early Years services. However, in the current climate of policy change and new ways of configuring and delivering services to young children, leaders have a significant responsibility to ensure their voices are heard.

Leadership task

Establishing and developing clear lines of communication with parents and strategies for involving them in decision-making, recognising that parents are not an homogenous group and there will need to be multiple opportunities and approaches to engaging them. Strategies for listening to children's views need to be established also and leaders have a responsibility to ensure that staff have the necessary skills and commitment to be effective in this aspect of the work. Early Years leaders also need to develop a public face, advocating for children and seeking to influence policy and practice locally and possibly nationally. Rodd (2006) suggests that this advocacy role can be achieved by:

➤ participation in professional organisations

➤ research and writing

➤ networking with other professionals

➤ becoming political and using the media.

From Rodd (2006: 234–9)

Characteristics of Early Years leaders

Although the traditional trait theories (that leaders have particular attributes that make them fit for leadership) have been to some extent superseded in this field by transformational theories which suggest any practitioner can have or develop leadership ability, there are some personal attributes and skills that leaders may benefit from possessing or developing.

Communication skills

In these complex contexts the ability to communicate effectively is a key skill for leaders. Effective communicators:

➤ communicate to clarify and extend understanding for all involved

➤ are responsive to the communication needs of others

➤ have a range of communication modes and styles to suit different others

➤ are confident and assertive in their communications without impinging on the rights of others

➤ manage their communication to avoid inappropriate emotional expression, unconsidered responses and thoughtless replies

➤ make time for others to communicate with them, seek non-communicators and support them to share, listen carefully and respond appropriately

➤ share personal information where appropriate, use humour to develop relationships and are warm and friendly to others.

Reflective skills

Increasingly, development of leaders has focused on their ability to understand their own behaviour and motivations and reflect on their own actions as a learning process. Reflective leaders:

➤ take time to consider their own actions and behaviour and use these reflections to modify and amend their future actions

➤ seek feedback on their leadership style and effectiveness and use this feedback to develop more effective practice

➤ seek training and development opportunities to support them in their leadership role

➤ use research and academic writing to develop their understanding of practice issues and the multi-professional leadership role

➤ ensure that they have their own support and mentoring needs met outside the team context

➤ encourage and support other team members to develop reflective practice and to seek and take advantage of training and development opportunities.

Flexibility and accommodating skills

Change has become the norm in children's services contexts, challenging the ability of all practitioners and professionals to keep abreast of new demands, ways of working and relationships. Leaders need to be flexible and able to meet the demands of change and support their teams to do the same. Flexible leaders:

➤ keep informed about new developments in policy and practice and ensure that they consider the implications of these within and beyond the setting or context

➤ network with others to maintain knowledge and understanding of the external context

➤ support their teams to understand new developments and their meaning for the setting or context

➤ are open to new approaches to the work and new ways of conceptualising the issues involved

➤ develop their understanding of the different team members' roles and professional backgrounds and look for the opportunities this variety can offer

➤ recognise that change may be a challenge to the team as whole and individuals in particular and can be supportive without losing site of new opportunities presented by change.

Professional skills

Leaders need to be able to support their team in their day-to-day work and their understanding of the tasks at hand and how to be effective in their roles. They need to give leadership in terms of effective practice, without impinging on the expertise and skills of others. Leaders demonstrate professional skills through:

➤ modelling effective practice with children, adults and other professionals

- disseminating information about the policies and working practices of the context or setting to all stakeholders
- supporting other team members where changes in practice are needed
- conveying the ethos of the setting or context in a variety of ways and supporting other team members to do this
- modelling good teamwork and team behaviour by being supportive and constructive in their relationships with team members
- learning from team members with different disciplinary backgrounds, filling gaps in their own knowledge and understanding and being willing to learn from others.

Support for developing multi-professional leadership capacity

Several authors on multi-professional leadership and Early Years leadership issues note that there are limited training and qualification opportunities for those involved in leadership roles in Early Years contexts, leaving some leaders in this field 'significantly under-prepared for their complex leadership role' (Aubrey, 2007: 13). In addition, there has been a lack of emphasis on this area of development until recent years and training opportunities and leadership capacity in the area remain limited but growing. However, the importance of effective leadership in this context cannot be underestimated. Rodd (2006:259) states:

The role of the leader and the manner in which that role is carried out has become central to the provision of high-quality services and to determining the level of professionalism that is accorded to the early childhood field. It is no longer acceptable for practitioners to be unprepared to exercise leadership effectively.

In addition, Aubrey (2007) points out that the challenge for Early Years leaders is to continue to improve quality in a policy context that is promoting increases in capacity for all children. As such, there is an ongoing need to build Early Years leadership capacity in the workforce and to ensure that this is based on multi-professional leadership qualifications and training to support leaders effectively in

the current context and to raise the profile of the field.

Qualifications and training

The National College of School Leadership (NCSL) has established the National Professional Qualification in Integrated Centre Leadership (NPQICL) course for Children's Centre leaders to support multi-professional leadership development. This course is aimed at supporting Children's Centre leaders to become reflective, flexible, confident and informed leaders able to meet the demands of changing team structures and ways of working. However, it is aimed only at Children's Centre leaders and as such reaches a limited number of practitioners in the field.

The Early Years Professional Status (EYPS) programme includes a focus on leadership issues and the practitioners achieving this status are assumed to take leadership roles in their setting. However, this programme is not available to all Early Years practitioners, requiring entry qualifications at Foundation Degree or degree level. In addition, Savage and Leeson (2007) comment that there may be insufficient theorising of leadership roles for the qualification to equip practitioners for effective leadership.

Sector-endorsed Foundation Degree courses in Early Years and similar subjects are a route into higher education for practitioners wishing to study part-time and continue working. It is common now to find that leadership modules are part of the core provision on Foundation Degrees in Early Years, reflecting the need to strengthen leadership skills in the Early Years sector across the workforce. These courses may be more widely available to practitioners, particularly where local authorities are willing to give financial support. However, there may be wide variations between courses in terms of the content and extent of leadership development, and the concepts that underpin this. Similarly, Honours Degrees in Early Years or Early Childhood are aimed at developing a graduate workforce in the Early Years sector. Many of these courses offer the opportunity to study leadership and management and to progress into leadership roles in Early Years settings.

Local authority development programmes and training opportunities may also be available to leaders. Access to, funding and availability of these may vary considerably between authorities. However, increasingly clusters or families of settings are supporting their own development through sharing the costs of training across a range of issues.

There is a substantial case for extending and clarifying leadership training and development opportunities in the Early Years sector and to making these opportunities available to a much wider section of the workforce. The Children's Workforce Development Council (CWDC) has a remit to develop the whole of the children's workforce including leadership and management aspects. However, a much clearer qualification and progression structure is needed across the children's workforce in order to achieve this. Previous efforts to clarify the qualifications structure have encountered difficulties with the sheer volume and complexity of existing qualifications. The Integrated Qualifications Framework promised for 2010 is an attempt to make the qualification structure clearer and to provide more opportunities for movement between different sectors in the children's workforce and for progression to higher level posts. It should enable qualifications in one sector of the children's workforce to become transferable to another.

Conclusion

Leaders of multi-professional teams in the Early Years sector face a number of significant challenges. Concepts and theories of leadership in Early Years are in a relatively early stage of development in themselves and yet as increasingly 'leadership' becomes synonymous with 'multi-professional leadership' new ways of viewing and configuring this role need to be developed. In addition, multi-professional approaches need to draw on a more robust evidence base in order to claim cost-effectiveness and improved quality of services to children and families. The demands of establishing and supporting multi-professional teams are becoming well documented, along with key factors contributing to success across the wide range of types and context for multi-professional teams in children's services. However, research needs to continue to recognise the diversity of contexts and settings and to reflect the different needs of teams within these. Finally, training and qualifications for leadership in multi-professional teams in Early Years services remains limited to a small sector of the workforce although the need to develop capacity in this area is growing.

Despite this, there is a growing body of research to suggest that Early Years leaders can be drawn successfully from across the workforce and that these leaders may be developing specific unique approaches to meet the needs of the services they work in.

How to move on in your research

Anning, A., Cottrell, D., Frost, N., Green, J. and Robinson, M. (2006), *Developing Multi-professional Teamwork for Integrated Children's Services.* Buckingham: Open University Press

This is one of the most significant pieces of research into multi-professional teamworking in children's services, providing important insights into the workings of such teams and factors which support working together.

Aubrey, C. (2007), *Leading and Managing in the Early Years.* London: Sage

A well-written and interesting piece of research into leadership in Early Years contexts.

Fitzgerald, D. and Kay, J. (2008), *Working Together in Children's Services.* Abingdon: David Fulton

A good initial text on multi-disciplinary service development in children's services.

Rodd, J. (2006) (3rd edition), *Leadership in Early Childhood.* Maidenhead: Open University Press

This continues to be one of the best texts on leadership in the Early Years available, covering a wide range of topics and regularly updated through new editions.

References

Anning, A., Cottrell, D., Frost, N., Green, J. and Robinson, M. (2006), *Developing Multi-professional Teamwork for Integrated Children's Services.* Buckingham: Open University Press

Atkinson, M., Wilkin, A., Stott, A. and Kinder, K. (2001), *Multi-agency Working: An Audit of Activity.* Slough: National Foundation for Educational Research

Atkinson, M., Wilkin, A., Stott, A. and Kinder, K. (2002), *Multi-agency Working: A Detailed Study.* Slough: National Foundation for Educational Research

Aubrey, C. (2007), *Leading and Managing in the Early Years.* London: Sage

Brown, K. and White, K. (2006), *Exploring the Evidence Base for Integrated Children's Services.* Scottish Executive Education Department. Last accessed on 8 January 2008 at http://www.scotland.gov.uk/Resource/Doc/90282/0021746.pdf

Cameron, C. (2003), 'An historical perspective on changing child care policy', in **Brannen, J. and Moss, P. (eds)**, *Rethinking Children's Care.* Buckingham: Open University Press

Chandler, T. (2006), 'Working in multi-disciplinary teams', in **Pugh, G. and Duffy, B. (eds) (4th edition)**, *Contemporary Issues in the Early Years.* London: Sage

DoH (1991), *Working Together Under the Children Act, 1989.* London: HMSO

ECM (2007a), *Every Child Matters: Change for Children Strategic Overview.* Last accessed on 7 January 2008 at http://www.everychildmatters.gov.uk/aims/strategicoverview/

ECM (2007b), *Every Child Matters: Change for Children Multi-Agency: Setting Up Multi-Agency Services.* Last accessed on 7 January 2008 at http://www.everychildmatters.gov.uk/deliveringservices/multiagencyworking/

ECM (2007c), *Every Child Matters: Change for Children Benefits of Multi-Agency Work.* Last accessed on 7 January 2008 at http://www.everychildmatters.gov.uk/deliveringservices/multiagencyworking/benefitsofmultiagency/

Fitzgerald, D. and Kay, J. (2008), *Working Together in Children's Services.* Abingdon: David Fulton

Frost, N. (2005), *Professionalism, Partnership and Joined-up Thinking.* Dartington: Research in Practice

Halsey, K., Gulliver, C., Johnson, A., Martin, K. and Kinder, K. (2006), *Evaluation of Behaviour and Education Support Teams.* London: DfES

Kagan, S. (1994), 'Leadership: Rethinking it – making it happen'. *Young Children*, Vol. 49, No. 5, pp50–54

Laming, H. (2003), *The Victoria Climbié Inquiry Report.* Last accessed on 4 February 2008 at http://www.victoria-climbie-inquiry.org.uk/

Moran, P., Jacobs, C., Bunn, A. and Bifulco, A. (2007), 'Multi-agency working: Implications for an early-intervention social work team'. *Child & Family Social Work*, Vol.12 (2), pp143–51

Ovretveit, J (1993), *Coordinating Community Care: Multidisciplinary Teams and Care Management.* Buckingham: Open University Press

Sloper, P. (2004), 'Facilitators and barriers for co-ordinated multi-agency services'. *Child Care, Health and Development*, Vol. 30 (6), pp571–80

Rodd, J. (2006) (3rd edition), *Leadership in Early Childhood.* Maidenhead: Open University Press

Rushmer, R. and Pallis, G. (2002), 'Inter-professional working: The wisdom of integrated working and the disaster of blurred boundaries'. *Public Money & Management*, 23 (1), pp.59–66

Savage, J. and Leeson, C. (2007), 'Leadership in early childhood settings', in Willan, J., Parker-Rees, R. and Savage, J. (eds) (2nd edition), *Early Childhood Studies.* Exeter: Learning Matters

Webb, R. and Vuillamy, G. (2004), *A Multi-Agency Approach to Reducing Disaffection and Exclusions from School.* DfES Research Report No. 568. University of York

Webb, R. and Vuillamy, G. (2001), 'Joining up the solutions: The rhetoric and practice of inter-agency co-operation'. *Children and Society*, 15, 315–32.

Useful websites

http://www.everychildmatters.gov.uk/deliveringservices/multiagencyworking/benefitsofmultiagency

Section on the ECM website that outlines some of the evidence that supports multi-agency approaches.

16 Research methods
Iain MacLeod-Brudenell

This chapter is designed to develop your skills in understanding the relationship between theory and practice in early childhood studies through focused research. It will encourage you to develop the insights gained in your practice experience and your own personal interests in Early Years.

Recognising and utilising your existing skills in observation and extending these into more formal research skills requires a commitment to being a researcher. What does research entail? What is a researcher? Firstly, research does require an openness of mind. Ideas and values that we hold may be challenged by our research findings. Secondly, a researcher in the field of education and care is usually a practitioner and it would be likely that research forms a basis for professional and personal reflection. This would be followed through with action to enhance practice.

There is a process to effective research, whether it is on a small scale and conducted with one child, or a larger scale survey. Careful organisation, clarity of purpose and recording will help to ensure that your efforts are tangible rather than transitory, or confused in outcome. Ensure that you read through the whole of this chapter before you start working on your research project!

This chapter addresses the following areas:

➤ Research: an overview
➤ Devising a research question
➤ The literature search: accessing information
➤ Planning your research study
➤ Research methods
➤ Using a research diary
➤ Ethical considerations
➤ Approaches to small-scale enquiry
➤ Analysis of data

By undertaking the suggested study within this chapter it is hoped that you will be able to:

1 make informed reflections upon an area you have selected to research

2 tackle an in-depth enquiry of relevant issues with confidence

3 understand how to secure an appropriate body of substantive and relevant knowledge

4 feel confident in formulating the questions you wish to address and implement appropriate means of securing answers to those questions

5 present and evaluate those answers as a means to identifying further questions to pose

6 evaluate the quality of your achievement.

Research: an overview

Research projects are commonly required of students in the second stage of a Foundation Degree course. They may be given any one of a number of different names, including:

➤ extended project
➤ special study
➤ focus study
➤ work-based project
➤ independent study.

Although such projects have different names, they perform the same purpose – to test your ability to conduct a small-scale research project. A focused research project helps you to pursue in greater depth issues that relate to your existing knowledge of younger children.

Some students will have prior experience of undertaking research as part of their courses leading to a Higher National Diploma or an Advanced Diploma in Childcare and Education; for others, this will be an entirely new experience.

Why research?

Research study within an Early Childhood Studies course is designed to enable you to learn, practise and develop a range of research techniques in order to aid your understanding of children.

Opportunities for focused study are usually selected from a personally chosen field of study. This may be an issue of professional interest that has been selected in order to help you to become a better or more effective practitioner, or it may be an area of personal interest that relates to a current and critical issue in early childhood studies.

What will tutors expect of you?

It is usual for students undertaking research studies to be supported but not directed by tutorial staff. They will expect you to be independent and to manage your time effectively. You will be expected to:

➤ have a clear idea of the topic you are researching
➤ develop lines of argument and justify your judgements by demonstrating your ability to present, evaluate, and interpret your research findings
➤ read widely
➤ incorporate references from your reading in your research study.

Glossary of terms

There are many terms used within research, which may be unfamiliar to you. They may appear to be 'jargon' and be unnecessarily complicated. To simplify your first steps in research it may be useful for you to refer to the following glossary of terms. As you gain confidence and extend your reading you will become familiar with the terms and realise just how basic the following explanations are!

Data The information gathered through research.

Epistemology Theorising about knowledge and how we can access it.

Ethics Consideration of possible effects of the research on those you are researching. Research ethics involves being clear about how you research, for example getting informed consent from those you interview, question and research.

Experimental approach A research approach that involves introducing changes.

Experimental design Designing an experiment. This will usually allow you to make at least one change to assess its effects on those you are researching; to control anything that may influence those you are researching; to organise and control the conditions of the experiment.

Field notes The data you gather formally and informally, such as the notes you make when you go out and research.

Focus group conversations A form of group interview in which data is gained from the interaction between participants.

Interpretation The process of drawing meanings from your research.

Interviews Asking questions of those you are researching. These may be structured, using a prescribed list of questions, or unstructured, a more loosely conducted interview where you allow the person you are interviewing to extend their thoughts as they wish.

Longitudinal research This form of research investigates change over a substantial period of time. It allows analysis based on the monitoring and recording of change.

Method The tools of data collection and the techniques used (such as interviews and observations).

Methodology The theoretical approach used to get knowledge through research. The methodology sets out the way of systematically getting knowledge.

Observational approach is one that is conducted with the researcher as an 'outsider'. Observational in this sense means that you do not intervene in the process.

Observation as a research method for eliciting data, finding out information. It can be participatory or non-participatory, structured or non-structured.

Participant observer The researcher can intervene and in this sense it can be experimental.

Praxis Practice informed by theory and theory informed by practice.

Reflexivity Reflexivity is being aware that you may have a bias in your approach to interpreting your research. It is important to be honest and reflect on personal factors which may affect the way you approach your research.

Questionnaire A means of gathering data from research subjects by using written questions, which should be unbiased, focused and carefully chosen.

Reliability The accuracy and consistency of research. Researchers strive to make the research as error-free as possible by using various means to check for accuracy and eliminate possible bias.

Replicating Repeating the experiment. This may happen for various reasons, for example as a means of checking for reliability of evidence or for comparative purposes.

Research methods The techniques you use to gain knowledge.

Sample This usually refers to a group of people who are the subject of research. The sample is taken to represent part of the whole. For example, a group of children in a Year 1 class may be used as the sample in a research project. Your findings may provide data which informs you in a more general way about other children in Year 1.

Triangulation Using, combining and comparing different forms of research method and/or different sources of information to arrive at a fuller understanding of an event.

Validity The endeavour to arrive at an accurate and 'truthful' outcome to the research.

Qualitative and quantitative research methods

There are two approaches that students of care and education are likely to use: qualitative or quantitative research methods. The former is the most frequently used as it enables students to have direct contact with the group that is the focus of the study, using a variety of research methods to gather data. In your reading of other literature on research you will find that each research approach has its supporters and critics. Try to make your own mind up and match the method with what you hope to achieve. We do not all get it right first time! Qualitative researchers are more likely to be concerned with interpreting observed behaviours. Quantitative researchers tend to be more interested in interpreting data gained by measurement.

Quantitative methods

These involve the collection of data that can be analysed statistically.

Supporters of this method argue that its key advantage is that data is objective. There is not necessarily a direct interaction with the group being researched; it is more likely that contact will be fairly formal and regulated. This distance does help to maintain objectivity. In studies of parents or practitioners, statistical data gathered by questionnaire may be very useful. All of the studies could be verified by undertaking replication of the research.

Quantitative methods often use surveys and questionnaires as a means of gathering data. The statistics are analysed and the results may provide a broad snapshot of the issue. When dealing with large groups of people this is the most cost-effective method of research in terms of time; it may be more expensive because there are other related costs such as postage, printing and telephone calls. If the sample is large and the study replicated it may be possible to identify patterns: of values, views, perceptions, actions and behaviour. Although surveys may be seen as an ideal way of ensuring objectivity in your research, this very much depends on the neutrality and objectivity of your survey questions. Questionnaires and interview schedules are not easy to construct and there is always a danger of bias. This will be expanded on further in this chapter in the section on questionnaires and interviews.

Measures

Measure is a term used to describe what you regard as being particularly important aspects of the research, a research measurement. What you choose to measure is of crucial importance. It could be an impression of children's reactions to particular stimuli, interaction between adult and child which would be subjective, your impression. It could be more objective if it is a measure of time; for example, when tracking children engaged in particular activities over a period of time. A measure should be consistent in approach. Whatever measures are used you must strive to ensure validity. In other words can your measures provide the same or similar results if they are undertaken at another time or by a different person?

Qualitative research

This focuses on asking questions about observed behaviour. It is likely that if you are following this approach to research you will be looking at a particular context, a setting for the research and at how those you are studying react or interact in that setting. Data in qualitative research is used to help understand

Case Study 1

Quantitative research approaches

Rashida has an interest in adoption and for her study selected to focus on an aspect of particular personal interest: attitudes towards adoption of children by lesbian couples. Rashida wished to gather accurate data and was concerned that honest responses would be more easily elicited if she could maintain anonymity. There were particular concerns about cultural and religious pressures. Quantitative research was undertaken using questionnaires, which were circulated to students on a number of other courses and at other universities. The courses selected were unrelated to childhood studies so that a more general impression of attitudes could be gained from a representative sample of the population. Rashida was more interested at this point of her studies in finding out general opinion than specific detail. The sample was restricted to students, mostly 'younger' students, and her selection of participants was based on pragmatic factors such as time, accessibility to groups of students and consideration of reliability, and who would return the completed questionnaires.

situations without necessarily arriving at a definitive explanation.

Because this approach seeks to understand a particular context or situation, a variety of methods are used in order to provide a broad and rich picture. Questionnaires, interviews and observations are often used to tease out understandings. These may be structured with a particular design such as case study or action research.

Gomm and Woods (1993) illustrate more fully the differences between qualitative and quantitative research. This text, although dated, provides useful examples of qualitative and quantitative approaches to educational research.

Case Study 2

Qualitative research approaches

Sam and her husband had recently successfully applied and been accepted to foster a young child. Their experience of this process had raised many questions for Sam. The links between the agencies involved, the preparation for parenthood and the self-examination and questioning relating to conflict of values in child-rearing practice had been contentious issues within the early stages of the process. Sam made contact with other families who were fostering and, through means of a diary, noted and reflected on the key developments. The research design was purposely left fairly open so that issues raised could be pursued in more detail. The methods used to gather data included informal and semi-structured interviews, observations and questionnaires. Sam's purpose was to find out if families engaged in this process encountered similar problems and issues and how they were tackled. The research journey was one of personal understanding as well as professional development.

Methods can be combined in research

In your research project you can combine methods. Quantitative data can be used in conjunction with data collected by qualitative methods. In Case Study 2, for example, Sam could have used statistical data relating to numbers of successful long-term fostering as a benchmark, larger numbers of foster carers could have been contacted and statistical data used to analyse geographical differences in provision. Sam decided to concentrate on a pragmatic approach and use face-to-face contact.

Often students new to research identify very quickly with one particular approach. Early childhood studies tend to veer towards the qualitative approach because this approach involves familiar methods such as observation and interview in order to find out about a specific group of people. These students are often less comfortable with statistics and generalisability.

The methods are different but each can support the other. In order to extend research findings into practice in more than one context, generalisability must be taken into account.

Some students have used the research project at stage two of a degree course as a pilot for their independent study in the honours year of their degree programme. For some, a qualitative approach was found to be useful as a starting point to examine live issues in their pilot. A quantitative approach was used in the final year when the research question had been answered, the theory was clear and could be tested with a wider-ranging sample.

It may be useful at this point to illustrate how a similar topic may be tackled from either perspective.

Case Study 3

Use of equipment in outdoor play

A quantitative approach may focus on the frequency of use of specific items of equipment. This may be conducted as a longitudinal study over a period of time to ascertain if there are patterns to usage. It may be a comparative study or a survey of use in a number of settings. A qualitative approach may focus on the use made of the equipment by individuals over a period of time to note any linkage with social development.

Activity 1

Accessing a research project

Aim High Stay Real: Outcomes for Children and Young People: The Views of Children, Parents and Practitioners (Sinclair, R., Cronin, K., Lanyon, C., et al., 2002) is a recent research publication that is very easy to read and demonstrates very effective use of qualitative research which incorporates elements of quantitative research methods in areas of early childhood. It would be useful to extend your understanding of this form of research by accessing a real research project through the internet or as a paper-based report.

There are also research reports on the websites listed at the end of this chapter which are easy to access and provide useful sources for comparison.

Purposes of research

Most practitioners would agree that there must be a 'purpose' to research. We all have our own view of a researcher. Some practitioners may, initially, view a researcher as a person who spends time studying a specialised, even narrow, aspect of childhood that has little relevance to everyday practice. With experience such practitioners would hopefully realise that the researcher is systematic in his or her study and that the end result of such study is new knowledge. All active and interested practitioners working with young children are 'researchers', but we may not be engaged in systematically recording and remembering what it is that we find out about children through our daily interactions with them.

When our research deals with people, gaining accurate information is often more complex than would first appear. How children relate to each other, to adults and to you may provide insights that were not anticipated. Children react to situations and construct meanings in different ways at different times. Noting how the reactions may differ, given the same opportunity at different times, provides insight into children's behaviours and emotional and cognitive development.

As we are researching children, careful consideration must be given to ethics. In schools and nurseries we are now used to taking care to observe confidentiality of information. In research that is written up names must be changed to maintain confidentiality (children, adult and the name of the research setting). Written permission to undertake the research must be obtained from an appropriate person before research is started; this may be a parent or carer, a manager or head teacher. In research, it is important to be objective in your interpretation. Statements must be supported by evidence.

Devising a research question

For some people, thinking of a topic to research may be easy. You may have an issue that has occupied your interest for some time. This may be a family interest or concern; you may have a member of your family, a young child whom you have supported in a particular way. Examples of research topics based on personal experiences include bereavement or the daily support of children with a health condition or disability. Some students may wish to closely examine an issue about which they have particularly strong views: putting the issue 'under the microscope'. There is a danger here that personal values may interfere with an objectivity of approach to the research. In these conditions you should engage in reflexivity. Reflexivity is the being aware that you may have a bias in your approach to interpreting your research. It is important to be honest and reflect on personal factors which may affect the way you approach your research. Ideas for research may arise from your lecture notes; possibly too many questions come to mind and you will need to prioritise your ideas. There are some students who appear to have difficulty in finding a subject to research. Some ideas for research are more appropriate than others in relation to your professional development. You may have ideas related to your own practical experience in the workplace but which you feel unable to tackle because there may be difficulties for you in your professional role. Such issues may be tackled using another setting or range of settings and gathering data by interview or questionnaire. You need to have in mind that whatever you choose can be subjected to very focused research and that it will have a clear and 'achievable' outcome. You will be researching with a real purpose. The time in which you undertake your study will be limited and you will wish to make best use of this.

Choosing an area for your research study

When you initially consider an area for research study your reasons for choosing one may include a range of factors. Some of these are illustrated in Figure 16.1.

The chosen area may have the potential to demonstrate your awareness of current and critical issues in education and care. It should most definitely be related to your own personal interest; you should enjoy the research! It should also inform and extend your professional knowledge and understanding and the professional practices associated with children.

The most interesting research reports are those that start with a clearly formulated question. Examples of starting points for research questions are shown in Figure 16.2.

Figure 16.1 Choosing an area for research: initial considerations

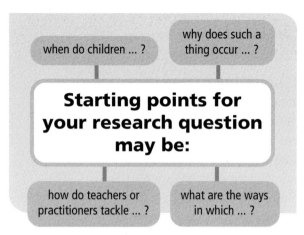

Figure 16.2 Your research question

Clarifying your research question

It is essential that you approach research with an open mind. You are not simply finding a means of justifying an opinion. The research question should indicate that you are reflexive and approaching the study with impartiality and objectivity. Your research question is very important, as it forms the key to the research design and each part of the research process. If it is too broad in approach you will find difficulty in focusing and although you may find some interesting strands of research you will become very frustrated when you are trying to make a clear and concise analysis of your study.

Key in your question onto your computer; print it out and keep it nearby as a reminder to help you to focus on the real issue. It will help you to remain on task. If your notes are written on disc you can add to and edit your text, formulate and modify your ideas, and plan more systematically. This will help you to draw out the main issues and it is a far more efficient use of your time than writing and rewriting notes by hand.

Keep your question clear and simple. The value of your study, for yourself and for others, depends on how well you formulate your question. The research study is easier to focus if the question is clear and unambiguous. Some people find it easier to talk about their ideas rather than writing them down straight

away and it is often useful at this point to identify a critical friend to help you with your study. This could be another student, someone you can trust to answer your questions in a straightforward way. It may be that you would find it helpful to work collaboratively with your critical friend to offer mutual support. Although you may be researching different areas, the recording process using research diaries will be similar. You do not have to share all your thoughts – but you may find talking through the issues raised by your research easier to record if you talk to someone about it. If you select a critical friend who demonstrates enthusiasm and an interest in your work they can prompt you into providing more detailed description of your findings – and vice versa!

Talking your ideas through with someone else should help you to clarify your ideas before you commit them to print. You could provide your critical friend with some questions as prompts to get you started. Some students find it useful to use a tape/digital recorder for conversations with their critical friend or just to record their own thoughts. It can be played back and notes made electronically.

Dos and don'ts
➤ Do focus on a research question.
➤ Do plan your time – be realistic.
➤ Do monitor and manage your time effectively.
➤ Do keep two copies of your work – one on the computer and one backed up to disc or memory stick.
➤ Don't delay the start of your work.
➤ Don't try to work in long stretches – work little and often (you will spot mistakes or lack of clarity more readily).
➤ Don't be too ambitious – choose a topic that can be completed within the timescale you have been allocated.

Figure 16.3 Research: some dos and don'ts

Your research question

1 Formulate your research question.

2 Find a critical friend.

3 Discuss your idea for the research question with your critical friend.

The literature search: accessing information

Once you have defined your research question you can then plan your reading and begin your literature search. This requires a systematic and disciplined approach. A very common mistake is for students to become diverted from their initial course and extend their reading beyond the confines of the research question. It is all too easy to find unanticipated areas of interest. Looking at other people's research reports is a valuable way of finding out about which aspects of your research question have been answered by others and what has been discovered and discussed. A thorough search of the literature will provide you with other leads for investigative reading. Often there may not be a direct reference to a research question in a book or article, but there may be references to follow up within the bibliography.

When you write up your research, you will need to show that you have made an effort to find out what has already been done in the area, and that you have taken account of it in your planning and carrying out the work. This is commonly written up in a section headed 'literature search'. Writing up the results of your search is often a really useful way of further clarifying your thoughts and moving your research question on. Doing this is a good way of leading up to making a clear statement of the research question and giving some theoretical backing to it. When making notes of your readings, make critical comments.

This does not mean negative comments! You are striving to analyse and to draw out the key points from your reading, which you will then compare and contrast.

You should avoid writing your literature review as a series of paragraphs, where a synopsis of each author's work is presented. If you follow this approach it appears as though you have just made notes on each author without reflecting on how views differ or relate to one another and how they help to answer the research question. Research is being constantly updated and therefore books can become outdated very quickly; to demonstrate your awareness of more recent developments in the field you must make use of journals and publications, newspapers, television, magazines and the internet. You may find that there is little available material on your chosen topic in academic literature, but that there is a wealth of material published on the internet through, for example, government websites.

As you undertake your reading you may find that someone else has already answered your question. Do not despair; you could use this existing research as a basis for your own. Examine the research report and modify it to meet your professional interests or needs. You could use a different research method or conduct it using a sample with very different characteristics.

Activity 3

Carrying out a literature search

You may make effective use of the literature if you draw from the full range of sources to answer your question.

1. What do academic authors think of the issue?
2. What is the latest research presented at conferences or published in academic journals? How is this impacting on practice and how is this described in professional magazines and journals?
3. What reports on the issue are presented to the public in newspapers or on television and radio?
4. What is on the internet that relates to your question?

You will need to sift through the materials available with care. The key to this section of your project is to demonstrate your familiarity with the subject. Draw out the important issues and relevant points from your reading. Consider why they are important and whether they convey specific knowledge or ideas.

Identify where issues are supported by evidence and whether the evidence is secured from primary or from secondary sources. Identify whether research reports contain original data and whether it incorporates reflection upon practice.

Set aside a regular time to do your reading – when you are not tired. Keep track of your references.

Citing references

You must check with your tutors for your university's approved referencing format. As you undertake your reading, copy your references and quotations and ensure that you take all bibliographical details. Figure 16.5 illustrates which information you should note, if you are going to quote from Coady's discussion of ethics, for example, which appears on page 68 in *Doing Early Childhood Research.*

Add all the details to your bibliography as you go along. Do not leave it until you have completed all of your reading. You can quote a page reference to a particular study like this (2001:68), where '2001' refers to the year the reference was published, and '68' refers to the page reference. This format is used in this book.

Publication	Points to note for reference purposes	
Rolfe, G., MacNaughton, S. and Siraj-Blatchford, I. (2001), *Doing Early Childhood Research*. Maidenhead: Open University Press	Author:	Coady, M.
	Date:	2001
	Title:	'Ethics in early childhood research' in MacNaughton, S., Rolfe, G. and Siraj-Blatchford, I. (Editors)
	Book Title:	*Doing Early Childhood Research*
	Place of Publication:	Maidenhead
	Publisher:	Open University Press
	Page Number:	p68

Figure 16.4 Example of points to note when citing references

Web search – using web-based resources

One of the things that it is really helpful to do early on in a research study is to find out what other people have already done in the area you are interested in.

1 There are several journals which focus on early childhood issues; download electronic copies of journal articles that relate to your study.

2 Government agencies publish research papers and project outcomes. Check to see if any of these add to your knowledge and understanding of your area of study.

3 Use keywords to search bibliographic catalogues for appropriate references to your topic.

Planning your research study

Planning your research is often referred to as 'designing'. Designing, when used in an art or design technology context, implies careful thought for the nature of what is produced, for the audience as well as the maker. Research design is similar to this. Careful consideration is given to how well the product meets the purpose; there is a measured response to the planning of time to craft the product. There is care in checking and monitoring that the product meets the defined need and, finally, that it is useful for others as well as you.

An early decision that you must make is whether you are going to design a project that will depend upon observation or be experimental in design. An observational approach will usually be conducted with the researcher as an 'outsider'. Observational in this sense means that you do not intervene in the process.

If the research is designed with care it will produce results that have validity. Without care in the design stage you will undoubtedly find that there are gaps in the process. Try to predict as much as possible in terms of the process. Research in education and care involves working with children, and working with

them can be very unpredictable. Children's behaviour can change if they know that they are being studied. Absence, weather conditions and age or development-related responses may have a bearing on what is, or is not, possible within a given time span. When making a longitudinal study of young children a number of factors may have a bearing on what is, or is not, possible in the time available for research. Unforeseen absence of a child at a critical time in the research time can have a devastating result. Plan for this possibility.

Make use of your computer in planning

Use your computer to help you to design your study. If your design is well organised it will help you to keep on track and ultimately you will finish with a product of which you are proud. If you rush the design you will encounter more problems than you should – and you may take longer to complete the study because you have overlooked something of importance.

Each section of the research question can be looked at separately. You will find that methods of tackling the research will spring to mind – note these on the computer as these may help you to form ideas for your methodology. You will focus on the target group; this should be saved as a document to be used as the possible sample. Cut and paste the answers on separate pages in your document and put these into appropriately titled folders: Sample and Methodology.

Making a submission

Your tutors will ask you to define your proposal in a submission that will be presented for approval. The format of the submission may differ from one university to another but will usually include the elements illustrated in Figure 16.5.

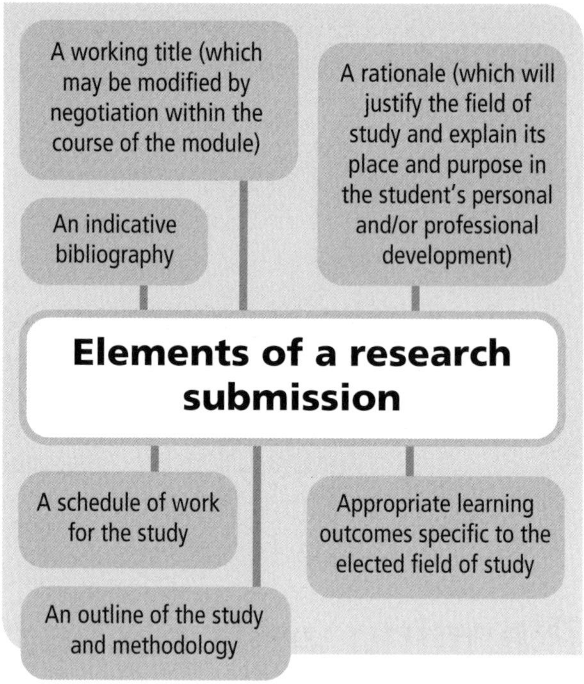

Figure 16.5 Elements of the research submission

Research methods

Guides on how to research may appear daunting for first-time researchers. The following sections address aspects of research methods in terms that are accessible to students in the second stage of a Foundation Degree. These are starting points and once you gain confidence you should make reference to the more formal guides to research indicated in the reading list at the end of this chapter.

The sample

It is hoped that your research will be useful to others: your colleagues at work, your fellow students or others who have an interest in your area of study. It is important that the sample (the group studied) represents a typical range of children or adults so that your findings could help to make general statements applicable to other similar groups. The size of the group will also have a bearing on the results. If you have a very small group then data must be very detailed to allow comparisons to be made with other groups. Your sample, its size and location will influence the research approach you will select.

Case Study 4

Using a small sample

Liz made a study of the provision of play for reception children in small rural schools. The study used responses from practitioners gained through use of questionnaires and telephone interviews to analyse data. Liz reflected upon provision generally and was able to identify factors that may affect the ability of small schools to provide play provision for reception-age children. Such factors related to size of groups, the location of school and the training of staff. Although a varied range of schools across the country were contacted and staff made a good response, the findings were limited. A small-scale piece of research, such as that undertaken by Liz, where there is little existing research literature available, is very valuable as a springboard for further personal research.

Observation as a research method

Observation as a research method can be participatory or non-participatory. As a participant observer you can intervene and in this sense it can be experimental. The experimental approach will involve introducing changes.

Case Study 5

An experimental study

Iram's experimental study was conducted in the home corner of a reception classroom. She began by looking at language and particularly the quality of spontaneous talk that was taking place. The home corner was, in Iram's words, 'the only place children could play without teacher control'. In designing her study, Iram considered varying and extending the 'props' that were available to children and to observe, record, monitor and evaluate the children's responses through language. The study was conducted over a year and was thus a longitudinal study of the context as well as of individual children.

Influence and control

As your research develops you will encounter a number of issues that relate to influence and control. For example, when you are working with children, either observing them from afar, or as a participant observer engaged with them more closely, your presence may influence them. You will know that when a video camera or a tape recorder is introduced to the class or group of children there is a reaction. Your presence as an observer may have a similar initial reaction: behaviour is different. You will also realise that after children have become accustomed to a video camera or a tape recorder behaviour reverts to more usual patterns. Build in time for children to become used to your new or different role. Be aware of the impact you may have on behaviour. Plan time to allow for settling down.

Case Study 6

Awareness of observer on behaviour

Craig's research project was undertaken in a small nursery school with children from a wide range of social and cultural backgrounds. Twenty languages were used within the nursery and the use and reticence or hesitancy in the use of spoken English was the focus of the project. Craig was given permission by parents and staff to tape-record children speaking. Initially, there were many problems: children were excited or curious when the tape recorder appeared; some were more hesitant; others were more than usually ebullient. Once children became accustomed to the tape recorder they reverted to usual behaviours – although some children did point out when the tape was running out! Over the next few weeks, Craig found that transcribing tapes was very time-consuming and that the quality of the recordings was affected by lots of unexpected extraneous noise. We tend to focus on other people's speech when listening to them and ignore much peripheral noise. Tape recorders do not do this! Craig had to find quieter areas in which to research and record. His presence in these new areas, where such activity had not previously taken place, raised more questions from children and another settling-down period was implemented.

Further reading: Lancaster, Y. and Broadbent, V. (2003), *Listening to Young Children*.

Validity

There are a number of ways of ensuring reliability and validity so that others may benefit from your research. You could collaborate with your critical friend and exchange roles, using each other's measures to test their reliability. You could ask another colleague in your workplace to use your measures. In practical terms, this is not often possible. In qualitative research, however, a valuable means of ensuring validity is through use of triangulation.

Triangulation involves getting another person's views or perceptions of an event being observed. Typically, in an Early Years setting this may involve asking another professional or a parent for their perspective on an event. You may also ask children. An observer makes an interpretation of what is observed, no matter how objective we strive to be.

Tape/digital recording has been used for purposes of triangulation when analysing language; however, visual cues and body language are, of course, unrecorded and interpretation is focused solely on verbal communications. Video is more accurate for purposes of analysis and confirmation of validity. The video can be analysed and findings confirmed or questioned. These forms of recording are now contentious and if you intend to use them you must carefully follow ethical practice.

Longitudinal research

You may possibly be expected to conduct your research over the full academic year. This provides for longer-term involvement in an Early Years context and for detailed research into the development of a child or a group of people. Longitudinal research has advantages in that it provides opportunity for a broad picture of an issue over time. The subtle complexities can be recorded and monitored with a degree of richness.

Long-term involvement in an Early Years context, which is constantly changing, requires the use of a variety of approaches to confirm data. Involving others in confirming your data, offering different perspectives, helps to provide a more rounded picture and to confirm reliability of your interpretation of events. When working with other adults in longitudinal studies, a problem may emerge in that participants change in their response to and involvement with the research, and misunderstandings may result. Keep people informed, fully involve them at all stages, not to the extent that they may feel that they are bombarded with information, but simply to update them about progress. Your 'contract' between yourself as the researcher and the other adults needs to remain open for negotiation.

People do change their minds; time and experience alters perception of events. In short-term research projects this is less of a problem than in longitudinal studies. Check your diary for any inconsistencies in people's responses or changes in perception. Be objective in your analysis of such issues and remember all notes should retain anonymity of the research subjects.

Activity 5

Choosing research methods

1   Match your research question to a research method.

2   Write a short justification as to why you have selected these methods rather than others.

3   Discuss your ideas for the research methods with your critical friend.

Using a research diary

One of the keys to a successful research project is good organisation and a most successful means of achieving this is to keep a research diary. Keeping a diary of your research process may be regarded as a task that places more stress on an already overworked student. This is not the case; a diary used well reduces stress levels because it keeps you on task and helps to keep ideas and actions in one place! It is one of the most useful tools for someone new to formal research. The diary is:

➤ a means of helping you to organise your ideas and thoughts

➤ a place to record your actions and to note your data

➤ a place to record the process

➤ a place to consider aspects of analysis.

As part of your employment, or within prior study, you will have developed skills in observing, recording and analysing children's development through writing case studies and making focused observations. Some of you will use recording methods in your workplace or placement as part of everyday practice. There is a requirement in many courses to keep a record of your perceptions of the taught modules and your workplace experience in a personal and professional log. The sequential focus of such activities prepares you for diary writing. You will find that keeping a research diary is easy to organise and it is an effective means of recording the detail required for effective reflection and analysis. The diary may also be used as an approach to research – a research method if the quality of the entries is carefully controlled and organised. The diary method fits well within a framework of qualitative research methods. Figure 16.6 illustrates the many uses of a diary.

The diary is a record of your research and can be used to provide a wide range of qualitative data to support your research study as shown in Figure 16.7.

Because you will be using the diary weekly, perhaps even daily, throughout your research project, opportunities will arise for you to recognise emergent patterns within your data. This may be, for example, in the ways children interact with adults, how adults question children or how children respond to particular contexts or stimuli within outdoor play.

Time spent on ensuring the quality of the diary will be rewarded. In some ways, a good research diary will be more valuable than other types of research methods in that it can present a series of sequential snapshots, it can reflect personal development and it can

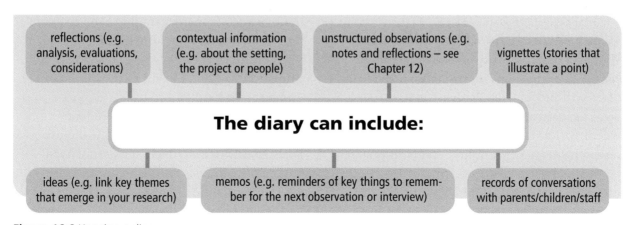

| reflections (e.g. analysis, evaluations, considerations) | contextual information (e.g. about the setting, the project or people) | unstructured observations (e.g. notes and reflections – see Chapter 12) | vignettes (stories that illustrate a point) |

The diary can include:

| ideas (e.g. link key themes that emerge in your research) | memos (e.g. reminders of key things to remember for the next observation or interview) | records of conversations with parents/children/staff |

Figure 16.6 Keeping a diary

Qualitative data to support your research study may include:	
A detailed record of your research process	Both factual and reflective.
A record of your personal development	Noting your ideas, your responses to your research and your reactions to incidents.
Relevant data	Records of conversations and informal interviews. Transcripts of taped conversations. Observational records.
A record of your responses	To your reading. Note bibliographical references.
An analysis of your reflections	The process of reflection over time.
A construction of your own theories and comparisons with others	Using your readings from the academic literature, websites, journals and the media.

Figure 16.7 Qualitative data you may include in your diary

show investigative strands in ways that are not possible through the use of questionnaire or interview.

In terms of personal development, the research diary is particularly important as it documents your perceptions and insights through the different stages of your research project. It should be noted here that the approach to writing the diary should be honest. It should note apparent failures as well as the successes. Reflection is concerned with analysing events and issues in ways that are not simply superficial or descriptive.

Recording the sequence of events is important so that events can be revisited and reflected upon in more detail and an overall picture may emerge.

What should the diary look like?

Writing a diary is a very personal matter and every writer develops his or her own style. The diary will include details that you may not want to share with others, as well as extracts which will be useful for essays and your research study. You will find that with practice you will develop your own ways of recording information. There may be sections where you use a form of note-taking, using bullet points or your own type of shorthand that

may be rewritten at a later date. You may use a particular form of layout or develop new ones. We have our own idiosyncrasies, but as long as you can understand and retrieve your thoughts and data from the diary this does not matter. You will rewrite the data recorded in your diary to meet the needs of different readers, in this case your research study tutor.

There is a temptation to use a ring binder because you can compile a compendium of different types of data; for example, annotated photographs and children's work, questionnaires and other data. The research diary could take this format or you could use a bound book. The advantage in using a bound book is that there will not then be the temptation to add or take away things from the sequential record. (You have the problem then of where to put all the extra materials. The additional materials you collect may be gathered in a file; this will form your archive.) There are no hard and fast rules so find a format that you can use with confidence. Whatever form the diary takes you should leave spaces or margins to make additional comments, analysis and reflections. These later entries could be made distinct by using a different colour of ink. You will find that strands begin to develop within your research;

these could be noted by using 'highlighters' of different colour.

Use your time effectively

Write diary entries regularly – and at a regular time. If you establish a habit it will be easier to maintain. You should quickly establish a pattern of writing your personal log at regular times. You should identify points to note within lectures, in your reading that relate to your study which you can reflect upon at home. Keep field notes in your practice setting. These could be made on sticky notes, on a clipboard or in any other format used within the setting for noting children's development. Transfer these notes to your diary at the end of the day and reflect upon them. At the end of the first term or semester, if you have not kept up to date with your diary entries, or if you have not done them at all, you may find it difficult to get started. Don't despair; start in a small way, and as soon as possible. Build up your confidence by setting small achievable targets and increase the frequency and detail of the diary entries over the next few weeks.

Making entries

As this research method is in diary format each entry should be organised in a systematic way. It is easier to follow and to track trends if you order your work. You will, of course, include the date and time of your observation or interaction. You should include contextual information; for example, where the research is taking place, what is happening, who is involved, the focus of the observation and anything else that seems important.

Although this is a personal document, it is useful to be disciplined in how you write your entries. You may wish to use headings. The system of numbering sections and paragraphs is particularly useful as this makes referencing sections of your work easier.

Activity 6

Your skills

1 Consider the skills that you are developing. These might include:
   ➤ interpersonal skills gained by talking to children, parents/carers and to other professionals
   ➤ skills in systematically recording observations and conversations.
2 Discuss your findings with your critical friend.
3 Write a short analysis of your personal development in research skills.

Ethical considerations

Children form a vulnerable group, and their rights need to be protected. Recent events have brought into question photographing and video filming of children. Some settings will not allow this; others will require parental permission. You will need to check carefully on the regulations in your setting. Your college or university may have specific guidelines for ethics in research, which you must follow.

In the absence of these, the following details should be followed.

Guidelines for ethical conduct in research

There are issues of consent in relation to children and you should indicate in the introduction to your study that you have observed ethical procedures. Your study

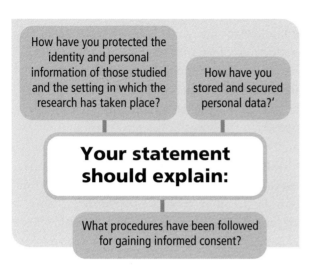

Inside the figure:

How have you protected the identity and personal information of those studied and the setting in which the research has taken place?

How have you stored and secured personal data?'

Your statement should explain:

What procedures have been followed for gaining informed consent?

Figure 16.8 An ethical protocol

should contain a statement indicating how you have ensured that the study is conducted in an ethical manner, an ethical protocol. Your statement should answer the questions shown in Figure 16.8 above.

You should be clear, honest and open about what you are hoping to achieve in your research. This should be conveyed to parents and carers in language that is clear and unambiguous. They should be able to give consent based on a clear understanding of the purpose of the research. You must be sensitive to the children. Their needs take priority over the research.

Further reading in the area of ethics may be required at some point in your research. Coady (2001) presents a clear focused discussion of a range of issues related to informed consent, deception in research, confidentiality and privacy and cultural issues.

Case Study 7

Organising your time

Claire has two children under five years of age. She works in a pre-school two days a week, Thursday and Friday, and attends university one day and one evening during term time. For her research, Claire has chosen a curriculum-related topic and she uses her weekly experience in the pre-school to undertake her research. She puts information on sticky notes during the sessions and writes up her findings as notes during lunch. She has to prepare for the Friday morning session at the end of Thursday afternoon and does not have time to record the afternoon findings until later in the evening, when her children are in bed. Saturday is a family day, so no university work is done until Sunday evening. Claire finds that working at this time is slow as she is very tired. She now sets aside some time during lunchtime on the day she is in university to write up her notes. Claire finds that after she has been to the evening session at university her mind is buzzing and she uses this time to write up her diary.

Approaches to small-scale enquiry

In this section the range of research methods will be explained in more depth. Consider which method will most effectively meet your research needs.

Experimental designs

In an experimental design, the experimenter introduces some sort of change and the effects of this are monitored. The aim is to find out whether this treatment (the change) has an effect on some outcome (the effects of the change). At the same time, the researcher tries to control other factors that might affect the outcome, to avoid the possibility that effects due to other factors are confused with effects caused by the treatment.

Observational designs

In an observational design, there is no change introduced by the researchers; they simply study 'things as they are'. It is still an issue, in an observational design, as to whether some degree of control is needed, for the same reasons as in experimental designs. It is important also to realise that observational designs are not the same as observation methods. Observation methods, that is, watching and recording behaviour, are widely used in Early Years research. They can be used in both experimental and observational studies, which is a bit confusing! The key point is that observational studies do not involve the researcher changing something to see what happens; if that is done, the study is by definition an experimental one.

Questionnaires

Questionnaires are a popular method of gathering data. Questionnaires ask questions. They look easy and quick to construct; but they are not. To write a questionnaire that will provide valid data, that is worthwhile research and that is not biased, takes time and effort. De Vaus (2002) offers a good guide to question formulation.

To check on accuracy and ensure validity of your findings you should test the results by using another method, such as interview. If the results match, you know they are likely to be more accurate than if you had relied on one method. We have all experienced being a recipient of a questionnaire; we therefore know the frustrations of having to select from a limited range of answers. It sometimes appears that the person who has devised the questionnaire already knows the answers and wants you to confirm them by ticking a box. It is easy to analyse data provided in a small range of boxes. The accuracy and value of the findings from such research depend on how the questions have been written. The interviewee may respond in a way that acknowledges you, changing the accuracy of the data in order to provide the answers the interviewee believes you wish to hear.

Gillham (2000) in *Developing a Questionnaire* provides a useful extended and detailed examination of the use of questionnaires within research.

Observation

Observation is used extensively as a method of obtaining information within Early Years settings (see Chapter 12). The familiarity of the use of observation to record, assess and monitor children's development provides security for practitioners. Using observation as a research tool is somewhat different in focus. Rather than observations being used to help your understanding of an individual child's progress and needs, you will observe, analyse and reflect upon wider issues.

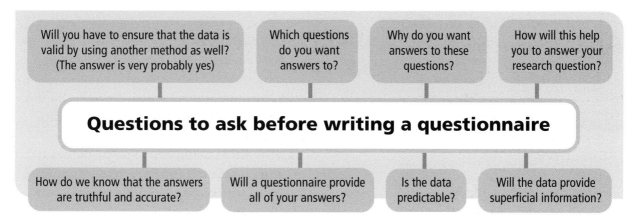

Figure 16.9 Writing a questionnaire: initial considerations

The presence of outsiders as observers may be intimidating. The possibility of the presence of an observer intentionally or unintentionally influencing the action is very real. Evidence obtained through observation is subject to personal interpretation.

It is not an easy technique to use effectively, as it is difficult in terms of concentration, in focusing on making decisions about what to record and in sustaining the level of quality if they are undertaken, as they should be, over a prolonged period of time.

Observation as a research method is most effective when used in combination with other methods. You can confirm what others tell you in interview through your own observation. Data from questionnaires may relate to context-based activities, which could be confirmed through observation.

Nason and Golding (1994), in a discussion of the comparative advantages and disadvantages of using observation methods, highlight time, expense and opportunity as key issues. You may wish to consider the questions highlighted in Figure 16.10.

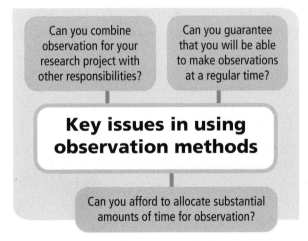

Figure 16.10 Using observation methods

Activity 7

Self-assessment exercise

Reflect on your first-hand observation of children. How has your prior experience, for example, participation in professional activities such as assessment of children, helped you to make measured judgements of children's capabilities and progress? Are these judgements entirely free from bias?

Interviews

Interviews may be a means of eliciting information from groups of people or individuals who would be reluctant to respond to questionnaires. Using interviews will provide more in-depth responses than a questionnaire; this will help to understand the issue rather than explain the extent of an issue. They are useful when combined with other methods to confirm validity of your data and your findings. They are easy to undertake and you can be sure of the response – unless something drastic happens to your tape recorder or pen.

There are two approaches to conducting interviews but between the two extremes there are many variations. Interviews may be unstructured or structured.

In an unstructured interview you may engage someone in conversation and focus on a number of key areas of questioning. You should record as much of the conversation as possible on paper (or laptop). When you have written up your interview you can check with the interviewee for their thoughts on the accuracy of your report. In some situations, particularly in semi-structured interviews, where there is an indication of the range of question topics, the interviewee may not object to you tape recording the conversation. This is valuable as a source of data, as the tape-recorded conversation can be transcribed and analysed.

In the interview schedule (your list of questions) ensure that the questions are not over-directive, that they are free from bias and that they allow the interviewees to speak 'with their own voice' and not be influenced by you. Be conscious of time if you use 'open' questions, which allow the interviewee free range to answer. If you use 'closed' questions with a narrow range of answers, take care to be unbiased. Interviews and questionnaires may cause people to become self-conscious. Are the answers that people give really what they think or what they believe?

Do answers to questions change depending upon the audience? Would someone say something to you, which they would not say within earshot of a manager? In an informal interview, the way in which a question is answered may be very different from the response provided in a written evaluation, which the manager may see. Some people prefer to write, others to talk.

Case Study 8

A survey of special needs

Dawn was undertaking a survey of special needs provision in a large national network of pre-school providers, which followed a specific philosophical approach to early childhood. The brochures provided by the organisation indicated that a special need was integrated into all teaching. Practice observed by Dawn indicated that this was the case and yet in questionnaires and interviews conducted with staff, responses indicated that there was no specific provision for children with special needs. There was clearly conflict between understanding of practice and practice within the workplace, communication of ideology and practice, and self-awareness of practice.

Case study approach

Many courses of early childhood studies use case study as a means of illustrating theory in practice, legislation and policy in action within a setting or context. Often such cases illustrate and examine relationships between members of a group, a family or interactions between agencies and families. A case study approach will look in detail at a particular group. For example, the study may focus on relationships within a group, interactions between members of the group. It may relate to responses or reactions by members of the group to outside agencies or the influence of such agencies on group members. As such interactions and relationships are complex, focusing on the group through a case study approach will enable you to gather rich and detailed data.

If your research question lends itself to a case study approach you will probably use a number of different methods to gather data. It therefore has the potential to give a more complete picture of a situation than most other research designs. Corroboration of the validity of data, the opportunity to test reliability of data, is one of the advantages to this approach. Several sources of data allow for cross-checking. Data from informal or semi-structured interviews can be compared with formal interview/questionnaire, observation and diary entries.

A case study can be a short project or a long-term, longitudinal study. Often case studies undertaken at stage two of a degree course result in findings that provide an exploratory platform for further study and can be extended into research for a longer and more tightly focused dissertation. The case could be used as a means of understanding a complex relationship or as a descriptive illustration of events, which are then tested in another setting or context. Case study research is covered in considerable detail by Stake (1994).

Revisions to the Code of Practice 2001

Bev is a special needs nursery nurse and works with a KS1 class. Her study focused on the revisions to the Code of Practice (2001), which required closer collaboration with parents than was previously expected. A case study approach offered opportunities for Bev to examine the documentation in detail, to compare this with practice in other countries (she has contacts in Australia) and to track the implementation of the Code of Practice with one child and her parents.

Focus group interviews

Focus group interviews are being increasingly used in social science research as a means of eliciting views through group conversation. While individual interviews with adults or children may appear intimidating, this may be less so when a group who know each other are interviewed through focused conversation. The key task for the researcher is to keep the group focused, to ensure that one person does not dominate the group and that those who are more hesitant to contribute may be encouraged to voice their reactions either within or outside of the group.

When using focus group conversations with children it as well to consider the following.

➤ Individual children may feel uncomfortable in the group.

➤ Individuals may influence the response made by others.

➤ Children (as well as adults) may respond in a way, or provide answers to questions which they feel the researcher wants to hear. Children and teachers in questioning or interview situations often feel that they are being 'tested'.

Lancaster and Broadbent (2003:46) provide an interesting checklist of strengths and limitations of focus group interviews with children.

Practitioners in Early Years settings relate well to cases as a means of professional development. Familiarity with issues raised in specific cases can be used to draw other colleagues into your research. They may be able to offer support and comment in a number of ways that will enhance your research. Comments may develop into conversations and then into informal interviews. A secondary development of using this approach may be to encourage practitioners in your workplace to review their own practice. If your project does develop into a more collaborative research project, it may well be that you could look at action research as a possible extension.

Action research

As an approach to small-scale research, action research appears well suited to the needs of a researcher conducting research in education and care settings. It is a very applied approach, one that links the research process closely to the Early Years context and has a practical purpose clearly visible to participants. It has often been used by groups of staff to review current practice and to introduce and implement new practices or procedures, a curriculum and professional development strategy. Action research is essentially a form of self-reflective enquiry, undertaken in order to improve practices. If you do wish to work with colleagues in this way you will find that your study will be reflective. It will address praxis, your own understanding of theory and practice, your own practice, and the relationships between context and practice.

Action research projects lead to change and have a focus on enabling participants to improve aspects of their own and their colleagues' practices. It is an experimental means of testing ideas and hunches, going through repeated cycles and changing each time.

It is essentially a collaborative activity, although often led by an individual. It is possible to undertake a small-scale research project as an action research project where you

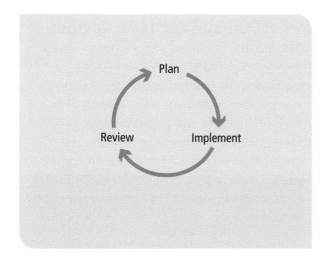

Figure 16.11 High/Scope cycle

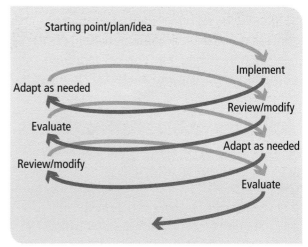

Figure 16.12 Action/research cycle

set up an experiment, implement it, analyse and refine it and implement it once more to measure any change.

There are similarities between the High/Scope Plan–Implement–Review cycle (Figure 16.11) and the action research cycle (Figure 16.12): Plan–Do–Review.

For further reading in this area two key texts are recommended, one by Elliott (1991), who is a key figure in the use of action research as an educational research tool, and the other by McNaughton (2001), who presents a clear and detailed discussion of the research method.

Analysis of data

You will now have researched the literature, selected and implemented your research project and have amassed a large amount of data. Sift carefully through your data. Mark with a specific colour those sections that are relevant. Put aside all those other interesting but not entirely relevant data!

Look at ways in which to present your material that conveys your findings clearly and unambiguously. Will this be as a series of charts, graphs or tables? If you have questionnaires, go through and identify similarities and differences of response.

Activity 8

Interpreting your findings

1 Check that you are taking care to look at your findings in an objective manner and that you can support your interpretations with evidence.

2 Check that you are taking care not to jump to conclusions and making observations or

statements within the research that will not stand scrutiny.

3 Check that you are not influencing the sample you are researching.

There may be no other alternative than to address each issue raised as a distinct entity in a separate paragraph. The key to a good presentation of data and analysis is to make it concise and clear.

Activity 9

Checking for clarity

1 Is there any evidence of bias in my observations, in my reflections or in my analysis? If so, what can I do to counteract my bias?

2 How subjective am I in my observations and reflections?

3 Have I left out any evidence that would not support my argument?

4 Have I checked my findings through triangulation?

5 Do my analysis and conclusions match the evidence provided by the data?

6 How useful is this research for others?

7 Are the findings generalisable or do they present understanding of issues?

Reflection and ideas for further research

It is often permissible and sometimes a requirement to conclude your study with a section that includes a reflection on your own development and ideas for further development of your area of research. Your research diary will provide you with ample material upon which to reflect. The following pointers may be helpful in constructing your conclusion.

Activity 10

Reflect on your development

1 What aspects of research have you particularly enjoyed?

2 What have you found difficult or demanding?

3 What new learning has taken place?

4 How could you improve your research skills?

5 How would you extend this research?

Conclusion

The purpose of this chapter has been to encourage you to engage in research and to feel confident in tackling some of the issues related to linking theory with practice. Coverage of the issues has been very brief. I hope that your enthusiasm for research has been fired!

How to move on in your research

Research commissioned by government sources may provide a particular political perspective on issues. However, as they are often undertaken by professional research teams, usually based in universities, further reading to elicit other approaches to the focus of the research project would demonstrate your ability to reflect on issues in greater depth. Government-sponsored research papers and reports are particularly interesting for purposes of reflective comparison between national education systems. Comparison may also be made with research reports commissioned by private early childhood providers such as the Pre-School Learning Alliance (http://www.pre-school.org.uk/research/research-projects) which is currently involved in a major European collaboration to identify successful social and educational policies for eliminating educational inequality among children.

References

Aubrey, C., David, T., Godfrey, R. and Thompson, L. (2000), *Researching Early Childhood Education: Debates and Issues in Methodology and Ethics*. London: Routledge Falmer
   This book provides an introduction to a range of issues relating to research in the Early Years.

Bell, J. (1999) (3rd edition), *Doing Your Research Project*. Maidenhead: Open University Press
   A sound basis for organising and undertaking a research project.

Blaxter, L., Hughes, C. and Tight, M. (1996), *How to Research*. Maidenhead: Open University Press
   A clearly written text which has proved popular with students.

Brooker, L. (2001) 'Interviewing children', in MacNaughton, S., Rolfe, G. and Siraj-Blatchford, I., *Doing Early Childhood Research*. Maidenhead: Open University Press
   A good starting point for reflection on direct research with children.

Coady, M. (2001), 'Ethics in early childhood research', in MacNaughton, S., Rolfe, G. and Siraj-Blatchford, I., *Doing Early Childhood Research* (pp64–72). Maidenhead: Open University Press.

Delamont, S. (1992), *Fieldwork in Educational Settings: Methods, Pitfalls and Perspectives*. London: Routledge Falmer
   A sound analysis of issues. Although the book is now rather dated, it remains a classic text.

Denscombe, M. (2003), *The Good Research Guide: For Small-scale Social Research Projects*. Maidenhead: Open University Press
   A clear and accessible text. It defines and clearly illustrates many research terms.

De Vaus, D.A (2002) (5th edition), *Surveys in Social Research*. London: Routledge
   This book offers a good guide to question formulation.

Edwards, A. and Talbot, R. (1999) (2nd edition), *The Hard-Pressed Researcher: A Research Handbook for the Caring Professions*. London: Longman
   A clear review of qualitative methods.

Elliott, J. (1991), *Action Research for Educational Change*. Maidenhead: Open University Press

Gillham, B. (2000), *Developing a Questionnaire*. London: Continuum
   A useful source for further reading about quantitative research.

Gomm, R. and Woods, P. (1993), *Educational Research in Action*. London: Paul Chapman
   Useful examples of qualitative and quantitative approaches to educational research.

Harrison, L. (2001), 'Quantitative designs and statistical analysis', in MacNaughton, S., Rolfe, G. and Siraj-Blatchford, I., *Doing Early Childhood Research* (pp93–16). Maidenhead: Open University Press.

Lancaster, Y. and Broadbent, V. (2003), *Listening to Young Children*. Maidenhead, Open University Press/McGraw-Hill
   A very useful preliminary text which I have found encourages the reader to challenge their own role and reflect upon their understanding and perceptions of children's 'talk'.

McNaughton, G. (2001), 'Action Research', in **MacNaughton, S., Rolfe, G. and Siraj-Blatchford, I.**, *Doing Early Childhood Research*. Maidenhead: Open University Press

MacNaughton, S., Rolfe, G. and Siraj-Blatchford, I. (2001), *Doing Early Childhood Research*. Maidenhead: Open University Press

This book has an emphasis on research that relates directly to early childhood. A very full range of issues are addressed in detail including research methods and analysis and the process of research.

Nason, J. and Golding, D. (1994) *in* **Cassell, C. and Symon (1994)** *Qualitative Methods in Organisational Research*. London: Sage

Roberts-Holmes. G. (2006), *Doing your Early Years Research Project*. London: Paul Chapman

A very accessible book which extends many of the points raised in this chapter.

Sinclair, R., Cronin, K., Lanyon, C., Stone, V. and Hulusi, A. (2002), *Aim High Stay Real*. National Children's Bureau/British Market Research Bureau: Qualitative and Children and Young People's Unit. London: Children and Young People's Unit. Available from mailbox@cypu.gsi.gov.uk or Children and Young People's Unit. 4E Caxton House, 6–12 Tothill Street, London SW1H 9NA. Ref No CYPUAHSR.

A good example of a research report relating to early childhood.

Stake, R. (1994), 'Case studies', **in Denzin, N. and Lincoln, Y. (eds)**, *Handbook of Qualitative Research*. London: Sage

Useful websites

www.bera.ac.uk/guidelines
British Educational Research Association (BERA) Ethical Guidelines.

www.bps.org.uk
British Psychological Society (BPS) Code of Conduct and Ethical Guidelines.

www.bids.ac.uk
International Bibliography of the Social Sciences (IBSS). A useful starting point.

www.pre-online.co.uk
PRE Online provides case study examples describing the practical application of research in and outside of the classroom, however its most useful articles are those which help in preparing for research.

www.montessori-ami.org/research/research.htm
This site provides access to research undertaken for, or related to, the Montessori ideal.

http://www.oecd.org
This site provides links to international research.

http://www.tlrp.org/pub/research.html
Provides links to reports of international Early Years research.

http://www.literacytrust.org.uk/Research/earlyreviews.html
Links to a number of Early Years project reports including links to government projects such as EPPE.

www.ioe.ac.uk/schools/ecpe/eppe/
Information related to major research projects in the Early Years in England.

Australia

www.education.gov.au/goved/go/pid/15

This is the link to the official Australian Government Early Years education research website. It also provides links to other international websites.

Canada

http://www.hrsdc.gc.ca/en/publications_ resources/research/categories/child_ development.shtml

A link to some early childhood research in Canada; very useful for purposes of comparison.

England

www.dfes.gov.uk/research/

The Department for Children, Schools and Families website provides a wide range of Early Years research reports can be downloaded. These cover areas such childminders, providers, Children's Centres, Nursery Schools.

http://www.surestart.gov.uk/research/

The research page of the Sure Start site provides links to much research material on all aspects of this massive educational development.

India

http://goidirectory.nic.in/education.htm

Interesting statistics are provided on this site (search for Early Years education on content of websites search engine).

Northern Ireland

www.deni.gov.uk

http://www.deni.gov.uk/index/32-statisticsandresearch_pg/32_statistics_and_ research-research_pg.htm

Provides a good, but limited range of research reports and briefings. For example, the 'Effective Pre-School Provision in Northern Ireland (EPPNI) Summary Report'.

This report has a comprehensive, if dated range of references; it also has a list of EPPNI 'Technical Papers' – very useful further reading which provides a good overview of the approach to pre-school education in Northern Ireland.

Republic of Ireland

http://www.cecde.ie/english/cecde_research. php

The Republic of Ireland Centre for Early Childhood Development and Education. Provides links to a wide range of Early Years research activity in Ireland.

http://www.education.ie

The Republic of Ireland Department of Education and Science website.

Scotland

www.scotland.gov.uk/Topics/Research/ Research/14478/SERD

Provides a link to Early Years educational research in Scotland.

New Zealand

http://www.minedu.govt.nz

This website provides links to a wide range of research project reports.

Index

Down's syndrome 80
duration observation 342
dynamical systems 74
dyslexia 156, 185

E

E Framework 56–7
Early Learning Partnerships
　　Project (ELPP) 386–7
Early Years Curriculum Group
　　(EYCG) 24
Early Years Foundation Stage
　　(EYFS) 303–7
　　across United Kingdom 306–7
　　aims 304
　　areas of learning 304–5
　　curriculum 44, 301–6
　　Every Child Matters
　　　　outcomes 86–7, 303, 304
　　health 235
　　Learning and Development
　　　　Principles 70
　　limitations 301–2, 305
　　planning principles 314
　　profile 302, 329
　　role of play 198–9, 207
Early Years practitioner see
　　practitioners; reflective
　　practice
ecological systems theory 74
education and childcare policy
　　378–87
　　influencing factors 378
education in early childhood
　　child-centred 24, 25
　　common aspects of theories 28
　　and crime 26
　　curriculum guidance 27
　　diverging opinions 26, 28
　　holistic approach 15, 16
　　Roman views 25
egocentrism 138
electronic communication 186–7
Emergency Protection Order
　　416, 419–20
emotional abuse 401–3
emotional intelligence 104
emotional literacy 104–9, 215
emotional and social
　　development 92–128, 238

enabling environment 122
　　influencing factors 109
　　innate emotions 96
　　primary and secondary
　　　　emotions 96
　　psychodynamic theories
　　　　93–5
　　smiling 98
empathy 116
environment, problem-solving
　　323–4
EpiPen 244
EPPE Project 44, 386
equality issues 316–17
Erikson, Erik 74, 93, 94–5
ethical issues
　　data-sharing 367
　　observations 331–2
event recording 341
Every Child Matters framework
　　364–7
　　Change for Children 281, 372
　　five outcomes 192, 365–6
　　Green Paper 365
　　influencing factors 364–5
　　parent and child
　　　　involvement 366
　　and safety 252
　　and vulnerable children 365,
　　　　366
experimental designs 470
extended school team 434–5
extended schools 351, 368,
　　370–1
　　and parent partnerships 275
　　play in 214
　　role of practitioners 43

F

facial expressions 60
　　and emotional development
　　　　95, 97
families
　　environmental influences
　　　　268–70
　　impact of change on 269
　　as systems 267–8
　　types 265–7
Family Nurse Partnership 374–5
fantasy play 195, 199

fats 241
febrile convulsions 251
fibre 242
fine motor skills 72, 85, 86
fire safety 254
first aid 258–9
Fisher, J. 24, 51, 65
focus group interviews 474
foetal alcohol syndrome 77–8
foetal development 75, 76–81
　　see also prenatal
　　　　development
food: healthy choices 70
　　see also healthy eating
food allergies 243–4
Food is Fun pyramid 247, 248
Forest Schools 215
formal operational stage 139
Foundation Stage Profile 302,
　　329
　　see also Early Years
　　　　Foundation Stage
Framework for Assessment of
　　Children in Need 424
frequency sampling 339–40
Freud, Sigmund 74, 93–4
friendships 116–21, 123
　　behaviourist approaches 118
　　changing patterns of 117
　　difficulties with 119
　　encouraging 118, 128
　　gender differences 118
　　as predictors of social
　　　　adjustment 120–1
　　skills used by children 118–19
Froebel, Friedrich William
　　17–20, 25, 30
　　influence on current practice
　　　　18–19
fully managed team 445

G

gardening in curriculum 33–4
genotype 69, 74
Gesell, Arnold 70, 73, 75
Goldschmied, E. 108, 166, 200,
　　201
government initiatives 37, 43
grasp reflex 83
Greenfield, S. 82–3

gross motor skills 72, 84, 85
growth
    defined 69
    milestones 70, 71
    see also physical
        development
Gunnar, M. 97, 102

responding to suspected abuse 412–15
safe environment 425–6
underpinning principles 411
see also child abuse; child protection
safety 252–9
accidents 254–9
adult-child ratios 257–8
fire 254
first aid 258–9
hygiene practices 254
legislation 253
scaffolding 145–6, 147, 158–9, 330
language development 167, 176, 178
and play 202
sensitive 146, 147
Scandinavian outdoor learning 198
schema 135, 136, 142, 158
Schon, D. 46, 52
school meals 32, 373, 374
schools
and child protection 411
role of Early Years practitioners 43
Scotland 16
accidental death by age group 255
children's mental health 237
curriculum 16, 27, 300, 306–7, 379
screening 375
antenatal 234–5
for disease 233–5, 238
pre-natal 332–3
self-description 110, 126–7
self-esteem 115, 123, 125, 316
and abuse 401
and competence 111
development of 109–16
domains of 112
encouraging positive 113–15, 127
measuring 111
and play 192
recognising low 113
role of caregivers 111, 112–13
self-fulfilling prophecy and behaviour 115

self-image 68
SEN children 317–19
entitlements 381–2
SEN Code of Practice 281–2, 317, 381–3
sensorimotor stage 137
sensory memory 151
separation anxiety 105, 106
services for children: historically 351–2
sexual abuse 403–5
sexual development 87, 88
Sheridan, Mary 70, 329
Shiffrin, R. 150
short-term memory 151, 156
Siegler, R. 154
Signalong 171, 172
signing systems 171–2
Siraj-Blatchford, J. 26, 27, 30, 134, 180
REPEY project 196, 311
sitters, standers and explorers 85
Skinner, B. 118, 165
Slobin, Dan I. 165
smacking issue 367, 399
Smilansky, S. 199, 200, 213
smiling 98, 125
smoking and prenatal development 78–9
social class classifications 223
social development and mealtimes 240
see also emotional and social development
social learning deficiency 118
social learning theory 118
social networking sites 186–7
social referencing 97
social skills 120–1, 126
socio-dramatic play 195, 199, 206, 213
sociometric observation 337, 342–3
somatosensory maps 83
special needs support assistants 43
see also SEN
speech development 172–3, 174
spina bifida 80–1
stakeholders and policy 355–6
Standard Occupational Classification 223

Steiner, Rudolf/schools 16, 17, 23, 30
conditions set 22–3
spiritual dimension 22, 23
stepfamilies 266–7
stepping reflex 83, 84
Story Sacks 65
stranger danger 224
stranger fear 105
study skills 1–13
goals 6
help and support 6–7
keyword search 38
note-taking 9
online materials 11–12
place to study 2
references 9–10, 11, 13
researching information 10–11
online 38
resources 2, 8
study calendar 5
taught sessions 8–9
time management 2–7
writing assignments 11–13
see also time management
Sturrock, G. 194
Stycar Sequences 329
Supervision Orders 421
Sure Start 16, 37, 228–9
involving parents 286
local programmes 229, 353–4, 384
role of practitioners 42
special needs guidance 383
see also Children's Centres
Sutton-Smith, B. 194
symbolic play 195, 199
systems theories 74

T

Tamis-Lemonda, C. 199, 201, 205
targets
and assessment 37
development 18, 305
five outcomes 368
health 229
obesity 373
and observation 330
teaching assistants 43

teams 62–3
  dimensions 62
  leadership of 443–50
  team building 62, 444
  within educational settings
    63
  see also multi-professional
    teams
teamwork
  effective and ineffective 63
  flexibility 442, 448
  skills for 442, 448–9
teeth, development of 84–5, 87
Ten Common Principles 24
Ten Year Childcare Strategy
    229, 377, 384
teratogens 76, 77–80
thalidomide 78
Thelen, E. 74
thinking skills, children's 315–
    16, 323–4
time management 2–7
  components of time 3, 4
  contingency plan 4
  prioritising time 3, 4, 7
  research study 469
time sampling 340
Together for Children (2007) 229
tracking observation 337–9
traditions in education and
    care 15, 16–17
training of practitioners 20
  McMillan 35
  Montessori method 21
  recognition of need for 44–5
  Steiner approach 23
transition to setting 108
  factors affecting child's
    experience 212

issues for children 210
issues for parents 209, 210
issues for practitioners 210
meeting different needs 212,
    213
pre-entry strategies 211
and reflective practice 211
relationship with parents
    211–12
strategies on entry 212
traveller children 212, 226
treasure basket play 166
Trevarthen, C. 102, 173
triangulation 455, 466

U

unconditional positive regard
    114–15, 126

V

validity of research 455
values 356–7
  and curriculum 380–1
  and team membership 441
  Waldorf/Steiner schools 23
vegetarian and vegan diets 243
verbal communication 59
vision, development of 84, 86
visual cliff 97
visual impairment and
    language 169
vitamins and minerals 242
Vygotsky, Lev 17, 133–4, 157,
    160, 330
  criticisms of 147

on language 166–7
on play 202
relevance of ideas 146–7
work of 143–6, 148
zone of proximal
    development 145, 159, 330

W

Waldorf Steiner schools 22–3
Wales 16
  children's mental health 237
  curriculum 27, 300–1, 306,
    379
walkers, talkers and pretenders
    86
Walters, R. 144
water intake 242–3
Wilderspin, Samuel 26
Winnicott, D.W. 194
Woodcock, M. 62
work-based learning 47–8
Workforce Reform 42, 367
working mothers 107
Working Together to Safeguard
    Children (2006) 363, 393,
    396, 421
World Health Organization
    growth standards 70, 71, 234
  and health 222, 227
writing assignments 11–13
written communication 60–1

Z

zone of proximal development
    145, 159, 330